These safety symbols are used in laboratory and field investigations in this book to indicate possible hazards. Learn the meaning of each symbol and refer to this page often. *Remember to wash your hands thoroughly after completing lab procedures.*

PROTECTIVE EQUIPMENT

Do not begin any lab without the proper protection equipment.

GOGGLES

Proper eye protection must be worn when performing or observing science activities which involve items or conditions as listed below.

APRON

Wear an approved apron when using substances that could stain, wet, or destroy cloth.

SOAP

Wash hands with soap and water before removing goggles and after all lab activities.

GLOVES

Wear gloves when working with biological materials, chemicals, animals, or materials that can stain or irritate hands.

LABORATORY HAZARDS

Symbols	Potential Hazards	Precaution	Response
DISPOSAL	contamination of classroom or environment due to improper disposal of materials such as chemicals and live specimens	• DO NOT dispose of hazardous materials in the sink or trash can. • Dispose of wastes as directed by your teacher.	• If hazardous materials are disposed of improperly, notify your teacher immediately.
EXTREME TEMPERATURE	skin burns due to extremely hot or cold materials such as hot glass, liquids, or metals; liquid nitrogen; dry ice	• Use proper protective equipment, such as hot mitts and/or tongs, when handling objects with extreme temperatures.	• If injury occurs, notify your teacher immediately.
SHARP OBJECTS	punctures or cuts from sharp objects such as razor blades, pins, scalpels, and broken glass	• Handle glassware carefully to avoid breakage. • Walk with sharp objects pointed downward, away from you and others.	• If broken glass or injury occurs, notify your teacher immediately.
ELECTRICAL	electric shock or skin burn due to improper grounding, short circuits, liquid spills, or exposed wires	• Check condition of wires and apparatus for fraying or uninsulated wires, and broken or cracked equipment. • Use only GFCI-protected outlets	• DO NOT attempt to fix electrical problems. Notify your teacher immediately.
CHEMICAL	skin irritation or burns, breathing difficulty, and/or poisoning due to touching, swallowing, or inhalation of chemicals such as acids, bases, bleach, metal compounds, iodine, poinsettias, pollen, ammonia, acetone, nail polish remover, heated chemicals, mothballs, and any other chemicals labeled or known to be dangerous	• Wear proper protective equipment such as goggles, apron, and gloves when using chemicals. • Ensure proper room ventilation or use a fume hood when using materials that produce fumes. • NEVER smell fumes directly. • NEVER taste or eat any material in the laboratory.	• If contact occurs, immediately flush affected area with water and notify your teacher. • If a spill occurs, leave the area immediately and notify your teacher.
FLAMMABLE	unexpected fire due to liquids or gases that ignite easily such as rubbing alcohol	• Avoid open flames, sparks, or heat when flammable liquids are present.	• If a fire occurs, leave the area immediately and notify your teacher.
OPEN FLAME	burns or fire due to open flame from matches, Bunsen burners, or burning materials	• Tie back loose hair and clothing. • Keep flame away from all materials. • Follow teacher instructions when lighting and extinguishing flames. • Use proper protection, such as hot mitts or tongs, when handling hot objects.	• If a fire occurs, leave the area immediately and notify your teacher.
ANIMAL SAFETY	injury to or from laboratory animals	• Wear proper protective equipment such as gloves, apron, and goggles when working with animals. • Wash hands after handling animals.	• If injury occurs, notify your teacher immediately.
BIOLOGICAL	infection or adverse reaction due to contact with organisms such as bacteria, fungi, and biological materials such as blood, animal or plant materials	• Wear proper protective equipment such as gloves, goggles, and apron when working with biological materials. • Avoid skin contact with an organism or any part of the organism. • Wash hands after handling organisms.	• If contact occurs, wash the affected area and notify your teacher immediately.
FUME	breathing difficulties from inhalation of fumes from substances such as ammonia, acetone, nail polish remover, heated chemicals, and mothballs	• Wear goggles, apron, and gloves. • Ensure proper room ventilation or use a fume hood when using substances that produce fumes. • NEVER smell fumes directly.	• If a spill occurs, leave area and notify your teacher immediately.
IRRITANT	irritation of skin, mucous membranes, or respiratory tract due to materials such as acids, bases, bleach, pollen, mothballs, steel wool, and potassium permanganate	• Wear goggles, apron, and gloves. • Wear a dust mask to protect against fine particles.	• If skin contact occurs, immediately flush the affected area with water and notify your teacher.
RADIOACTIVE	excessive exposure from alpha, beta, and gamma particles	• Remove gloves and wash hands with soap and water before removing remainder of protective equipment.	• If cracks or holes are found in the container, notify your teacher immediately.

INDIANA

GRADE 8

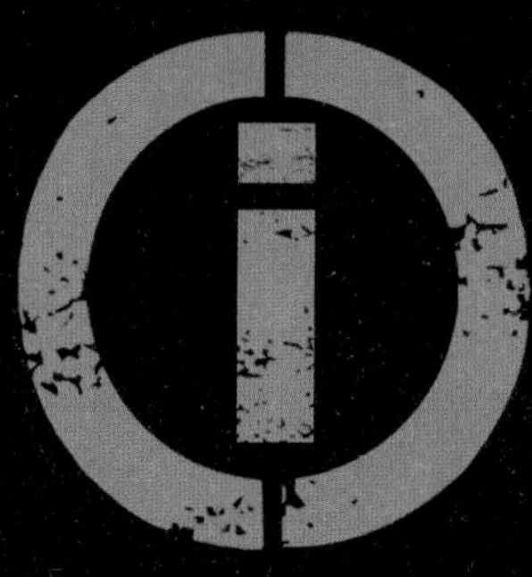

Glencoe

Your online portal to everything you need

connectED.mcgraw-hill.com

Look for these icons to access exciting digital resources

Audio

Review

Inquiry

WebQuest

Assessment

Concepts in Motion

McGraw Hill Education

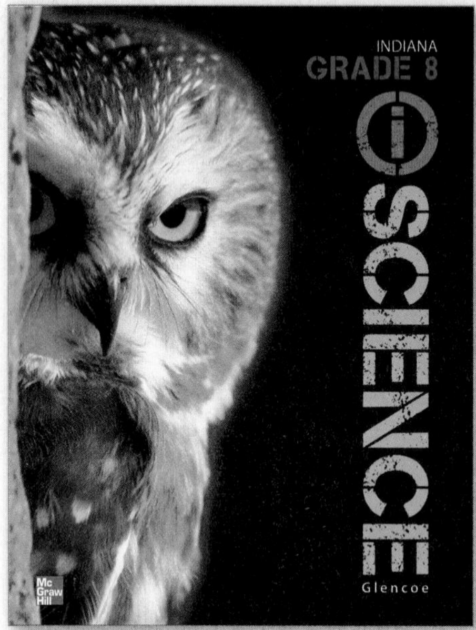

Northern Saw-Whet Owl, *Aegolius acadicus*
This small owl is nocturnal and, therefore, seldom is seen. It is only about 17 cm–22 cm in length and has a wingspan of about 50 cm–56 cm. Its habitat includes short conifers and dense thickets across most of the United States and southern Canada.

The McGraw·Hill Companies

Education

Send all inquiries to:
McGraw-Hill Education
8787 Orion Place
Columbus, OH 43240-4027

ISBN: 978-0-07-888036-0
MHID: 0-07-888036-X

Printed in the United States of America.

3 4 5 6 7 8 9 10 QDB/QDB 15 14 13 12 11

Contents in Brief

Indiana's Academic Standards for Science, Grade 8 Correlated to *Indiana* ⓘ *Science Grade 8*

Process Standards	Pages
The Nature of Science **Students gain scientific knowledge by observing the natural and constructed world, performing and evaluating investigations and communicating their findings. These principles should guide student work and be integrated into the curriculum along with the content standards on a daily basis.**	
8.NS.1 Make predictions and develop testable questions based on research and prior knowledge.	NOS 6, NOS 22–NOS 29, 5, 8, 44, 122, 140–141, 198, 238, 254, 256–257, 300–301, 315, 327, 378–379, 418–419, 468
8.NS.2 Plan and carry out investigations as a class, in small groups or independently often over a period of several class lessons.	NOS 13, 66–67, 90, 174–175, 189, 256–257, 315, 342–343, 456–457
8.NS.3 Collect quantitative data with appropriate tools or technologies and use appropriate units to label numerical data.	NOS 14–NOS 16, NOS 18–NOS 19, 66–67, 122, 130, 151, 162, 168, 220–221, 256–257, 269, 315, 327, 399, 439, 475
8.NS.4 Incorporate variables that can be changed, measured or controlled.	NOS 23, NOS 28, 44, 66–67, 91, 94, 174–175, 232, 238, 327
8.NS.5 Use the principles of accuracy and precision when making measurement.	NOS 16, 58, 66–67, 83, 140–141, 151, 168, 172, 174–175, 256–257, 269, 399
8.NS.6 Test predictions with multiple trials	44, 90, 94, 122, 140–141, 189, 198, 209, 238, 327, 468
8.NS.7 Keep accurate records in a notebook during investigations.	NOS 18, NOS 22–NOS 29, 9, 14, 26, 41, 45, 50, 56, 58, 60, 63, 66–67, 77, 85, 95, 100, 126, 130, 137, 160, 168, 172, 174–175, 190, 203, 205, 207, 209, 214, 220–221, 231, 239, 241, 251, 256–257, 283, 289, 298, 300–301, 311, 317, 327, 335, 357, 369, 373, 389, 401, 408, 410, 412, 429, 437, 439, 445, 449, 456–457, 475, 490, 492–493
8.NS.8 Analyze data, using appropriate mathematical manipulation as required, and use it to identify patterns and make inferences based on these patterns.	NOS 16–NOS 17, 8, 66–67, 83, 90, 130, 189, 254, 281, 291, 300–301, 315, 389, 437
8.NS.9 Evaluate possible causes for differing results (valid data).	22, 90, 113, 125, 130, 151, 162, 174–175, 220–221, 238, 256–257, 325, 327, 437, 449, 467, 475
8.NS.10 Compare the results of an experiment with the prediction.	8, 140–141, 162, 189, 198, 256–257, 269, 315, 327
8.NS.11 Communicate findings using graphs, charts, maps and models through oral and written reports.	NOS 7, NOS 27–NOS 28, 22, 44, 66–67, 140–141, 184–185, 256–257, 283, 289, 315, 342–343, 352–353, 378–379, 389, 418–419, 437, 456–457, 492–493
The Design Process: **As citizens of the constructed world, students will participate in the design process. Students will learn to use materials and tools safely and employ the basic principles of the engineering design process in order to find a solution to a problem.**	
8.DP.1 Identify a need or problem that needs to be solved.	NOS 12–NOS 13, NOS 30–NOS 31, 5, 66–67, 300–301, 315, 318, 342–343, 492–493
8.DP.2 Brainstorm potential solutions.	NOS 12–NOS 13, NOS 19, NOS 30–NOS 31, 5, 66–67, 300–301, 315, 342–343, 492–493
8.DP.3 Document the design throughout the entire design process so that it can be replicated in a portfolio/notebook with drawings including labels.	NOS 12–NOS 13, NOS 19, NOS 30–NOS 31, 5, 66–67, 300–301, 315, 342–343, 492–493

Indiana's Academic Standards for Science, Grade 8 Correlated to *Indiana* ⓘ *Science Grade 8*

Process Standards	Pages
8.DP.4 Select a solution to the need or problem.	NOS 12–NOS 13, NOS 19, NOS 30–NOS 31, 5, 66–67, 315, 342–343, 492–493
8.DP.5 Select the most appropriate materials to develop a solution that meets the need.	NOS 12–NOS 13, NOS 30–NOS 31, 5, 66–67, 342–343, 492–493
8.DP.6 Create a solution through a prototype.	NOS 12–NOS 13, NOS 19, NOS 30–NOS 31, 66–67, 76, 134, 162, 300–301, 315, 342–343, 492–493
8.DP.7 Test and evaluate how well the solution meets the goal.	NOS 12–NOS 13, NOS 19, NOS 30–NOS 31, 66–67, 342–343, 492–493
8.DP.8 Evaluate and test the design using measurement.	NOS 12–NOS 13, NOS 30–NOS 31, 66–67, 300–301, 315, 342–343
8.DP.9 Present evidence using mathematical representation (graphs, data tables).	NOS 12–NOS 13, NOS 30–NOS 31, 66–67, 300–301, 342–343, 492–493
8.DP.10 Communicate the solution including evidence using mathematical representations (graphs, data tables), drawings or prototype.	NOS 12–NOS 13, NOS 30–NOS 31, 66–67, 300–301, 318, 342–343
8.DP.11 Redesign to improve the solution based on how well the solution meets the need.	NOS 12–NOS 13, NOS 19, NOS 30–NOS 31, 66–67, 315, 342–343, 492–493
Standard 1: Physical Science	**Pages**
Core Standard **Describe how atomic structure determines chemical properties and how atoms and molecules interact.**	
8.1.1 Explain that all matter is composed of particular arrangements of atoms of approximately one hundred elements.	9, 11–14, 19
8.1.2 Understand that elements are organized on the periodic table based on atomic number.	77–82
8.1.3 Explain how the arrangement of atoms and molecules determines chemical properties of substances.	126, 128–129, 136–138
8.1.4 Describe the structure of an atom and relate the arrangement of electrons to how that atom interacts with other atoms.	23–28, 118–122, 127–128, 134–137
8.1.5 Explain that atoms join together to form molecules and compounds and illustrate with diagrams the relationship between atoms and compounds and/or molecules.	10–12, 17, 30–31, 127–130, 136–138
8.1.6 Explain that elements and compounds have characteristic properties such as density, boiling points and melting points that remain unchanged regardless of the sample size.	86–91, 97–100, 128–129, 136–138
8.1.7 Explain that chemical changes occur when substances react and form one or more different products, whose physical and chemical properties are different from those of the reactants.	151–153, 162–164
8.1.8 Demonstrate that in a chemical change, the total numbers of each kind of atom in the product are the same as in the reactants and that the total mass of the reacting system is conserved.	153, 156–158, 163–164

Indiana's Academic Standards for Science, Grade 8 Correlated to *Indiana* ⓘ *Science Grade 8*

Standard 2: Earth and Space Systems	Pages
Core Standard **Explain how the sun's energy heats the air, land, and water driving the processes that result in wind, ocean currents, and the water cycle.**	
Core Standard **Describe how human activities have changed the land, water, and atmosphere.**	
8.2.1 Recognize and demonstrate how the sun's energy drives convection in the atmosphere and in bodies of water, which results in ocean currents and weather patterns.	198–203, 207–210, 239–243, 285–289
8.2.2 Describe and model how water moves through the earth's crust, atmosphere, and oceans in a cyclic way, as liquid, vapor, and solid.	234–235, 250–254, 268, 272–273, 285–287, 289
8.2.3 Describe the characteristics of ocean currents and identify their effects on weather patterns.	285–289
8.2.4 Describe the physical and chemical composition of the atmosphere at different elevations.	191–194, 214–218, 250–254
8.2.5 Describe the conditions that cause Indiana weather and weather-related events such as tornadoes, lake effect snow, blizzards, thunderstorms, and flooding.	239–247
8.2.6 Identify, explain, and discuss some effects human activities have on the biosphere, such as air, soil, light, noise and water pollution.	214–218, 292–298, 313, 317–323, 327–331, 335–340
8.2.7 Recognize that some of Earth's resources are finite and describe how recycling, reducing consumption and the development of alternatives can reduce the rate of their depletion.	312–313, 322–323, 331–332, 340
8.2.8 Explain that human activities, beginning with the earliest herding and agricultural activities, have drastically changed the environment and have affected the capacity of the environment to support native species. Explain current efforts to reduce and eliminate these impacts and encourage sustainability.	292–298, 313, 317–323, 327–331, 335–340

Standard 3: Life Science	Pages
Core Standard **Understand the predictability of characteristics being passed from parents to offspring.**	
Core Standard **Explain how a particular environment selects for traits that increase the likelihood of survival and reproduction by individuals bearing those traits.**	
8.3.1 Explain that reproduction is essential for the continuation of every species and is the mechanism by which all organisms transmit genetic information.	357, 369, 390–395
8.3.2 Compare and contrast the transmission of genetic information in sexual and asexual reproduction.	357–365, 369–376

Indiana's Academic Standards for Science, Grade 8 Correlated to *Indiana* ⓘ*Science Grade 8*

Process Standards	Pages
8.3.3 Explain that genetic information is transmitted from parents to offspring mostly by chromosomes.	358, 399–406
8.3.4 Understand the relationship between deoxyribonucleic acid (DNA), genes, and chromosomes.	410–416
8.3.5 Identify and describe the difference between inherited traits and physical and behavioral traits that are acquired or learned.	400
8.3.6 Observe anatomical structures of a variety of organisms and describe their similarities and differences. Use the data collected to organize the organisms into groups and predict their relatedness.	452, 468–471, 475–481, 485–490
8.3.7 Recognize and explain that small genetic differences between parents and offspring can accumulate in successive generations so that descendants may be different from their ancestors.	441–442
8.3.8 Examine traits of individuals within a population of organisms that may give them an advantage in survival and reproduction in a given environment or when the environment changes.	443–444, 456–457
8.3.9 Describe the effect of environmental changes on populations of organisms when their adaptive characteristics put them at a disadvantage for survival. Describe how extinction of a species can ultimately result.	434, 456–457
8.3.10 Recognize and describe how new varieties of organisms have come about from selective breeding.	365, 445
Standard 4: Science, Technology and Engineering	**Pages**
Core Standard **Identify the appropriate materials to be used to solve a problem based on their specific properties and characteristics.**	
8.4.1 Understand how the strength of attractive forces between particles in a material helps to explain many physical properties of the material, such as why different materials exist as gases, liquids or solids at a given temperature.	42–46, 50–55
8.4.2 Rank the strength of attractions between the particles of room-temperature materials.	42, 43, 44, 46, 71, 73
8.4.3 Investigate the properties (mechanical, chemical, electrical, thermal, magnetic, and optical) of natural and engineered materials.	5, 14, 58, 63, 91, 95, 100, 160, 168, 172, 174–175

Indiana's Academic Standards for Science, Grade 8 Correlated to *Indiana* ⓘ *Science Grade 8*

Standard 4: Science, Technology and Engineering	Pages
Core Standard **Identify the appropriate materials to be used to solve a problem based on their specific properties and characteristics.**	
8.4.1 Understand how the strength of attractive forces between particles in a material helps to explain many physical properties of the material, such as why different materials exist as gases, liquids or solids at a given temperature.	42–46, 50–55
8.4.2 Rank the strength of attractions between the particles of room-temperature materials.	42, 43, 44, 46, 71, 73
8.4.3 Investigate the properties (mechanical, chemical, electrical, thermal, magnetic, and optical) of natural and engineered materials.	14, 58, 63, 91, 95, 100, 160, 168, 172, 174–175

Indiana Authorship and Review Team

Author
William D. Rogers, DA
Professor of Biology
Ball State University
Muncie, IN

Consultant
Cheryl Wistrom, PhD
Associate Professor of Chemistry
Saint Joseph's College
Rensselaer, IN

Reviewers
Jane E.M. Buckingham
Teacher
Crispus Attucks Medical Magnet High School
Indianapolis, IN

Ginger Shirley
Our Lady of Providence Junior–Senior High School
Clarksville, IN

Tony Spoors
Switzerland County Middle School
Vevay, IN

Nancy A. Stearns
Switzerland County Middle School
Vevay, IN

Driftwood River, Bartholomew County

Authors and Contributors

Authors

American Museum of Natural History
New York, NY

Michelle Anderson, MS
Lecturer
The Ohio State University
Columbus, OH

Juli Berwald, PhD
Science Writer
Austin, TX

John F. Bolzan, PhD
Science Writer
Columbus, OH

Rachel Clark, MS
Science Writer
Moscow, ID

Patricia Craig, MS
Science Writer
Bozeman, MT

Randall Frost, PhD
Science Writer
Pleasanton, CA

Lisa S. Gardiner, PhD
Science Writer
Denver, CO

Jennifer Gonya, PhD
The Ohio State University
Columbus, OH

Mary Ann Grobbel, MD
Science Writer
Grand Rapids, MI

Whitney Crispen Hagins, MA, MAT
Biology Teacher
Lexington High School
Lexington, MA

Carole Holmberg, BS
Planetarium Director
Calusa Nature Center and Planetarium, Inc.
Fort Myers, FL

Tina C. Hopper
Science Writer
Rockwall, TX

Jonathan D. W. Kahl, PhD
Professor of Atmospheric Science
University of Wisconsin-Milwaukee
Milwaukee, WI

Nanette Kalis
Science Writer
Athens, OH

S. Page Keeley, MEd
Maine Mathematics and Science Alliance
Augusta, ME

Cindy Klevickis, PhD
Professor of Integrated Science and Technology
James Madison University
Harrisonburg, VA

Kimberly Fekany Lee, PhD
Science Writer
La Grange, IL

Michael Manga, PhD
Professor
University of California, Berkeley
Berkeley, CA

Devi Ried Mathieu
Science Writer
Sebastopol, CA

Elizabeth A. Nagy-Shadman, PhD
Geology Professor
Pasadena City College
Pasadena, CA

William D. Rogers, DA
Professor of Biology
Ball State University
Muncie, IN

Donna L. Ross, PhD
Associate Professor
San Diego State University
San Diego, CA

Marion B. Sewer, PhD
Assistant Professor
School of Biology
Georgia Institute of Technology
Atlanta, GA

Julia Meyer Sheets, PhD
Lecturer
School of Earth Sciences
The Ohio State University
Columbus, OH

Michael J. Singer, PhD
Professor of Soil Science
Department of Land, Air and Water Resources
University of California
Davis, CA

Karen S. Sottosanti, MA
Science Writer
Pickerington, Ohio

Paul K. Strode, PhD
I.B. Biology Teacher
Fairview High School
Boulder, CO

Jan M. Vermilye, PhD
Research Geologist
Seismo-Tectonic Reservoir Monitoring (STRM)
Boulder, CO

Judith A. Yero, MA
Director
Teacher's Mind Resources
Hamilton, MT

Dinah Zike, MEd
Author, Consultant, Inventor of Foldables
Dinah Zike Academy; Dinah-Might Adventures, LP
San Antonio, TX

Margaret Zorn, MS
Science Writer
Yorktown, VA

Consulting Authors

Alton L. Biggs
Biggs Educational Consulting
Commerce, TX

Ralph M. Feather, Jr., PhD
Assistant Professor
Department of Educational Studies and Secondary Education
Bloomsburg University
Bloomsburg, PA

Douglas Fisher, PhD
Professor of Teacher Education
San Diego State University
San Diego, CA

Edward P. Ortleb
Science/Safety Consultant
St. Louis, MO

Series Consultants

Science

Solomon Bililign, PhD
Professor
Department of Physics
North Carolina Agricultural and Technical State University
Greensboro, NC

John Choinski
Professor
Department of Biology
University of Central Arkansas
Conway, AR

Anastasia Chopelas, PhD
Research Professor
Department of Earth and Space Sciences
UCLA
Los Angeles, CA

David T. Crowther, PhD
Professor of Science Education
University of Nevada, Reno
Reno, NV

A. John Gatz
Professor of Zoology
Ohio Wesleyan University
Delaware, OH

Sarah Gille, PhD
Professor
University of California San Diego
La Jolla, CA

David G. Haase, PhD
Professor of Physics
North Carolina State University
Raleigh, NC

Janet S. Herman, PhD
Professor
Department of Environmental Sciences
University of Virginia
Charlottesville, VA

David T. Ho, PhD
Associate Professor
Department of Oceanography
University of Hawaii
Honolulu, HI

Ruth Howes, PhD
Professor of Physics
Marquette University
Milwaukee, WI

Jose Miguel Hurtado, Jr., PhD
Associate Professor
Department of Geological Sciences
University of Texas at El Paso
El Paso, TX

Monika Kress, PhD
Assistant Professor
San Jose State University
San Jose, CA

Mark E. Lee, PhD
Associate Chair & Assistant Professor
Department of Biology
Spelman College
Atlanta, GA

Linda Lundgren
Science writer
Lakewood, CO

Keith O. Mann, PhD
Ohio Wesleyan University
Delaware, OH

Charles W. McLaughlin, PhD
Adjunct Professor of Chemistry
Montana State University
Bozeman, MT

Katharina Pahnke, PhD
Research Professor
Department of Geology and Geophysics
University of Hawaii
Honolulu, HI

Jesús Pando, PhD
Associate Professor
DePaul University
Chicago, IL

Hay-Oak Park, PhD
Associate Professor
Department of Molecular Genetics
Ohio State University
Columbus, OH

David A. Rubin, PhD
Associate Professor of Physiology
School of Biological Sciences
Illinois State University
Normal, IL

Toni D. Sauncy
Assistant Professor of Physics
Department of Physics
Angelo State University
San Angelo, TX

Series Consultants, continued

Malathi Srivatsan, PhD
Associate Professor of Neurobiology
College of Sciences and Mathematics
Arkansas State University
Jonesboro, AR

Cheryl Wistrom, PhD
Associate Professor of Chemistry
Saint Joseph's College
Rensselaer, IN

Reading

ReLeah Cossett Lent
Author/Educational Consultant
Blue Ridge, GA

Math

Vik Hovsepian
Professor of Mathematics
Rio Hondo College
Whittier, CA

Series Reviewers

Thad Boggs
Mandarin High School
Jacksonville, FL

Catherine Butcher
Webster Junior High School
Minden, LA

Erin Darichuk
West Frederick Middle School
Frederick, MD

Joanne Hedrick Davis
Murphy High School
Murphy, NC

Anthony J. DiSipio, Jr.
Octorara Middle School
Atglen, PA

Adrienne Elder
Tulsa Public Schools
Tulsa, OK

Carolyn Elliott
Iredell-Statesville Schools
Statesville, NC

Christine M. Jacobs
Ranger Middle School
Murphy, NC

Jason O. L. Johnson
Thurmont Middle School
Thurmont, MD

Felecia Joiner
Stony Point Ninth Grade Center
Round Rock, TX

Joseph L. Kowalski, MS
Lamar Academy
McAllen, TX

Brian McClain
Amos P. Godby High School
Tallahassee, FL

Von W. Mosser
Thurmont Middle School
Thurmont, MD

Ashlea Peterson
Heritage Intermediate Grade Center
Coweta, OK

Nicole Lenihan Rhoades
Walkersville Middle School
Walkersvillle, MD

Maria A. Rozenberg
Indian Ridge Middle School
Davie, FL

Barb Seymour
Westridge Middle School
Overland Park, KS

Ginger Shirley
Our Lady of Providence Junior-Senior High School
Clarksville, IN

Curtis Smith
Elmwood Middle School
Rogers, AR

Sheila Smith
Jackson Public School
Jackson, MS

Sabra Soileau
Moss Bluff Middle School
Lake Charles, LA

Tony Spoores
Switzerland County Middle School
Vevay, IN

Nancy A. Stearns
Switzerland County Middle School
Vevay, IN

Kari Vogel
Princeton Middle School
Princeton, MN

Alison Welch
Wm. D. Slider Middle School
El Paso, TX

Linda Workman
Parkway Northeast Middle School
Creve Coeur, MO

Online Guide

connectED.mcgraw-hill.com

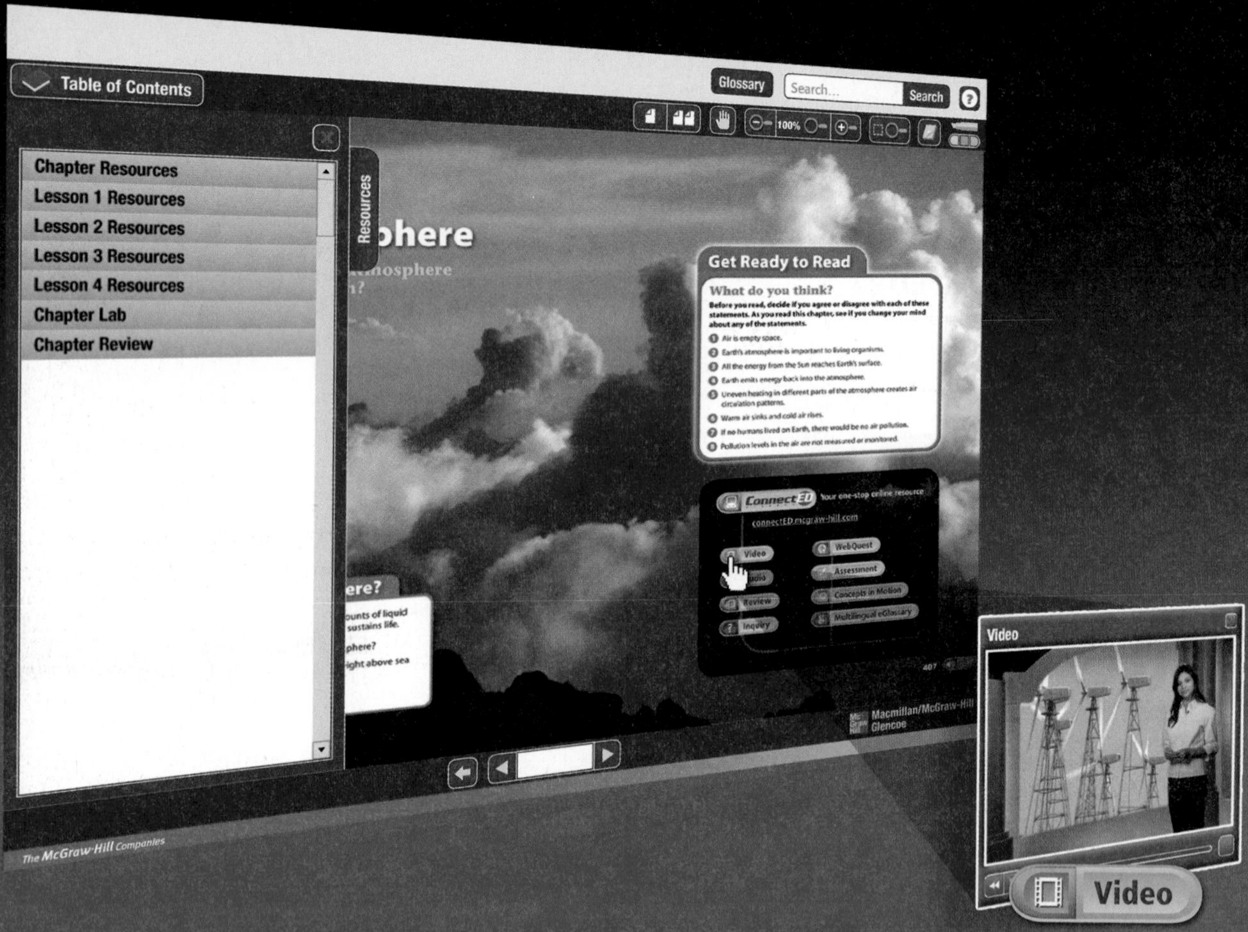

Your Digital Science Portal

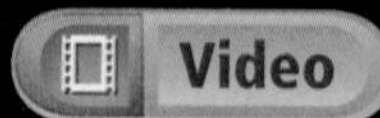

See the science in real life through these exciting videos.

Click the link and you can listen to the text while you follow along.

Try these interactive tools to help you review the lesson concepts.

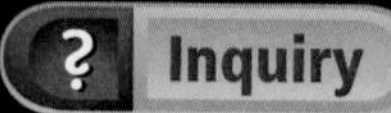

Explore concepts through hands-on and virtual labs.

These web-based challenges relate the concepts you're learning about to the latest news and research.

Digital and Print Solutions

The icons in your online student edition link you to interactive learning opportunities. Browse your online student book to find more.

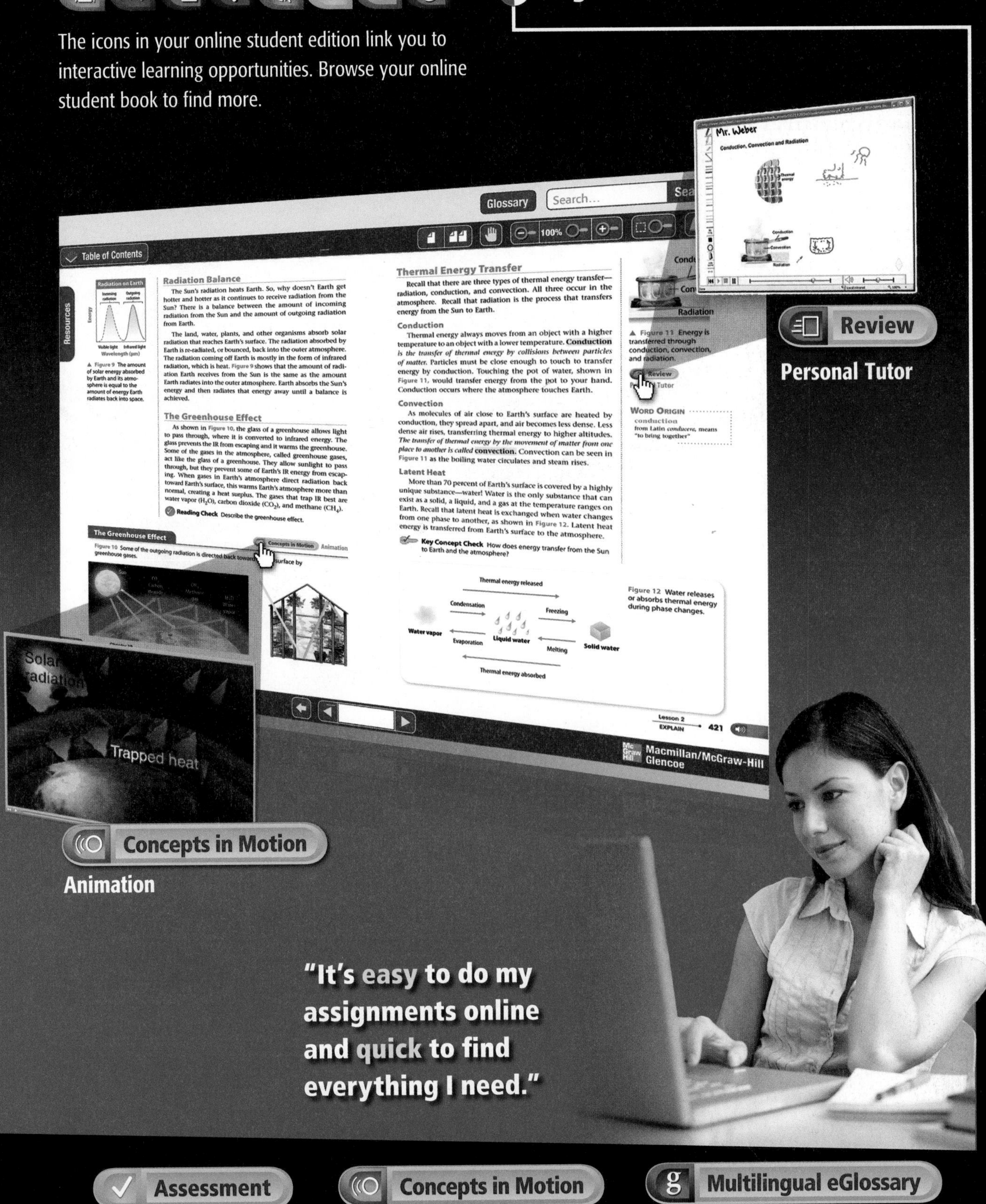

Assessment

Check how well you understand the concepts with online quizzes and practice questions.

Concepts in Motion

The textbook comes alive with animated explanations of important concepts.

Multilingual eGlossary

Read key vocabulary in 13 languages.

Treasure Hunt

Your science book has many features that will aid you in your learning. Some of these features are listed below. You can use the activity at the right to help you find these and other special features in the book.

- THE BIG IDEA can be found at the start of each chapter.
- The Reading Guide at the start of each lesson lists **Key Concepts,** vocabulary terms, and online supplements to the content.
- ConnectED icons direct you to online resources such as animations, personal tutors, math practices, and quizzes.
- Inquiry Labs and Skill Practices are in each chapter.
- Your FOLDABLES® help organize your notes.

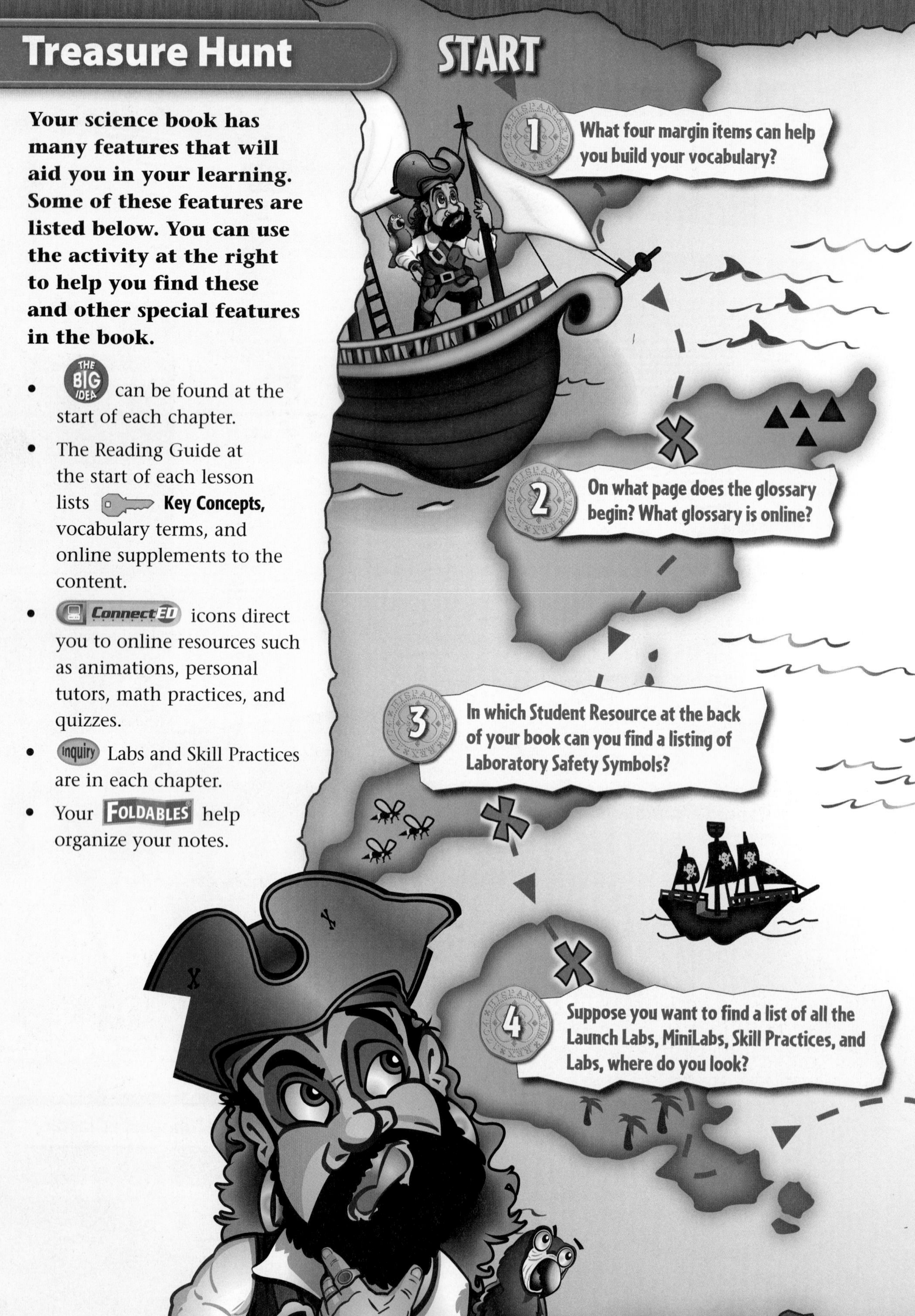

START
1 What four margin items can help you build your vocabulary?
2 On what page does the glossary begin? What glossary is online?
3 In which Student Resource at the back of your book can you find a listing of Laboratory Safety Symbols?
4 Suppose you want to find a list of all the Launch Labs, MiniLabs, Skill Practices, and Labs, where do you look?

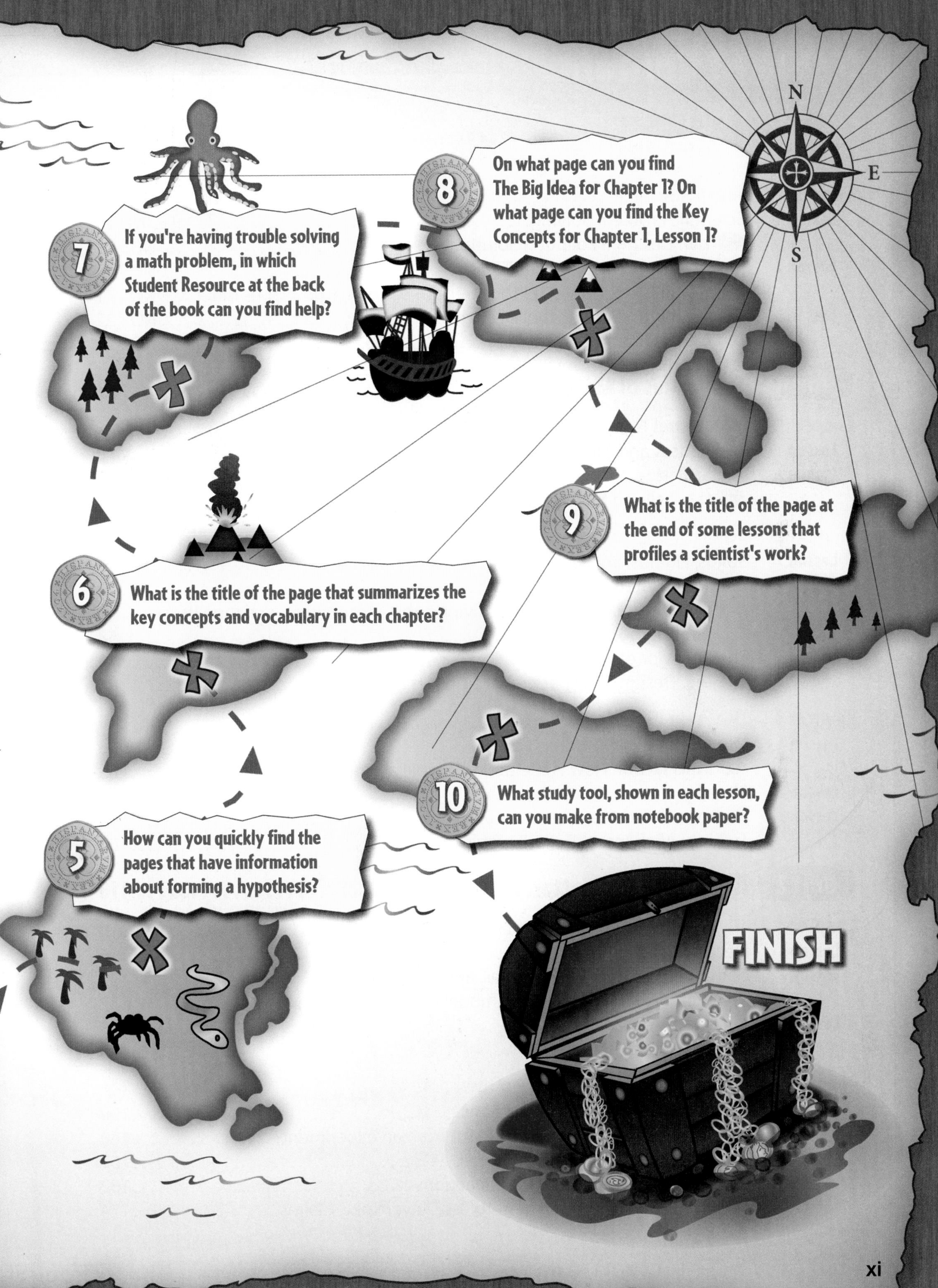
N
E
S
8
On what page can you find The Big Idea for Chapter 1? On what page can you find the Key Concepts for Chapter 1, Lesson 1?
7
If you're having trouble solving a math problem, in which Student Resource at the back of the book can you find help?
9
What is the title of the page at the end of some lessons that profiles a scientist's work?
6
What is the title of the page that summarizes the key concepts and vocabulary in each chapter?
10
What study tool, shown in each lesson, can you make from notebook paper?
5
How can you quickly find the pages that have information about forming a hypothesis?
FINISH

Table of Contents

Student Resources

Inquiry

Inquiry Launch Labs

Inquiry MiniLabs

Inquiry Skill Practice

Inquiry Labs

Features

GREEN SCIENCE

HOW IT WORKS

SCIENCE & SOCIETY

CAREERS in SCIENCE

TABLE OF CONTENTS

Scientific Problem Solving

THE BIG IDEA What is scientific inquiry?

Inquiry Sci-Fi Movie Scene?

This might look like a weird spaceship docking in a science-fiction movie. However, it is actually the back of an airplane engine being tested in a huge wind tunnel. An experiment is an important part of scientific investigations.

- Why is an experiment important?
- Does experimentation occur in all branches of science?
- What is scientific inquiry?

Nature of SCIENCE

This chapter begins your study of the nature of science, but there is even more information about the nature of science in this book. Each unit begins by exploring an important topic that is fundamental to scientific study. As you read these topics, you will learn even more about the nature of science.

Patterns	**Unit 1**
Models	**Unit 2**
Systems	**Unit 3**
Technology	**Unit 4**
History	**Unit 5**

Lesson 1 Scientific Inquiry

Reading Guide

Key Concepts
ESSENTIAL QUESTIONS

- What are some steps used during scientific inquiry?
- What are the results of scientific inquiry?
- What is critical thinking?

Vocabulary

science p. NOS 4
observation p. NOS 6
inference p. NOS 6
hypothesis p. NOS 6
prediction p. NOS 6
scientific theory p. NOS 8
scientific law p. NOS 8
technology p. NOS 9
critical thinking p. NOS 10

Academic Standards for Science

Covers: 8.NS.1, 8.NS.11, 8.DP.1, 8.DP.2, 8.DP.3, 8.DP.4, 8.DP.5, 8.DP.6, 8.DP.7, 8.DP.8, 8.DP.9, 8.DP.10, 8.DP.11

Understanding Science

A clear night sky is one of the most beautiful sights on Earth. The stars seem to shine like a handful of diamonds scattered on black velvet. Why do stars seem to shine more brightly some nights than others?

Did you know that when you ask questions, such as the one above, you are practicing science? **Science** *is the investigation and exploration of natural events and of the new information that results from those investigations.* Like a scientist, you can help shape the future by accumulating knowledge, developing new technologies, and sharing ideas with others.

Throughout history, people of many different backgrounds, interests, and talents have made scientific contributions. Sometimes they overcame a limited educational background and excelled in science. One example is Marie Curie, shown in **Figure 1.** She was a scientist who won two Nobel prizes in the early 1900s for her work with radioactivity. As a young student, Marie was not allowed to study at the University of Warsaw in Poland because she was a woman. Despite this obstacle, she made significant contributions to science.

Figure 1 Modern medical procedures such as X-rays, radioactive cancer treatments, and nuclear-power generation are some of the technologies made possible because of the pioneering work of Marie Curie and her associates.

Branches of Science

Scientific study is organized into several branches, or parts. The three branches that you will study in middle school are physical science, Earth science, and life science. Each branch focuses on a different part of the natural world.

WORD ORIGIN

science
from Latin *scientia,* means "knowledge" or "to know"

Physical Science

Physical science, or physics and chemistry, is the study of matter and energy. The physicist shown here is adjusting an instrument that measures radiation from the Big Bang. Physical scientists ask questions such as

- What happens to energy during chemical reactions?
- How does gravity affect roller coasters?
- What makes up protons, neutrons, and electrons?

Earth Science

Earth scientists study the many processes that occur on Earth and deep within Earth. This scientist is collecting a water sample in southern Mexico.

Earth scientists ask questions such as

- What are the properties of minerals?
- How is energy transferred on Earth?
- How do volcanoes form?

Life Science

Life scientists study all organisms and the many processes that occur in them. The life scientist shown is studying the avian flu virus.

Life scientists ask questions such as

- How do plant cells and animal cells differ?
- How do animals survive in the desert?
- How do organisms in a community interact?

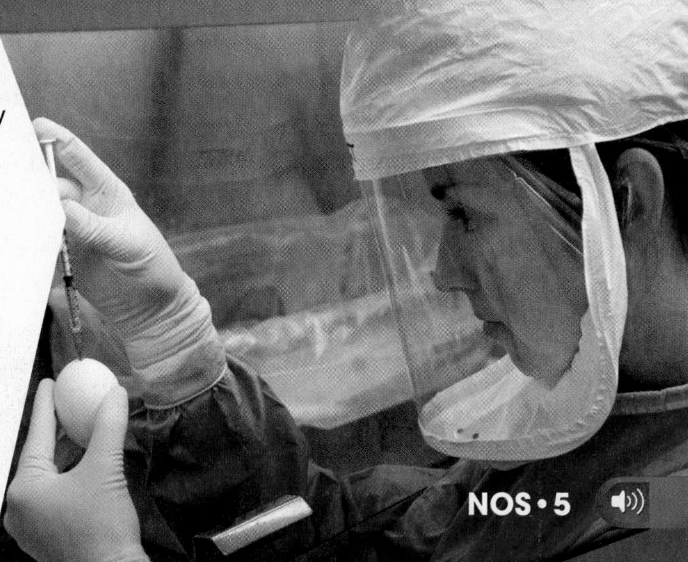

What is Scientific Inquiry?

When scientists conduct investigations, they often want to answer questions about the natural world. To do this, they use scientific inquiry—a series of skills used to answer questions. You might have heard these steps called "the scientific method." However, there is no one scientific method. In fact, the skills that scientists use to conduct an investigation can be used in any order. One possible sequence is shown in **Figure 2.** Like a scientist, you perform scientific investigations every day, and you will do investigations throughout this course.

 **Reading Check** What is scientific inquiry?

Ask Questions

Imagine warming yourself near a fireplace or a campfire? As you throw twigs and logs onto the fire, you see that fire releases smoke and light. You also feel the warmth of the thermal energy being released. These are **observations**—*the results of using one or more of your senses to gather information and taking note of what occurs.* Observations often lead to questions. You ask yourself, "When logs burn, what happens to the wood? Do the logs disappear? Do they change in some way?"

When observing the fire, you might recall from an earlier science course that matter can change form, but it cannot be created or destroyed. Therefore, you infer that the logs do not just disappear. They must undergo some type of change. An **inference** *is a logical explanation of an observation that is drawn from prior knowledge or experience.*

Hypothesize and Predict

After making observations and inferences, you decide to investigate further. Like a scientist, you might develop a **hypothesis**—*a possible explanation for an observation that can be tested by scientific investigations.* Your hypothesis about what happens to the logs might be: When logs burn, new substances form because matter cannot be destroyed.

When scientists state a hypothesis, they often use it to make predictions to help test their hypothesis. *A* **prediction** *is a statement of what will happen next in a sequence of events.* Scientists make predictions based on what information they think they will find when testing their hypothesis. For instance, based on your hypothesis, you might predict that if logs burn, then the substances that make up the logs change into other substances.

Figure 2 There are many possible steps in the process of scientific inquiry, and they can be performed in a variety of different sequences.

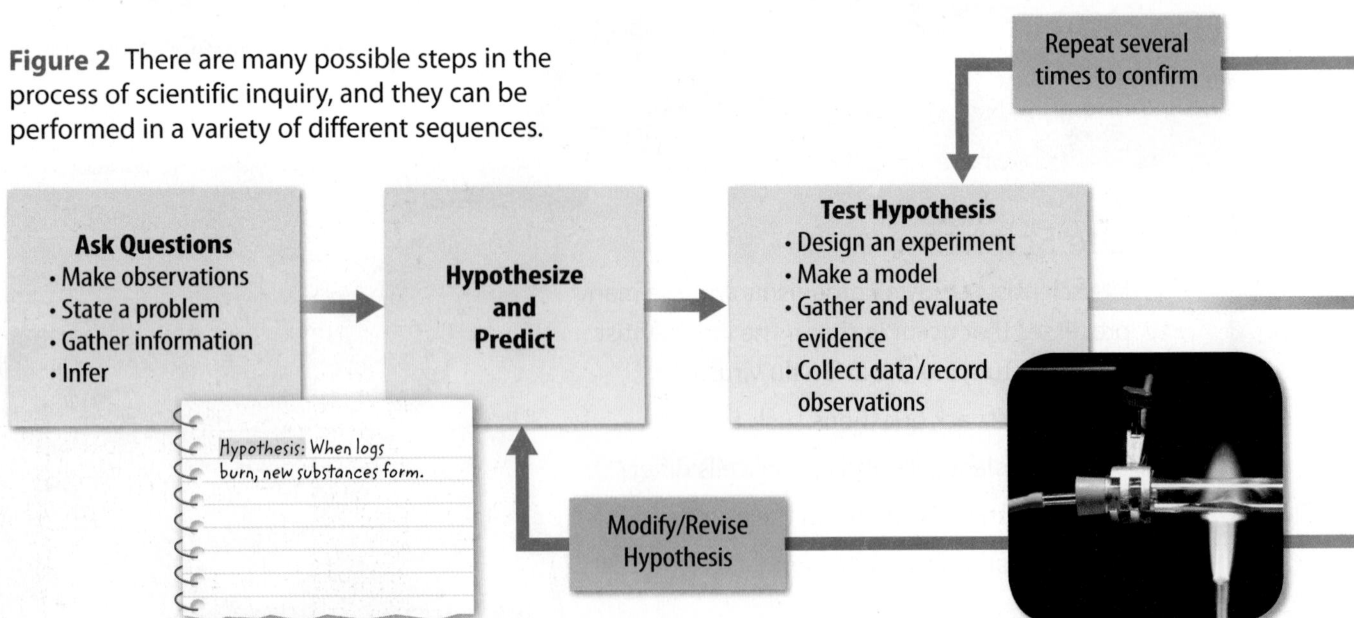

Test Hypothesis and Analyze Results

How could you test your hypothesis? When you test a hypothesis, you often test your predictions. If a prediction is confirmed, then it supports your hypothesis. If your prediction is not confirmed, you might modify your hypothesis and retest it.

To test your predictions and hypothesis, you could design an experiment to find out what substances make up wood. Then you could determine what makes up the ash, the smoke, and other products that formed after the burning process. You also could research this topic and possibly find answers on reliable science Web sites or in science books.

After doing an experiment or research, you need to analyze your results and findings. You might make additional inferences after reviewing your data. If you find that new substances actually do form when wood burns, your hypothesis is supported. If new products do not form, your hypothesis is not supported. Some methods of testing a hypothesis and analyzing results are shown in **Figure 2.**

Draw Conclusions

After analyzing your results, you can begin to draw conclusions about your investigation. A conclusion is a summary of the information gained from testing a hypothesis. Like a scientist does, you should test and retest your hypothesis several times to make sure the results are consistent.

Communicate Results

Sharing the results of a scientific inquiry is an important part of science. By exchanging information, scientists can evaluate and test others' work and make faster progress in their own research. Exchanging information is one way of making scientific advances as quickly as possible and keeping scientific information accurate. During your investigation, if you do research on the Internet or in science books, you use information that someone else communicated. Scientists exchange information in many ways, as shown below in **Figure 2.**

Key Concept Check What are some steps used during scientific inquiry?

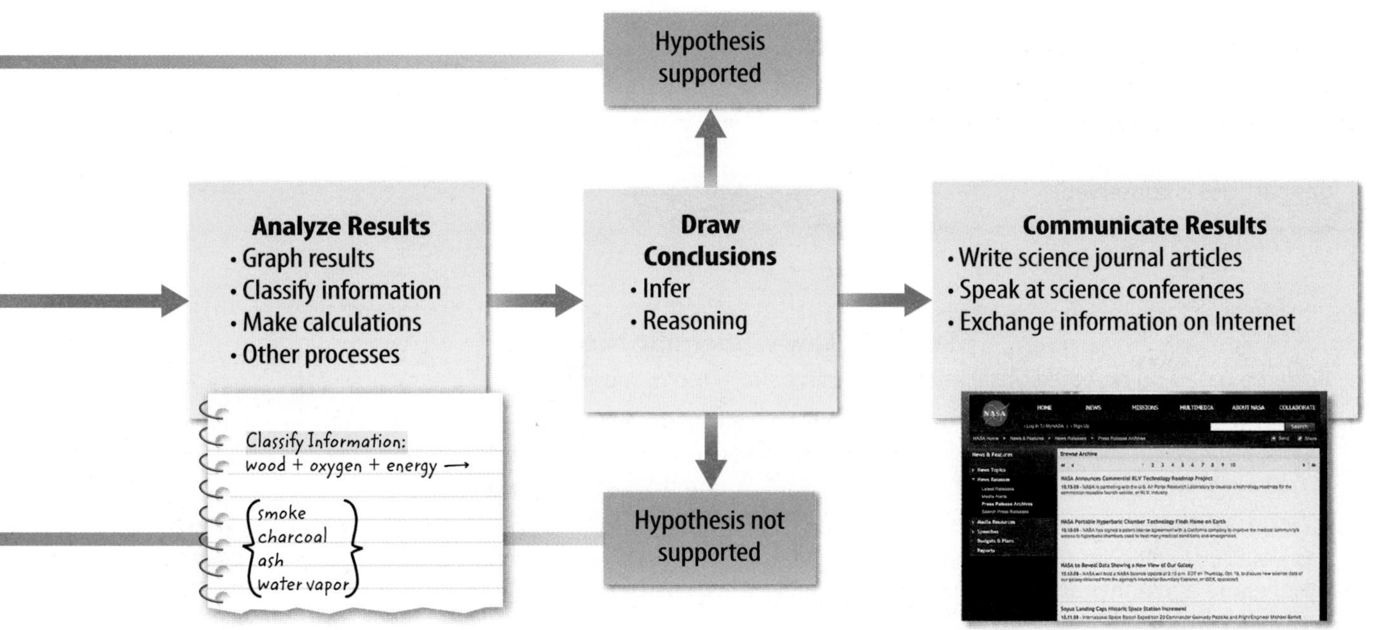

Unsupported or Supported Hypotheses

What happens if a hypothesis is not supported by an investigation? Was the scientific investigation a failure and a waste of time? Absolutely not! Even when a hypothesis is not supported, you gain valuable information. You can revise your hypothesis and test it again. Each time you test a hypothesis, you learn more about the topic you are studying.

Scientific Theory

When a hypothesis (or a group of closely related hypotheses) is supported through many tests over many years, a scientific theory can develop. A **scientific theory** *is an explanation of observations or events that is based on knowledge gained from many observations and investigations.*

A scientific theory does not develop from just one hypothesis, but from many hypotheses that are connected by a common idea. The kinetic molecular theory described below explains the behavior and energy of particles that make up a gas.

Scientific Law

A scientific law is different from a societal law, which is an agreement on a set of behaviors. A **scientific law** *is a rule that describes a repeatable pattern in nature.* A scientific law does not explain why or how the pattern happens, it only states that it will happen. For example, if you drop a ball, it will fall towards the ground every time. This is a repeated pattern that relates to the law of universal gravitation. The law of conservation of energy, described below, is also a scientific law.

Kinetic Molecular Theory

The kinetic molecular theory explains how particles that make up a gas move in constant, random motions. A particle moves in a straight line until it collides with another particle or with the wall of its container.

The kinetic molecular theory also assumes that the collisions of particles in a gas are elastic collisions. An elastic collision is a collision in which no kinetic energy is lost. Therefore, kinetic energy among gas particles is conserved.

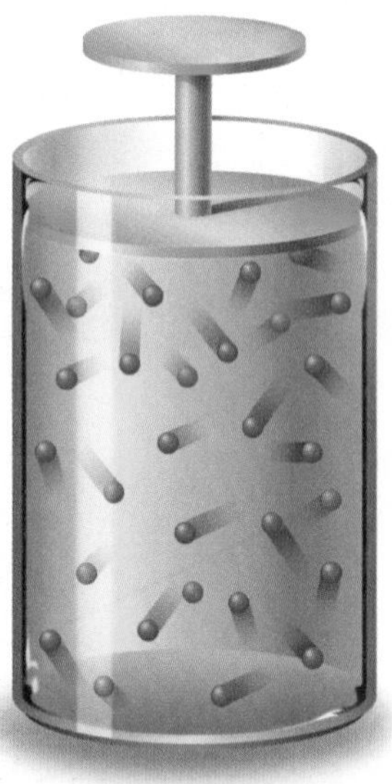

Law of Conservation of Energy

The law of conservation of energy states that in any chemical reaction or physical change, energy is neither created nor destroyed. The total energy of particles before and after collisions is the same.

However, this scientific law, like all scientific laws, does not explain *why* energy is conserved. It simply states that energy *is* conserved.

Scientific Law v. Scientific Theory

Both are based on repeated observations and can be rejected or modified.

A scientific law states that an event *will* occur. For example, energy will be conserved when particles collide. It does not explain why an event will occur or how it will occur. Scientific laws work under specific conditions in nature. A law stands true until an observation is made that does not follow the law.

A scientific theory is an explanation of *why* or *how* an event occurred. For example, collisions of particles of a gas are elastic collisions. Therefore, no kinetic energy is lost. A theory can be rejected or modified if someone observes an event that disproves the theory. A theory will never become a law.

Results of Scientific Inquiry

Why do you and others ask questions and investigate the natural world? Just as scientific questions vary, so do the results of science. Most often, the purpose of a scientific investigation is to develop new materials and technology, discover new objects, or find answers to questions, as shown below.

 **Key Concept Check** What are the results of scientific inquiry?

New Materials and Technology

Every year, corporations and governments spend millions of dollars on research and design of new materials and technologies. **Technology** *is the practical use of scientific knowledge, especially for industrial or commercial use.* For example, scientists hypothesize and predict how new materials will make bicycles and cycling gear lighter, more durable, and more aerodynamic. Using wind tunnels, scientists test these new materials to see whether they improve the cyclist's performance. If the cyclist's performance improves, their hypotheses are supported. If the performance does not improve or it doesn't improve enough, scientists will revise their hypotheses and conduct more tests.

New Objects or Events

Scientific investigations also lead to newly discovered objects or events. For example, NASA's *Hubble Space Telescope* captured this image of two colliding galaxies. They have been nicknamed the mice, because of their long tails. The tails are composed of gases and young, hot blue stars. If computer models are correct, these galaxies will combine in the future and form one large galaxy.

Answers to Questions

Often scientific investigations are launched to answer *who, what, when, where,* or *how* questions. For example, research chemists investigate new substances, such as substances found in mushrooms and bacteria, as shown on the right. New drug treatments for cancer, HIV, and other diseases might be found using new substances. Other scientists look for clues about what causes diseases, whether they can be passed from person to person, and when the disease first appeared.

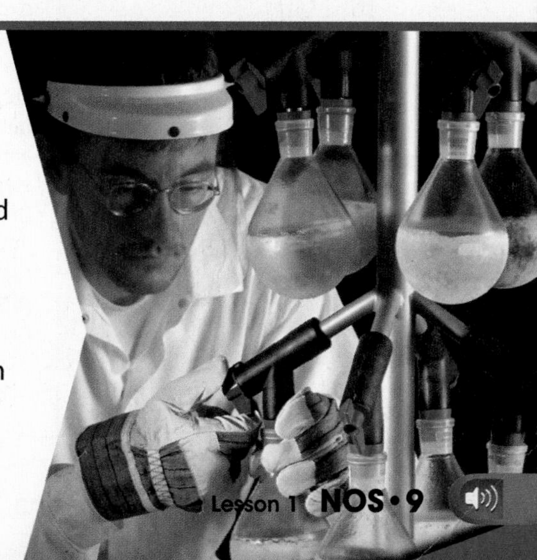

FOLDABLES®

Create a two-tab book and label it as shown. Use it to discuss the importance of evaluating scientific information.

Why is it important to...

...be scientifically literate?	...use critical thinking?

Evaluating Scientific Information

Do you ever you read advertisements, articles, or books that claim to contain scientifically proven information? Are you able to determine if the information is actually true and scientific instead of pseudoscientific (information incorrectly represented as scientific)? Whether you are reading printed media or watching commercials on TV, it is important that you are skeptical, identify facts and opinions, and think critically about the information. **Critical thinking** *is comparing what you already know with the information you are given in order to decide whether you agree with it.*

Key Concept Check What is critical thinking?

Be A Rock Star!

Do you dream of being a rock star?

Sing, dance, and play guitar like a rock star with the new Rocker-rific Spotlight. A new scientific process developed by Rising Star Laboratories allows you to overcome your lack of musical talent and enables you to perform like a real rock star.

This amazing new light actually changes your voice quality and enhances your brain chemistry so that you can sing, dance, and play a guitar like a professional rock star. Now, there is no need to practice or pay for expensive lessons. The Rocker-rific Spotlight does the work for you.

Dr. Sammy Truelove says, "Never before has lack of talent stopped someone from achieving his or her dreams of being a rock star. This scientific breakthrough transforms people with absolutely no talent into amazing rock stars in just minutes. Of the many patients that I have tested with this product, no one has failed to achieve his or her dreams."

Disclaimer: This product was tested on laboratory rats and might not work for everyone.

Skepticism
Have you heard the saying, if it sounds too good to be true, it probably is? To be skeptical is to doubt the truthfulness of something. A scientifically literate person can read information and know that it misrepresents the facts. Science often is self-correcting because someone usually challenges inaccurate information and tests scientific results for accuracy.

Identifying Facts and Misleading Information
Misleading information often is worded to sound like scientific facts. A scientifically literate person can recognize fake claims and quickly determine when information is false.

Critical Thinking
Use critical thinking skills to compare what you know with the new information given to you. If the information does not sound reliable, either research and find more information about the topic or dismiss the information as unreliable.

Identify Opinions
An opinion is a personal view, feeling, or claim about a topic. Opinions cannot be proven true or false. And, an opinion might contain inaccurate information.

Science cannot answer all questions.

It might seem that scientific inquiry is the best way to answer all questions. But there are some questions that science cannot answer. Questions that deal with beliefs, values, personal opinions, and feelings cannot be answered scientifically. This is because it is impossible to collect scientific data on these topics.

Science cannot answer questions such as

- Which video game is the most fun to play?
- Are people kind to others most of the time?
- Is there such a thing as good luck?

Figure 3 Always follow safety procedures when doing scientific investigations. If you have questions, ask your teacher.

Safety in Science

Scientists know that using safe procedures is important in any scientific investigation. When you begin scientific inquiry, you should always wear protective equipment, as shown in **Figure 3.** You also should learn the meaning of safety symbols, listen to your teacher's instructions, and learn to recognize potential hazards. For more information, consult the Science Skills Handbook at the back of this book.

Lesson 1 Review

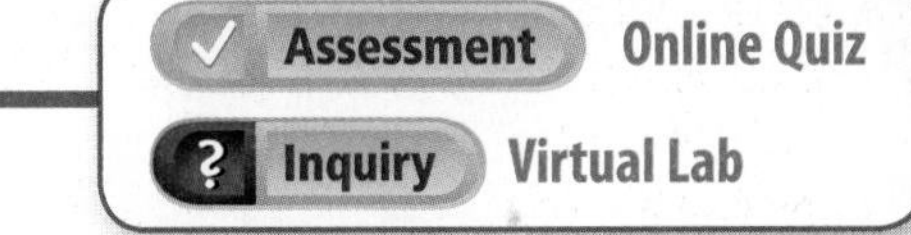

Use Vocabulary

1. **Define** *technology* in your own words.
2. **Use the term** *observation* in a sentence.

Understand Key Concepts 

3. Which action is NOT a way to test a hypothesis?
   A. analyze results
   B. design an experiment
   C. make a model
   D. gather and evaluate evidence
4. **Describe** three examples of the results of scientific inquiry.
5. **Give an example** of a time when you practiced critical thinking.

Interpret Graphics

6. **Compare** Copy and fill in the graphic organizer below. List some examples of how to communicate the results of scientific inquiry.

Critical Thinking

7. **Summarize** Your classmate writes the following as a hypothesis:

   Red is a beautiful color.

   Write a brief explanation to your classmate explaining why this is not a hypothesis.

Science & Engineering

The Design Process

Create a Solution to a Problem

Scientists investigate and explore natural events and then interpret data and share information learned from those investigations. How do engineers differ from scientists? Engineers design, construct, and maintain things that do not occur in nature. Look around. The results of engineering include cell phones, bicycles, contact lenses, roller coasters, computers, cars, and buildings. Science involves the practice of scientific inquiry, but engineering involves The Design Process—a set of methods used to create solutions to problems or needs.

What do a water park and a water tower have in common? Both are designed for a purpose. A water tower is an elevated water container that uses pressure to supply water to buildings. Some water towers even have creative designs. Engineers design water parks to provide entertainment to people. However, engineers must design water parks to meet specific safety regulations.

The Design Process

1. Identify a Problem or Need

Determine a problem or need
- Document all questions, research, and procedures throughout the process

2. Research and Develop Solutions

- Brainstorm possible solutions
- Research any existing solutions that address the problem or need
- Suggest limitations of the solutions

3. Construct a Prototype

- Develop possible solutions
- Estimate materials, costs, resources, and time to develop the solutions
- Select the best possible solution
- Construct a prototype

4. Test and Evaluate Solutions

- Use models to test the solution
- Use graphs, charts, and tables to evaluate results
- Analyze the process and evaluate strengths and weaknesses in solution

5. Communicate Results and Redesign

- Communicate your design process and results to others
- Redesign and modify solution
- Construct final solution

It's Your Turn

Design a Pollution Solution

You are a water-pollution specialist working for Pollution Solutions, Inc. For your job, you travel all over the world, examine various water-pollution problems, and design and engineer devices to solve water-pollution crises. You have just received an urgent call to analyze and solve a water crisis.

Identify the Problem

You know that clean water is essential for life on Earth and that polluted water can cause harm. What is the source of your water crisis? What type of pollution is present? Is it thermal or industrial pollution? Or is it sewage, acid rain, litter, nuclear waste, eutrophication, or underground storage tanks? How can the solution treat the pollution, restore clean water, and protect humans and the environment? How can future pollution be avoided? Record in your Science Journal your problem and questions with possible solutions.

Research Existing Solutions

Begin answering your questions by researching types of water pollution, the sources, and the solutions. Choose one type of water pollution to address in this crisis. Note any limitations to possible solutions, such as cost, size, materials, location, time, or other restraints.

Brainstorm Possible Solutions

Record ideas to develop solutions to water pollution in varying environments and locations. Note materials and equipment necessary for clean water devices. Also include the estimated cost and time of development and construction. Because this has been identified as a crisis, time is very short for developing a solution and constructing an antipollution device.

Construct a Prototype

Draw several plans to address your problem. Use simple materials to construct a scale model of your water-pollution solution. Check the scale of the dimensions of each element for accuracy to guarantee a viable water-pollution solution.

Test and Evaluate Solutions

Test your model to help guarantee an effective and safe solution. Use graphs, charts, and tables to record and evaluate the process and identify strengths and weaknesses in your solutions.

Communicate Your Results and Redesign Your Pollution Solution

Communicate your design process and solution to peers using visual displays and models. Discuss and critique your working pollution solution. Do further research and testing, if necessary. Redesign and modify your solution to meet design objectives. Then, construct a model of your final water-pollution solution.

Lesson 2

Measurement and Scientific Tools

Reading Guide

Key Concepts

ESSENTIAL QUESTIONS

- Why did scientists create the International System of Units (SI)?
- Why is scientific notation a useful tool for scientists?
- How can tools, such as graduated cylinders and triple-beam balances, assist physical scientists?

Vocabulary

description p. NOS 12

explanation p. NOS 12

International System of Units (SI) p. NOS 13

scientific notation p. NOS 15

percent error p. NOS 15

Academic Standards for Science

Covers: 8.NS.3, 8.NS.5, 8.NS.7, 8.NS.8, 8.DP.2, 8.DP.3, 8.DP.4, 8.DP.6, 8.DP.7, 8.DP.11

Description and Explanation

Suppose you work for a company that tests cars to see how they perform during accidents, as shown in **Figure 4.** You might use various scientific tools to measure the acceleration of cars as they crash into other objects.

A **description** *is a spoken or written summary of observations.* The measurements you record are descriptions of the results of the crash tests. Later, your supervisor asks you to write a report that interprets the measurements you took during the crash tests. *An* **explanation** *is an interpretation of observations.* As you write your explanation, you make inferences about why the crashes damaged the vehicles in specific ways.

Notice that there is a difference between a description and an explanation. When you describe something, you report your observations. When you explain something, you interpret your observations.

The International System of Units

Different parts of the world use different systems of measurements. This can cause confusion when people who use different systems communicate their measurements. This confusion was eliminated in 1960 when a new system of measurement was adopted. *The internationally accepted system of measurement is the* **International System of Units (SI).**

Key Concept Check Why did scientists create the International System of Units?

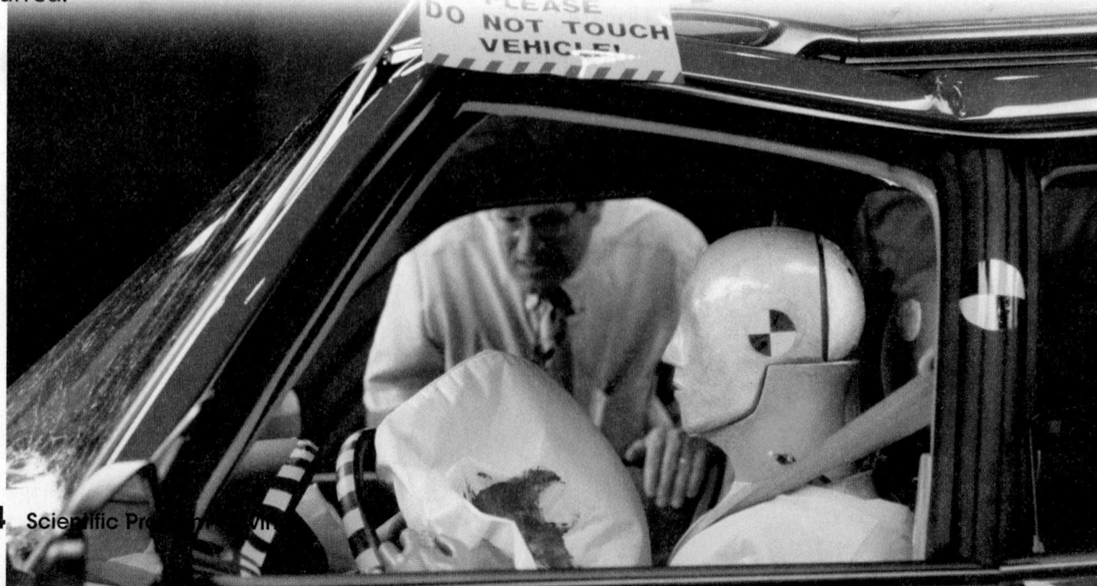

Figure 4 A description of an event details what you observed. An explanation explains why or how the event occurred.

SI Base Units

When you take measurements during scientific investigations and labs in this course, you will use the SI system. The SI system uses standards of measurement, called base units, as shown in **Table 1.** Other units used in the SI system that are not base units are derived from the base units. For example, the liter, used to measure volume, was derived from the base unit for length.

SI Unit Prefixes

In older systems of measurement, there usually was no common factor that related one unit to another. The SI system eliminated this problem.

The SI system is based on multiples of ten. Any SI unit can be converted to another by multiplying by a power of ten. Factors of ten are represented by prefixes, as shown in **Table 2.** For example, the prefix *milli-* means 0.001 or 10^{-3}. So, a milliliter is 0.001 L, or 1/1,000 L. Another way to say this is: 1 L is 1,000 times greater than 1 mL.

Converting Among SI Units

It is easy to convert from one SI unit to another. You either multiply or divide by a factor of ten. You also can use proportion calculations to make conversions. An example of how to convert between SI units is shown in **Figure 5.**

Concepts in Motion Interactive Table

Table 1 SI Base Units

Quantity Measured	Unit (symbol)
Length	meter (m)
Mass	kilogram (kg)
Time	second (s)
Electric current	ampere (A)
Temperature	kelvin (K)
Substance amount	mole (mol)
Light intensity	candela (cd)

Table 2 Prefixes

Prefix	Meaning
Mega- (M)	1,000,000 or (10^6)
Kilo- (k)	1,000 or (10^3)
Hecto- (h)	100 or (10^2)
Deka- (da)	10 or (10^1)
Deci- (d)	0.1 or $\left(\frac{1}{10}\right)$ or (10^{-1})
Centi- (c)	0.01 or $\left(\frac{1}{100}\right)$ or (10^{-2})
Milli- (m)	0.001 or $\left(\frac{1}{1,000}\right)$ or (10^{-3})
Micro- (μ)	0.000001 or $\left(\frac{1}{1,000,000}\right)$ or (10^{-6})

Figure 5 The rock in the photograph has a mass of 17.5 grams. Convert that measurement to kilograms. ▼

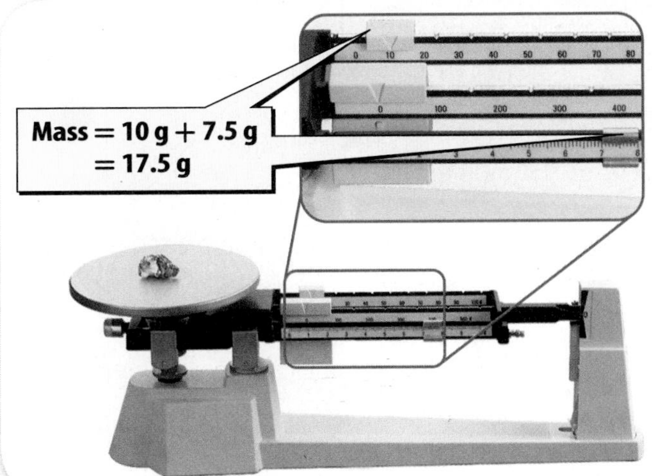

1. Determine the correct relationship between grams and kilograms. There are 1,000 g in 1 kg.

$$\frac{1\text{ kg}}{1{,}000\text{ g}}$$

$$\frac{x}{17.5\text{ g}} = \frac{1\text{ kg}}{1{,}000\text{ g}}$$

$$x = \frac{(17.5\not{g})(1\text{ kg})}{1{,}000\not{g}};\ x = 0.0175\text{ kg}$$

2. Check your units. The unit *grams* divides in the equation, so the answer is 0.0175 kg.

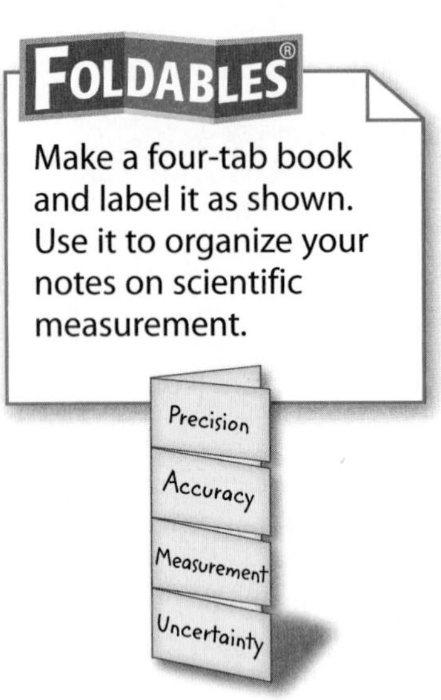
FOLDABLES
Make a four-tab book and label it as shown. Use it to organize your notes on scientific measurement.
Precision
Accuracy
Measurement
Uncertainty

Table 3 Student Density and Error Data
(Accepted value: Density of sodium chloride, 21.7 g/cm³)

	Student A	Student B	Student C
	Density	Density	Density
Trial 1	23.4 g/cm³	18.9 g/cm³	21.9 g/cm³
Trial 2	23.5 g/cm³	27.2 g/cm³	21.4 g/cm³
Trial 3	23.4 g/cm³	29.1 g/cm³	21.3 g/cm³
Mean	23.4 g/cm³	25.1 g/cm³	21.5 g/cm³

Measurement and Uncertainty

You might be familiar with the terms *precision* and *accuracy*. In science, these terms have different meanings. Precision is a description of how similar or close repeated measurements are to each other. Accuracy is a description of how close a measurement is to an accepted value.

The difference between precision and accuracy is illustrated in **Table 3.** Students were asked to find the density of sodium chloride (NaCl). In three trials, each student measured the volume and the mass of NaCl. Then, they calculated the density for each trial and calculated the mean, or average. Student A's measurements are the most precise because they are closest to each other. Student C's measurements are the most accurate because they are closest to the scientifically accepted value. Student B's measurements are neither precise nor accurate. They are not close to each other or to the accepted value.

WORD ORIGIN
notation
from Latin *notationem,* means "a marking or explanation"

Tools and Accuracy

No measuring tool provides a perfect measurement. All measurements have some degree of uncertainty. Some tools or instruments produce more accurate measurements, as shown in **Figure 6.**

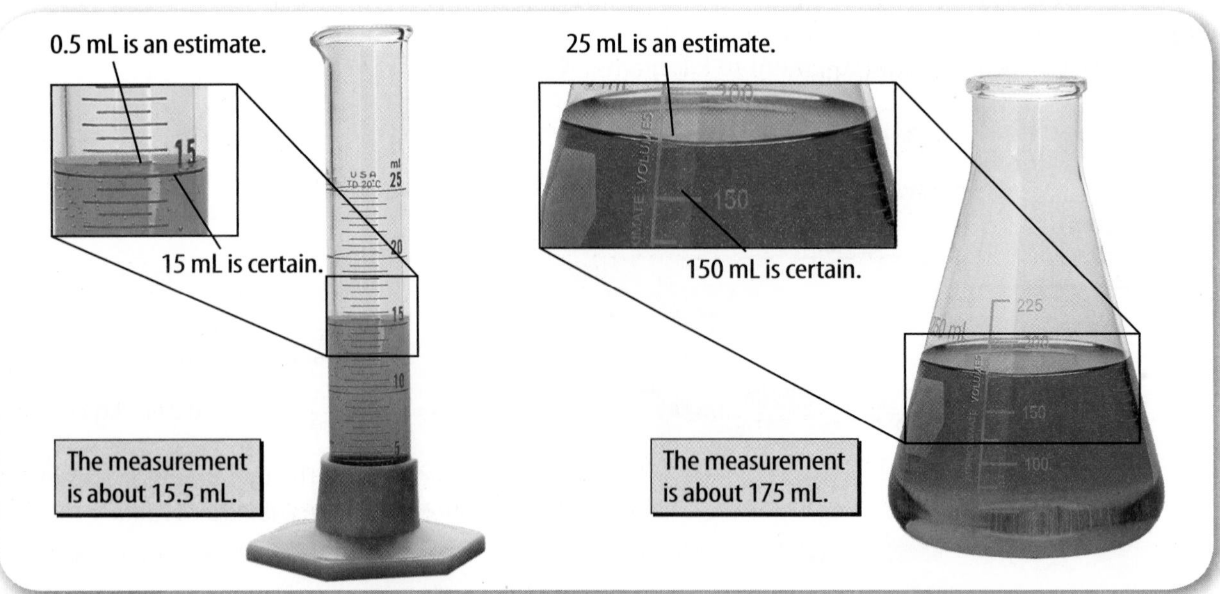
0.5 mL is an estimate.
15 mL is certain.
The measurement is about 15.5 mL.
25 mL is an estimate.
150 mL is certain.
The measurement is about 175 mL.

Figure 6 The graduated cylinder is graduated in 1-mL increments. The beaker is graduated in, or divided into, 50-mL increments. Liquid measurements taken with the graduated cylinder have greater accuracy.

Scientific Notation

Suppose you are writing a report that includes Earth's distance from the Sun—149,600,000 km—and the density of the Sun's lower atmosphere—0.000000028 g/cm^3. These numbers take up too much space in your report, so you use **scientific notation**—*a method of writing or displaying very small or very large numbers in a short form.* To write the numbers above in scientific notation, use the steps in the beige box on the right.

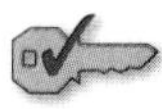
Key Concept Check Why is scientific notation a useful tool for scientists?

Percent Error

The densities recorded in **Table 3** are experimental values because they were calculated during an experiment. Each of these values has some error because the accepted value for table salt density is 21.65 g/cm^3. Percent error can help you determine the size of your experimental error. **Percent error** *is the expression of error as a percentage of the accepted value.*

How to Write in Scientific Notation

1. Write the original number.
   - **A. 149,600,000**
   - **B. 0.000000028**
2. Move the decimal point to the right or the left to make the number between 1 and 10. Count the number of decimal places moved and note the direction.
   - **A. 1.49600000** = 8 places to the left
   - **B. 00000002.8** = 8 places to the right
3. Rewrite the number deleting all extra zeros to the right or to the left of the decimal point.
   - **A. 1.496**
   - **B. 2.8**
4. Write a multiplication symbol and the number *10* with an exponent. The exponent should equal the number of places that you moved the decimal point in step 2. If you moved the decimal point to the left, the exponent is positive. If you moved the decimal point to the right, the exponent is negative.
   - **A.** 1.496×10^8
   - **B.** 2.8×10^{-8}

Math Skills — Percent Error

Solve for Percent Error A student in the laboratory measures the boiling point of water at 97.5°C. If the accepted value for the boiling point of water is 100.0°C, what is the percent error?

1. This is what you know: **experimental value = 97.5°C**; **accepted value = 100.0°C**
2. This is what you need to find: percent error
3. Use this formula:

$$\text{percent error} = \frac{|\textbf{experimental value} - \textbf{accepted value}|}{\textbf{accepted value}} \times 100\%$$

4. Substitute the known values into the equation and perform the calculations

$$\text{percent error} = \frac{|97.5° - 100.0°|}{100.0°} \times 100\% = 2.50\%$$

Review
- **Math Practice**
- **Personal Tutor**

Practice

Calculate the percent error if the experimental value of the density of gold is 18.7 g/cm^3 and the accepted value is 19.3 g/cm^3.

Scientific Tools

As you conduct scientific investigations, you will use tools to make measurements. The tools listed here are some of the tools commonly used in science. For more information about the correct use and safety procedures for these tools, see the Science Skills Handbook at the back of this book.

◀ Science Journal

Use a science journal to record observations, write questions and hypotheses, collect data, and analyze the results of scientific inquiry. All scientists record the information they learn while conducting investigations. Your journal can be a spiral-bound notebook, a loose-leaf binder, or even just a pad of paper.

Balances ▶

A balance is used to measure the mass of an object. Units often used for mass are kilograms (kg), grams (g), and milligrams (mg). Two common types of balances are the electronic balance and the triple-beam balance. In order to get the most accurate measurements when using a balance, it is important to calibrate the balance often.

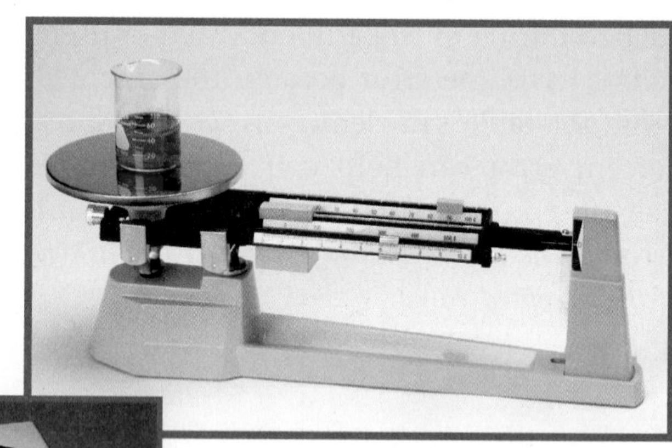

◀ Glassware

Laboratory glassware is used to hold or measure the volume of liquids. Flasks, beakers, test tubes, and graduated cylinders are just some of the different types of glassware available. Volume usually is measured in liters (L) and milliliters (mL).

Thermometers ▶

A thermometer is used to measure the temperature of substances. Although Kelvin is the SI unit of measurement for temperature, in the science classroom, you often measure temperature in degrees Celsius (°C). Never stir a substance with a thermometer because it might break. If a thermometer does break, tell your teacher immediately. Do not touch the broken glass or the liquid inside the thermometer.

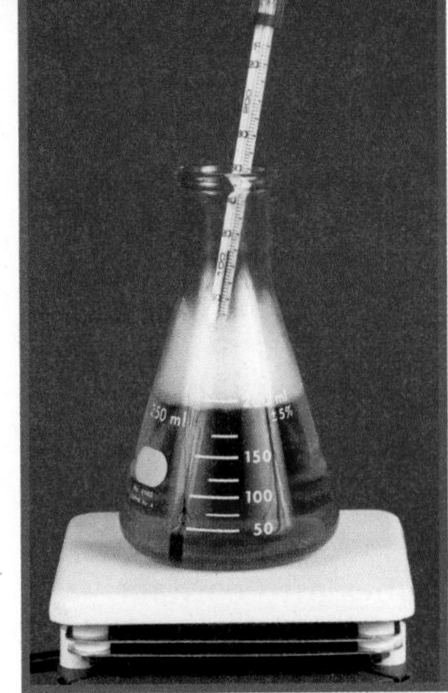

◀ Calculators

A hand-held calculator is a scientific tool that you might use in math class. But you also can use it in the lab and in the field (real situation outside the lab) to make quick calculations using your data.

Computers ▼

For today's students, it is difficult to think of a time when scientists—or anyone—did not use computers in their work. Scientists can collect, compile, and analyze data more quickly using a computer. Scientists use computers to prepare research reports and to share their data and ideas with investigators worldwide.

Hardware refers to the physical components of a computer, such as the monitor and the mouse. Computer software refers to the programs that are run on computers, such as word processing, spreadsheet, and presentation programs.

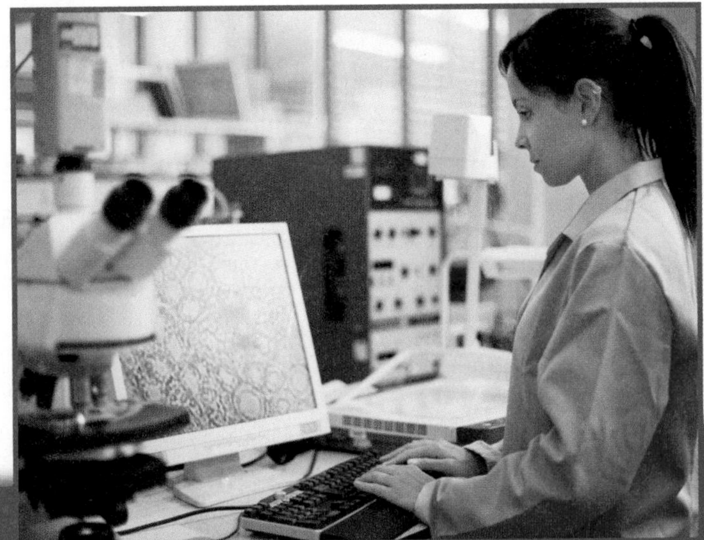

Electronic probes can be attached to computers and handheld calculators to record measurements. There are probes for collecting different kinds of information, such as temperature and the speed of objects.

Key Concept Check How can scientific tools, such as graduated cylinders and triple-beam balances, assist scientists?

Additional Tools Used by Physical Scientists

You can use pH paper to quickly estimate the acidity of a liquid substance. The paper changes color when it comes into contact with an acid or a base.

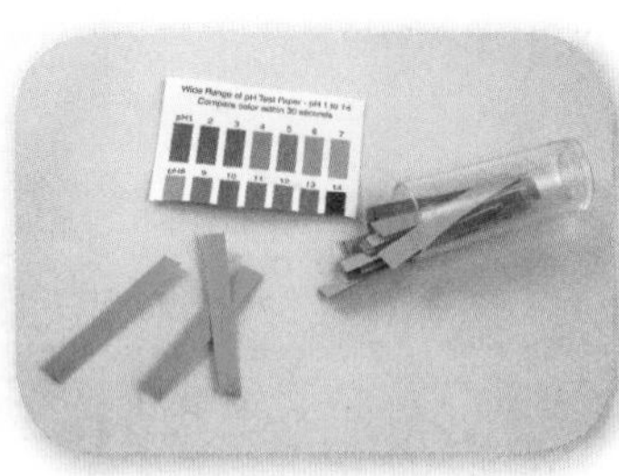

Scientists use stopwatches to measure the time it takes for an event to occur. The SI unit for time is seconds (s). However, for longer events, the units *minutes (min)* and *hours (h)* can be used.

A hot plate is a small heating device that can be placed on a table or desk. Hot plates are used to heat substances in the laboratory.

You use a spring scale to measure the weight or the amount of force applied to an object. The SI unit for weight is the newton (N).

Lesson 2 Review

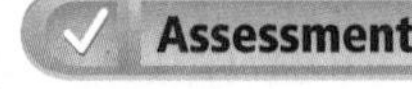

Online Quiz

Use Vocabulary

1. A spoken or written summary of observations is a(n) ________, while a(n) ________ is an interpretation of observations.

Understand Key Concepts

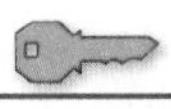

2. Which type of glassware would you use to measure the volume of a liquid?
   A. beaker
   B. flask
   C. graduated cylinder
   D. test tube

3. **Summarize** why a scientist measuring the diameter of an atom or the distance to the Moon would use scientific notation.

4. **Explain** why scientists use the International System of Units (SI).

Interpret Graphics

5. **Identify** Copy and fill in the graphic organizer below listing some scientific tools that you could use to collect data.

Critical Thinking

6. **Explain** why precision and accuracy should be reported in a scientific investigation.

Math Skills

Math Practice

7. Calculate the percent error if the experimental value for the density of zinc is 9.95 g/cm^3. The accepted value is 7.13 g/cm^3.

45 minutes

How do geometric shapes differ in strength?

If you look at a bridge, a building crane, or the framework of a tall building, you will notice that various geometric shapes make up the structure. In this activity, you will observe the strength of several geometric shapes in terms of their rigidity, or resistance to changing their shape.

Materials

plastic straws

scissors

ruler

string

Safety

Learn It

When scientists make hypotheses, they often then **predict** that an event will occur based on their hypothesis.

Try It

1. Read and complete a lab safety form.
2. You are going to construct a triangle and a square using straws. Predict which shape will be more resistant to changing shape and write your prediction in your Science Journal.
3. Measure and cut the straws into seven segments, each 6 cm long.
4. Measure and cut one 20-cm and one 30-cm length of string.
5. Thread the 30-cm length of string through four straw segments. Bend the corners to form a square. Tie the ends of the string together in a double knot to complete the square.
6. Thread the 20-cm string through three of the straw segments. Bend to form a triangle. Tie the ends of the string together to complete the triangle.
7. Test the strength of the square by gently trying to change its shape. Repeat with the triangle. Record your observations.
8. Propose several ways to make the weaker shape stronger. Draw diagrams showing how to modify the shape to make it more rigid.
9. Test your hypothesis. If necessary, refine your hypothesis and retest it. Repeat this step until you make the shape stronger.

Apply It

10. Look at the photograph at to the left. Which of your tested shapes is used the most? Based on your observations, why is this shape used?
11. What modifications made your shape stronger? Why?
12. **Key Concept** How might a scientist use a model to test a hypothesis?

Lesson 3 Case Study

Reading Guide

Key Concepts
ESSENTIAL QUESTIONS

- Why are evaluation and testing important in the design process?
- How is scientific inquiry used in a real-life scientific investigation?

Vocabulary

variable p. NOS 21
constant p. NOS 21
independent variable p. NOS 21
dependent variable p. NOS 21
experimental group p. NOS 21
control group p. NOS 21
qualitative data p. NOS 24
quantitative data p. NOS 24

Academic Standards for Science

Covers: 8.NS.1, 8.NS.4, 8.NS.7, 8.NS.11, 8.DP.1, 8.DP.2, 8.DP.3, 8.DP.4, 8.DP.5, 8.DP.6, 8.DP.7, 8.DP.8, 8.DP.9, 8.DP.10, 8.DP.11

The Minneapolis Bridge Failure

On August 1, 2007, the center section of the Interstate-35W (I-35W) bridge in Minneapolis, Minnesota, suddenly collapsed. A major portion of the bridge fell more than 30 m into the Mississippi River, as shown in **Figure 7.** There were more than 100 cars and trucks on the bridge at the time, including a school bus carrying over 50 students.

The failure of this 8-lane, 581-m long interstate bridge came as a surprise to almost everyone. Drivers do not expect a bridge to drop out from underneath them. The design and engineering processes that bridges undergo are supposed to ensure that bridge failures do not happen.

Controlled Experiments

After the 2007 bridge collapse, investigators had to determine why the bridge failed. To do this, they needed to use scientific inquiry, which you read about in Lesson 1. The investigators designed controlled experiments to help them answer questions and test their hypotheses. A controlled experiment is a scientific investigation that tests how one factor affects another. You might conduct controlled experiments to help discover answers to questions, to test a hypotheses, or to collect data.

Figure 7 A portion of the Interstate-35W bridge in Minneapolis, Minnesota, collapsed in August 2007. Several people were killed, and many more were injured.

Identifying Variables and Constants

When conducting an experiment, you must identify factors that can affect the experiment's outcome. *A* **variable** *is any factor that can have more than one value.* In controlled experiments, there are two kinds of variables. *The* **independent variable** *is the factor that you want to test. It is changed by the investigator to observe how it affects a dependent variable. The* **dependent variable** *is the factor you observe or measure during an experiment.* **Constants** *are the factors in an experiment that do not change.*

You can change the independent variable to observe how it affects the dependent variable. Without constants, two independent variables could change at the same time, and you would not know which variable affected the dependent variable.

Experimental Groups

A controlled experiment usually has at least two groups. *The* **experimental group** *is used to study how a change in the independent variable changes the dependent variable. The* **control group** *contains the same factors as the experimental group, but the independent variable is not changed.* Without a control, it is impossible to know whether your experimental observations result from the variable you are testing or some other factor.

This case study will explore how the investigators used scientific inquiry to determine why the bridge collapsed. Notebooks in the margin identify what a scientist might write in a science journal. The blue boxes contain additional helpful information that you might use.

Simple Beam Bridges

Before you read about the bridge-collapse investigation, think about the structure of bridges. The simplest type of bridge is a beam bridge, as shown in **Figure 8.** This type of bridge has one horizontal beam across two supports. A beam bridge often is constructed across small creeks. A disadvantage of beam bridges is that they tend to sag in the middle if they are too long.

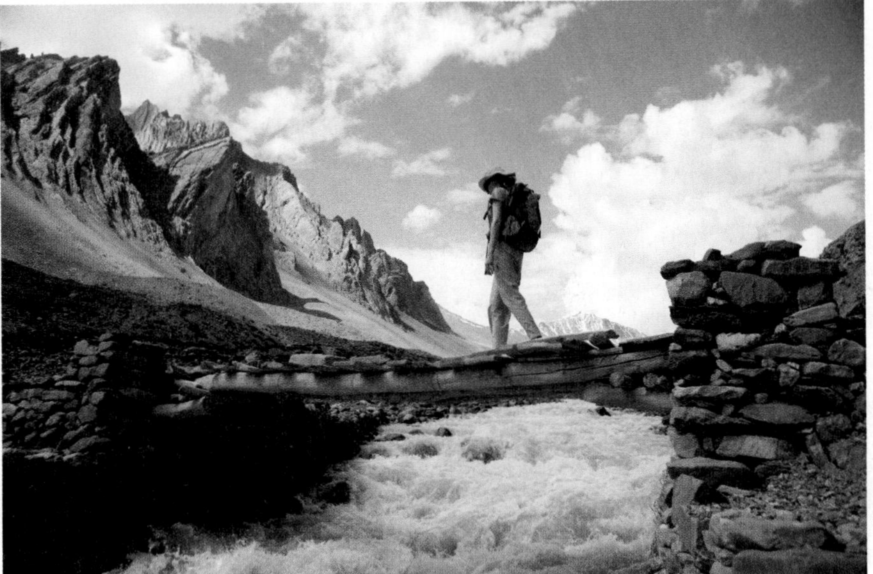

Figure 8 Simple beam bridges span short distances, such as small creeks.

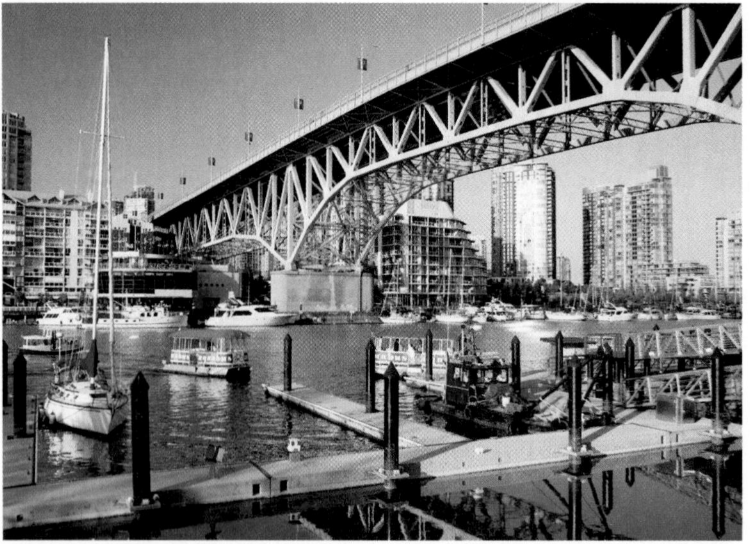

Figure 9 Truss bridges can span long distances and are strengthened by a series of interconnecting triangles called trusses. ▶

Truss Bridges

A truss bridge, shown in **Figure 9,** often spans long distances. This type of bridge is supported only at its two ends, but an assembly of interconnected triangles, or trusses, strengthens it. The I-35W bridge, shown in **Figure 10,** was a truss bridge designed in the early 1960s. The I-35W bridge was designed with straight beams connected to triangular and vertical supports. These supports held up the deck of the bridge, or the roadway. The beams in the bridge's deck and the supports came together at structures known as gusset plates, shown below on the right. These steel plates joined the triangular and vertical truss elements to the overhead roadway beams. These beams ran along the deck of the bridge. This area, where the truss structure connects to the roadway portion of the bridge at a gusset plate, also is called a node.

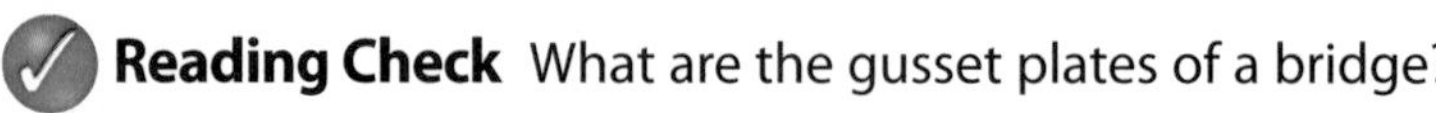

Reading Check What are the gusset plates of a bridge?

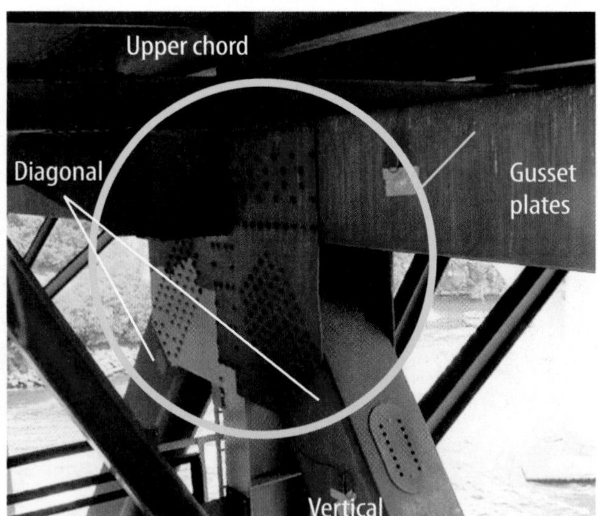

Figure 10 Trusses were a major structural element of the I-35W bridge. The gusset plates at each node in the bridge, shown on the right, are critical pieces that hold the bridge together. ▼

Figure 11 The collapsed bridge was further damaged by rescue workers trying to recover victims of the accident.

Scientists often observe and gather information about an object or an event before proposing a hypothesis. This information is recorded or filed for the investigation.

Observations:
- Recovered parts of the collapsed bridge
- A video showing the sequence of events as the bridge fails and falls into the river

Bridge Failure Observations

After the I-35W bridge collapsed, shown in **Figure 11**, the local sheriff's department handled the initial recovery of the collapsed bridge structure. Finding, freeing, and identifying victims was a high priority, and unintentional damage to the collapsed bridge occurred in the process. However, investigators eventually recovered the entire structure.

The investigators labeled each part with the location where it was found. They also noted the date when they removed each piece. Investigators then moved the pieces to a nearby park. There, they placed the pieces in their relative original positions. Examining the reassembled structure, investigators found physical evidence they needed to determine where the breaks in each section occurred.

The investigators found more clues in a video. A motion-activated security camera recorded the bridge collapse. The video showed about 10 seconds of the collapse, which revealed the sequence of events that destroyed the bridge. Investigators used this video to help pinpoint where the collapse began.

Asking Questions

One or more factors could have caused the bridge to fail. Was the original bridge design faulty? Were bridge maintenance and repair poor or lacking? Was there too much weight on the bridge at the time of the collapse? Each of these questions was studied to determine why the bridge collapsed. Did one or a combination of these factors cause the bridge to fail?

Asking questions and seeking answers to those questions is a way that scientists formulate hypotheses.

When gathering information or collecting data, scientists might perform an experiment, create a model, gather and evaluate evidence, or make calculations.

Qualitative data: A thicker layer of concrete was added to the bridge to reinforce rods.

Quantitative data: The concrete increased the load on the bridge by 13.4 percent.

The modifications in 1998 increased the load on the bridge by 6.1 percent.

At the time of the collapse in 2007, the load on the bridge increased by another 20 percent.

Gathering Information and Data

Investigators reviewed the modifications made to the bridge since it opened in 1967. In 1977, engineers noticed that salt used to deice the bridge during winter weather was causing the reinforcement rods in the roadway to weaken. To protect the rods, engineers applied a thicker layer of concrete to the surface of the bridge roadway. Analysis after the collapse revealed that this extra concrete increased the dead load on the bridge by about 13.4 percent. A load can be a force applied to the structure from the structure itself (dead load) or from temporary loads such as traffic, wind gusts, or earthquakes (live load). Investigators recorded this qualitative and quantitative data. **Qualitative data** *uses words to describe what is observed.* **Quantitative data** *uses numbers to describe what is observed.*

In 1998, additional modifications were made to the bridge. The bridge that was built in the 1960s did not meet current safety standards. Analysis showed that the changes made to the bridge during this renovation further increased the dead load on the bridge by about 6.1 percent.

An Early Hypothesis

At the time of the collapse in 2007, the bridge was undergoing additional renovations. Four piles of sand, four piles of gravel, a water tanker filled with over 11,000 L of water, a cement tanker, a concrete mixer, and other equipment, supplies, and workers were assembled on the bridge. In addition to these renovation materials, normal vehicle traffic was on the bridge. Did these renovations, materials, and traffic overload the bridge, causing the center section to collapse as shown in **Figure 12?** Only a thorough analysis could answer this question.

Figure 12 The center section of the bridge broke away and fell into the river.

A hypothesis is a possible explanation for an observation that can be tested by scientific investigations.

Hypothesis: The bridge failed because it was overloaded.

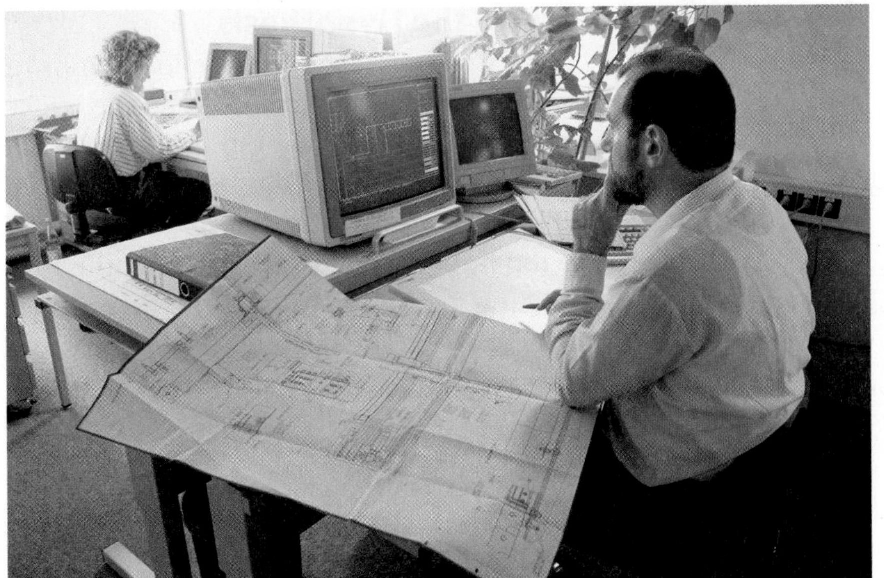

Figure 13 Engineers used computer models to study the structure and loads on the bridge.

Computer Modeling

The analysis of the bridge was conducted using computer-modeling software, as shown in **Figure 13.** Using computer software, investigators entered data from the Minnesota bridge into a computer. The computer performed numerous mathematical calculations. After thorough modeling and analysis, it was determined that the bridge was not overloaded.

Revising the Hypothesis

Evaluations conducted in 1999 and 2003 provided additional clues as to why the bridge might have failed. As part of the study, investigators took numerous pictures of the bridge structure. The photos revealed bowing of the gusset plates at the eleventh node from the south end of the bridge. Investigators labeled this node *U10.* Gusset plates are designed to be stronger than the structural parts they connect. It is possible that the bowing of the plates indicated a problem with the gusset plate design. Previous inspectors and engineers missed this warning sign.

Hypothesis:
~~1. The bridge failed because it was overloaded.~~
2. The gusset plates failed, which lead to the bridge collapse.

The accident investigators found that some recovered gusset plates were fractured, while others were not damaged. If the bridge had been properly constructed, none of the plates should have failed. But inspection showed that some of the plates failed very early in the collapse.

After evaluating the evidence, the accident investigators formulated the hypothesis that the gusset plates failed, which lead to the bridge collapse. Now investigators had to test this hypothesis.

Test the Hypothesis:

- Compare the load on the bridge when it collapsed with the load limits of the bridge at each of the main gusset plates.
- Determine the demand-to-capacity ratios for the main gusset plates.
- Calculate the appropriate thicknesses of the U10 gusset plates.

Independent Variables: actual load on bridge and load bridge was designed to handle

Dependent Variable: demand-to-capacity ratio

Testing the Hypothesis

The investigators knew the load limits of the bridge. To calculate the load on the bridge when it collapsed, they estimated the combined weight of the bridge and the traffic on the bridge. The investigators divided the load on the bridge when it collapsed by the load limits of the bridge to find the demand-to-capacity ratio. The demand-to-capacity ratio provides a measure of a structure's safety.

Analyzing Results

As investigators calculated the demand-to-capacity ratios for each of the main gusset plates, they found that the ratios were particularly high for the U10 node. The U10 plate, shown in **Figure 14,** failed earliest in the bridge collapse. **Table 4** shows the demand-to-capacity ratios for a few of the gusset plates at some nodes. A value greater than 1 means the structure is unsafe. Notice how high the ratios are for the U10 gusset plate compared to the other plates.

Further calculations showed that the U10 plates were not thick enough to support the loads they were supposed to handle. They were about half the thickness they should have been.

Key Concept Check Why are evaluation and testing important in the design process?

Figure 14 The steel plates, or gusset plates, at the U10 node were too thin for the loads the bridge carried.

Table 4 Node-Gusset Plate Analysis

Gusset Plate	Thickness (cm)	Demand-to-Capacity Ratios for the Upper-Node Gusset Plates					
		Horizontal loads			Vertical loads		
U8	3.5	0.05	0.03	0.07	0.31	0.46	0.20
U10	1.3	1.81	1.54	1.83	1.70	1.46	1.69
U12	2.5	0.11	0.11	0.10	0.71	0.37	1.15

Drawing Conclusions

Over the years, modifications to the I-35W bridge added more load to the bridge. On the day of the accident, traffic and the concentration of construction vehicles and materials added still more load. Investigators concluded that if the U10 gusset plates were properly designed, they would have supported the added load. When the investigators examined the original records for the bridge, they were unable to find any detailed gusset plate specifications. They could not determine whether undersized plates were used because of a mistaken calculation or some other error in the design process. The only thing that they could conclude with certainty was that undersized gusset plates could not reliably hold up the bridge.

The Federal Highway Administration and the National Transportation Safety Board published the results of their investigations. These published reports now provide scientists and engineers with valuable information they can use in future bridge designs. These reports are good examples of why it is important for scientists and engineers to publish their results and to share information.

Analyzing Results: The U10 gusset plates should have been twice as thick as they were to support the bridge.

Conclusions: The bridge failed because the gusset plates were not properly designed and they could not carry the load that they were supposed to carry.

Key Concept Check Give three examples of the scientific inquiry process that was used in this investigation.

Lesson 3 Review

Assessment Online Quiz

Use Vocabulary

1. **Distinguish** between qualitative data and quantitative data.
2. **Contrast** *variable, independent variable,* and *dependent variable.*

Understand Key Concepts

3. Constants are necessary in a controlled experiment because, without constants, you would not know which variable affected the
   A. control group.
   B. experimental group.
   C. dependent variable.
   D. independent variable.
4. **Give an example** of a situation in your life in which you depend on adequate testing and evaluation in a product design to keep you safe.

Interpret Graphics

5. **Summarize** Copy and fill in the flow chart below and summarize the sequence of scientific inquiry steps that was used in one part of the case study.

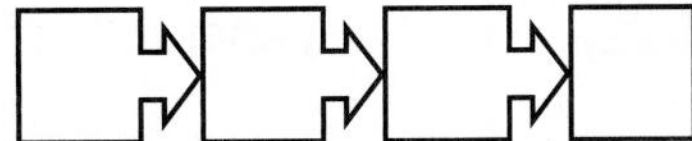

Critical Thinking

6. **Analyze** how the scientific inquiry process differs when engineers design a product, such as a bridge, and when they investigate design failure.
7. **Evaluate** why the gusset plates were such a critical piece in the bridge design.
8. **Recommend** ways that bridge designers and inspectors can prevent future bridge collapses.

1–2 class periods

Build and Test a Bridge

Materials

plastic straws

ruler

scissors

cotton string

cardboard

Also needed: notebook paper, books or other masses, balance (with a capacity of at least 2 kg)

Safety

In the Skill lab, you observed the relative strengths of two different geometric shapes. In the case study about the bridge collapse, you learned how scientists used scientific inquiry to determine the cause of the bridge collapse. In this investigation, you will combine geometric shapes to build model bridge supports. Then you will use scientific inquiry to determine the maximum load that your bridge will hold.

Ask a Question

What placement of supports produces the strongest bridge?

Make Observations

1. Read and complete a lab safety form.
2. Cut the straws into 24 6-cm segments.
3. Thread three straw segments onto a 1-m piece of string. Slide the segments toward one end of the string. Double knot the string to form a triangle. There should be very little string showing between the segments.
4. Thread the long end of the remaining string through two more straw segments. Double knot the string to one unattached corner to form another triangle. Cut off the remaining string, leaving at least a 1 cm after the knot. Use the string and one more straw segment to form a tetrahedron, as shown below.
5. Use the remaining string and straw segments to build three more tetrahedrons.
6. Set the four tetrahedrons on a piece of paper. They will serve as supports for your bridge deck, a 20-cm x 30-cm piece of cardboard.
7. With your teammates, decide where you will place the tetrahedrons on the paper to best support a load placed on the bridge deck.

Form a Hypothesis

8. Form a hypothesis about where you will place your tetrahedrons and why that placement will support the most weight. Recall that a hypothesis is an explanation of an observation.

Test Your Hypothesis

9. Test your hypothesis by placing the tetrahedrons in your chosen locations on the paper. Lay the cardboard "bridge deck" over the top.
10. Use a balance to find the mass of a textbook. Record the mass in your Science Journal.
11. Gently place the textbook on the bridge deck. Continue to add massed objects until your bridge collapses. Record the total mass that collapsed the bridge.
12. Examine the deck and supports. Look for possible causes of bridge failure.

Analyze and Conclude

13. **Analyze** Was your hypothesis supported? How do you know?
14. **Compare and Contrast** Study the pictures of bridges in Lesson 3. How does the failure of your bridge compare to the failure of the I-35W bridge?
15. **The Big Idea** What steps of scientific inquiry did you use in this activity? What would you do next to figure out how to make a stronger bridge?

Communicate Your Results

Compare your results with those of several other teams. Discuss the placement of your supports and any other factors that may cause your bridge to fail.

Extension

Try building your supports with straw segments that are shorter (4 cm long) and longer (8 cm long). Test your bridges in the same way with each size of support.

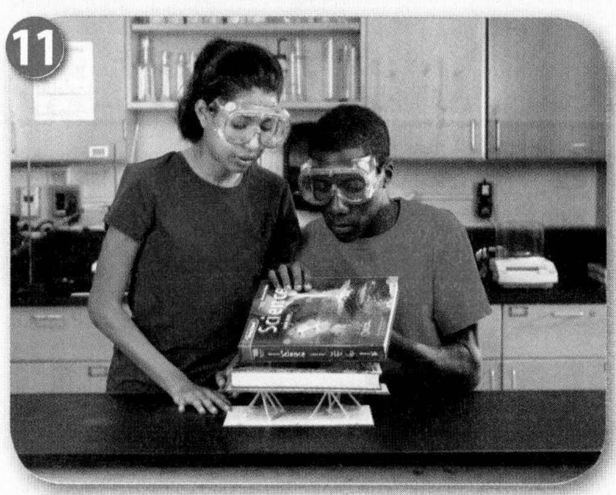

11

Lab Tips

- ☑ When building your tetrahedrons, make sure to double knot all connections and pull them tight. When you are finished, test each tetrahedron by pressing lightly on the top point.
- ☑ When adding the books to the bridge deck, place the books gently on top of the pile. Do not drop them.

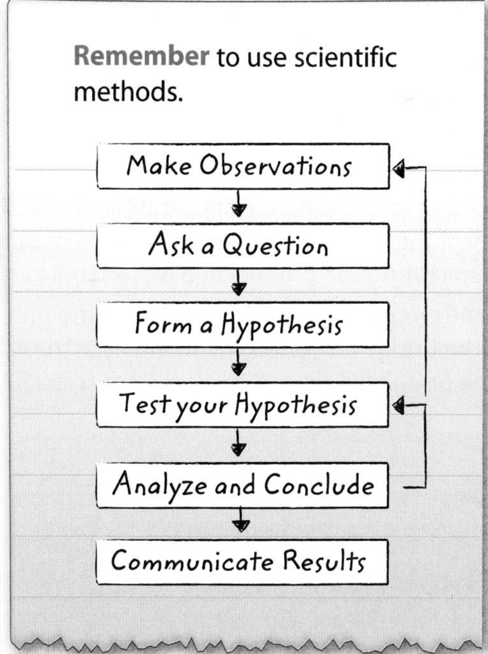

Study Guide and Review

Scientific inquiry is a collection of methods that scientists use in different combinations to perform scientific investigations.

Key Concepts Summary

Lesson 1: Scientific Inquiry

- Some steps used during scientific inquiry are making **observations** and **inferences,** developing a **hypothesis,** analyzing results, and drawing conclusions. These steps, among others, can be performed in any order.
- There are many results of scientific inquiry, and a few possible outcomes are the development of new materials and new technology, the discovery of new objects and events, and answers to basic questions.
- **Critical thinking** is comparing what you already know about something to new information and deciding whether or not you agree with the new information.

Vocabulary

science p. NOS 4
observation p. NOS 6
inference p. NOS 6
hypothesis p. NOS 6
prediction p. NOS 6
scientific theory p. NOS 8
scientific law p. NOS 8
technology p. NOS 9
critical thinking p. NOS 10

Lesson 2: Measurement and Scientific Tools

- Scientists developed one universal system of units, the **International System of Units (SI),** to improve communication among scientists.
- **Scientific notation** is a useful tool for writing large and small numbers in a shorter form.
- Tools such as graduated cylinders and triple-beam balances make scientific investigation easier, more accurate, and repeatable.

Vocabulary

description p. NOS 12
explanation p. NOS 12
International System of Units (SI) p. NOS 12
scientific notation p. NOS 15
percent error p. NOS 15

Lesson 3: Case Study—The Minneapolis Bridge Failure

- Evaluation and testing are important in the design process for the safety of the consumer and to keep costs of building or manufacturing the product at a reasonable level.
- Scientific inquiry was used throughout the process of determining why the bridge collapsed, including hypothesizing potential reasons for the bridge failure and testing those hypotheses.

Vocabulary

variable p. NOS 21
independent variable p. NOS 21
dependent variable p. NOS 21
constants p. NOS 21
qualitative data p. NOS 21
quantitative data p. NOS 21
experimental group p. NOS 24
control group p. NOS 24

Use Vocabulary

1. The ________ contains the same factors as the experimental group, but the independent variable is not changed.
2. The expression of error as a percentage of the accepted value is ________.
3. The process of studying nature at all levels and the collection of information that is accumulated is ________.
4. The ________ are the factors in the experiment that stay the same.

Understand Key Concepts 

5 Which is NOT an SI base unit?

A. kilogram

B. liter

C. meter

D. second

6 While analyzing results from an investigation, a scientist calculates a very small number that he or she wants to make easier to use. Which does the scientist use to record the number?

A. explanation

B. inference

C. scientific notation

D. scientific theory

7 Which is NOT true of a scientific law?

A. It can be modified or rejected.

B. It states that an event will occur.

C. It explains why an event will occur.

D. It is based on repeated observations.

8 Which tool would a scientist use to find the mass of a small steel rod?

A. balance

B. computer

C. hot plate

D. thermometer

Critical Thinking

9 **Write** a brief description of the activity shown in the photo.

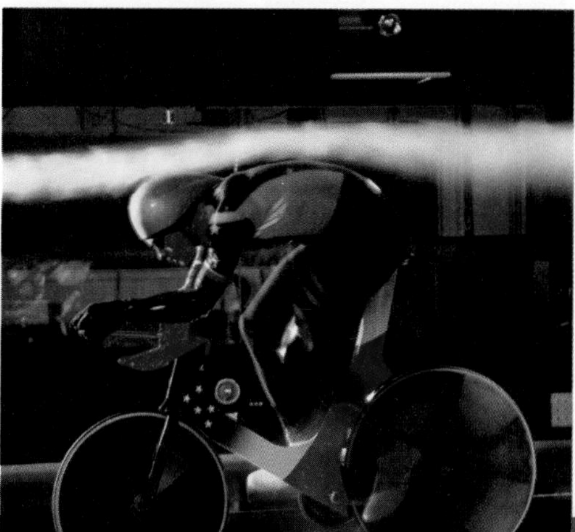

Writing in Science

10 **Write** a five-sentence paragraph that gives examples of how critical thinking, skepticism, and identifying facts and opinions can help you in your everyday life. Be sure to include a topic sentence and concluding sentence in your paragraph.

REVIEW THE BIG IDEA

11 What is scientific inquiry? Explain why it is a constantly changing process.

12 Which part of scientific inquiry does this photo demonstrate?

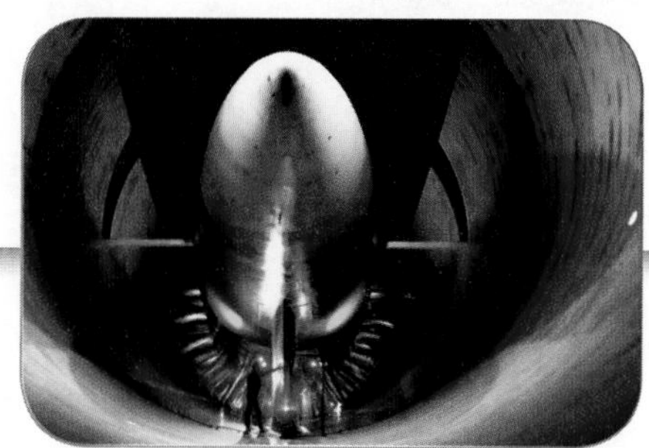

Math Skills

Review
Math Practice

13 The accepted scientific value for the density of sucrose is 1.59 g/cm^3. You perform three trials to measure the density of sucrose, and your data is shown in the table below. Calculate the percent error for each trial.

Trial	Density	Percent Error
Trial 1	1.55 g/cm^3	
Trial 2	1.60 g/cm^3	
Trial 3	1.58 g/cm^3	

Unit 1 Properties of Matter

Sent to her room, Molly Cool dreams of escaping.
If only she could change state and become a liquid, she could flow under the bedroom door and down the stairs...
...then flow to the fireplace where the heat would turn her into vapor and she could escape up the chimney.
I'm free!
Hello birds!

1000 B.C. 1700 1800

350 B.C.
Greek philosopher Aristotle defines an element as "one of those bodies into which other bodies can decompose, and that itself is not capable of being divided into another."

1704
Isaac Newton proposes that atoms attach to each other by some type of force.

1869
Dmitri Mendeleev publishes the first version of the periodic table.

1874
G. Johnstone Stoney proposes the existence of the electron, a subatomic particle that carries a negative electric charge, after experiments in electrochemistry.

1897
J.J. Thompson demonstrates the existence of the electron, proving Stoney's claim.

Look at all the houses!
Dinner tiiiime!
By changing state once more to become plasma, she could be back in time for dinner...
...And no one would ever know!

1900

1950

1907
Physicists Hans Geiger and Ernest Marsden, under the direction of Ernest Rutherford, conduct the famous gold foil experiment. Rutherford concludes that the atom is mostly empty space and that most of the mass is concentrated in the atomic nucleus.

1918
Ernest Rutherford reports that the hydrogen nucleus has a positive charge, and he names it the proton.

1932
James Chadwick discovers the neutron, a subatomic particle with no electric charge and a mass slightly larger than a proton.

Inquiry
Visit ConnectED for this unit's STEM activity.

Technology

Figure 1 Nature cannot easily recycle many human-made materials. Much of our trash remains in landfills for years. Scientists are developing materials that degrade quickly. This will help decrease the amount of pollution..

Scientists use technology to develop materials with desirable properties. **Technology** is the practical use of scientific knowledge, especially for industrial or commercial use. In the late 1800s, scientists developed the first plastic material, called celluloid, from cotton. Celluloid quickly gained popularity for use as photographic film. In the 20th century, scientists developed other plastic materials, such as polystyrene, rayon, and nylon. These new materials were inexpensive, durable, lightweight, and could be molded into any shape.

New technologies can come with problems. For example, many plastics are made from petroleum and contain harmful chemicals. The high pressures and temperatures needed to produce plastics require large amounts of energy. Bacteria and fungi that easily break down natural materials do not easily decompose plastics. Often, plastics accumulate in landfills where they can remain for hundreds, or even thousands, of years, as shown in **Figure 1.**

Types of Materials

Figure 2 Some organisms produce materials with properties that are useful to people. Scientists are trying to replicate these materials for new technologies.

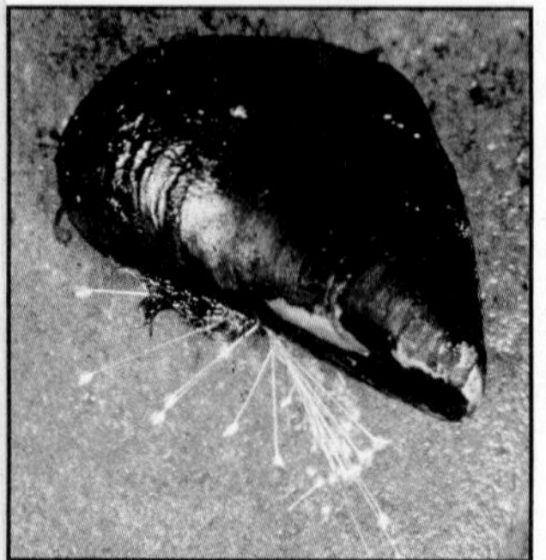

◀ Most human-made adhesives attach to some surfaces, but not others. Mussels, which are similar to clams, produce a "superglue" that is stronger than anything people can make. It also works on any surface, wet or dry. Chemists are trying to develop a technology that will replicate the mussel glue. This glue would provide solutions to difficult problems: Ships could be repaired under water. The glue also would work on teeth and could be used to set broken bones.

Abalone and other mollusks construct a protective shell from proteins and seawater. The material is four times stronger than human-made metal alloys and ceramics. Using technology, scientists are working to duplicate this material. They hope to use the new product in many ways, including hip and elbow replacements. Automakers could use these strong, lightweight materials for automobile body panels. ▶

Consider the Possibilities!

Chemists are looking to nature for ideas for new materials. For example, some sea sponges have skeletons that beam light deep inside the animal, similar to the way fiber-optic cables work. A bacterium from a snail-like nudibranch contains compounds that stop other sea creatures from growing on the nudibranch's back. These compounds could be used in paints to stop creatures from forming a harmful crust on submerged parts of boats and docks. Chrysanthemum flowers produce a product that keeps ticks and mosquitoes away. **Figure 2** includes other organisms that produce materials with remarkable properties.

Chemists and biologists are teaming up to understand, and hopefully replicate, the processes that organisms use to survive. Hopefully, these process can lead to technologies and materials with unique properties that are helpful to people.

MiniLab

15 minutes

How would you use it?

How would you use an adhesive that could stick to any surface? Invent a new purpose for mussel "superglue"!

1. Work with a partner to develop three tasks that could be accomplished using products produced by an organism.
2. Select one of your ideas, and develop it into an invention. Draw pictures of your new invention and explain how it works.
3. Write an advertisement for your invention including a description of the role of the material from nature used in your product.

Analyze and Conclude

1. **Explain** What task or problem did your invention solve?
2. **Infer** How did a material from an organism help you develop your invention?

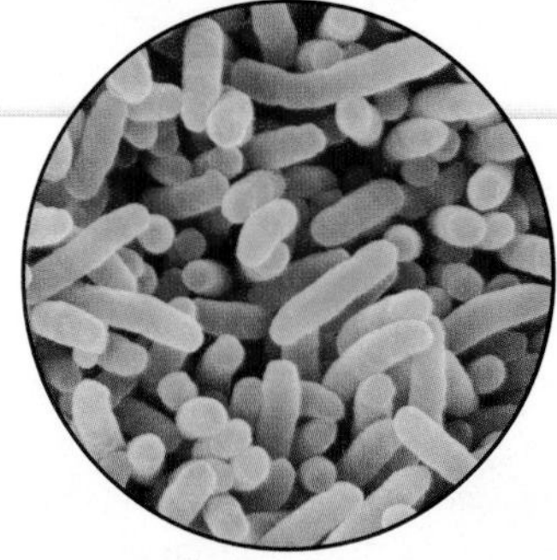

◀ A British company has developed bacteria that produce large amounts of hydrogen gas when fed a diet of sugar. Chemists are working to produce tanks of these microorganisms that produce enough hydrogen to replace other fuels used to heat homes. Bacteria may become the power plants of the future.

Under a microscope, the horn of a rhinoceros looks much like the material used to make the wings of a Stealth aircraft. However, the rhino horn is self-healing. Picture a car with technologically advanced fenders similar to the horn of a rhinoceros; such a car could repair itself if it were in a fender-bender! ▶

◀ Spider silk begins as a liquid inside the spider's body. When ejected through openings, called spinnerets, it becomes similar to a plastic thread. However, its properties include strength five times greater than steel, stretchability greater than nylon, and toughness better than the material in bulletproof vests! Chemists are using technology to make a synthetic spider silk. They hope to someday use the material for cables strong enough to support a bridge or as reinforcing fibers in aircraft bodies some day.

Chapter 1

Matter and Atoms

THE BIG IDEA **How does the classification of matter depend on atoms?**

Inquiry Tiny Parts?

From a distance, you might think this looks like a normal picture, but what happens when you look closely? Tiny photographs arranged in a specific way make a new image that looks very different from the individual pictures. The new image depends on the parts and the way they are arranged. Similarly, all the matter around you depends on its parts and the way they are arranged.

- How would the image be different if the individual pictures were arranged in another way?
- How does the image depend on the individual parts?

Get Ready to Read

What do you think?

Before you read, decide if you agree or disagree with each of these statements. As you read this chapter, see if you change your mind about any of the statements.

1. Things that have no mass are not matter.
2. The arrangement of particles is the same throughout a mixture.
3. An atom that makes up gold is exactly the same as an atom that makes up aluminum.
4. An atom is mostly empty space.
5. If an atom gains electrons, the atom will have a positive charge.
6. Each electron is a cloud of charge that surrounds the center of an atom.

Your one-stop online resource

connectED.mcgraw-hill.com

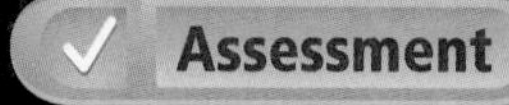

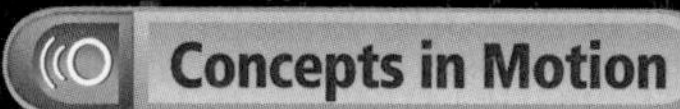

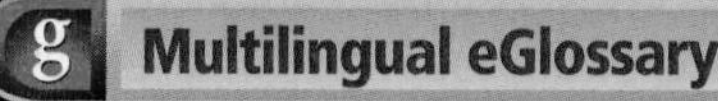

Lesson 1

Reading Guide

Key Concepts
ESSENTIAL QUESTIONS

- What is the relationship among atoms, elements, and compounds?
- How are some mixtures different from solutions?
- How do mixtures and compounds differ?

Vocabulary

matter p. 9
atom p. 9
substance p. 10
element p. 11
molecule p. 11
compound p. 12
mixture p. 14
heterogeneous mixture p. 15
homogeneous mixture p. 16

Multilingual eGlossary

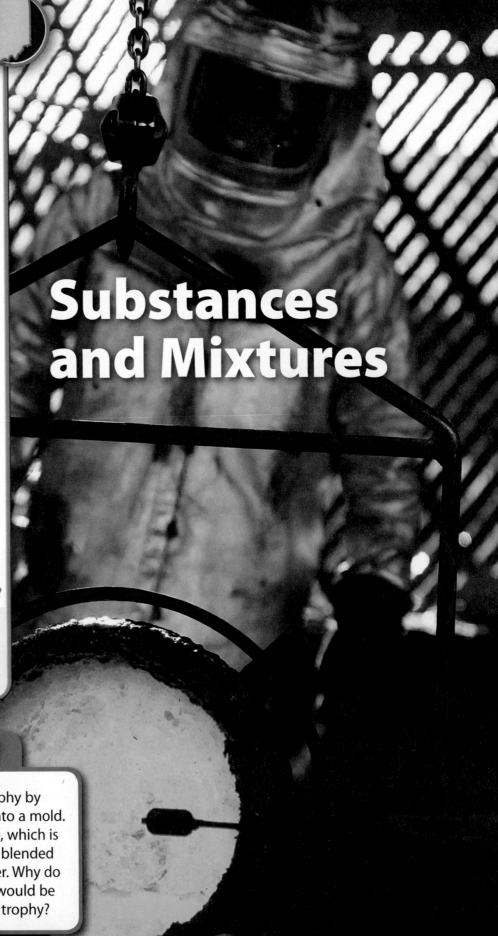

Video

- BrainPOP®
- What's Science Got to do With It?

Academic Standards for Science

Covers: 8.1.1, 8.1.5, 8.4.3, 8.NS.1, 8.NS.7, 8.NS.8, 8.NS.10

Substances and Mixtures

Inquiry Is it pure?

This worker is making a trophy by pouring hot, liquid metal into a mold. The molten metal is bronze, which is a mixture of several metals blended to make the trophy stronger. Why do you think a bronze trophy would be stronger than a pure metal trophy?

Launch Lab

10 minutes

Can you always see the parts of materials?

If you eat a pizza, you can see the cheese, the pepperoni, and the other parts it is made from. Can you always see the individual parts when you mix materials?

1. Read and complete a lab safety form.
2. Observe the **materials** at the eight stations your teacher has set up.
3. Record in your Science Journal the name and a short description of each material.

Think About This

1. **Classify** Which materials have easily identifiable parts?
2. **Key Concept** Is it always easy to see the parts of materials that are mixed? Explain.

What is matter?

Imagine how much fun it would be to go windsurfing! As the force of the wind pushes the sail, you lean back to balance the board. You feel the heat of the Sun and the spray of water against your face. Whether you are windsurfing on a lake or sitting at your desk in a classroom, everything around you is made of matter. **Matter** *is anything that has mass and takes up space.* Matter is everything you can see, such as water and trees. It is also some things you cannot see, such as air. You know that air is matter because you can feel its mass when it blows against your skin. You can see that it takes up space when it inflates a sail or a balloon.

Anything that does not have mass or volume is not matter. Types of energy, such as heat, sound, and electricity, are not matter. Forces, such as magnetism and gravity, also are not forms of matter.

What is matter made of?

The matter around you, including all solids, liquids, and gases, is made of atoms. *An* **atom** *is a small particle that is the building block of matter.* In this chapter, you will read that an atom is made of even smaller particles. There are many types of atoms. Each type of atom has a different number of smaller particles. You also will read that atoms can combine with each other in many ways. It is the many kinds of atoms and the ways they combine that form the different types of matter.

Reading Check Why are there so many types of matter?

WORD ORIGIN

atom
from Greek *atomos*, means "uncut"

Figure 1 You can classify matter as a substance or a mixture. ▼

Matter
- Anything that has mass and takes up space
- Most matter is made up of atoms.

Substances
- Matter with a composition that is always the same

Mixtures
- Matter that can vary in composition

Classifying Matter

Because all the different types of matter around you are made of atoms, they must have characteristics in common. But why do all types of matter look and feel different? How is the matter that makes up a pure gold ring similar to the matter that makes up your favorite soda or even the matter that makes up your body? How are these types of matter different?

As the chart in **Figure 1** shows, scientists place matter into one of two groups—substances or mixtures. Pure gold is in one group. Soda and your body are in the other. What determines whether a type of matter is a substance or a mixture? The difference is in the composition.

What is a substance?

What is the difference between a gold ring and a can of soda? What is the difference between table salt and trail mix? Pure gold is always made up of the same type of atom, but soda is not. Similarly, table salt, or sodium chloride, is always made up of the same types of atoms, but trail mix is not. This is because sodium chloride and gold are substances. *A* **substance** *is matter with a composition that is always the same.* A certain substance always contains the same kinds of atoms in the same combination. Soda and trail mix are another type of matter that you will read about later in this lesson.

Because gold is a substance, anything that is pure gold will have the same composition. Bars of gold are made of the same atoms as those in a pure gold ring, as shown in **Figure 2.** And, since sodium chloride is a substance, if you are salting your food in Alaska or in Ohio, the atoms that make up the salt will be the same. If the composition of a given substance changes, you will have a new substance.

 **Reading Check** Why is gold classified as a substance?

Figure 2 A substance always contains the same kinds of atoms bonded in the same way. ▼

Substances

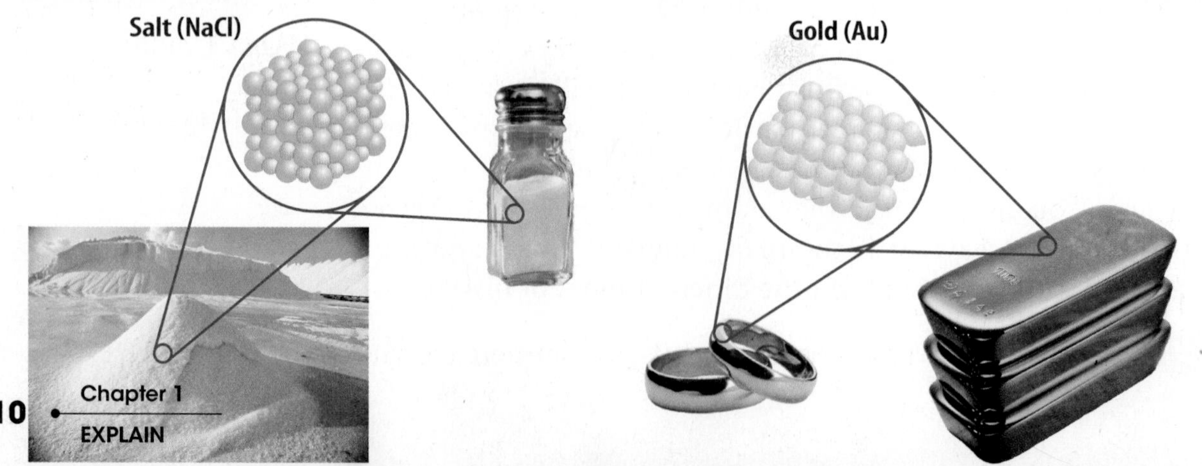

Elements

Some substances, such as gold, are made of only one kind of atom. Others, such as sodium chloride, are made of more than one kind. *An* **element** *is a substance made of only one kind of atom.* All atoms of an element are alike, but atoms of one element are different from atoms of other elements. For example, the element gold is made of only gold atoms, and all gold atoms are alike. But gold atoms are different from silver atoms, oxygen atoms, and atoms of every other element.

 **Key Concept Check** How are atoms and elements related?

What is the smallest part of an element? If you could break down an element into its smallest part, that part would be one atom. Most elements, such as carbon and silver, consist of a large group of individual atoms. Some elements, such as hydrogen and bromine, consist of molecules. *A* **molecule** (MAH lih kyewl) *is two or more atoms that are held together by chemical bonds and act as a unit.* Examples of elements made of individual atoms and molecules are shown in **Figure 3.**

Elements on the Periodic Table You probably can name many elements, such as carbon, gold, and oxygen. Did you know that there are about 115 elements? As shown in **Figure 4,** each element has a symbol, such as C for carbon, Au for gold, and O for oxygen. The periodic table printed in the back of this book gives other information about each element. You will learn more about elements in the next lesson.

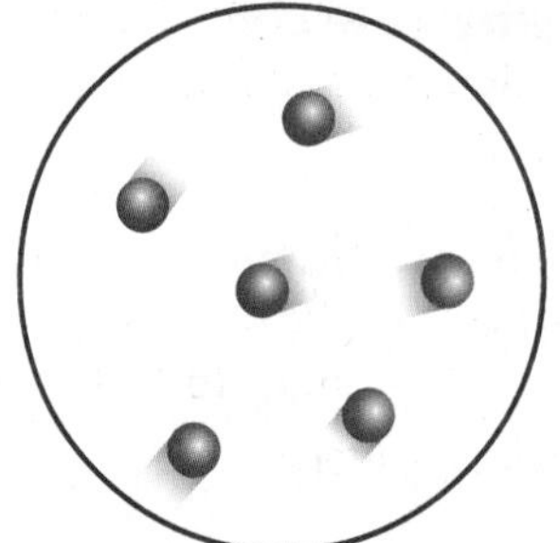

Individual atoms

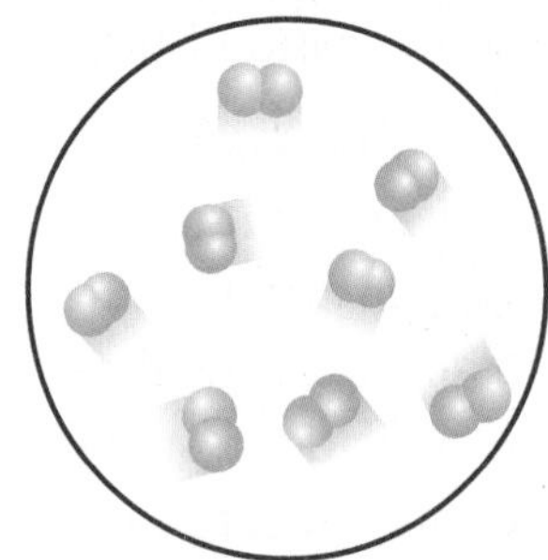

Molecules

Figure 3 The smallest part of all elements is an atom. In some elements, the atoms are grouped into molecules.

Elements

Concepts in Motion Animation

Figure 4 Element symbols have either one or two letters. Temporary symbols have three letters.

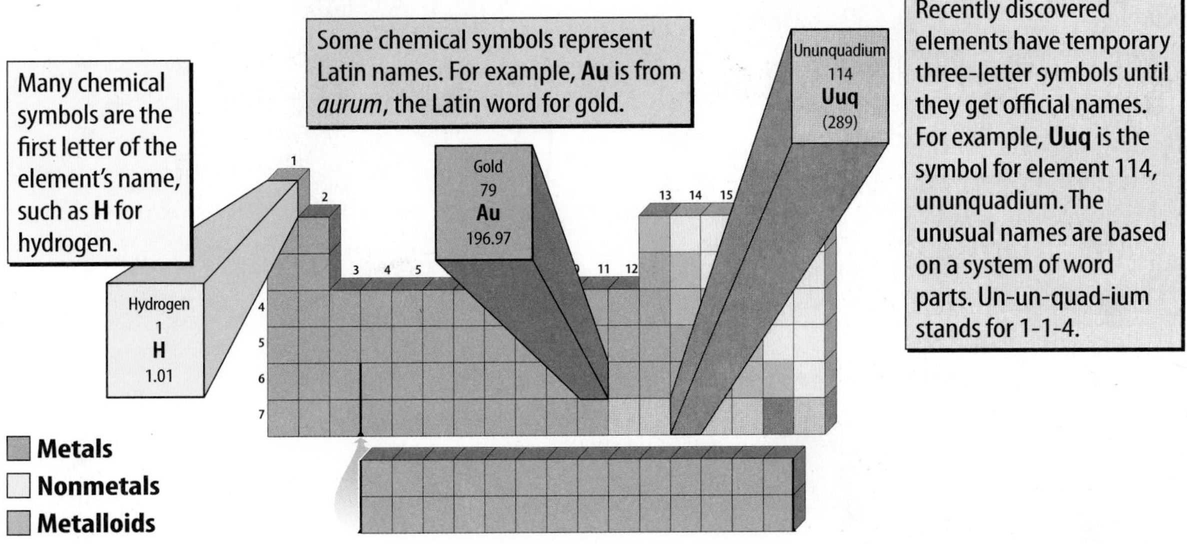

Many chemical symbols are the first letter of the element's name, such as **H** for hydrogen.
Some chemical symbols represent Latin names. For example, **Au** is from *aurum*, the Latin word for gold.
Recently discovered elements have temporary three-letter symbols until they get official names. For example, **Uuq** is the symbol for element 114, ununquadium. The unusual names are based on a system of word parts. Un-un-quad-ium stands for 1-1-4.
Hydrogen
1
H
1.01
Gold
79
Au
196.97
Ununquadium
114
Uuq
(289)
Metals
Nonmetals
Metalloids

Visual Check What color are the blocks used for elements that have not yet been verified?

Compounds

Does it surprise you to learn that there are only about 115 different elements? After all, if you think about all the different things you see each day, you could probably name many more types of matter than this. Why are there so many kinds of matter when there are only about 115 elements? Most matter is made of atoms of different types of elements bonded together.

A **compound** *is a substance made of two or more elements that are chemically joined in a specific combination.* Because each compound is made of atoms in a specific combination, a compound is a substance. Pure water (H_2O) is a compound because every sample of pure water contains atoms of hydrogen and oxygen in the same combination—two hydrogen atoms to every oxygen atom. There are many types of matter because elements can join to form compounds.

Molecules Recall that a molecule is two or more atoms that are held together by chemical bonds and that act as a unit. Is a molecule the smallest part of a compound? For many compounds, this is true. Many compounds exist as molecules. An example is water. In water, two hydrogen atoms and one oxygen atom always exist together and act as a unit. Carbon dioxide (CO_2) and table sugar ($C_6H_{12}O_6$) are also examples of compounds that are made of molecules.

However, as shown in **Figure 5,** some compounds are not made of molecules. In some compounds, such as table salt, or sodium chloride, no specific atoms travel together as a unit. However, table salt (NaCl) is still a substance because it always contains only sodium (Na) and chlorine (Cl) atoms.

 **Key Concept Check** How do elements and compounds differ?

Figure 5  Sugar particles are molecules because they always travel together as a unit. Salt particles do not travel together as a unit.

Sugar

Salt

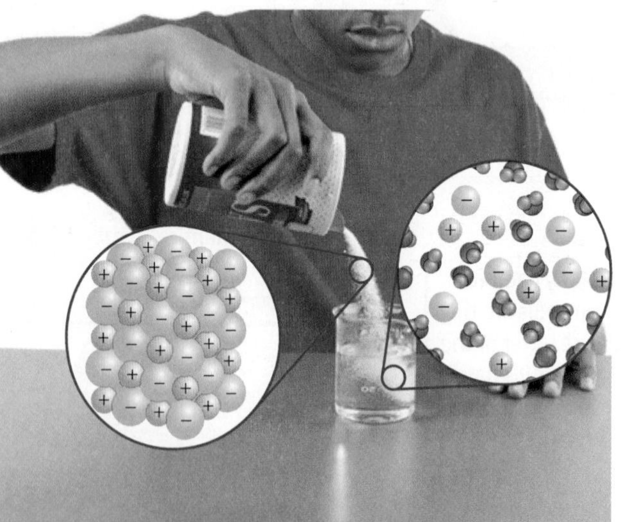

Visual Check What happens to the salt particles when the boy mixes the salt in the water? What do you think would happen if the water evaporated?

Properties of Compounds How would you describe sodium chloride, or table salt? The properties of a compound, such as table salt, are usually different from the properties of the elements from which it is made. Table salt, for example, is made of the elements sodium and chlorine. Sodium is a soft metal, and chlorine is a poisonous green gas. These properties are much different from the table salt you sprinkle on food!

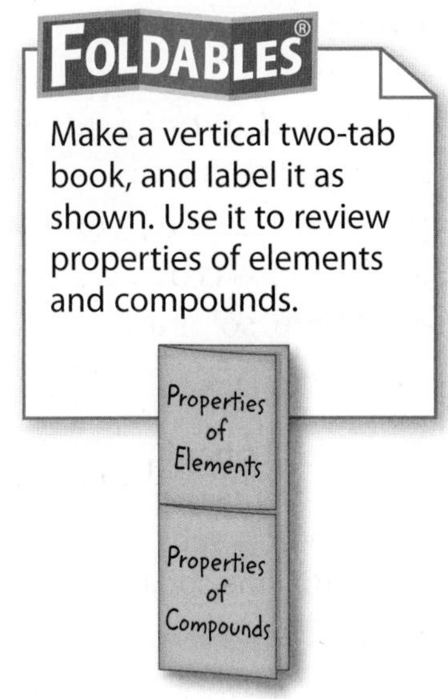

FOLDABLES®
Make a vertical two-tab book, and label it as shown. Use it to review properties of elements and compounds.
Properties of Elements
Properties of Compounds

Chemical Formulas Just as elements have chemical symbols, compounds have chemical formulas. A formula includes the symbols of each element in the compound. It also includes small numbers, called subscripts, that show the ratio of the elements in the compound. You can see the formulas for some compounds in **Table 1.**

Different Combinations of Atoms Sometimes the same elements combine to form different compounds. For example, nitrogen and oxygen can form six different compounds. The chemical formulas are N_2O, NO, N_2O_3, NO_2, N_2O_4, and N_2O_5. They contain the same elements, but because the combinations of atoms are different, each compound has different properties, as shown in **Table 1.**

Table 1 Atoms can combine in different ways and form different compounds.

Table 1

Formula and Molecular Structure	Properties/Uses
N_2O Nitrous oxide	colorless gas used as an anesthetic
NO_2 Nitrogen dioxide	brown gas, toxic, air pollutant
N_2O_3 Dinitrogen trioxide	blue liquid

Figure 6 It's hard to tell which is in the glass—pure water (a substance) or lemon-lime soda (a mixture).

What is a mixture?

By looking at the glass of clear liquid in **Figure 6,** can you tell whether it is lemon-lime soda or water? Lemon-lime soda is almost clear, and someone might confuse it with water, which is a substance. Recall that a substance is matter with a composition that is always the same. However, sodas are a combination of substances such as water, carbon dioxide, sugar, and other compounds. In fact, most solids, liquids, and gases you see each day are mixtures. *A* **mixture** *is matter that can vary in composition.* It is made of two or more substances that are blended but are not chemically bonded.

What would happen if you added more sugar to a glass of soda? You would still have soda, but it would be sweeter. Changing the amount of one substance in a mixture does not change the identity of the mixture or its individual substances.

Air and tap water are also mixtures. Air is a mixture of nitrogen, oxygen, and other substances. However, the composition of air can vary. Air in a scuba tank usually contains more oxygen and less of the other substances. Tap water might look like pure water, but it is a mixture of pure water (H_2O) and small amounts of other substances. Since the substances that make up tap water are not bonded together, the composition of tap water can vary. This is true for all mixtures.

Inquiry MiniLab

20 minutes

How do elements, compounds, and mixtures differ?

The elements in a compound cannot be separated easily. However, you often can use the properties of the substances in a mixture to separate them.

1. Read and complete a lab safety form.
2. Observe samples of **sand** and **iron filings** with a **magnifying lens.** Record your observations in your Science Journal.
3. Combine the sand and iron filings in a **clear cup.** Stir with a **toothpick.** Observe the mixture with the magnifying lens. Record your observations.
4. Cover one end of a **magnet** with **plastic wrap.** Stir the mixture with the covered magnet. Record your observations.

Analyze and Conclude

1. **Classify** The formula for sand is SiO_2. The symbol for iron is Fe. Use this to classify each as an element, a compound, or a mixture.
2. **Key Concept** What are two ways you could tell from your observations that the combination of sand and iron filings is a mixture and not a substance?

Types of Mixtures

How do trail mix, soda, and air differ? One difference is that trail mix is a solid, soda is a liquid, and air is a gas. This tells you that a mixture can be any state of matter. Another difference is that you can see the **individual** parts that make up trail mix, but you cannot see the parts that make up soda or air. This is because trail mix is a different type of mixture than soda and air. There are two types of mixtures—heterogeneous (he tuh roh JEE nee us) and homogeneous (hoh muh JEE nee us). The prefix *hetero-* means "different," and the prefix *homo-* means "the same." Heterogeneous and homogeneous mixtures differ in how evenly the substances that compose them are mixed.

ACADEMIC VOCABULARY
individual
(adjective) single; separate

Heterogeneous Mixtures

Suppose you take a bag of trail mix and pour it into two identical bowls. What might you notice? At first glance, each bowl appears the same. However, if you look closely, you might notice that one bowl has more nuts and another bowl has more raisins. The contents of the bowls differ because trail mix is a heterogeneous mixture. *A* **heterogeneous mixture** *is a mixture in which the substances are not evenly mixed.* Therefore, if you take two samples from the same mixture, such as trail mix, the samples might have different amounts of the individual substances. The mixtures shown in **Figure 7** are examples of heterogeneous mixtures.

Reading Check Explain why vegetable soup is classified as a heterogeneous mixture.

Figure 7 The different parts of a heterogeneous mixture are not evenly mixed.

Heterogeneous Mixtures

The numbers of peanuts, pretzels, raisins, and other types of food in trail mix could change, and it still would be trail mix.

You know that granite is a heterogeneous mixture because you can see the different minerals from which it is made.

With a microscope, you would be able to see that smoke is a heterogeneous mixture of gas and solid particles.

▲ **Figure 8** Salt is soluble in water. Pepper is insoluble in water. The pepper and water is a mixture, but not a solution.

Homogeneous Mixtures

If you pour soda into two glasses, the amounts of water, carbon dioxide, sugar, and other substances in the mixture would be the same in both glasses. Soda is an example of a **homogeneous mixture**—*a mixture in which two or more substances are evenly mixed, but not bonded together.*

Evenly Mixed Parts In a homogeneous mixture, the substances are so small and evenly mixed that you cannot see the boundaries between substances in the mixture. Brass, a mixture of copper and zinc, is a homogeneous mixture because the copper atoms and the zinc atoms are evenly mixed. You cannot see the boundaries between the different types of substances, even under most microscopes. Lemonade and air are also examples of homogeneous mixtures for the same reason.

Solution Another name for a homogeneous mixture is a solution. A solution is made of two parts—a solvent and one or more solutes. The solvent is the substance that is present in the largest amount. The solutes dissolve, or break apart, and mix evenly in the solvent. In **Figure 8,** water is the solvent, and salt is the solute. Salt is soluble in water. Notice also in the figure that pepper does not dissolve in water. No solution forms between pepper and water. Pepper is insoluble in water.

Other examples of solutions are described in **Figure 9.** Note that all three states of matter—solid, liquid, and gas—can be a solvent or a solute in a solution.

Key Concept Check How are some mixtures different from solutions?

Figure 9  Solids, liquids, and gases can combine to make solutions. ▼

Homogeneous Mixtures

A trumpet is made of brass, a solution of solid copper and solid zinc.

The natural gas used in a gas stove is a solution of methane, ethane, and other gases.

This ammonia cleaner is a solution of water and ammonia gas.

Compounds v. Mixtures

Think again about putting trail mix into two bowls. If you put more peanuts in one of the bowls, you still have trail mix in both bowls. Since the substances that make up a mixture are not bonded, adding more of one substance does not change the identity or the properties of the mixture. It also does not change the identity or the properties of each individual substance. In a heterogeneous mixture of peanuts, raisins, and pretzels, the properties of the individual parts don't change if you add more peanuts. The peanuts and the raisins don't bond together and become something new.

Similarly, in a solution such as soda or air, the substances do not bond together and form something new. Carbon dioxide, water, sugar, and other substances in soda are mixed together. Nitrogen, oxygen, and other substances in air also keep their separate properties because air is a mixture. If it were a compound, the parts would be bonded and would not keep their separate properties.

Key Concept Check How do mixtures and compounds differ?

Compounds and Solutions Differ

Compounds and solutions are alike in that they both look like pure substances. Look back at the lemon-lime soda and the water in **Figure 6.** The soda is a solution. A solution might look like a substance because the elements and the compounds that make up a solution are evenly mixed. However, compounds and solutions differ in one important way. The atoms that make up a given compound are bonded together. Therefore, the composition of a given compound is always the same. Changing the composition results in a new compound.

However, the substances that make up a solution, or any other mixture, are not bonded together. Therefore, adding more of one substance will not change the composition of the solution. It will just change the ratio of the substances in the solution. These differences are described in **Table 2.**

Table 2 Differences Between Solutions and Compounds

	Solutions	Compound
Composition	Made up of substances (elements and compounds) evenly mixed together; the composition can vary in a given mixture.	Made up of atoms bonded together; the combination of atoms is always the same in a given compound.
Changing the composition	The solution is still the same with similar properties. However, the relative amounts of substances might be different.	Changing the composition of a compound has changes into a new compound with new properties.
Properties of parts	The substances keep their own properties when they are mixed.	The properties of the compound are different from the properties of the atoms that make it up.

Separating Mixtures

Have you ever picked something you did not like off a slice of pizza? If you have, you have separated a mixture. Because the parts of a mixture are not combined chemically, you can use a physical process, such as removing them by hand, to separate the mixture. The identity of the parts does not change. Separating the parts of a compound is more difficult. The elements that make up a compound are combined chemically. Only a **chemical change** can separate them.

Review Vocabulary

chemical change
a change in matter in which the substances that make up the matter change into other substances with different chemical and physical properties

Separating Heterogeneous Mixtures Separating the parts of a pizza is easy because the pizza has large, solid parts. Two other ways to separate heterogeneous mixtures are shown in **Figure 10.** The strainer in the figure filters larger rocks from the mixture of rocks and dirt. The oil and vinegar is also a heterogeneous mixture because the oil floats on the vinegar. You can separate this mixture by carefully removing the floating oil.

Other properties also might be useful for separating the parts. For example, if one of the parts is magnetic, you could use a magnet to remove it. In a mixture of solid powders, you might dissolve one part in water and then pour it out, leaving the other part behind. In each case, to separate a heterogeneous mixture, you use differences in the physical properties of the parts.

Reading Check Name three methods of separating heterogeneous mixtures.

Figure 10 You can separate heterogeneous and homogeneous mixtures.

Visual Check How could you separate the small rocks and dirt that passed through the strainer on the left?

Separating Mixtures

A strainer removes large parts of the heterogeneous mixture of rocks and sediment. Only small rocks and dirt fall through.

In this heterogeneous mixture of oil and vinegar, the oil floats on the vinegar. You can separate them by lifting off the oil.

Making rock candy is a way of separating a solution. Solid sugar crystals form as a mixture of hot water and sugar cools.

Separating Homogeneous Mixtures Imagine trying to separate soda into water, carbon dioxide, sugar, and other substances it is made from. Because the parts are so small and evenly mixed, separating a homogeneous mixture such as soda can be difficult. However, you can separate some homogeneous mixtures by boiling or evaporation. For example, if you leave a bowl of sugar water outside on a hot day, the water will evaporate, leaving the sugar behind. An example of separating a homogeneous mixture by making rock candy is shown in **Figure 10.**

Visualizing Classification of Matter

Think about all the types of matter you have read about in this lesson. As shown in **Figure 11,** matter can be classified as either a substance or a mixture. Substances are either elements or compounds. The two kinds of mixtures are homogeneous mixtures and heterogeneous mixtures. Notice that all substances and mixtures are made of atoms. Matter is classified according to the types of atoms and the arrangement of atoms in matter. In the next lesson, you will study the structure of atoms.

Figure 11 You can classify matter based on its characteristics.

Classifying Matter

Matter
- Anything that has mass and takes up space
- Most matter on Earth is made up of atoms.
- Two classifications of matter: substances and mixtures

Substances
- Matter with a composition that is always the same
- Two types of substances: elements and compounds

Element
- Consists of just one type of atom
- Organized on the periodic table
- Each element has a chemical symbol.

Compound
- Two or more types of atoms bonded together
- Properties are different from the properties of the elements that make it up
- Each compound has a chemical formula.

Substances physically combine to form mixtures.

Mixtures can be separated into substances by physical methods.

Mixtures
- Matter that can vary in composition
- Substances are not bonded together.
- Two types of mixtures: heterogeneous and homogeneous

Heterogeneous Mixture
- Two or more substances unevenly mixed
- Different substances are visible by an unaided eye or a microscope.

Homogeneous Mixture—Solution
- Two or more substances evenly mixed
- Different substances cannot be seen even by a microscope.

Lesson 1 Review

Assessment Online Quiz
Inquiry Virtual Lab

Visual Summary

An element is a substance made of only one kind of atom.

The substances that make up a mixture are blended but not chemically bonded.

Homogeneous mixtures have the same makeup of substances throughout a given sample.

FOLDABLES®

Use your lesson Foldable to review the lesson. Save your Foldable for the project at the end of the chapter.

What do you think NOW?

You first read the statements below at the beginning of the chapter.

1. Things that have no mass are not matter.
2. The arrangement of particles is the same throughout a mixture.
3. An atom that makes up gold is exactly the same as an atom that makes up aluminum.

Did you change your mind about whether you agree or disagree with the statements? Rewrite any false statements to make them true.

Use Vocabulary

1. A small particle that is the building block of matter is a(n) ________.
2. **Use the term** *substance* in a sentence.
3. **Define** *molecule* in your own words.

Understand Key Concepts 

4. **Describe** the relationship among atoms, elements, and compounds.
5. Silver nitrate, $AgNO_3$, is which type of matter?
   - **A.** element
   - **B.** compound
   - **C.** heterogeneous mixture
   - **D.** homogeneous mixture
6. **Explain** how some mixtures are different from solutions.

Interpret Graphics

7. **Observe** Does the model at the right represent a mixture or a substance? How do you know?

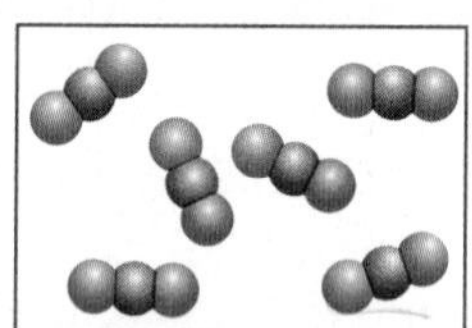

8. **Organize Information** Copy and fill in the graphic organizer below with details about substances and mixtures.

Substances	Mixtures

Critical Thinking

9. **Design** a method to separate a mixture of sugar, sand, and bits of iron.
10. **Decide** During a science investigation, a sample of matter breaks down into two kinds of atoms. Was the original sample an element or a compound? Explain.

Crude Oil

HOW IT WORKS

Separating Out Gasoline

Have you ever wondered where the gasoline used in automobiles comes from? Gasoline is part of a mixture of fuels called crude oil. How can workers separate gasoline from this mixture?

One way to separate a mixture is by boiling it. Crude oil is separated by a process called fractional distillation. First, the oil is boiled and allowed to cool. As the crude oil cools, each part changes from a gas to a liquid at a different temperature. Workers catch each fuel just as it changes back to a liquid. Eventually the crude oil is refined into all its useful parts.

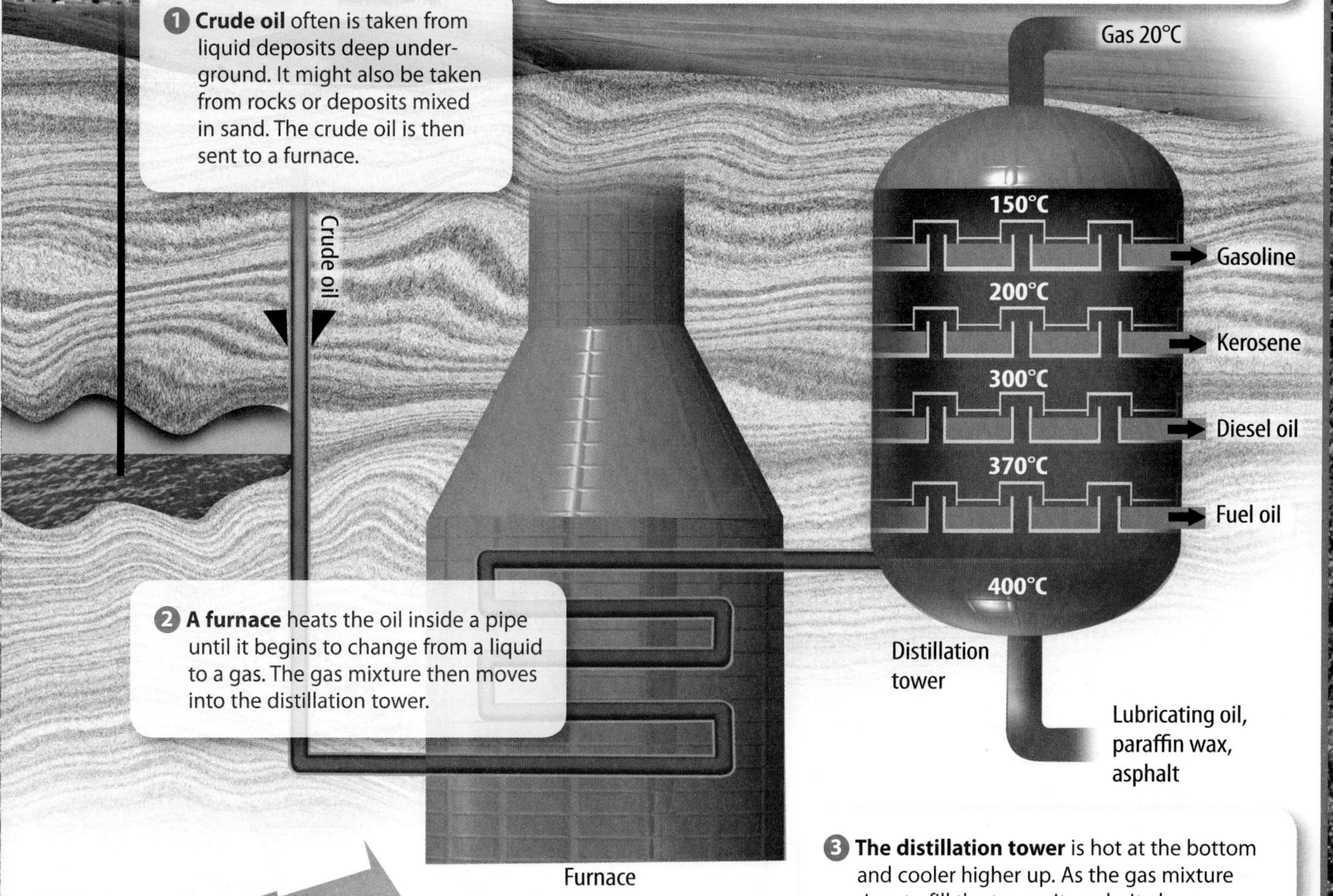

1 **Crude oil** often is taken from liquid deposits deep underground. It might also be taken from rocks or deposits mixed in sand. The crude oil is then sent to a furnace.

Crude oil

2 **A furnace** heats the oil inside a pipe until it begins to change from a liquid to a gas. The gas mixture then moves into the distillation tower.

Furnace

Gas 20°C

150°C

Gasoline

200°C

Kerosene

300°C

Diesel oil

370°C

Fuel oil

400°C

Distillation tower

Lubricating oil, paraffin wax, asphalt

3 **The distillation tower** is hot at the bottom and cooler higher up. As the gas mixture rises to fill the tower, it cools. It also passes over trays at different levels. Each fuel in the mixture changes to a liquid when it cools to a temperature that matches its boiling point. Gasoline changes to a liquid at the level in the tower at 150°C. A tray then catches the gasoline and moves it away.

It's Your Turn

CREATE A POSTER Blood is a mixture, too. Donated blood often is refined in laboratories to separate it into parts. What are those parts? What are they used for? How are they separated? Find the answers, and create a poster based on your findings.

Lesson 2

Reading Guide

Key Concepts
ESSENTIAL QUESTIONS

- Where are protons, neutrons, and electrons located in an atom?
- How is the atomic number related to the number of protons in an atom?
- What effect does changing the number of particles in an atom have on the atom's identity?

Vocabulary

nucleus p. 24
proton p. 24
neutron p. 24
electron p. 24
electron cloud p. 25
atomic number p. 26
isotope p. 27
ion p. 27

Academic Standards for Science

8.1.4 Describe the structure of an atom and relate the arrangement of electrons to how that atom interacts with other atoms.

8.1.5 Explain that atoms join together to form molecules and compounds and illustrate with diagrams the relationship between atoms and compounds and/or molecules.

Also covers: 8.NS.7, 8.NS.9, 8.NS.11

The Structure of Atoms

What makes them different?

This ring is made of two of the most beautiful materials in the world—diamond and gold. Diamond is a clear, sparkling crystal made of only carbon atoms. Gold is a shiny, yellow metal made of only gold atoms. How can they be so different if each is made of just one type of atom? The structure of atoms makes significant differences in materials.

Launch Lab

20 minutes

How can you make different things from the same parts?

Atoms are all made of the same parts. Atoms can be different from each other because they have different numbers of these parts. In this lab, you will investigate how you can make things that are different from each other even though you use the same parts to make them.

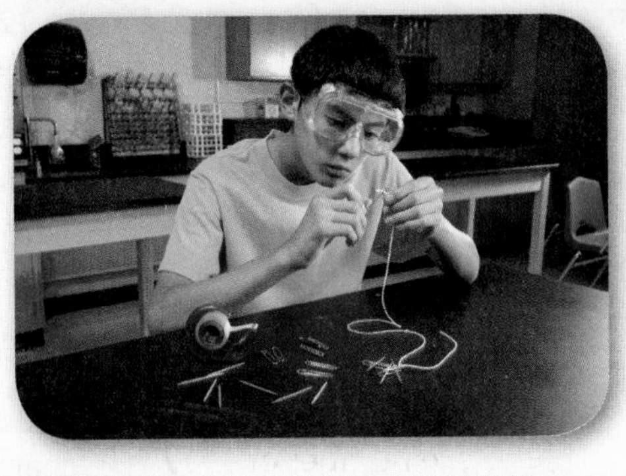

1. Read and complete a lab safety form.
2. Think about how you can join **paper clips, toothpicks,** and **string** to make different types of objects. You must use at least one of each item, but not more than five of any kind.
3. Make the object. Use **tape** to connect the items.
4. Plan and make two more objects using the same three items, varying the numbers of each item.
5. In your Science Journal, describe how each of the objects you made are alike and different.

Think About This

1. **Observe** What do the objects you made have in common? In what ways are they different?
2. **Key Concept** What effect do you think increasing or decreasing the number of items you used would have on the objects you made?

The Parts of an Atom

Now that you have read about ways to classify matter, you can probably recognize the different types you see each day. You might see pure elements, such as copper and iron, and you probably see many compounds, such as table salt. Table salt is a compound because it contains the atoms of two different elements—sodium and chlorine—in a specific combination. You also probably see many mixtures. The silver often used in jewelry is a homogeneous mixture of metals that are evenly mixed, but not bonded together.

As you read in Lesson 1, the many types of matter are possible because there are about 115 different elements. Each element is made up of a different type of atom. Atoms can combine in many different ways. They are the basic parts of matter.

What makes the atoms of each element different? Atoms are made of several types of tiny particles. The number of each of these particles in an atom is what makes atoms different from each other. It is what makes so many types of matter possible.

Reading Check What makes the atoms of different elements different from each other?

FOLDABLES®

Make a vertical two-column chart book. Label it as shown. Use it to organize information about the particles in an atom.

The Nucleus—Protons and Neutrons

The basic structure of all atoms is the same. As shown in **Figure 12,** an atom has a center region with a positive **charge.** One or more negatively charged particles move around this center region. *The* **nucleus** *is the region at the center of an atom that contains most of the mass of the atom.* Two kinds of particles make up the nucleus. *A* **proton** *is a positively charged particle in the nucleus of an atom. A* **neutron** *is an uncharged particle in the nucleus of an atom.*

SCIENCE USE V. COMMON USE
charge
Science Use an electrical property of some objects that determines whether the object is positive, negative, or neutral
Common Use buying something with a credit card

Reading Check Why does a nucleus always have a positive charge?

WORD ORIGIN
proton
from Greek *protos,* means "first"

Electrons

Atoms have no electric charge unless they change in some way. Therefore, there must be a negative charge that balances the positive charge of the nucleus. *An* **electron** *is a negatively charged particle that occupies the space in an atom outside the nucleus.* Electrons are so small and move so quickly that scientists are unable to tell exactly where a given electron is located at any specific time. Therefore, scientists describe their positions around the nucleus as a cloud rather than specific points. A model of an atom and its parts is shown in **Figure 12.**

Key Concept Check Where are protons, neutrons, and electrons located in an atom?

Figure 12 All atoms have a positively charged nucleus surrounded by one or more electrons.

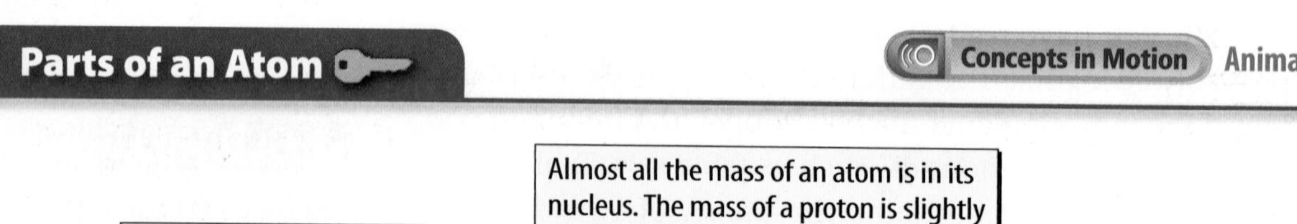
Parts of an Atom
Concepts in Motion
Animation

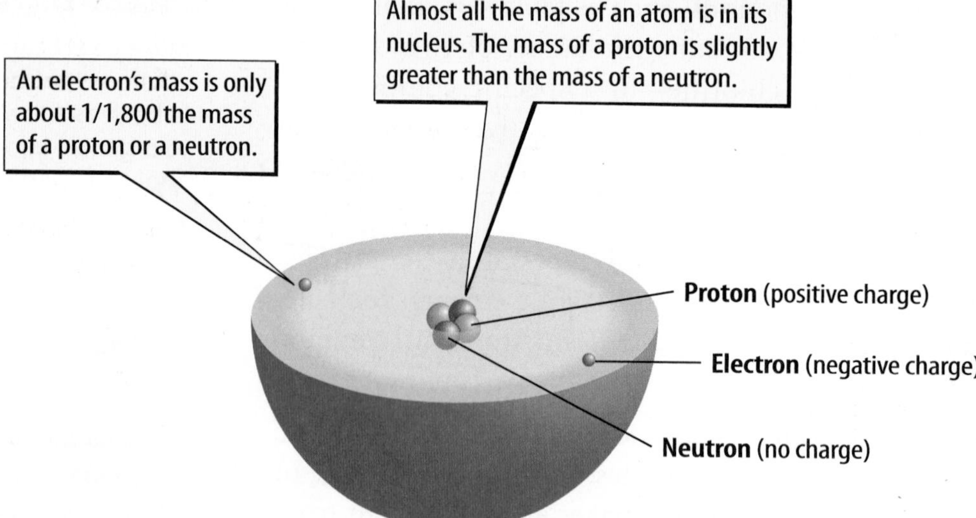
An electron's mass is only about 1/1,800 the mass of a proton or a neutron.
Almost all the mass of an atom is in its nucleus. The mass of a proton is slightly greater than the mass of a neutron.
Proton (positive charge)
Electron (negative charge)
Neutron (no charge)

Visual Check How many protons and how many electrons does this atom have?

An Electron Cloud Drawings of an atom, such as the one in **Figure 13,** often show electrons circling the nucleus like planets orbiting the Sun. Scientists have conducted experiments that show the movement of electrons is more complex than this. The modern idea of an atom is called the electron-cloud model. *An* **electron cloud** *is the region surrounding an atom's nucleus where one or more electrons are most likely to be found.* It is important to understand that an electron is not a cloud of charge. An electron is one tiny particle. An electron cloud is mostly empty space. At any moment in time, electrons are located at specific points within that area.

Electron Energy You have read that electrons are constantly moving around the nucleus in a region called the electron cloud. However, some electrons are closer to the nucleus than others. Electrons occupy certain areas around the nucleus according to their energy, as shown in **Figure 13.** Electrons close to the nucleus are strongly attracted to it and have less energy. Electrons farther from the nucleus are less attracted to it and have more energy.

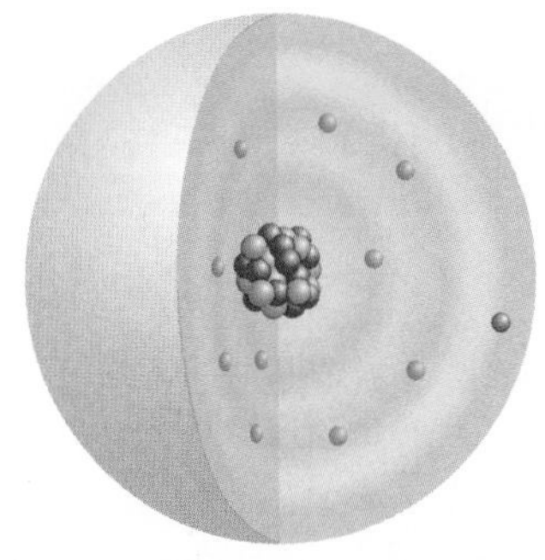

▲ **Figure 13** Electrons farther from the nucleus have more energy.

Personal Tutor

The Size of Atoms

It might be difficult to visualize an atom, but every solid, liquid, and gas is made of millions and millions of atoms. Your body, your desk, and the air you breathe are all made of tiny atoms. To understand how small an atom is, look at **Figure 14.** Suppose you could increase the size of everything around you. If you could multiply the width of an atom by 100 million, or 1×10^8, it would be the size of an orange. An orange would then increase to the size of Earth!

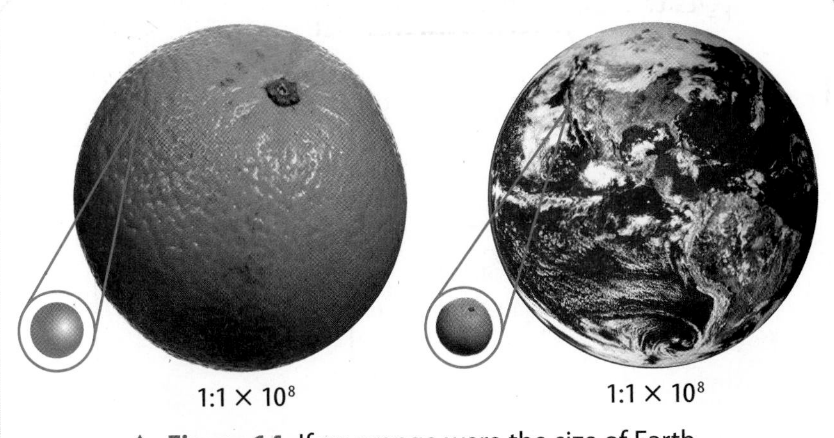

▲ **Figure 14** If an orange were the size of Earth, then an atom would be the size of an orange.

Math Skills

Use Scientific Notation

Scientists write very large and very small numbers using scientific notation. A gram of carbon has about 50,000,000,000,000,000,000 atoms. Express this in scientific notation.

1. Move the decimal until one nonzero digit remains on the left:

   5.0000000000000000000

2. Count the places you moved. Here it is 19 left.
3. Show that number as a power of 10. The exponent is negative if the decimal moves right and positive if it moves left. Answer: 5×10^{19}
4. Reverse the process to change scientific notation back to a whole number.

Practice

The diameter of a carbon atom is 2.2×10^{-8} cm. Write this as a whole number.

- **Math Practice**
- **Personal Tutor**

MiniLab 20 minutes

How can you model atoms?

You can use models to study parts of atoms.

Element	Protons	Neutrons	Electrons
Boron	5	6	
		5	4
Carbon		6	6
	2	2	
Nitrogen	7	6	

1. Read and complete a lab safety form.
2. Copy the table above into your Science Journal. Fill in the blanks in the table. ⚠ *Do not eat any food you use for a lab.*
3. Use pieces of **toothpicks** and **colored marshmallows** to model the nucleus of an atom of each element. Use pink for protons and green for neutrons.
4. On a desk, use yellow marshmallows to surround each nucleus with electrons.

Analyze and Conclude

1. **Decide** Which model element's atomic number is greatest? How do you know?
2. **Key Concept** What would change if the last model element had eight protons?

Differences in Atoms

In some ways atoms are alike. Each has a positively charged nucleus surrounded by a negatively charged electron cloud. But atoms can differ from each other in several ways. Atoms can have different numbers of protons, neutrons, or electrons.

Protons and Atomic Number

Look at the periodic table in the back of this book. In each block, the number under the element name shows how many protons each atom of the element has. For example, each oxygen atom has eight protons. *The* **atomic number** *is the number of protons in the nucleus of an atom of an element.* If there are 12 protons in the nucleus of an atom, that element's atomic number is 12. Examine **Figure 15.** Notice that the atomic number of magnesium is the whole number above its symbol. The atomic number of carbon is 6. This means that each carbon atom has 6 protons.

Every element in the periodic table has a different atomic number. You can identify an element if you know either its atomic number or the number of protons its atoms have. If an atom has a different number of protons, it is a different element.

Key Concept Check How is the atomic number related to the number of protons in an atom?

Figure 15 An atomic number is the number of protons in each atom of the element.

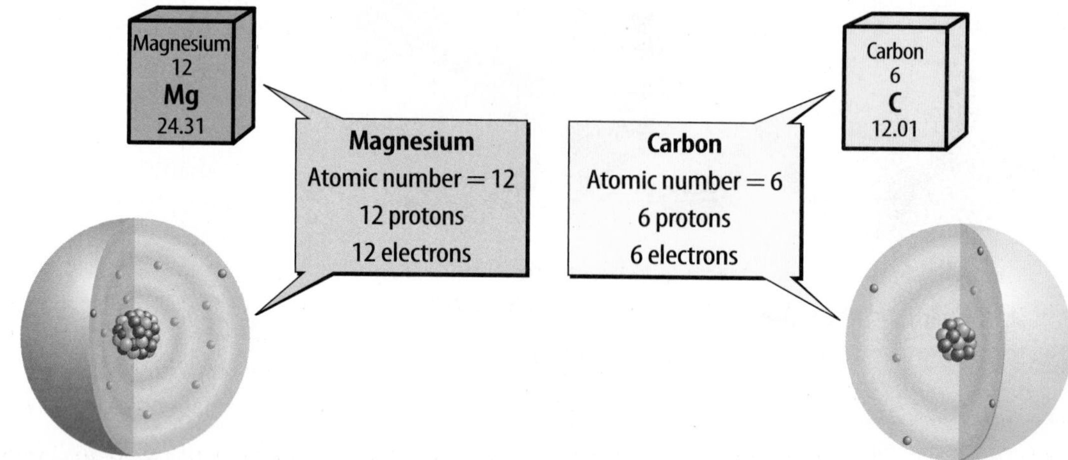

Lesson 2 Review

Assessment | Online Quiz

Visual Summary

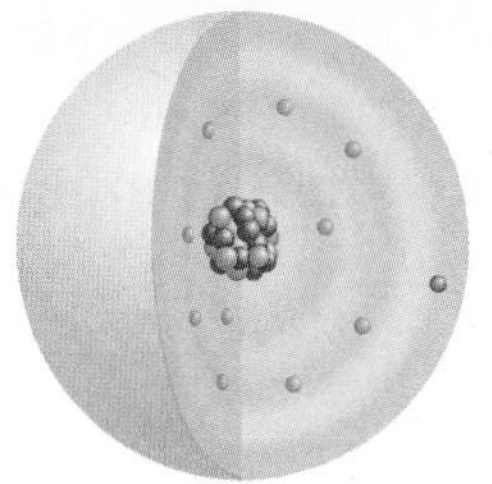

All matter is made of atoms. Atoms are made of protons, electrons, and neutrons.

An orange is about 100 million times wider than an atom.

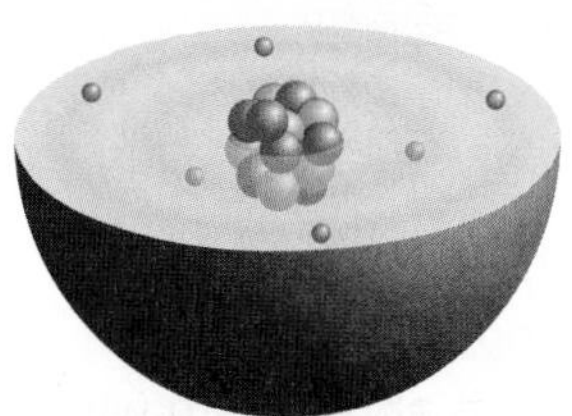

Atoms of the same element can have different numbers of neutrons.

FOLDABLES®

Use your lesson Foldable to review the lesson. Save your Foldable for the project at the end of the chapter.

What do you think NOW?

You first read the statements below at the beginning of the chapter.

4. An atom is mostly empty space.

5. If an atom gains electrons, the atom will have a positive charge.

6. Each electron is a cloud of charge that surrounds the center of an atom.

Did you change your mind about whether you agree or disagree with the statements? Rewrite any false statements to make them true.

Use Vocabulary

1. **Distinguish** between a proton and a neutron.
2. An atom that has lost one or more electrons is a(n) ________.
3. **Use the term** *isotope* in a complete sentence.

Understand Key Concepts 

4. Which is located outside the nucleus of an atom?

   A. electron
   B. ion
   C. neutron
   D. proton

5. **Identify** the element that has nine protons.
6. **Explain** how atomic number relates to the number of particles in an atom's nucleus.

Interpret Graphics

7. **Organize** Copy and fill in the graphic organizer below to summarize what you have learned about the parts, the sizes, and the differences of atoms.

Properties of Atoms	
Parts	
Size	
Differences	

Critical Thinking

8. **Decide** Can you tell which element an atom is if you know its charge and the number of electrons it has? Explain.

Math Skills

Review — Math Practice

9. The diameter of an atomic nucleus is about 0.0000000000000016 cm. Express this number in scientific notation.
10. The mass of a hydrogen atom is about 1.67×10^{-27} kg. Express this as a whole number.

50 minutes

Balloon Molecules

Materials

balloons

tape

black marker

index cards

Safety

Knowing how atoms join to form the smallest parts of a compound can be useful. It can sometimes help you predict properties of compounds. It also can help you understand how compounds combine to form mixtures. In this lab, you will connect small balloons to make models of molecules.

Question

How do atoms combine to make molecules?

Procedure

1. Read and complete a lab safety form.
2. Look at the molecule models in the table below. Each molecule is made of two or more atoms. Each type of atom is drawn in a different color.
3. Notice that a water molecule—H_2O—consists of two hydrogen atoms and one oxygen atom.
4. Inflate three balloons as models of the three atoms that make up a water molecule. Choose one color for the two hydrogen atoms and a different color for the oxygen atom. Inflate each balloon until it is about 4 cm wide.
5. Look at the shape of the water molecule in the table. Use tape to connect your model atoms in that shape.
6. Use a black marker to write *H* on each hydrogen balloon and *O* on the oxygen balloon.
7. Write *Water H_2O* on an index card, and place the card next to your model.

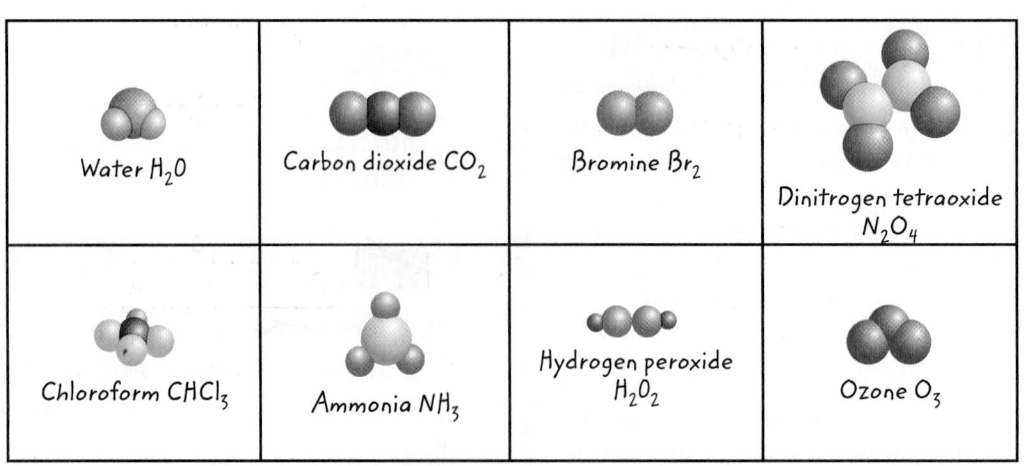

8 Look at the molecules in the table. Choose three molecules that you would like to model. Notice the types of atoms that make up the molecules you have chosen to model.

9 Choose a different color balloon for each type of atom. If possible, use the same colors for hydrogen and oxygen that you used for your water molecule.

10 Use tape to connect the atoms in the same arrangements shown in the table. Then use a marker to write the chemical symbol of each element on the balloon for that type of atom.

11 Label an index card for each molecule, just as you did for the water molecule. Display each of your models together.

Analyze and Conclude

12 **Analyze** Which, if any, of the molecules you modeled represent the smallest particles of a substance? Which, if any, represent the smallest particles of an element? Explain.

13 **The Big Idea** How do the molecules you modeled depend on atoms?

Communicate Your Results

Use a digital camera to take photographs of each model you made. Then, use the photos to make a computer presentation explaining the atoms that join to make each molecule you modeled.

Inquiry Extension

Make models for the other compounds shown in this chapter, including any that you did not previously make in the table on the previous page. Remember that the smallest parts of some compounds, such as NaCl, are not molecules because the same atoms do not always travel together. You can still model these particles as long as you keep in mind that they are not called molecules.

10

Lab Tips

- When making your models, it is best to have all the balloons inflated to the same size, but keep in mind that real atoms have different diameters.
- Press down lightly when writing the chemical symbols on the model atoms to avoid popping the balloons.

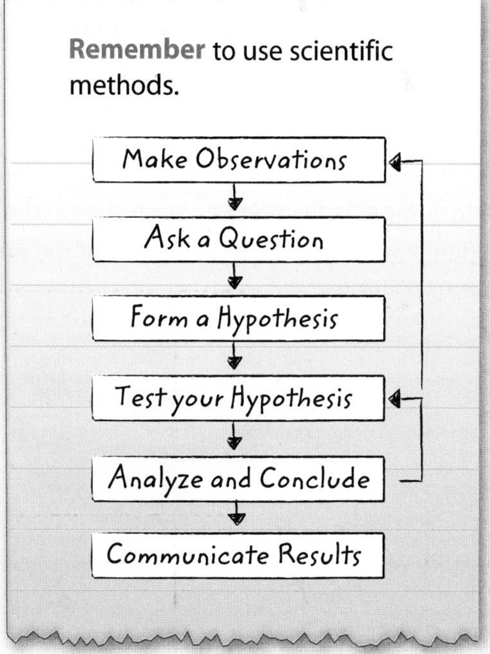

Chapter 1 Study Guide

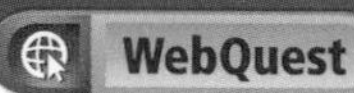

Matter is classified according to the type and arrangement of atoms from which it is made.

Key Concepts Summary

Lesson 1: Substances and Mixtures

- An **atom** is a building block of **matter.** An **element** is matter made of only one type of atom. A **compound** is a **substance** that contains two or more elements.
- A **heterogeneous mixture** is not a solution because the substances that make up a heterogeneous mixture are not evenly mixed. The substances that make up a solution, or a **homogeneous mixture,** are evenly mixed.
- **Mixtures** differ from compounds in their composition, whether their parts join, and the properties of their parts.

Vocabulary

matter p. 9
atom p. 9
substance p. 10
element p. 11
molecule p. 11
compound p. 12
mixture p. 14
heterogeneous mixture p. 15
homogeneous mixture p. 16

Lesson 2: The Structure of Atoms

- The center of an atom is the **nucleus.** The nucleus contains **protons** and **neutrons. Electrons** occupy the space in an atom outside the nucleus.
- The identity of an atom is determined by its **atomic number.** The atomic number is the number of protons in the atom.
- The identity of an atom stays the same if the number of neutrons or electrons changes.

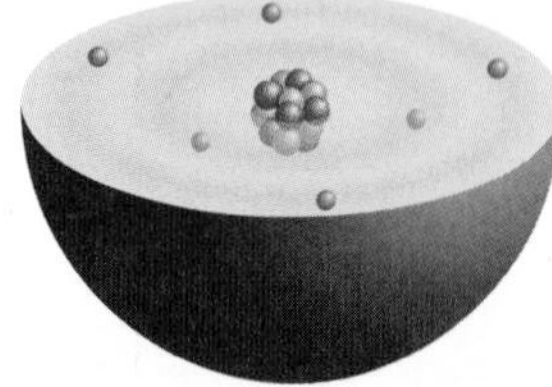

Vocabulary

nucleus p. 24
proton p. 24
neutron p. 24
electron p. 24
electron cloud p. 25
atomic number p. 26
isotope p. 27
ion p. 27

Study Guide

Review

- Personal Tutor
- Vocabulary eGames
- Vocabulary eFlashcards

FOLDABLES® Chapter Project

Assemble your lesson Foldables as shown to make a Chapter Project. Use the project to review what you have learned in this chapter.

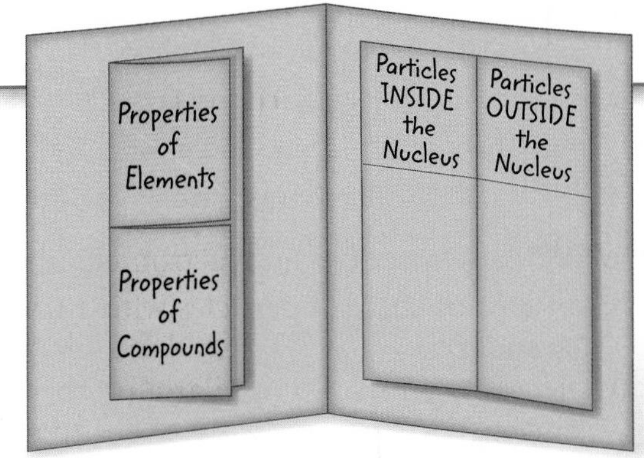

Use Vocabulary

1. A particle that consists of two or more atoms bonded together is a(n) ________.
2. A salad is an example of a(n) ________ because it is a mixture in which you can easily remove the individual parts.
3. Matter is classified as a(n) ________ if it is made of two or more substances that are physically blended but are not chemically bonded.
4. A positively charged particle in the nucleus of an atom is a(n) ________.
5. Almost all of the mass of an atom is found in the ________ of an atom.
6. If a chlorine atom gains an electron, it becomes a(n) ________ of chlorine.

Link Vocabulary and Key Concepts

Concepts in Motion Interactive Concept Map

Copy this concept map, and then use vocabulary terms from the previous page to complete the concept map.

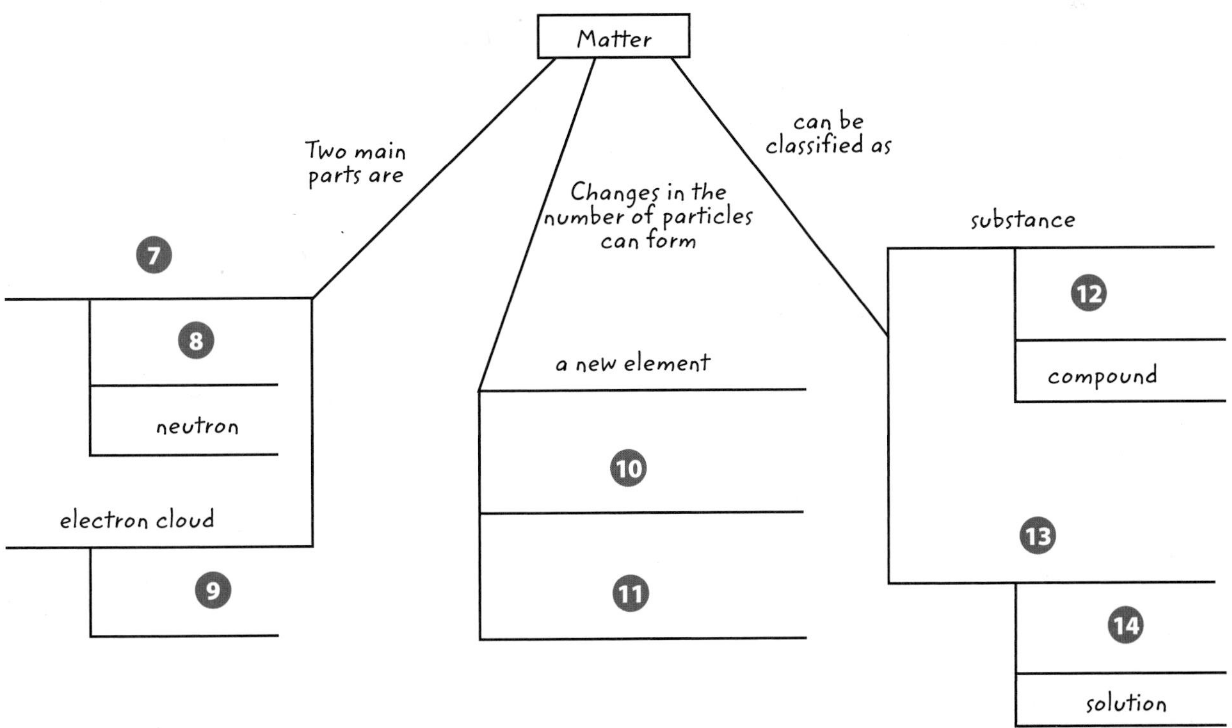

Chapter 1 Review

Understand Key Concepts 

1. Which is a substance?
   - A. fruit salad
   - B. granola cereal
   - C. spaghetti
   - D. table salt

2. Which is the best model for a homogeneous mixture?

   A.
   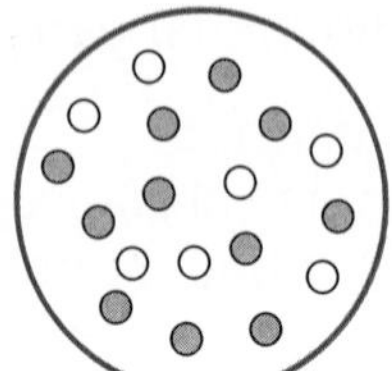

   B.
   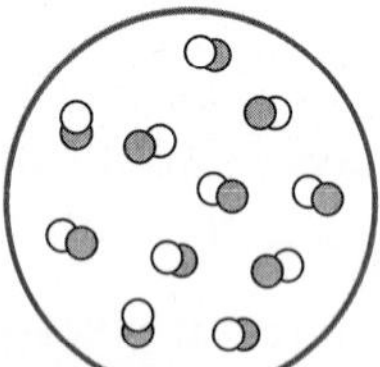

   C.
   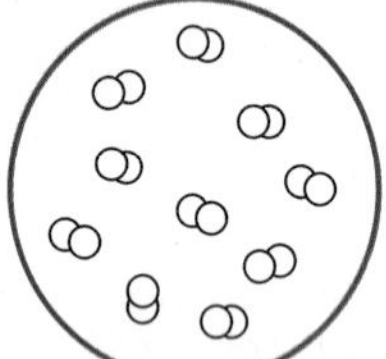

   D.
   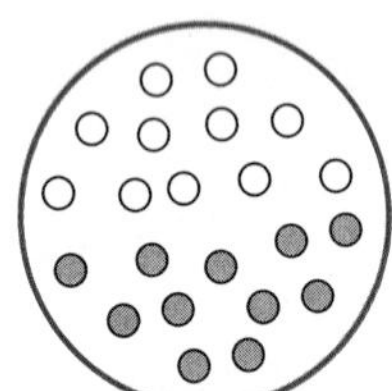

3. Which is a property of all atoms?
   - A. more electrons than protons
   - B. a nucleus with a positive charge
   - C. a positively charged electron cloud
   - D. same number of protons as neutrons

4. Which is another name for a solution?
   - A. element
   - B. compound
   - C. heterogeneous mixture
   - D. homogeneous mixture

5. Which would you most likely be able to separate into its parts by filtering?
   - A. heterogeneous mixture of two liquids
   - B. heterogeneous mixture of two solids
   - C. homogeneous mixture of two liquids
   - D. homogeneous mixture of two solids

6. Where is almost all the mass of an atom located?
   - A. in the electrons
   - B. in the neutrons
   - C. in the nucleus
   - D. in the protons

7. Which best describes an electron cloud?
   - A. an area of charged particles with a fixed boundary
   - B. electrons on a fixed path around the nucleus
   - C. mostly empty space with tiny charged particles in it
   - D. a solid mass of charge around the nucleus

8. Which is true about carbon-12 compared with carbon-13?
   - A. Carbon-12 has more neutrons.
   - B. Carbon-12 has more protons.
   - C. Carbon-13 has more neutrons.
   - D. Carbon-13 has more protons.

9. Look at the periodic table block below for potassium. How many electrons does an uncharged atom of potassium have?

   - A. 19
   - B. 20
   - C. 39
   - D. 40

Assessment
Online Test Practice

Critical Thinking

10 **Classify** Look at the illustration below. Is this a model of a substance or a mixture? How do you know?

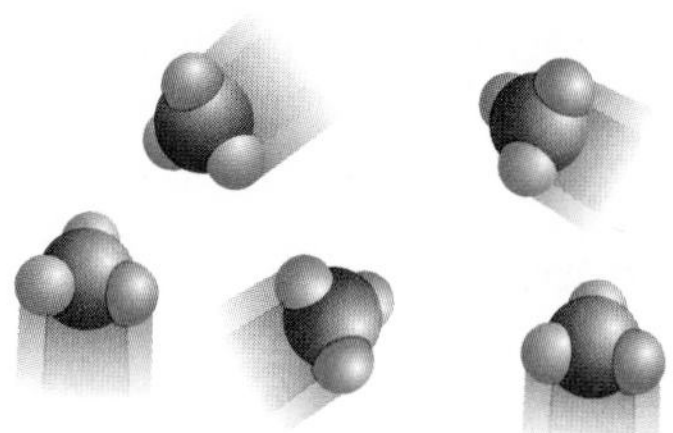

11 **Deduce** Each atom of protium has one proton, no neutrons, and one electron. Each atom of deuterium has one proton, two neutrons, and one electron. Are these the same or different elements? Why?

12 **Decide** Suppose you mix several liquids in a jar. After a few minutes, the liquids form layers. Is this a homogeneous mixture or a heterogeneous mixture? Why?

13 **Describe** a method for separating a mixture of salt water.

14 **Generalize** Consider the substances N_2O_5, H_2, CH_4, H_2O, KCl, and O_2. Is it possible to tell just from the symbols and the numbers which are elements and which are compounds? Explain.

15 **Suggest** how you can define an electron cloud differently from the chapter.

16 **Analyze** A substance has an atomic number of 80. How many protons and electrons do atoms of the substance have? What is the substance?

Writing in Science

17 **Write** a paragraph in which you explain the modern atomic model to an adult who has never heard of it before. Include two questions he or she might ask, and write answers to the questions.

REVIEW THE BIG IDEA

18 Explain how compounds, elements, heterogeneous mixtures, homogeneous mixtures, matter, and substances are related.

19 The photograph below depends on its parts. This is similar to the relationship of matter and atoms. How does the classification of matter depend on atoms?

Math Skills

Math Practice

Use Scientific Notation

20 The mass of one carbon atom is 0.00000000000000000000001994 g. Express this number in scientific notation.

21 The mass of an electron is about 9.11×10^{-31} kg. Write this as a whole number.

22 In 1 L of hydrogen gas, there are about 54,000,000,000,000,000,000,000 hydrogen atoms. Express the number of atoms using scientific notation.

23 Particles in chemistry are often described by the unit mole. One mole is defined as about 6.022×10^{23} particles. Write this as a whole number.

24 The mass of hydrogen-3, tritium, is about 5.01×10^{-27} kg. Write this as a whole number.

Standardized Test Practice

Record your answers on the answer sheet provided by your teacher or on a sheet of paper.

Multiple Choice

Use the figure below to answer questions 1 and 2.

1 How many atoms are in the particle?

A 1

B 2

C 3

D 5

2 Which kind of matter might contain only this type of particle?

A a compound

B an element

C a heterogeneous mixture

D a homogeneous mixture

3 Which class of matter is the least evenly mixed?

A compounds

B heterogeneous mixtures

C homogeneous mixtures

D solutions

4 Which correctly describes a compound but not a mixture?

A All the atoms are of the same element.

B All the molecules have at least two atoms.

C The combination of substances never changes.

D The substances can be separated without breaking bonds.

5 A girl pours a spoonful of sugar into a glass of warm water. She stirs the water until the sugar disappears. When she tastes the water, she notices that it is now sweet. Which describes the kind of matter in the glass?

A a compound

B an element

C a solution

D a substance

6 How could you separate a mixture of stone and wooden beads that are all the same size?

A Add water to the mixture and skim off the wooden beads, which float.

B Heat the mixture until the stone beads melt.

C Strain the mixture to separate out the stone beads.

D Use a magnet to pull out the wooden beads.

Use the figure below to answer question 7.

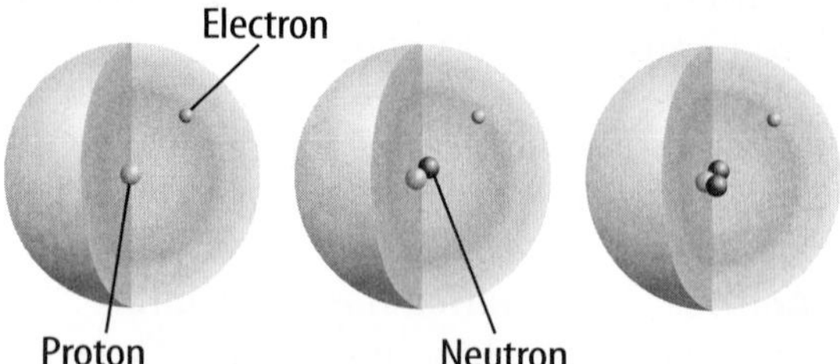

7 The figure shows models of three different atoms. What can you conclude about the three models shown in the figure?

A They all show positive ions.

B They all show negative ions.

C They all show the same element.

D They all show the same isotope.

8 What is the atomic number of an atom that has 2 electrons, 3 protons, and 4 neutrons?

A 2

B 3

C 4

D 7

Use the table below to answer questions 9 and 10.

	Number of Protons	Number of Neutrons	Number of Electrons
A	8	8	8
B	8	8	10
C	8	9	8
D	9	10	9

9 The table shows the numbers of protons, neutrons, and electrons for four atoms. Which atom has a negative charge?

A A

B B

C C

D D

10 Which of the atoms is a different element than the others?

A A

B B

C C

D D

Constructed Response

11 How do protons, electrons, and neutrons differ in charge and location in the atom?

Use the figures below to answer questions 12 and 13.

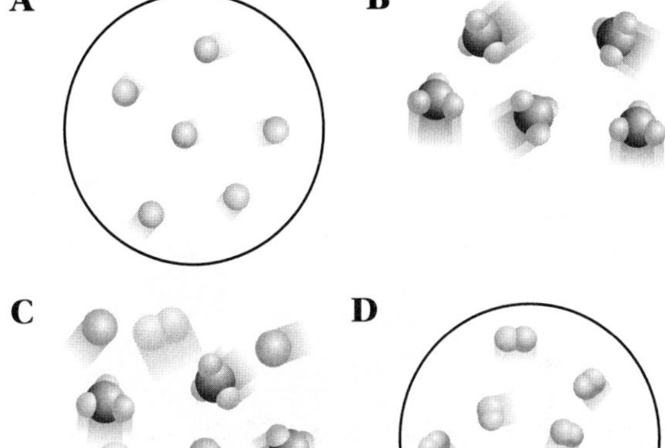

12 Classify each model A–D as either an element, a compound, or a mixture. Explain your reasoning for each answer.

13 Imagine that samples A and D were reacted and formed a compound. Then imagine that the same samples were combined to form a mixture. How would the two combinations differ?

14 Suppose a neutral atom has 5 protons, 5 neutrons, and 5 electrons. List the number of protons, electrons, and neutrons for the following.

a. a positive ion of the same element

b. a negative ion of the same element

c. a neutral isotope of the same element

NEED EXTRA HELP?														
If You Missed Question...	1	2	3	4	5	6	7	8	9	10	11	12	13	14
Go to Lesson...	1	1	1	1	1	1	2	2	2	2	1	1	2	2

Chapter 2

States of Matter

THE BIG IDEA

What physical changes and energy changes occur as matter goes from one state to another?

Inquiry Liquid Glass?

When you look at this blob of molten glass, can you envision it as a beautiful vase? The solid glass was heated in a furnace until it formed a molten liquid. Air is blown through a pipe to make the glass hollow and give it form.

- Can you identify a solid, a liquid, and a gas in the photo?
- What physical changes and energy changes do you think occurred when the glass changed state?

Get Ready to Read

What do you think?

Before you read, decide if you agree or disagree with each of these statements. As you read this chapter, see if you change your mind about any of the statements.

1. Particles moving at the same speed make up all matter.
2. The particles in a solid do not move.
3. Particles of matter have both potential energy and kinetic energy.
4. When a solid melts, thermal energy is removed from the solid.
5. Changes in temperature and pressure affect gas behavior.
6. If the pressure on a gas increases, the volume of the gas also increases.

Your one-stop online resource

connectED.mcgraw-hill.com

 Video

 WebQuest

 Audio

Assessment

 Review

Concepts in Motion

 Inquiry

 Multilingual eGlossary

Lesson 1

Solids, Liquids, and Gases

Reading Guide

Key Concepts
ESSENTIAL QUESTIONS

- How do particles move in solids, liquids, and gases?
- How are the forces between particles different in solids, liquids, and gases?

Vocabulary

solid p. 43
liquid p. 44
viscosity p. 44
surface tension p. 45
gas p. 46
vapor p. 46

Multilingual eGlossary

Academic Standards for Science

8.4.1 Understand how the strength of attractive forces between particles in a material helps to explain many physical properties of the material, such as why different materials exist as gases, liquids or solids at a given temperature.

8.4.2 Rank the strength of attractions between the particles of room-temperature materials.

Also covers: 8.NS.1, 8.NS.4, 8.NS.6, 8.NS.7, 8.NS.11

Inquiry Giant Bubbles?

Giant bubbles can be made from a solution of water, soap, and a syrupy liquid called glycerine. These liquids change the properties of water. Soap changes water's surface tension. Glycerine changes the evaporation rate. How do surface tension and evaporation work?

Launch Lab

10 minutes

How can you see particles in matter? 

It's sometimes difficult to picture how tiny objects, such as the particles that make up matter, move. However, you can use other objects to model the movement of these particles.

1. Read and complete a lab safety form.
2. Place about 50 **copper pellets** into a **plastic petri dish.** Place the cover on the dish, and secure it with **tape.**
3. Hold the dish by the edges. Gently vibrate the dish from side to side no more than 1–2 mm. Observe the pellets. Record your observations in your Science Journal.
4. Repeat step 3, vibrating the dish less than 1 cm from side to side.
5. Repeat step 3, vibrating the dish 3–4 cm from side to side.

Think About This

1. If the pellets represent particles in matter, what do you think the shaking represents?
2. In which part of the experiment do you think the pellets were like a liquid? Explain.
3.  **Key Concept** If the pellets represent molecules of water, what do you think are the main differences among molecules of ice, water, and vapor?

Describing Matter

Take a closer look at the photo on the previous page. Do you see **matter?** The three most common forms, or states, of matter on Earth are solids, liquids, and gases. The giant bubble contains air, which is a mixture of gases. The ocean water and the soap mixture used to make the bubble are liquids. The sand, sign, and boards are a few of the solids in the photo.

Review Vocabulary

matter
anything that takes up space and has mass

There is a fourth state of matter, plasma, that is not shown in this photo. Plasma is high-energy matter consisting of positively and negatively charged particles. Plasma is the most common state of matter in space. It also is in lightning flashes, fluorescent lighting, and stars, including the Sun.

There are many ways to describe matter. You can describe the state, the color, the texture, and the odor of matter using your senses. You also can describe matter using measurements, such as mass, volume, and density. Mass is the amount of matter in an object. The units for mass are often grams (g) or kilograms (kg). Volume is the amount of space that a sample of matter occupies. The units for liquid volume are usually liters (L) or milliliters (mL). The units for solid volume are usually cubic centimeters (cm^3) or cubic meters (m^3). Density is a quantity calculated by dividing an object's mass by its volume. The units of density are usually g/cm^3 or g/mL.

Particles in Motion

Have you ever wondered what makes something a solid, a liquid, or a gas? Two main factors that determine the state of matter are particle motion and particle forces.

Particles, such as atoms, ions, or molecules, moving in different ways make up all matter. The particles in some matter are close together and vibrate back and forth. In other matter, they are farther apart. Sometimes, particles slide past each other or move freely and spread out. Regardless of how close particles are to each other, they all have random motion. Random motion is movement in all directions and at different speeds. If particles are free to move, they move in straight lines until they collide with something. Collisions usually change the speed and direction of the particles' movements.

FOLDABLES®
Use a sheet of notebook paper to make a three-tab Foldable as shown. Record information about each state of matter under the tabs.
Solid
Liquid
Gas

Forces Between Particles

Recall that atoms that make up matter contain positively charged protons and negatively charged electrons. There is a force of attractions between these oppositely charged particles, as shown in **Figure 1.**

You just read that the particles that make up matter move at all speeds and in all directions. If the motion of particles slows, the particles move closer together. This is because the attraction between them pulls them toward each other. Strong attractive forces hold particles close together. As the motion of particles increases, particles move farther apart. The attractive forces between particles get weaker. The spaces between them increase and the particles can slip past one another. As the motion of particles continues to increase, they move even farther apart. Eventually, the distance between particles is so great that there is little or no attractive forces between the particles. The particles move randomly and spread out. As you continue to read, you will learn how particle motion and particle forces determine whether matter is a solid, a liquid, or a gas.

Figure 1 The forces between particles of matter and the movement of particles determine the physical state of matter.

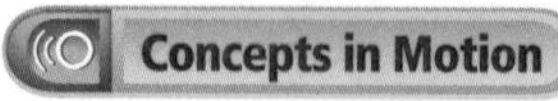

Animation

Particles move slowly and can only vibrate in place. Therefore, the attractive forces between particles are strong.

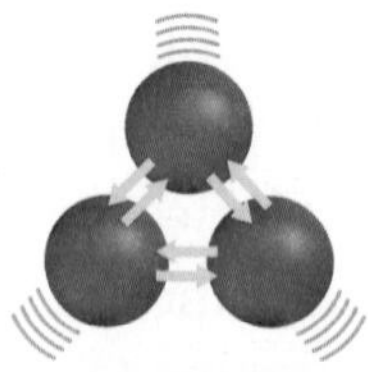

Particles move faster and slip past each other. The distance between particles increases. Therefore, the attractive forces between particles are weaker.

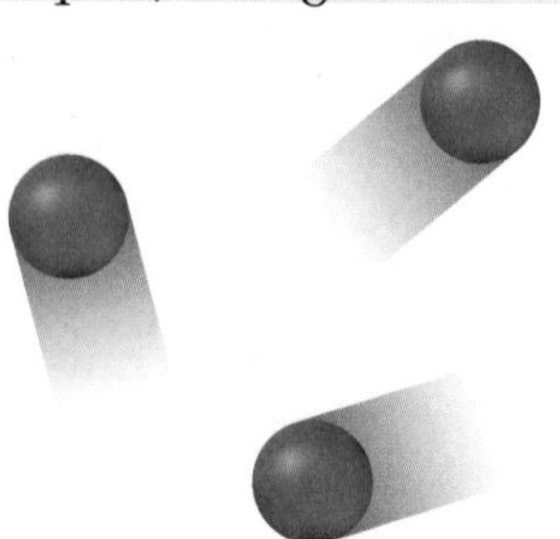

Particles move fast. The distance between the particles is great, and therefore, the attractive forces between particles are very weak.

Solids

If you had to describe a solid, what would you say? You might say, a **solid** *is matter that has a definite shape and a definite volume.* For example, if the skateboard in **Figure 2** moves from one location to another, the shape and volume of it do not change.

Particles in a Solid

Why doesn't a solid change its shape and volume? Notice in **Figure 2** how the particles in a solid are close together. The particles are very close to their neighboring particles. That's because the attractive forces between the particles are strong and hold them close together. The strong attractive forces and slow motion of the particles keep them tightly held in their positions. The particles simply vibrate back and forth in place. This arrangement gives solids a definite shape and volume.

Key Concept Check Describe the movement of particles in a solid and the forces between them.

Types of Solids

All solids are not the same. For example, a diamond and a piece of charcoal don't look alike. However, they are both solids made of only carbon atoms. A diamond and a lump of charcoal both contain particles that strongly attract each other and vibrate in place. What makes them different is the arrangement of their particles. Notice in **Figure 3** that the arrangement of particles in a diamond is different from that in charcoal. A diamond is a crystalline solid. It has particles arranged in a specific, repeating order. Charcoal is an amorphous solid. It has particles arranged randomly. Different particle arrangements give these materials different properties. For example, a diamond is a hard material, and charcoal is a brittle material.

Reading Check What is the difference between crystalline and amorphous solids?

Solid Particle Movement

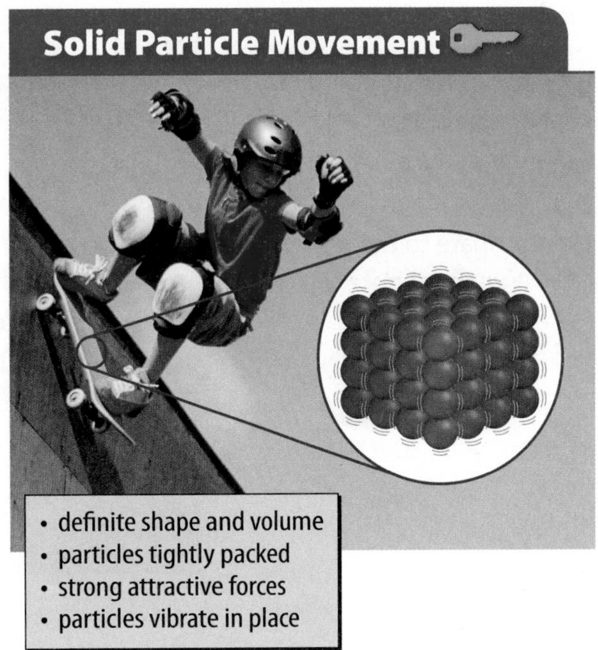

- definite shape and volume
- particles tightly packed
- strong attractive forces
- particles vibrate in place

▲ **Figure 2** The particles in a solid have strong attractive forces and vibrate in place.

Figure 3 Carbon is a solid that can have different particle arrangements. ▼

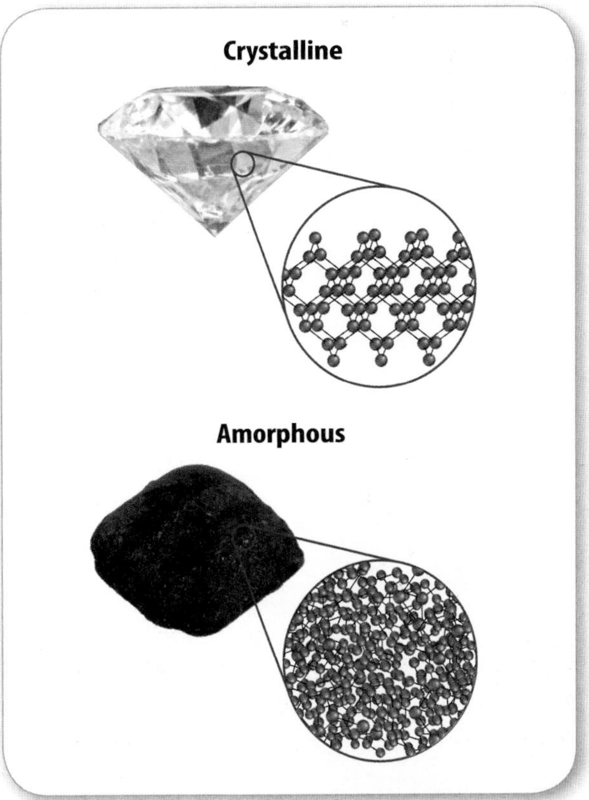

Figure 4 The motion of particles in a liquid causes the particles to move slightly farther apart. ▶

Visual Check How does the spacing among these particles compare to the particle spacing in **Figure 2?**

Liquid Particle Movement
• no definite shape, has definite volume
• particles free to move past other particles
• attractive forces weaker than those in solids

Liquids

You have probably seen a waterfall, such as the one in **Figure 4.** Water is a liquid. *A* **liquid** *is matter with a definite volume but no definite shape.* Liquids flow and can take the shape of their containers. The container for this water is the riverbed.

WORD ORIGIN
viscosity
from Latin *viscum,* means "sticky"

Particles in a Liquid

How can liquids change their shape? The particle motion in the liquid state of a material is faster than the particle motion in the solid state. This increased particle motion causes the particles to move slightly farther apart. As the particles move farther apart, the attractive forces between the particles decrease. The weaker attractive forces allow particles to slip past one another. They also enable liquids to flow and take the shape of their containers.

Viscosity

If you have ever poured or dipped honey, as shown in **Figure 5,** you have experienced a liquid with a high viscosity. **Viscosity** (vihs KAW sih tee) *is a measurement of a liquid's resistance to flow.* Honey has high viscosity, while water has low viscosity. Viscosity is due to particle mass, particle shape, and the strength of the attraction between the particles of a liquid. In general, the stronger the attractive forces between particles, the higher the viscosity. For many liquids, viscosity decreases as the liquid becomes warmer. The mass and shape of a particle also affects its ability to slip past other particles. More massive particles tend to move more slowly. Particles with complex shapes, such as long chains, also have high viscosity because the particles have difficulty slipping past one another.

Figure 5 Honey has a high viscosity. ▼

Figure 6 The surface tension of water enables this spider to walk on the surface of a lake.

Surface Tension

How can the nursery web spider in **Figure 6** walk on water? Believe it or not, it is because of the interactions between molecules.

The blowout in **Figure 6** shows the attractive forces between water molecules. Water molecules below the surface are surrounded on all sides by other water molecules. Therefore, they have attractive forces, or pulls, in all directions. The attraction between similar molecules, such as water molecules, is called cohesion.

Water molecules at the surface of a liquid do not have liquid water molecules above them. As a result, they experience a greater downward pull, and the surface particles become tightly stretched like the head of a drum. Molecules at the surface of a liquid have **surface tension,** *the uneven forces acting on the particles on the surface of a liquid.* Surface tension allows a spider to walk on water. In general, the stronger the attractive forces between particles, the greater the surface tension of the liquid.

Recall the giant bubbles at the beginning of the chapter. The thin water-soap film surrounding the bubbles forms because of surface tension between the particles.

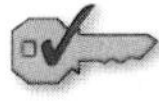 **Key Concept Check** Describe the movement of particles in a liquid and the forces between them.

20 minutes

How can you make bubble films?

Have you ever observed surface tension? Which liquids have greater surface tension?

1. Read and complete a lab safety form.
2. Place about 100 mL of cool water in a **small bowl.** Lower a **wire bubble frame** into the bowl, and gently lift it. Use a **magnifying lens** to observe the edges of the frame. Write your observations in your Science Journal.
3. Add a full **dropper** of **liquid dishwashing soap** to the water. Stir with a **toothpick** until mixed. Lower the frame into the mixture and lift it out. Record your observations.
4. Use a toothpick to break the bubble film on one side of the thread. Observe.

Analyze and Conclude

1. **Recognize Cause and Effect** Explain what caused the thread to form an arc when half the bubble film broke.
2. **Key Concept** Explain why pure water doesn't form bubbles. What happens to the forces between water molecules when you add soap?

Gas Particle Movement

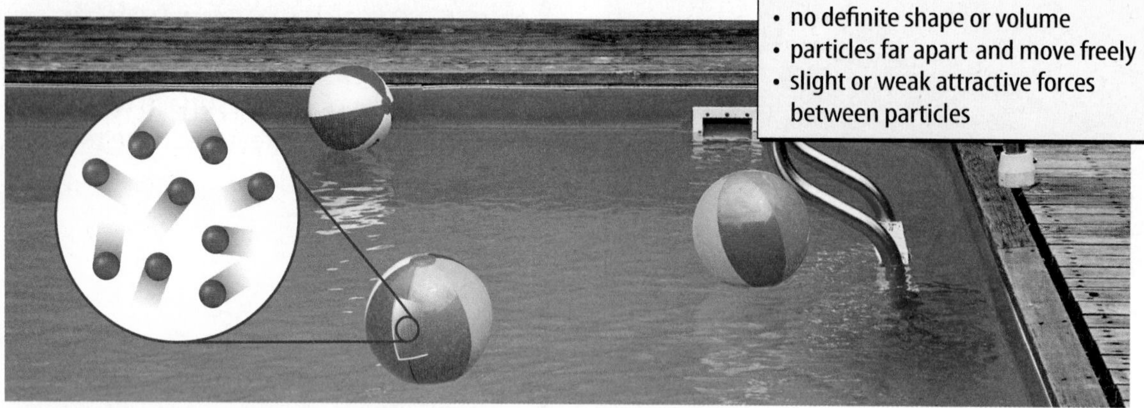

• no definite shape or volume
• particles far apart and move freely
• slight or weak attractive forces between particles

Figure 7 The particles in a gas are far apart, and there is little or no attractive forces are between particles.

Visual Check What are gas particles likely to hit as they move?

Gases

Look at the photograph in **Figure 7.** Where is the gas? *A* **gas** *is matter that has no definite volume and no definite shape.* It is not easy to identify the gas because you cannot see it. However, gas particles are inside and outside the inflatable balls. Air is a mixture of gases, including nitrogen, oxygen, argon, and carbon dioxide.

Reading Check What is a gas, and what is another object that contains a gas?

Particles in a Gas

Why don't gases have definite volumes or definite shapes like solids and liquids? Compare the particles in **Figures 2, 4,** and **7.** Notice how the distance between particles differs. As the particles move faster, such as when matter goes from the solid state to the liquid state, the particles move farther apart. When the particles in matter move even faster, such as when matter goes from the liquid state to the gas state, the particles move even farther apart. When the distances between particles changes, the attractive forces between the particles also changes.

Forces Between Particles

As a type of matter goes from the solid state to the liquid state, the distance between the particles increases and the attractive forces between the particles decreases. When the same matter goes from the liquid state to the gas state, the particles are even farther apart and the attractive forces between the particles are weak or absent. As a result, the particles spread out to fill their container. Because gas particles lack attractive forces between particles, they have no definite shape or definite volume.

Vapor

Have you ever heard the term *vapor? The gas state of a substance that is normally a solid or a liquid at room temperature is called* **vapor.** For example, water is normally a liquid at room temperature. When it is a gas state, such as in air, it is called water vapor. Other substances that can form a vapor are rubbing alcohol, iodine, mercury, and gasoline.

Key Concept Check How do particles move and interact in a gas?

Lesson 1 Review

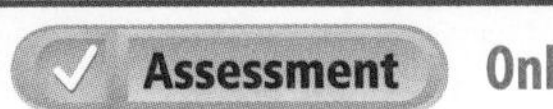

Visual Summary

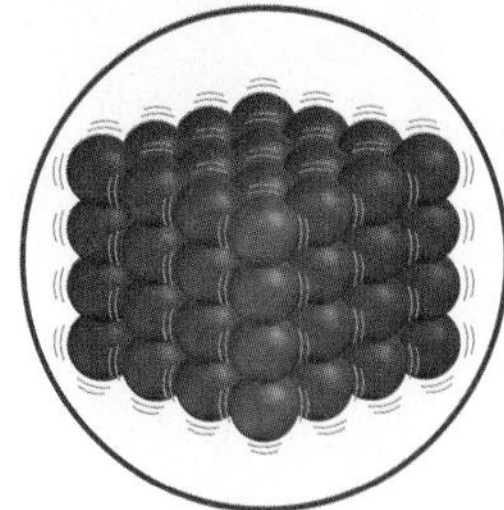

The particles that make up a solid can only vibrate in place. The particles are close together, and there are strong forces among them.

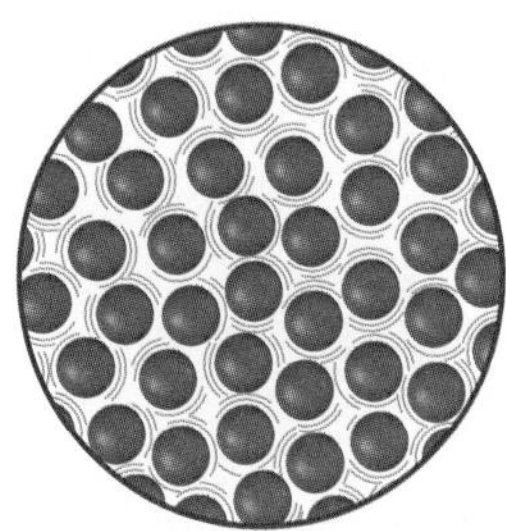

The particles that make up a liquid are far enough apart that particles can flow past other particles. The forces among these particles are weaker than those in a solid.

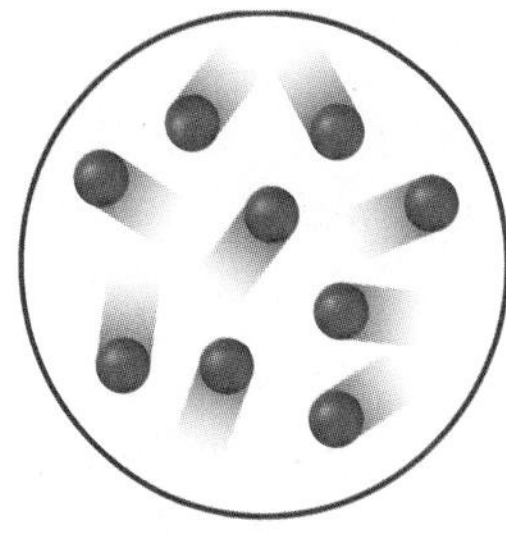

The particles that make up a gases are far apart. There is little or no attraction among the particles.

FOLDABLES®

Use your lesson Foldable to review the lesson. Save your Foldable for the project at the end of the chapter.

What do you think NOW?

You first read the statements below at the beginning of the chapter.

1. Particles moving at the same speed make up all matter.
2. The particles in a solid do not move.

Did you change your mind about whether you agree or disagree with the statements? Rewrite any false statements to make them true.

Use Vocabulary

1. A measurement of how strongly particles attract one another at the surface of a liquid is ______.
2. **Define** *solid, liquid,* and *gas* in your own words.
3. A measurement of a liquid's resistance to flow is known as ______.

Understand Key Concepts 

4. Which state of matter rarely is found on Earth?
   - **A.** gas
   - **B.** liquid
   - **C.** plasma
   - **D.** solid
5. **Compare** particle movement in solids, liquids, and gases.
6. **Compare** the forces between particles in a liquid and in a gas.

Interpret Graphics

7. **Explain** why the particles at the surface in the image below have surface tension while the particles below the surface do not.

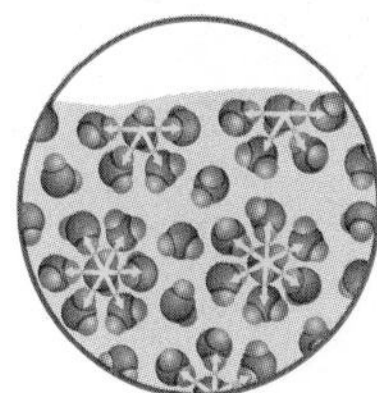

8. **Summarize** Copy and fill in the graphic organizer to compare two types of solids.

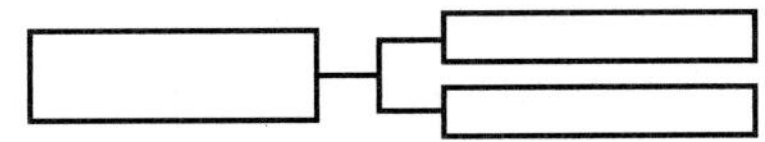

Critical Thinking

9. **Hypothesize** how you could change the viscosity of a cold liquid, and explain why your idea would work.
10. **Summarize** the relationship between the motion of particles and attractive forces between particles.

HOW IT WORKS

Freeze-Drying Foods

Have you noticed that the berries you find in some breakfast cereals are lightweight and dry—much different from the berries you get from the market or the garden?

Fresh fruit would spoil quickly if it were packaged in breakfast cereal, so fruits in cereals are often freeze-dried. When liquid is returned to the freeze-dried fruit, its physical properties more closely resemble fresh fruit. Freeze-drying, or lyophilization (lie ah fuh luh ZAY shun), is the process in which a solvent (usually water) is removed from a solid. During this process, a frozen solvent changes to a gas without going through the liquid state. Freeze-dried foods are lightweight and long-lasting. Astronauts have been using freeze-dried food during space travel since the 1960s.

How Freeze-Drying Works

1 Machines called freeze-dryers are used to freeze-dry foods and other products. Fresh or cooked food is flash-frozen, changing moisture in the food to a solid.

2 The frozen food is placed in a large vacuum chamber, where moisture is removed. Heat is applied to accelerate moisture removal. Condenser plates remove vaporized solvent from the chamber and convert the frozen food to a freeze-dried solid.

3 Freeze-dried food is sealed in oxygen- and moisture-proof packages to ensure stability and freshness. When the food is rehydrated, it returns to its near-normal state of weight, color, and texture.

ASTRONAUT
Ice Cream
NET WT .7 OZ (19g)

It's Your Turn

PREDICT/DISCOVER What kinds of products besides food are freeze-dried? Use library or internet resources to learn about other products that undergo the freeze-drying process. Discuss the benefits or drawbacks of freeze-drying.

Lesson 2

Changes in State

Reading Guide

Key Concepts
ESSENTIAL QUESTIONS

- How is temperature related to particle motion?
- How are temperature and thermal energy different?
- What happens to thermal energy when matter changes from one state to another?

Vocabulary

kinetic energy p. 50
temperature p. 50
thermal energy p. 51
vaporization p. 53
evaporation p. 54
condensation p. 54
sublimation p. 54
deposition p. 54

Academic Standards for Science

8.4.1 Understand how the strength of attractive forces between particles in a material helps to explain many physical properties of the material, such as why different materials exist as gases, liquids or solids at a given temperature.

Also covers: 8.NS.5, 8.NS.7

Inquiry Spring Thaw?

When you look at a snowman, you probably don't think about states of matter. However, water is one of the few substances that you frequently observe in three states of matter at Earth's temperatures. What energy changes are involved when matter changes state?

Launch Lab

10 minutes

Do liquid particles move?

If you look at a glass of milk sitting on a table, it appears to have no motion. But appearances can be deceiving!

1. Read and complete a lab safety form.
2. Use a **dropper,** and place one drop of **2 percent milk** on a **glass slide.** Add a **cover slip.**
3. Place the slide on a **microscope** stage, and focus on low power. Focus on a single globule of fat in the milk. Observe the motion of the globule for several minutes. Record your observations in your Science Journal.

Think About This

1. Describe the motion of the fat globule.
2. What do you think caused the motion of the globule?
3. **Key Concept** What do you think would happen to the motion of the fat globule if you warmed the milk? Explain.

Kinetic and Potential Energy

When snow begins to melt after a snowstorm, all three states of water are present. The snow is a solid, the melted snow is a liquid, and the air above the snow and ice contains water vapor, a gas. What causes particles to change state?

Kinetic Energy

Recall that the particles that make up matter are in constant motion. These particles have **kinetic energy,** *the energy an object has due to its motion.* The faster particles move, the more kinetic energy they have. Within a given substance, such as water, particles in the solid state have the least amount of kinetic energy. This is because they only vibrate in place. Particles in the liquid state move faster than particles in the solid state. Therefore, they have more kinetic energy. Particles in the gaseous state move very quickly and have the most kinetic energy of particles of a given substance.

Temperature *is a measure of the average kinetic energy of all the particles in an object.* Within a given substance, a temperature increase means that the particles, on average, are moving at greater speeds, or have a greater average kinetic energy. For example, water molecules at 25°C are generally moving faster and have more kinetic energy than water molecules at 10°C.

Key Concept Check How is temperature related to particle motion?

Potential Energy

In addition to kinetic energy, particles have potential energy. Potential energy is stored energy due to the interactions between particles or objects. For example, when you pick up a ball and then let it go, the gravitational force between the ball and Earth causes the ball to fall toward Earth. Before you let the ball go, it has potential energy.

Potential energy typically increases when objects get farther apart and decreases when they get closer together. The basketball in the top part of **Figure 8** is farther off the ground than it is in the bottom part of the figure. The farther an object is from Earth's surface, the greater the gravitational potential energy. As the ball gets closer to the ground, the potential energy decreases.

You can think of the potential energy of particles in a similar way. The chemical potential energy is due to the position of the particles relative to other particles. The chemical potential energy of particles increases and decreases as the distances between particles increases or decreases. The particles in the top part of **Figure 8** are farther apart than the particles in the bottom part. The particles that are farther apart have greater chemical potential energy.

Thermal Energy

Thermal energy *is the total potential and kinetic energies of an object.* You can change an object's state of matter by adding or removing thermal energy. When you add thermal energy to an object, the particles either move faster (increased kinetic energy) or get farther apart (increased potential energy) or both. The opposite is true when you remove thermal energy from an object. If enough thermal energy is added or removed, a change of state can occur.

Key Concept Check How do thermal energy and temperature differ?

Figure 8 The potential energy of the ball depends on the distance between the ball and Earth. The potential energy of particles in matter depends on the distances between the particles.

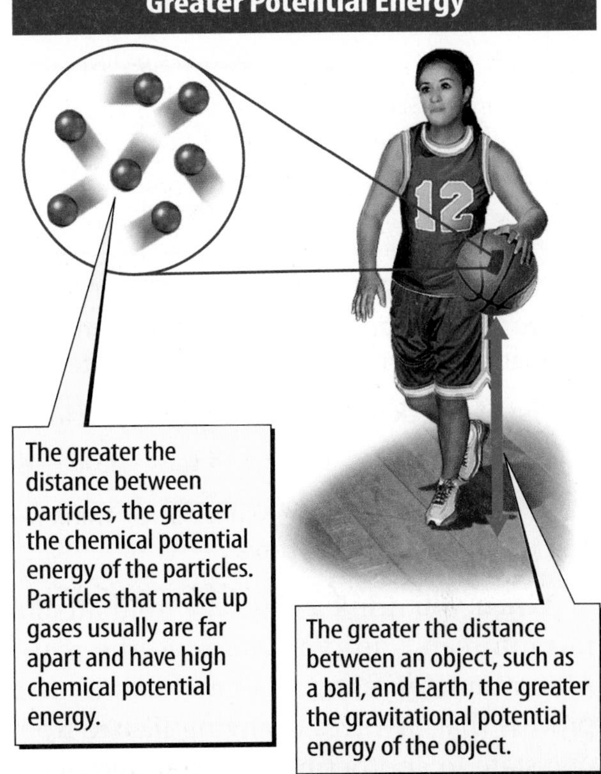

Greater Potential Energy
12
The greater the distance between particles, the greater the chemical potential energy of the particles. Particles that make up gases usually are far apart and have high chemical potential energy.
The greater the distance between an object, such as a ball, and Earth, the greater the gravitational potential energy of the object.

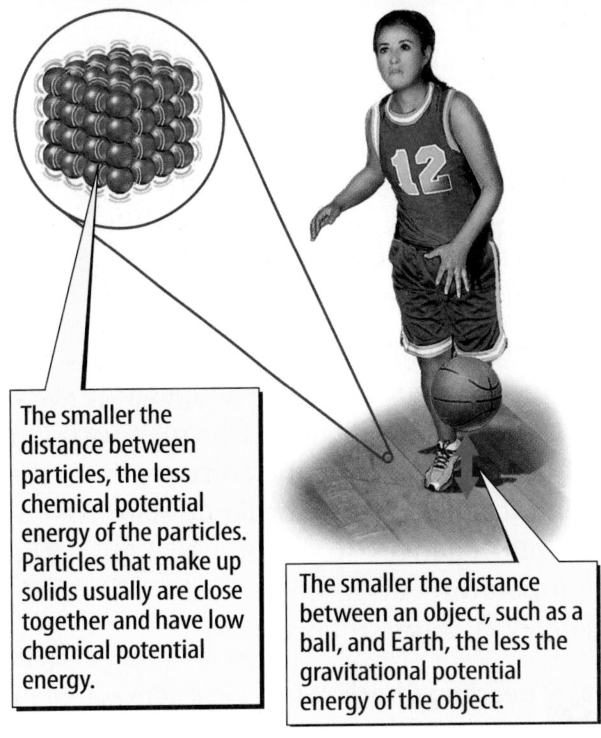

Less Potential Energy
12
The smaller the distance between particles, the less chemical potential energy of the particles. Particles that make up solids usually are close together and have low chemical potential energy.
The smaller the distance between an object, such as a ball, and Earth, the less the gravitational potential energy of the object.

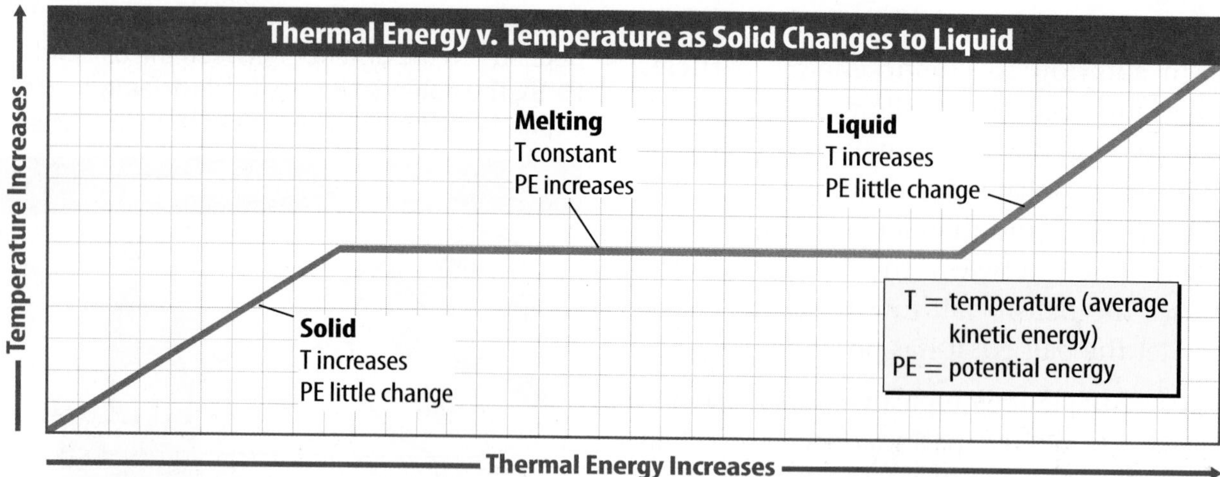

Figure 9 Adding thermal energy to matter causes the particles that make up the matter to increase in kinetic energy, potential energy, or both.

Visual Check During melting, which factor remains constant?

Solid to Liquid or Liquid to Solid

When you drink a beverage from an aluminum can, do you recycle the can? Aluminum recycling is one example of a process that involves changing matter from one state to another by adding or removing thermal energy.

Melting

The first part of the recycling process involves melting aluminum cans. To change matter from a solid to a liquid, thermal energy must be added. The graph in **Figure 9** shows the relationship between increasing temperature and increasing thermal energy (potential energy + kinetic energy).

At first, both the thermal energy and the temperature increase. The temperature stops increasing when it reaches the melting point of the matter, the temperature at which the solid state changes to the liquid state. As aluminum changes from solid to liquid, the temperature does not change. However, energy changes still occur.

Reading Check What is added to matter to change it from a solid to a liquid?

Energy Changes

What happens when a solid reaches its melting point? Notice the line on the graph is horizontal. This means that the temperature, or average kinetic energy, stops increasing. However, the amount of thermal energy continues to increase. How is this possible?

Once a solid reaches its melting point, the average speed of particles does not change, but the distance between the particles does change. The particles move farther apart and potential energy increases. Once a solid completely melts, the addition of thermal energy will cause the kinetic energy of the particles to increase again, as shown by a temperature increase.

Freezing

After the aluminum melts, it is poured into molds to cool. As the aluminum cools, thermal energy leaves it. Freezing is a process that is the reverse of melting. The temperature at which matter changes from the liquid state to the solid state is its freezing point. To observe the temperature and thermal energy changes that occur to hot aluminum blocks, move from right to left on the graph in **Figure 9.**

During evaporation, a liquid vaporizes only at its surface.
During boiling, a liquid vaporizes at its surface and within the liquid.
Bubbles, or vaporized particles, rise to the top of the liquid and escape from the container.

▲ **Figure 10** Boiling and evaporation are two kinds of vaporization.

Visual Check Why doesn't the evaporation flask have bubbles below the surface?

Personal Tutor

Liquid to Gas or Gas to Liquid

When you heat water, do you ever notice how bubbles begin to form at the bottom and rise to the surface? The bubbles contain water vapor, a gas. *The change in state of a liquid into a gas is* **vaporization.** **Figure 10** shows two types of vaporization—evaporation and boiling.

Boiling

Vaporization that occurs within a liquid is called boiling. The temperature at which boiling occurs in a liquid is called its boiling point. In **Figure 11,** notice the energy changes that occur during this process. The kinetic energy of particles increases until the liquid reaches its boiling point.

At the boiling point, the potential energy of particles begins increasing. The particles move farther apart until the attractive forces no longer hold them together. At this point, the liquid changes to a gas. When boiling ends, if thermal energy continues to be added, the kinetic energy of the gas particles begins to increase again. Therefore, the temperature begins to increase again as shown on the graph.

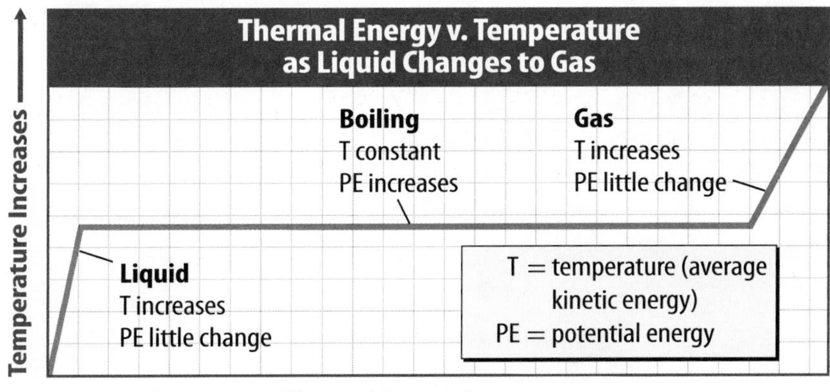

◀ **Figure 11** When thermal energy is added to a liquid, kinetic energy and potential energy changes occur.

WORD ORIGIN
evaporation
from Latin *evaporare,* means "disperse in steam or vapor"

Evaporation

Unlike boiling, **evaporation** *is vaporization that occurs only at the surface of a liquid.* Liquid in an open container will vaporize, or change to a gas, over time due to evaporation.

Condensation

Boiling and evaporation are processes that change a liquid to a gas. A reverse process also occurs. When a gas loses enough thermal energy, the gas changes to a liquid, or condenses. *The change of state from a gas to a liquid is called* **condensation.** Overnight, water vapor often condenses on blades of grass, forming dew.

Solid to Gas or Gas to Solid

Is it possible for a solid to become a gas without turning to a liquid first? Yes, in fact, dry ice does. Dry ice, as shown in **Figure 12,** is solid carbon dioxide. It turns immediately into a gas when thermal energy is added to it. The process is called sublimation. **Sublimation** *is the change of state from a solid to a gas without going through the liquid state.* As dry ice sublimes, it cools and condenses the water vapor in the surrounding air, creating a thick fog.

SCIENCE USE V. COMMON USE
deposition
Science Use the change of state of a gas to a solid without going through the liquid state

Common Use giving a legal testimony under oath

The opposite of sublimation is deposition. **Deposition** *is the change of state of a gas to a solid without going through the liquid state.* For deposition to occur, thermal energy has to be removed from the gas. You might see deposition in autumn when you wake up and there is frost on the grass. As water vapor loses thermal energy, it changes into a solid known as frost.

Reading Check Why are sublimation and deposition unusual changes of state?

Figure 12 Dry ice sublimes—goes directly from the solid state to the gas state—when thermal energy is added. Frost is an example of the opposite process—deposition.

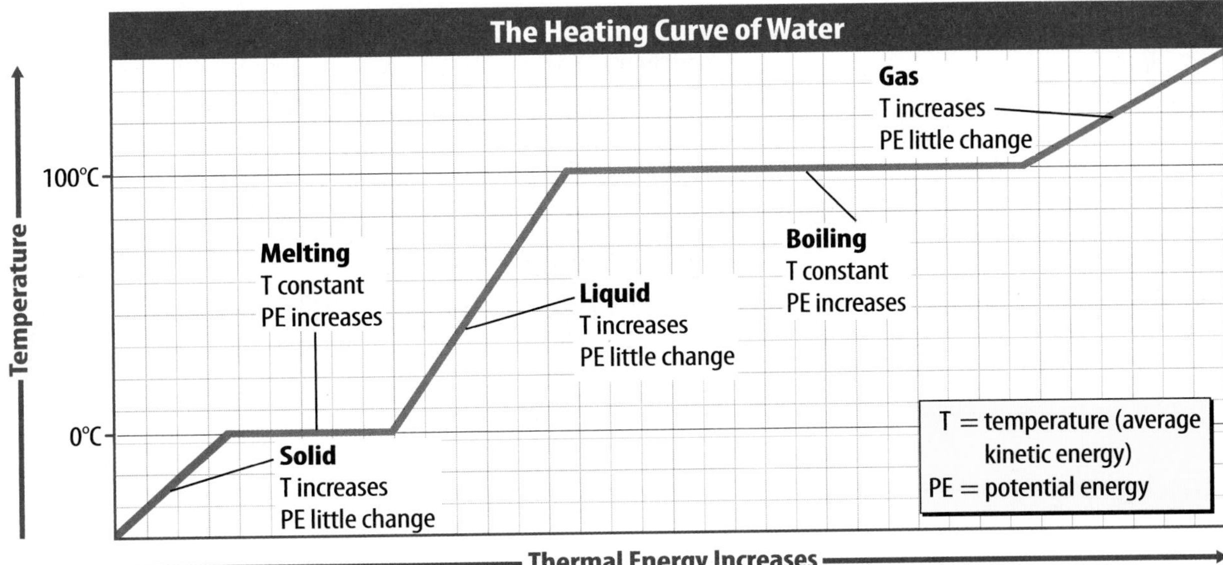

Figure 13 Water undergoes energy changes and state changes as thermal energy is added and removed.

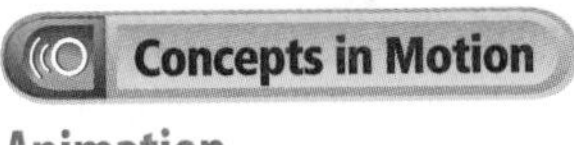

Animation

States of Water

Water is the only substance that exists naturally as a solid, a liquid, and a gas within Earth's temperature range. To better understand the energy changes during a change in state, it is helpful to study the heating curve of water, as shown in **Figure 13.**

Adding Thermal Energy

Suppose you place a beaker of ice on a hot plate. The hot plate transfers thermal energy to the beaker and then to the ice. The temperature of the ice increases. Recall that this means the average kinetic energy of the water molecules increases.

At 0°C, the melting point of water, the water molecules vibrate so rapidly that they begin to move out of their places. At this point, added thermal energy only increases the distance between particles and decreases attractive forces—melting occurs. Once melting is complete, the average kinetic energy of the particles (temperature) begins to increase again as more thermal energy is added.

When water reaches 100°C, the boiling point, liquid water begins to change to water vapor. Again, kinetic energy is constant as vaporization occurs. When the change of state is complete, the kinetic energy of molecules increases once more, and so does the temperature.

Key Concept Check Describe the changes in thermal energy as water goes from a solid to a liquid.

Removing Thermal Energy

The removal of thermal energy is the reverse of the process shown in **Figure 13.** Cooling water vapor changes the gas to a liquid. Cooling the water further changes it to ice.

FOLDABLES®

Fold a sheet of notebook paper to make a four-tab Foldable as shown. Label the tabs, define the terms, and record what you learn about each term under the tabs.

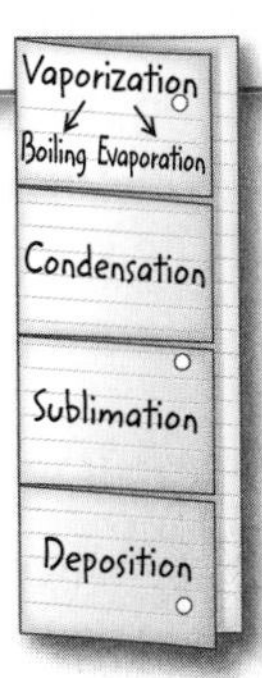

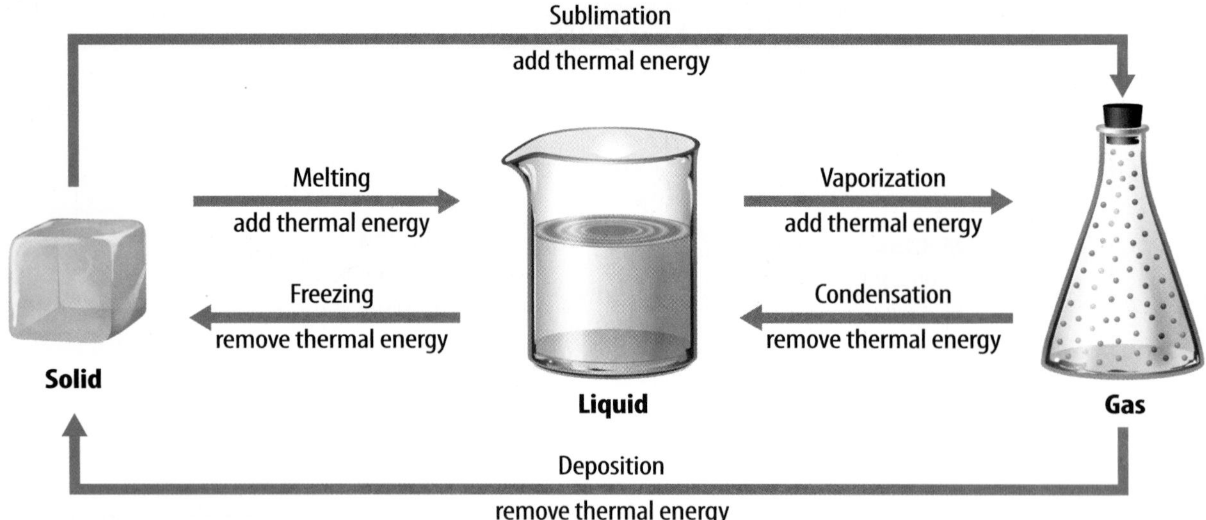

Figure 14 For a change of state to occur, thermal energy must move into or out of matter.

Animation

Conservation of Mass and Energy

The diagram in **Figure 14** illustrates the energy changes that occur as thermal energy is added or removed from matter. Notice that opposite processes, melting and freezing and vaporization and condensation, are shown. When matter changes state, matter and energy are always conserved.

When water vaporizes, it appears to disappear. If the invisible gas is captured and its mass added to the remaining mass of the liquid, you would see that matter is conserved. This is also true for energy. Surrounding matter, such as air, often absorbs thermal energy. If you measured all the thermal energy, you would find that energy is conserved.

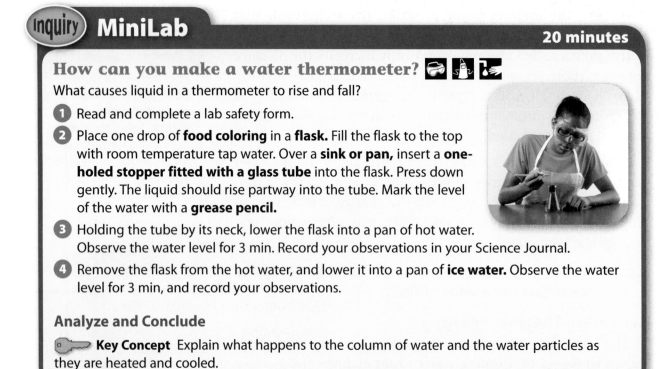

Inquiry MiniLab

20 minutes

How can you make a water thermometer?

What causes liquid in a thermometer to rise and fall?

1. Read and complete a lab safety form.
2. Place one drop of **food coloring** in a **flask.** Fill the flask to the top with room temperature tap water. Over a **sink or pan,** insert a **one-holed stopper fitted with a glass tube** into the flask. Press down gently. The liquid should rise partway into the tube. Mark the level of the water with a **grease pencil.**
3. Holding the tube by its neck, lower the flask into a pan of hot water. Observe the water level for 3 min. Record your observations in your Science Journal.
4. Remove the flask from the hot water, and lower it into a pan of **ice water.** Observe the water level for 3 min, and record your observations.

Analyze and Conclude

Key Concept Explain what happens to the column of water and the water particles as they are heated and cooled.

Lesson 2 Review

✓ Assessment Online Quiz

Visual Summary

All matter has thermal energy. Thermal energy is the sum of potential and kinetic energy.

When thermal energy is added to a liquid, vaporization can occur.

When enough thermal energy is removed from matter, a change of state can occur.

FOLDABLES®

Use your lesson Foldable to review the lesson. Save your Foldable for the project at the end of the chapter.

What do you think NOW?

You first read the statements below at the beginning of the chapter.

3. Particles of matter have both potential energy and kinetic energy.

4. When a solid melts, thermal energy is removed from the solid.

Did you change your mind about whether you agree or disagree with the statements? Rewrite any false statements to make them true.

Use Vocabulary

1. The measure of average kinetic energy of the particles in a material is ___________.
2. **Define** *kinetic energy* and *thermal energy* in your own words.
3. The change of a liquid into a gas is known as ___________.

Understand Key Concepts 

4. The process that is opposite of condensation is known as
   - **A.** deposition.
   - **B.** freezing.
   - **C.** melting.
   - **D.** vaporization.
5. **Explain** how temperature and particle motion are related.
6. **Describe** the relationship between temperature and thermal energy.
7. **Generalize** the changes in thermal energy when matter increases in temperature and then changes state.

Interpret Graphics

8. **Describe** what is occurring below.

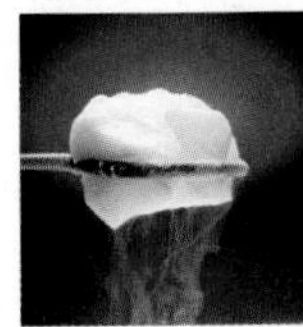

9. **Summarize** Copy and fill in the graphic organizer below to identify the two types of vaporization that can occur in matter.

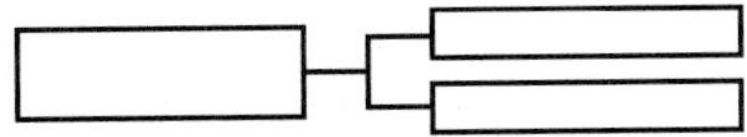

Critical Thinking

10. **Summarize** the energy and state changes that occur when freezing rain falls and solidifies on a wire fence.
11. **Compare** the amount of thermal energy needed to melt a solid and the amount of thermal energy needed to freeze the same liquid.

How does dissolving substances in water change its freezing point?

Materials

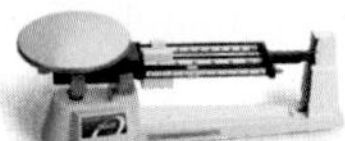
triple-beam balance

beaker

foam cup

50-mL graduated cylinder

distilled water

Also needed: ice-salt slush, test tubes, thermometers

Safety

You know that when thermal energy is removed from a liquid, the particles move more slowly. At the freezing point, the particles move so slowly that the attractive forces pull them together to form a solid. What happens if the water contains particles of another substance, such as salt? You will form a hypothesis and test the hypothesis to find out.

Learn It

To **form a hypothesis** is to propose a possible explanation for an observation that is testable by a scientific investigation. You **test the hypothesis** by conducting a scientific investigation to see whether the hypothesis is supported.

Try It

1. Read and complete a lab safety form.
2. Form a hypothesis that answers the question in the title of the lab. Write your hypothesis in your Science Journal.
3. Copy the data table in your Science Journal.
4. Use a triple-beam balance to measure 5 g of table salt (NaCl). Dissolve the 5 g of table salt in 50 mL of distilled water.
5. Place 40 mL of distilled water in one large test tube. Place 40 mL of the salt-water mixture in a second large test tube.
6. Measure and record the temperature of the liquids in each test tube.
7. Place both test tubes into a large foam cup filled with crushed ice-salt slush. Gently rotate the thermometers in the test tubes. Record the temperature in each test tube every minute until the temperature remains the same for several minutes.

Apply It

8. How does the data tell you when the freezing point of the liquid has been reached?
9. Was your hypothesis supported? Why or why not?
10. **Key Concept** Explain your observations in terms of how temperature affects particle motion and how a liquid changes to a solid.

Water	Time (min)	0	1	2	3	4	5	6	7	8
	Temperature (°C)									
Salt water	Time (min)	0	1	2	3	4	5	6	7	8
	Temperature (°C)									

Lesson 3

The Behavior of Gases

Reading Guide

Key Concepts
ESSENTIAL QUESTIONS

- How does the kinetic molecular theory describe the behavior of a gas?
- How are temperature, pressure, and volume related in Boyle's law?
- How is Boyle's law different from Charles's law?

Vocabulary

kinetic molecular theory p. 60

pressure p. 61

Boyle's law p. 62

Charles's law p. 63

Multilingual eGlossary

Video

What's Science Got to do With It?

Academic Standards for Science

8.4.3 Investigate the properties (mechanical, chemical, electrical, thermal, magnetic, and optical) of natural and engineered materials.

Also covers: 8.NS.2, 8.NS.3, 8.NS.4, 8.NS.5, 8.NS.7, 8.NS.8, 8.NS.11, 8.DP.1, 8.DP.2, 8.DP.3, 8.DP.4, 8.DP.5, 8.DP.6, 8.DP.7, 8.DP.8, 8.DP.9, 8.DP.10, 8.DP.11

Inquiry Survival Gear?

Why do some pilots wear oxygen masks? Planes fly at high altitudes where the atmosphere has a lower pressure and gas molecules are less concentrated. If the pressure is not adjusted inside the airplane, a pilot must wear an oxygen mask to inhale enough oxygen to keep the body functioning.

Launch Lab

15 minutes

Are volume and pressure of a gas related?

Pressure affects gases differently than it affects solids and liquids. How do pressure changes affect the volume of a gas?

1. Read and complete a lab safety form.
2. Stretch and blow up a **small balloon** several times.
3. Finally, blow up the balloon to a diameter of about 5 cm. Twist the neck, and stretch the mouth of the balloon over the opening of a **plastic bottle. Tape** the neck of the balloon to the bottle.
4. Squeeze and release the bottle several times while observing the balloon. Record your observations in your Science Journal.

Think About This

1. Why doesn't the balloon deflate when you attach it to the bottle?
2. What caused the balloon to inflate when you squeezed the bottle?
3. **Key Concept** Using this lab as a reference, do you think pressure and volume of a gas are related? Explain.

Understanding Gas Behavior

Pilots do not worry as much about solids and liquids at high altitudes as they do gases. That is because gases behave differently than solids and liquids. Changes in temperature, pressure, and volume affect the behavior of gases more than they affect solids and liquids.

Academic Vocabulary

theory
(noun) an explanation of things or events that is based on knowledge gained from many observations and investigations

The explanation of particle behavior in solids, liquids, and gases is based on the kinetic molecular theory. *The* **kinetic molecular theory** *is an explanation of how particles in matter behave.* Some basic ideas in this theory are

- small particles make up all matter;
- these particles are in constant, random motion;
- the particles collide with other particles, other objects, and the walls of their container;
- when particles collide, no energy is lost.

You have read about most of these, but the last two statements are very important in explaining how gases behave.

Key Concept Check How does the kinetic molecular theory describe the behavior of a gas?

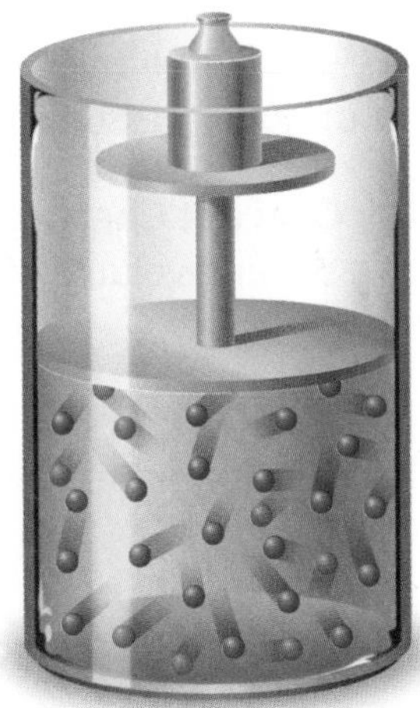

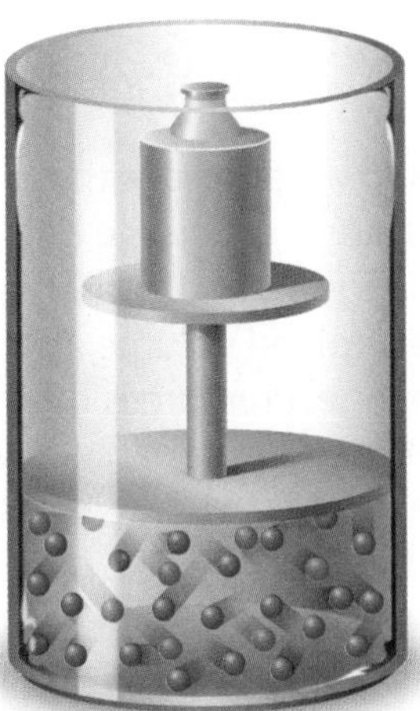

Figure 15 As weight on the plunger increases, pressure inside the cylinder increases. As pressure increases, the volume of the gas decreases.

What is pressure?

Particles in gases move constantly. As a result of this movement, gas particles constantly collide with other particles and their container. When particles collide with their container, pressure results. **Pressure** *is the amount of force applied per unit of area.* For example, gas in a cylinder, as shown in **Figure 15,** might contain trillions of gas particles. These particles exert forces on the cylinder each time they strike it. When the plunger moves down because of the weight on it, pressure inside the cylinder increases. The space between particles decreases, and the gas is compressed. The empty spaces between particles make gases compressible.

Pressure and Volume

Figure 15 also shows the relationship between pressure and volume of gas at a constant temperature. What happens to pressure if the volume of a container changes? Notice that when the volume is greater, the particles have more room to move. This additional space results in fewer collisions within the cylinder, and pressure is less. The gas particles in the middle cylinder have even less volume and more pressure. In the cylinder on the right, the pressure is greater because the volume is less. The particles collide with the container more frequently. Because of the greater number of collisions within the container, pressure is greater.

WORD ORIGIN

pressure
from Latin *pressura,* means "to press"

FOLDABLES®

Fold a sheet of notebook paper to make a three-tab Foldable and label as shown. Use your Foldable to compare two important gas laws.

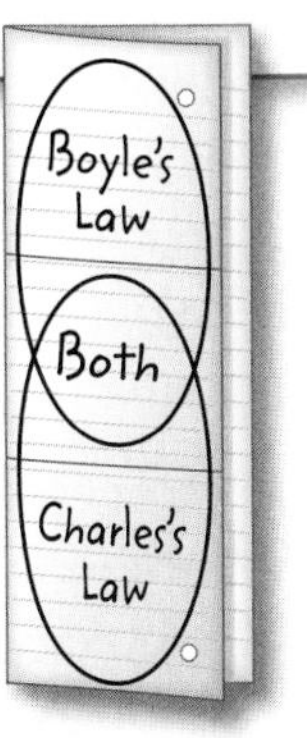

Math Skills 

Solve Equations

Boyle's law can be stated by the equation

$$V_2 = \frac{P_1V_1}{P_2}$$

P_1 and V_1 represent the pressure and volume before a change. P_2 and V_2 are the pressure and volume after a change. Pressure is often measured in kilopascals (kPa). For example, what is the final volume of a gas with an initial volume of **50.0 mL** if the pressure increases from **600.0 kPa** to **900.0 kPa**?

1. Replace the terms in the equation with the actual values.

$$V_2 = \frac{(600.0 \text{ kPa})(50.0 \text{ mL})}{(900.0 \text{ kPa})}$$

2. Cancel units, multiply, and then divide.

$$V_2 = \frac{(600.0 \cancel{\text{kPa}})(50.0 \text{ mL})}{(900.0 \cancel{\text{kPa}})}$$

$$V_2 = 33.3 \text{ mL}$$

Practice

What is the final volume of a gas with an initial volume of 100.0 mL if the pressure decreases from 500.0 kPa to 250.0 kPa?

- Math Practice
- Personal Tutor

Boyle's Law

You read that the pressure and volume of a gas are related. Robert Boyle (1627–1691), a British scientist, was the first to describe this property of gases. **Boyle's law** *states that pressure of a gas increases if the volume decreases and pressure of a gas decreases if the volume increases, when temperature is constant.* This law can be expressed mathematically as shown to the left.

Key Concept Check What is the relationship between pressure and volume of a gas if temperature is constant?

Boyle's Law in Action

You have probably felt Boyle's law in action if you have ever traveled in an airplane. While on the ground, the air pressure inside your middle ear and the pressure of the air surrounding you are equal. As the airplane takes off and begins to increase in altitude, the air pressure of the surrounding air decreases. However, the air pressure inside your middle ear does not decrease. The trapped air in your middle ear increases in volume, which can cause pain. These pressure changes also occur when the plane is landing. You can equalize this pressure difference by yawning or chewing gum.

Graphing Boyle's Law

This relationship is shown in the graph in **Figure 16.** Pressure is on the *x*-axis, and volume is on the *y*-axis. Notice that the line decreases in value from left to right. This shows that as the pressure of a gas increases, the volume of the gas decreases.

Figure 16 The graph shows that as pressure increases, volume decreases. This is true only if the temperature of the gas is constant.

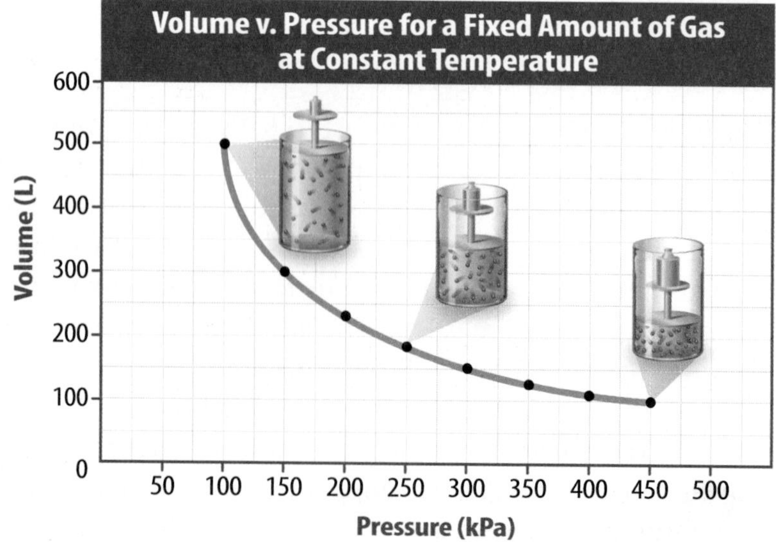

Figure 17 As the temperature of a gas increases, the kinetic energy of the particles increases. The particles move farther apart, and volume increases.

Temperature and Volume

Pressure and volume changes are not the only factors that affect gas behavior. Changing the temperature of a gas also affects its behavior, as shown in **Figure 17.** The gas in the cylinder on the left has a low temperature. The average kinetic energy of the particles is low, and they move closer together. The volume of the gas is less. When thermal energy is added to the cylinder, the gas particles move faster and spread farther apart. This increases the pressure from gas particles, which push up the plunger. This increases the volume of the container.

Charles's Law

Jacque Charles (1746–1823) was a French scientist who described the relationship between temperature and volume of a gas. **Charles's law** *states that the volume of a gas increases with increasing temperature, if the pressure is constant.* Charles's practical experience with gases was most likely the result of his interest in balloons. Charles and his colleague were the first to pilot and fly a hydrogen-filled balloon in 1783.

Key Concept Check How is Boyle's law different from Charles's law?

Inquiry MiniLab — 20 minutes

How does temperature affect the volume?

You can observe Charles's law in action using a few lab supplies.

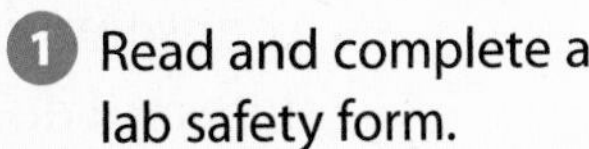

1. Read and complete a lab safety form.

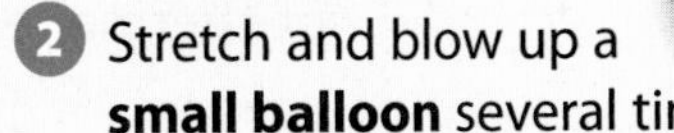

2. Stretch and blow up a **small balloon** several times.

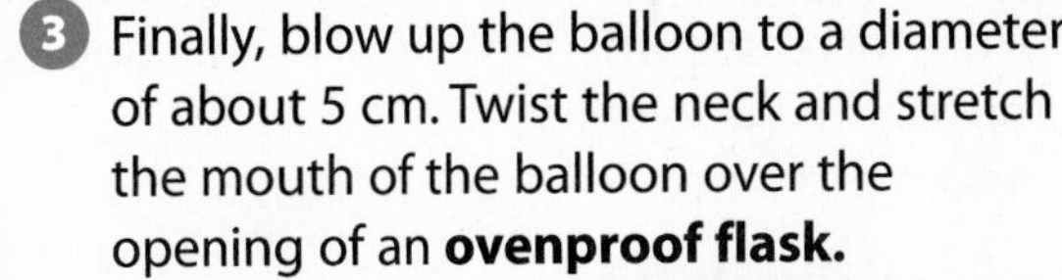

3. Finally, blow up the balloon to a diameter of about 5 cm. Twist the neck and stretch the mouth of the balloon over the opening of an **ovenproof flask.**
4. Place the flask on a cold **hot plate.** Turn on the hot plate to low, and gradually heat the flask. Record your observations in your Science Journal.
5. ⚠ Use **tongs** to remove the flask from the hot plate. Allow the flask to cool for 5 min. Record your observations.
6. Place the flask in a **bowl of ice water.** Record your observations.

Analyze and Conclude

Key Concept What is the effect of temperature changes on the volume of a gas?

Charles's Law in Action

You have probably seen Charles's law in action if you have ever taken a balloon outside on a cold winter day. Why does a balloon appear slightly deflated when you take it from a warm place to a cold place? When the balloon is in cold air, the temperature of the gas inside the balloon decreases. Recall that a decrease in temperature is a decrease in the average kinetic energy of particles. As a result, the gas particles slow down and begin to get closer together. Fewer particles hit the inside of the balloon. The balloon appears partially deflated. If the balloon is returned to a warm place, the kinetic energy of the particles increases. More particles hit the inside of the balloon and push it out. The volume increases.

Reading Check What happens when you warm a balloon?

Graphing Charles's Law

The relationship described in Charles's law is shown in the graph of several gases in **Figure 18.** Temperature is on the *x*-axis and volume is on the *y*-axis. Notice that the lines are straight and represent increasing values. Each line in the graph is extrapolated to −273°C. *Extrapolated* means the graph is extended beyond the observed data points. This temperature also is referred to as 0 K (kelvin), or absolute zero. This temperature is theoretically the lowest possible temperature of matter. At absolute zero, all particles are at the lowest possible energy state and do not move. The particles contain a minimal amount of thermal energy (potential energy + kinetic energy).

Key Concept Check Which factors must be constant in Boyle's law and in Charles's law?

Figure 18 The volume of a gas increases when the temperature increases at constant pressure.

Visual Check What do the dashed lines mean?

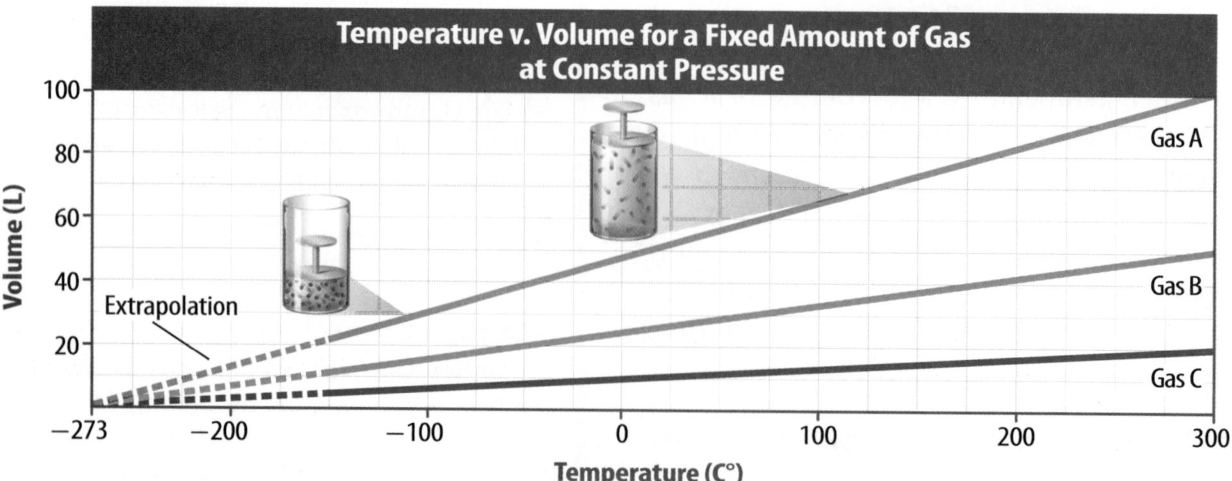

Lesson 3 Review

Assessment Online Quiz
? Inquiry Virtual Lab

Visual Summary

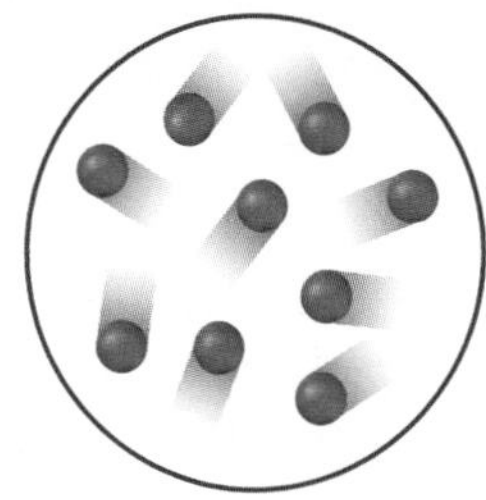

The explanation of particle behavior in solids, liquids, and gases is based on the kinetic molecular theory.

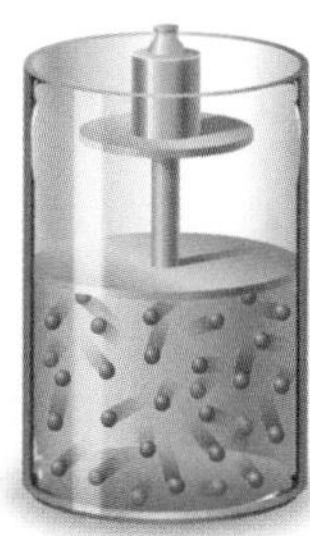

As volume of a gas decreases, the pressure increases when at constant temperature.

At constant pressure, as the temperature of a gas increases, the volume also increases.

FOLDABLES®

Use your lesson Foldable to review the lesson. Save your Foldable for the project at the end of the chapter.

What do you think NOW?

You first read the statements below at the beginning of the chapter.

5. Changes in temperature and pressure affect gas behavior.

6. If the pressure on a gas increases, the volume of the gas also increases.

Did you change your mind about whether you agree or disagree with the statements? Rewrite any false statements to make them true.

Use Vocabulary

1 **List** the basic ideas of the kinetic molecular theory.

2 ________ is force applied per unit area.

Understand Key Concepts 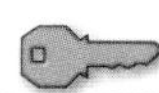

3 Which is held constant when a gas obeys Boyle's law?

A. motion
B. pressure
C. temperature
D. volume

4 **Describe** how the kinetic molecular theory explains the behavior of a gas.

5 **Contrast** Charles's law with Boyle's law.

6 **Explain** how temperature, pressure, and volume are related in Boyle's law.

Interpret Graphics

7 **Explain** what happens to the particles to the right when more weights are added?

8 **Identify** Copy and fill in the graphic organizer below to list three factors that affect gas behavior.

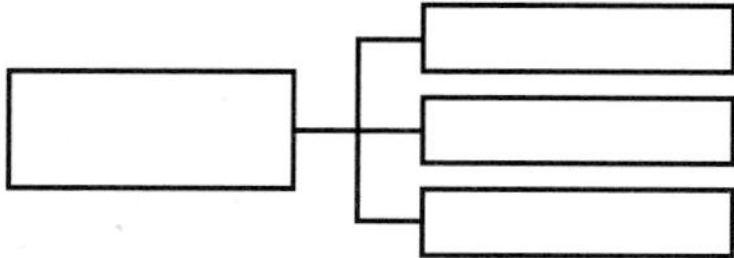

Critical Thinking

9 **Describe** what would happen to the pressure of a gas if the volume of the gas doubles while at a constant temperature.

Math Skills

Math Practice

10 **Calculate** The pressure on 400 mL of a gas is raised from 20.5 kPa to 80.5 kPa. What is the final volume of the gas?

Lab

1–2 Class Periods

Design an Experiment to Collect Data

In this chapter, you have learned about the relationship between the motion of particles in matter and change of state. How might you use your knowledge of particles in real life? Suppose that you work for a state highway department in a cold climate. Your job is to test three products. You must determine which is the most effective in melting existing ice, the best at keeping melted ice from refreezing, and the best product to buy.

Question

How can you compare the products? What might make one product better than another? Consider how you can describe and compare the effect of each product on both existing ice and the freezing point of water. Think about controls, variables, and the equipment you have available.

Procedure

1. Read and complete a lab safety form.
2. In your Science Journal, write a set of procedures you will use to answer your questions. Include the materials and steps you will use to test the effect of each product on existing ice and on the freezing point of water. How will you record your data? Draw any data tables, such as the example below, that you might need. Have your teacher approve your procedures.

Distilled Water	Time (min)	0	1	2	3	4	5	6	7	8
	Temperature (°C)									
Product A	Time (min)	0	1	2	3	4	5	6	7	8
	Temperature (°C)									
Product B	Time (min)	0	1	2	3	4	5	6	7	8
	Temperature (°C)									
Product C	Time (min)	0	1	2	3	4	5	6	7	8
	Temperature (°C)									

3. Begin by observing and recording your observations on how each product affects ice. Does it make ice melt or melt faster?
4. Test the effect of each product on the freezing point of water. Think about how you will ensure that each product is tested in the same way.
5. Add any additional tests you think you might need to make your recommendation.

Materials

triple-beam balance

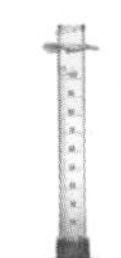

50-mL graduated cylinders

beakers

test tubes

thermometers

distilled water

Also needed: ice, salt

Safety

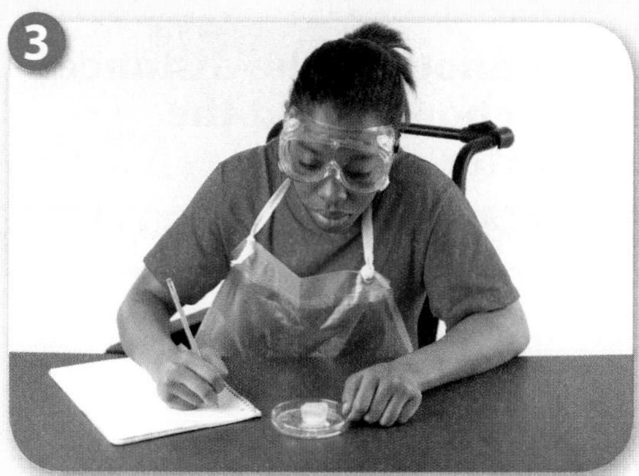

Analyze and Conclude

6. **Analyze the data** you have collected. Which product was most effective in melting existing ice? How do you know?
7. **Determine** which product was most effective in lowering the freezing point of water.
8. **Draw or make a model** to show the effect of dissolved solids on water molecules.
9. **Recognize Cause and Effect** In terms of particles, what causes dissolved solids to lower the freezing point of water?
10. **Draw Conclusions** In terms of particles, why are some substances more effective than others in lowering the freezing point of water?
11. **The Big Idea** Why is the kinetic molecular theory important in understanding how and why matter changes state?

Communicate Your Results

You are to present your recommendations to the road commissioners. Create a graphic presentation that clearly displays your results and justifies your recommendations about which product to buy.

Extension

In some states, road crews spray liquid deicer on the roads. If your teacher approves, you may enjoy testing liquids, such as alcohol, corn syrup, or salad oil.

Lab Tips

- To ensure fair testing, add the same mass of each product to the ice cubes at the same time.
- Be sure to add the same mass of each solid to the same volume of water. About 1 g of solid in 10 mL of water is a good ratio.
- Keep adding crushed ice/salt slush to the cup so that the liquid in the test tubes remains below the surface.

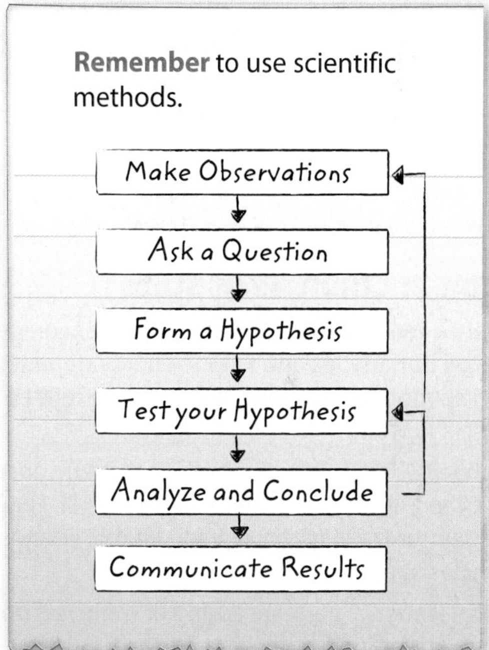

Chapter 2 Study Guide

As matter changes from one state to another, the distances and the forces between the particles change, and the amount of thermal energy in the matter changes.

Key Concepts Summary

Lesson 1: Solids, Liquids, and Gases

- Particles vibrate in **solids.** They move faster in **liquids** and even faster in **gases.**
- The force of attraction among particles decreases as matter goes from a solid, to a liquid, and finally to a gas.

Solid

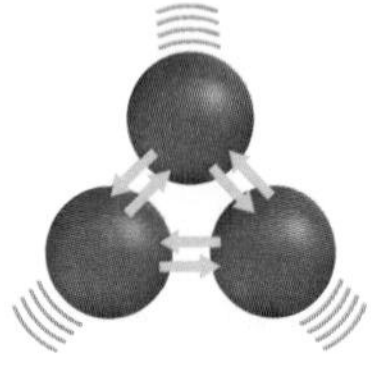

Liquid

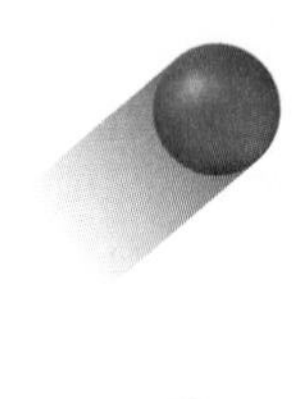

Gas

Vocabulary

solid p. 43
liquid p. 44
viscosity p. 44
surface tension p. 45
gas p. 46
vapor p. 46

Lesson 2: Changes in State

- Because **temperature** is defined as the average **kinetic energy** of particles and kinetic energy depends on particle motion, temperature is directly related to particle motion.
- **Thermal energy** includes both the kinetic energy and the potential energy of particles in matter. However, temperature is only the average kinetic energy of particles in matter.
- Thermal energy must be added or removed from matter for a change of state to occur.

Vocabulary

kinetic energy p. 50
temperature p. 50
thermal energy p. 51
vaporization p. 53
evaporation p. 54
condensation p. 54
sublimation p. 54
deposition p. 54

Lesson 3: The Behavior of Gases

- The **kinetic molecular theory** states basic assumptions that are used to describe particles and their interactions in gases and other states of matter.
- **Pressure** of a gas increases if the volume decreases, and pressure of a gas decreases if the volume increases, when temperature is constant.
- **Boyle's law** describes the behavior of a gas when pressure and volume change at constant temperature. **Charles's law** describes the behavior of a gas when temperature and volume change, and pressure is constant.

Vocabulary

kinetic molecular theory p. 60
pressure p. 61
Boyle's Law p. 62
Charles's Law p. 63

Review
- Personal Tutor
- Vocabulary eGames
- Vocabulary eFlashcards

FOLDABLES® Chapter Project

Assemble your lesson Foldables as shown to make a Chapter Project. Use the project to review what you have learned in this chapter.

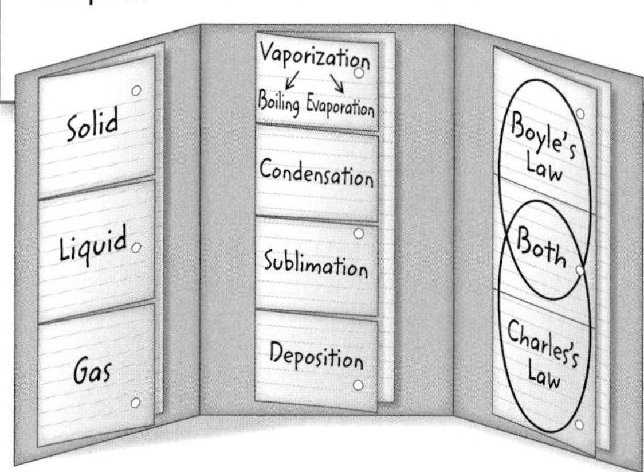

Use Vocabulary

Replace the underlined word with the correct term.

1. Matter with a definite shape and a definite volume is known as a <u>gas</u>.
2. <u>Surface tension</u> is a measure of a liquid's resistance to flow.
3. The gas state of a substance that is normally a solid or a liquid at room temperature is a <u>pressure</u>.
4. <u>Boiling</u> is vaporization that occurs at the surface of a liquid.
5. <u>Boyle's law</u> is an explanation of how particles in matter behave.
6. When graphing a gas obeying <u>Boyle's law</u>, the line will be a straight line with a positive slope.

Link Vocabulary and Key Concepts

Concepts in Motion Interactive Concept Map

Copy this concept map, and then use vocabulary terms from the previous page to complete the concept map.

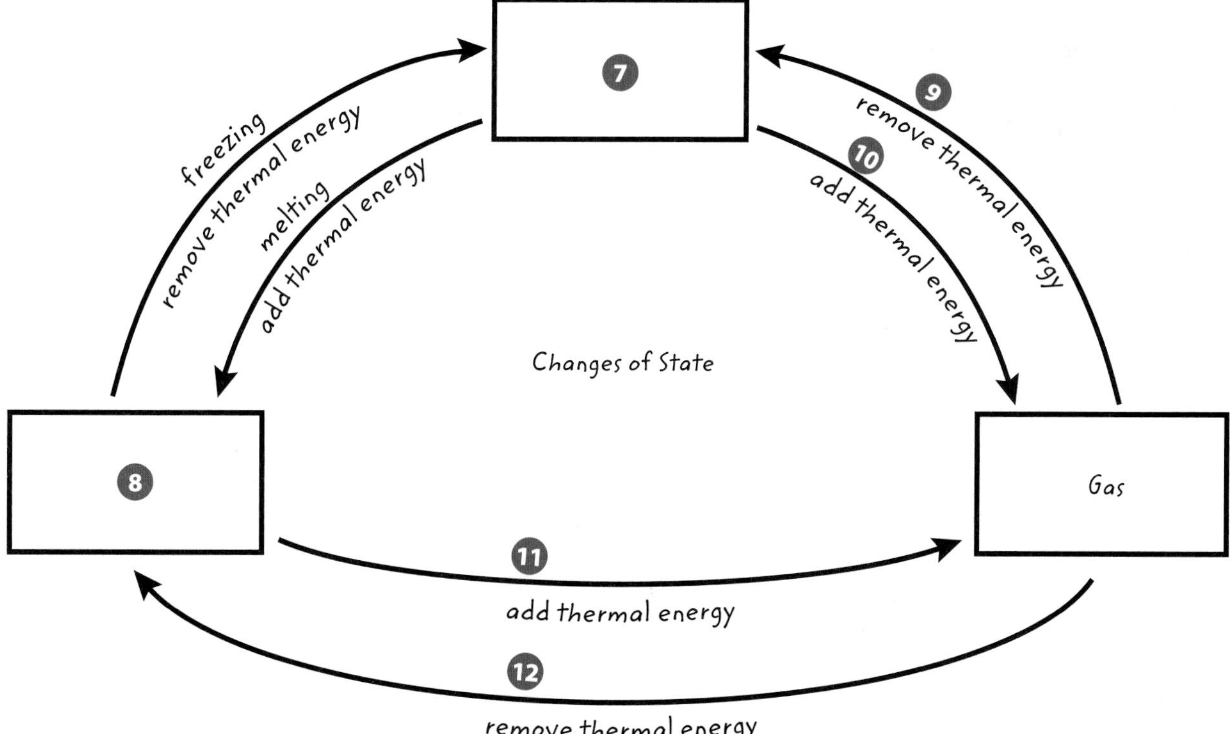

Chapter 2 Review

Understand Key Concepts 

1. What would happen if you tried to squeeze a gas into a smaller container?
   A. The attractive forces between the particles would increase.
   B. The force of the particles would prevent you from doing it.
   C. The particles would have fewer collisions with the container.
   D. The repulsive forces of the particles would pull on the container.

2. Which type of motion in the figure below best represents the movement of gas particles?

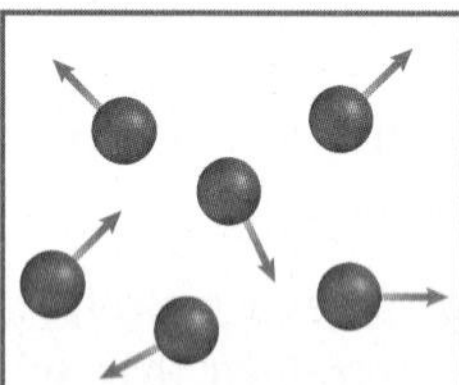

Motion 1

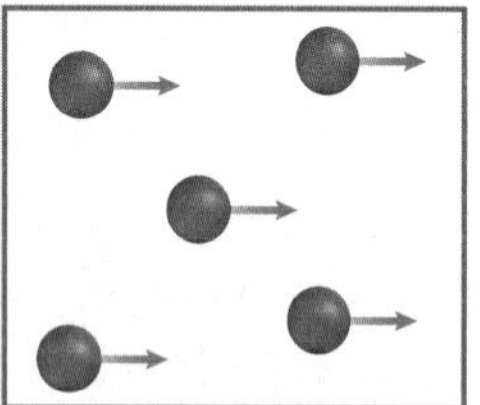

Motion 2

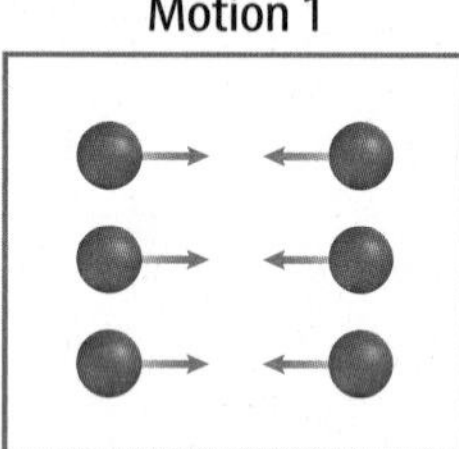

Motion 3

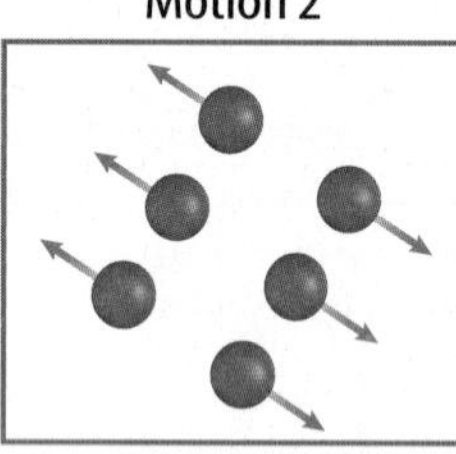

Motion 4

   A. motion 1
   B. motion 2
   C. motion 3
   D. motion 4

3. A pile of snow slowly disappears into the air, even though the temperature remains below freezing. Which process explains this?
   A. condensation
   B. deposition
   C. evaporation
   D. sublimation

4. Which unit is a density unit?
   A. cm^3
   B. cm^3/g
   C. g
   D. g/cm^3

5. Which is a form of vaporization?
   A. condensation
   B. evaporation
   C. freezing
   D. melting

6. When a needle is placed on the surface of water, it floats. Which idea best explains why this happens?
   A. Boyle's law
   B. molecular theory
   C. surface tension
   D. viscosity theory

7. In which material would the particles be most closely spaced?
   A. air
   B. brick
   C. syrup
   D. water

Use the graph below to answer questions 8 and 9.

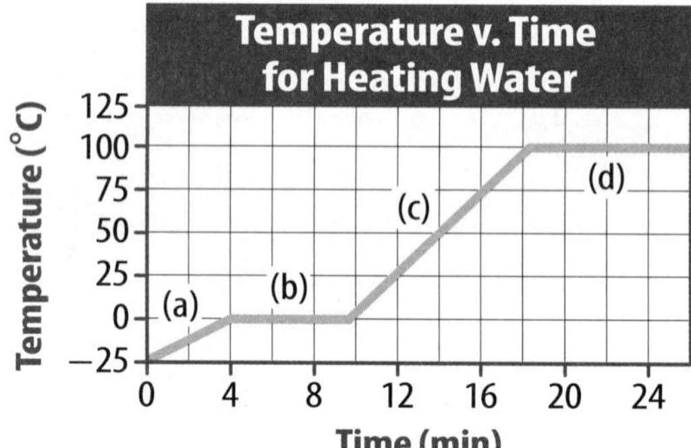

8. Which area of the graph above shows melting of a solid?
   A. a
   B. b
   C. c
   D. d

9. Which area or areas of the graph above shows a change in the potential energy of the particles?
   A. a
   B. a and c
   C. b and d
   D. c

Critical Thinking

10. **Explain** how the distances between particles in a solid, a liquid, and a gas help determine the densities of each.

11. **Describe** what would happen to the volume of a balloon if it were submerged in hot water.

12. **Assess** The particles of an unknown liquid have very weak attractions for other particles in the liquid. Would you expect the liquid to have a high or low viscosity?

13. **Rank** the strength of attraction between the particles that make up the gas in an oxygen tank, a rock, and juice, all at room temperature.

14. **Evaluate** Each beaker below contains the same amount of water. The thermometers show the temperature in each beaker. Explain the kinetic energy differences in each beaker.

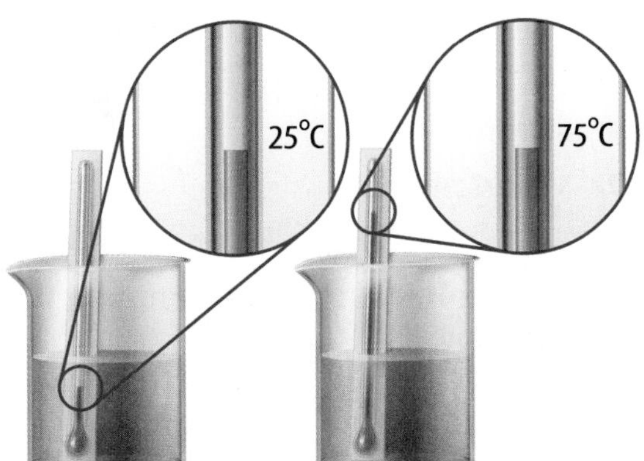

15. **Summarize** A glass with a few milliliters of water is placed on a counter. No one touches the glass. Explain what happens to the water after a few days.

Writing in Science

16. **Write** a paragraph that describes how you could determine the melting point of a substance from its heating or cooling curve.

REVIEW THE BIG IDEA

17. During springtime in Alaska, frozen rivers thaw and boats can navigate the rivers again. What physical changes and energy changes occur to the ice molecules when ice changes to water? Explain the process in which water in the river changes to water vapor.

18. In the photo below, explain how the average kinetic energy of the particles change as the molten glass cools. What instrument could you use to verify the change in the average kinetic energy of the particles?

Math Skills

Math Practice

Solve Equations

19. The pressure on 1 L of a gas at a pressure of 600 kPa is lowered to 200 kPa. What is the final volume of the gas?

20. A gas has a volume of 30 mL at a pressure of 5000 kPa. What is the volume of the gas if the pressure is lowered to 1,250 kPa?

Standardized Test Practice

Record your answers on the answer sheet provided by your teacher or on a separate sheet of paper.

Multiple Choice

1 Which property applies to matter that consists of particles vibrating in place?

- **A** has a definite shape
- **B** takes the shape of the container
- **C** flows easily at room temperature
- **D** Particles are far apart.

Use the figure below to answer questions 2 and 3.

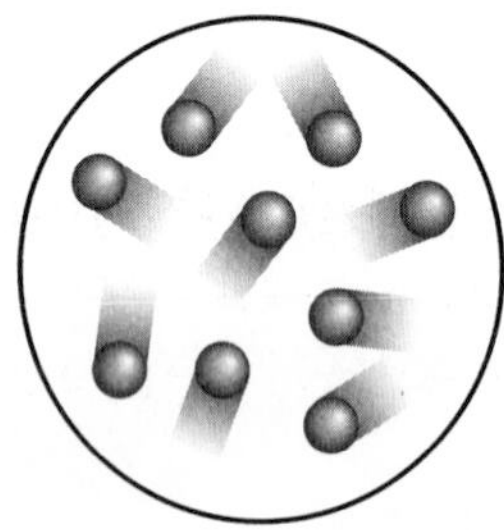

2 Which state of matter is represented above?

- **A** amorphous solid
- **B** crystalline solid
- **C** gas
- **D** liquid

3 Which best describes the attractive forces between particles shown in the figure?

- **A** The attractive forces keep the particles vibrating in place.
- **B** The particles hardly are affected by the attractive forces.
- **C** The attractive forces keep the particles close together but still allow movement.
- **D** The particles are locked in their positions because of the attractive forces between them.

4 What happens to matter as its temperature increases?

- **A** The average kinetic energy of its particles decreases.
- **B** The average thermal energy of its particles decreases.
- **C** The particles gain kinetic energy.
- **D** The particles lose potential energy.

Use the figure to answer question 5.

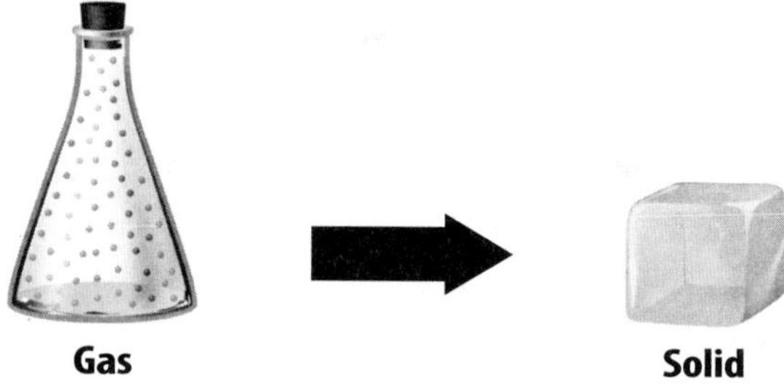

5 Which process is represented in the figure?

- **A** deposition
- **B** freezing
- **C** sublimation
- **D** vaporization

6 Which is a fundamental assumption of the kinetic molecular theory?

- **A** All atoms are composed of subatomic particles.
- **B** The particles of matter move in predictable paths.
- **C** No energy is lost when particles collide with one another.
- **D** Particles of matter never come into contact with one another.

7 Which is true of the thermal energy of particles?

A Thermal energy includes the potential and the kinetic energy of the particles.

B Thermal energy is the same as the average kinetic energy of the particles.

C Thermal energy is the same as the potential energy of particles.

D Thermal energy is the same as the temperature of the particles.

Use the graph below to answer question 8.

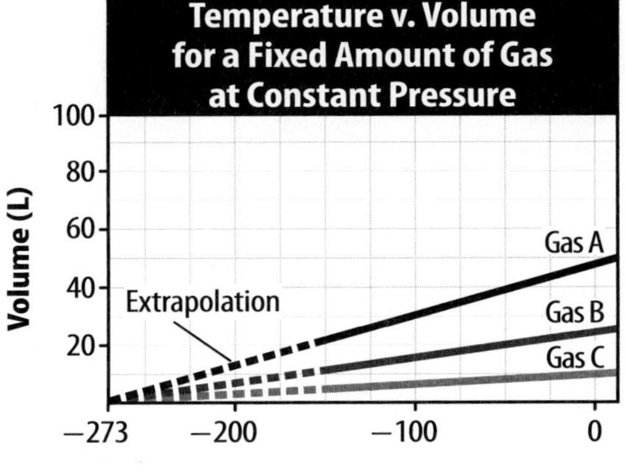

8 Which relationship is shown in the graph?

A Boyle's law

B Charles's law

C kinetic molecular theory

D definition of thermal energy

Constructed Response

9 Some people say that something that does not move very quickly is "as slow as molasses in winter." What property of molasses is described by the saying? Based on the saying, how do you think this property changes with temperature?

Use the graph to answer questions 10 and 11.

A scientist measured the temperature of a sample of frozen mercury as thermal energy is added to the sample. The graph below shows the results.

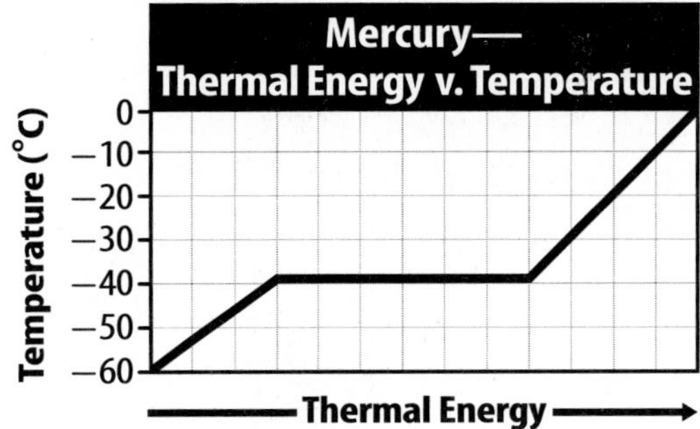

10 At what temperature does mercury melt? How do you know?

11 Describe the motion and arrangement of mercury atoms while the temperature is constant.

12 Atmospheric pressure is greater at the base of a mountain than at its peak. A hiker drinks from a water bottle at the top of a mountain. The bottle is capped tightly. At the base of the mountain, the water bottle has collapsed slightly. What happened to the gas inside the bottle? Assume constant temperature. Explain.

NEED EXTRA HELP?												
If You Missed Question...	1	2	3	4	5	6	7	8	9	10	11	12
Go to Lesson...	1	1	1	2	2	3	2	3	1	1	2	3

Chapter 3

The Periodic Table

THE BIG IDEA

How is the periodic table used to classify and provide information about all known elements?

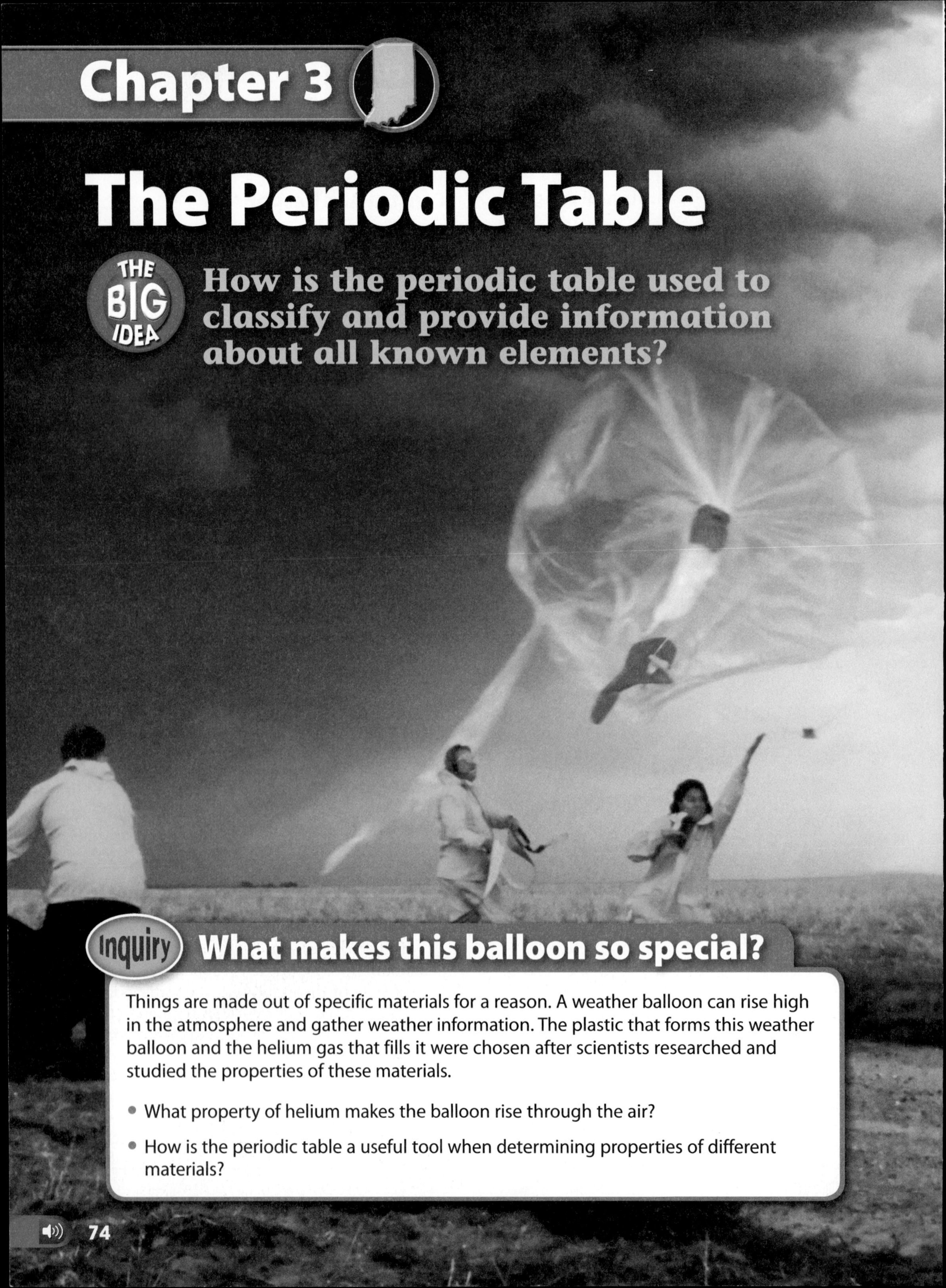

Inquiry What makes this balloon so special?

Things are made out of specific materials for a reason. A weather balloon can rise high in the atmosphere and gather weather information. The plastic that forms this weather balloon and the helium gas that fills it were chosen after scientists researched and studied the properties of these materials.

- What property of helium makes the balloon rise through the air?
- How is the periodic table a useful tool when determining properties of different materials?

Get Ready to Read

What do you think?

Before you read, decide if you agree or disagree with each of these statements. As you read this chapter, see if you change your mind about any of the statements.

1. The elements on the periodic table are arranged in rows in the order they were discovered.
2. The properties of an element are related to the element's location on the periodic table.
3. Fewer than half of the elements are metals.
4. Metals are usually good conductors of electricity.
5. Most of the elements in living things are nonmetals.
6. Even though they look very different, oxygen and sulfur share some similar properties.

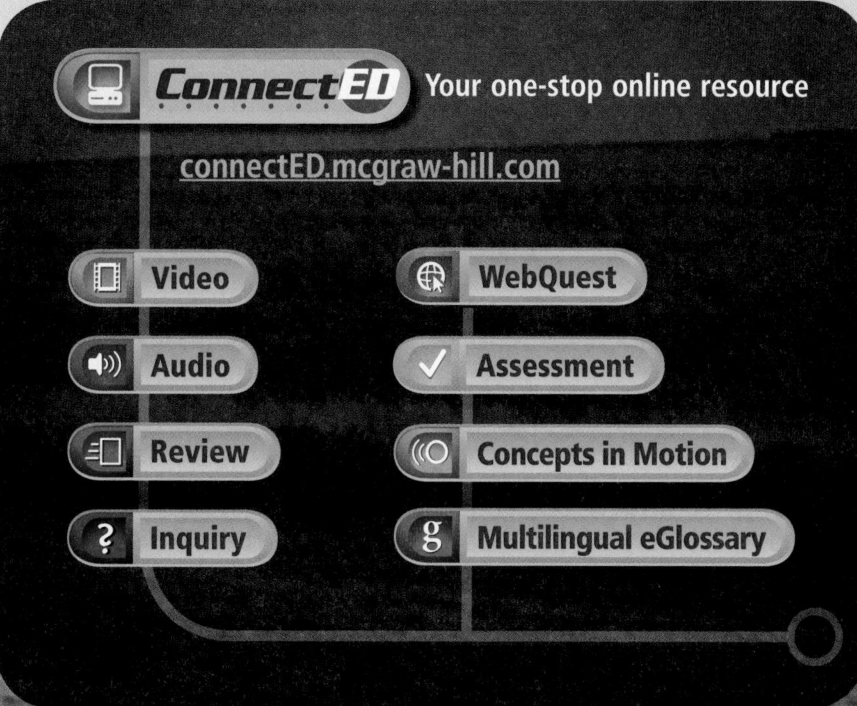

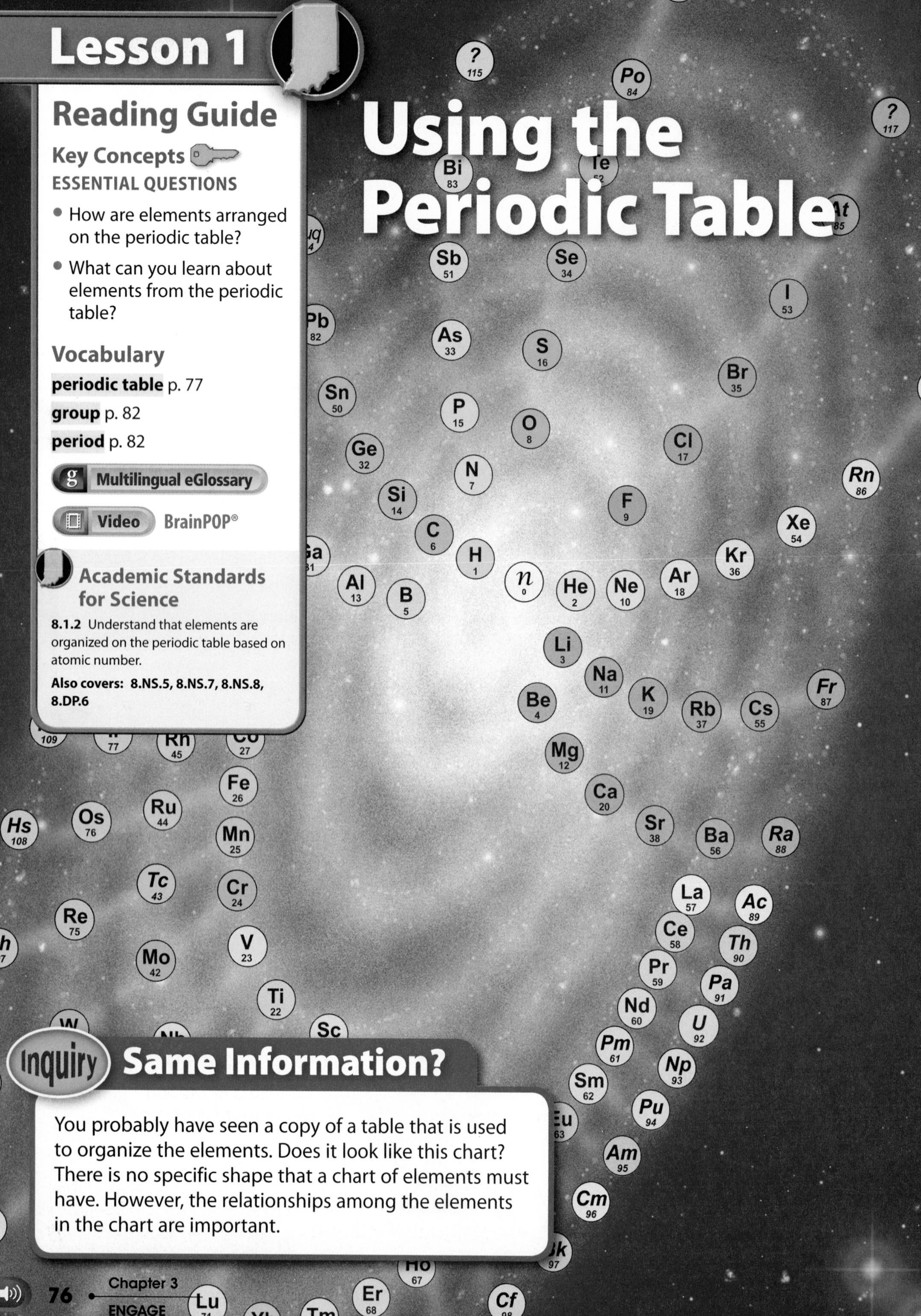

Lesson 1

Reading Guide

Key Concepts

ESSENTIAL QUESTIONS

- How are elements arranged on the periodic table?
- What can you learn about elements from the periodic table?

Vocabulary

periodic table p. 77

group p. 82

period p. 82

Multilingual eGlossary

Video BrainPOP®

Academic Standards for Science

8.1.2 Understand that elements are organized on the periodic table based on atomic number.

Also covers: 8.NS.5, 8.NS.7, 8.NS.8, 8.DP.6

Using the Periodic Table

Inquiry Same Information?

You probably have seen a copy of a table that is used to organize the elements. Does it look like this chart? There is no specific shape that a chart of elements must have. However, the relationships among the elements in the chart are important.

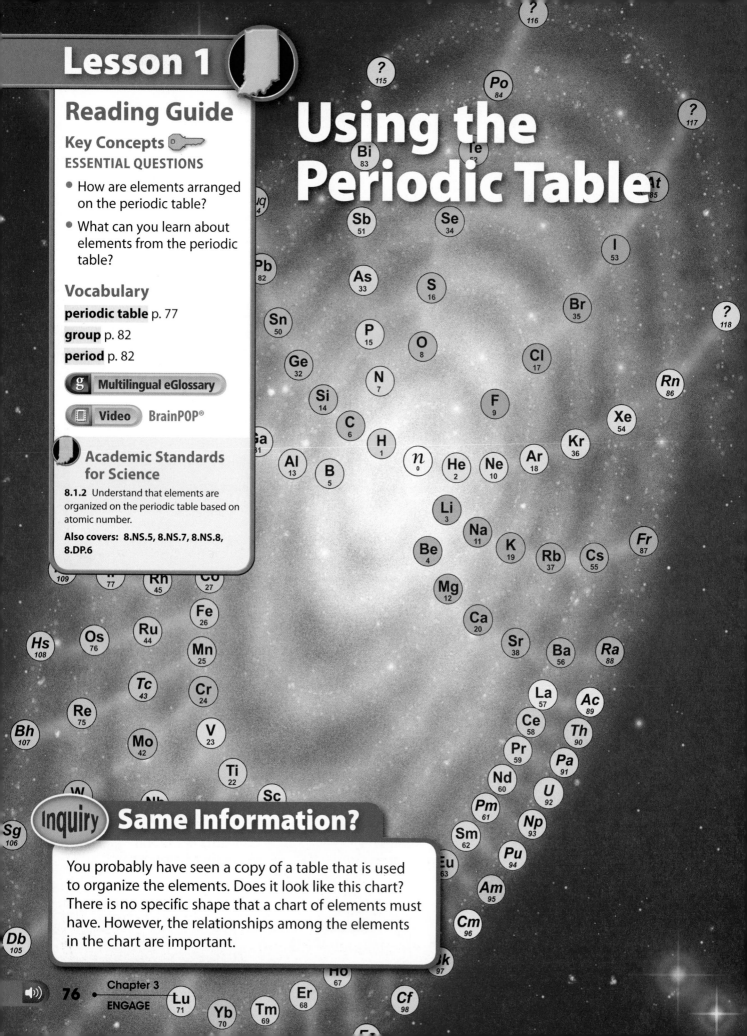

Launch Lab

15 minutes

How can objects be organized?

What would it be like to shop at a grocery store where all the products are mixed up on the shelves? Maybe cereal is next to the dish soap and bread is next to the canned tomatoes. It would take a long time to find the groceries that you needed. How does organizing objects help you to find and use what you need?

1. Read and complete a lab safety form.
2. Empty the **interlocking plastic bricks** from the **plastic bag** onto your desk and observe their properties. Think about ways you might group and sequence the bricks so that they are organized.
3. Organize the bricks according to your plan.
4. Compare your pattern of organization with those used by several other students.

Think About This

1. Describe in your Science Journal the way you grouped your bricks. Why did you choose that way of grouping?
2. Describe how you sequenced the bricks.
3. **Key Concept** How does organizing things help you to use them more easily?

What is the periodic table?

The "junk drawer" in **Figure 1** is full of pens, notepads, rubber bands, and other supplies. It would be difficult to find a particular item in this messy drawer. How might you organize it? First, you might dump the contents onto the counter. Then you could sort everything into piles. Pens and pencils might go into one pile. Notepads and paper go into another. Organizing the contents of the drawer makes it easier to find the things you need, also shown in **Figure 1.**

Just as sorting helped to organize the objects in the junk drawer, sorting can help scientists organize information about the elements. Recall that there are more than 100 elements, each with a unique set of physical and chemical properties.

Scientists use a table called the periodic (pihr ee AH dihk) table to organize elements. *The* **periodic table** *is a chart of the elements arranged into rows and columns according to their physical and chemical properties.* It can be used to determine the relationships among the elements.

In this chapter, you will read about how the periodic table was developed. You will also read about how you can use the periodic table to learn about the elements.

Figure 1 Sorting objects by their similarities makes it easier to find what you need.

Developing a Periodic Table

In 1869 a Russian chemist and teacher named Dimitri Mendeleev (duh MEE tree • men duh LAY uf) was working on a way to classify elements. At that time, more than 60 elements had been discovered. He studied the physical properties such as density, color, melting point, and atomic mass of each element. Mendeleev also noted chemical properties such as how each element reacted with other elements. Mendeleev arranged the elements in a list using their atomic masses. He noticed that the properties of the elements seemed to repeat in a pattern.

When Mendeleev placed his list of elements into a table, he arranged them in rows of increasing atomic mass. Elements with similar properties were grouped the same column. The columns in his table are like the piles of sorted objects in your junk drawer. Both contain groups of things with similar properties.

Reading Check What physical property did Mendeleev use to place the elements in rows on the periodic table?

Patterns in Properties

The term *periodic* means "repeating pattern." For example, seasons and months are periodic because they follow a repeating pattern every year. The days of the week are periodic since they repeat every seven days.

What were some of the repeating patterns Mendeleev noticed in his table? Melting point is one property that shows a repeating pattern. Recall that melting point is the temperature at which a solid changes to a liquid. The blue line in **Figure 2** represents the melting points of the elements in row 2 of the periodic table. Notice that the melting point of carbon is higher than the melting point of lithium. However, the melting point of fluorine, at the far right of the row, is lower than that of carbon. How do these melting points show a pattern? Look at the red line in **Figure 2.** This line represents the melting points of the elements in row 3 of the periodic table. The melting points follow the same increasing and then decreasing pattern as the blue line, or row 2. Boiling point and reactivity also follow a periodic pattern.

A Periodic Property

Figure 2 Melting points increase, then decrease, across a period on the periodic table.

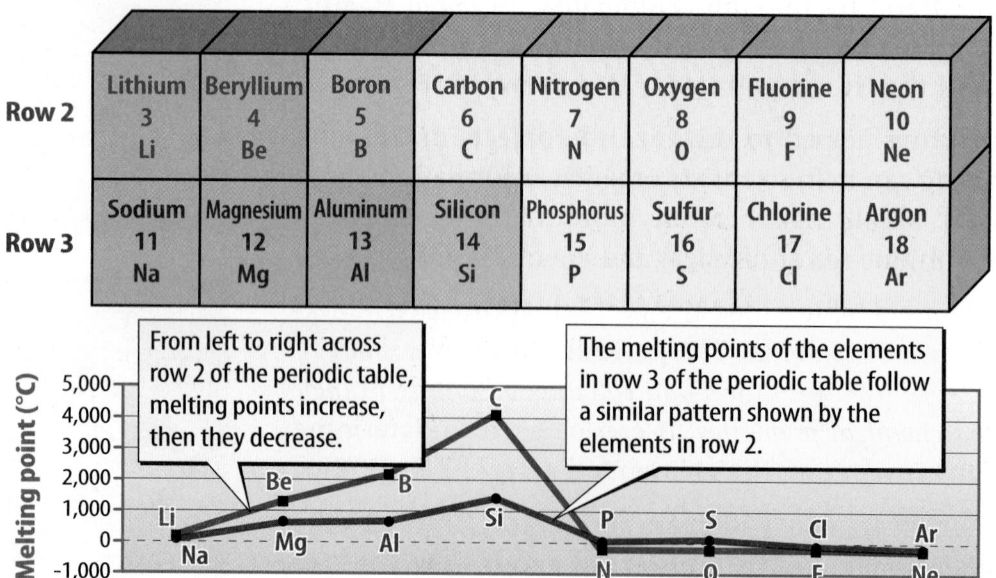

Predicting Properties of Undiscovered Elements

When Mendeleev arranged all known elements by increasing atomic mass, there were large gaps between some elements. He predicted that scientists would discover elements that would fit into these spaces. Mendeleev also predicted that the properties of these elements would be similar to the known elements in the same columns. Both of his predictions turned out to be true.

Changes to Mendeleev's Table

Mendeleev's periodic table enabled scientists to relate the properties of the known elements to their position on the table. However, the table had a problem—some elements seemed out of place. Mendeleev believed that the atomic masses of certain elements must be invalid because the elements appeared in the wrong place on the periodic table. For example, Mendeleev placed tellurium before iodine despite the fact that tellurium has a greater atomic mass than iodine. He did so because iodine's properties more closely resemble those of fluorine and chlorine, just as copper's properties are closer to those of silver and gold, as shown in **Figure 3.**

FOLDABLES®

Use four sheets of paper to make a top-tab book. Use it to organize your notes about the development of the periodic table.

History | Why It Changed | Today's Table | The Periodic Table

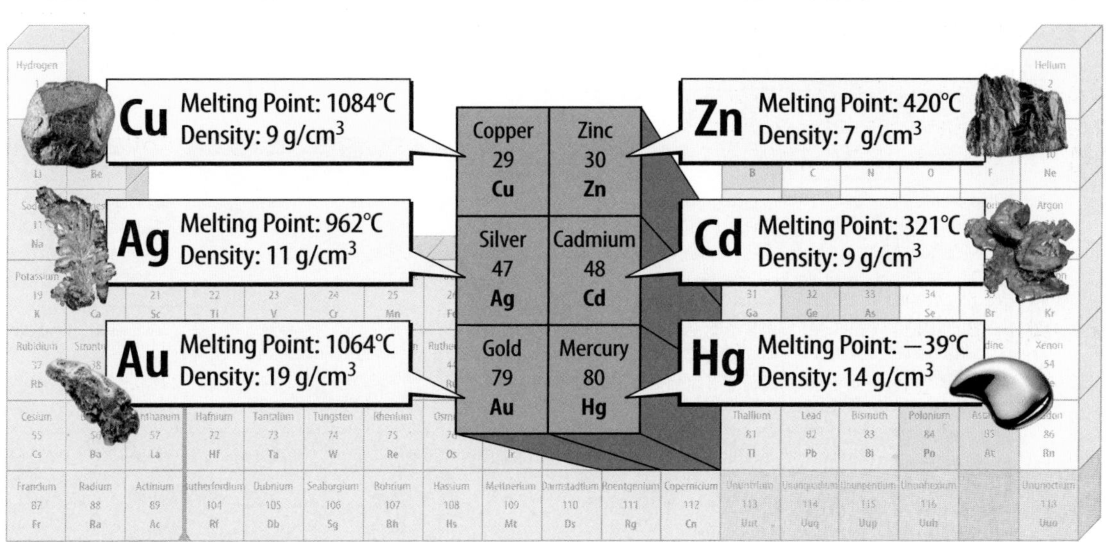

Figure 3 On today's periodic table, copper is in the same column as silver and gold. Zinc is in the same column as cadmium and mercury.

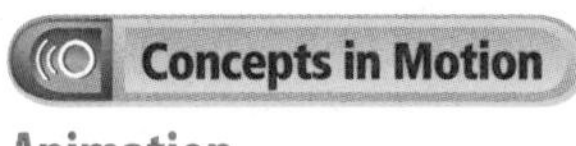

Animation

The Importance of Atomic Number

In the early 1900s, the scientist Henry Moseley solved the problem with Mendeleev's table. Moseley found that if elements were listed according to increasing atomic number instead of listing atomic mass, columns would contain elements with similar properties. Recall that the atomic number of an element is the number of protons in the nucleus of each of that element's atoms.

Key Concept Check What determines where an element is located on the periodic table you use today?

Science Use v. Common Use

period

Science Use the completion of a cycle; a row on the periodic table

Common Use a point used to mark the end of a sentence; a time frame

Today's Periodic Table

You can identify many of the properties of an element from its placement on the **periodic** table. The table, as shown in **Figure 4,** is organized into columns, rows, and blocks, which are based on certain patterns of properties. In the next two lessons, you will learn how an element's position on the periodic table can help you interpret the element's physical and chemical properties.

Figure 4 The periodic table is used to organize elements according to increasing atomic number and properties.

Concepts in Motion Animation

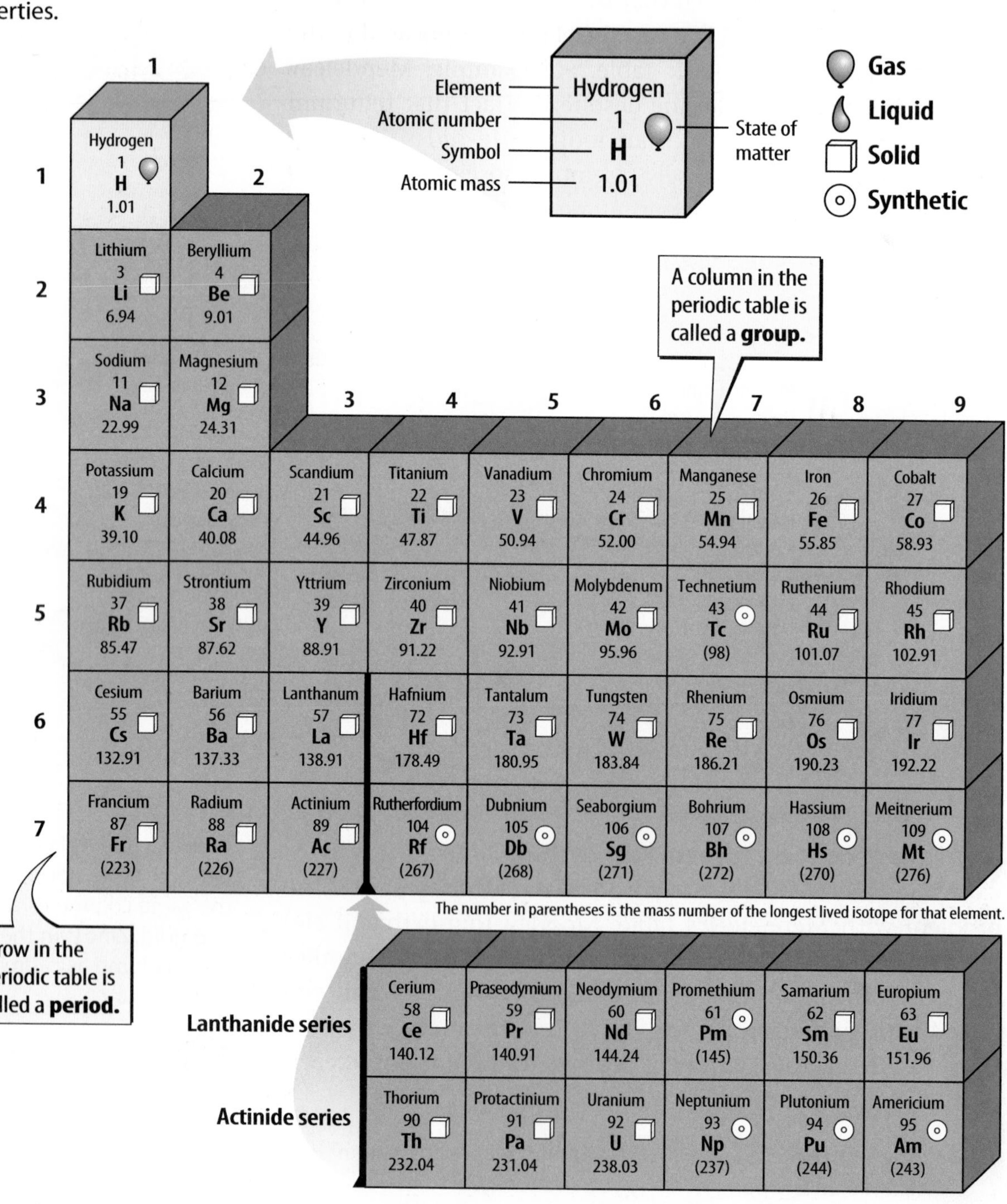

What is on an element key?

The element key shows an element's chemical symbol, atomic number, and atomic mass. The key also contains a symbol that shows the state of matter at room temperature. Look at the element key for helium in **Figure 5.** Helium is a gas at room temperature. Some versions of the periodic table give additional information, such as density, conductivity, or melting point.

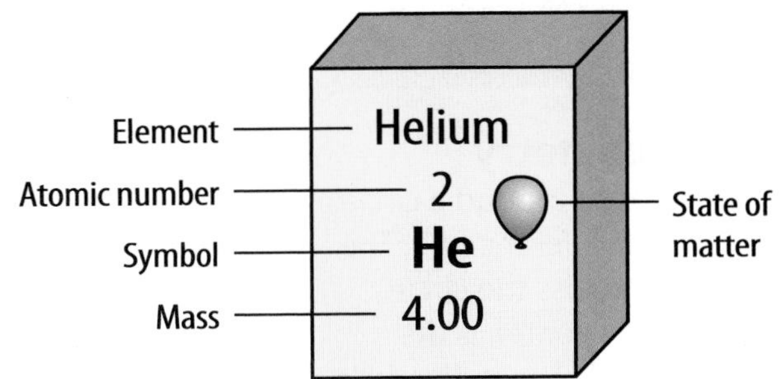

Figure 5 An element key shows important information about each element.

Visual Check What does this key tell you about helium?

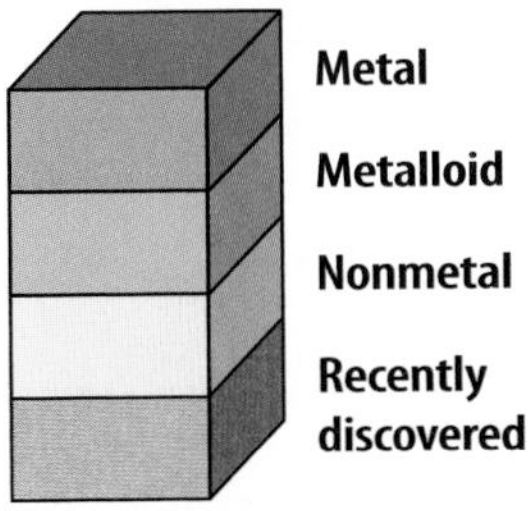

Metal

Metalloid

Nonmetal

Recently discovered

10	11	12	13	14	15	16	17	18
								Helium 2 He 4.00
			Boron 5 B 10.81	Carbon 6 C 12.01	Nitrogen 7 N 14.01	Oxygen 8 O 16.00	Fluorine 9 F 19.00	Neon 10 Ne 20.18
			Aluminum 13 Al 26.98	Silicon 14 Si 28.09	Phosphorus 15 P 30.97	Sulfur 16 S 32.07	Chlorine 17 Cl 35.45	Argon 18 Ar 39.95
Nickel 28 Ni 58.69	Copper 29 Cu 63.55	Zinc 30 Zn 65.38	Gallium 31 Ga 69.72	Germanium 32 Ge 72.64	Arsenic 33 As 74.92	Selenium 34 Se 78.96	Bromine 35 Br 79.90	Krypton 36 Kr 83.80
Palladium 46 Pd 106.42	Silver 47 Ag 107.87	Cadmium 48 Cd 112.41	Indium 49 In 114.82	Tin 50 Sn 118.71	Antimony 51 Sb 121.76	Tellurium 52 Te 127.60	Iodine 53 I 126.90	Xenon 54 Xe 131.29
Platinum 78 Pt 195.08	Gold 79 Au 196.97	Mercury 80 Hg 200.59	Thallium 81 Tl 204.38	Lead 82 Pb 207.20	Bismuth 83 Bi 208.98	Polonium 84 Po (209)	Astatine 85 At (210)	Radon 86 Rn (222)
Darmstadtium 110 Ds (281)	Roentgenium 111 Rg (280)	Copernicium 112 Cn (285)	Ununtrium * 113 Uut (284)	Ununquadium * 114 Uuq (289)	Ununpentium * 115 Uup (288)	Ununhexium * 116 Uuh (293)		Ununoctium * 118 Uuo (294)

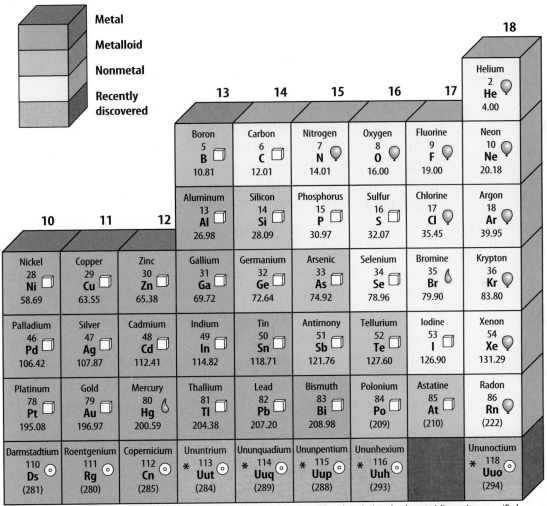

* The names and symbols for elements 113-116 and 118 are temporary. Final names will be selected when the elements' discoveries are verified.

Gadolinium 64 Gd 157.25	Terbium 65 Tb 158.93	Dysprosium 66 Dy 162.50	Holmium 67 Ho 164.93	Erbium 68 Er 167.26	Thulium 69 Tm 168.93	Ytterbium 70 Yb 173.05	Lutetium 71 Lu 174.97
Curium 96 Cm (247)	Berkelium 97 Bk (247)	Californium 98 Cf (251)	Einsteinium 99 Es (252)	Fermium 100 Fm (257)	Mendelevium 101 Md (258)	Nobelium 102 No (259)	Lawrencium 103 Lr (262)

Math Skills

Use Geometry

The distance around a circle is the circumference (C). The distance across the circle, through its center, is the diameter (d). The radius (r) is half of the diameter. The circumference divided by the diameter for any circle is equal to π (pi), or 3.14. The formula for determining the circumference is:

$$C = \pi d \text{ or } C = 2\pi r$$

For example, an iron (Fe) atom has a radius of **126 pm** (picometers; 1 picometer = one-trillionth of a meter) The circumference of an iron atom is:

$C = 2 \times 3.14 \times 126$ **pm**

$C =$ **791 pm**

Practice

The radius of a uranium (U) atom is 156 pm. What is its circumference?

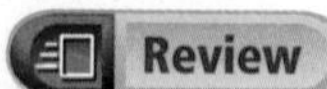

- Math Practice
- Personal Tutor

Groups

A **group** *is a column on the periodic table.* Elements in the same group have similar chemical properties and react with other elements in similar ways. There are patterns in the physical properties of a group such as density, melting point, and boiling point. The groups are numbered 1–18, as shown in **Figure 4.**

Key Concept Check What can you infer about the properties of two elements in the same group?

Periods

The rows on the periodic table are called **periods.** The atomic number of each element increases by one as you read from left to right across each period. The physical and chemical properties of the elements also change as you move left to right across a period.

Metals, Nonmetals, and Metalloids

Almost three-fourths of the elements on the periodic table are metals. Metals are on the left side and in the middle of the table. Individual metals have some properties that differ, but all metals are shiny and conduct thermal energy and electricity.

With the exception of hydrogen, nonmetals are located on the right side of the periodic table. The properties of nonmetals differ from the properties of metals. Many nonmetals are gases, and they do not conduct thermal energy or electricity.

Between the metals and the nonmetals on the periodic table are the metalloids. Metalloids have properties of both metals and nonmetals. **Figure 6** shows an example of a metal, a metalloid, and a nonmetal.

Figure 6 In period 3, magnesium is a metal, silicon is a metalloid, and sulfur is a nonmetal.

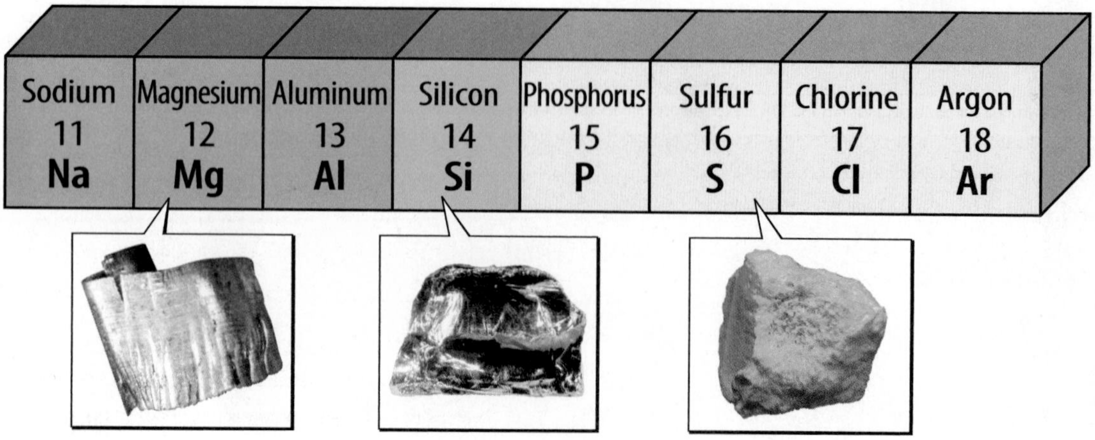

Sodium 11 Na
Magnesium 12 Mg
Aluminum 13 Al
Silicon 14 Si
Phosphorus 15 P
Sulfur 16 S
Chlorine 17 Cl
Argon 18 Ar

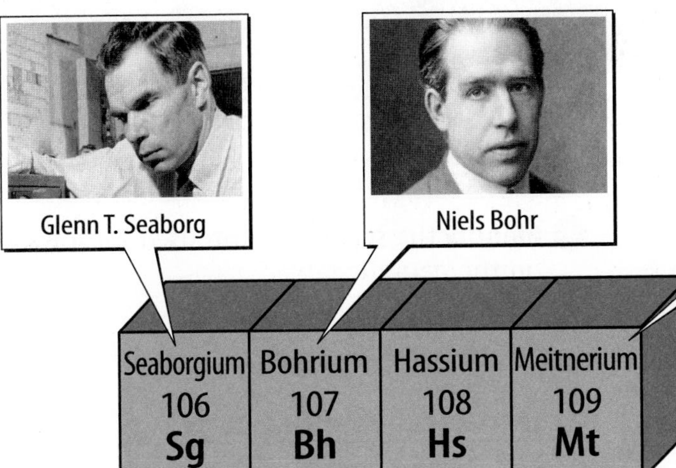

Figure 7 Three of these synthetic elements are named to honor important scientists.

How Scientists Use the Periodic Table

Even today, new elements are created in laboratories, named, and added to the present-day periodic table. Four of these elements are shown in **Figure 7.** These elements are all synthetic, or made by people, and do not occur naturally on Earth. Sometimes scientists can create only a few atoms of a new element. Yet scientists can use the periodic table to predict the properties of new elements they create. Look back at the periodic table in **Figure 4.** What group would you predict to contain element 117? You would probably expect element 117 to be in group 17 and to have similar properties to other elements in the group. Scientists hope to one day synthesize element 117.

The periodic table contains more than 100 elements. Each element has unique properties that differ from the properties of other elements. But each element also shares similar properties with nearby elements. The periodic table shows how elements relate to each other and fit together into one organized chart. Scientists use the periodic table to understand and predict elements' properties. You can, too.

Reading Check How is the periodic table used to predict the properties of an element?

Inquiry MiniLab 20 minutes

How does atom size change across a period?

One pattern seen on the periodic table is in the radius of different atoms. The figure below shows how atomic radius is measured.

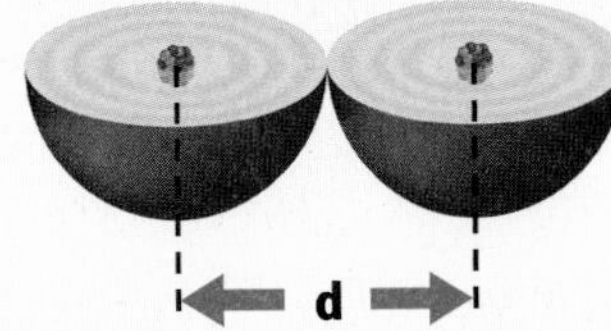

Atomic radius $= \frac{1}{2}$d

1. Read and complete a lab safety form.
2. Using **scissors** and **card stock paper,** cut seven 2-cm × 4-cm rectangles. Using a **marker,** label each rectangle with the atomic symbol of each of the first seven elements in period 2. Obtain the radius for each atom from your teacher.
3. Using a **ruler,** cut **plastic straws** to the same number of millimeters as each atomic radius given in picometers. For example, if the atomic radius is 145 pm, cut a straw 145 mm long.
4. **Tape** each of the labeled rectangles to the top of its appropriate straw.
5. Insert the straws into **modeling clay** according to increasing atomic number.

Analyze and Conclude

1. **Describe** the pattern you see in your model.
2. **Key Concept** Predict the pattern of atomic radii of the elements in period 4.

Lesson 1 Review

Assessment Online Quiz
Inquiry Virtual Lab

Visual Summary

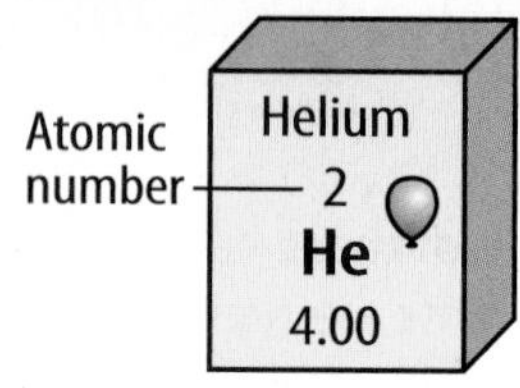

On the periodic table, elements are arranged according to increasing atomic number and similar properties.

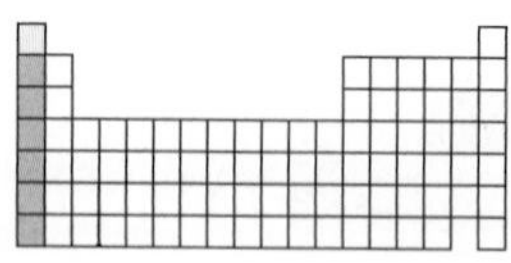

A column of the periodic table is called a group. Elements in the same group have similar properties.

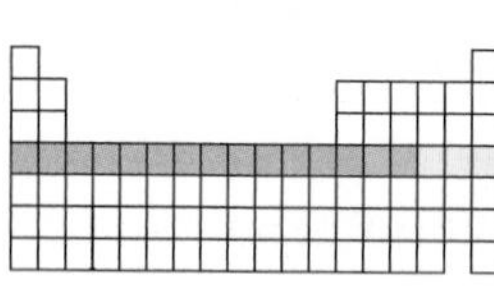

A row of the periodic table is called a period. Properties of elements repeat in the same pattern from left to right across each period.

FOLDABLES®

Use your lesson Foldable to review the lesson. Save your Foldable for the project at the end of the chapter.

What do you think NOW?

You first read the statements below at the beginning of the chapter.

1. The elements on the periodic table are arranged in rows in the order they were discovered.

2. The properties of an element are related to the element's location on the periodic table.

Did you change your mind about whether you agree or disagree with the statements? Rewrite any false statements to make them true.

Use Vocabulary

1. **Identify** the scientific term used for rows on the periodic table.
2. **Name** the scientific term used for columns on the periodic table.

Understand Key Concepts

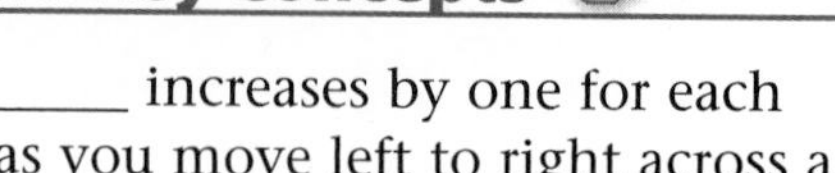

3. The ________ increases by one for each element as you move left to right across a period.
4. What does the decimal number in an element key represent?
   - **A.** atomic mass
   - **B.** atomic number
   - **C.** chemical symbol
   - **D.** state of matter

Interpret Graphics

5. **Classify** each marked element, 1 and 2, as a metal, a nonmetal, or a metalloid.

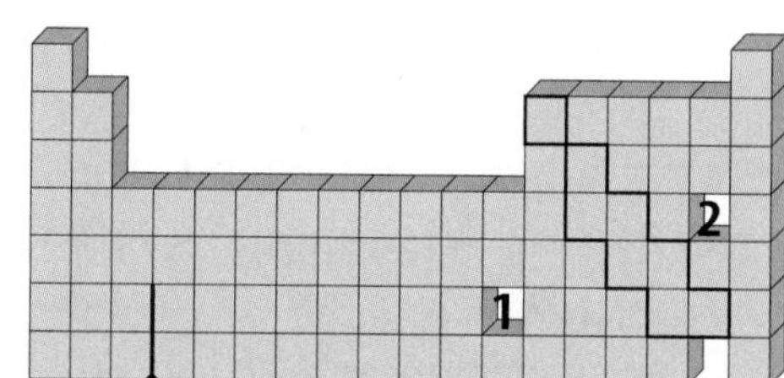

6. **Identify** Copy and fill in the graphic organizer below to identify the color-coded regions of the periodic table.

Critical Thinking

7. **Predict** Look at the perioidic table and predict three elements that have lower melting points than calcium (Ca).

Math Skills

Math Practice

8. Carbon (C) and silicon (Si) are in group 4 of the periodic table. The atomic radius of carbon is 77 pm and sulfur is 117 pm. What is the circumference of each atom?

Identify Patterns

25 minutes

How is the periodic table arranged?

Materials

20 cards

What would happen if schools did not assign students to grades or classes? How would you know where to go on the first day of school? What if your home did not have an address? How could you tell someone where you live? Life becomes easier with organization. The following activity will help you discover how elements are organized on the periodic table.

Learn It

Patterns help you make sense of the world around you. The days of the week follow a pattern, as do the months of the year. **Identifying a pattern** involves organizing things into similar groups and then sequencing the things in the same way in each group.

Try It

1. Obtain cards from your teacher. Turn the cards over so the sides with numbers are facing up.
2. Separate the cards into three or more piles. All of the cards in a pile should have a characteristic in common.
3. Organize each pile into a pattern. Use all of the cards.
4. Lay out the cards into rows and columns based on their characteristics and patterns.

Apply It

5. Describe in your Science Journal the patterns you used to organize your cards. Do other patterns exist in your arrangement?
6. Are there gaps in your arrangement? Can you describe what a card in one of those gaps would look like?
7. **Key Concept** What characteristics of elements might you use to organize them in a similar pattern?

Lesson 2

Metals

Reading Guide

Key Concepts
ESSENTIAL QUESTIONS

- What elements are metals?
- What are the properties of metals?

Vocabulary

metal p. 87
luster p. 87
ductility p. 88
malleability p. 88
alkali metal p. 89
alkaline earth metal p. 89
transition element p. 90

Multilingual eGlossary

Academic Standards for Science

8.1.6 Explain that elements and compounds have characteristic properties such as density, boiling points and melting points that remain unchanged regardless of the sample size.

8.4.3 Investigate the properties (mechanical, chemical, electrical, thermal, magnetic, and optical) of natural and engineered materials.

Also covers: 8.NS.2, 8.NS.4, 8.NS.6, 8.NS.8, 8.NS.9

Inquiry Where does it strike?

Lightning strikes the top of the Empire State Building approximately 100 times a year. Why does lightning hit the top of this building instead of the city streets or buildings below? Metal lightning rods allow electricity to flow through them more easily than other materials do. Lightning moves through these materials and the building is not harmed.

Launch Lab

20 minutes

What properties make metals useful?

The properties of metals determine their uses. Copper conducts thermal energy, which makes it useful for cookware. Aluminum has low density, so it is used in aircraft bodies. What other properties make metals useful?

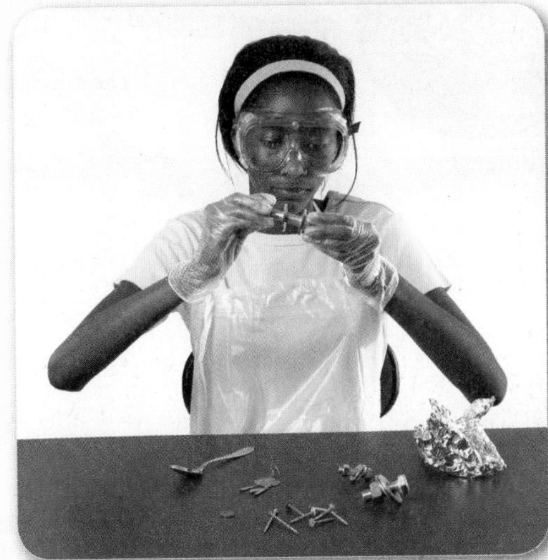

1. Read and complete a lab safety form.
2. With your group, observe the **metal objects** in your **container.** For each object, discuss what properties allow the metal to be used in that way.
3. Observe the **photographs of gold and silver jewelry.** What properties make these two metals useful in jewelry?
4. Examine **other objects around the room** that you think are made of metal. Do they share the same properties as the objects in your container? Do they have other properties that make them useful?

Think About This

1. What properties do all the metals share? What properties are different?
2. **Key Concept** In your Science Journal, list at least four properties of metals that determine their uses.

What is a metal?

What do stainless steel knives and forks, copper wire, aluminum foil, and gold jewelry have in common? They are all made from metals.

As you read in Lesson 1, most of the elements on the periodic table are metals. In fact, of all the known elements, more than three-quarters are metals. With the exception of hydrogen, all of the elements in groups 1–12 on the periodic table are metals. In addition, some of the elements in groups 13–15 are metals. To be a metal, an element must have certain properties.

Key Concept Check How does the position of an element on the periodic table allow you to determine if the element is a metal?

Physical Properties of Metals

Recall that physical properties are characteristics used to describe or identify something without changing its makeup. All metals share certain physical properties.

A **metal** *is an element that is generally shiny. It is easily pulled into wires or hammered into thin sheets. A metal is a good conductor of electricity and thermal energy.* Gold exhibits the common properties of metals.

Luster and Conductivity People use gold for jewelry because of its beautiful color and metallic luster. **Luster** *describes the ability of a metal to reflect light.* Gold is also a good conductor of thermal energy and electricity. However, gold is too expensive to use in normal electrical wires or metal cookware. Copper is often used instead.

Properties of Metals

Figure 8 Gold has many uses based on its properties.

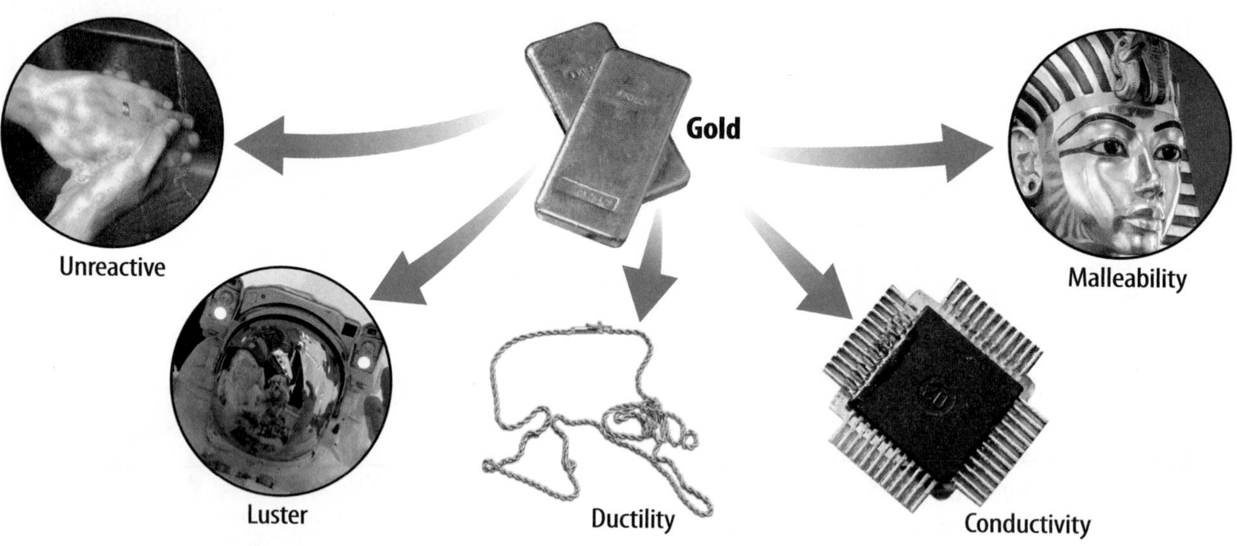

Visual Check Analyze why the properties shown in each photo are an advantage to using gold.

WORD ORIGIN

ductility
from Latin *ductilis,* means "may be led or drawn"

REVIEW VOCABULARY

density
the mass per unit volume of a substance

FOLDABLES®

Make a two-tab book. Label it as shown. Use it to record information about the properties of metals.

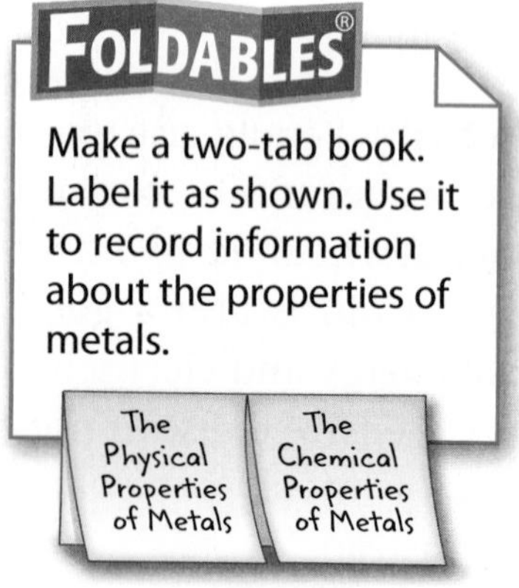

Ductility and Malleability Gold is the most ductile metal. **Ductility** (duk TIH luh tee) *is the ability to be pulled into thin wires.* A piece of gold with the mass of a paper clip can be pulled into a wire that is more than 3 km long.

Malleability (ma lee uh BIH luh tee) *is the ability of a substance to be hammered or rolled into sheets.* Gold is so malleable that it can be hammered into thin sheets. A pile of a million thin sheets would be only as high as a coffee mug.

Other Physical Properties of Metals In general the **density,** strength, boiling point, and melting point of a metal are greater than those of other elements. Except for mercury, all metals are solid at room temperature. Many uses of a metal are determined by the metal's physical properties, as shown in **Figure 8.**

Key Concept Check What are some physical properties of metals?

Chemical Properties of Metals

Recall that a chemical property is the ability or inability of a substance to change into one or more new substances. The chemical properties of metals can differ greatly. However, metals in the same group usually have similar chemical properties. For example, gold and other elements in group 11 do not easily react with other substances.

Group 1: Alkali Metals

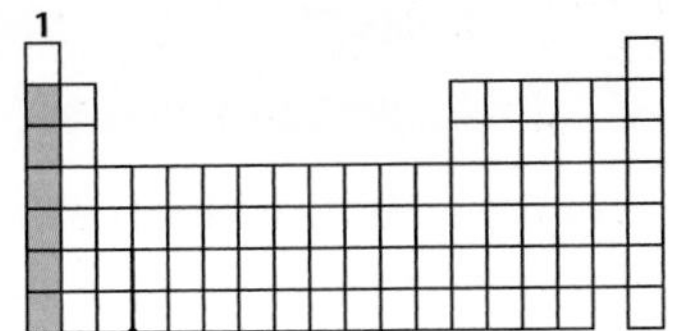

The elements in group 1 are called **alkali** (AL kuh li) **metals.** The alkali metals include lithium, sodium, potassium, rubidium, cesium, and francium.

Because they are in the same group, alkali metals have similar chemical properties. Alkali metals react quickly with other elements, such as oxygen. Therefore, in nature, they occur only in compounds. Pure alkali metals must be stored so that they do not come in contact with oxygen and water vapor in the air. **Figure 9** shows potassium and sodium reacting with water.

Alkali metals also have similar physical properties. Pure alkali metals have a silvery appearance. As shown in **Figure 9,** they are soft enough to cut with a knife. The alkali metals also have the lowest densities of all metals. A block of pure sodium metal could float on water because of its very low density.

Figure 9 Alkali metals react violently with water. They are also soft enough to be cut with a knife.

Concepts in Motion
Animation

Potassium

Sodium

Lithium

Group 2: Alkaline Earth Metals

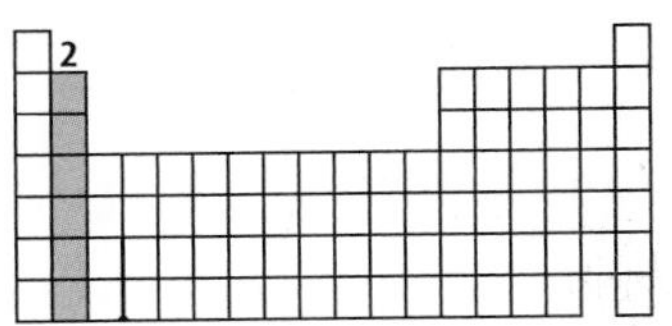

The elements in group 2 on the periodic table are called **alkaline** (AL kuh lun) **earth metals.** These metals are beryllium, magnesium, calcium, strontium, barium, and radium.

Alkaline earth metals also react quickly with other elements. However, they do not react as quickly as the alkali metals do. Like the alkali metals, pure alkaline earth metals do not occur naturally. Instead, they combine with other elements and form compounds. The physical properties of the alkaline earth metals are also similar to those of the alkali metals. Alkaline earth metals are soft and silvery. They also have low density, but they have greater density than alkali metals.

Reading Check Which element reacts faster with oxygen—barium or potassium?

Transition Elements

Concepts in Motion Animation

Figure 10 Transition elements are in blocks at the center of the periodic table. Many colorful materials contain small amounts of transition elements.

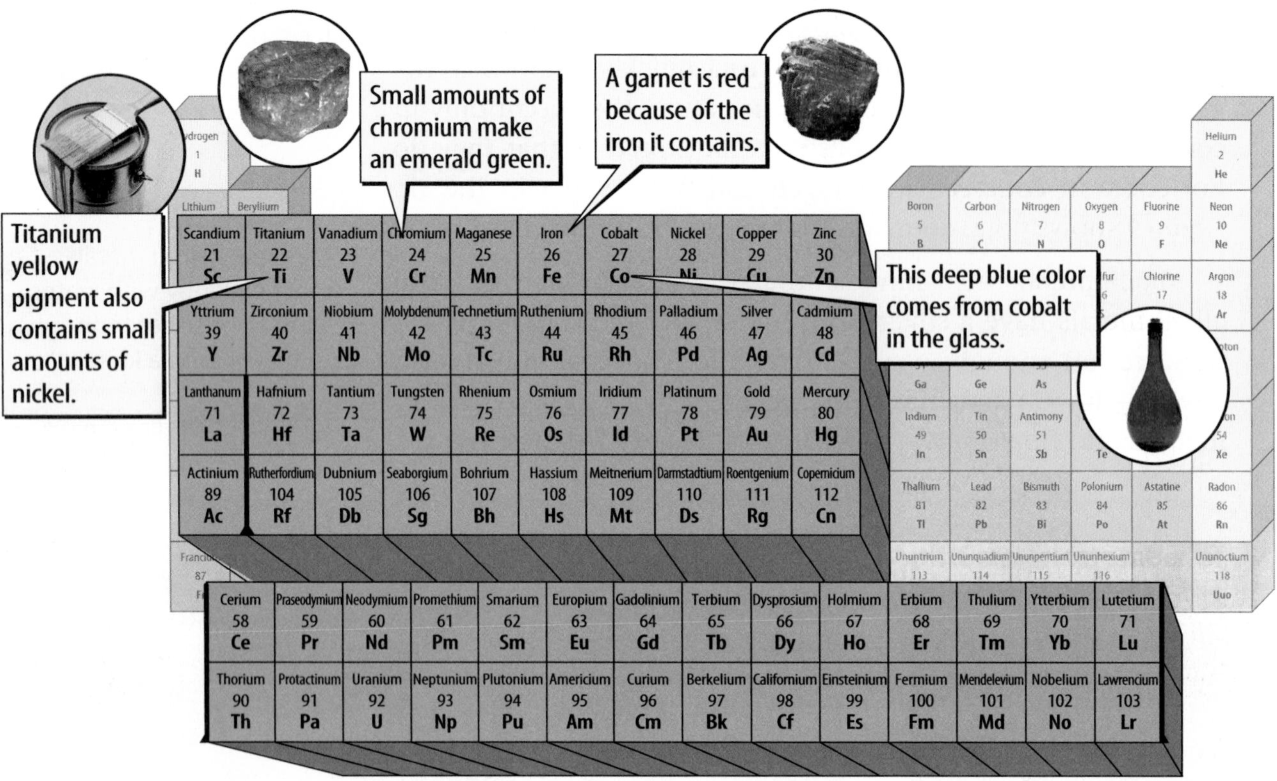

Groups 3–12: Transition Elements

The elements in groups 3–12 are called **transition elements.** The transition elements are in two blocks on the periodic table. The main block is in the center of the periodic table. The other block includes the two rows at the bottom of the periodic table, as shown in **Figure 10.**

Properties of Transition Elements

All transition elements are metals. They have higher melting points, greater strength, and higher densities than the alkali metals and the alkaline earth metals. Transition elements also react less quickly with oxygen. Some transition elements can exist in nature as free elements. An element is a free element when it occurs in pure form, not in a compound.

Uses of Transition Elements

Transition elements in the main block of the periodic table have many important uses. Because of their high densities, strength, and resistance to corrosion, transition elements such as iron make good building materials. Copper, silver, nickel, and gold are used to make coins. These metals are also used for jewelry, electrical wires, and many industrial applications.

Main-block transition elements can react with other elements and form many compounds. Many of these compounds are colorful. Artists use transition-element compounds in paints and pigments. The color of many gems, such as garnets and emeralds, comes from the presence of small amounts of transition elements, as illustrated in **Figure 10.**

Lanthanide and Actinide Series

Two rows of transition elements are at the bottom of the periodic table, as shown in **Figure 10.** These elements were removed from the main part of the table so that periods 6 and 7 were not longer than the other periods. If these elements were included in the main part of the table, the first row, called the lanthanide series, would stretch between lanthanum and halfnium. The second row, called the actinide series, would stretch between actinium and rutherfordium.

Some lanthanide and actinide series elements have valuable properties. For example, lanthanide series elements are used to make strong magnets. Plutonium, one of the actinide series elements, is used as a fuel in some nuclear reactors.

Inquiry MiniLab **20 minutes**

How well do materials conduct thermal energy?

How well a material conducts thermal energy can often determine its use.

1. Read and complete a lab safety form.
2. Have your teacher add about 200 mL of very **hot water** to a **250-mL beaker.**
3. Place **rods of metal, plastic, glass, and wood** in the water for 30 seconds.
4. Set four large **ice cubes** on a sheet of **paper towel.** Use **tongs** to quickly remove each rod from the hot water. Place the heated end of the rod on an ice cube.
5. After 30 seconds, remove the rods and examine the ice cubes.

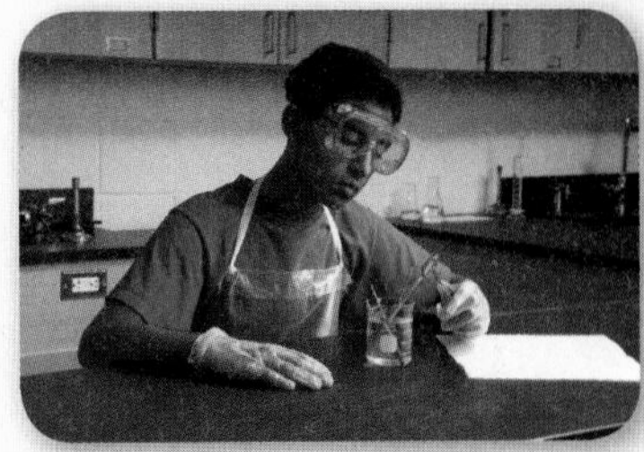

Analyze and Conclude

1. **Conclude** What can you conclude about how well metals conduct thermal energy?
2. **Key Concept** Cookware is often made of metal. What property of metals makes them useful for this purpose?

Patterns in Properties of Metals

Recall that the properties of elements follow repeating patterns across the periods of the periodic table. In general, elements increase in metallic properties such as luster, malleability, and electrical conductivity from right to left across a period, as shown in **Figure 11.** The elements on the far right of a period have no metallic properties at all. Potassium (K), the element on the far left in period 4, has the highest luster, is the most malleable, and conducts electricity better than all the elements in this period.

There are also patterns within groups. Metallic properties tend to increase as you move down a group, also shown in **Figure 11.** You could predict that the malleability of gold is greater than the malleability of either silver or copper because it is below these two elements in group 11.

Reading Check Where would you expect to find elements on the periodic table with few or no metallic properties?

Figure 11 Metallic properties of elements increase as you move to the left and down on the periodic table.

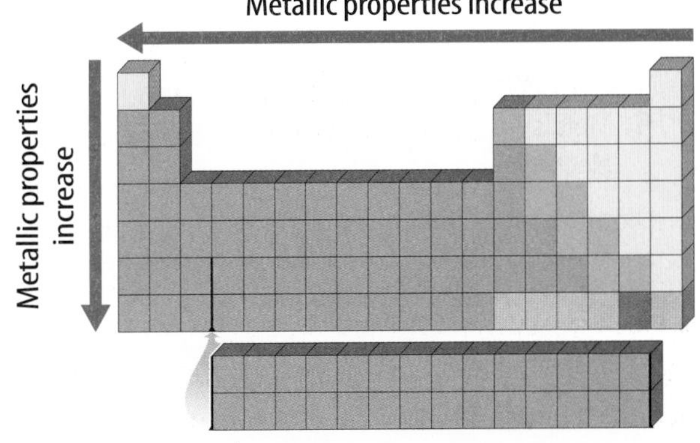

Lesson 2 Review

Visual Summary

Properties of metals include conductivity, luster, malleability, and ductility.

Alkali metals and alkaline earth metals react easily with other elements. These metals make up groups 1 and 2 on the periodic table.

Transition elements make up groups 3–12 and the lanthanide and actinide series on the periodic table.

FOLDABLES®

Use your lesson Foldable to review the lesson. Save your Foldable for the project at the end of the chapter.

What do you think NOW?

You first read the statements below at the beginning of the chapter.

3. Fewer than half of the elements are metals.

4. Metals are usually good conductors of electricity.

Did you change your mind about whether you agree or disagree with the statements? Rewrite any false statements to make them true.

Use Vocabulary

1. **Use the term** *luster* in a sentence.
2. **Identify** the property that makes copper metal ideal for wiring.
3. Elements that have the lowest densities of all the metals are called ________.

Understand Key Concepts 

4. **List** the physical properties that most metals have in common.
5. Which is a chemical property of transition elements?
   A. brightly colored
   B. great ductility
   C. denser than alkali metals
   D. reacts little with oxygen
6. **Organize** the following metals from least metallic to most metallic: barium, zinc, iron, and strontium.

Interpret Graphics

7. **Examine** this section of the periodic table. What metal will have properties most similar to those of chromium (Cr)? Why?

Vanadium 23 V	Chromium 24 Cr	Maganese 25 Mn
Niobium 41 Nb	Molybdenum 42 Mo	Technetium 43 Tc

Critical Thinking

8. **Investigate** your classroom and locate five examples of materials made from metal.
9. **Evaluate** the physical properties of potassium, magnesium, and copper. Select the best choice to use for a building project. Explain why this metal is the best building material to use.

Fireworks

SCIENCE & SOCIETY

Metals add variety to color.

About 1,000 years ago, the Chinese discovered the chemical formula for gunpowder. Using this formula, they invented the first fireworks. One of the primary ingredients in gunpowder is saltpeter, or potassium nitrate. Find potassium on the periodic table. Notice that potassium is a metal. How does the chemical behavior of a metal contribute to a colorful fireworks show?

Purple: mix of strontium and copper compounds

Blue: copper compounds

Yellow: sodium compounds

Gold: iron burned with carbon

White-hot: barium-oxygen compounds or aluminum or magnesium burn

Orange: calcium compounds

Green: barium compounds

Red: strontium and lithium compounds

Metal compounds contribute to the variety of colors you see at a fireworks show. Recall that metals have special chemical and physical properties. Compounds that contain metals also have special properties. For example, each metal turns a characteristic color when burned. Lithium, an alkali metal, forms compounds that burn red. Copper compounds burn blue. Aluminum and magnesium burn white.

It's Your Turn

FORM AN OPINION Fireworks contain metal compounds. Are they bad for the environment or for your health? Research the effects of metals on human health and on the environment. Decide if fireworks are safe to use a holiday celebrations.

Lesson 3

Reading Guide

Key Concepts
ESSENTIAL QUESTIONS

- Where are nonmetals and metalloids on the periodic table?
- What are the properties of nonmetals and metalloids?

Vocabulary

nonmetal p. 95
halogen p. 97
noble gas p. 98
metalloid p. 99
semiconductor p. 99

Multilingual eGlossary

Academic Standards for Science

8.1.6 Explain that elements and compounds have characteristic properties such as density, boiling points and melting points that remain unchanged regardless of the sample size.

8.4.3 Investigate the properties (mechanical, chemical, electrical, thermal, magnetic, and optical) of natural and engineered materials.

Also covers: 8.NS.4, 8.NS.6, 8.NS.7

Nonmetals and Metalloids

Inquiry Why don't they melt?

What do you expect to happen to something when a flame is placed against it? As you can see, the nonmetal material this flower sits on protects the flower from the flame. Some materials conduct thermal energy. Other materials, such as this one, do not.

Launch Lab

20 minutes

What are some properties of nonmetals?

You now know what the properties of metals are. What properties do nonmetals have?

1. Read and complete a lab safety form.
2. Examine pieces of **copper, carbon, aluminum,** and **sulfur.** Describe the appearance of these elements in your Science Journal.
3. Use a **conductivity tester** to check how well these elements conduct electricity. Record your observations.
4. Wrap each element sample in a **paper towel.** Carefully hit the sample with a **hammer.** Unwrap the towel and observe the sample. Record your observations.

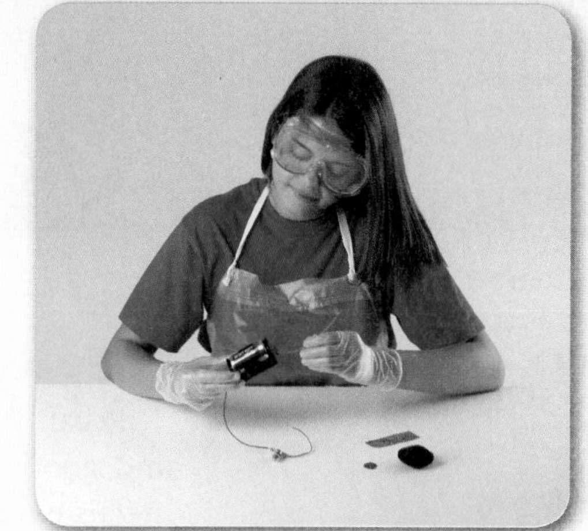

Think About This

1. Locate these elements on the periodic table. From their locations, which elements are metals? Which elements are nonmetals?
2. **Key Concept** Using your results, compare the properties of metals and nonmetals.
3. **Key Concept** What property of a nonmetal makes it useful to insulate electrical wires?

The Elements of Life

Would it surprise you to learn that more than 96 percent of the mass of your body comes from just four elements? As shown in **Figure 12,** all four of these elements—oxygen, carbon, hydrogen, and nitrogen—are nonmetals. **Nonmetals** *are elements that have no metallic properties.*

Of the remaining elements in your body, the two most common elements also are nonmetals—phosphorus and sulfur. These six elements form the compounds in proteins, fats, nucleic acids, and other large molecules in your body and in all other living things.

Reading Check What are the six most common elements in the human body?

Figure 12 Like other living things, this woman's mass comes mostly from nonmetals.

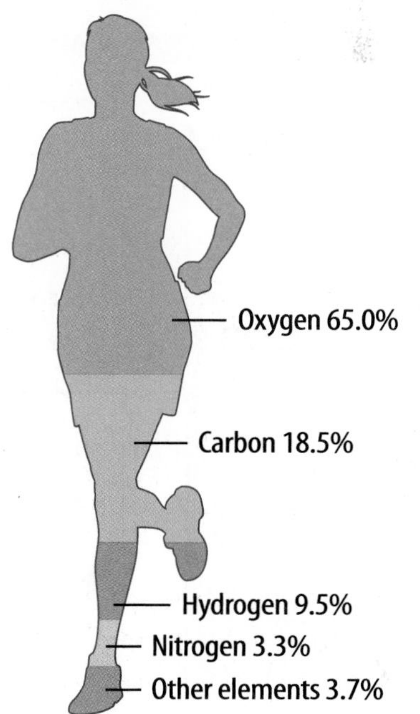

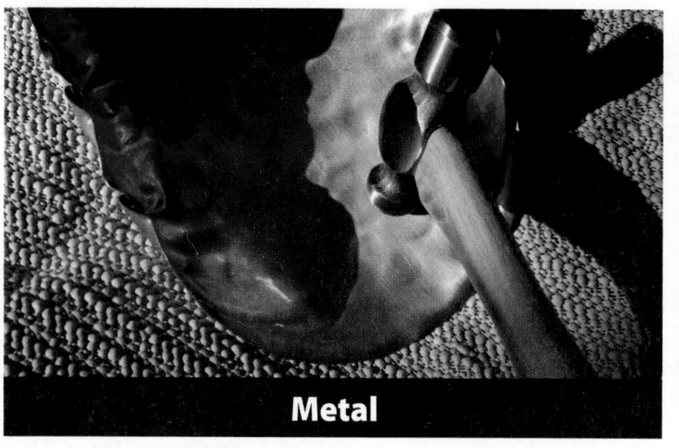

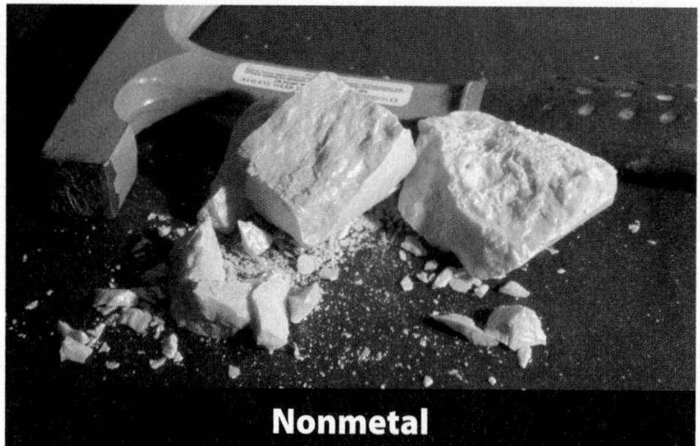

▲ **Figure 13** Solid metals, such as copper, are malleable. Solid nonmetals, such as sulfur, are brittle.

How are nonmetals different from metals?

Recall that metals have luster. They are ductile, malleable, and good conductors of electricity and thermal energy. All metals except mercury are solids at room temperature.

The properties of nonmetals are different from those of metals. Many nonmetals are gases at room temperature. Those that are solid at room temperature have a dull surface, which means they have no luster. Because nonmetals are poor conductors of electricity and thermal energy, they are good insulators. For example, nose cones on space shuttles are insulated from the intense thermal energy of reentry by a material made from carbon, a nonmetal. **Figure 13** and **Figure 14** show several properties of nonmetals.

Key Concept Check What properties do nonmetals have?

Figure 14 Nonmetals have properties that are different from those of metals. Phosphorus and carbon are dull, brittle solids that do not conduct thermal energy or electricity. ▼

Properties of Nonmetals 

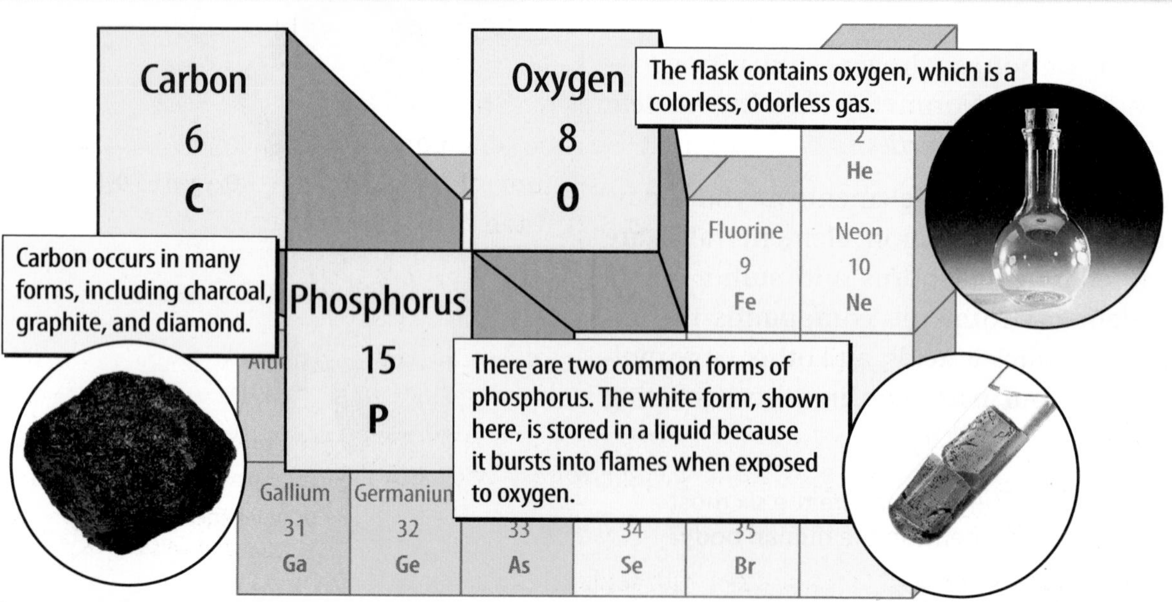

Carbon
6
C
Oxygen
8
O
The flask contains oxygen, which is a colorless, odorless gas.
He
Fluorine
9
Fe
Neon
10
Ne
Carbon occurs in many forms, including charcoal, graphite, and diamond.
Phosphorus
15
P
There are two common forms of phosphorus. The white form, shown here, is stored in a liquid because it bursts into flames when exposed to oxygen.
Gallium
31
Ga
Germanium
32
Ge
33
As
34
Se
35
Br

Visual Check Compare the properties of oxygen to those of carbon and phosphorus.

Figure 15 These glass containers each hold a halogen gas. Although they are different colors in their gaseous state, they react similarly with other elements.

Visual Check Compare the colors of these halogens.

Nonmetals in Groups 14–16

Look back at the periodic table in **Figure 4.** Notice that groups 14–16 contain metals, nonmetals, and metalloids. The chemical properties of the elements in each group are similar. However, the physical properties of the elements can be quite different.

Carbon is the only nonmetal in group 14. It is a solid that has different forms. Carbon is in most of the compounds that make up living things. Nitrogen, a gas, and phosphorus, a solid, are the only nonmetals in group 15. These two elements form many different compounds with other elements, such as oxygen. Group 16 contains three nonmetals. Oxygen is a gas that is essential for many organisms. Sulfur and selenium are solids that have the physical properties of other solid nonmetals.

FOLDABLES®

Fold a sheet of paper to make a table with three columns and three rows. Label it as shown. Use it to organize information about nonmetals and metalloids.

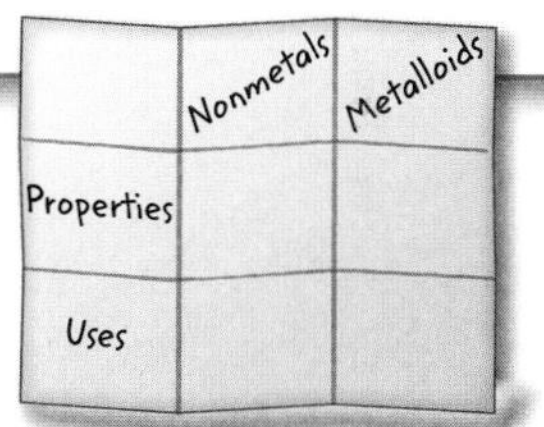

Group 17: The Halogens

An element in group 17 of the periodic table is called a **halogen** (HA luh jun). **Figure 15** shows the halogens fluorine, chlorine, bromine, and iodine. The term *halogen* refers to an element that can react with a metal and form a salt. For example, chlorine gas reacts with solid sodium and forms sodium chloride, or table salt. Calcium chloride is another salt often used on icy roads.

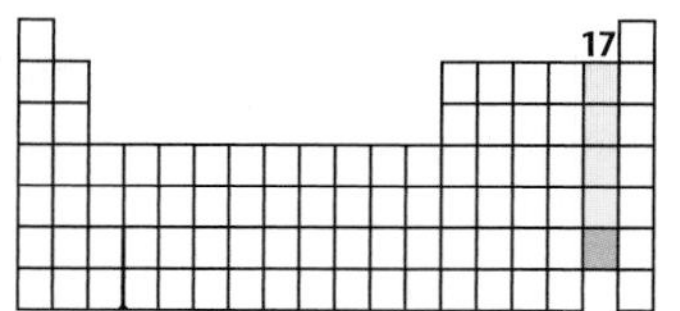

Halogens react readily with other elements and form compounds. They react so readily that halogens only can occur naturally in compounds. They do not exist as free elements. They even form compounds with other nonmetals, such as carbon. In general, the halogens are less reactive as you move down the group.

Word Origin
halogen
from Greek *hals,* means "salt"; and *–gen,* means "to produce"

Reading Check Will bromine react with sodium? Explain your answer.

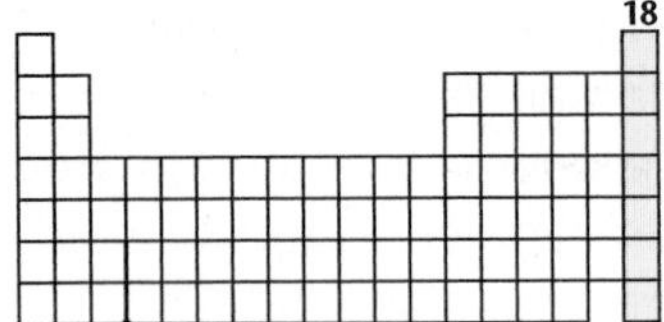

Group 18: The Noble Gases

The elements in group 18 are known as the **noble gases.** The elements helium, neon, argon, krypton, xenon, and radon are the noble gases. Unlike the halogens, the only way elements in this group react with other elements is under special conditions in a laboratory. These elements were not yet discovered when Mendeleev **constructed** his periodic table because they do not form compounds naturally. Once they were discovered, they fit into a group at the far right side of the table.

ACADEMIC VOCABULARY

construct
(verb) to make by combining and arranging parts

Hydrogen

Figure 16 shows the element key for hydrogen. Of all the elements, hydrogen has the smallest atomic mass. It is also the most common element in the universe.

Is hydrogen a metal or a nonmetal? Hydrogen is most often classified as a nonmetal because it has many properties like those of nonmetals. For example, like some nonmetals, hydrogen is a gas at room temperature. However, hydrogen also has some properties similar to those of the group 1 alkali metals. In its liquid form, hydrogen conducts electricity just like a metal does. In some chemical reactions, hydrogen reacts as if it were an alkali metal. However, under conditions on Earth, hydrogen usually behaves like a nonmetal.

Reading Check Why is hydrogen usually classified as a nonmetal?

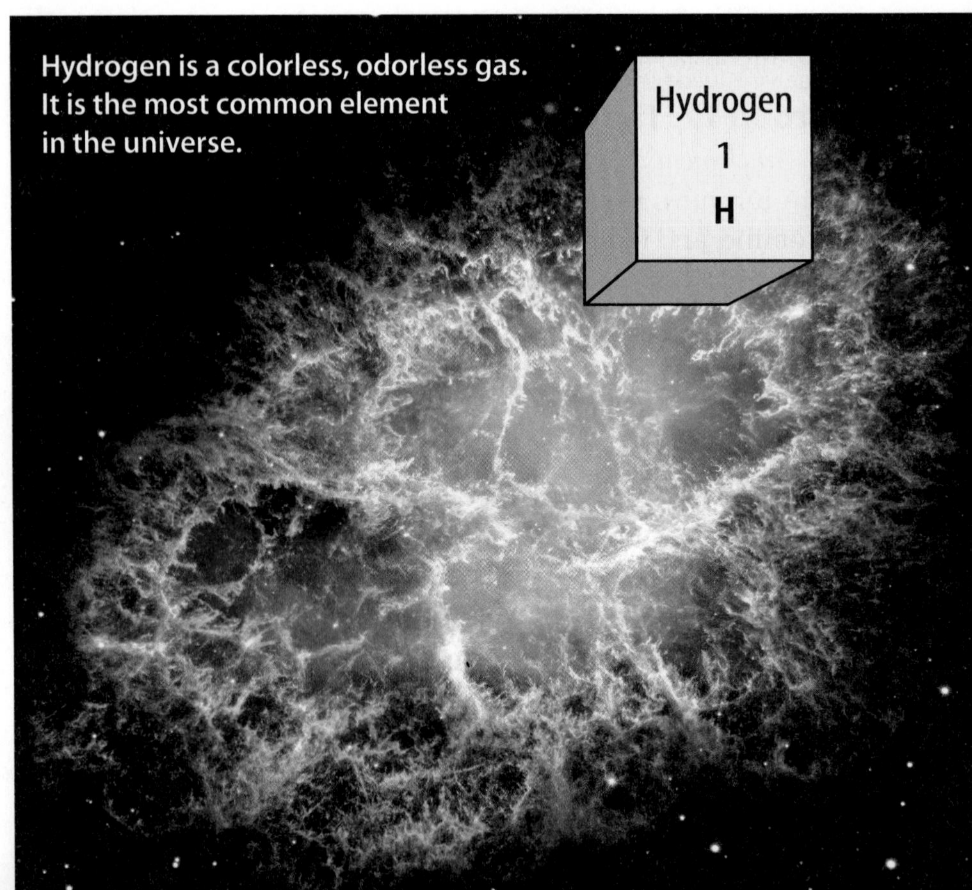

Hydrogen is a colorless, odorless gas.
It is the most common element
in the universe.
Hydrogen
1
H

Figure 16 More than 90 percent of all the atoms in the universe are hydrogen atoms. Hydrogen is the main fuel for the nuclear reactions that occur in stars.

Metalloids

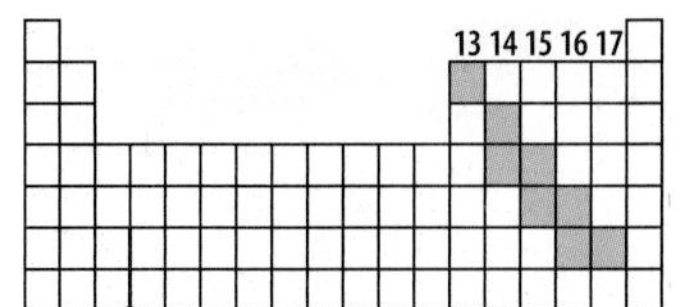

Between the metals and the nonmetals on the periodic table are elements known as metalloids. *A* **metalloid** (MEH tul oyd) *is an element that has physical and chemical properties of both metals and nonmetals.* The elements boron, silicon, germanium, arsenic, antimony, tellurium, polonium, and astatine are metalloids. Silicon is the most abundant metalloid in the universe. Most sand is made of a compound containing silicon. Silicon is also used in many different products, some of which are shown in **Figure 17.**

Key Concept Check Where are metalloids on the periodic table?

Semiconductors

Recall that metals are good conductors of thermal energy and electricity. Nonmetals are poor conductors of thermal energy and electricity but are good insulators. A property of metalloids is the ability to act as a semiconductor. *A* **semiconductor** *conducts electricity at high temperatures, but not at low temperatures.* At high temperatures, metalloids act like metals and conduct electricity. But at lower temperatures, metalloids act like nonmetals and stop electricity from flowing. This property is useful in electronic devices such as computers, televisions, and solar cells.

WORD ORIGIN

semiconductor
from Latin *semi-*, means "half"; and *conducere,* means "to bring together"

Figure 17 The properties of silicon make it useful for many different products.

Uses of Silicon

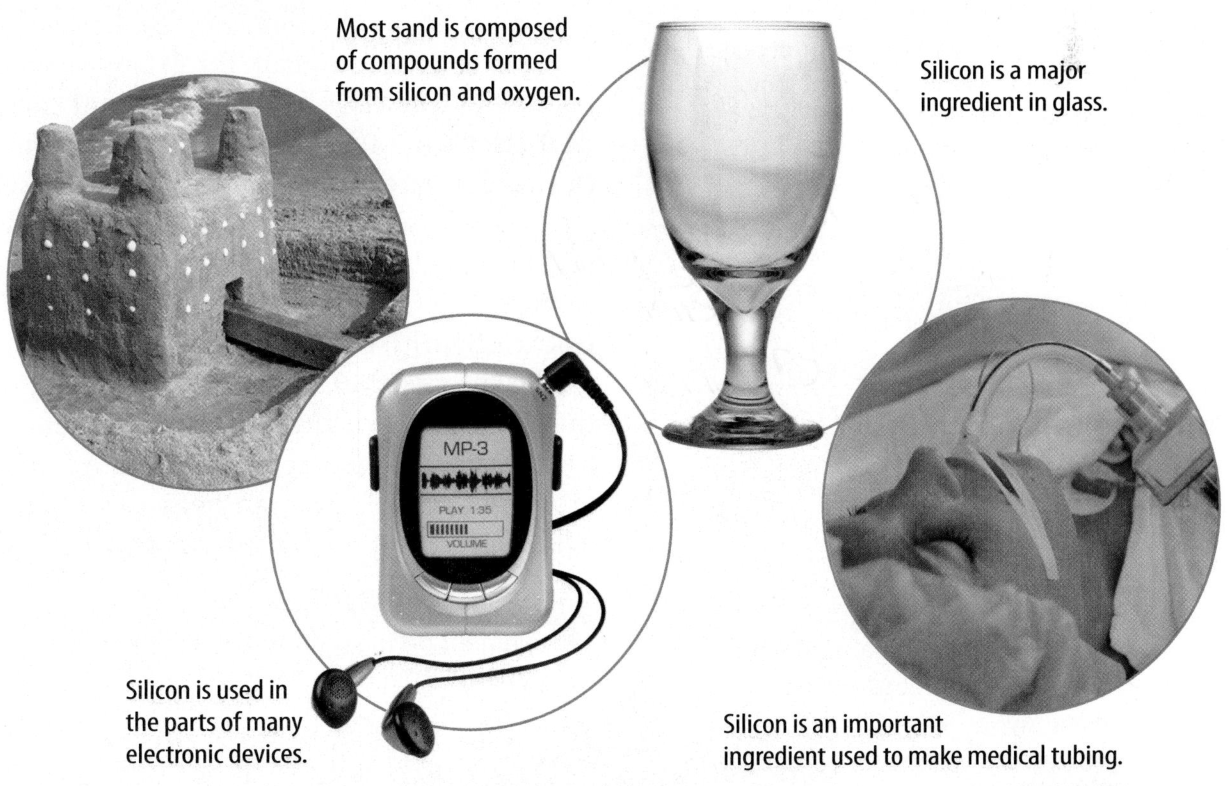

Most sand is composed of compounds formed from silicon and oxygen.

Silicon is a major ingredient in glass.

Silicon is used in the parts of many electronic devices.

Silicon is an important ingredient used to make medical tubing.

Figure 18 This microchip conducts electricity at high temperatures using a semiconductor.

Review **Personal Tutor**

Inquiry MiniLab 15 minutes

Which insulates better?

In this lab, you will compare how well a metal bowl and a nonmetal ball containing a mixture of nonmetals conduct thermal energy.

1. Read and complete a lab safety form.
2. Pour very **warm water** into a **pitcher.**
3. Pour half of the warm water into a **metal bowl.** In your Science Journal, describe how the outside of the bowl feels.
4. Inflate a **beach ball** until it is one-third full. Mold the partially filled beach ball into the shape of a bowl. Pour the remaining warm water into your beach ball bowl. Feel the outside of the bowl. Describe how it feels.

Analyze and Conclude

1. **Explain** the difference in the outside temperatures of the two bowls.
2. **Predict** the results of putting ice in each of the bowls.
3.  **Key Concept** Make a statement about how well a nonmetal conducts thermal energy.

Properties and Uses of Metalloids

Pure silicon is used in making semiconductor devices for computers and other electronic products. Germanium is also used as a semiconductor. However, metalloids have other uses, as shown in **Figure 18.** Pure silicon and Germanium are used in semiconductors. Boron is used in water softeners and laundry products. Boron also glows bright green in fireworks. Silicon is one of the most abundant elements on Earth. Sand, clay, and many rocks and minerals are made of silicon compounds.

Metals, Nonmetals, and Metalloids

You have read that all metallic elements have common characteristics, such as malleability, conductivity, and ductility. However, each metal has unique properties that make it different from other metals. The same is true for nonmetals and metalloids. How can knowing the properties of an element help you evaluate its uses?

Look again at the periodic table. An element's position on the periodic table tells you a lot about the element. By knowing that sulfur is a nonmetal, for example, you know that it breaks easily and does not conduct electricity. You would not choose sulfur to make a wire. You would not try to use oxygen as a semiconductor or sodium as a building material. You know that transition elements are strong, malleable, and do not react easily with oxygen or water. These metals make good building materials because they are strong, malleable, and less reactive than other elements. Understanding the properties of elements can help you decide which element to use in a given situation.

Reading Check Why would you not use an element on the right side of the periodic table as a building material?

Lesson 3 Review

Assessment Online Quiz

Visual Summary

A nonmetal is an element that has no metallic properties. Solid nonmetals are dull, brittle, and do not conduct thermal energy or electricity.

Halogens and noble gases are nonmetals. These elements are found in group 17 and group 18 of the periodic table.

Metalloids have some metallic properties and some nonmetallic properties. The most important use of metalloids is as semiconductors.

FOLDABLES®

Use your lesson Foldable to review the lesson. Save your Foldable for the project at the end of the chapter.

What do you think NOW?

You first read the statements below at the beginning of the chapter.

5. Most of the elements in living things are nonmetals.

6. Even though they look very different, oxygen and sulfur share some similar properties.

Did you change your mind about whether you agree or disagree with the statements? Rewrite any false statements to make them true.

Use Vocabulary

1. **Distinguish** between a nonmetal and a metalloid.
2. An element in group 17 of the periodic table is called a(n) ________.
3. An element in group 18 of the periodic table is called a(n) ________.

Understand Key Concepts 

4. The ability of a halogen to react with a metal to form a salt is an example of a ________ property.
   - **A.** chemical
   - **B.** noble gas
   - **C.** periodic
   - **D.** physical
5. **Classify** each of the following elements as a metal, a nonmetal, or a metalloid: boron, carbon, aluminum, and silicon.
6. **Infer** which group you would expect to contain element 117. Use the periodic table to help you answer this question.

Interpret Graphics

7. **Sequence** nonmetals, metals, and metalloids in order from left to right across the periodic table by copying and completing the graphic organizer below.

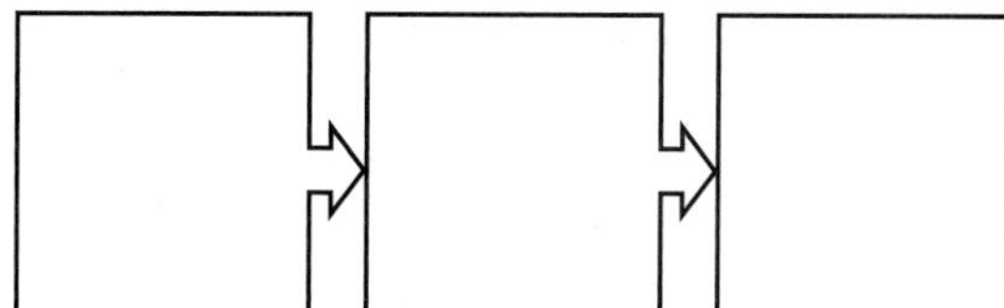

Critical Thinking

8. **Hypothesize** how your classroom would be different if there were no metalloids.
9. **Analyze** why hydrogen is sometimes classified as a metal.
10. **Determine** whether there would be more nonmetals in group 14 or in group 16. Explain your answer.

Alien Insect Periodic Table

Materials

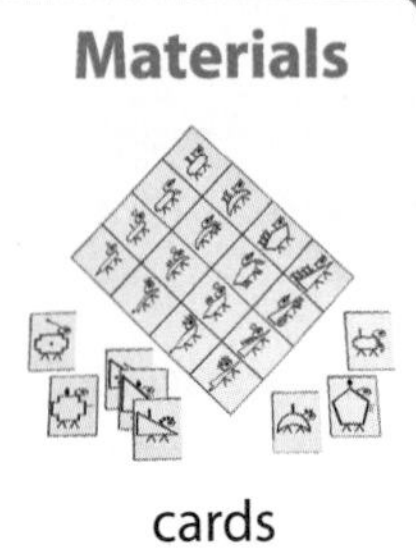

cards

The periodic table classifies elements according to their properties. In this lab, you will model the procedure used to develop the periodic table. Your model will include developing patterns using pictures of alien insects. You will then use your patterns to predict what missing alien insects look like.

Question

How can I arrange objects into patterns by using their properties?

Procedure

1. Obtain a set of alien insect pictures. Spread them out so you can see all of them. Observe the pictures with a partner. Look for properties that you might use to organize the pictures.
2. Make a list of properties you might use to group the alien insects. These properties are those that a number of insects have in common.
3. Make a list of properties you might use to sequence the insects. These properties change from one insect to the next in some pattern.
4. With your partner, decide what pattern you will use to arrange the alien insects in an organized rectangular block. All the insects in a vertical column, or group, must be the same in some way. They must also share some feature that changes regularly as you move down the group. All the aliens in a horizontal row, or period, must be the same in some way and must also share some feature that changes regularly as you move across the period.

4

5 Arrange your insects as you planned. Two insects are missing from your set. Leave empty spaces in your rectangular block for these pictures. When you have finished arranging your insects, have the teacher check your pattern.

6 Write a description of the properties you predict each missing alien insect will have. Then draw a picture of each missing insect.

Analyze and Conclude

7 **Explain** Could you have predicted the properties of the missing insects without placing the others in a pattern? Why or why not?

8 **The Big Idea** How is your arrangement similar to the one developed by Mendeleev for elements? How is it different?

9 **Infer** What properties can you use to predict the identity of one missing insect? What do you not know about that insect?

Communicate Your Results

Create a slide show presentation that demonstrates, step by step, how you grouped and sequenced your insects and predicted the properties of the missing insects. Show your presentation to students in another class.

Inquiry Extension

How could you change the insects so that they better represent the properties of elements, such as atomic mass?

Lab Tips

- ☑ A property is any observable characteristic that you can use to distinguish between objects.
- ☑ A pattern is a consistent plan or model used as a guide for understanding or predicting something.

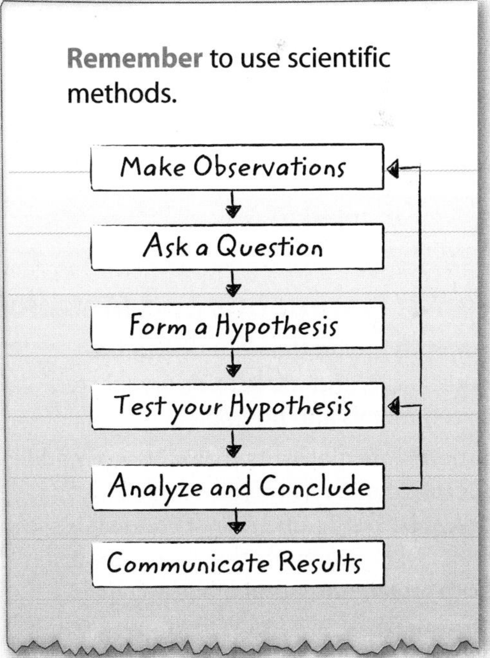

Chapter 3 Study Guide

Elements are organized on the periodic table according to increasing atomic number and similar properties.

Key Concepts Summary

Lesson 1: Using the Periodic Table

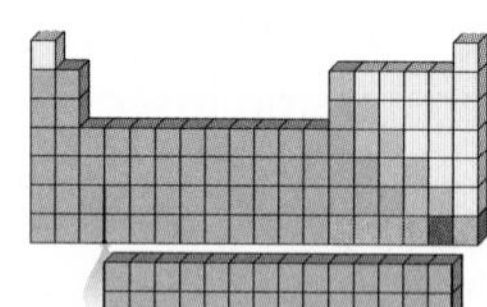

- Elements are organized on the **periodic table** by increasing atomic number and similar properties.
- Elements in the same **group,** or column, of the periodic table have similar properties.
- Elements' properties change across a **period,** which is a row of the periodic table.
- Each element key on the periodic table provides the name, symbol, atomic number, and atomic mass for an element.

Vocabulary

periodic table p. 77
group p. 82
period p. 82

Lesson 2: Metals

- **Metals** are located on the left and middle side of the periodic table.
- Metals are elements that have **ductility, malleability, luster,** and conductivity.
- The **alkali metals** are in group 1 of the periodic table, and the **alkaline earth metals** are in group 2.
- **Transition elements** are metals in groups 3–12 of the periodic table, as well as the lanthanide and actinide series.

Vocabulary

metal p. 87
luster p. 87
ductility p. 88
malleability p. 88
alkali metal p. 89
alkaline earth metal p. 89
transition element p. 90

Lesson 3: Nonmetals and Metalloids

- **Nonmetals** are on the right side of the periodic table, and **metalloids** are located between metals and nonmetals.
- Nonmetals are elements that have no metallic properties. Solid nonmetals are dull in appearance, brittle, and do not conduct electricity. Metalloids are elements that have properties of both metals and nonmetals.
- Some metalloids are **semiconductors.**
- Elements in group 17 are called **halogens,** and elements in group 18 are **noble gases.**

Vocabulary

nonmetal p. 95
halogen p. 97
noble gas p. 98
metalloid p. 99
semiconductor p. 99

Review
- Personal Tutor
- Vocabulary eGames
- Vocabulary eFlashcards

FOLDABLES® Chapter Project

Assemble your lesson Foldables as shown to make a Chapter Project. Use the project to review what you have learned in this chapter.

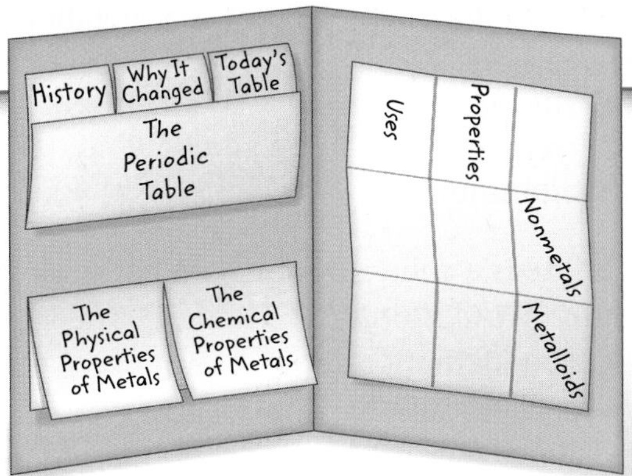

Use Vocabulary

1. The element magnesium (Mg) is in ________ 3 of the periodic table.
2. An element that is shiny, is easily pulled into wires or hammered into thin sheets, and is a good conductor of electricity and heat is a(n) ________.
3. Copper is used to make wire because it has the property of ________.
4. An element that is sometimes a good conductor of electricity and sometimes a good insulator is a(n) ________.
5. An element that is a poor conductor of heat and electricity but is a good insulator is a(n) ________.

Link Vocabulary and Key Concepts

Concepts in Motion Interactive Concept Map

Copy this concept map, and then use vocabulary terms from the previous page to complete the concept map.

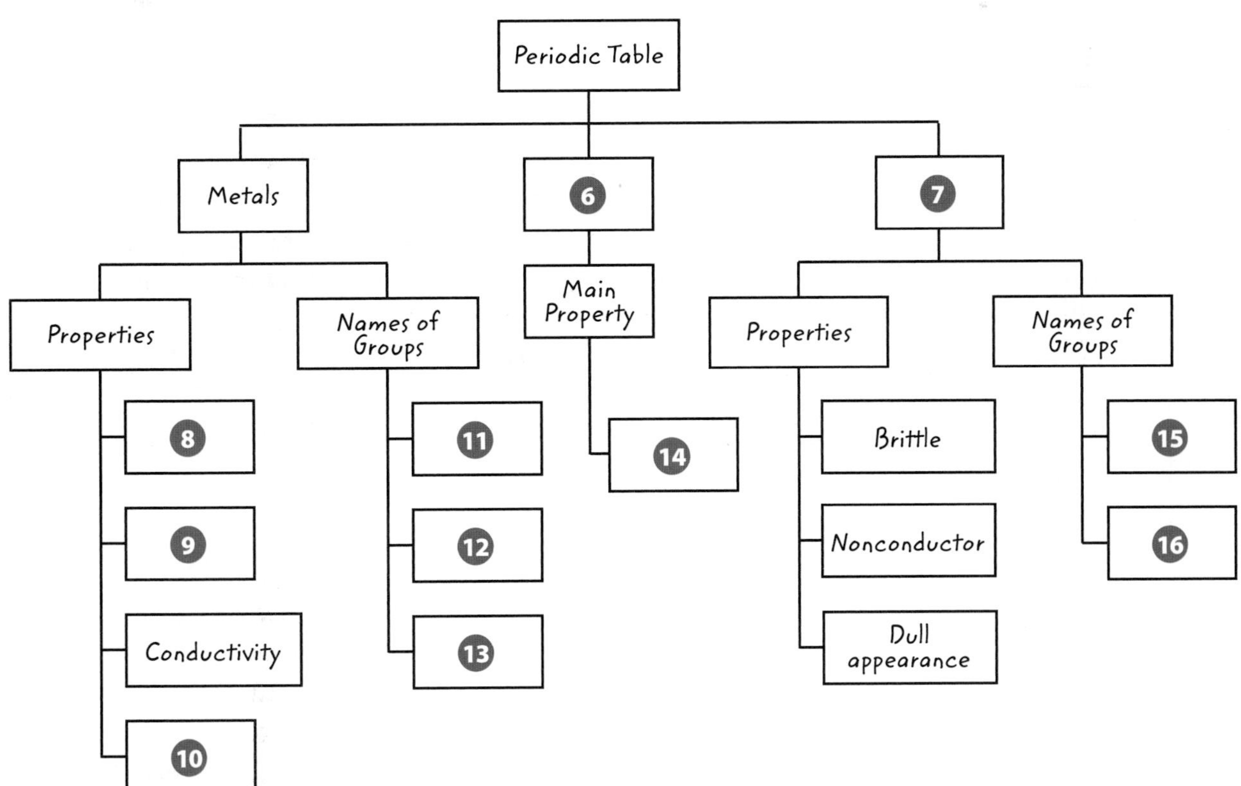

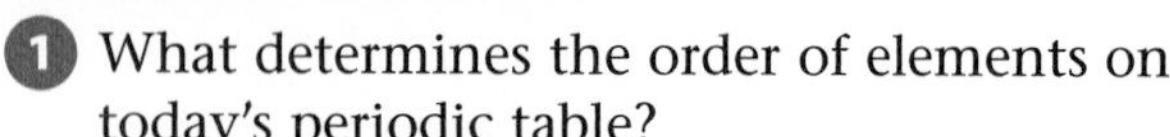

Chapter 3 Review

Understand Key Concepts

1 What determines the order of elements on today's periodic table?

A. increasing atomic mass
B. decreasing atomic mass
C. increasing atomic number
D. decreasing atomic number

2 The element key for nitrogen is shown below.

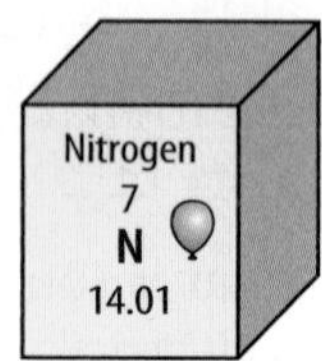

From this key, determine the atomic mass of nitrogen.

A. 7
B. 7.01
C. 14.01
D. 21.01

3 Look at the periodic table in Lesson 1. Which of the following lists of elements forms a group on the periodic table?

A. Li, Be, B, C, N, O, F, and Ne
B. He, Ne, Ar, Kr, Xe, and Rn
C. B, Si, As, Te, and At
D. Sc, Ti, V, Cr, Mn, Fe, Co, Cu, Ni, and Zn

4 Which is NOT a property of metals?

A. brittleness
B. conductivity
C. ductility
D. luster

5 What are two properties that make a metal a good choice to use as wire in electronics?

A. conductivity, malleability
B. ductility, conductivity
C. luster, malleability
D. malleability, high density

6 Where are most metals on the periodic table?

A. on the left side only
B. on the right side only
C. in the middle only
D. on the left side and in the middle

7 Look at the periodic table in Lesson 1 and determine which element is a metalloid.

A. carbon
B. silicon
C. oxygen
D. aluminum

8 Iodine is a solid nonmetal. What is one property of iodine?

A. conductivity
B. dull appearance
C. malleability
D. ductility

9 The following table lists some information about certain elements in group 17.

Element Symbol	Atomic Number	Melting Point (°C)	Boiling Point (°C)
F	9	−233	−187
Cl	17	−102	−35
Br	35	−7.3	59
I	53	114	183

Which statement describes what happens to these elements as atomic number increases?

A. Both melting point and boiling point decrease.
B. Melting point increases and boiling point decreases.
C. Melting point decreases and boiling point increases.
D. Both melting point and boiling point increase.

Assessment
Online Test Practice

Critical Thinking

10 **Recommend** an element to use to fill bottles that contain ancient paper. The element should be a gas at room temperature, should be denser than helium, and should not easily react with other elements.

11 **Apply** Why is mercury the only metal to have been used in thermometers?

12 **Evaluate** the following types of metals as a choice to make a Sun reflector: alkali metals, alkaline earth metals, or transition metals. The metal cannot react with water or oxygen and must be shiny and strong.

13 The figure below shows a pattern of densities.

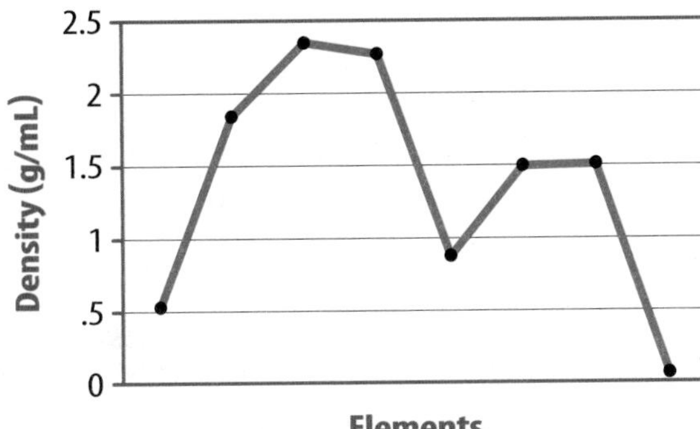

Infer whether you are looking at a graph of elements within a group or across a period. Explain your answer.

14 **Contrast** aluminum and nitrogen. Show why aluminum is a metal and nitrogen is not.

15 **Classify** A student sorted six elements. He placed iron, silver, and sodium in group A. He placed neon, oxygen, and nitrogen in group B. Name one other element that fits in group A and another element that belongs in group B. Explain your answer.

Writing in Science

16 **Write** a plan that shows how a metal, a nonmetal, and a metalloid could be used when constructing a building.

REVIEW

17 Explain how atomic number and properties are used to determine where element 115 is placed on the periodic table.

18 The photo below shows how the properties of materials determine their uses. How can the periodic table be used to help you find elements with properties similar to that of helium?

Math Skills

Math Practice

Use Geometry

19 The table below shows the atomic radii of three elements in group 1 on the periodic table.

Element	Atomic radius
Li	152 pm
Na	186 pm
K	227 pm

a. What is the circumference of each atom?

b. Rubidium (Rb) is the next element in Group 1. What would you predict about the radius and circumference of a rubidium atom?

Standardized Test Practice

Record your answers on the answer sheet provided by your teacher or on a sheet of paper.

Multiple Choice

1 Where are most nonmetals located on the periodic table?

A in the bottom row

B on the left side and in the middle

C on the right side

D in the top row

Use the figure below to answer question 2.

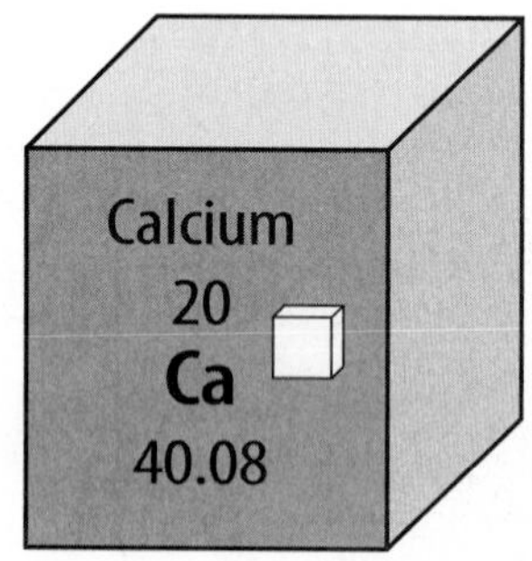

2 What is the atomic mass of calcium?

A 20

B 40.08

C $40.08 \div 20$

D $40.08 + 20$

3 Which element is most likely to react with potassium?

A bromine

B calcium

C nickel

D sodium

4 Which group of elements can act as semiconductors?

A halogens

B metalloids

C metals

D noble gases

Use the table below about group 13 elements to answer question 5.

Element Symbol	Atomic Number	Density (g/cm^3)	Atomic Mass
B	5	2.34	10.81
Al	13	2.70	26.98
Ga	31	5.90	69.72
In	49	7.30	114.82

5 How do density and atomic mass change as atomic number increases?

A Density and atomic mass decrease.

B Density and atomic mass increase.

C Density decreases and atomic mass increases.

D Density increases and atomic mass decreases.

6 Which elements have high densities, strength, and resistance to corrosion?

A alkali metals

B alkaline earth metals

C metalloids

D transition elements

7 Which is a property of a metal?

A It is brittle.

B It is a good insulator.

C It has a dull appearance.

D It is malleable.

Assessment
Online Standardized Test Practice

Use the figure below to answer questions 8 and 9.

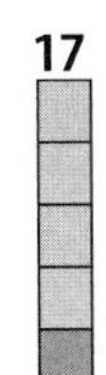

8 The figure shows a group in the periodic table. What is the name of this group of elements?

A halogens
B metalloids
C metals
D noble gases

9 Which is a property of these elements?

A They are conductors.
B They are semiconductors.
C They are nonreactive with other elements.
D They react easily with other elements.

10 What is one similarity among elements in a group?

A atomic mass
B atomic weight
C chemical properties
D practical uses

Constructed Response

Use the figure below to answer questions 11 and 12.

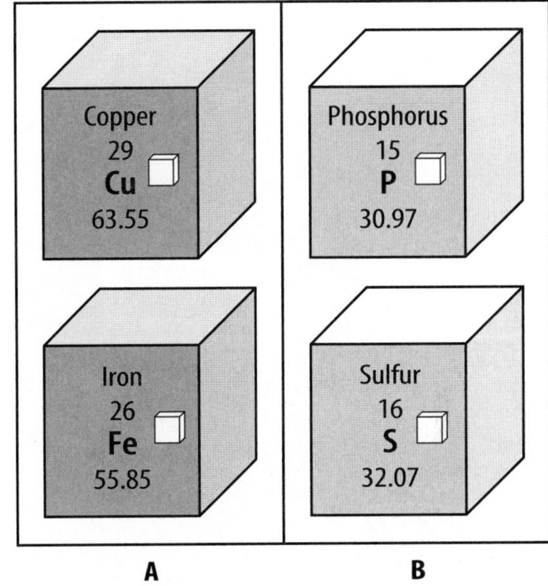

11 Groups A and B each contain two elements. Identify each group as metals, nonmetals, or metalloids. Would silicon belong to one of these groups? Why or why not?

12 Which group in the figure above yields the strongest building elements? Why?

13 How does the periodic table of elements help scientists today?

14 What connection does the human body have with the elements on the periodic table?

NEED EXTRA HELP?														
If You Missed Question...	1	2	3	4	5	6	7	8	9	10	11	12	13	14
Go to Lesson...	1	1	3	3	1	2	2	3	3	1	2, 3	2	1	3

Unit 2

INTERACTIONS OF MATTER

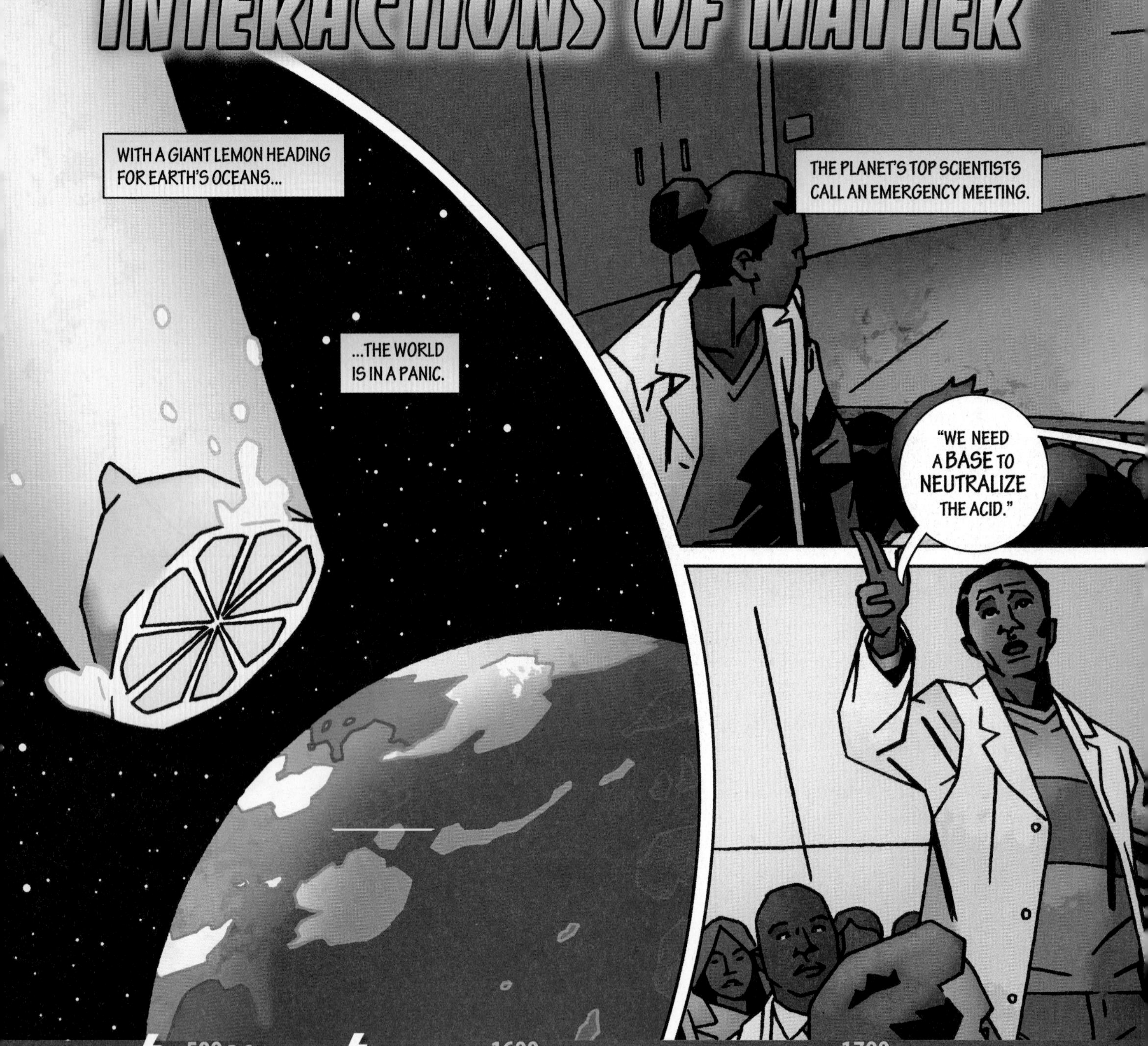

WITH A GIANT LEMON HEADING FOR EARTH'S OCEANS...
...THE WORLD IS IN A PANIC.
THE PLANET'S TOP SCIENTISTS CALL AN EMERGENCY MEETING.
"WE NEED A BASE TO NEUTRALIZE THE ACID."

500 B.C. 1600 1700

1000 B.C.
Chemistry is considered more of an art than a science. Chemical arts include the smelting of metals and the making of drugs, dyes, iron, and bronze.

1661
A clear distinction is made between chemistry and alchemy when *The Sceptical Chymist* is published by Robert Boyle. Modern chemistry begins to emerge.

1789
Antoine Lavoisier, the "father of modern chemistry," clearly outlines the law of conservation of mass.

1803
John Dalton publishes his atomic theory, which states that all matter is composed of atoms, which are small and indivisible and can join together to form chemical compounds. Dalton is considered the originator of modern atomic theory.

1869
The first periodic table is published by Dmitri Mendeleev. The table arranges elements into vertical columns and horizontal rows and is arranged by atomic number.

1953
James Watson and Francis Crick develop the double-helix model of DNA. This discovery leads to a spike in research of the biochemistry of life.

1983
Kary Mullis devises the polymerase chain reaction (PCR), a technique for copying a small portion of DNA in a lab environment. PCR can be used to synthesize specific pieces of DNA and makes the sequencing of DNA of organisms possible.

? Inquiry
Visit ConnectED for this unit's STEM activity.

Health and Science

Have an upset stomach? Chew on some charcoal. Have a headache? Rub a little peppermint oil on your temples. As shown in **Figure 1**, people have used chemicals to fix physical ailments for thousands of years, long before the development of the first medicines. Many cures were discovered by accident. People did not understand why the cures worked, only that they did work.

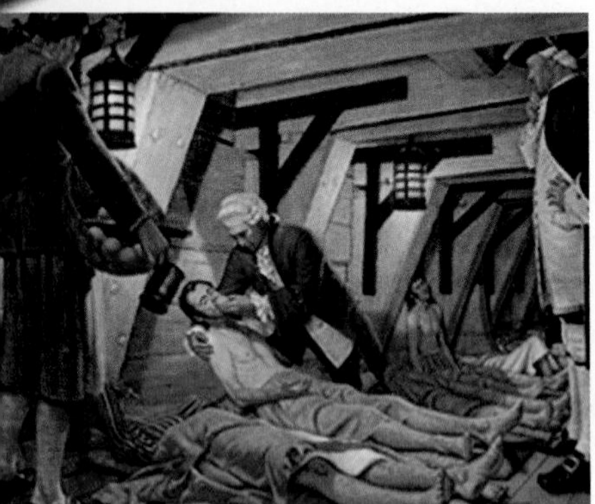

▲ **Figure 1** Thousands of years ago, people believed that evil spirits were responsible for illness. They often treated the physical symptoms with herbs or other natural materials.

Asking Questions About Health

Over time, people asked questions about which cures worked and which cures did not work. They made observations, recorded their findings, and had discussions about cures with other people. This process was the start of the scientific investigation of health. **Health** is the overall condition of an organism or group of organisms at any given time. Early studies focused on treating the physical parts of the body. The study of how chemicals interact in organisms did not come until much later. Recognizing that chemicals can affect health opened a whole new field of study known as biochemistry. The time line in **Figure 2** shows some of the medical and chemical discoveries people made that led to the development of medicines that save lives.

Figure 2 The time line shows several significant discoveries and developments in the history of medicine. ▼

4,200 years ago Clay tablets describe using sesame oil on wounds to treat infection.

3,500 years ago An ancient papyrus described how Egyptians applied moldy bread to wounds to prevent infection.

More than 3,300 years later, scientists found that a chemical in mold broke down the cell membranes of bacteria, killing them. Similar discoveries led to the development of antibiotics.

2,500 years ago Hippocrates, known as the "Father of Medicine," is the first physician known to separate medical knowledge from myth and superstition.

Year 900 The first pharmacy opened in Persia, which is now Iraq.

1740s A doctor found that the disease called scurvy was caused by a lack of Vitamin C.

Early explorers on long sea voyages often lost their teeth or developed deadly sores. Ships could not carry many fruits and vegetables, which contain Vitamin C, because they spoil quickly. Scientists suspect that many early explorers might have died because their diets did not include the proper vitamins.

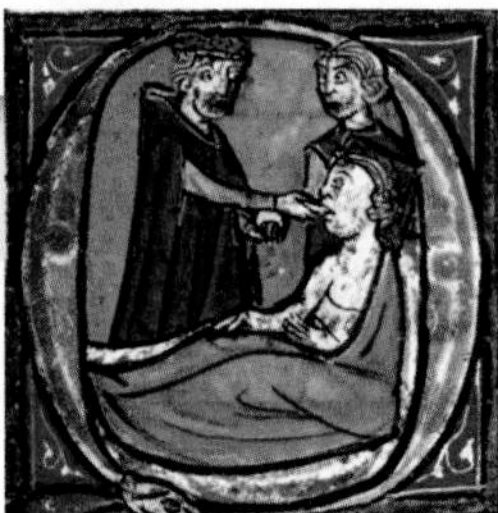

Benefits and Risks of Medicines

Scientists might recognize that a person's body is missing a necessary chemical, but that does not mean they can always fix the problem. For example, people used to get necessary vitamins and minerals by eating natural, whole foods. Today, food processing destroys many nutrients. Foods last longer, but they do not provide all the nutrients the body needs.

Researchers still do not understand the role of many chemicals in the body. Taking a medicine to fix one problem sometimes causes others, called side effects. Some side effects can be worse than the original problem. For example, antibiotics kill some disease-causing bacteria. However, widespread use of antibiotics has resulted in "super bugs"—bacteria that are resistant to treatment.

Histamines are chemicals that have many functions in the body, including regulating sleep and decreasing sensitivity to allergens. However, low levels of histamines have been linked to some serious illnesses. Many medicines have long-term effects on health. Before you take a medicine, you should recognize that you are adding a chemical to your body. You should be as informed as possible about any possible side effects.

Inquiry MiniLab

15 minutes

Is everyone's chemistry the same?

Each person's body is a unique "chemical factory." Why might using the same medicine to treat illness not work exactly the same way in everyone?

1. Read and complete a lab safety form.
2. Place a strip of **pH paper** on your tongue. Immediately place the paper in a **self-sealing plastic bag.**
3. Compare the color of your paper to the **color guide.** Record the pH in your Science Journal.
4. Record your pH on a class chart for comparison.

Analyze and Conclude

1. **Organize Data** What was the range of pH values among your classmates?
2. **Predict** How might differences in pH affect how well a medicine works in different people?

1770s The first vaccination is developed and administered.

1800s Nitrous oxide is first used as an anesthetic by dentists.

1920s Insulin is identified as the missing hormone in people with diabetes.

Scientists studying digestion in dogs noticed that ants were attracted to the urine of a dog whose pancreas had been removed. They determined the dog's urine contained sugar, which attracted ants. Eventually, scientists discovered that diabetes resulted from a lack of insulin, a chemical produced in the pancreas that regulates blood sugar. Today, some people with diabetes wear an insulin pump that monitors their blood sugar and delivers insulin to their bodies.

1920s Penicillin is discovered, but not developed for treatment of disease until the mid-1940s.

2000s First vaccine to target a cause of cancer

Chapter 4

Elements and Chemical Bonds

THE BIG IDEA **How do elements join together to form chemical compounds?**

Inquiry How do they combine?

How many different words could you type using just the letters on a keyboard? The English alphabet has only 26 letters, but a dictionary lists hundreds of thousands of words using these letters! Similarly only about 115 different elements make all kinds of matter.

- How do so few elements form so many different kinds of matter?
- Why do you think different types of matter have different properties?
- How are atoms held together to produce different types of matter?

Get Ready to Read

What do you think?

Before you read, decide if you agree or disagree with each of these statements. As you read this chapter, see if you change your mind about any of the statements.

1. Elements rarely exist in pure form. Instead, combinations of elements make up most of the matter around you.
2. Chemical bonds that form between atoms involve electrons.
3. The atoms in a water molecule are more chemically stable than they would be as individual atoms.
4. Many substances dissolve easily in water because opposite ends of a water molecule have opposite charges.
5. Losing electrons can make some atoms more chemically stable.
6. Metals are good electrical conductors because they tend to hold onto their valence electrons very tightly.

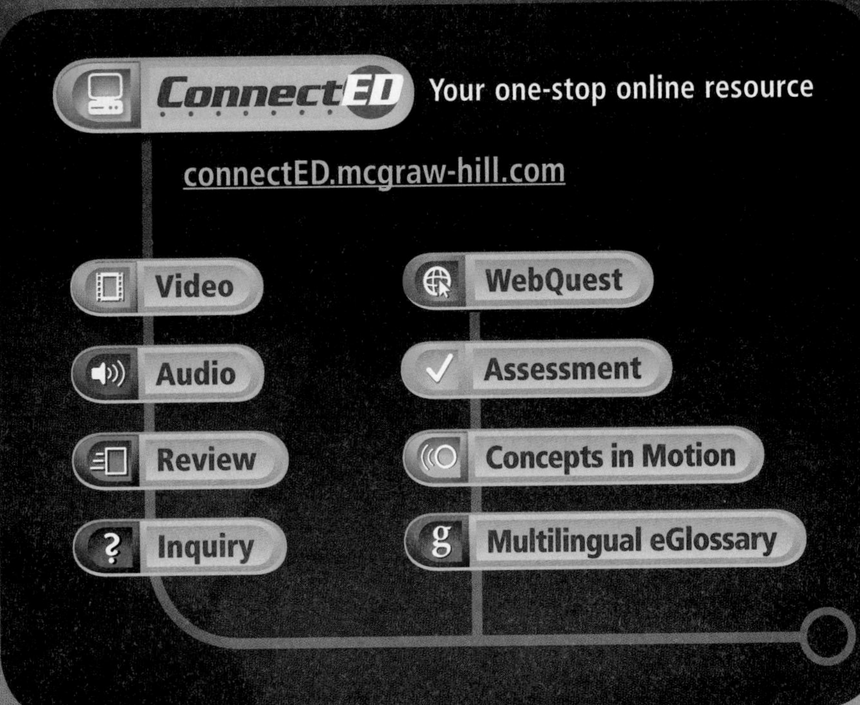

Lesson 1

Reading Guide

Key Concepts
ESSENTIAL QUESTIONS

- How is an electron's energy related to its distance from the nucleus?
- Why do atoms gain, lose, or share electrons?

Vocabulary

chemical bond p. 118
valence electron p. 120
electron dot diagram p. 121

Multilingual eGlossary

Video BrainPOP®

Academic Standards for Science

8.1.4 Describe the structure of an atom and relate the arrangement of electrons to how that atom interacts with other atoms.

Also covers: 8.NS.1, 8.NS.4, 8.NS.6, 8.NS.9

Electrons and Energy Levels

Inquiry Are pairs more stable?

Rowing can be hard work, especially if you are part of a racing team. The job is made easier because the rowers each pull on the water with a pair of oars. How do pairs make the boat more stable?

Launch Lab

20 minutes

How is the periodic table organized?

How do you begin to put together a puzzle of a thousand pieces? You first sort similar pieces into groups. All edge pieces might go into one pile. All blue pieces might go into another pile. Similarly, scientists placed the elements into groups based on their properties. They created the periodic table, which organizes information about all the elements.

1. Obtain six **index cards** from your teacher. Using one card for each element name, write the names *beryllium, sodium, iron, zinc, aluminum,* and *oxygen* at the top of a card.
2. Open your textbook to the periodic table printed on the inside back cover. Locate the element key for each element written on your cards.
3. For each element, find the following information and write it on the index card: symbol, atomic number, atomic mass, state of matter, and element type.

Think About This

1. What do the elements in the blue blocks have in common? In the green blocks? In the yellow blocks?
2. **Key Concept** Each element in a column on the periodic table has similar chemical properties and forms bonds in similar ways. Based on this, for each element you listed on a card, name another element on the periodic table that has similar chemical properties.

The Periodic Table

Imagine trying to find a book in a library if all the books were unorganized. Books are organized in a library to help you easily find the information you need. The periodic table is like a library of information about all chemical elements.

A copy of the periodic table is on the inside back cover of this book. The table has more than 100 blocks—one for each known element. Each block on the periodic table includes basic properties of each element such as the element's state of matter at room temperature and its atomic number. The atomic number is the number of protons in each atom of the element. Each block also lists an element's atomic mass, or the average mass of all the different isotopes of that element.

Periods and Groups

You can learn about some properties of an element from its position on the periodic table. Elements are organized in periods (rows) and groups (columns). The periodic table lists elements in order of atomic number. The atomic number increases from left to right as you move across a period. Elements in each group have similar chemical properties and react with other elements in similar ways. In this lesson, you will read more about how an element's position on the periodic table can be used to predict its properties.

Reading Check How is the periodic table organized?

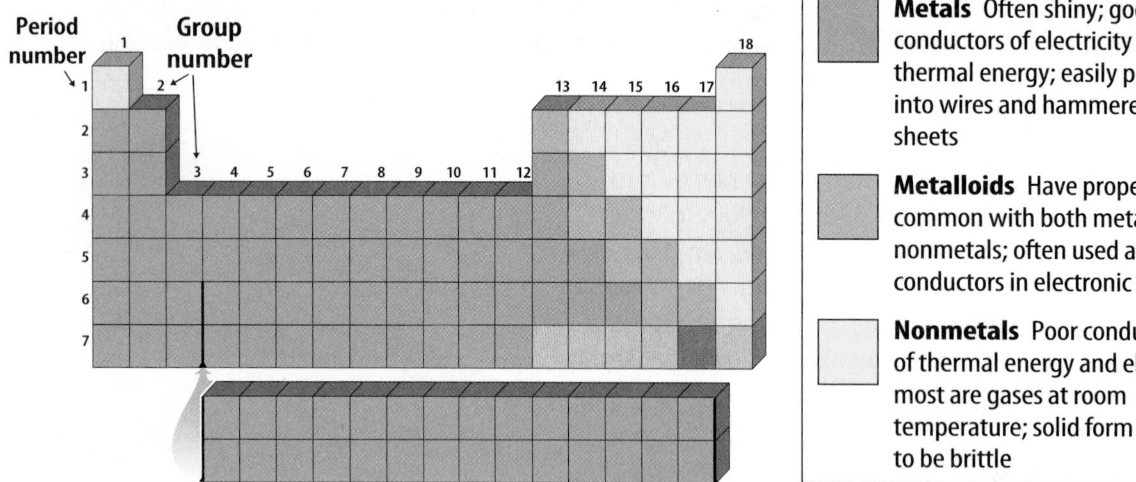

▲ **Figure 1** Elements on the periodic table are classified as metals, nonmetals, or metalloids.

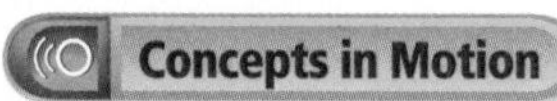

Animation

Metals, Nonmetals, and Metalloids

The three main regions of elements on the periodic table are shown in **Figure 1.** Except for hydrogen, elements on the left side of the table are metals. Nonmetals are on the right side of the table. Metalloids form the narrow stair-step region between metals and nonmetals.

Reading Check Where are metals, nonmetals, and metalloids on the periodic table?

REVIEW VOCABULARY

compound
matter that is made up of two or more different kinds of atoms joined together by chemical bonds

Atoms Bond

In nature, pure elements are rare. Instead, atoms of different elements chemically combine and form **compounds.** Compounds make up most of the matter around you, including living and nonliving things. There are only about 115 elements, but these elements combine and form millions of compounds. Chemical bonds hold them together. *A* **chemical bond** *is a force that holds two or more atoms together.*

Electron Number and Arrangement

Recall that atoms contain protons, neutrons, and electrons, as shown in **Figure 2.** Each proton has a positive charge; each neutron has no charge; and each electron has a negative charge. The atomic number of an element is the number of protons in each atom of that element. In a neutral (uncharged) atom, the number of protons equals the number of electrons.

The exact position of electrons in an atom cannot be determined. This is because electrons are in constant motion around the nucleus. However, each electron is usually in a certain area of space around the nucleus. Some are in areas close to the nucleus, and some are in areas farther away.

Figure 2 Protons and neutrons are in an atom's nucleus. Electrons move around the nucleus. ▼

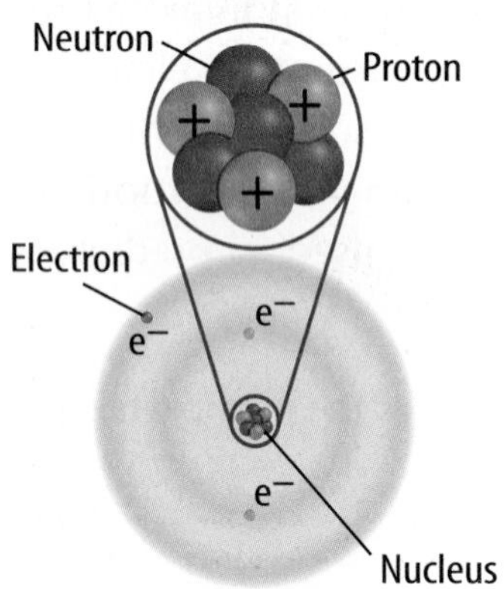

Electrons and Energy Different electrons in an atom have different amounts of energy. An electron moves around the nucleus at a distance that corresponds to its amount of energy. Areas of space in which electrons move around the nucleus are called energy levels. Electrons closest to the nucleus have the least amount of energy. They are in the lowest energy level. Electrons farthest from the nucleus have the greatest amount of energy. They are in the highest energy level. The energy levels of an atom are shown in **Figure 3.** Notice that only two electrons can be in the lowest energy level. The second energy level can hold up to eight.

Key Concept Check How is an electron's energy related to its position in an atom?

Electrons and Bonding Imagine two magnets. The closer they are to each other, the stronger the attraction of their opposite ends. Negatively charged electrons have a similar attraction to the positively charged nucleus of an atom. The electrons in energy levels closest to the nucleus of the same atom have a strong attraction to that nucleus. However, electrons farther from that nucleus are weakly attracted to it. They can easily be attracted to the nucleus of other atoms. This attraction between the positive nucleus of one atom and the negative electrons of another atom is what creates a chemical bond.

FOLDABLES®

Make two quarter-sheet note cards from a sheet of paper. Use them to organize your notes on valence electrons and electron dot diagrams.

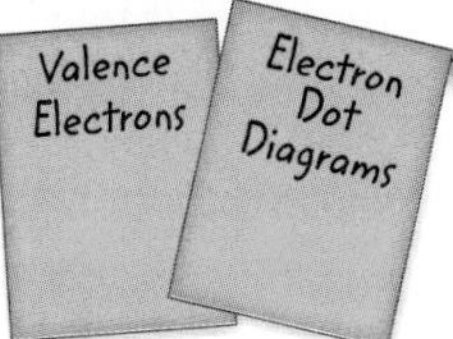

Figure 3 Electrons are in certain energy levels within an atom.

Electron Energy Levels

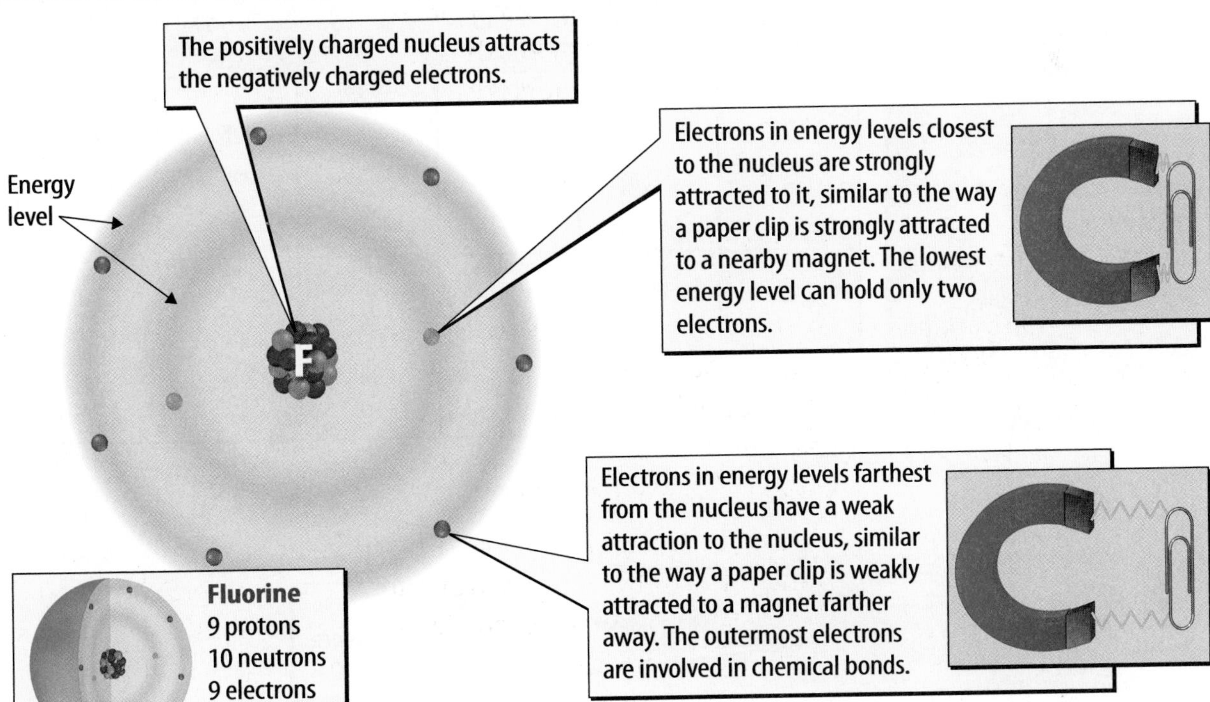

The positively charged nucleus attracts the negatively charged electrons.
Energy level
F
Electrons in energy levels closest to the nucleus are strongly attracted to it, similar to the way a paper clip is strongly attracted to a nearby magnet. The lowest energy level can hold only two electrons.
Electrons in energy levels farthest from the nucleus have a weak attraction to the nucleus, similar to the way a paper clip is weakly attracted to a magnet farther away. The outermost electrons are involved in chemical bonds.
Fluorine
9 protons
10 neutrons
9 electrons

Valence Electrons

You have read that electrons farthest from their nucleus are easily attracted to the nuclei of nearby atoms. These outermost electrons are the only electrons involved in chemical bonding. Even atoms that have only a few electrons, such as hydrogen or lithium, can form chemical bonds. This is because these electrons are still the outermost electrons and are exposed to the nuclei of other atoms. A **valence electron** *is an outermost electron of an atom that participates in chemical bonding.* Valence electrons have the most energy of all electrons in an atom.

Word Origin

valence
from Latin *valentia*, means "strength, capacity"

The number of valence electrons in each atom of an element can help determine the type and the number of bonds it can form. How do you know how many valence electrons an atom has? The periodic table can tell you. Except for helium, elements in certain groups have the same number of valence electrons. **Figure 4** illustrates how to use the periodic table to determine the number of valence electrons in the atoms of groups 1, 2, and 13–18. Determining the number of valence electrons for elements in groups 3–12 is more complicated. You will learn about these groups in later chemistry courses.

Figure 4 You can use the group numbers at the top of the columns to determine the number of valence electrons in atoms of groups 1, 2, and 13–18.

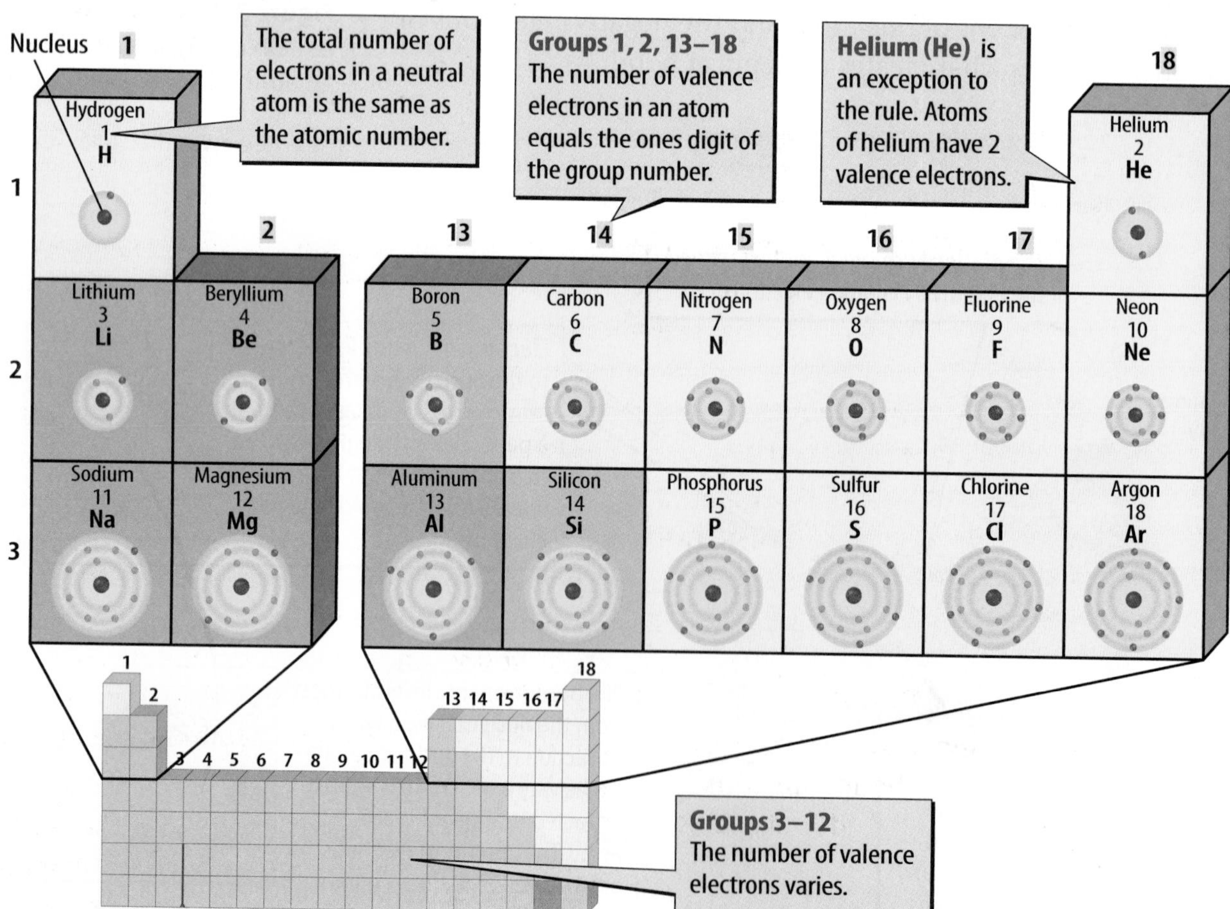

Visual Check How many valence electrons does an atom of phosphorous (P) have?

Writing and Using Electron Dot Diagrams

Figure 5 Electron dot diagrams show the number of valence electrons in an atom.

Steps for writing a dot diagram	Beryllium	Carbon	Nitrogen	Argon
1 Identify the element's group number on the periodic table.	2	14	15	18
2 Identify the number of valence electrons. • This equals the ones digit of the group number.	2	4	5	8
3 Draw the electron dot diagram. • Place one dot at a time on each side of the symbol (top, right, bottom, left). Repeat until all dots are used.	Be·	·C·	·N·	:Ar:
4 Determine if the atom is chemically stable. • An atom is chemically stable if all dots on the electron dot diagram are paired.	Chemically Unstable	Chemically Unstable	Chemically Unstable	Chemically Stable
5 Determine how many bonds this atom can form. • Count the dots that are unpaired.	2	4	3	0

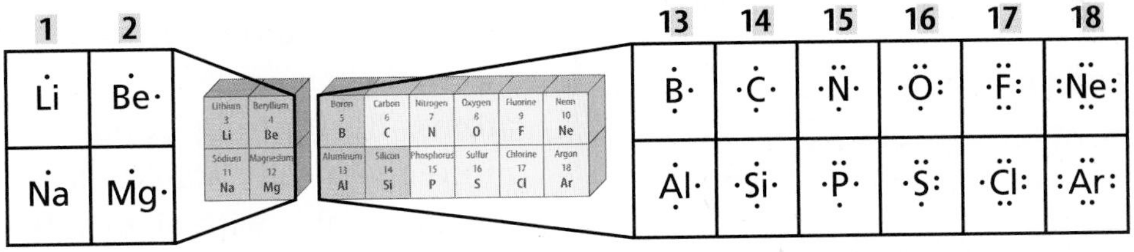

1	2	13	14	15	16	17	18
Li	Be·	B·	·C·	·N·	·O:	·F:	:Ne:
Na	Mg·	Al·	·Si·	·P·	·S:	·Cl:	:Ar:

Electron Dot Diagrams

In 1916 an American Chemist named Gilbert Lewis developed a method to show an element's valence electrons. He developed the **electron dot diagram,** *a model that represents valence electrons in an atom as dots around the element's chemical symbol.*

Electron dot diagrams can help you predict how an atom will bond with other atoms. Dots, representing valence electrons, are placed one-by-one on each side of an element's chemical symbol until all the dots are used. Some dots will be paired up, others will not. The number of unpaired dots is often the number of bonds an atom can form. The steps for writing dot diagrams are shown in **Figure 5.**

Reading Check Why are electron dot diagrams useful?

Recall that each element in a group has the same number of valence electrons. As a result, every element in a group has the same number of dots in its electron dot diagram.

Notice in **Figure 5** that an argon atom, Ar, has eight valence electrons, or four pairs of dots, in the diagram. There are no unpaired dots. Atoms with eight valence electrons do not easily react with other atoms. They are chemically stable. Atoms that have between one and seven valence electrons are reactive, or chemically unstable. These atoms easily bond with other atoms and form chemically stable compounds.

Atoms of hydrogen and helium have only one energy level. These atoms are chemically stable with two valence electrons.

Inquiry MiniLab 20 minutes

How does an electron's energy relate to its position in an atom?

Electrons in energy levels closest to the nucleus are strongly attracted to it. You can use paper clips and a magnet to model a similar attraction.

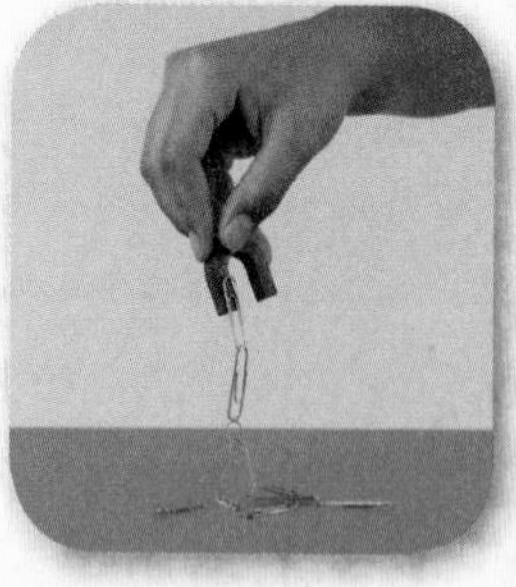

1. Read and complete a lab safety form.
2. Pick up a **paper clip** with a **magnet.** Use the first paper clip to pick up another one.
3. Continue picking up paper clips in this way until you have a chain of paper clips and no more will attach.
4. Gently pull off the paper clips one by one.

Analyze and Conclude

1. **Observe** Which paper clip was the easiest to remove? Which was the most difficult?
2. **Use Models** In what way do the magnet and the paper clips act as a model for an atom?
3. **Key Concept** How does an electron's position in an atom affect its ability to take part in chemical bonding?

Noble Gases

The elements in Group 18 are called noble gases. With the exception of helium, noble gases have eight valence electrons and are chemically stable. Chemically stable atoms do not easily react, or form bonds, with other atoms. The electron structures of two noble gases—neon and helium—are shown in **Figure 6.** Notice that all dots are paired in the dot diagrams of these atoms.

Stable and Unstable Atoms

Atoms with unpaired dots in their electron dot diagrams are reactive, or chemically unstable. For example, nitrogen, shown in **Figure 6,** has three unpaired dots in its electron dot diagram, and it is reactive. Nitrogen, like many other atoms, becomes more stable by forming chemical bonds with other atoms.

When an atom forms a bond, it gains, loses, or shares valence electrons with other atoms. By forming bonds, atoms become more chemically stable. Recall that atoms are most stable with eight valence electrons. Therefore, atoms with less than eight valence electrons form chemical bonds and become stable. In Lessons 2 and 3, you will read which atoms gain, lose, or share electrons when forming stable compounds.

Key Concept Check Why do atoms gain, lose, or share electrons?

Figure 6 Atoms gain, lose, or share valence electrons and become chemically stable.

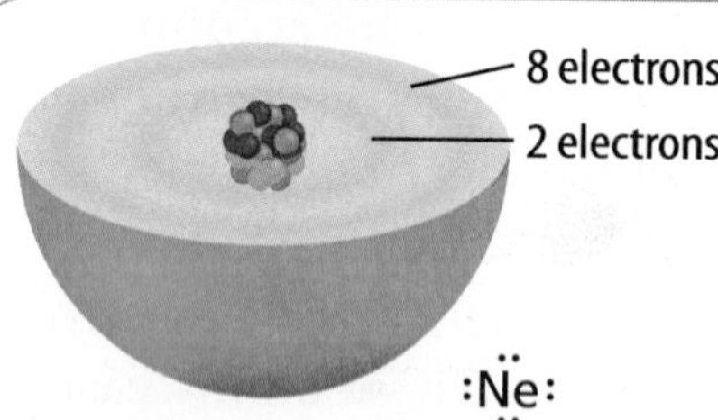

Neon has 10 electrons: 2 inner electrons and 8 valence electrons. A neon atom is chemically stable because it has 8 valence electrons. All dots in the dot diagram are paired.

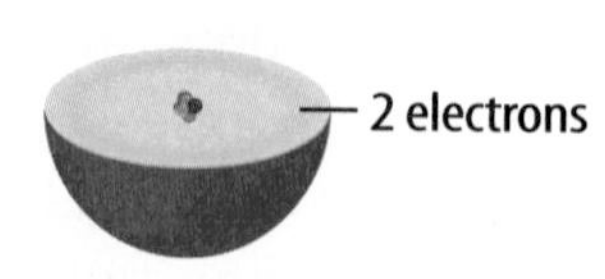

Helium has 2 electrons. Because an atom's lowest energy level can hold only 2 electrons, the 2 dots in the dot diagram are paired. Helium is chemically stable.

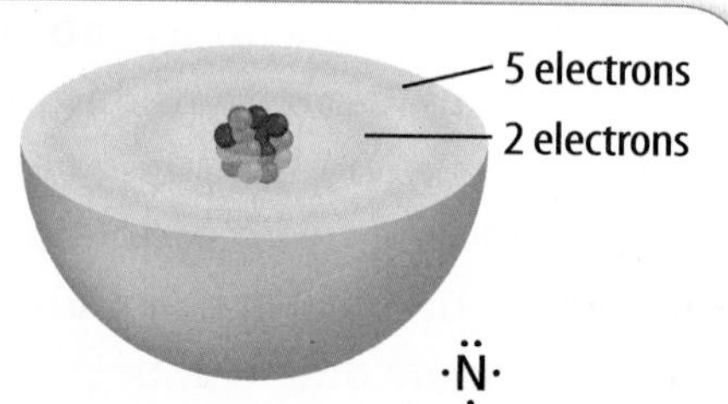

Nitrogen has 7 electrons: 2 inner electrons and 5 valence electrons. Its dot diagram has 1 pair of dots and 3 unpaired dots. Nitrogen atoms become more stable by forming chemical bonds.

Lesson 1 Review

Assessment Online Quiz

Inquiry Virtual Lab

Visual Summary

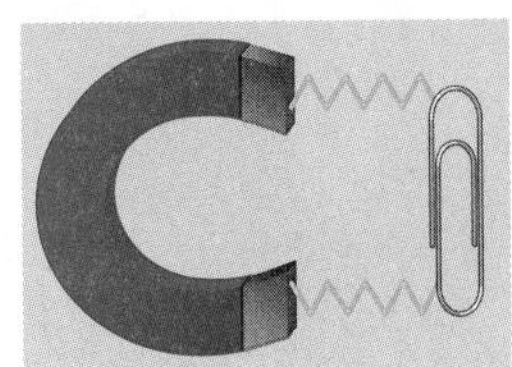

Electrons are less strongly attracted to a nucleus the farther they are from it, similar to the way a magnet attracts a paper clip.

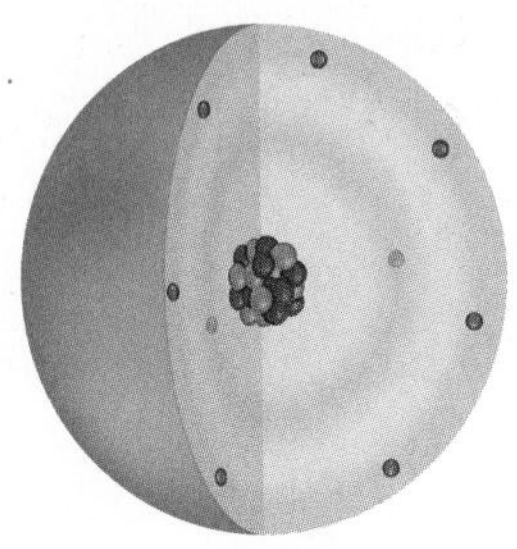

Electrons in atoms are in energy levels around the nucleus. Valence electrons are involved in chemical bonding.

All noble gases, except He, have four pairs of dots in their electron dot diagrams. Noble gases are chemically stable.

FOLDABLES®

Use your lesson Foldable to review the lesson. Save your Foldable for the project at the end of the chapter.

What do you think NOW?

You first read the statements below at the beginning of the chapter.

1. Elements rarely exist in pure form. Instead, combinations of elements make up most of the matter around you.
2. Chemical bonds that form between atoms involve electrons.

Did you change your mind about whether you agree or disagree with the statements? Rewrite any false statements to make them true.

Use Vocabulary

1. **Use the term** *chemical bond* in a complete sentence.
2. **Define** *electron dot diagram* in your own words.
3. The electrons of an atom that participate in chemical bonding are called ________.

Understand Key Concepts 

4. **Identify** the number of valence electrons in each atom: calcium, carbon, and sulfur.
5. Which part of the atom is shared, gained, or lost when forming a chemical bond?
   A. electron
   B. neutron
   C. nucleus
   D. proton
6. **Draw** electron dot diagrams for oxygen, potassium, iodine, nitrogen, and beryllium.

Interpret Graphics

7. **Determine** the number of valence electrons in each diagram shown below.

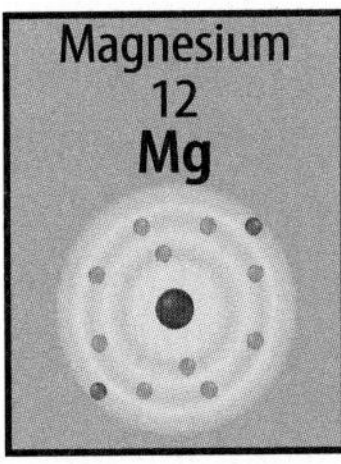

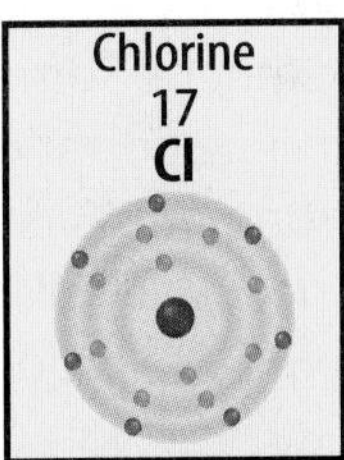

8. **Organize Information** Copy and fill in the graphic organizer below to describe one or more details for each concept: electron energy, valence electrons, stable atoms.

Concept	Description

Critical Thinking

9. **Compare** krypton and bromine in terms of chemical stability.
10. **Decide** An atom of nitrogen has five valence electrons. How could a nitrogen atom become more chemically stable?

GREEN SCIENCE

New Green Airships

The Difference of One Valence Electron

Faster than ocean liners and safer than airplanes, airships used to be the best way to travel. The largest, the *Hindenburg*, was nearly the size of the *Titanic*. To this day, no larger aircraft has ever flown. So, what happened to the giant airship? The answer lies in a valence electron.

The builders of the *Hindenburg* filled it with a lighter-than-air gas, hydrogen, so that it would float. Their plan was to use helium, a noble gas. However, helium was scarce. They knew hydrogen was explosive, but it was easier to get. For nine years, hydrogen airships floated safely back and forth across the Atlantic. But in 1937, disaster struck. Just before it landed, the *Hindenburg* exploded in flames. The age of the airship was over.

H

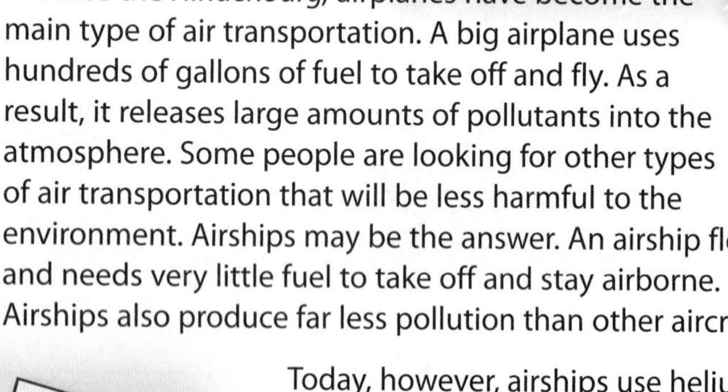

Since the *Hindenburg,* airplanes have become the main type of air transportation. A big airplane uses hundreds of gallons of fuel to take off and fly. As a result, it releases large amounts of pollutants into the atmosphere. Some people are looking for other types of air transportation that will be less harmful to the environment. Airships may be the answer. An airship floats and needs very little fuel to take off and stay airborne. Airships also produce far less pollution than other aircraft.

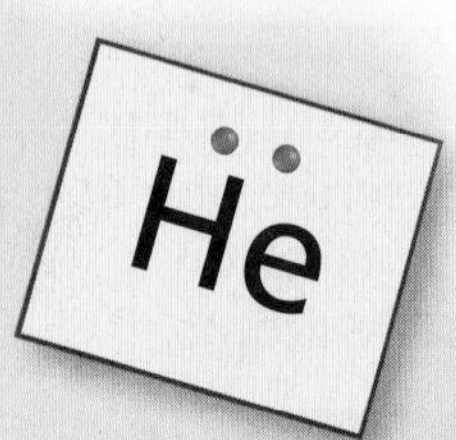

Today, however, airships use helium not hydrogen. With two valence electrons instead of one, as hydrogen has, helium is unreactive. Thanks to helium's chemical stability, someday you might be a passenger on a new, luxurious, but not explosive, version of the *Hindenburg*.

▲ **A new generation of big airships might soon be hauling freight and carrying passengers.**

It's Your Turn

RESEARCH Precious documents deteriorate with age as their surfaces react with air. Parchment turns brown and crumbles. Find out how our founding documents have been saved from this fate by noble gases.

Lesson 2

Compounds, Chemical Formulas, and Covalent Bonds

Reading Guide

Key Concepts
ESSENTIAL QUESTIONS

- How do elements differ from the compounds they form?
- What are some common properties of a covalent compound?
- Why is water a polar compound?

Vocabulary

covalent bond p. 127
molecule p. 128
polar molecule p. 129
chemical formula p. 130

Academic Standards for Science

8.1.3 Explain how the arrangement of atoms and molecules determines chemical properties of substances.

8.1.4 Describe the structure of an atom and relate the arrangement of electrons to how that atom interacts with other atoms.

8.1.5 Explain that atoms join together to form molecules and compounds and illustrate with diagrams the relationship between atoms and compounds and/or molecules.

8.1.6 Explain that elements and compounds have characteristic properties such as density, boiling points and melting points that remain unchanged regardless of the sample size.

Also covers: 8.NS.3, 8.NS.6, 8.NS.7, 8.NS.8, 8.NS.9

Inquiry How do they combine?

A jigsaw puzzle has pieces that connect in a certain way. The pieces fit together by sharing tabs with other pieces. All of the pieces combine and form a complete puzzle. Like pieces of a puzzle, atoms can join together and form a compound by sharing electrons.

Inquiry Launch Lab

20 minutes

How is a compound different from its elements?

The sugar you use to sweeten foods at home is probably sucrose. Sucrose contains the elements carbon, hydrogen, and oxygen. How does table sugar differ from the elements that it contains?

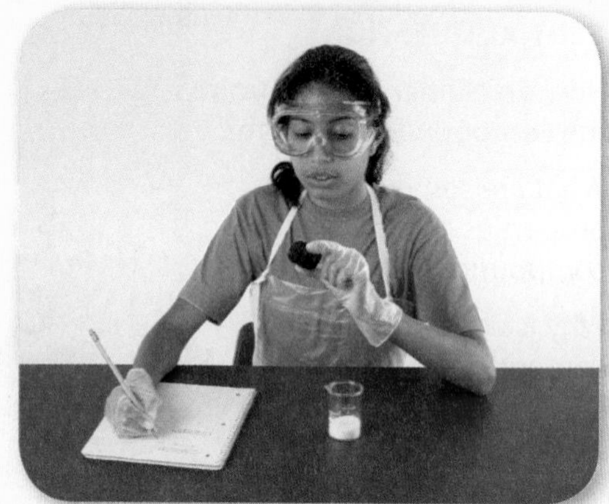

1. Read and complete a lab safety form.
2. Air is a mixture of several gases, including oxygen and hydrogen. Charcoal is a form of carbon. Write some properties of oxygen, hydrogen, and carbon in your Science Journal.
3. Obtain from your teacher a piece of **charcoal** and a **beaker** with **table sugar** in it.
4. Observe the charcoal. In your Science Journal, describe the way it looks and feels.
5. Observe the table sugar in the beaker. What does it look and feel like? Record your observations.

Think About This

1. Compare and contrast the properties of charcoal, hydrogen, and oxygen.
2. **Key Concept** How do you think the physical properties of carbon, hydrogen, and oxygen change when they combined to form sugar?

From Elements to Compounds

Have you ever baked cupcakes? First, combine flour, baking soda, and a pinch of salt. Then, add sugar, eggs, vanilla, milk, and butter. Each ingredient has unique physical and chemical properties. When you mix the ingredients together and bake them, a new product results—cupcakes. The cupcakes have properties that are different from the ingredients.

In some ways, compounds are like cupcakes. Recall that a compound is a substance made up of two or more different elements. An element is made of one type of atom, but compounds are chemical combinations of different types of atoms. Compounds and the elements that make them up often have different properties, such as density, melting point, and boiling point. The properties of elements and compounds are unique and remain unchanged regardless of the size of the sample.

Chemical **bonds** join atoms together. Recall that a chemical bond is a force that holds atoms together in a compound. In this lesson, you will learn that atoms can form bonds by sharing valence electrons.

Key Concept Check How is a compound different from the elements that compose it?

Science Use v. Common Use

bond

Science Use a force that holds atoms together in a compound

Common Use a close personal relationship between two people

Covalent Bonds

Review Personal Tutor

Figure 7 A covalent bond forms when two nonmetal atoms share electrons.

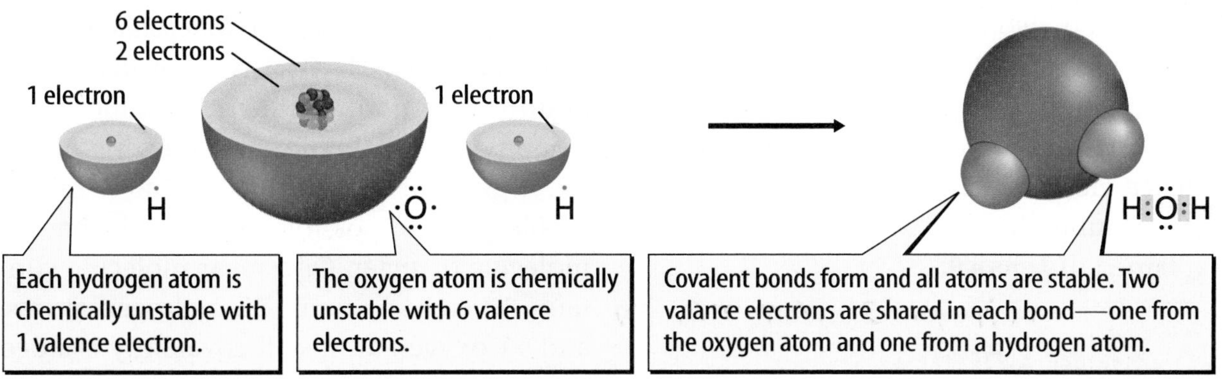

6 electrons
2 electrons
1 electron
1 electron
H
O
H
H:O:H
Each hydrogen atom is chemically unstable with 1 valence electron.
The oxygen atom is chemically unstable with 6 valence electrons.
Covalent bonds form and all atoms are stable. Two valance electrons are shared in each bond—one from the oxygen atom and one from a hydrogen atom.

Covalent Bonds—Electron Sharing

As you read in Lesson 1, one way that atoms can become more chemically stable is by sharing valence electrons. When unstable, nonmetal atoms bond together, they bond by sharing valence electrons. *A* **covalent bond** *is a chemical bond formed when two atoms share one or more pairs of valence electrons.* The atoms then form a stable covalent compound.

A Noble Gas Electron Arrangement

Look at the reaction between hydrogen and oxygen in **Figure 7.** Before the reaction, each hydrogen atom has one valence electron. The oxygen atom has six valence electrons. Recall that most atoms are chemically stable with eight valence electrons—the same electron arrangement as a noble gas. An atom with less than eight valence electrons becomes stable by forming chemical bonds until it has eight valence electrons. Therefore, an oxygen atom forms two bonds to become stable. A hydrogen atom is stable with two valence electrons. It forms one bond to become stable.

Shared Electrons

If the oxygen atom and each hydrogen atom share their unpaired valence electrons, they can form two covalent bonds and become a stable covalent compound. Each covalent bond contains two valence electrons—one from the hydrogen atom and one from the oxygen atom. Since these electrons are shared, they count as valence electrons for both atoms in the bond. Each hydrogen atom now has two valence electrons. The oxygen atom now has eight valence electrons, since it bonds to two hydrogen atoms. All three atoms have the electron arrangement of a noble gas and the compound is stable.

FOLDABLES®

Make three quarter-sheet note cards from a sheet of paper to organize information about single, double, and triple covalent bonds.

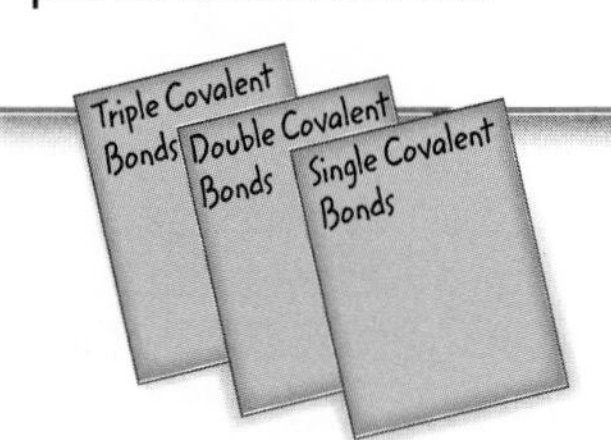

Double and Triple Covalent Bonds

As shown in **Figure 8,** a single covalent bond exists when two atoms share one pair of valence electrons. A double covalent bond exists when two atoms share two pairs of valence electrons. Double bonds are stronger than single bonds. A triple covalent bond exists when two atoms share three pairs of valence electrons. Triple bonds are stronger than double bonds. Multiple bonds are explained in **Figure 8.**

Covalent Compounds

When two or more atoms share valence electrons, they form a stable covalent compound. The covalent compounds carbon dioxide, water, and sugar are very different, but they also share similar properties. Covalent compounds usually have low melting points and low boiling points. They are usually gases or liquids at room temperature, but they can also be solids. Covalent compounds are poor conductors of thermal energy and electricity.

Molecules

The chemically stable unit of a covalent compound is a molecule. *A* **molecule** *is a group of atoms held together by covalent bonding that acts as an independent unit.* Table sugar ($C_{12}H_{22}O_{11}$) is a covalent compound. One grain of sugar is made up of trillions of sugar molecules. Imagine breaking a grain of sugar into the tiniest microscopic particle possible. You would have a molecule of sugar. One sugar molecule contains 12 carbon atoms, 22 hydrogen atoms, and 11 oxygen atoms all covalently bonded together. The only way to further break down the molecule would be to chemically separate the carbon, hydrogen, and oxygen atoms. These atoms alone have very different properties from the compound sugar.

Key Concept Check What are some common properties of covalent compounds?

Multiple Bonds

Figure 8 The more valence electrons that two atoms share, the stronger the covalent bond is between the atoms .

When two hydrogen atoms bond, they form a single covalent bond.

One Single Covalent Bond

H· + ·H ⟶ H:H

In a single covalent bond, 1 pair of electrons is shared between two atoms. Each H atom shares 1 valence electron with the other.

When one carbon atom bonds with two oxygen atoms, two double covalent bonds form.

Two Double Covalent Bonds

·Ö: + ·Ċ· + ·Ö: ⟶ :O::C::O:

In a double covalent bond, 2 pairs of electrons are shared between two atoms. One O atom and the C atom each share 2 valence electrons with the other.

When two nitrogen atoms bond, they form a triple covalent bond.

One Triple Covalent Bond

·N· + ·N· ⟶ :N⋮⋮N:

In a triple covalent bond, 3 pairs of electrons are shared between two atoms. Each N atom shares 3 valence electrons with the other.

Visual Check Is the bond stronger between atoms in hydrogen gas (H_2) or nitrogen gas (N_2)? Why?

Water and Other Polar Molecules

In a covalent bond, one atom can attract the shared electrons more strongly than the other atom can. Think about the valence electrons shared between oxygen and hydrogen atoms in a water molecule. The oxygen atom attracts the shared electrons more strongly than each hydrogen atom does. As a result, the shared electrons are pulled closer to the oxygen atom, as shown in **Figure 9.** Since electrons have a negative charge, the oxygen atom has a partial negative charge. The hydrogen atoms have a partial positive charge. *A molecule that has a partial positive end and a partial negative end because of unequal sharing of electrons is a* **polar molecule.**

WORD ORIGIN

polar
from Latin *polus,* means "pole"

The charges on a polar molecule affect its properties. Sugar, for example, dissolves easily in water because both sugar and water are polar. The negative end of a water molecule pulls on the positive end of a sugar molecule. Also, the positive end of a water molecule pulls on the negative end of a sugar molecule. This causes the sugar molecules to separate from one another and mix with the water molecules.

 **Key Concept Check** Why is water a polar compound?

Nonpolar Molecules

A hydrogen molecule, H_2, is a nonpolar molecule. Because the two hydrogen atoms are identical, their attraction for the shared electrons is equal. The carbon dioxide molecule, CO_2, in **Figure 9** is also nonpolar. A nonpolar compound will not easily dissolve in a polar compound, but it will dissolve in other nonpolar compounds. Oil is an example of a nonpolar compound. It will not dissolve in water. Have you ever heard someone say "like dissolves like"? This means that polar compounds can dissolve in other polar compounds. Similarly, nonpolar compounds can dissolve in other nonpolar compounds.

Figure 9 Atoms of a polar molecule share their valence electrons unequally. Atoms of a nonpolar molecule share their valence electrons equally.

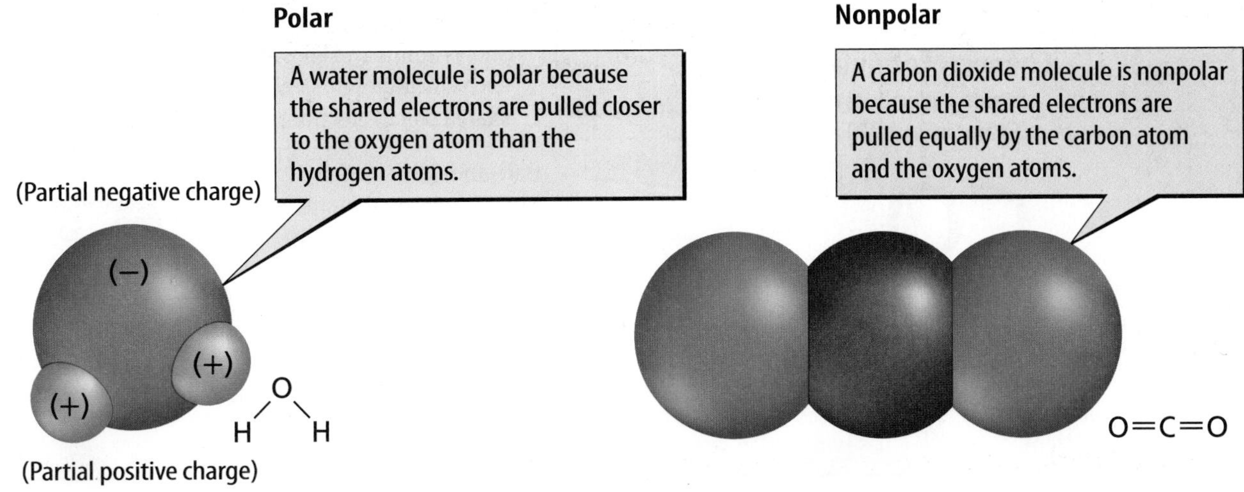
Polar
A water molecule is polar because the shared electrons are pulled closer to the oxygen atom than the hydrogen atoms.
(Partial negative charge)
(–)
(+)
(+)
O
H H
(Partial positive charge)
Nonpolar
A carbon dioxide molecule is nonpolar because the shared electrons are pulled equally by the carbon atom and the oxygen atoms.
O=C=O

Inquiry MiniLab 20 minutes

How do compounds form?

Use building blocks to model ways in which elements combine to form compounds.

1. Examine various types of **interlocking plastic blocks.** Notice that the blocks have different numbers of holes and pegs. Attaching one peg to one hole represents a shared pair of electrons.
2. Draw the electron dot diagrams for carbon, nitrogen, oxygen, and hydrogen in your Science Journal. Based on the diagrams, decide which block should represent an atom of each element.
3. Use the blocks to make models of H_2, CO_2, NH_3, H_2O, and CH_4. All pegs on the largest block must fit into a hole, and no blocks can stick out over the edge of a block, either above or below it.

Analyze and Conclude

1. **Explain** how you decided which type of block should be assigned to each type of atom.
2.  **Key Concept** Name at least one way that your models show the difference between a compound and the elements that combine and form the compound.

Chemical Formulas and Molecular Models

How do you know which elements make up a compound? *A* **chemical formula** *is a group of chemical symbols and numbers that represent the elements and the number of atoms of each element that make up a compound.* Just as a recipe lists ingredients, a chemical formula lists the elements in a compound. For example, the chemical formula for carbon dioxide shown in **Figure 10** is CO_2. The formula uses chemical symbols that show which elements are in the compound. Notice that CO_2 is made up of carbon (C) and oxygen (O). A subscript, or small number after a chemical symbol, shows the number of atoms of each element in the compound. Carbon dioxide (CO_2) contains two atoms of oxygen bonded to one atom of carbon.

A chemical formula describes the types of atoms in a compound or a molecule, but it does not explain the shape or appearance of the molecule. There are many ways to model a molecule. Each one can show the molecule in a different way. Common types of models for CO_2 are shown in **Figure 10.**

Reading Check What information is given in a chemical formula?

Figure 10 Chemical formulas and molecular models provide information about molecules.

Chemical Formula

A carbon dioxide molecule is made up of carbon (C) and oxygen (O) atoms.

A symbol without a subscript indicates one atom. Each molecule of carbon dioxide has one carbon atom.

The subscript 2 indicates two atoms of oxygen. Each molecule of carbon dioxide has two oxygen atoms.

Dot Diagram
- Shows atoms and valence electrons

:Ö::C::Ö:

Structural Formula
- Shows atoms and lines; each line represents one shared pair of electrons

O=C=O

Ball-and-Stick Model
- Balls represent atoms and sticks represent bonds; used to show bond angles

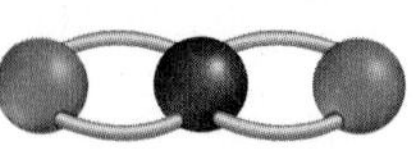

Space-Filling Model
- Spheres represent atoms; used to show three-dimensional arrangement of atoms

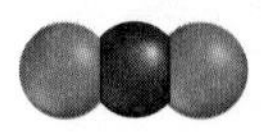

Lesson 2 Review

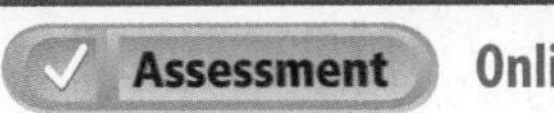

Visual Summary

CO_2

A chemical formula is one way to show the elements that make up a compound.

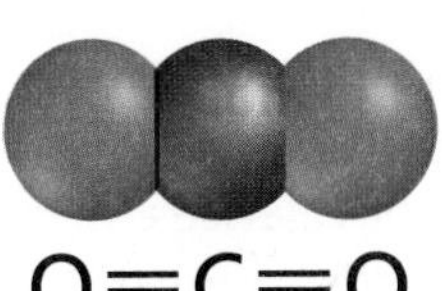

A covalent bond forms when atoms share valence electrons. The smallest particle of a covalent compound is a molecule.

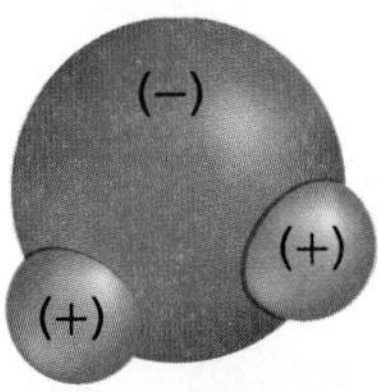

Water is a polar molecule because the oxygen and hydrogen atoms unequally share electrons.

FOLDABLES®

Use your lesson Foldable to review the lesson. Save your Foldable for the project at the end of the chapter.

What do you think NOW?

You first read the statements below at the beginning of the chapter.

3. The atoms in a water molecule are more chemically stable than they would be as individual atoms.

4. Many substances dissolve easily in water because opposite ends of a water molecule have opposite charges.

Did you change your mind about whether you agree or disagree with the statements? Rewrite any false statements to make them true.

Use Vocabulary

1. **Define** *covalent bond* in your own words.
2. The group of symbols and numbers that shows the types and numbers of atoms that make up a compound is a ________.
3. **Use the term** *molecule* in a complete sentence.

Understand Key Concepts 

4. **Contrast** Name at least one way water (H_2O) is different from the elements that make up water.
5. **Explain** why water is a polar molecule.
6. A sulfur dioxide molecule has one sulfur atom and two oxygen atoms. Which is its correct chemical formula?

   A. SO_2
   B. $(SO)_2$
   C. S_2O_2
   D. S_2O

Interpret Graphics

7. **Examine** the electron dot diagram for chlorine below.

In chlorine gas, two chlorine atoms join to form a Cl_2 molecule. How many pairs of valence electrons do the atoms share?

8. **Compare and Contrast** Copy and fill in the graphic organizer below to identify at least one way polar and nonpolar molecules are similar and one way they are different.

Polar and Nonpolar Molecules	
Similarities	
Differences	

Critical Thinking

9. **Develop** an analogy to explain the unequal sharing of valence electrons in a water molecule.

Skill Practice Model

25 minutes

How can you model compounds?

Materials

colored pencils

Chemists use models to explain how electrons are arranged in an atom. Electron dot diagrams are models used to show how many valence electrons an atom has. Electron dot diagrams are useful because they can help predict the number and type of bond an atom will form.

Learn It

In science, **models** are used to help you visualize objects that are too small, too large, or too complex to understand. A model is a representation of an object, idea, or event.

Try It

1. Use the periodic table to write the electron dot diagrams for hydrogen, oxygen, carbon, and silicon.
2. Using your electron dot diagrams from step 1, write electron dot diagrams for the following compounds: H_2O, CO, CO_2, SiO_2, C_2H_2, and CH_4. Use colored pencils to differentiate the electrons for each atom. Remember that all the above atoms, except hydrogen and helium, are chemically stable when they have eight valence electrons. Hydrogen and helium are chemically stable with two valence electrons.

Apply It

3. Based on your model, describe silicon's electron dot diagram and arrangement of valence electrons before and after it forms the compound SiO_2.
4. **Key Concept** Which of the covalent compounds you modeled contain double bonds? Which contain triple bonds?

2

1	2
Hydrogen 1 H	
Lithium 3 Li	Beryllium 4 Be
Sodium 11 Na	Magnesium 12 Mg
Potassium 19 K	Calcium 20 Ca
Rubidium 37 Rb	Strontium 38 Sr
Cesium 55 Cs	Barium 56 Ba
Francium 87 Fr	Radium 88 Ra

13	14	15	16	17	18
					Helium 2 He
Boron 5 B	Carbon 6 C	Nitrogen 7 N	Oxygen 8 O	Fluorine 9 F	Neon 10 Ne
Aluminum 13 Al	Silicon 14 Si	Phosphorus 15 P	Sulfur 16 S	Chlorine 17 Cl	Argon 18 Ar
Gallium 31 Ga	Germanium 32 Ge	Arsenic 33 As	Selenium 34 Se	Bromine 35 Br	Krypton 36 Kr
Indium 49 In	Tin 50 Sn	Antimony 51 Sb	Tellurium 52 Te	Iodine 53 I	Xenon 54 Xe
Thallium 81 Tl	Lead 82 Pb	Bismuth 83 Bi	Polonium 84 Po	Astatine 85 At	Radon 86 Rn

Lesson 3

Ionic and Metallic Bonds

Reading Guide

Key Concepts 

ESSENTIAL QUESTIONS

- What is an ionic compound?
- How do metallic bonds differ from covalent and ionic bonds?

Vocabulary

ion p. 134

ionic bond p. 136

metallic bond p. 137

Multilingual eGlossary

Academic Standards for Science

8.1.3 Explain how the arrangement of atoms and molecules determines chemical properties of substances.

8.1.4 Describe the structure of an atom and relate the arrangement of electrons to how that atom interacts with other atoms.

8.1.5 Explain that atoms join together to form molecules and compounds and illustrate with diagrams the relationship between atoms and compounds and/or molecules.

8.1.6 Explain that elements and compounds have characteristic properties such as density, boiling points and melting points that remain unchanged regardless of the sample size.

Also covers: 8.NS.1, 8.NS.5, 8.NS.6, 8.NS.7, 8.NS.10, 8.NS.11, 8.DP.6

Inquiry What is this?

This scene might look like snow along a shoreline, but it is actually thick deposits of salt on a lake. Over time, tiny amounts of salt dissolved in river water that flowed into this lake and built up as water evaporated. Salt is a compound that forms when elements form bonds by gaining or losing valence electrons, not sharing them.

Inquiry Launch Lab

15 minutes

How can atoms form compounds by gaining and losing electrons?

Metals on the periodic table often lose electrons when forming stable compounds. Nonmetals often gain electrons.

1. Read and complete a lab safety form.
2. Make two model atoms of sodium, and one model atom each of calcium, chlorine, and sulfur. To do this, write each element's chemical symbol with a **marker** on a **paper plate.** Surround the symbol with small balls of **clay** to represent valence electrons. Use one color of clay for the metals (groups 1 and 2 elements) and another color of clay for nonmetals (groups 16 and 17 elements).
3. To model sodium sulfide (Na_2S), place the two sodium atoms next to the sulfur atom. To form a stable compound, move each sodium atom's valence electron to the sulfur atom.
4. Form as many other compound models as you can by removing valence electrons from the groups 1 and 2 plates and placing them on the groups 16 and 17 plates.

Think About This

1. What other compounds were you able to form?
2. **Key Concept** How do you think your models are different from covalent compounds?

FOLDABLES

Make two quarter-sheet note cards as shown. Use the cards to summarize information about ionic and metallic compounds.

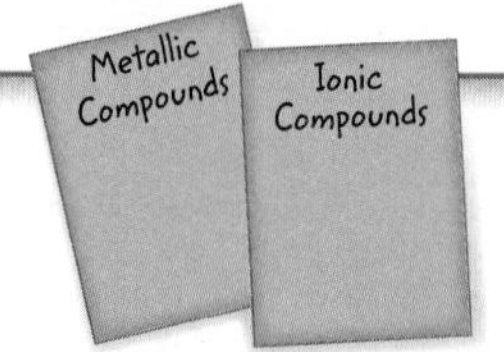

Understanding Ions

As you read in Lesson 2, the atoms of two or more nonmetals form compounds by sharing valence electrons. However, when a metal and a nonmetal bond, they do not share electrons. Instead, one or more valence electrons transfers from the metal atom to the nonmetal atom. After electrons transfer, the atoms bond and form a chemically stable compound. Transferring valence electrons results in atoms with the same number of valence electrons as a noble gas.

When an atom loses or gains a valence electron, it becomes an ion. *An* **ion** *is an atom that is no longer electrically neutral because it has lost or gained valence electrons.* Because electrons have a negative charge, losing or gaining an electron changes the overall charge of an atom. An atom that loses valence electrons becomes an ion with a positive charge. This is because the number of electrons is now less than the number of protons in the atom. An atom that gains valence electrons becomes an ion with a negative charge. This is because the number of protons is now less than the number of electrons.

Word Origin

ion
from Greek *ienai,* means "to go"

Reading Check Why do atoms that a gain electrons become an ion with a negative charge?

Losing Valence Electrons

Look at the periodic table on the inside back cover of this book. What information about sodium (Na) can you infer from the periodic table? Sodium is a metal. Its atomic number is 11. This means each sodium atom has 11 protons and 11 electrons. Sodium is in group 1 on the periodic table. Therefore, sodium atoms have one valence electron, and they are chemically unstable.

Metal atoms, such as sodium, become more stable when they lose valence electrons and form a chemical bond with a nonmetal. If a sodium atom loses its one valence electron, it would have a total of ten electrons. Which element on the periodic table has atoms with ten electrons? Neon (Ne) atoms have a total of ten electrons. Eight of these are valence electrons. When a sodium atom loses one valence electron, the electrons in the next lower energy level are now the new valence electrons. The sodium atom then has eight valence electrons, the same as the noble gas neon and is chemically stable.

Gaining Valence Electrons

In Lesson 2, you read that nonmetal atoms can share valence electrons with other nonmetal atoms. Nonmetal atoms can also gain valence electrons from metal atoms. Either way, they achieve the electron arrangement of a noble gas. Find the nonmetal chlorine (Cl) on the periodic table. Its atomic number is 17. Atoms of chlorine have seven valence electrons. If a chlorine atom gains one valence electron, it will have eight valence electrons. It will also have the same electron arrangement as the noble gas argon (Ar).

When a sodium atom loses a valence electron, it becomes a positively charged ion. This is shown by a plus (+) sign. When a chlorine atom gains a valence electron, it becomes a negatively charged ion. This is shown by a negative (–) sign. **Figure 11** illustrates the process of a sodium atom losing an electron and a chlorine atom gaining an electron.

Reading Check Are atoms of a group 16 element more likely to gain or lose valence electrons?

Losing and Gaining Electrons

Concepts in Motion Animation

Figure 11 Sodium atoms have a tendency to lose a valence electron. Chlorine atoms have a tendency to gain a valence electron.

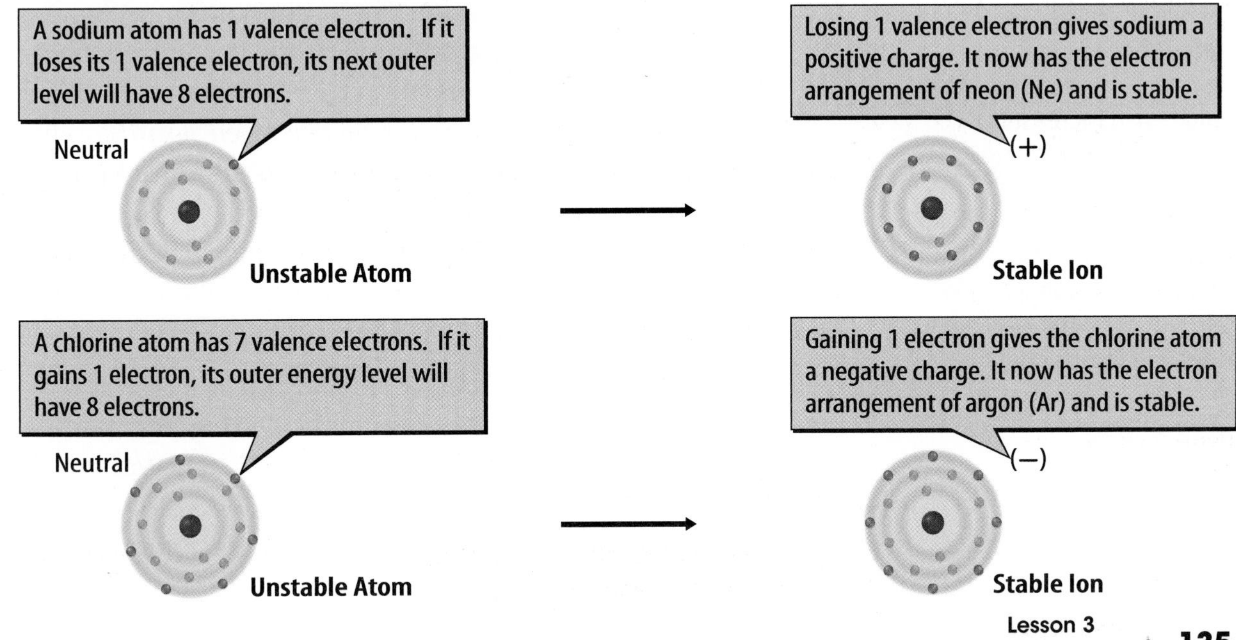

A sodium atom has 1 valence electron. If it loses its 1 valence electron, its next outer level will have 8 electrons.
Neutral
Unstable Atom
Losing 1 valence electron gives sodium a positive charge. It now has the electron arrangement of neon (Ne) and is stable.
(+)
Stable Ion
A chlorine atom has 7 valence electrons. If it gains 1 electron, its outer energy level will have 8 electrons.
Neutral
Unstable Atom
Gaining 1 electron gives the chlorine atom a negative charge. It now has the electron arrangement of argon (Ar) and is stable.
(–)
Stable Ion

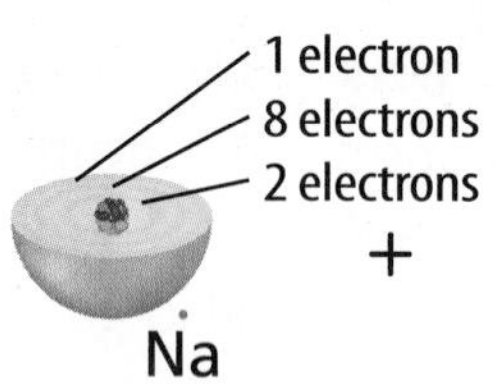

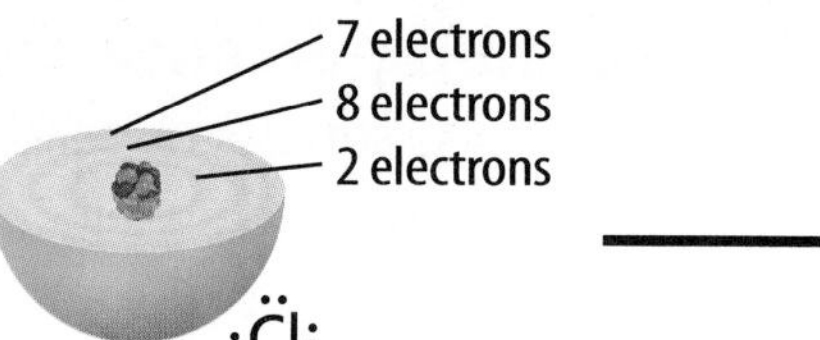

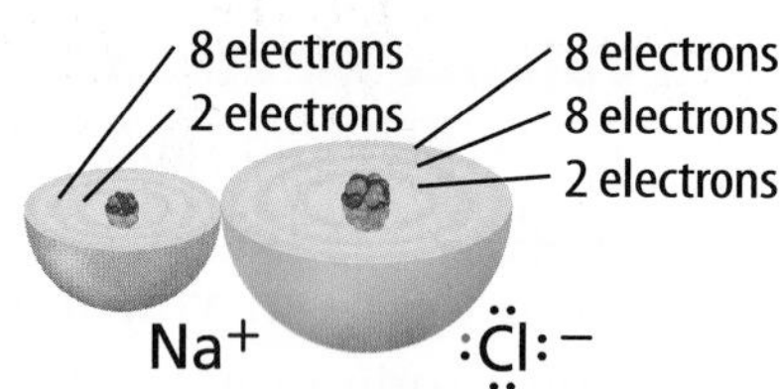

Sodium and chlorine atoms are stable when they have eight valence electrons. A sodium atoms loses one valence electron and becomes stable. A chlorine atom gains one valence electron and becomes stable.

The positively charged sodium ion and the negatively charged chlorine ion attract each other. Together they form a strong ionic bond.

Figure 12 An ionic bond forms between Na and Cl when an electron transfers from Na to Cl.

Concepts in Motion Animation

Determining an Ion's Charge

Atoms are electrically neutral because they have the same number of protons and electrons. Once an atom gains or loses electrons, it becomes a charged ion. For example, the atomic number for nitrogen (N) is 7. Each N atom has 7 protons and 7 electrons and is electrically neutral. However, an N atom often gains 3 electrons when forming an ion. The N ion then has 10 electrons. To determine the charge, subtract the number of electrons in the ion from the number of protons.

$$7 \text{ protons} - 10 \text{ electrons} = -3 \text{ charge}$$

A nitrogen ion has a −3 charge. This is written as N^{3-}.

Ionic Bonds—Electron Transferring

Recall that metal atoms typically lose valence electrons and nonmetal atoms typically gain valence electrons. When forming a chemical bond, the nonmetal atoms gain the electrons lost by the metal atoms. Take a look at **Figure 12.** In NaCl, or table salt, a sodium atom loses a valence electron. The electron is transferred to a chlorine atom. The sodium atom becomes a positively charged ion. The chlorine atom becomes a negatively charged ion. These ions attract each other and form a stable ionic compound. *The attraction between positively and negatively charged ions in an ionic compound is an* **ionic bond.**

Key Concept Check What holds ionic compounds together?

Ionic Compounds

Ionic compounds are usually solid and brittle at room temperature. They also have relatively high melting and boiling points. Many ionic compounds dissolve in water. Water that contains dissolved ionic compounds is a good conductor of electricity. This is because an electrical charge can pass from ion to ion in the solution.

Math Skills

Use Percentage

An atom's radius is measured in picometers (pm), 1 trillion times smaller than a meter. When an atom becomes an ion, its radius increases or decreases. For example, a Na atom has a radius of **186 pm**. A Na^+ ion has a radius of **102 pm**. By what percentage does the radius change?

Subtract the atom's radius from the ion's radius.

$$102 \text{ pm} - 186 \text{ pm} = -84 \text{ pm}$$

Divide the difference by the atom's radius.

$$-84 \text{ pm} \div 186 \text{ pm} = -0.45$$

Multiply the answer by 100 and add a % sign.

$$-0.45 \times 100 = -45\%$$

A negative value is a decrease in size. A positive value is an increase.

Practice

The radius of an oxygen (O) atom is 73 pm. The radius of an oxygen ion (O^{2-}) is 140 pm. By what percentage does the radius change?

Review

- Math Practice
- Personal Tutor

Comparing Ionic and Covalent Compounds

Recall that in a covalent bond, two or more nonmetal atoms share electrons and form a unit, or molecule. Covalent compounds, such as water, are made up of many molecules. However, when nonmetal ions bond to metal ions in an ionic compound, there are no molecules. Instead, there is a large collection of oppositely charged ions. All of the ions attract each other and are held together by ionic bonds.

Metallic Bonds—Electron Pooling

Recall that metal atoms typically lose valence electrons when forming compounds. What happens when metal atoms bond to other metal atoms? Metal atoms form compounds with one another by combining, or pooling, their valence electrons. *A* **metallic bond** *is a bond formed when many metal atoms share their pooled valence electrons.*

The pooling of valence electrons in aluminum is shown in **Figure 13.** The aluminum atoms lose their valence electrons and become positive ions, indicated by the plus (+) signs. The negative (–) signs indicate the valence electrons, which move from ion to ion. Valence electrons in metals are not bonded to one atom. Instead, a "sea of electrons" surrounds the positive ions.

Key Concept Check How do metal atoms bond with one another?

Figure 13 Valence electrons move among all the aluminum (Al) ions.

Inquiry MiniLab 20 minutes

How many ionic compounds can you make?

You have read that in ionic bonding, metal atoms transfer electrons to nonmetal atoms.

1. Copy the table below into your Science Journal.

Group	Elements	Type	Dot Diagram
1	Li, Na, K	Metal	$\dot{X}$
2	Be, Mg, Ca	Metal	
14	C	Nonmetal	
15	N, P	Nonmetal	
16	O, S	Nonmetal	
17	F, Cl	Nonmetal	

2. Fill in the last column with the correct dot diagram for each group. Color the dots of the metal atoms with a **red marker** and the dots of the nonmetal atoms with a **blue marker.**
3. Using the information in your table, create five different ionic bonds. Write (a) the equation for the electron transfer and (b) the formula for each compound. For example:

a. $Na + Na + \cdot\ddot{O}: \longrightarrow Na^+ + Na^+ + :\ddot{O}:^{2-}$

b. Na_2O

Analyze and Conclude

1. **Explain** What happens to the metal and nonmetal ions after the electrons have been transferred?
2. **Key Concept** Describe the ionic bonds that hold the ions together in your compounds.

Academic Vocabulary

conduct
(verb) to serve as a medium through which something can flow

Table 1 Bonds can form when atoms share valence electrons, transfer valence electrons, or pool valence electrons.

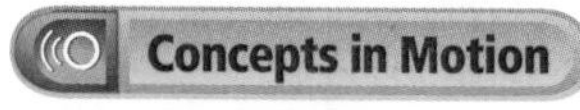

Interactive Table

Properties of Metallic Compounds

Metals are good conductors of thermal energy and electricity. Because the valence electrons can move from ion to ion, they can easily **conduct** an electric charge. When a metal is hammered into a sheet or drawn into a wire, it does not break. The metal ions can slide past one another in the electron sea and move to new positions. Metals are shiny because the valence electrons at the surface of a metal interact with light. **Table 1** compares the covalent, ionic, and metallic bonds that you studied in this chapter.

Reading Check How does valence electron pooling explain why metals can be hammered into a sheet?

Table 1 Covalent, Ionic, and Metallic Bonds

Type of Bond	What is bonding?	Properties of Compounds
Covalent (−) (+) (+) Water	nonmetal atoms; nonmetal atoms	• gas, liquid, or solid • low melting and boiling points • often not able to dissolve in water • poor conductors of thermal energy and electricity • dull appearance
Ionic Na^+ Cl^- Salt	nonmetal ions; metal ions	• solid crystals • high melting and boiling points • dissolves in water • solids are poor conductors of thermal energy and electricity • ionic compounds in water solutions conduct electricity
Metallic Al^+ Aluminum	metal ions; metal ions	• usually solid at room temperature • high melting and boiling points • do not dissolve in water • good conductors of thermal energy and electricity • shiny surface • can be hammered into sheets and pulled into wires

Predict

5 If you place an iron nail in the vinegar-salt solution, predict what changes will occur to the nail.

Test Your Prediction

6 Use sandpaper to clean two nails. Place one nail in the vinegar-salt solution, and place the other nail on a clean paper towel. You will compare the dry nail to the one in the solution and observe changes as they occur.

7 Every 5 minutes observe the nail in the solution and record your observations in your Science Journal. Remember to use the dry nail to help detect changes in the wet nail. Use a stopwatch or a clock with a second hand to measure the time. Keep the nail in the solution for 25 minutes

8 After 25 minutes, use a plastic spoon to remove the nail from the solution. Dispose of all materials as directed by your teacher.

Analyze and Conclude

9 **Compare and Contrast** What changes occurred when you placed the dull pennies in the vinegar-salt solution?

10 **Recognize Cause and Effect** What changes occurred to the nail in the leftover solution? Infer why these changes occurred.

11 **The Big Idea** Give two examples of how elements chemically combine and form compounds in this lab.

Communicate Your Results

Create a chart suitable for display summarizing this lab and your results.

Inquiry Extension

The Statue of Liberty is made of copper. Research why the statue is green.

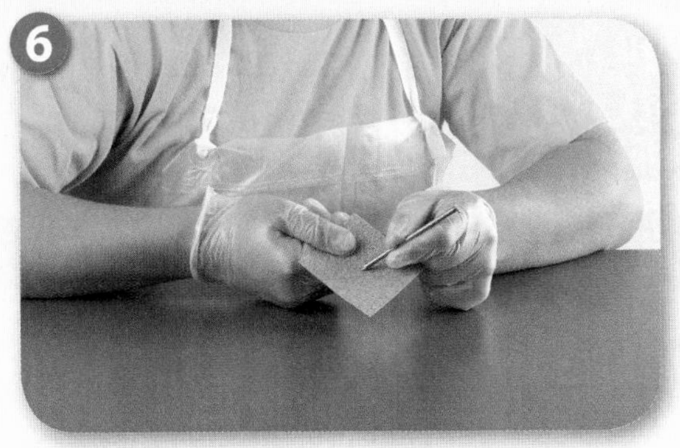

Lab Tips

- Be sure the pennies are separated when they are in the vinegar-salt solution. You may need to stir them with the plastic spoon.
- Use the plastic spoon to bring the nail out of the solution when checking for changes.

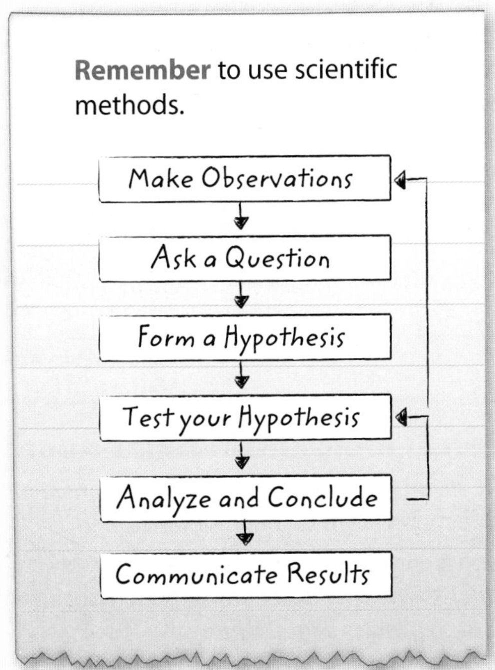

Chapter 4 Study Guide

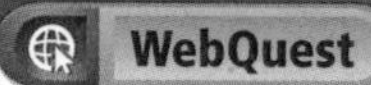

Elements can join together by sharing, transferring, or pooling electrons to make chemical compounds.

Key Concepts Summary	Vocabulary
Lesson 1: Electrons and Energy Levels • Electrons with more energy are farther from the atom's nucleus and are in a higher energy level. • Atoms with fewer than eight **valence electrons** gain, lose, or share valence electrons and form stable compounds. Atoms in stable compounds have the same electron arrangement as a noble gas. 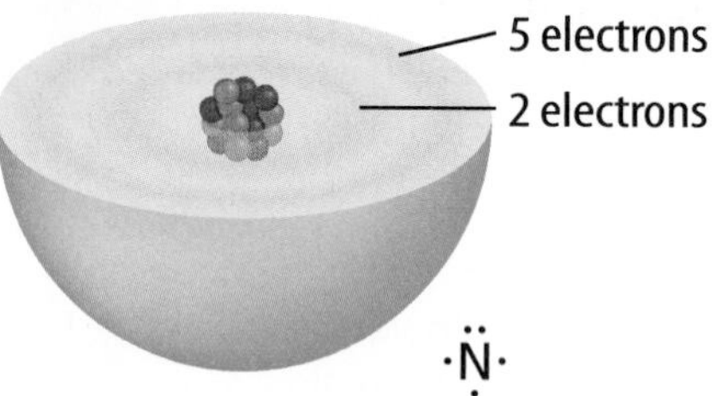 	**chemical bond** p. 118 **valence electron** p. 120 **electron dot diagram** p. 121
Lesson 2: Compounds, Chemical Formulas, and Covalent Bonds • A compound and the elements it is made from have different chemical and physical properties. • A **covalent bond** forms when two nonmetal atoms share valence electrons. Common properties of covalent compounds include low melting points and low boiling points. They are usually gas or liquid at room temperature and poor conductors of electricity. • Water is a polar compound because the oxygen atom pulls more strongly on the shared valence electrons than the hydrogen atoms do. 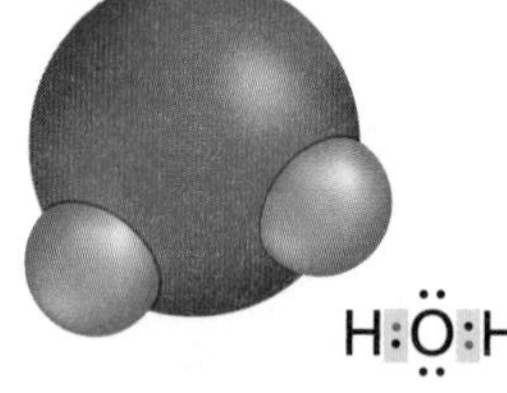 	**covalent bond** p. 127 **molecule** p. 128 **polar molecule** p. 129 **chemical formula** p. 130
Lesson 3: Ionic and Metallic Bonds • **Ionic bonds** form when valence electrons move from a metal atom to a nonmetal atom. • An ionic compound is held together by ionic bonds, which are attractions between positively and negatively charged **ions.** • A **metallic bond** forms when valence electrons are pooled among many metal atoms. 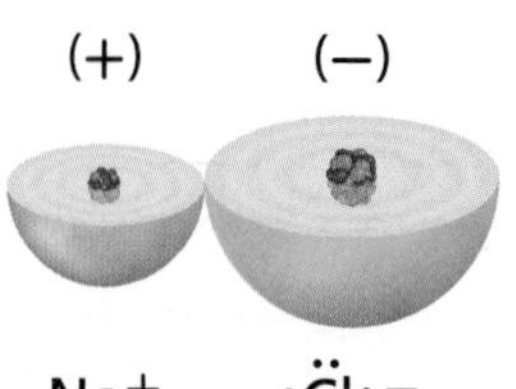 	**ion** p. 134 **ionic bond** p. 136 **metallic bond** p. 137

- Personal Tutor
- Vocabulary eGames
- Vocabulary eFlashcards

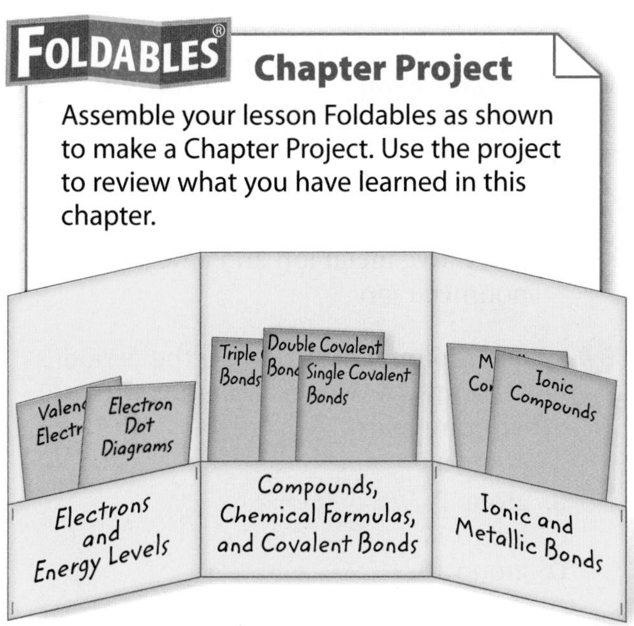

Use Vocabulary

1. The force that holds atoms together is called a(n) ________.
2. You can predict the number of bonds an atom can form by drawing its ________.
3. The nitrogen and hydrogen atoms that make up ammonia (NH_3) are held together by a(n) ________ because the atoms share valence electrons unequally.
4. Two hydrogen atoms and one oxygen atom together are a ________ of water.
5. A positively charged sodium ion and a negatively charged chlorine ion are joined by a(n) ________ to form the compound sodium chloride.

Link Vocabulary and Key Concepts

Copy this concept map, and then use vocabulary terms from the previous page and other terms from the chapter to complete the concept map.

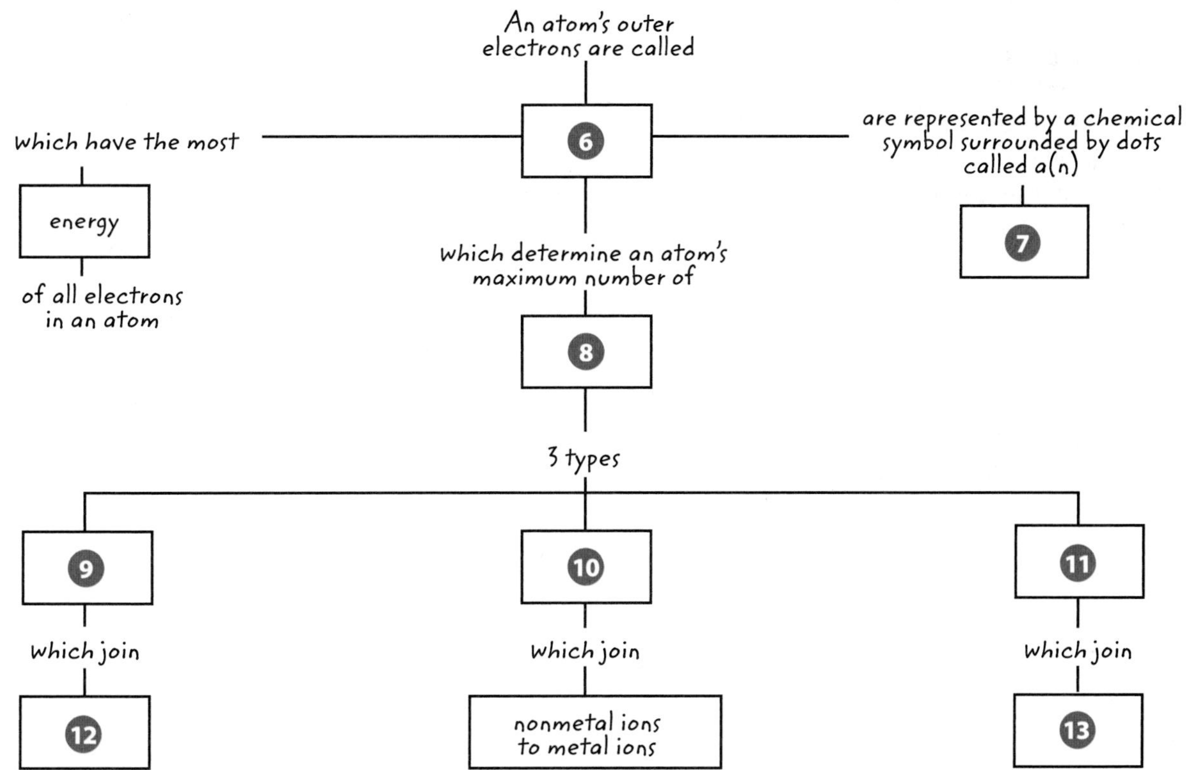

Chapter 4 Review

Understand Key Concepts

1. Atoms lose, gain, or share electrons and become as chemically stable as
   A. an electron.
   B. an ion.
   C. a metal.
   D. a noble gas.

2. Which is the correct electron dot diagram for boron, one of the group 13 elements?
   A. 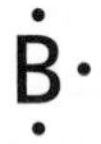
   B. 
   C. 
   D. 

3. If an electron transfers from one atom to another atom, what type of bond will most likely form?
   A. covalent
   B. ionic
   C. metallic
   D. polar

4. What change would make an atom represented by this diagram have the same electron arrangement as a noble gas?

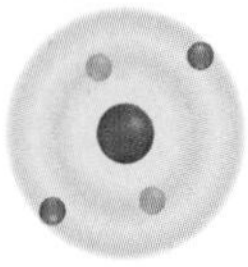

   A. gaining two electrons
   B. gaining four electrons
   C. losing two electrons
   D. losing four electrons

5. What would make bromine, a group 17 element, more similar to a noble gas?
   A. gaining one electron
   B. gaining two electrons
   C. losing one electron
   D. losing two electrons

6. Which would most likely be joined by an ionic bond?
   A. a positive metal ion and a positive nonmetal ion
   B. a positive metal ion and a negative nonmetal ion
   C. a negative metal ion and a positive nonmetal ion
   D. a negative metal ion and a negative nonmetal ion

7. Which group of elements on the periodic table forms covalent compounds with other nonmetals?
   A. group 1
   B. group 2
   C. group 17
   D. group 18

8. Which best describes an atom represented by this diagram?

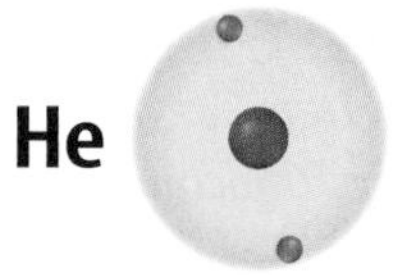

   A. It is likely to bond by gaining six electrons.
   B. It is likely to bond by losing two electrons.
   C. It is not likely to bond because it is already stable.
   D. It is not likely to bond because it has too few electrons.

9. How many dots would a dot diagram for selenium, one of the group 16 elements, have?
   A. 6
   B. 8
   C. 10
   D. 16

Assessment
Online Test Practice

Critical Thinking

10 **Classify** Use the periodic table to classify the elements potassium (K), bromine (Br), and argon (Ar) according to how likely their atoms are to do the following.

a. lose electrons to form positive ions
b. gain electrons to form negative ions
c. neither gain nor lose electrons

11 **Describe** the change that is shown in this illustration. How does this change affect the stability of the atom?

$$\cdot\ddot{\text{N}}\cdot \longrightarrow :\ddot{\text{N}}:^{3-}$$

12 **Analyze** One of your classmates draws an electron dot diagram for a helium atom with two dots. He tells you that these dots mean each helium atom has two unpaired electrons and can gain, lose, or share electrons to have four pairs of valence electrons and become stable. What is wrong with your classmate's argument?

13 **Explain** why the hydrogen atoms in a hydrogen gas molecule (H_2) form nonpolar covalent bonds but the oxygen and hydrogen atoms in water molecules (H_2O) form polar covalent bonds.

14 **Contrast** Why is it possible for an oxygen atom to form a double covalent bond, but it is not possible for a chlorine atom to form a double covalent bond?

Writing in Science

15 **Compose** a poem at least ten lines long that explains ionic bonding, covalent bonding, and metallic bonding.

REVIEW THE BIG IDEA

16 Which types of atoms pool their valence electrons to form a "sea of electrons"?

17 Describe a way in which elements joining together to form chemical compounds is similar to the way the letters on a computer keyboard join together to form words.

Math Skills

Review
Math Practice

Element	Atomic Radius	Ionic Radius
Potassium (K)	227 pm	133 pm
Iodine (I)	133 pm	216 pm

18 What is the percent change when an iodine atom (I) becomes an ion (I^-)?

19 What is the percent change when a potassium atom (K) becomes an ion (K^+)?

Standardized Test Practice

Record your answers on the answer sheet provided by your teacher or on a sheet of paper.

Multiple Choice

1 Which information does the chemical formula CO_2 NOT give you?

A number of valence electrons in each atom

B ratio of atoms in the compound

C total number of atoms in one molecule of the compound

D type of elements in the compound

Use the diagram below to answer question 2.

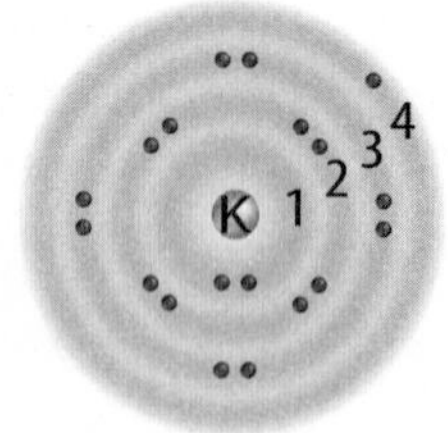

2 The diagram above shows a potassium atom. Which is the second-highest energy level?

A 1

B 2

C 3

D 4

3 What is shared in a metallic bond?

A negatively charged ions

B neutrons

C pooled valence electrons

D protons

4 Which is a characteristic of most nonpolar compounds?

A conduct electricity poorly

B dissolve easily in water

C solid crystals

D shiny surfaces

Use the diagram below to answer question 5.

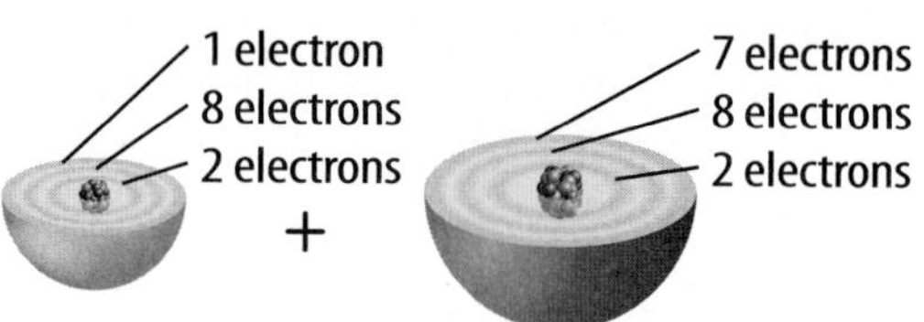

5 The atoms in the diagram above are forming a bond. Which represents that bond?

A

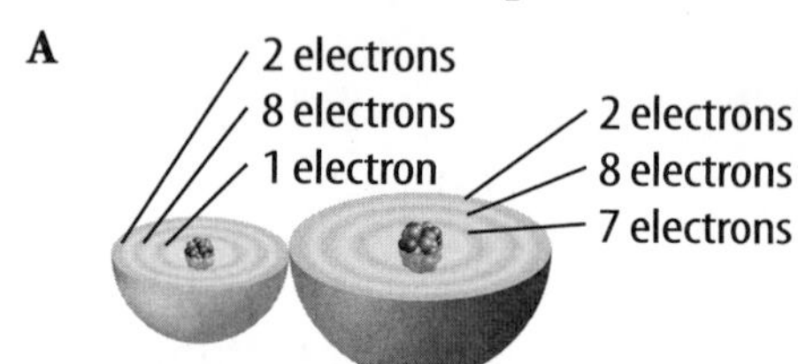

B

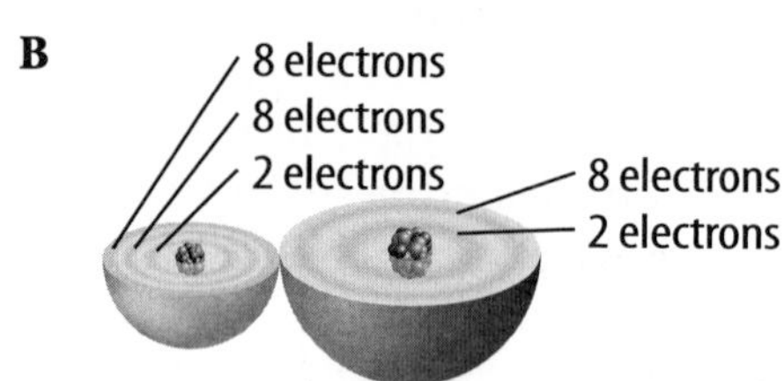

C

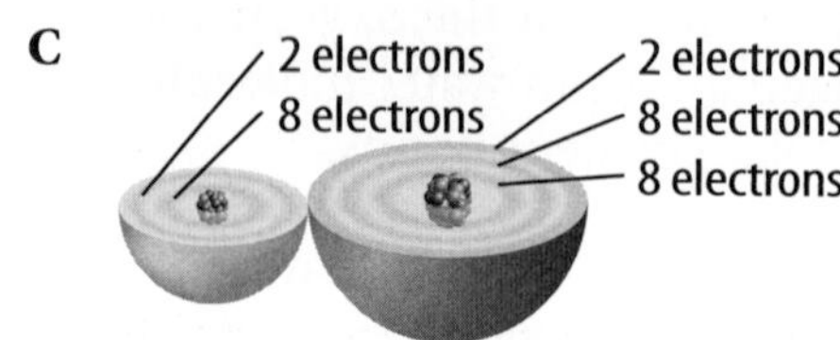

D

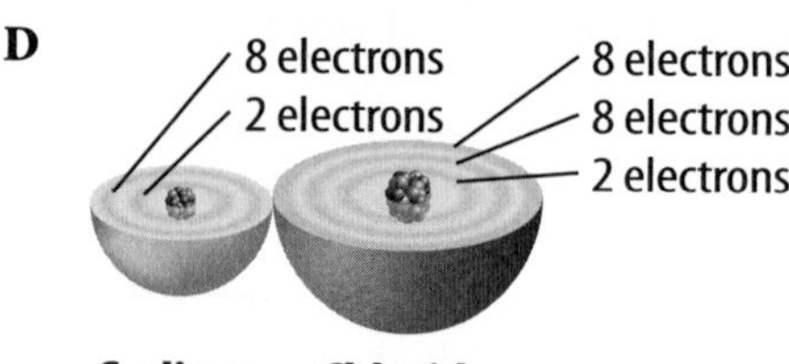

6 Covalent bonds typically form between the atoms of elements that share

A nuclei.

B oppositely charged ions.

C protons.

D valence electrons.

Use the diagram below to answer question 7.

Water Molecule

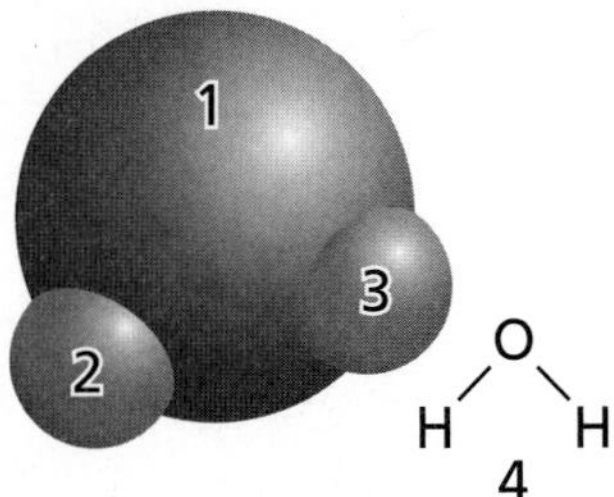

7 In the diagram above, which shows an atom with a partial negative charge?

A 1

B 2

C 3

D 4

8 Which compound is formed by the attraction between negatively and positively charged ions?

A bipolar

B covalent

C ionic

D nonpolar

9 The atoms of noble gases do NOT bond easily with other atoms because their valence electrons are

A absent.

B moving.

C neutral.

D stable.

Constructed Response

Use the table below to answer question 10.

Property	Rust	Iron	Oxygen
Color			Clear
Solid, liquid, or gas			
Strength		Strong	Does NOT apply
Usefulness			

10 Rust is a compound of iron and oxygen. Compare the properties of rust, iron, and oxygen by filling in the missing cells in the table above. What can you conclude about the properties of compounds and their elements?

Use the diagram below to answer questions 11 and 12.

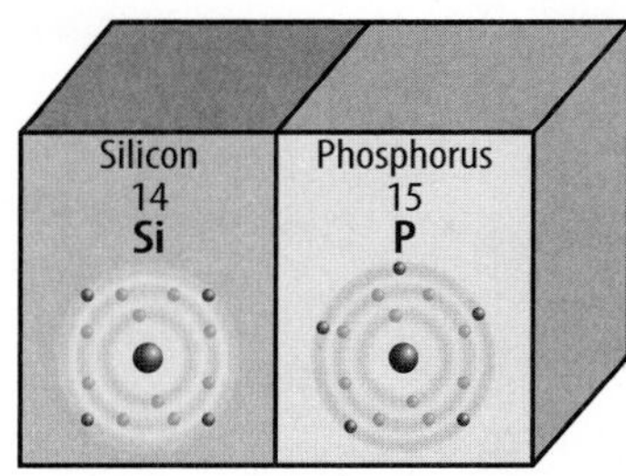

11 In the diagram, how are valence electrons illustrated? How many valence electrons does each element have?

12 Describe a stable electron configuration. For each element above, how many electrons are needed to make a stable electron configuration?

NEED EXTRA HELP?												
If You Missed Question...	1	2	3	4	5	6	7	8	9	10	11	12
Go to Lesson...	2	1	3	3	3	2	2	3	1	2	1	1

Chapter 5

Chemical Reactions and Equations

THE BIG IDEA What happens to atoms and energy during a chemical reaction?

Inquiry How does it work?

An air bag deploys in less than the blink of an eye. How does the bag open so fast? At the moment of impact, a sensor triggers a chemical reaction between two chemicals. This reaction quickly produces a large amount of nitrogen gas. This gas inflates the bag with a pop.

- A chemical reaction can produce a gas. How is this different from a gas produced when a liquid boils?
- Where do you think the nitrogen gas that is in an air bag comes from? Do you think any of the chemicals in the air bag contain the element nitrogen?
- What do you think happens to atoms and energy during a chemical reaction?

Get Ready to Read

What do you think?

Before you read, decide if you agree or disagree with each of these statements. As you read this chapter, see if you change your mind about any of the statements.

1. If a substance bubbles, you know a chemical reaction is occurring.
2. During a chemical reaction, some atoms are destroyed and new atoms are made.
3. Reactions always start with two or more substances that react with each other.
4. Water can be broken down into simpler substances.
5. Reactions that release energy require energy to get started.
6. Energy can be created in a chemical reaction.

ConnectED Your one-stop online resource

connectED.mcgraw-hill.com

- Video
- Audio
- Review
- Inquiry
- WebQuest
- Assessment
- Concepts in Motion
- Multilingual eGlossary

Lesson 1

Reading Guide

Key Concepts
ESSENTIAL QUESTIONS

- What are some signs that a chemical reaction might have occurred?
- What happens to atoms during a chemical reaction?
- What happens to the total mass in a chemical reaction?

Vocabulary

chemical reaction p. 151
chemical equation p. 154
reactant p. 155
product p. 155
law of conservation of mass p. 156
coefficient p. 158

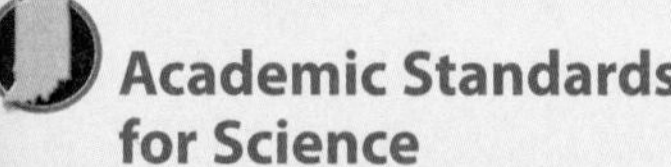

Academic Standards for Science

Covers: 8.1.7, 8.1.8, 8.4.3, 8.NS.3, 8.NS.5, 8.NS.6, 8.NS.7, 8.NS.9

Understanding Chemical Reactions

Inquiry Does it run on batteries?

Flashes of light from fireflies dot summer evening skies in many parts of the United States. But, firefly light doesn't come from batteries. Fireflies make light using a process called bioluminescence (bi oh lew muh NE cents). In this process, chemicals in the firefly's body combine in a two-step process and make new chemicals and light.

Inquiry Launch Lab

15–20 minutes

Where did it come from?

Does a boiled egg have more mass than a raw egg? What happens when liquids change to a solid?

1. Read and complete a lab safety form.
2. Use a **graduated cylinder** to add 25 mL of **solution A** to a **self-sealing plastic bag.** Place a **stoppered test tube** containing **solution B** into the bag. Be careful not to dislodge the stopper.
3. Seal the bag completely, and wipe off any moisture on the outside with a **paper towel.** Place the bag on the **balance.** Record the total mass in your Science Journal.
4. Without opening the bag, remove the stopper from the test tube and allow the liquids to mix. Observe and record what happens.
5. Place the sealed bag and its contents back on the balance. Read and record the mass.

Think About This

1. What did you observe when the liquids mixed? How would you account for this observation?
2. Did the mass of the bag's contents change? If so, could the change have been due to the precision of the balance, or did the matter in the bag change its mass? Explain.
3. **Key Concept** Do you think matter was gained or lost in the bag? How can you tell?

Changes in Matter

When you put liquid water in a freezer, it changes to solid water, or ice. When you pour brownie batter into a pan and bake it, the liquid batter changes to a solid, too. In both cases, a liquid changes to a solid. Are these changes the same?

Physical Changes

Recall that matter can undergo two types of changes—chemical or physical. A physical change does not produce new substances. The substances that exist before and after the change are the same, although they might have different physical properties. This is what happens when liquid water freezes. Its physical properties change from a liquid to a solid, but the water, H_2O, does not change into a different substance. Water molecules are always made up of two hydrogen atoms bonded to one oxygen atom regardless of whether they are solid, liquid, or gas.

Chemical Changes

Recall that during a chemical change, one or more substances change into new substances. The starting substances and the substances produced have different physical and chemical properties. For example, when brownie batter bakes, a chemical change occurs. Many of the substances in the baked brownies are different from the substances in the batter. As a result, baked brownies have physical and chemical properties that are different from those of brownie batter.

A chemical change also is called a chemical reaction. These terms mean the same thing. *A* **chemical reaction** *is a process in which atoms of one or more substances rearrange to form one or more new substances.* In this lesson, you will read what happens to atoms during a reaction and how these changes can be described using equations.

Reading Check What types of properties change during a chemical reaction?

Signs of a Chemical Reaction

How can you tell if a chemical reaction has taken place? You have read that the substances before and after a reaction have different properties. You might think that you could look for changes in properties as a sign that a reaction occurred. In fact, changes in the physical properties of color, state of matter, and odor are all signs that a chemical reaction might have occurred. Another sign of a chemical reaction is a change in energy. If substances get warmer or cooler or if they give off light or sound, it is likely that a reaction has occurred. Some signs that a chemical reaction might have occurred are shown in **Figure 1.**

However, these signs are not proof of a chemical change. For example, bubbles appear when water boils. But, bubbles also appear when baking soda and vinegar react and form carbon dioxide gas. How can you be sure that a chemical reaction has taken place? The only way to know is to study the chemical properties of the substances before and after the change. If they have different chemical properties, then the substances have undergone a chemical reaction.

Key Concept Check What are some signs that a chemical reaction might have occurred?

Figure 1 You can detect a chemical reaction by looking for changes in properties and changes in energy of the substances that reacted.

Change in Properties

Change in color

Bright copper changes to green when the copper reacts with certain gases in the air.

Formation of bubbles

Bubbles of carbon dioxide form when baking soda is added to vinegar.

Change in odor

When food burns or rots, a change in odor is a sign of chemical change.

Formation of a precipitate

A precipitate is a solid formed when two liquids react.

Change in Energy

Warming or cooling

Thermal energy is either given off or absorbed during a chemical change.

Release of light

A firefly gives off light as the result of a chemical change.

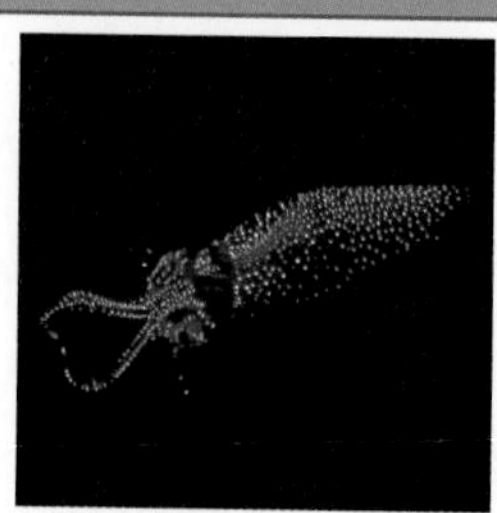

What happens in a chemical reaction?

During a chemical reaction, one or more substances react and form one or more new substances. How are these new substances formed?

Atoms Rearrange and Form New Substances

To understand what happens in a reaction, first review substances. Recall that there are two types of substances—elements and compounds. Substances have a fixed arrangement of atoms. For example, in a single drop of water, there are trillions of oxygen and hydrogen atoms. However, all of these atoms are arranged in the same way—two atoms of hydrogen are bonded to one atom of oxygen. If this arrangement changes, the substance is no longer water. Instead, a different substance forms with different physical and chemical properties. This is what happens during a chemical reaction. Atoms of elements or compounds rearrange and form different elements or compounds.

Bonds Break and Bonds Form

How does the rearrangement of atoms happen? Atoms rearrange when **chemical bonds** between atoms break. Recall that constantly moving particles make up all substances, including solids. As particles move, they collide with one another. If the particles collide with enough energy, the bonds between atoms can break. The atoms separate, rearrange, and new bonds can form. The reaction that forms hydrogen and oxygen from water is shown in **Figure 2.** Adding electric energy to water molecules can cause this reaction. The added energy causes bonds between the hydrogen atoms and the oxygen atoms to break. After the bonds between the atoms in water molecules break, new bonds can form between pairs of hydrogen atoms and between pairs of oxygen atoms.

REVIEW VOCABULARY

chemical bond
an attraction between atoms when electrons are shared, transferred, or pooled

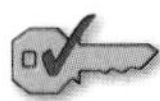 **Key Concept Check** What happens to atoms during a chemical reaction?

Figure 2 Notice that no new atoms are created in a chemical reaction. The existing atoms rearrange and form new substances.

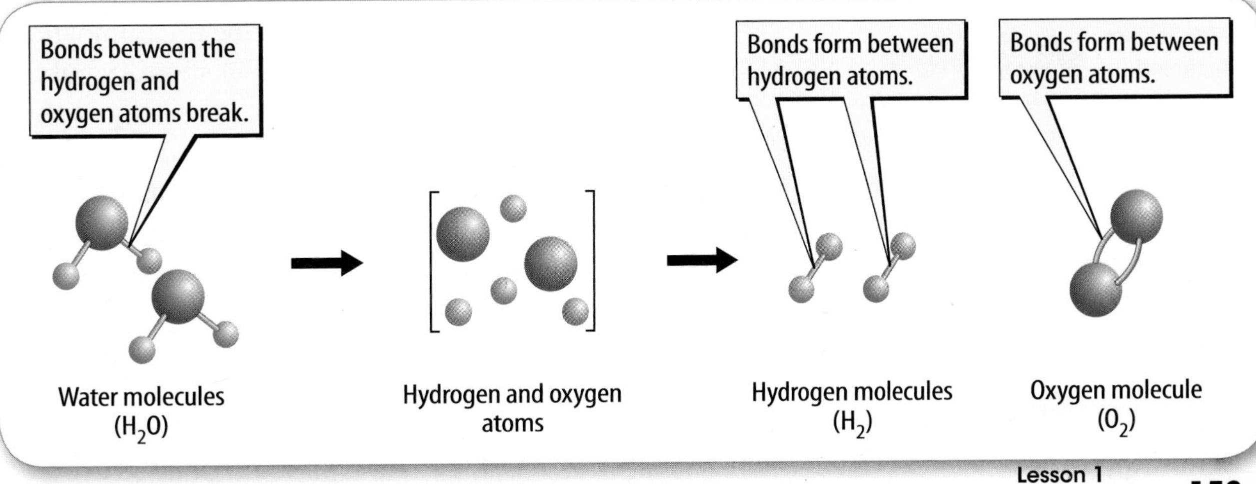
Bonds between the hydrogen and oxygen atoms break.
Bonds form between hydrogen atoms.
Bonds form between oxygen atoms.
Water molecules (H_2O)
Hydrogen and oxygen atoms
Hydrogen molecules (H_2)
Oxygen molecule (O_2)

Table 1 Symbols and Formulas of Some Elements and Compounds

Substance	Formula	# of atoms
Carbon	C	C: 1
Copper	Cu	Cu: 1
Cobalt	Co	Co: 1
Oxygen	O_2	O: 2
Hydrogen	H_2	H: 2
Chlorine	Cl_2	Cl: 2
Carbon dioxide	CO_2	C: 1 O: 2
Carbon monoxide	CO	C: 1 O: 1
Water	H_2O	H: 2 O: 1
Hydrogen peroxide	H_2O_2	H: 2 O: 2
Glucose	$C_6H_{12}O_6$	C: 6 H: 12 O: 6
Sodium chloride	NaCl	Na: 1 Cl: 1
Magnesium hydroxide	$Mg(OH)_2$	Mg: 1 O: 2 H: 2

Table 1 Symbols and subscripts describe the type and number of atoms in an element or a compound.

Visual Check Describe the number of atoms in each element in the following: C, Co, CO, and CO_2.

Concepts in Motion Interactive Table

Chemical Equations

Suppose your teacher asks you to produce a specific reaction in your science laboratory. How might your teacher describe the reaction to you? He or she might say something such as "react baking soda and vinegar to form sodium acetate, water, and carbon dioxide." It is more likely that your teacher will describe the reaction in the form of a chemical equation. *A* **chemical equation** *is a description of a reaction using element symbols and chemical formulas.* Element symbols represent elements. Chemical formulas represent compounds.

Element Symbols

Recall that symbols of elements are shown in the periodic table. For example, the symbol for carbon is C. The symbol for copper is Cu. Each element can exist as just one atom. However, some elements exist in nature as diatomic molecules—two atoms of the same element bonded together. A formula for one of these diatomic elements includes the element's symbol and the subscript *2*. A subscript describes the number of atoms of an element in a compound. Oxygen (O_2) and hydrogen (H_2) are examples of diatomic molecules. Some element symbols are shown above the blue line in **Table 1.**

Chemical Formulas

When atoms of two or more different elements bond, they form a compound. Recall that a chemical formula uses elements' symbols and subscripts to describe the number of atoms in a compound. If an element's symbol does not have a subscript, the compound contains only one atom of that element. For example, carbon dioxide (CO_2) is made up of one carbon atom and two oxygen atoms. Remember that two different formulas, no matter how similar, represent different substances. Some chemical formulas are shown below the blue line in **Table 1.**

Writing Chemical Equations

A chemical equation includes both the substances that react and the substances that are formed in a chemical reaction. *The starting substances in a chemical reaction are* **reactants.** *The substances produced by the chemical reaction are* **products.** **Figure 3** shows how a chemical equation is written. Chemical formulas are used to describe the reactants and the products. The reactants are written to the left of an arrow, and the products are written to the right of the arrow. Two or more reactants or products are separated by a plus sign. The general structure for an equation is:

reactant + reactant → product + product

When writing chemical equations, it is important to use correct chemical formulas for the reactants and the products. For example, suppose a certain chemical reaction produces carbon dioxide and water. The product carbon dioxide would be written as CO_2 and not as CO. CO is the formula for carbon monoxide, which is not the same compound as CO_2. Water would be written as H_2O and not as H_2O_2, the formula for hydrogen peroxide.

Inquiry MiniLab — 10 minutes

How does an equation represent a reaction?

Sulfur dioxide (SO_2) and oxygen (O_2) react and form sulfur trioxide (SO_3). How does an equation represent the reaction?

1. Read and complete a lab safety form.
2. Use **yellow modeling clay** to model two atoms of sulfur. Use **red modeling clay** to model six atoms of oxygen.
3. Make two molecules of SO_2 with a sulfur atom in the middle of each molecule. Make one molecule of O_2. Sketch the models in your Science Journal.
4. Rearrange atoms to form two molecules of SO_3. Place a sulfur atom in the middle of each molecule. Sketch the models in your Science Journal.

Analyze and Conclude

1. **Identify** the reactants and the products in this chemical reaction.
2. **Write** a chemical equation for this reaction.
3. **Explain** What do the letters represent in the equation? The numbers?
4. **Key Concept** In terms of chemical bonds, what did you model by pulling molecules apart and building new ones?

Figure 3 An equation is read much like a sentence. This equation is read as "carbon plus oxygen produces carbon dioxide."

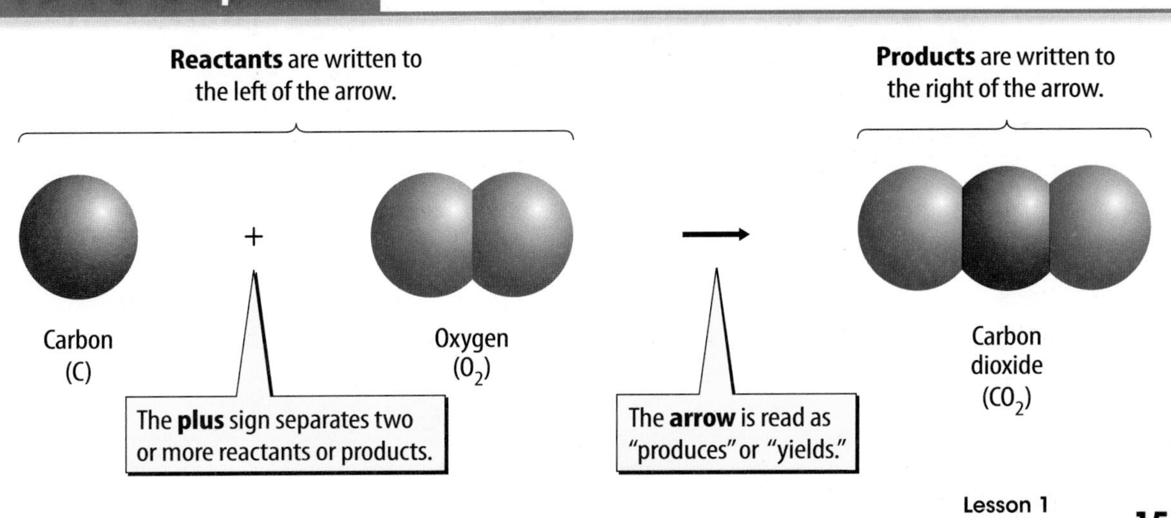

Parts of an Equation
Reactants are written to the left of the arrow.
Products are written to the right of the arrow.
+
→
Carbon (C)
Oxygen (O_2)
Carbon dioxide (CO_2)
The plus sign separates two or more reactants or products.
The arrow is read as "produces" or "yields."

WORD ORIGIN

product
from Latin *producere,* means "bring forth"

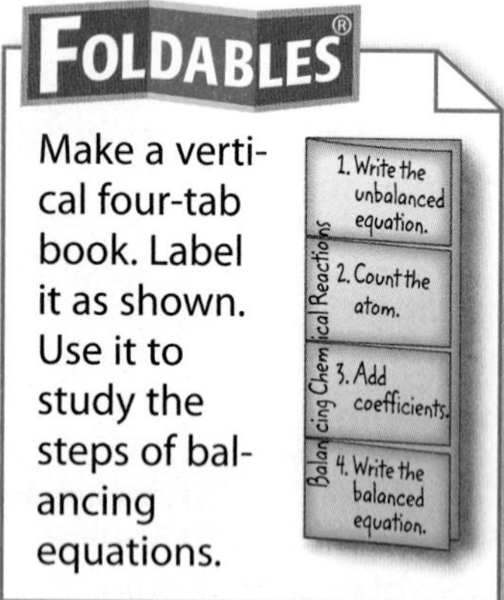
FOLDABLES
Balancing Chemical Reactions
1. Write the unbalanced equation.
2. Count the atom.
3. Add coefficients.
4. Write the balanced equation.

Make a vertical four-tab book. Label it as shown. Use it to study the steps of balancing equations.

Conservation of Mass

A French chemist named Antoine Lavoisier (AN twan • luh VWAH see ay) (1743–1794) discovered something interesting about chemical reactions. In a series of experiments, Lavoisier measured the masses of substances before and after a chemical reaction inside a closed container. He found that the total mass of the reactants always equaled the total mass of the **products.** Lavoisier's results led to the law of conservation of mass. *The* **law of conservation of mass** *states that the total mass of the reactants before a chemical reaction is the same as the total mass of the products after the chemical reaction.*

Atoms are conserved.

The discovery of atoms provided an explanation for Lavoisier's observations. Mass is conserved in a reaction because atoms are conserved. Recall that during a chemical reaction, bonds break and new bonds form. However, atoms are not destroyed, and no new atoms form. All atoms at the start of a chemical reaction are present at the end of the reaction. **Figure 4** shows that mass is conserved in the reaction between baking soda and vinegar.

Key Concept Check What happens to the total mass of the reactants in a chemical reaction?

Figure 4 As this reaction takes place, the mass on the balance remains the same, showing that mass is conserved.

Conservation of Mass

The baking soda is contained in a balloon. The balloon is attached to a flask that contains vinegar.

When the balloon is tipped up, the baking soda pours into the vinegar. The reaction forms a gas that is collected in the balloon.

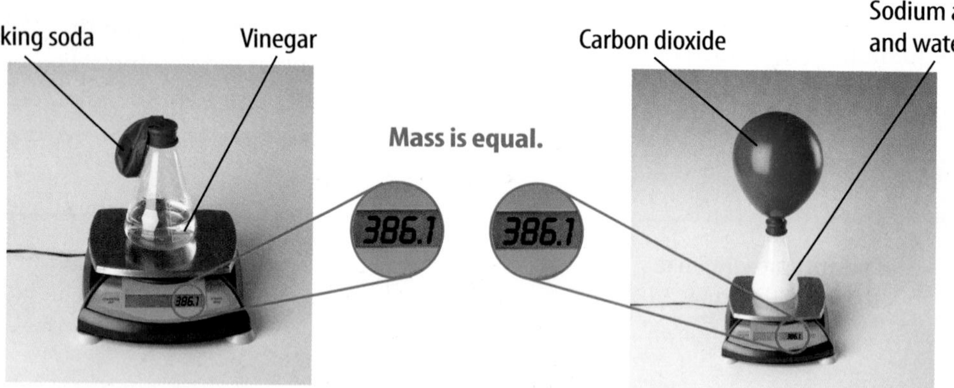
Baking soda
Vinegar
Mass is equal.
386.1
386.1
Carbon dioxide
Sodium acetate and water

baking soda + **vinegar** → **sodium acetate** + **water** + **carbon dioxide**

$NaHCO_3$ + $HC_2H_3O_2$ → $NaC_2H_3O_2$ + H_2O + CO_2

$NaHCO_3$	$HC_2H_3O_2$		$NaC_2H_3O_2$	H_2O	CO_2
1 Na: ●	4 H: ●●●●	**Atoms are equal.**	1 Na: ●	2 H: ●●	1 C: ●
1 H: ●	2 C: ●●		2 C: ●●	1 O: ●	2 O: ●●
1 C: ●	2 O: ●●		3 H: ●●●		
3 O: ●●●			2 O: ●●		

Is an equation balanced?

How does a chemical equation show that atoms are conserved? An equation is written so that the number of atoms of each element is the same, or balanced, on each side of the arrow. The equation showing the reaction between carbon and oxygen that produces carbon dioxide is shown below. Remember that oxygen is written as O_2 because it is a diatomic molecule. The formula for carbon dioxide is CO_2.

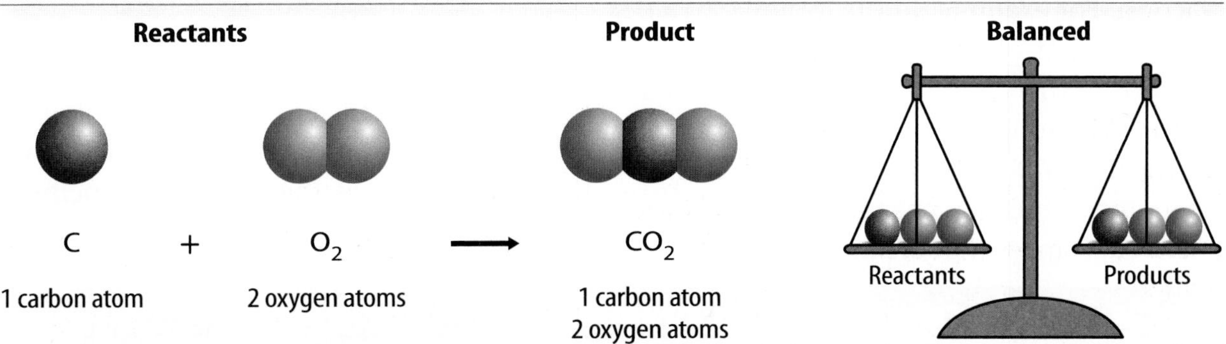

Is there the same number of carbon atoms on each side of the arrow? Yes, there is one carbon atom on the left and one on the right. Carbon is balanced. Is oxygen balanced? There are two oxygen atoms on each side of the arrow. Oxygen also is balanced. The atoms of all elements are balanced. Therefore, the equation is balanced.

You might think a balanced equation happens automatically when you write the symbols and formulas for reactants and products. However, this usually is not the case. For example, the reaction between hydrogen (H_2) and oxygen (O_2) that forms water (H_2O) is shown below.

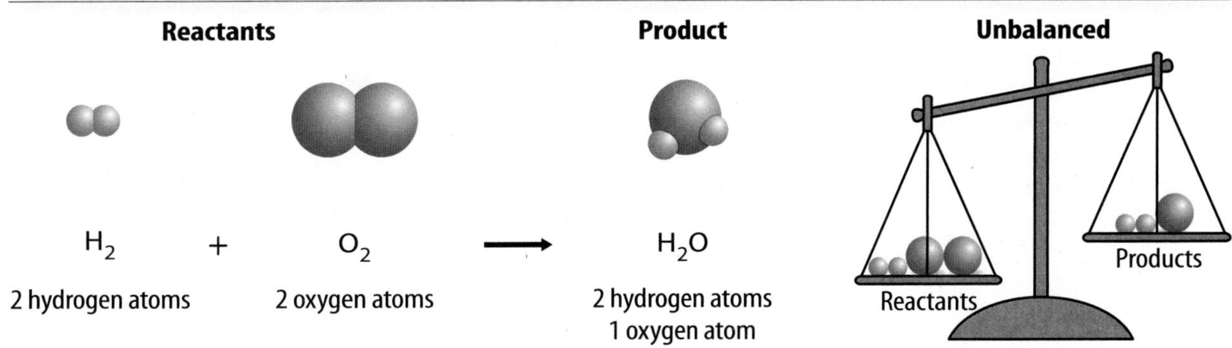

Count the number of hydrogen atoms on each side of the arrow. There are two hydrogen atoms in the product and two in the reactants. They are balanced. Now count the number of oxygen atoms on each side of the arrow. Did you notice that there are two oxygen atoms in the reactants and only one in the product? Because they are not equal, this equation is not balanced. To accurately represent this reaction, the equation needs to be balanced.

Balancing Chemical Equations

When you balance a chemical equation, you count the atoms in the reactants and the products and then add coefficients to balance the number of atoms. *A* **coefficient** *is a number placed in front of an element symbol or chemical formula in an equation.* It is the number of units of that substance in the reaction. For example, in the formula $2H_2O$, the *2* in front of H_2O is a coefficient, This means that there are two molecules of water in the reaction. Only coefficients can be changed when balancing an equation. Changing subscripts changes the identities of the substances that are in the reaction.

If one molecule of water contains two hydrogen atoms and one oxygen atom, how many H and O atoms are in two molecules of water ($2H_2O$)? Multiply each by 2.

2×2 H atoms = 4 H atoms
2×1 O atom = 2 O atoms

When no coefficient is present, only one unit of that substance takes part in the reaction. **Table 2** shows the steps of balancing a chemical equation.

Table 2 Balancing a Chemical Equation

Step	Equation
1 Write the unbalanced equation. Make sure that all chemical formulas are correct.	$H_2 + O_2 \rightarrow H_2O$ *reactants* → *products*
2 Count atoms of each element in the reactants and in the products. **a.** Note which, if any, elements have a balanced number of atoms on each side of the equation. Which atoms are not balanced? **b.** If all of the atoms are balanced, the equation is balanced.	$H_2 + O_2 \rightarrow H_2O$ *reactants*: H = 2, O = 2 *products*: H = 2, O = 1
3 Add coefficients to balance the atoms. **a.** Pick an element in the equation that is not balanced, such as oxygen. Write a coefficient in front of a reactant or a product that will balance the atoms of that element. **b.** Recount the atoms of each element in the reactants and the products. Note which atoms are not balanced. Some atoms that were balanced before might no longer be balanced. **c.** Repeat step 3 until the atoms of each element are balanced.	$H_2 + O_2 \rightarrow 2H_2O$ *reactants*: H = 2, O = 2 *products*: H = 4, O = 2 $2H_2 + O_2 \rightarrow 2H_2O$ *reactants*: H = 4, O = 2 *products*: H = 4, O = 2
4 Write the balanced chemical equation including the coefficients.	$2H_2 + O_2 = 2H_2O$

Visual Check In row 2 above, which element is not balanced? In the top of row 3, which element is not balanced?

Lesson 1 Review

Assessment Online Quiz

Visual Summary

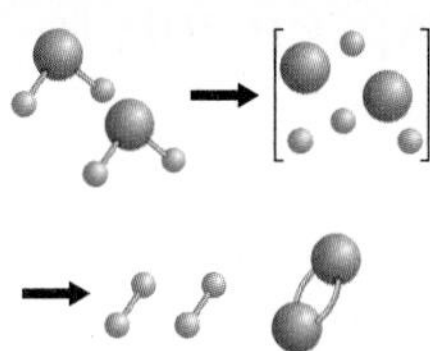

A chemical reaction is a process in which bonds break and atoms rearrange, forming new bonds.

$2H_2 + O_2 \rightarrow 2H_2O$

A chemical equation uses symbols to show reactants and products of a chemical reaction.

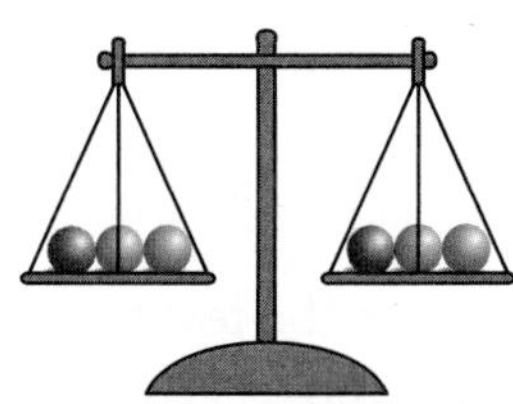

The mass and the number of each type of atom do not change during a chemical reaction. This is the law of conservation of mass.

FOLDABLES®

Use your lesson Foldable to review the lesson. Save your Foldable for the project at the end of the chapter.

What do you think NOW?

You first read the statements below at the beginning of the chapter.

1. If a substance bubbles, you know a chemical reaction is occurring.
2. During a chemical reaction, some atoms are destroyed and new atoms are made.

Did you change your mind about whether you agree or disagree with the statements? Rewrite any false statements to make them true.

Use Vocabulary

1. **Define** *reactants* and *products*.

Understand Key Concepts 

2. Which is a sign of a chemical reaction?
   - **A.** chemical properties change
   - **B.** physical properties change
   - **C.** a gas forms
   - **D.** a solid forms
3. **Explain** why subscripts cannot change when balancing a chemical equation.
4. **Infer** Is the reaction below possible? Explain why or why not.

$$H_2O + NaOH \rightarrow NaCl + H_2$$

Interpret Graphics

5. **Describe** the reaction below by listing the bonds that break and the bonds that form.

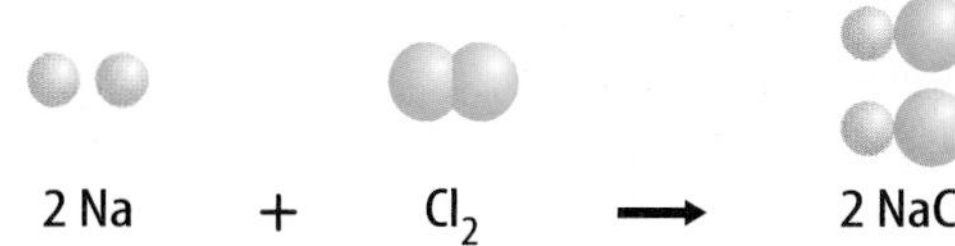

6. **Interpret** Copy and complete the table to determine if this equation is balanced:

$$CH_4 + 2O_2 \rightarrow CO_2 + 2H_2O$$

Is this reaction balanced? Explain.

Type of Atom	Number of Atoms in the Balanced Chemical Equation	
	Reactants	Products

Critical Thinking

7. Balance this chemical equation. Hint: Balance Al last and then use a multiple of 2 and 3.

$$Al + HCl \rightarrow AlCl_3 + H_2$$

Inquiry Skill Practice **Follow a Procedure** 40 minutes

What can you learn from an experiment?

Materials

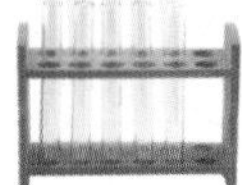

test tubes and rack

ammonium hydroxide (NH_4OH)

ALUMINUM FOIL

aluminum foil

sodium bicarbonate ($NaHCO_3$)

Also needed: copper foil, tongs, salt water, copper sulfate solution ($CuSO_4$), 25-mL graduated cylinder, Bunsen burner, plastic spoon, toothpick, ring stand and clamp, splints, matches, paper towel

Safety

Observing reactions allows you to compare different types of changes that can occur. You can then design new experiments to learn more about reactions.

Learn It

If you have never done a test before, it is helpful to **follow a procedure.** A procedure tells you which materials to use and what steps to take.

Try It

1. Read and complete a safety form.
2. Copy the table into your Science Journal. During each procedure, record observations in the table.

3a. Dip a strip of aluminum foil into salt water in a test tube for about 1 min to remove the coating.

3b. Place 5 mL of copper sulfate solution in a test tube. Lift the aluminum foil from the salt water. Drop it into the test tube of copper sulfate so that the bottom part is in the liquid. Look for evidence of a chemical change. Set the test tube in a rack, and do the other procedures.

4. Use tongs to hold a small piece of copper foil in a flame for 3 min. Set the foil on a heat-proof surface, and allow it to cool. Use a toothpick to examine the product.
5. Place a spoonful of sodium bicarbonate in a dry test tube. Clamp the tube to a ring stand at a 45° angle. Point the mouth of the tube away from people. Move a burner flame back and forth under the tube. Observe the reaction. Test for carbon dioxide with a lighted wood splint.
6. Add 1 drop of ammonium hydroxide to a test tube containing 5 mL of copper sulfate solution.
7. Pour the liquid from the test tube in step 3b into a clean test tube. Dump the aluminum onto a paper towel. Record your observations of both the liquid and the solid.

Apply It

8. Using the table, write a balanced equation for each reaction.
9. Why did the color of the copper sulfate disappear in step 3b?
10. **Key Concept** How can you tell the difference between types of reactions by the number and type of reactants and products?

Step	Reactants	Products	Observations and Evidence of Chemical Reaction
3 + 7	$Al + CuSO_4$	$Cu + Al_2(SO_4)_3$	
4	$Cu + O_2$	CuO	
5	$NaHCO_3$	$CO_2 + Na_2CO_3 + H_2O$	
6	$NH_4OH + CuSO_4$	$(NH_4)_2SO_4 + CU(OH)_2$	

Lesson 2

Reading Guide

Key Concepts

ESSENTIAL QUESTIONS

- How can you recognize the type of chemical reaction by the number or type of reactants and products?
- What are the different types of chemical reactions?

Vocabulary

synthesis p. 163
decomposition p. 163
single replacement p. 164
double replacement p. 164
combustion p. 164

Multilingual eGlossary

Video

What's Science Got to do With It?

Academic Standards for Science

8.1.7 Explain that chemical changes occur when substances react and form one or more different products, whose physical and chemical properties are different from those of the reactants.

8.1.8 Demonstrate that in a chemical change, the total numbers of each kind of atom in the product are the same as in the reactants and that the total mass of the reacting system is conserved.

Also covers: 8.NS.3, 8.NS.9, 8.NS.10, 8.NS.11, 8.DP.6

Types of Chemical Reactions

Inquiry Where did it come from?

When lead nitrate, a clear liquid, combines with potassium iodide, another clear liquid, a yellow solid appears instantly. Where did it come from? Here's a hint—the name of the solid is lead iodide. Did you guess that parts of each reactant combined and formed it? You'll learn about this and other types of reactions in this lesson.

15 minutes

What combines with what?

The reactants and the products in a chemical reaction can be elements, compounds, or both. In how many ways can these substances combine?

1. Read and complete a lab safety form.
2. Divide a **sheet of paper** into four equal sections labeled *A, B, Y,* and *Z.* Place **red paper clips** in section A, **yellow clips** in section B, **blue clips** in section Y, and **green clips** in section Z.
3. Use another sheet of paper to copy the table shown to the right. Turn the paper so that a long edge is at the top. Print *REACTANTS ⟶ PRODUCTS* across the top then complete the table.
4. Using the paper clips, model the equations listed in the table. Hook the clips together to make diatomic elements or compounds. Place each clip model onto your paper over the matching written equation.
5. As you read this lesson, match the types of equations to your paper clip equations.

	REACTANTS	→	PRODUCTS
1	AY	→	A + Y
2	B + Z	→	BZ
3	$2A_2 + Y_2$	→	$2A_2Y$
4	A + BY	→	B + AY
5	Z + BY	→	Y + BZ
6	AY + BZ	→	AZ + BY

Think About This

1. Which equation represents hydrogen combining with oxygen and forming water? How do you know?
2. **Key Concept** How could you use the number and type of reactants to identify a type of chemical reaction?

Patterns in Reactions

If you have ever used hydrogen peroxide, you might have noticed that it is stored in a dark bottle. This is because light causes hydrogen peroxide to change into other substances. Maybe you have seen a video of an explosion demolishing an old building, like in **Figure 5.** How is the reaction with hydrogen peroxide and light similar to a building demolition? In both, one reactant breaks down into two or more products.

The breakdown of one reactant into two or more products is one of four major types of chemical reactions. Each type of chemical reaction follows a unique pattern in the way atoms in reactants rearrange to form products. In this lesson, you will read how chemical reactions are classified by recognizing patterns in the way the atoms recombine.

Figure 5 When dynamite explodes, it chemically changes into several products and releases energy.

Types of Chemical Reactions

There are many different types of reactions. It would be impossible to memorize them all. However, most chemical reactions fit into four major categories. Understanding these categories of reactions can help you predict how compounds will react and what products will form.

Synthesis

A **synthesis** (SIHN thuh sus) *is a type of chemical reaction in which two or more substances combine and form one compound.* In the synthesis reaction shown in **Figure 6,** magnesium (Mg) reacts with oxygen (O_2) in the air and forms magnesium oxide (MgO). You can recognize a synthesis reaction because two or more reactants form only one product.

Decomposition

In a **decomposition** *reaction, one compound breaks down and forms two or more substances.* You can recognize a decomposition reaction because one reactant forms two or more products. For example, hydrogen peroxide (H_2O_2), shown in **Figure 6,** decomposes and forms water (H_2O) and oxygen gas (O_2). Notice that decomposition is the reverse of synthesis.

Key Concept Check How can you tell the difference between synthesis and decomposition reactions?

FOLDABLES®

Make a horizontal four-door book. Label it as shown. Use it to organize your notes about the different types of chemical reactions.

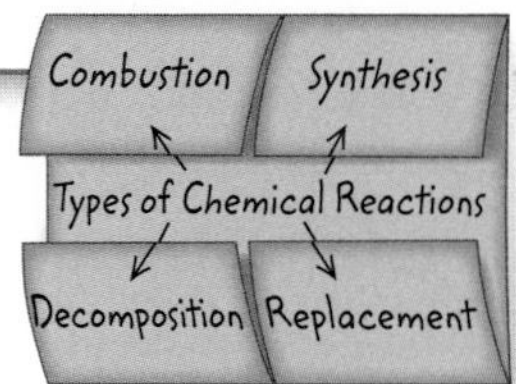

WORD ORIGIN

synthesis
from Greek *syn-*, means "together"; and *tithenai,* means "put"

Figure 6 Synthesis and decomposition reactions are opposites of each other.

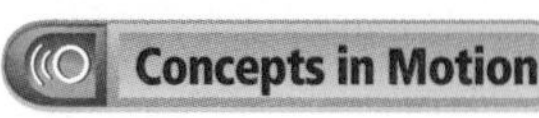

Animation

Synthesis and Decomposition Reactions

Synthesis Reactions

Examples:

$2Na + Cl_2 \rightarrow 2NaCl$

$2H_2 + O_2 \rightarrow 2H_2O$

$H_2O + SO_3 \rightarrow H_2SO_4$

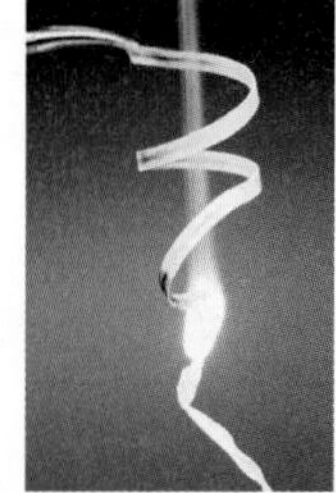

$2Mg$ magnesium $+$ O_2 oxygen $\rightarrow$ $2MgO$ magnesium oxide

Decomposition Reactions

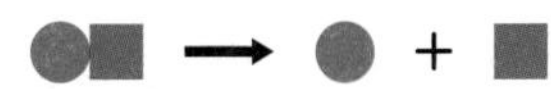

Examples:

$CaCO_3 \rightarrow CaO + CO_2$

$2H_2O \rightarrow 2H_2 + O_2$

$2KClO_3 \rightarrow 2KCl + 3O_2$

$2H_2O_2$ hydrogen peroxide $\rightarrow$ $2H_2O$ water $+$ O_2 oxygen

Replacement Reactions

Single Replacement

Examples:
$Fe + CuSO_4 \rightarrow FeSO_4 + Cu$
$Zn + 2HCl + ZnCl_2 + H_2$

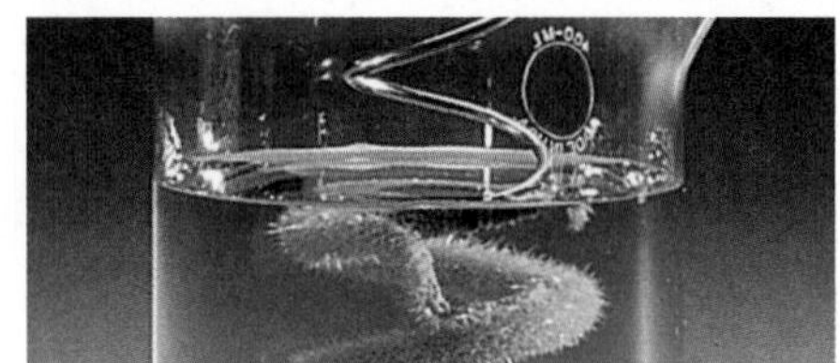

$2AgNO_3$ silver nitrate + Cu copper $\rightarrow$ $Cu(NO_3)_2$ copper nitrate + $2Ag$ silver

Double Replacement

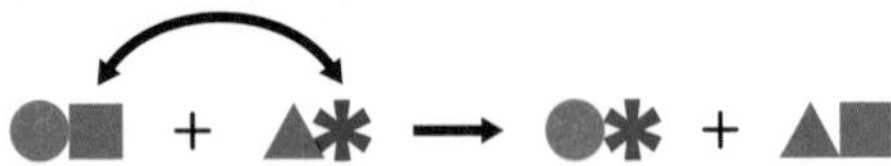

Examples:
$NaCl + AgNO_3 \rightarrow NaNO_3 + AgCl$
$HCl + FeS \rightarrow FeCl_2 + H_2S$

$Pb(NO_3)_2$ lead nitrate + $2KI$ potassium iodide $\rightarrow$ $2KNO_3$ potassium nitrate + PbI_2 lead iodide

▲ **Figure 7** In each of these reactions, an atom or group of atoms replaces another atom or group of atoms.

Combustion Reactions

substance + $O_2 \rightarrow$ substance(s)

C_3H_8 propane + $5O_2$ oxygen $\rightarrow$ $3CO_2$ carbon dioxide + $4H_2O$ water

Example:
$2C_4H_{10} + 13O_2 \rightarrow 8CO_2 + 10H_2O$

▲ **Figure 8** Combustion reactions always contain oxygen (O_2) as a reactant and often produce carbon dioxide (CO_2) and water (H_2O).

Replacement

In a replacement reaction, an atom or group of atoms replaces part of a compound. There are two types of replacement reactions. *In a* **single-replacement** *reaction, one element replaces another element in a compound.* In this type of reaction, an element and a compound react and form a different element and a different compound. *In a* **double-replacement** *reaction, the negative ions in two compounds switch places, forming two new compounds.* In this type of reaction, two compounds react and form two new compounds. **Figure 7** describes these replacement reactions.

Combustion

Combustion *is a chemical reaction in which a substance combines with oxygen and releases energy.* This energy usually is released as thermal energy and light energy. For example, burning is a common combustion reaction. The burning of fossil fuels, such as the propane (C_3H_8) shown in **Figure 8,** produces the energy we use to cook food, power vehicles, and light cities.

Key Concept Check What are the different types of chemical reactions?

Lesson 2 Review

Assessment Online Quiz
Inquiry Virtual Lab

Visual Summary

Chemical reactions are classified according to patterns seen in their reactants and products.

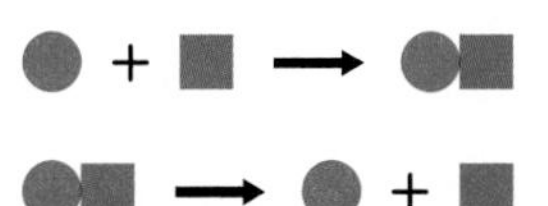

In a synthesis reaction, there are two or more reactants and one product. A decomposition reaction is the opposite of a synthesis reaction.

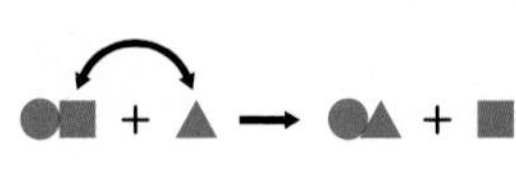

In replacement reactions, an element, or elements, in a compound is replaced with another element or elements.

FOLDABLES®

Use your lesson Foldable to review the lesson. Save your Foldable for the project at the end of the chapter.

What do you think NOW?

You first read the statements below at the beginning of the chapter.

3. Reactions always start with two or more substances that react with each other.

4. Water can be broken down into simpler substances.

Did you change your mind about whether you agree or disagree with the statements? Rewrite any false statements to make them true.

Use Vocabulary

1. **Contrast** synthesis and decomposition reactions using a diagram.
2. A reaction in which parts of two substances switch places and make two new substances is a(n) ________.

Understand Key Concepts 

3. **Classify** the reaction shown below.

$$2Na + Cl_2 \rightarrow 2NaCl$$

A. combustion
B. decomposition
C. single replacement
D. synthesis

4. Write a balanced equation that produces Na and Cl_2 from NaCl. Classify this reaction.
5. **Classify** In which two groups of reactions can this reaction be classified?

$$2SO_2 + O_2 \rightarrow 2SO_3$$

Interpret Graphics

6. **Complete** this table to identify four types of chemical reactions and the patterns shown by the reactants and the products.

Type of Reaction	Pattern of Reactants and Products
Synthesis	at least two reactants; one product

Critical Thinking

7. **Design** a poster to illustrate single- and double-replacement reactions.
8. **Infer** The combustion of methane (CH_4) produces energy. Where do you think this energy comes from?

HOW IT WORKS

How does a light stick work?

What makes it glow?

Glowing neon necklaces, bracelets, or sticks—chances are you've worn or used them. Light sticks—also known as glow sticks—come in brilliant colors and provide light without electricity or batteries. Because they are lightweight, portable, and waterproof, they provide an ideal light source for campers, scuba divers, and other activities in which electricity is not readily available. Light sticks also are useful in emergency situations in which an electric current from battery-powered lights could ignite a fire.

Light sticks give off light because of a chemical reaction that happens inside the tube. During the reaction, energy is released as light. This is known as chemiluminescence (ke mee lew muh NE sunts).

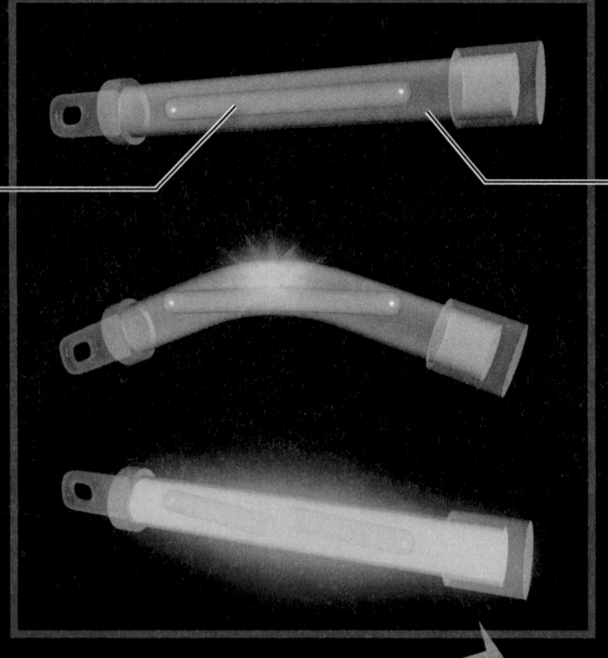

A light stick consists of a plastic tube with a glass tube inside it. Hydrogen peroxide fills the glass tube..

A solution of phenyl oxalate ester and fluorescent dye surround the glass tube.

When you bend the outer plastic tube, the inner glass tube breaks, causing the hydrogen peroxide, ester, and dye to mix together.

When the solutions mix together, they react. Energy produced by the reaction causes the electrons in the dye to produce light.

It's Your Turn

RESEARCH AND REPORT Research bioluminescent organisms, such as fireflies and sea animals. How is the reaction that occurs in these organisms similar to or different from that in a glow stick? Work in small groups, and present your findings to the class.

Lesson 3

Reading Guide

Key Concepts
ESSENTIAL QUESTIONS

- Why do chemical reactions always involve a change in energy?
- What is the difference between an endothermic reaction and an exothermic reaction?
- What factors can affect the rate of a chemical reaction?

Vocabulary

endothermic p. 169
exothermic p. 169
activation energy p. 170
catalyst p. 172
enzyme p. 172
inhibitor p. 172

Multilingual eGlossary

Academic Standards for Science

8.4.3 Investigate the properties (mechanical, chemical, electrical, thermal, magnetic, and optical) of natural and engineered materials.

Also covers: 8.NS.2, 8.NS.3, 8.NS.4, 8.NS.5, 8.NS.7, 8.NS.8

Energy Changes and Chemical Reactions

Inquiry Energy from Bonds?

A deafening roar, a blinding light, and the power to lift 2 million kg—what is the source of all this energy? Chemical bonds in the fuel store all the energy needed to launch a space shuttle. Chemical reactions release the energy in these bonds.

20 minutes

Where's the heat?

Does a chemical change always produce a temperature increase?

1. Read and complete a lab safety form.
2. Copy the table into your Science Journal.
3. Use a **graduated cylinder** to measure 25 mL of **citric acid solution** into a **foam cup.** Record the temperature with a **thermometer**.
4. Use a **plastic spoon** to add a rounded spoonful of **solid sodium bicarbonate** to the cup. Stir.
5. Use a **clock** or **stopwatch** to record the temperature every 15 s until it stops changing. Record your observations during the reaction.
6. Add 25 mL of **sodium bicarbonate solution** to a **second foam cup.** Record the temperature. Add a spoonful of **calcium chloride**. Repeat step 5.

Time	Temperature (°C)	
	Citric Acid Solution	Sodium Bicarbonate Solution
Starting temp.		
15 s		
30 s		
45 s		
1 min		
1 min, 15 s		
1 min, 30 s		
1 min, 45 s		
2 min		
2 min, 15 sec		

Think About This

1. What evidence do you have that the changes in the two cups were chemical reactions?
2. What happened to the temperature in the two cups? How would you explain the changes?
3. **Key Concept** Based on your observations and past experience, would a change in temperature be enough to convince you that a chemical change had taken place? Why or why not? What else could cause a temperature change?

Energy Changes

What is about 1,500 times heavier than a typical car and 300 times faster than a roller coaster? Do you need a hint? The energy it needs to move this fast comes from a chemical reaction that produces water. If you guessed a space shuttle, you are right!

It takes a large amount of energy to launch a space shuttle. The shuttle's main engines burn almost 2 million L of liquid hydrogen and liquid oxygen. This chemical reaction produces water vapor and a large amount of energy. The energy produced heats the water vapor to high temperatures, causing it to expand rapidly. When the water expands, it pushes the shuttle into orbit. Where does all this energy come from?

Chemical Energy in Bonds

Recall that when a chemical reaction occurs, chemical bonds in the reactants break and new chemical bonds form. Chemical bonds contain a form of energy called chemical energy. Breaking a bond absorbs energy from the surroundings. The formation of a chemical bond releases energy to the surroundings. Some chemical reactions release more energy than they absorb. Some chemical reactions absorb more energy than they release. You can feel this energy change as a change in the temperature of the surroundings. Keep in mind that in all chemical reactions, energy is conserved.

Key Concept Check Why do chemical reactions involve a change in energy?

Endothermic Reactions—Energy Absorbed

Have you ever heard someone say that the sidewalk was hot enough to fry an egg? To fry, the egg must absorb energy. *Chemical reactions that absorb thermal energy are* **endothermic** *reactions.* For an endothermic reaction to continue, energy must be constantly added.

reactants + thermal energy → products

In an endothermic reaction, more energy is required to break the bonds of the reactants than is released when the products form. Therefore, the overall reaction absorbs energy. The reaction on the left in **Figure 9** is an endothermic reaction.

Exothermic Reactions—Energy Released

Most chemical reactions release energy as opposed to absorbing it. *An* **exothermic** *reaction is a chemical reaction that releases thermal energy.*

reactants → products + thermal energy

In an exothermic reaction, more energy is released when the products form than is required to break the bonds in the reactants. Therefore, the overall reaction releases energy. The reaction shown on the right in **Figure 9** is exothermic.

Key Concept Check What is the difference between an endothermic reaction and an exothermic reaction?

FOLDABLES®

Make a vertical three-tab Venn book. Label it as shown. Use it to compare and contrast energy in chemical reactions.

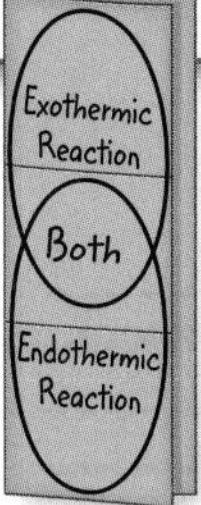
Exothermic Reaction
Both
Endothermic Reaction

WORD ORIGIN

exothermic
from Greek *exo-*, means "outside"; and *therm,* means "heat"

Figure 9 Whether a reaction is endothermic or exothermic depends on the amount of energy contained in the bonds of the reactants and the products.

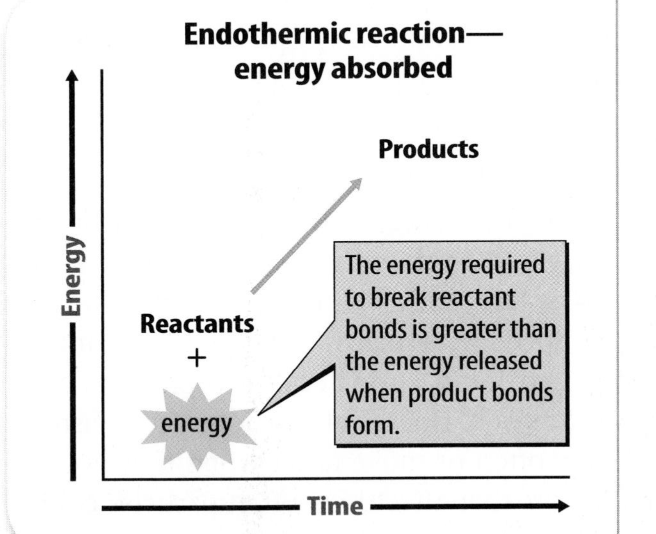
Endothermic reaction—
energy absorbed
Products
Reactants
+
energy
The energy required to break reactant bonds is greater than the energy released when product bonds form.
Energy
Time

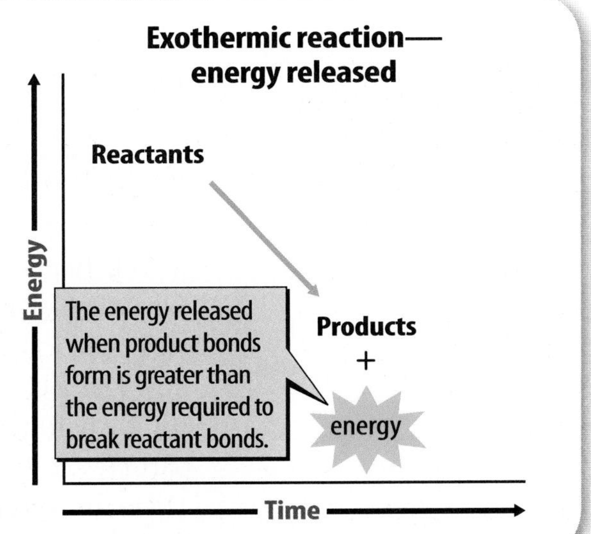
Exothermic reaction—
energy released
Reactants
Products
+
energy
The energy released when product bonds form is greater than the energy required to break reactant bonds.
Energy
Time

Visual Check Why does one arrow point upward and the other arrow point downward in these diagrams?

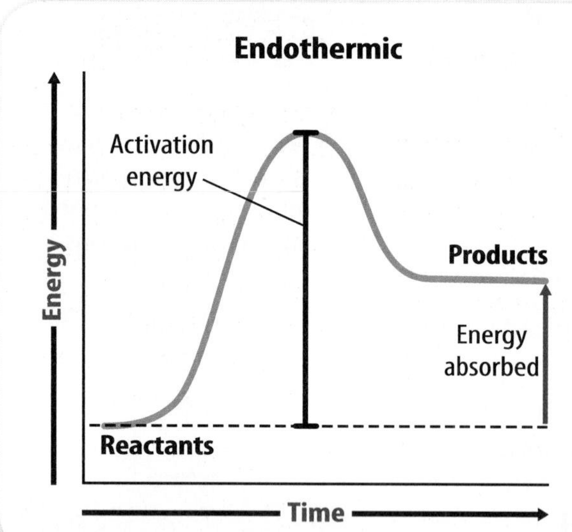

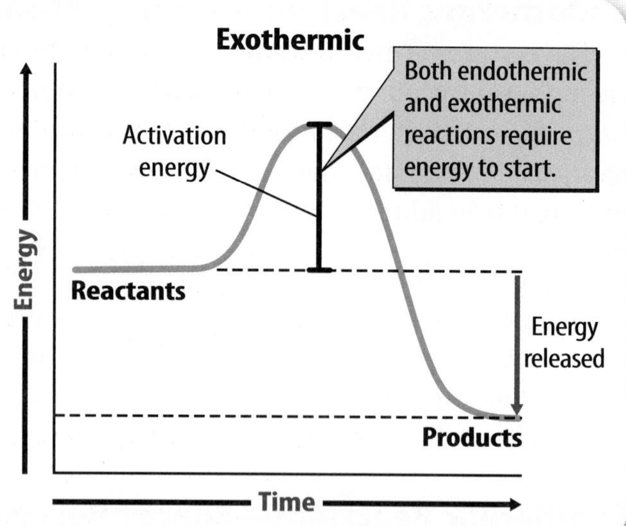

Figure 10  Both endothermic and exothermic reactions require activation energy to start the reaction.

Visual Check How can a reaction absorb energy to start but still be exothermic?

Activation Energy

You might have noticed that some chemical reactions do not start by themselves. For example, a newspaper does not burn when it comes into contact with oxygen in air. However, if a flame touches the paper, it starts to burn.

All reactions require energy to start the breaking of bonds. This energy is called activation energy. **Activation energy** *is the minimum amount of energy needed to start a chemical reaction.* Different reactions have different activation energies. Some reactions, such as the rusting of iron, have low activation energy. The energy in the surroundings is enough to start these reactions. If a reaction has high activation energy, more energy is needed to start the reaction. For example, wood requires the thermal energy of a flame to start burning. Once the reaction starts, it releases enough energy to keep the reaction going. **Figure 10** shows the role activation energy plays in endothermic and exothermic reactions.

Reaction Rates

Some chemical reactions, such as the rusting of a bicycle wheel, happen slowly. Other chemical reactions, such as the explosion of fireworks, happen in less than a second. The rate of a reaction is the speed at which it occurs. What controls how fast a chemical reaction occurs? Recall that particles must collide before they can react. Chemical reactions occur faster if particles collide more often or move faster when they collide. There are several factors that affect how often particles collide and how fast particles move.

Reading Check How do particle collisions relate to reaction rate?

Surface Area

Surface area is the amount of exposed, outer area of a solid. Increased surface area increases reaction rate because more particles on the surface of a solid come into contact with the particles of another substance. For example, if you place a piece of chalk in vinegar, the chalk reacts slowly with the acid. This is because the acid contacts only the particles on the surface of the chalk. But, if you grind the chalk into powder, more chalk particles contact the acid, and the reaction occurs faster.

Temperature

Imagine a crowded hallway. If everyone in the hallway were running, they would probably collide with each other more often and with more energy than if everyone were walking. This is also true when particles move faster. At higher temperatures, the average speed of particles is greater. This speeds reactions in two ways. First, particles collide more often. Second, collisions with more energy are more likely to break chemical bonds.

Concentration and Pressure

Think of a crowded hallway again. Because the concentration of people is higher in the crowded hallway than in an empty hallway, people probably collide more often. Similarly, increasing the concentration of one or more reactants increases collisions between particles. More collisions result in a faster reaction rate. In gases, an increase in pressure pushes gas particles closer together. When particles are closer together, more collisions occur. Factors that affect reaction rate are shown in **Figure 11.**

Math Skills 

Use Geometry

The surface area (SA) of one side of a 1-cm cube is 1 cm × 1 cm, or 1 cm^2. The cube has 6 equal sides. Its total SA is 6 × 1 cm^2, or 6 cm^2. What is the total SA of the two solids made when the cube is cut in half?

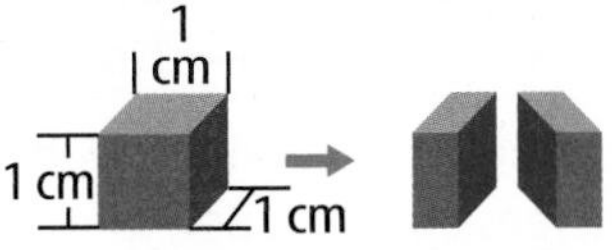

1. The new surfaces made each have an area of 1 cm × 1 cm = 1 cm^2.
2. Multiply the area by the number of new surfaces. 2 × 1 cm^2 = 2 cm^2 The total SA is 8 cm^2.

Practice

Calculate the amount of SA gained when a 2-cm cube is cut in half.

- Math Practice
- Personal Tutor

Figure 11  Several factors can affect reaction rate.

Slower Reaction Rate

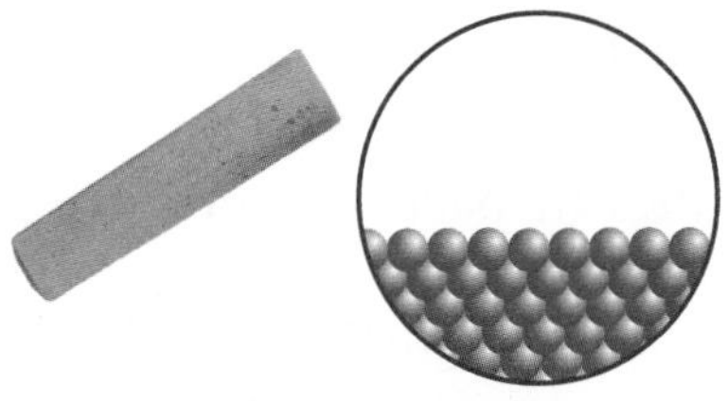

Less surface area

Lower temperature

Lower concentration

Faster Reaction Rate

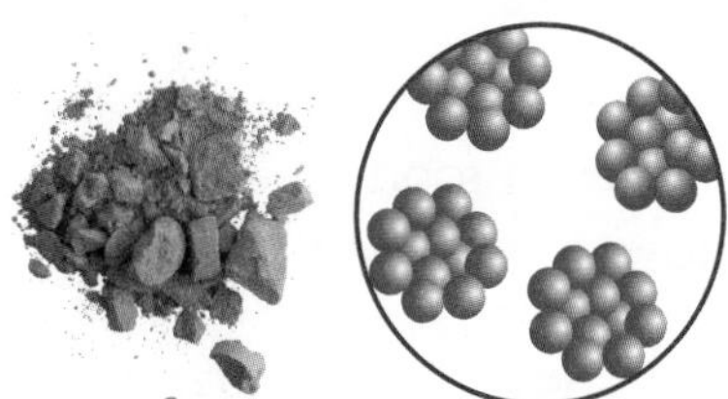

More surface area

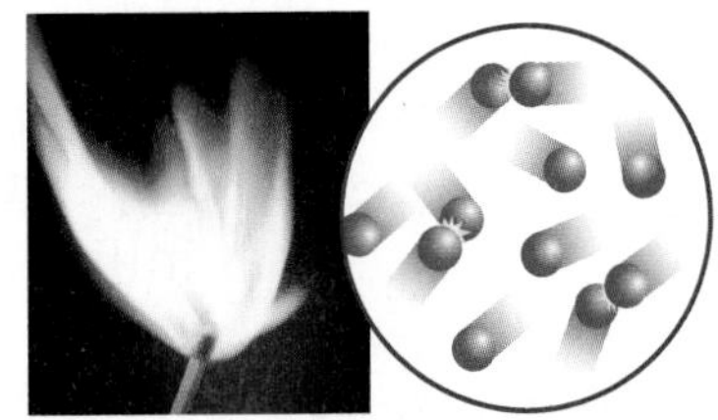

Higher temperature

Higher concentration

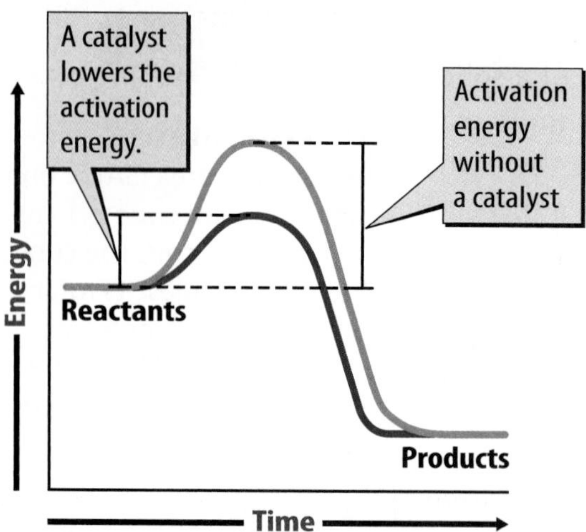

Figure 12 The blue line shows how a catalyst can increase the reaction rate.

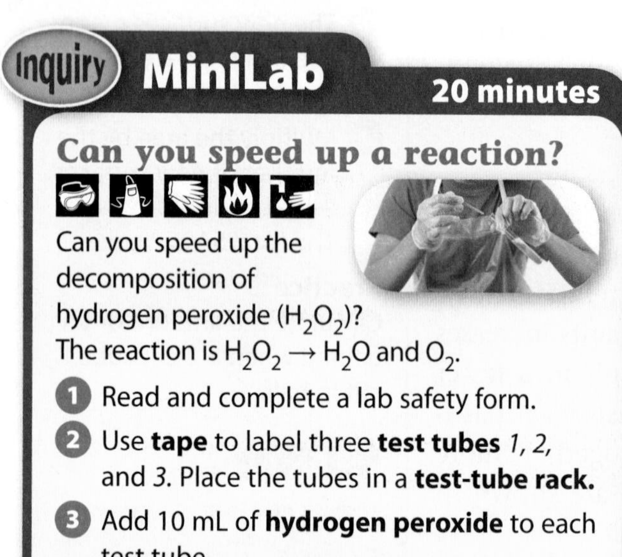

Inquiry MiniLab

20 minutes

Can you speed up a reaction?

Can you speed up the decomposition of hydrogen peroxide (H_2O_2)? The reaction is $H_2O_2 \rightarrow H_2O$ and O_2.

1. Read and complete a lab safety form.
2. Use **tape** to label three **test tubes** *1, 2,* and *3.* Place the tubes in a **test-tube rack.**
3. Add 10 mL of **hydrogen peroxide** to each test tube.
4. Observe tube 1 for changes. Add a small piece of **raw potato** to tube 2. Record observations in your Science Journal.
5. Add a pinch of **dry yeast** to tube 3. Shake the tube gently. Record observations.
6. Use **matches** to light a **wood splint,** then blow it out, leaving a glowing tip. One at a time, hold each test tube at a 45° angle and insert the glowing splint into the tube just above the liquid. Record your observations.

Analyze and Conclude

1. **Draw Conclusions** What was the chemical reaction when the potato and yeast were added?
2. **Key Concept** Why is the reaction in tube 3 faster than in the other two tubes?

Catalysts

A **catalyst** *is a substance that increases reaction rate by lowering the activation energy of a reaction.* One way catalysts speed reactions is by helping reactant particles contact each other more often. Look at **Figure 12.** Notice that the activation energy of the reaction is lower with a catalyst than it is without a catalyst. A catalyst isn't changed in a reaction, and it doesn't change the reactants or products. Also, a catalyst doesn't increase the amount of reactant used or the amount of product that is made. It only makes a given reaction happen faster. Therefore, catalysts are not considered reactants in a reaction.

You might be surprised to know that your body is filled with catalysts called enzymes. *An* **enzyme** *is a catalyst that speeds up chemical reactions in living cells.* For example, the enzyme protease (PROH tee ays) breaks the protein molecules in the food you eat into smaller molecules that can be absorbed by your intestine. Without enzymes, these reactions would occur too slowly for life to exist.

Inhibitors

Recall than an enzyme is a molecule that speeds reactions in organisms. However, some organisms, such as bacteria, are harmful to humans. Some medicines contain molecules that attach to enzymes in bacteria. This keeps the enzymes from working properly. If the enzymes in bacteria can't work, the bacteria die and can no longer infect a human. The active ingredients in these medicines are called inhibitors. *An* **inhibitor** *is a substance that slows, or even stops, a chemical reaction.* Inhibitors can slow or stop the reactions caused by enzymes.

Inhibitors are also important in the food industry. Preservatives in food are substances that inhibit, or slow down, food spoilage.

Key Concept Check What factors can affect the rate of a chemical reaction?

Lesson 3 Review

Assessment Online Quiz

Visual Summary

Endothermic

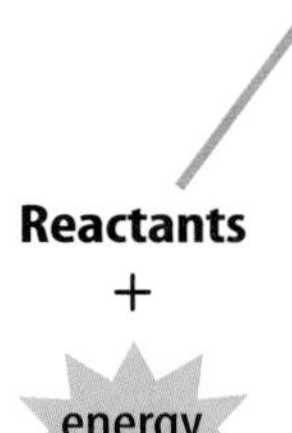

Chemical reactions that release energy are exothermic, and those that absorb energy are endothermic.

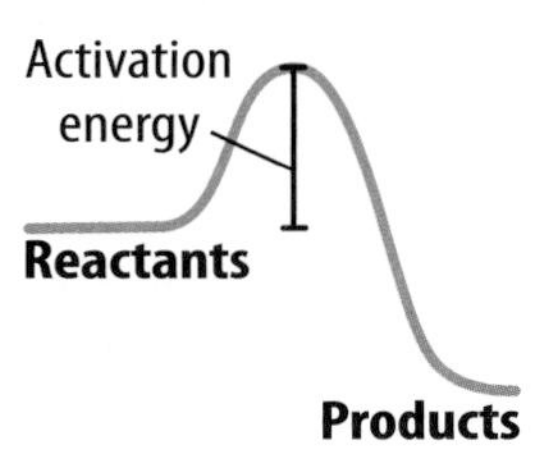

Activation energy must be added to a chemical reaction for it to proceed.

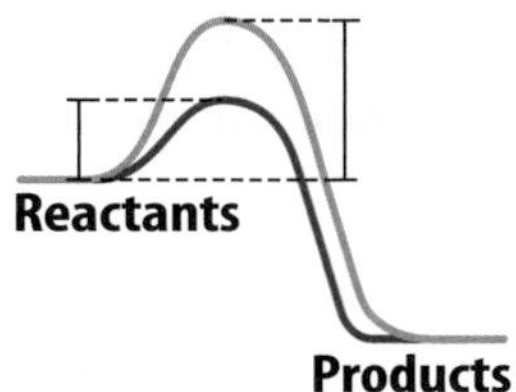

Catalysts, including enzymes, speed up chemical reactions. Inhibitors slow them down.

FOLDABLES®

Use your lesson Foldable to review the lesson. Save your Foldable for the project at the end of the chapter.

What do you think NOW?

You first read the statements below at the beginning of the chapter.

5. Reactions that release energy require energy to get started.

6. Energy can be created in a chemical reaction.

Did you change your mind about whether you agree or disagree with the statements? Rewrite any false statements to make them true.

Use Vocabulary

1 The smallest amount of energy required by reacting particles for a chemical reaction to begin is the ________.

Understand Key Concepts 

2 How does a catalyst increase reaction rate?

A. by increasing the activation energy
B. by increasing the amount of reactant
C. by increasing the contact between particles
D. by increasing the space between particles

3 **Contrast** endothermic and exothermic reactions in terms of energy.

4 **Explain** When propane burns, heat and light are produced. Where does this energy come from?

Interpret Graphics

5 **List** Copy and complete the graphic organizer to describe four ways to increase the rate of a reaction.

Critical Thinking

6 **Infer** Explain why keeping a battery in a refrigerator can extend its life.

7 **Infer** Explain why a catalyst does not increase the amount of product that can form.

Math Skills

Math Practice

8 An object measures 1 cm × 1 cm × 3 cm.

a. What is the surface area of the object?
b. What is the total surface area if you cut the object into three equal pieces?

2 class periods

Design an Experiment to Test Advertising Claims

Materials

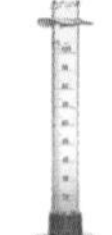

graduated cylinder

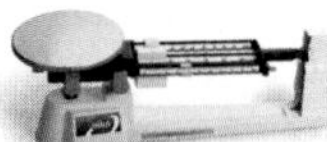

balance

droppers

baking soda

plastic spoon

Also needed: various brands of liquid and solid antacids (both regular and maximum strength), beakers, universal indicator in dropper bottle, 0.1M HCl solution, stirrers

Safety

Antacids contain compounds that react with excess acid in your stomach and prevent a condition called heartburn. Suppose you work for a laboratory that tests advertising claims about antacids. What kinds of procedures would you follow? How would you decide which antacid is the most effective?

Ask a Question

Ask a question about the claims that you would like to investigate. For example: what does *most effective* mean? What would make an antacid the strongest?

Make Observations

1. Read and complete a lab safety form.
2. Study the selection of antacids available for testing. You will use a 0.1M HCl solution to simulate stomach acid. Use the questions below to discuss with your lab partners which advertising claim you might test and how you might test it.
3. In your Science Journal, write a procedure for each variable that you will test to answer your question. Include the materials and steps you will use to test each variable. Place the steps of each procedure in order. Have your teacher approve your procedures.
4. Make a chart or table to record observations during your experiments.

Questions
Which advertising claim will I test? What question am I trying to answer?
What will be the independent and the dependent variables for each test? Recall that the independent variable is the variable that is changed. A dependent variable changes when you change the independent variable.
What variables will be held constant in each test?
How many different procedures will I use, and what equipment will I need?
How much of each antacid will I use? How many antacids will I test?
How will I use the indicator?
How many times will I do each test?
How will I record the data and observations?
What will I analyze to form a conclusion?

Form a Hypothesis

5 Write a hypothesis for each variable. Your hypothesis should identify the independent variable and state why you think changing the variable will alter the effectiveness of an antacid tablet.

Test Your Hypothesis

6 On day 2, use the available materials to perform your experiments. Accurately record all observations and data for each test.

7 Add any additional tests you think you need to answer your questions.

8 Examine the data you have collected. If the data are not conclusive, what other tests can you do to provide more information?

9 Write all your observations and measurements in your Science Journal. Use tables to record any quantitative data.

Analyze and Conclude

10 **Infer** What do you think advertisers mean when they say their product is most effective?

11 **Draw Conclusions** If you needed an antacid, which one would you use, based on the limited information provided from your experiments? Explain your reasoning.

12 **Analyze** Would breaking an antacid tablet into small pieces before using it make it more effective? Why or why not?

13 **The Big Idea** How does understanding chemical reactions enable you to analyze products and their claims?

Communicate Your Results

Combine your data with other teams. Compare the results and conclusions. Discuss the validity of advertising claims for each brand of antacid.

Research over-the-counter antacids that were once available by prescription only. Do they work in the same way as the antacids you tested? Explain.

2

Lab Tips

- Think about how you might measure the amount of acid the tablet neutralizes. Would you add the tablet to the acid or the acid to the tablet? What does the indicator show you?
- Try your tests on a small scale before using the full amounts to see how much acid you might need.
- Always get your teacher's approval before trying any new test.

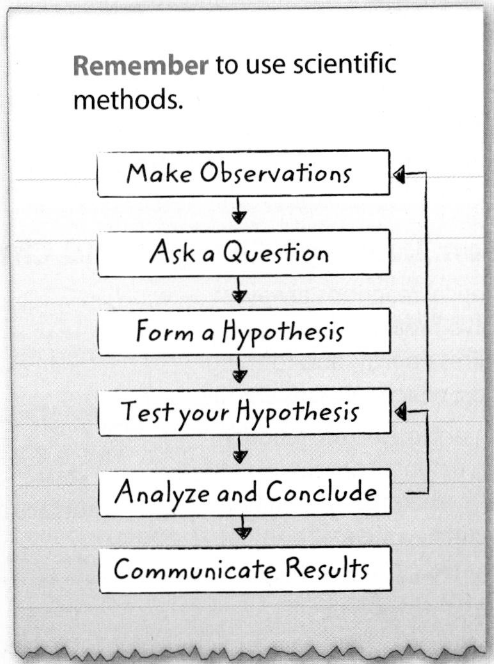

Chapter 5 Study Guide

Atoms are neither created nor destroyed in chemical reactions. Energy can be released when chemical bonds form or absorbed when chemical bonds are broken.

Key Concepts Summary

Lesson 1: Understanding Chemical Reactions

- There are several signs that a **chemical reaction** might have occurred, including a change in temperature, a release of light, a release of gas, a change in color or odor, and the formation of a solid from two liquids.
- In a chemical reaction, atoms of **reactants** rearrange and form **products.**
- The total mass of all the reactants is equal to the total mass of all the products in a reaction.

Reactants			Products		
1 Na: ●	4 H: ●●●●	Atoms are equal.	1 Na: ●	2 H: ●●	1 C: ●
1 H: ●	2 C: ●●		2 C: ●●	1 O: ●	2 O: ●●
1 C: ●	2 O: ●●		3 H: ●●●		
3 O: ●●●			2 O: ●●		

Lesson 2: Types of Chemical Reactions

- Most chemical reactions fit into one of a few main categories—synthesis, decomposition, combustion, and single- or double-replacement.
- **Synthesis** reactions create one product. **Decomposition** reactions start with one reactant. **Single-** and **double-replacement** reactions involve replacing one element or group of atoms with another element or group of atoms. **Combustion** reactions involve a reaction between one reactant and oxygen, and they release thermal energy.

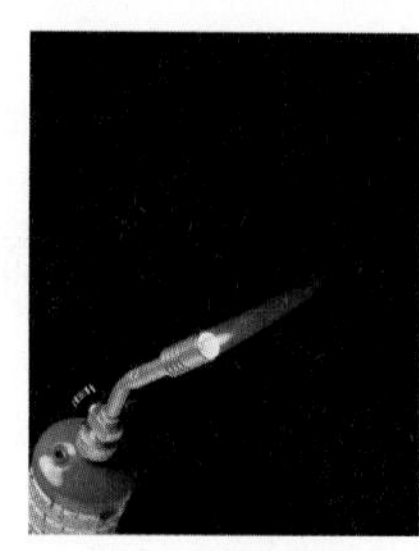

Lesson 3: Energy Changes and Chemical Reactions

- Chemical reactions always involve breaking bonds, which requires energy, and forming bonds, which releases energy.
- In an **endothermic** reaction, the reactants contain less energy than the products. In an **exothermic** reaction, the reactants contain more energy than the products.

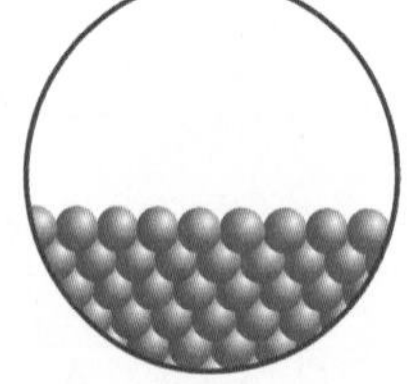

Less surface area

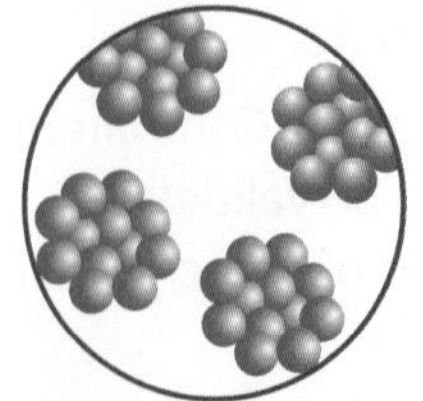

More surface area

- The rate of a chemical reaction can be increased by increasing the surface area, the temperature, or the concentration of the reactants or by adding a **catalyst.**

Vocabulary

chemical reaction p. 151
chemical equation p. 154
reactant p. 155
product p. 155
law of conservation of mass p. 156
coefficient p. 158

synthesis p. 163
decomposition p. 163
single replacement p. 164
double replacement p. 164
combustion p. 164

endothermic p. 169
exothermic p. 169
activation energy p. 170
catalyst p. 172
enzyme p. 172
inhibitor p. 172

Review

- Personal Tutor
- Vocabulary eGames
- Vocabulary eFlashcards

FOLDABLES® Chapter Project

Assemble your lesson Foldables as shown to make a Chapter Project. Use the project to review what you have learned in this chapter.

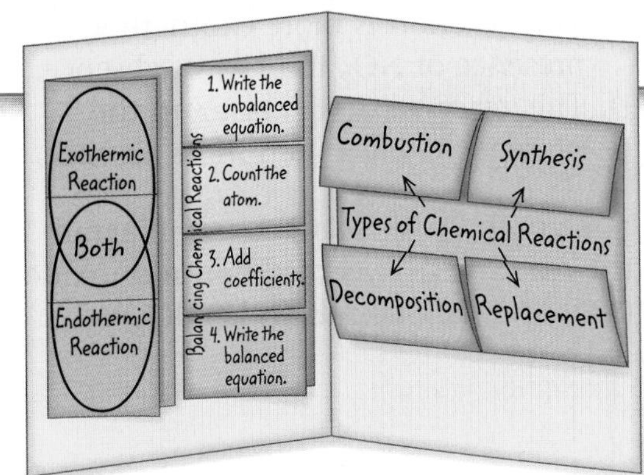

Use Vocabulary

1. When water forms from hydrogen and oxygen, water is the ________.
2. A(n) ________ uses symbols instead of words to describe a chemical reaction.
3. In a(n) ________ reaction, one element replaces another element in a compound.
4. When Na_2CO_3 is heated, it breaks down into CO_2 and Na_2O in a(n) ________ reaction.
5. The chemical reactions that keep your body warm are ________ reactions.
6. Even exothermic reactions require ________ to start.

Link Vocabulary and Key Concepts

Concepts in Motion Interactive Concept Map

Copy this concept map, and then use vocabulary terms from the previous page and other terms from the chapter to complete the concept map.

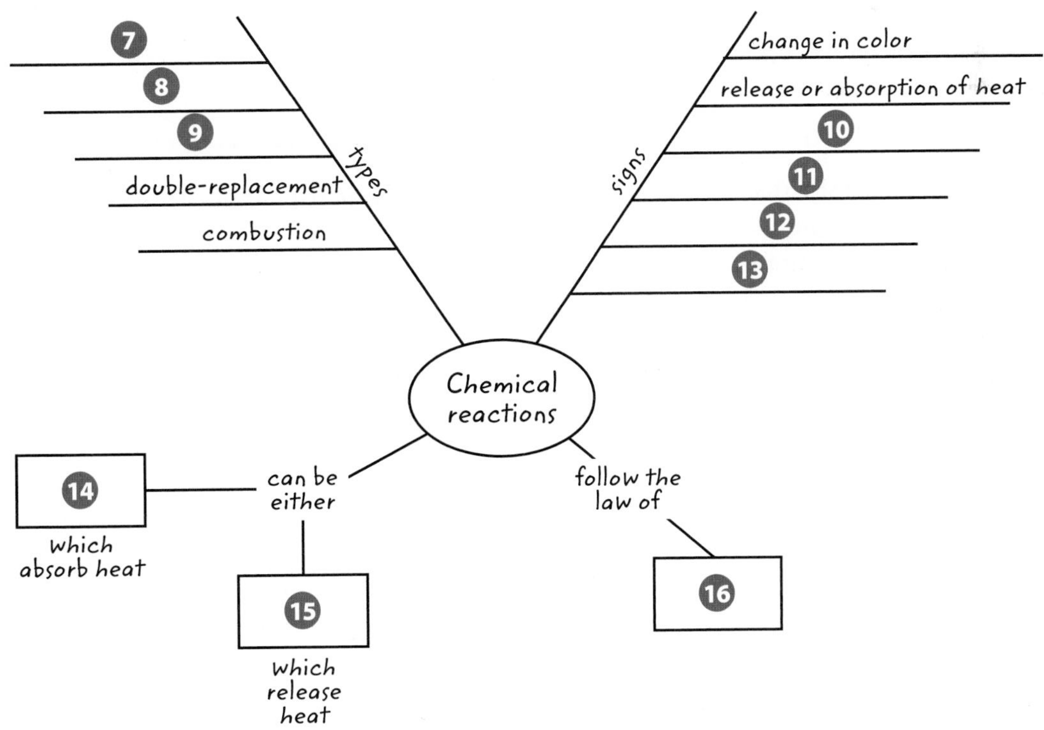

Chapter 5 Review

Understand Key Concepts

1. How many carbon atoms react in this equation?

$$2C_4H_{10} + 13O_2 \rightarrow 8CO_2 + 10H_2O$$

A. 2
B. 4
C. 6
D. 8

2. The chemical equation below is unbalanced.

$$Zn + HCl \rightarrow ZnCl_2 + H_2$$

Which is the correct balanced chemical equation?

A. $Zn + H_2Cl_2 \rightarrow ZnCl_2 + H_2$
B. $Zn + HCl \rightarrow ZnCl + H$
C. $2Zn + 2HCl \rightarrow ZnCl_2 + H_2$
D. $Zn + 2HCl \rightarrow ZnCl_2 + H_2$

3. When iron combines with oxygen gas and forms rust, the total mass of the products

A. depends on the reaction conditions.
B. is less than the mass of the reactants.
C. is the same as the mass of the reactants.
D. is greater than the mass of the reactants.

4. Potassium nitrate forms potassium oxide, nitrogen, and oxygen in certain fireworks.

$$4KNO_3 \rightarrow 2K_2O + 2N_2 + 5O_2$$

This reaction is classified as a

A. combustion reaction.
B. decomposition reaction.
C. single-replacement reaction.
D. synthesis reaction.

5. Which type of reaction is the reverse of a decomposition reaction?

A. combustion
B. synthesis
C. double-replacement
D. single-replacement

6. The compound NO_2 can act as a catalyst in the reaction that converts ozone (O_3) to oxygen (O_2) in the upper atmosphere. Which statement is true?

A. More oxygen is created when NO_2 is present.
B. NO_2 is a reactant in the chemical reaction that converts O_3 to O_2.
C. This reaction is more exothermic in the presence of NO_2 than in its absence.
D. This reaction occurs faster in the presence of NO_2 than in its absence.

7. The graph below is an energy diagram for the reaction between carbon monoxide (CO) and nitrogen dioxide (NO_2).

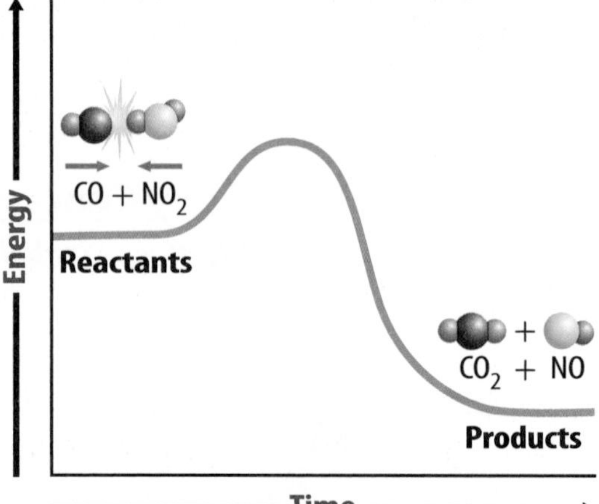

Which is true about this reaction?

A. More energy is required to break reactant bonds than is released when product bonds form.
B. Less energy is required to break reactant bonds than is released when product bonds form.
C. The bonds of the reactants do not require energy to break because the reaction releases energy.
D. The bonds of the reactants require energy to break, and therefore the reaction absorbs energy.

Assessment

Online Test Practice

Critical Thinking

8 **Predict** The diagram below shows two reactions—one with a catalyst (blue) and one without a catalyst (orange).

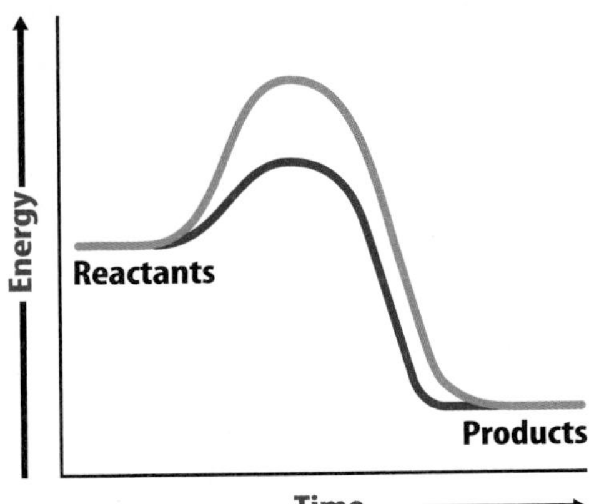

How would the blue line change if an inhibitor were used instead of a catalyst?

9 **Analyze** A student observed a chemical reaction and collected the following data:

Observations before the reaction	A white powder was added to a clear liquid.
Observations during the reaction	The reactants bubbled rapidly in the open beaker.
Mass of reactants	4.2 g
Mass of products	4.0 g

The student concludes that mass was not conserved in the reaction. Explain why this is not a valid conclusion. What might explain the difference in mass?

10 **Explain Observations** How did the discovery of atoms explain the observation that the mass of the products always equals the mass of the reactants in a reaction?

Writing in Science

11 **Write instructions** that explain the steps in balancing a chemical equation. Use the following equation as an example.

$$MnO_2 + HCl \rightarrow MnCl_2 + H_2O + Cl_2$$

REVIEW THE BIG IDEA

12 Explain how atoms and energy are conserved in a chemical reaction.

13 When a car air bag inflates, sodium azide (NaN_3) decomposes and produces nitrogen gas (N_2) and another product. What element does the other product contain? How do you know?

Math Skills

Math Practice

Use Geometry

14 What is the surface area of the cube shown below? What would the total surface area be if you cut the cube into 27 equal cubes?

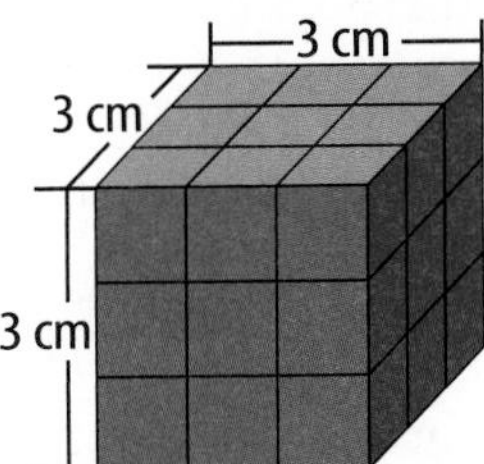

15 Suppose you have ten cubes that measure 2 cm on each side.

a. What is the total surface area of the cubes?

b. What would the surface area be if you glued the cubes together to make one object that is two cubes wide, one cube high, and five cubes long? Hint: draw a picture of the final cube and label the length of each side.

Standardized Test Practice

Record your answers on the answer sheet provided by your teacher or on a sheet of paper.

Multiple Choice

1 How can you verify that a chemical reaction has occurred?

A Check the temperature of the starting and ending substances.

B Compare the chemical properties of the starting substances and ending substances.

C Look for a change in state.

D Look for bubbling of the starting substances.

Use the figure below to answer questions 2 and 3.

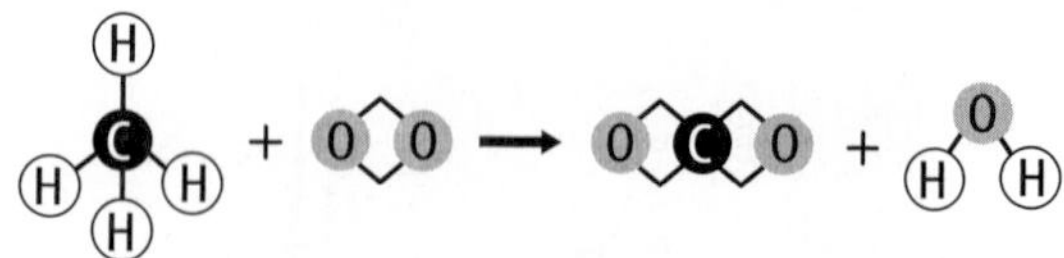

2 The figure above shows models of molecules in a chemical reactions. Which substances are reactants in this reaction?

A CH_4 and CO_2

B CH_4 and O_2

C CO_2 and H_2O

D O_2 and H_2O

3 Which equation shows that atoms are conserved in the reaction?

A $CH_4 + O_2 \longrightarrow CO_2 + H_2O$

B $CH_4 + O_2 \longrightarrow CO_2 + 2H_2O$

C $CH_4 + 2O_2 \longrightarrow CO_2 + 2H_2O$

D $2CH_4 + O_2 \longrightarrow 2CO_2 + H_2O$

4 Which occurs before new bonds can form during a chemical reaction?

A The atoms in the original substances are destroyed.

B The bonds between atoms in the original substances are broken.

C The atoms in the original substances are no longer moving.

D The bonds between atoms in the original substances get stronger.

Use the figure below to answer question 5.

5 The figure above uses shapes to represent a chemical reaction. What kind of chemical reaction does the figure represent?

A decomposition

B double-replacement

C single-replacement

D synthesis

6 Which type of chemical reaction has only one reactant?

A decomposition

B double-replacement

C single-replacement

D synthesis

7 Which element is always a reactant in a combustion reaction?

A carbon

B hydrogen

C nitrogen

D oxygen

Use the figure below to answer question 8.

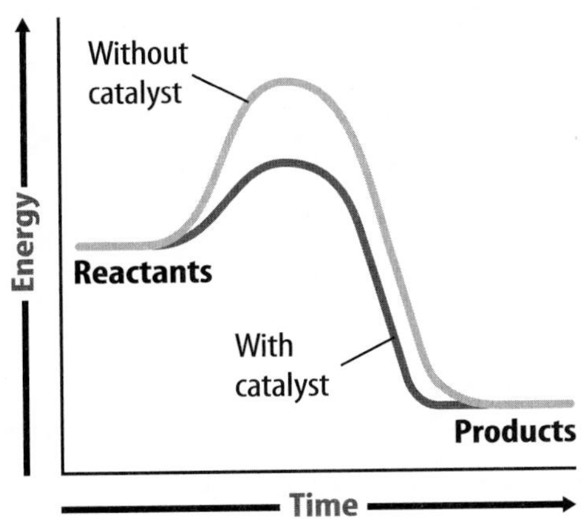

8 The figure above shows changes in energy during a reaction. The lighter line shows the reaction without a catalyst. The darker line shows the reaction with a catalyst. Which is true about these two reactions?

- **A** The reaction with the catalyst is more exothermic than the reaction without the catalyst.
- **B** The reaction with the catalyst requires less activation energy than the reaction without the catalyst.
- **C** The reaction with the catalyst requires more reactants than the reaction without the catalyst.
- **D** The reaction with the catalyst takes more time than the reaction without the catalyst.

Constructed Response

9 Explain the role of energy in chemical reactions.

10 How does a balanced chemical equation illustrate the law of conservation of mass?

11 Many of the reactions that occur when something decays are decomposition reactions. What clues show that this type of reaction is taking place? What happens during a decomposition reaction?

Use the figure below to answer questions 12 and 13.

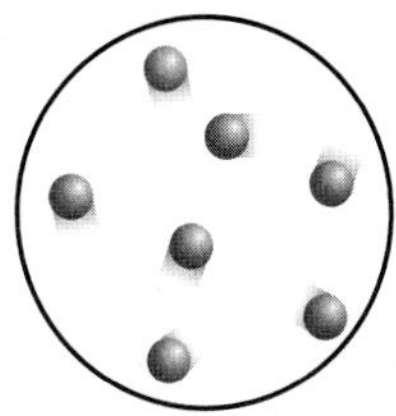

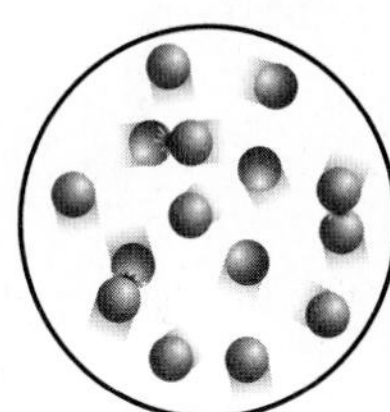

12 Compare the two gas samples represented in the figure in terms of pressure and concentration.

13 Describe the conditions that would increase the rate of a reaction.

NEED EXTRA HELP?													
If You Missed Question...	1	2	3	4	5	6	7	8	9	10	11	12	13
Go to Lesson...	1	1	1	1	2	2	2	3	3	1	2	3	3

Unit 3

Weather and Climate

1441
Prince Munjong of Korea invents the first rain gauge to gather and measure the amount of liquid precipitation over a period of time.

1450
The first anemometer, a tool to measure wind speed, is developed by Leone Battista Alberti.

1643
Italian physicist Evangelista Torricelli invents the barometer to measure pressure in the air. This tool improves meteorology, which relied on simple sky observations.

1714
German physicist Daniel Fahrenheit develops the mercury thermometer, making it possible to measure temperature.

1752
Swedish astronomer Andres Celsius proposes a centigrade temperature scale where 0° is the freezing point of water and 100° is the boiling point of water.

1800 1900 2000

1806
Francis Beaufort creates a system for naming wind speeds and aptly names it the Beaufort Wind Force Scale. This scale is used mainly to classify sea conditions.

1960
TIROS 1, the world's first weather satellite, is sent into space equipped with a TV camera.

1964
The U.S. National Severe Storms Laboratory begins experimenting with the use of Doppler radar for weather-monitoring purposes.

2006
Meteorologists hold 8,800 jobs in the United States alone. These scientists work in government and private agencies, in research services, on radio and television stations, and in education.

Inquiry
Visit ConnectED for this unit's **STEM** activity.

Lesson 1

Describing Earth's Atmosphere

Reading Guide

Key Concepts
ESSENTIAL QUESTIONS

- How did Earth's atmosphere form?
- What is Earth's atmosphere made of?
- What are the layers of the atmosphere?
- How do air pressure and temperature change as altitude increases?

Vocabulary

atmosphere p. 189
water vapor p. 190
troposphere p. 192
stratosphere p. 192
ozone layer p. 192
ionosphere p. 193

Multilingual eGlossary

Academic Standards for Science

8.2.4 Describe the physical and chemical composition of the atmosphere at different elevations.

Also covers: 8.NS.2, 8.NS.6, 8.NS.7, 8.NS.9, 8.NS.10

Inquiry Why is the atmosphere important?

What would Earth be like without its atmosphere? Earth's surface would be scarred with craters created from the impact of meteorites. Earth would experience extreme daytime-to-nighttime temperature changes. How would changes in the atmosphere affect life? What effect would atmospheric changes have on weather and climate?

Launch Lab

20 minutes

Where does air apply pressure?

With the exception of Mercury, most planets in the solar system have some type of atmosphere. However, Earth's atmosphere provides what the atmospheres of other planets cannot: oxygen and water. Oxygen, water vapor, and other gases make up the gaseous mixture in the atmosphere called air. In this activity, you will explore air's effect on objects on Earth's surface.

1. Read and complete a lab safety form.
2. Add **water** to a **cup** until it is two-thirds full.
3. Place a large **index card** over the opening of the cup so that it is completely covered.
4. Hold the cup over a tub or a large bowl.
5. Place one hand on the index card to hold it in place as you quickly turn the cup upside down. Remove your hand.

Think About This

1. What happened when you turned the cup over?
2. How did air play a part in your observation?
3. **Key Concept** How do you think these results might differ if you repeated the activity in a vacuum?

Importance of Earth's Atmosphere

The photo on the previous page shows Earth's atmosphere as seen from space. How would you describe the atmosphere? *The* **atmosphere** (AT muh sfihr) *is a thin layer of gases surrounding Earth.* Earth's atmosphere is hundreds of kilometers high. However, when compared to Earth's size, it is about as thick as an apple's skin is to an apple.

The atmosphere contains the oxygen, carbon dioxide, and water necessary for life on Earth. Earth's atmosphere also acts like insulation on a house. It helps keep temperatures on Earth within a range in which living organisms can survive. Without it, daytime temperatures would be extremely high and nighttime temperatures would be extremely low.

The atmosphere helps protect living organisms from some of the Sun's harmful rays. It also helps protect Earth's surface from being struck by meteors. Most meteors that fall toward Earth burn up before reaching Earth's surface. Friction with the atmosphere causes it to burn. Only the very largest meteors strike Earth.

Reading Check Why is Earth's atmosphere important to life on Earth?

WORD ORIGIN

atmosphere
from Greek *atmos*, means "vapor"; and Latin *sphaera*, means "sphere"

Origins of Earth's Atmosphere

Most scientists agree that when Earth formed, it was a ball of molten rock. As Earth slowly cooled, its outer surface hardened. Erupting volcanoes emitted hot gases from Earth's interior. These gases surrounded Earth forming an atmosphere.

Ancient Earth's atmosphere was thought to be water vapor with a little carbon dioxide (CO_2) and nitrogen. **Water vapor** *is water in its gaseous form.* This ancient atmosphere did not have enough oxygen to support life as we know it. As Earth and its atmosphere cooled, the water vapor condensed into **liquid.** Rain fell and then evaporated from Earth's surface repeatedly for thousands of years. Eventually, water accumulated on Earth's surface, forming oceans. Most of the original CO_2 that dissolved in rain is in rocks on the ocean floor. Today the atmosphere has more nitrogen than CO_2.

REVIEW VOCABULARY
liquid
matter with a definite volume but no definite shape that can flow from one place to another

Earth's first organisms could undergo photosynthesis, which changed the atmosphere. Recall that photosynthesis uses light energy to produce sugar and oxygen from carbon dioxide and water. The organisms removed CO_2 from the atmosphere and released oxygen into it. Eventually the levels of CO_2 and oxygen supported the development of other organisms.

Key Concept Check How did Earth's present atmosphere form?

Inquiry MiniLab

20 minutes

Why does the furniture get dusty?

Have you ever noticed that furniture gets dusty? The atmosphere is one source for dirt and dust particles. Where can you find dust in your classroom?

1. Read and complete a lab safety form.
2. Choose a place in your classroom to collect a sample of dust.
3. Using a **duster,** collect dust from about a 50-cm^2 area.
4. Examine the duster with a **magnifying lens.** Observe any dust particles. Some might be so small that they only make the duster look gray.
5. Record your observations in your Science Journal.
6. Compare your findings with those of other members of your class.

Analyze and Conclude

1. **Analyze** how the area surrounding your collection site might have influenced how much dust you observed on the duster.
2. **Infer** the source of the dust.
3. **Key Concept** Other than gases and water droplets, predict what Earth's atmosphere might contain.

Figure 1 Oxygen and nitrogen make up most of the atmosphere, with the other gases making up only 1 percent. ▼

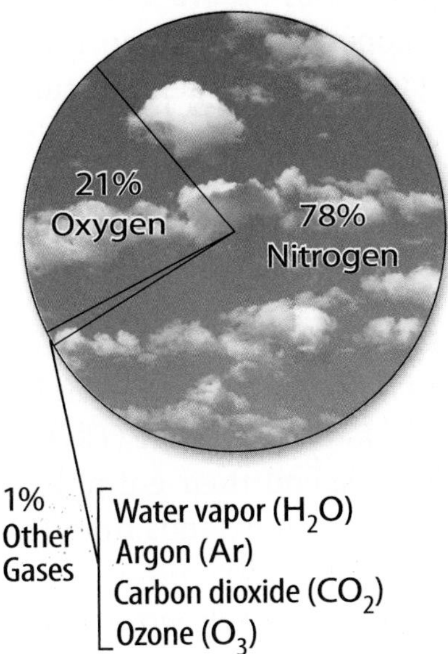

1% Other Gases
- Water vapor (H_2O)
- Argon (Ar)
- Carbon dioxide (CO_2)
- Ozone (O_3)

Visual Check What percent of the atmosphere is made up of oxygen and nitrogen?

▲ **Figure 2** One way solid particles enter the atmosphere is from volcanic eruptions.

Composition of the Atmosphere

Today's atmosphere is mostly made up of invisible gases, including nitrogen, oxygen, and carbon dioxide. Some solid and liquid particles, such as ash from volcanic eruptions and water droplets, are also present.

Gases in the Atmosphere

Study **Figure 1**. Which gas is the most abundant in Earth's atmosphere? Nitrogen makes up about 78 percent of Earth's atmosphere. About 21 percent of Earth's atmosphere is oxygen. Other gases, including argon, carbon dioxide, and water vapor, make up the remaining 1 percent of the atmosphere.

The amounts of water vapor, carbon dioxide, and ozone vary. The concentration of water vapor in the atmosphere ranges from 0 to 4 percent. Carbon dioxide is 0.038 percent of the atmosphere. A small amount of ozone is at high altitudes. Ozone also occurs near Earth's surface in urban areas.

Solids and Liquids in the Atmosphere

Tiny solid particles are also in Earth's atmosphere. Many of these, such as pollen, dust, and salt, can enter the atmosphere through natural processes. **Figure 2** shows another natural source of particles in the atmosphere—ash from volcanic eruptions. Some solid particles enter the atmosphere because of human activities, such as driving vehicles that exhaust soot.

The most common liquid particles in the atmosphere are water droplets. Although microscopic in size, water droplets are visible when they form clouds. Other atmospheric liquids include acids that result when volcanoes erupt and fossil fuels are burned. Sulfur dioxide and nitrous oxide combine with water vapor in the air and form the acids.

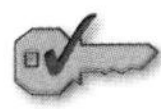

Key Concept Check What is Earth's atmosphere made of?

Layers of Atmosphere

Concepts in Motion Animation

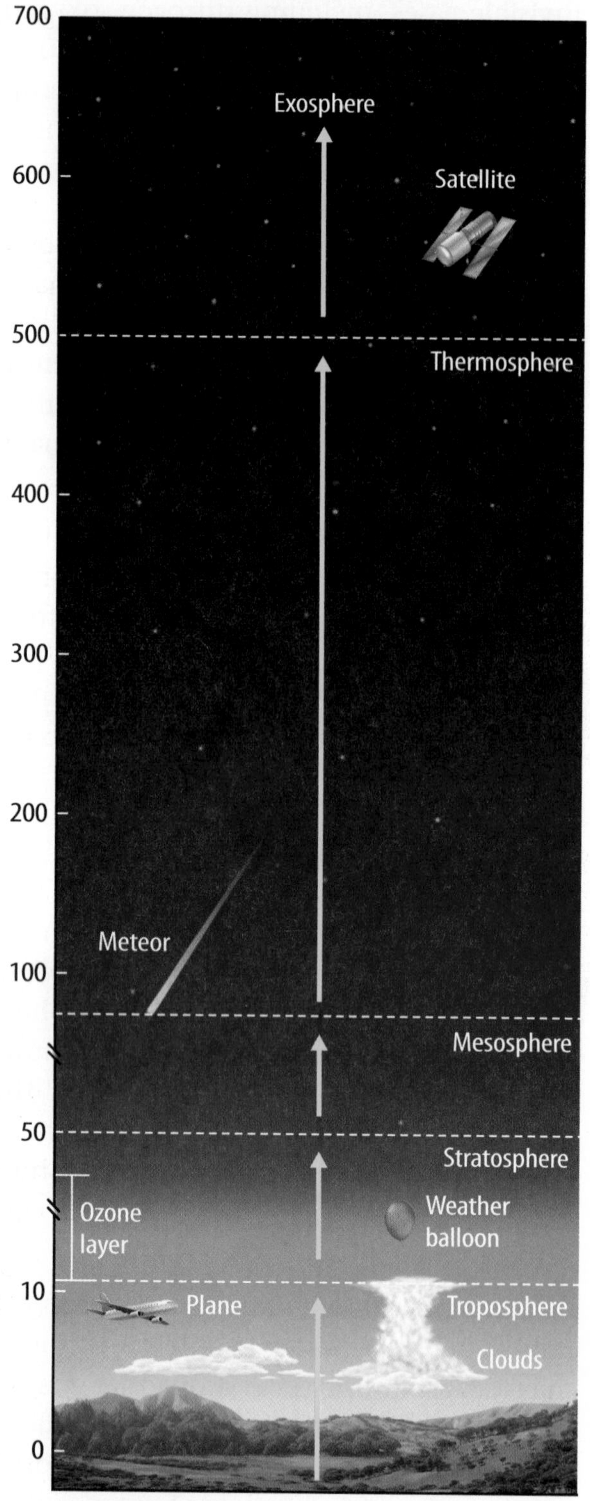

(km)
700
Exosphere
600
Satellite
500
Thermosphere
400
300
200
Meteor
100
Mesosphere
50
Stratosphere
Ozone layer
Weather balloon
10
Plane
Troposphere
Clouds
0

Figure 3 Scientists divide Earth's atmosphere into different layers.

Visual Check In which layer of the atmosphere do planes fly?

Layers of the Atmosphere

The atmosphere has several different layers, as shown in **Figure 3.** Each layer has unique properties, including the composition of gases and how temperature changes with altitude. Notice that the scale between 0–100 km in **Figure 3** is not the same as the scale from 100–700 km. This is so all the layers can be shown in one image.

Troposphere

The atmospheric layer closest to Earth's surface is called the **troposphere** (TRO puh sfihr). Most people spend their entire lives within the troposphere. It extends from Earth's surface to altitudes between 8–15 km. Its name comes from the Greek word *tropos,* which means "change." The temperature in the troposphere decreases as you move away from Earth. The warmest part of the troposphere is near Earth's surface. This is because most sunlight passes through the atmosphere and warms Earth's surface. The warmth is radiated to the troposphere, causing weather.

 **Reading Check** Describe the troposphere.

Stratosphere

The atmospheric layer directly above the troposphere is the **stratosphere** (STRA tuh sfihr). The stratosphere extends from about 15 km to about 50 km above Earth's surface. The lower half of the stratosphere contains the greatest amount of ozone gas. *The area of the stratosphere with a high concentration of ozone is referred to as the* **ozone layer.** The presence of the ozone layer causes increasing stratospheric temperatures with increasing altitude.

An ozone (O_3) molecule differs from an oxygen (O_2) molecule. Ozone has three oxygen atoms instead of two. This difference is important because ozone absorbs the Sun's ultraviolet rays more effectively than oxygen does. Ozone protects Earth from ultraviolet rays that can kill plants, animals, and other organisms and cause skin cancer in humans.

Mesosphere and Thermosphere

As shown in **Figure 3,** the mesosphere extends from the stratosphere to about 85 km above Earth. The thermosphere can extend from the mesopshere to more than 500 km above Earth. Combined, these layers are much broader than the troposphere and the stratosphere, yet only 1 percent of the atmosphere's gas molecules are found in the mesosphere and the thermosphere. Most meteors burn up in these layers instead of striking Earth.

The Ionosphere *The* **ionosphere** *is a region within the mesosphere and thermosphere that contains ions.* Between 60 km and 500 km above Earth's surface, the ionosphere's ions reflect AM radio waves transmitted at ground level. After sunset when ions recombine, this reflection increases. **Figure 4** shows how AM radio waves can travel long distances, especially at night, by bouncing off Earth and the ionosphere.

FOLDABLES®

Make a vertical four-tab book using the titles shown. Use it to record similarities and differences among these four layers of the atmosphere. Fold the top half over the bottom and label the outside *Layers of the Atmosphere.*

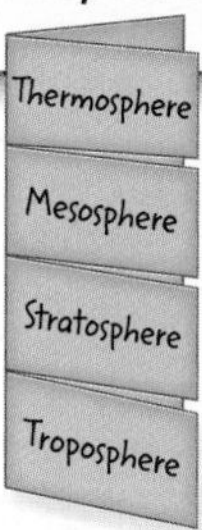

Radio Waves and the Ionosphere

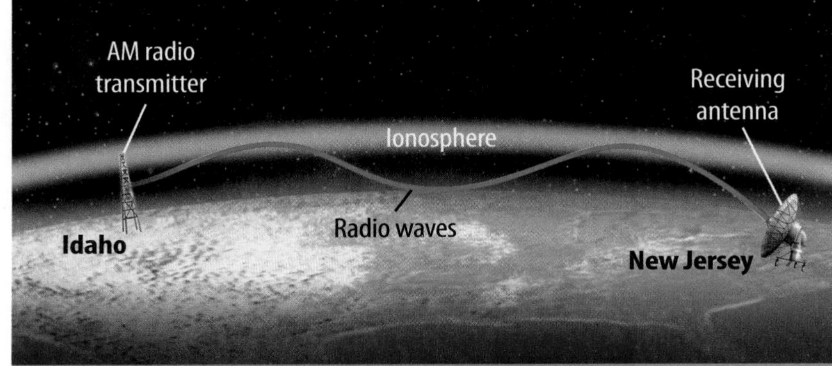

Figure 4 Radio waves can travel long distances in the atmosphere.

Auroras The ionosphere is where stunning displays of colored lights called auroras occur, as shown in **Figure 5.** Auroras are most frequent in the spring and fall, but are best seen when the winter skies are dark. Auroras occur when ions from the Sun strike air molecules, causing them to emit vivid colors of light. People who live in the higher latitudes, nearer to the North Pole and the South Pole, are most likely to see auroras.

▲ **Figure 5** Auroras occur in the ionosphere.

Exosphere

The exosphere is the atmospheric layer farthest from Earth's surface. Here, pressure and density are so low that individual gas molecules rarely strike one another. The molecules move at incredibly fast speeds after absorbing the Sun's radiation. Since there is no definite edge to the atmosphere, molecules can escape the pull of gravity and travel into space.

 **Key Concept Check** What are the layers of the atmosphere?

Figure 6 Molecules in the air are closer together near Earth's surface than they are at higher altitudes. ▼

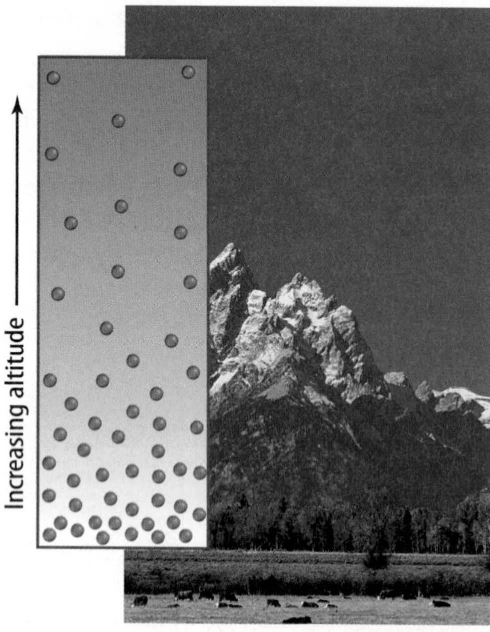

Air Pressure and Altitude

Gravity is the force that pulls all objects toward Earth. When you stand on a scale, you can read your weight. This is because gravity is pulling you toward Earth. Gravity also pulls the atmosphere toward Earth. The pressure that a column of air exerts on anything below it is called air pressure. Gravity's pull on air increases its density. At higher altitudes, the air is less dense. **Figure 6** shows that air pressure is greatest near Earth's surface because the air molecules are closer together. This dense air exerts more force than the less dense air near the top of the atmosphere. Mountain climbers sometimes carry oxygen tanks at high altitudes because fewer oxygen molecules are in the air at high altitudes.

Reading Check How does air pressure change as altitude increases?

Figure 7 Temperature differences occur within the layers of the atmosphere. ▼

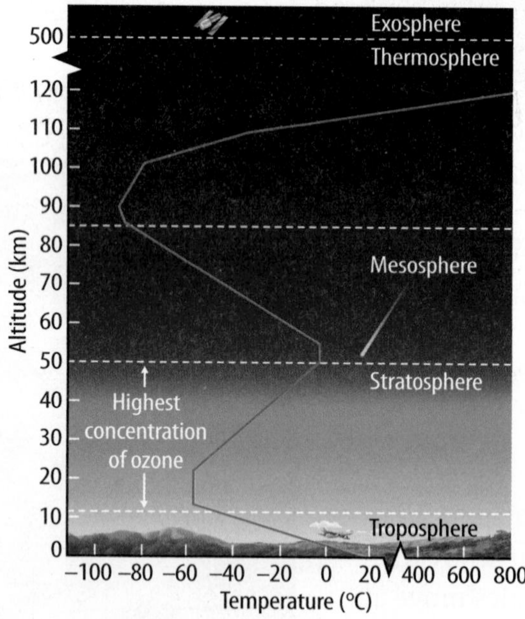

Visual Check Which temperature pattern is most like the troposphere's?

Temperature and Altitude

Figure 7 shows how temperature changes with altitude in the different layers of the atmosphere. If you have ever been hiking in the mountains, you have experienced the temperature cooling as you hike to higher elevations. In the troposphere, temperature decreases as altitude increases. Notice that the opposite effect occurs in the stratosphere. As altitude increases, temperature increases. This is because of the high concentration of ozone in the stratosphere. Ozone absorbs energy from sunlight, which increases the temperature in the stratosphere.

In the mesosphere, as altitude increases, temperature again decreases. In the thermosphere and exosphere, temperatures increase as altitude increases. These layers receive large amounts of energy from the Sun. This energy is spread across a small number of particles, creating high temperatures.

Key Concept Check How does temperature change as altitude increases?

Lesson 1 Review

Assessment Online Quiz

Inquiry Virtual Lab

Visual Summary

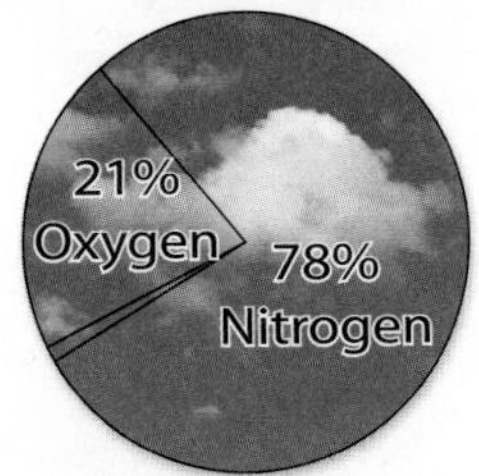

Earth's atmosphere consists of gases that make life possible.

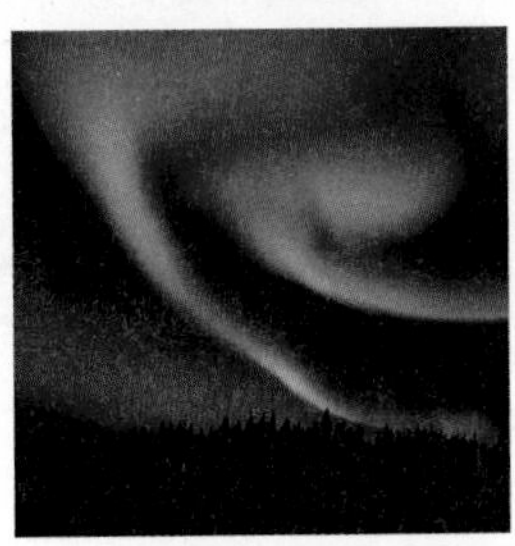

Layers of the atmosphere include the troposphere, the stratosphere, the mesosphere, the thermosphere, and the exosphere.

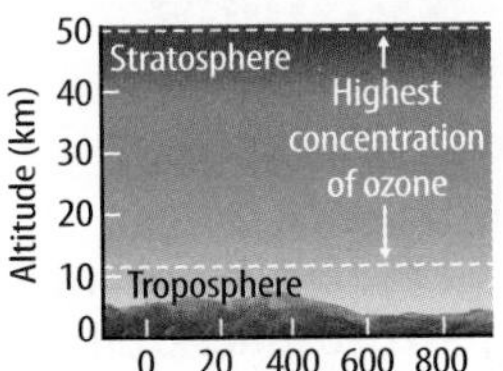

The ozone layer is the area in the stratosphere with a high concentration of ozone.

FOLDABLES®

Use your lesson Foldable to review the lesson. Save your Foldable for the project at the end of the chapter.

What do you think NOW?

You first read the statements below at the beginning of the chapter.

1. Air is empty space.
2. Earth's atmosphere is important to living organisms.

Did you change your mind about whether you agree or disagree with the statements? Rewrite any false statements to make them true.

Use Vocabulary

1. The ________ is a thin layer of gases surrounding Earth.
2. The area of the stratosphere with a high concentration of ozone is referred to as the ________.
3. **Define** Using your own words, define *water vapor.*

Understand Key Concepts 

4. Which atmospheric layer is closest to Earth's surface?
   - **A.** mesosphere
   - **B.** stratosphere
   - **C.** thermosphere
   - **D.** troposphere
5. **Identify** the two atmospheric layers in which temperature decreases as altitude increases.

Interpret Graphics

6. **Contrast** Copy and fill in the graphic organizer below to contrast the composition of gases in Earth's early atmosphere and its present-day atmosphere.

Atmosphere	Gases
Early	
Present-day	

7. **Determine** the relationship between air pressure and the water in the glass in the photo below.

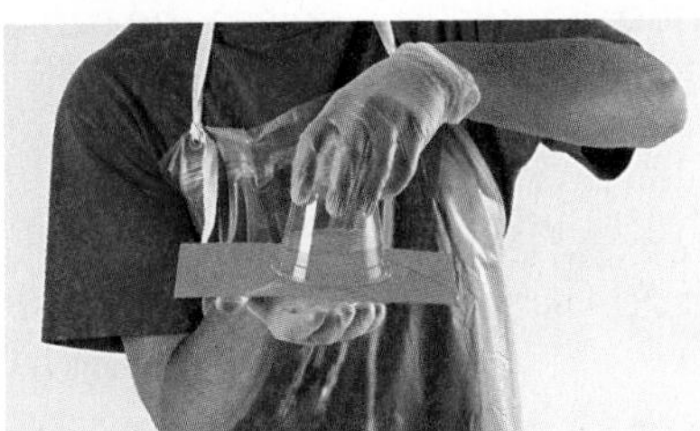

Critical Thinking

8. **Explain** three ways the atmosphere is important to living things.

CAREERS in SCIENCE

AMERICAN MUSEUM OF NATURAL HISTORY

A Crack in Earth's Shield

Scientists discover an enormous hole in the ozone layer that protects Earth.

The ozone layer is like sunscreen, protecting Earth from the Sun's ultraviolet rays. But not all of Earth is covered. Every spring since 1985, scientists have been monitoring a growing hole in the ozone layer above Antarctica.

This surprising discovery was the outcome of years of research from Earth and space. The first measurements of polar ozone levels began in the 1950s, when a team of British scientists began launching weather balloons in Antarctica. In the 1970s, NASA started using satellites to measure the ozone layer from space. Then, in 1985 a close examination of the British team's records indicated a large drop in ozone levels during the Antarctic spring. The levels were so low that the scientists checked and rechecked their instruments before they reported their findings. NASA scientists quickly confirmed the discovery—an enormous hole in the ozone layer over the entire continent of Antarctica. They reported that the hole might have originated as far back as 1976.

Human-made compounds found mostly in chemicals called chlorofluorocarbons, or CFCs, are destroying the ozone layer. During cold winters, molecules released from these compounds are transformed into new compounds by chemical reactions on ice crystals that form in the ozone layer over Antarctica. In the spring, warming by the Sun breaks down the new compounds and releases chlorine and bromine. These chemicals break apart ozone molecules, slowly destroying the ozone layer.

In 1987, CFCs were banned in many countries around the world. Since then, the loss of ozone has slowed and possibly reversed, but a full recovery will take a long time. One reason is that CFCs stay in the atmosphere for more than 40 years. Still, scientists predict the hole in the ozone layer will eventually mend.

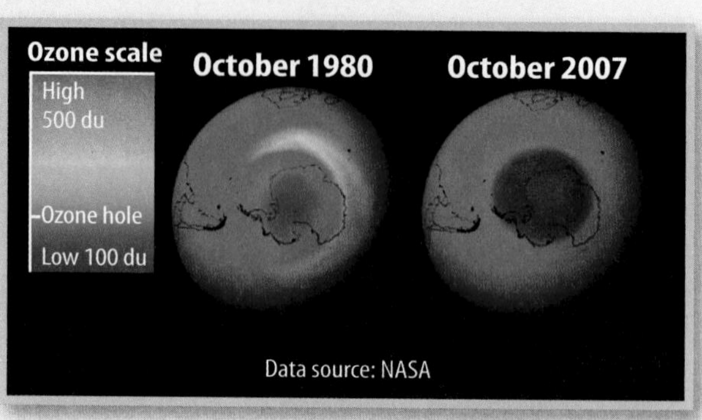

▲ **A hole in the ozone has developed over Antarctica.**

Global Warming and the Ozone

Drew Shindell is a NASA scientist investigating the connection between the ozone layer in the stratosphere and the buildup of greenhouse gases throughout the atmosphere. Surprisingly, while these gases warm the troposphere, they are actually causing temperatures in the stratosphere to become cooler. As the stratosphere cools above Antarctica, more clouds with ice crystals form—a key step in the process of ozone destruction. While the buildup of greenhouse gases in the atmosphere may slow the recovery, Shindell still thinks that eventually the ozone layer will heal itself.

It's Your Turn

NEWSCAST Work with a partner to develop three questions about the ozone layer. Research to find the answers. Take the roles of reporter and scientist. Present your findings to the class in a newscast format.

Lesson 2

Energy Transfer in the Atmosphere

Reading Guide

Key Concepts 
ESSENTIAL QUESTIONS

- How does energy transfer from the Sun to Earth and the atmosphere?
- How are air circulation patterns within the atmosphere created?

Vocabulary

radiation p. 198
conduction p. 201
convection p. 201
stability p. 202
temperature inversion p. 203

g Multilingual eGlossary

Academic Standards for Science

8.2.1 Recognize and demonstrate how the sun's energy drives convection in the atmosphere and in bodies of water, which results in ocean currents and weather patterns.

Also covers: 8.NS.1, 8.NS.6, 8.NS.7, 8.NS.10

Inquiry What's really there?

Mirages are created as light passes through layers of air that have different temperatures. How does energy create the reflections? What other effects does energy have on the atmosphere?

Inquiry Launch Lab

15 minutes

What happens to air as it warms?

Earth receives light energy from the Sun, which is converted to thermal energy on Earth. Thermal energy powers the weather systems that impact your everyday life.

1. Read and complete a lab safety form.
2. Turn on a **lamp** with an incandescent lightbulb.
3. Place your hands under the light near the lightbulb. What do you feel?
4. Dust your hands with **powder.**
5. Place your hands below the lightbulb and clap them together once.
6. Observe what happens to the particles.

Think About This

1. How might the energy in step 3 move from the lightbulb to your hand?
2. How did the particles move when you clapped your hands?
3. **Key Concept** How did particle motion show you how the air was moving?

Energy from the Sun

The Sun's energy travels 148 million km to Earth in only 8 minutes. How does the Sun's energy get to Earth? It reaches Earth through the **process** of radiation. **Radiation** *is the transfer of energy by electromagnetic waves.* Ninety-nine percent of the radiant energy from the Sun consists of visible light, ultraviolet light, and infrared radiation.

ACADEMIC VOCABULARY
process
(noun) an ordered series of actions

Visible Light

The majority of sunlight is visible light. Recall that visible light is light that you can see. The atmosphere is like a window to visible light, allowing it to pass through. At Earth's surface it is converted to thermal energy, commonly called heat.

Near-Visible Wavelengths

The wavelengths of ultraviolet (UV) light and infrared radiation (IR) are just beyond the range of visibility to human eyes. UV light has short wavelengths and can break chemical bonds. Excess exposure to UV light will burn human skin and can cause skin cancer. Infrared radiation (IR) has longer wavelengths than visible light. You can sense IR as thermal energy or warmth. As energy from the Sun is absorbed by Earth, it is radiated back as IR.

Reading Check Contrast visible and ultraviolet light.

Energy on Earth

As the Sun's energy passes through the atmosphere, some of it is absorbed by gases and particles, and some of it is reflected back into space. As a result, not all the energy coming from the Sun reaches Earth's surface.

Absorption

Study **Figure 8.** Gases and particles in the atmosphere absorb about 20 percent of incoming solar radiation. Oxygen, ozone, and water vapor all absorb incoming ultraviolet light. Water and carbon dioxide in the troposphere absorb some infrared radiation from the Sun. Earth's atmosphere does not absorb visible light. Visible light must be converted to infrared radiation before it can be absorbed.

Reflection

Bright surfaces, especially clouds, **reflect** incoming radiation. Study **Figure 8** again. Clouds and other small particles in the air reflect about 25 percent of the Sun's radiation. Some radiation travels to Earth's surface and is then reflected by land and sea surfaces. Snow-covered, icy, or rocky surfaces are especially reflective. As shown in **Figure 8,** this accounts for about 5 percent of incoming radiation. In all, about 30 percent of incoming radiation is reflected into space. This means that, along with the 20 percent of incoming radiation that is absorbed in the atmosphere, Earth's surface only receives and absorbs about 50 percent of incoming solar radiation.

Science Use v. Common Use

reflect

Science Use to return light, heat, sound, etc., after it strikes a surface

Common Use to think quietly and calmly

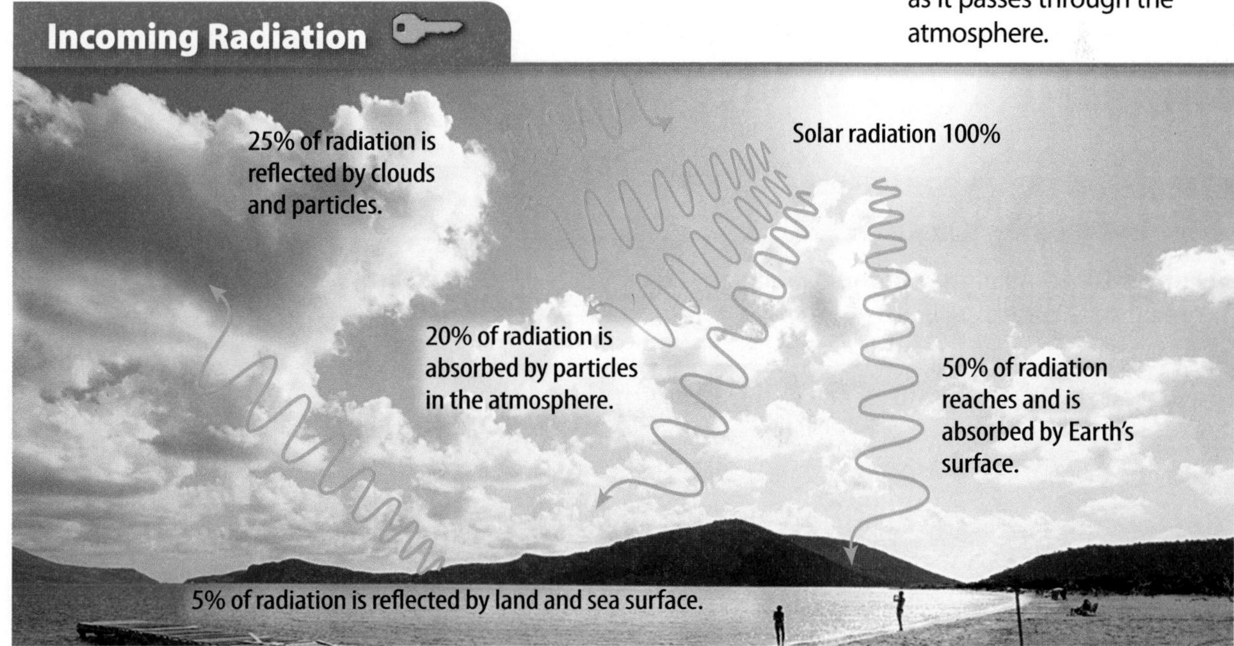
Incoming Radiation
25% of radiation is reflected by clouds and particles.
Solar radiation 100%
20% of radiation is absorbed by particles in the atmosphere.
50% of radiation reaches and is absorbed by Earth's surface.
5% of radiation is reflected by land and sea surface.

Figure 8 Some of the energy from the Sun is reflected or absorbed as it passes through the atmosphere.

Visual Check What percent of incoming radiation is absorbed by gases and particles in the atmosphere?

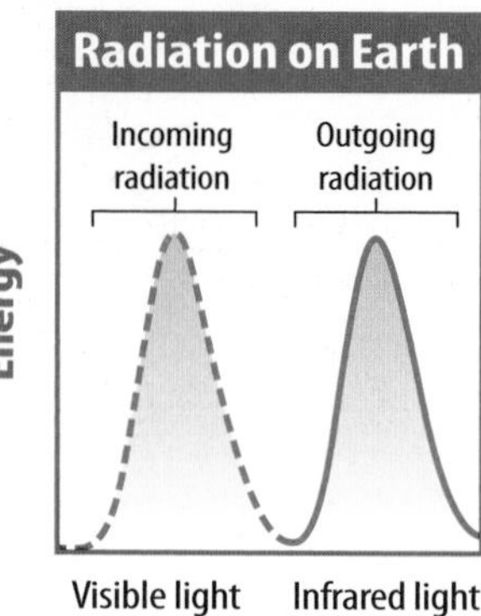

▲ **Figure 9** The amount of solar energy absorbed by Earth and its atmosphere is equal to the amount of energy Earth radiates back into space.

Radiation Balance

The Sun's radiation heats Earth. So, why doesn't Earth get hotter and hotter as it continues to receive radiation from the Sun? There is a balance between the amount of incoming radiation from the Sun and the amount of outgoing radiation from Earth.

The land, water, plants, and other organisms absorb solar radiation that reaches Earth's surface. The radiation absorbed by Earth is re-radiated, or bounced, back into the outer atmosphere. The radiation coming off Earth is mostly in the form of infrared radiation, which is heat. **Figure 9** shows that the amount of radiation Earth receives from the Sun is the same as the amount Earth radiates into the outer atmosphere. Earth absorbs the Sun's energy and then radiates that energy away until a balance is achieved.

The Greenhouse Effect

As shown in **Figure 10,** the glass of a greenhouse allows light to pass through, where it is converted to infrared energy. The glass prevents the IR from escaping and it warms the greenhouse. Some of the gases in the atmosphere, called greenhouse gases, act like the glass of a greenhouse. They allow sunlight to pass through, but they prevent some of Earth's IR energy from escaping. When gases in Earth's atmosphere direct radiation back toward Earth's surface, this warms Earth's atmosphere more than normal, creating a heat surplus. The gases that trap IR best are water vapor (H_2O), carbon dioxide (CO_2), and methane (CH_4).

Reading Check Describe the greenhouse effect.

The Greenhouse Effect

Animation

Figure 10 Some of the outgoing radiation is directed back toward Earth's surface by greenhouse gases.

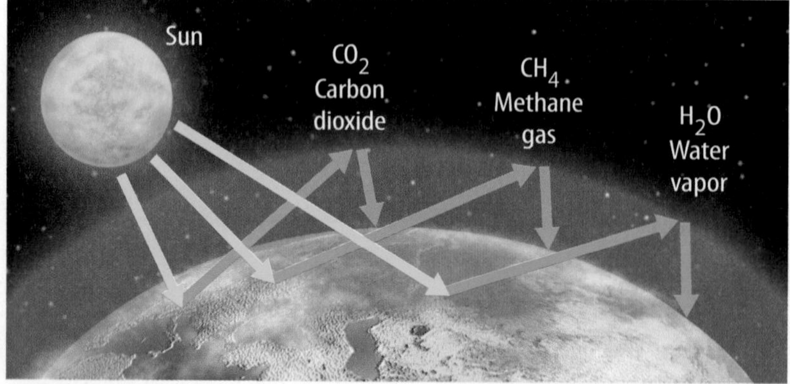

Thermal Energy Transfer

Recall that there are three types of thermal energy transfer—radiation, conduction, and convection. All three occur in the atmosphere. Recall that radiation is the process that transfers energy from the Sun to Earth.

Conduction

Thermal energy always moves from an object with a higher temperature to an object with a lower temperature. **Conduction** *is the transfer of thermal energy by collisions between particles of matter.* Particles must be close enough to touch to transfer energy by conduction. Touching the pot of water, shown in **Figure 11,** would transfer energy from the pot to your hand. Conduction occurs where the atmosphere touches Earth.

Convection

As molecules of air close to Earth's surface are heated by conduction, they spread apart, and air becomes less dense. Less dense air rises, transferring thermal energy to higher altitudes. *The transfer of thermal energy by the movement of matter from one place to another is called* **convection.** Convection can be seen in **Figure 11** as the boiling water circulates and steam rises.

Latent Heat

More than 70 percent of Earth's surface is covered by a highly unique substance—water! Water is the only substance that can exist as a solid, a liquid, and a gas at the temperature ranges on Earth. Recall that latent heat is exchanged when water changes from one phase to another, as shown in **Figure 12.** Latent heat energy is transferred from Earth's surface to the atmosphere.

Key Concept Check How does energy transfer from the Sun to Earth and the atmosphere?

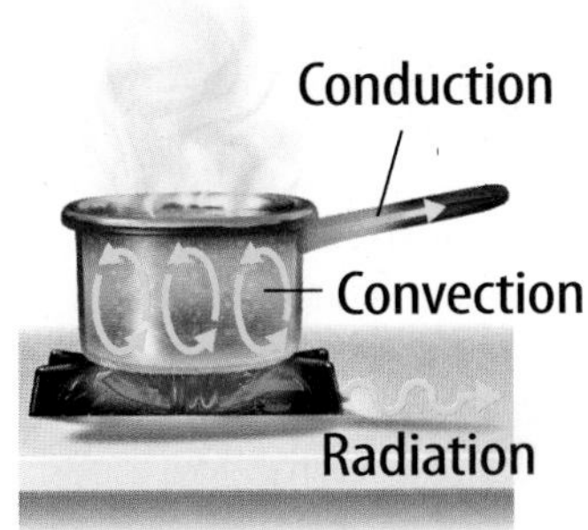

▲ **Figure 11** Energy is transferred through conduction, convection, and radiation.

Personal Tutor

Word Origin

conduction
from Latin *conducere,* means "to bring together"

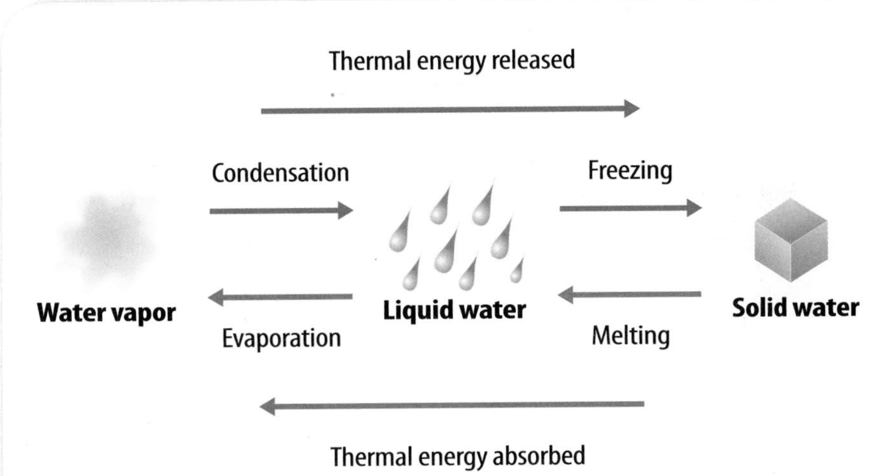

Figure 12 Water releases or absorbs thermal energy during phase changes.

FOLDABLES®

Fold a sheet of paper to make a four-column, four-row table and label as shown. Use it to record information about thermal energy transfer.

Energy Transfer by	Description	Everyday Example	Effect on the Atmosphere
Radiation			
Convection			
Conduction			

Circulating Air

Figure 13 Rising warm air is replaced by cooler, denser air that sinks beside it.

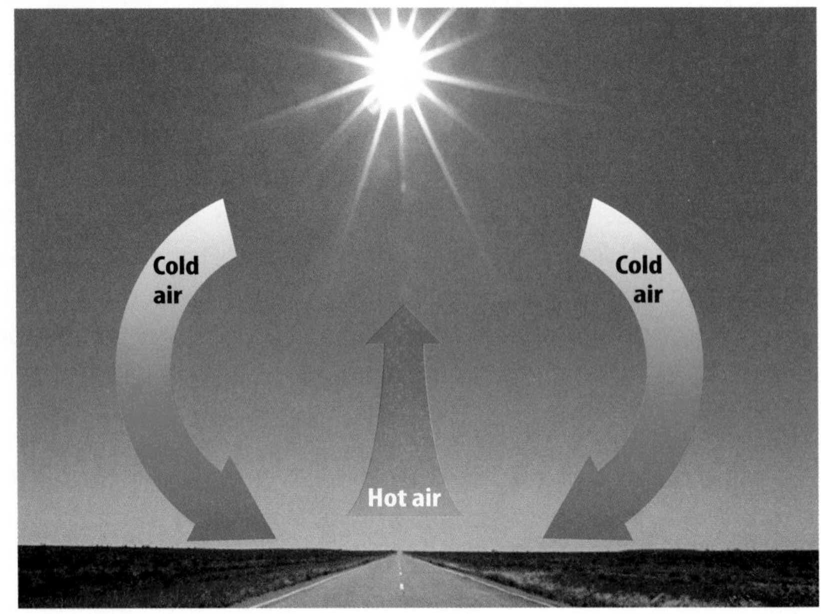

Circulating Air

You've read that energy is transferred through the atmosphere by convection. On a hot day, air that is heated becomes less dense. This creates a pressure difference. Cool, denser air pushes the warm air out of the way. The warm air is replaced by the more dense air, as shown in **Figure 13.** The warm air is often pushed upward. Warmer, rising air is always accompanied by cooler, sinking air.

Air is constantly moving. For example, wind flowing into a mountain range rises and flows over it. After reaching the top, the air sinks. This up-and-down motion sets up an atmospheric phenomenon called a mountain wave. The upward moving air within mountain waves creates lenticular (len TIH kyuh lur) clouds, shown in **Figure 14.** Circulating air affects weather and climate around the world.

Figure 14 Lens-shaped, lenticular clouds form when air rises within a "mountain wave." ▼

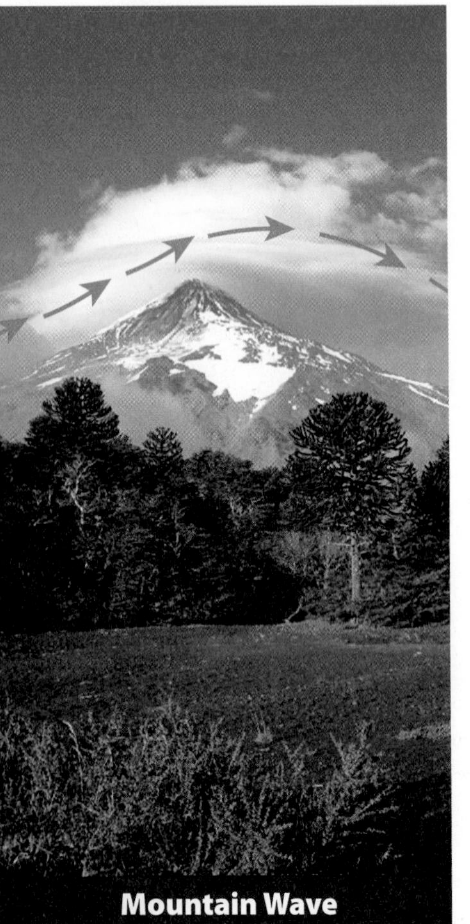

Key Concept Check How are air circulation patterns within the atmosphere created?

Stability

When you stand in the wind, your body forces some of the air to move above you. The same is true for hills and buildings. Conduction and convection also cause air to move upward. **Stability** *describes whether circulating air motions will be strong or weak.* When air is unstable, circulating motions are strong. During stable conditions, circulating motions are weak.

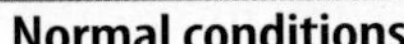
Normal conditions

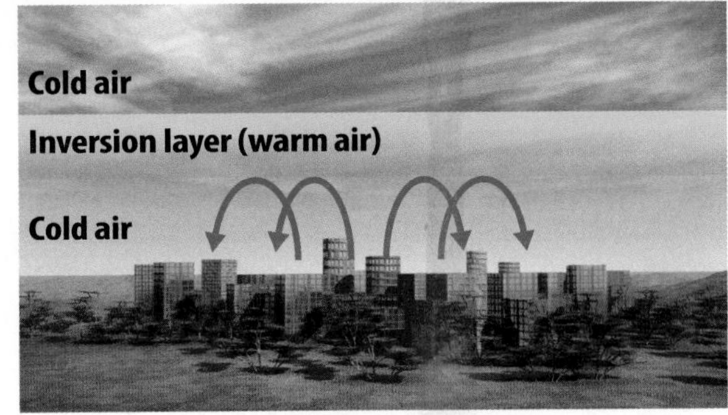

Temperature inversion

Figure 15 A temperature inversion occurs when cooler air is trapped beneath warmer air.

Visual Check How do conditions during a temperature inversion differ from normal conditions?

Unstable Air and Thunderstorms Unstable conditions often occur on warm, sunny afternoons. During unstable conditions, ground-level air is much warmer than higher-altitude air. As warm air rises rapidly in the atmosphere, it cools and forms large, tall clouds. Latent heat, released as water vapor changes from a gas to a liquid, adds to the instability, and produces a thunderstorm.

Reading Check Relate unstable air to the formation of thunderstorms.

Stable Air and Temperature Inversions Sometimes ground-level air is nearly the same temperature as higher-altitude air. During these conditions, the air is stable, and circulating motions are weak. A temperature inversion can occur under these conditions. *A* **temperature inversion** *occurs in the troposphere when temperature increases as altitude increases.* During a temperature inversion, a layer of cooler air is trapped by a layer of warmer air above it, as shown in **Figure 15.** Temperature inversions prevent air from mixing and can trap pollution in the air close to Earth's surface.

Inquiry MiniLab

20 minutes

Can you identify a temperature inversion?

You've read that a temperature inversion is a reversal of normal temperature conditions in the troposphere. What do data from a temperature inversion look like on a graph?

Analyze and Conclude

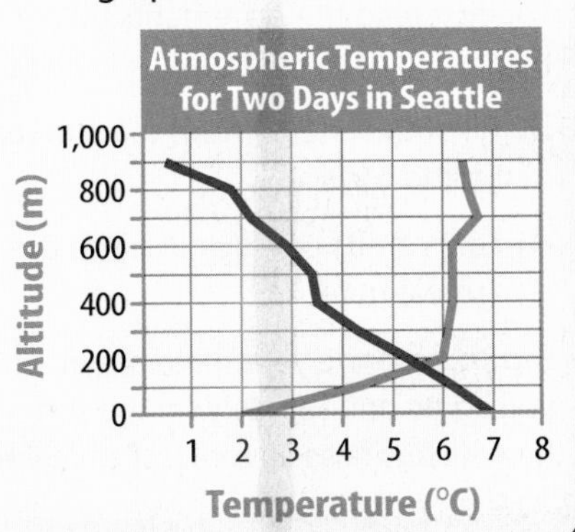

1. **Describe** the information presented in the graph. How do the graph's lines differ?
2. **Analyze** Which graph line represents normal conditions in the troposphere? Which represents a temperature inversion? Explain your answers in your Science Journal.
3. **Key Concept** From the graph, what pattern does a temperature inversion have?

Lesson 2 Review

✓ Assessment Online Quiz

Visual Summary

Not all radiation from the Sun reaches Earth's surface.

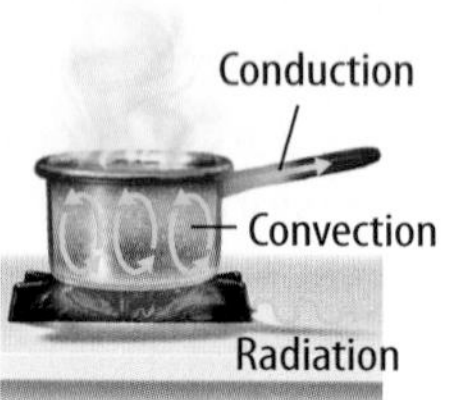

Thermal energy transfer in the atmosphere occurs through radiation, conduction, and convection.

Temperature inversion

Temperature inversions prevent air from mixing and can trap pollution in the air close to Earth's surface.

FOLDABLES®

Use your lesson Foldable to review the lesson. Save your Foldable for the project at the end of the chapter.

What do you think NOW?

You first read the statements below at the beginning of the chapter.

3. All of the energy from the Sun reaches Earth's surface.

4. Earth emits energy back into the atmosphere.

Did you change your mind about whether you agree or disagree with the statements? Rewrite any false statements to make them true.

Use Vocabulary

1 The property of the atmosphere that describes whether circulating air motions will be strong or weak is called ________.

2 **Define** *conduction* in your own words.

3 ________ is the transfer of thermal energy by the movement of matter from one place to another.

Understand Key Concepts 

4 Which statement is true?

- **A.** The Sun's energy is completely blocked by Earth's atmosphere.
- **B.** The Sun's energy passes through the atmosphere without warming it significantly.
- **C.** The Sun's IR energy is absorbed by greenhouse gases.
- **D.** The Sun's energy is primarily in the UV range.

5 **Distinguish** between conduction and convection.

Interpret Graphics

6 **Explain** how greenhouses gases affect temperatures on Earth.

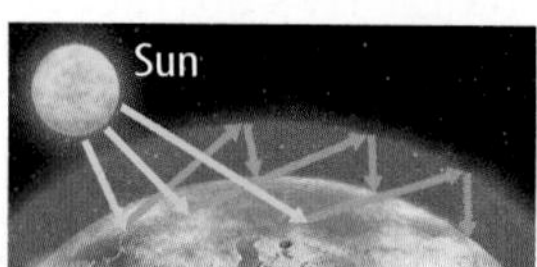

7 **Sequence** Copy and fill in the graphic organizer below to describe how energy from the Sun is absorbed in Earth's atmosphere.

Energy Absorption → [ ] / [ ]

Critical Thinking

8 **Suggest** a way to keep a parked car cool on a sunny day.

9 **Relate** temperature inversions to air stability.

Can you conduct, convect, and radiate?

After solar radiation reaches Earth, the molecules closest to Earth transfer thermal energy from molecule to molecule by conduction. The newly warmed air becomes less dense and moves through the process of convection.

Materials

candle

metal rod

glass rod

wooden dowel

500-mL beaker

ice

bowls (2)

lamp

glass cake pan

food coloring

250-mL beaker

Safety

Learn It

When you **compare and contrast** two or more things, you look for similarities and differences between them. When you **compare** two things, you look for the similarities, or how they are the same. When you **contrast** them, you look for how they are different from each other.

Try It

1. Read and complete a lab safety form.
2. Drip a small amount of melted candle wax onto one end of a metal rod, a glass rod, and a wooden dowel.
3. Place a 500-mL beaker on the lab table. Have your teacher add 350 mL of very hot water. Place the ends of the rods without candle wax in the water. Set aside.
4. Place an ice cube into each of two small bowls labeled A and B.
5. Place bowl A under a lamp with a 60- or 75-watt lightbulb. Place the light source 10 cm above the bowl. Turn on the lamp. Set bowl B aside.
6. Fill a glass cake pan with room-temperature water to a level of 2 cm. Put 2–3 drops of red food coloring into a 250-mL beaker of very hot water. Put 2–3 drops of blue food coloring into a 250-mL beaker of very cold water and ice cubes. Carefully pour the hot water into one end of the pan. Slowly pour the very cold water into the same end of the pan. Observe what happens from the side of the pan. Record your observations in your Science Journal.
7. Observe the candle wax on the rods in the hot water and the ice cubes in the bowls.

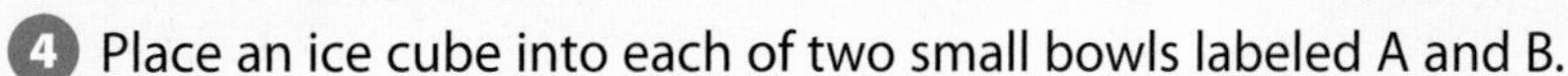

Apply It

8. What happened to the candle wax? Identify the type of energy transfer.
9. Which ice cube melted the most in the bowls? Identify the type of energy transfer that melted the ice.
10. Compare and contrast how the hot and cold water behaved in the pan. Identify the type of energy transfer.
11. **Key Concept** Explain how each part of the lab models radiation, conduction, or convection.

Lesson 3

Air Currents

Reading Guide

Key Concepts
ESSENTIAL QUESTIONS

- How does uneven heating of Earth's surface result in air movement?
- How are air currents on Earth affected by Earth's spin?
- What are the main wind belts on Earth?

Vocabulary

wind p. 207
trade winds p. 209
westerlies p. 209
polar easterlies p. 209
jet stream p. 209
sea breeze p. 210
land breeze p. 210

Multilingual eGlossary

Video

What's Science Got to do With It?

Academic Standards for Science

8.2.1 Recognize and demonstrate how the sun's energy drives convection in the atmosphere and in bodies of water, which results in ocean currents and weather patterns.

Also covers: 8.NS.6, 8.NS.7

Inquiry How does air push these blades?

If you have ever ridden a bicycle into a strong wind, you know the movement of air can be a powerful force. Some areas of the world have more wind than others. What causes these differences? What makes wind?

Launch Lab

15 minutes

Why does air move?

Early sailors relied on wind to move their ships around the world. Today, wind is used as a renewable source of energy. In the following activity, you will explore what causes air to move.

1. Read and complete a lab safety form.
2. Inflate a **balloon.** Do not tie it. Hold the neck of the balloon closed.
3. Describe how the inflated balloon feels.
4. Open the neck of the balloon without letting go of the balloon. Record your observations of what happens in your Science Journal.

Think About This

1. What caused the inflated balloon surface to feel the way it did when the neck was closed?
2. What caused the air to leave the balloon when the neck was opened?
3. **Key Concept** Why didn't outside air move into the balloon when the neck was opened?

Global Winds

There are great wind belts that circle the globe. The energy that causes this massive movement of air originates at the Sun. However, wind patterns can be global or local.

Unequal Heating of Earth's Surface

The Sun's energy warms Earth. However, the same amount of energy does not reach all of Earth's surface. The amount of energy an area gets depends largely on the Sun's angle. For example, energy from the rising or setting Sun is not very intense. But Earth heats up quickly when the Sun is high in the sky.

In latitudes near the equator—an area referred to as the tropics—sunlight strikes Earth's surface at a high angle—nearly 90°—year round. As a result, in the tropics there is more sunlight per unit of surface area. This means that the land, the water, and the air at the equator are always warm.

At latitudes near the North Pole and the South Pole, sunlight strikes Earth's surface at a low angle. Sunlight is now spread over a larger surface area than in the tropics. As a result, the poles receive very little energy per unit of surface area and are cooler.

Recall that differences in density cause warm air to rise. Warm air puts less pressure on Earth than cooler air. Because it's so warm in the tropics, air pressure is usually low. Over colder areas, such as the North Pole and the South Pole, air pressure is usually high. This difference in pressure creates wind. **Wind** *is the movement of air from areas of high pressure to areas of low pressure.* Global wind belts influence both climate and weather on Earth.

Key Concept Check How does uneven heating of Earth's surface result in air movement?

Figure 16 Three cells in each hemisphere move air through the atmosphere.

Visual Check Which wind belt do you live in?

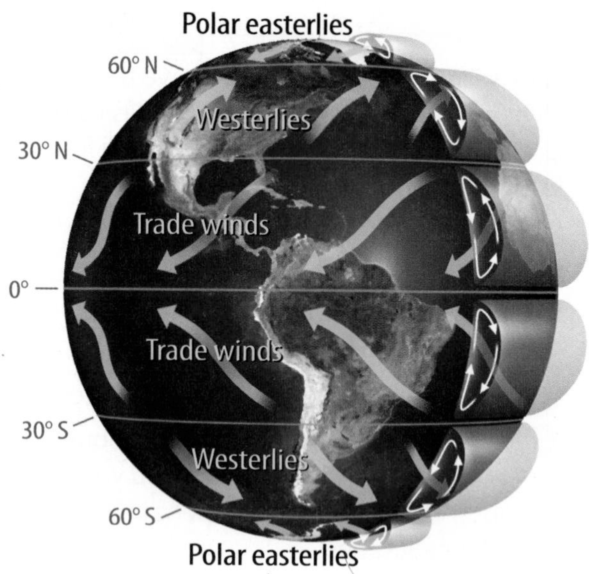

Global Wind Belts

Figure 16 shows the three-cell model of circulation in Earth's atmosphere. In the Northern Hemisphere, hot air in the cell nearest the equator moves to the top of the troposphere. There, the air moves northward until it cools and moves back to Earth's surface near 30° latitude. Most of the air in this convection cell then returns to Earth's surface near the equator.

The cell at the highest northern latitudes is also a convection cell. Air from the North Pole moves toward the equator along Earth's surface. The cooler air pushes up the warmer air near 60° latitude. The warmer air then moves northward and repeats the cycle. The cell between 30° and 60° latitude is not a convection cell. Its motion is driven by the other two cells, in a motion similar to a pencil that you roll between your hands. Three similar cells exist in the Southern Hemisphere. These cells help generate the global wind belts.

FOLDABLES®

Make a shutterfold. As illustrated, draw Earth and the three cells found in each hemisphere on the inside of the shutterfold. Describe each cell and explain the circulation of Earth's atmosphere. On the outside, label the global wind belts.

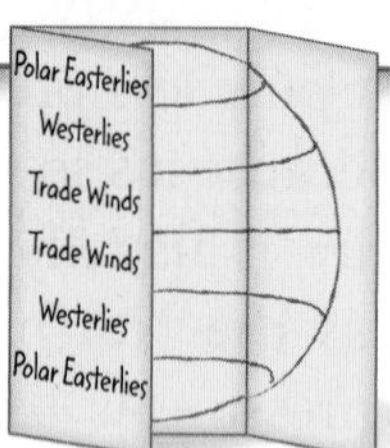

The Coriolis Effect

What happens when you throw a ball to someone across from you on a moving merry-go-round? The ball appears to curve because the person catching the ball has moved. Similarly, Earth's rotation causes moving air and water to appear to move to the right in the Northern Hemisphere and to the left in the Southern Hemisphere. This is called the Coriolis effect. The contrast between high and low pressure and the Coriolis effect creates distinct wind patterns, called prevailing winds.

Key Concept Check How are air currents on Earth affected by Earth's spin?

Prevailing Winds

The three global cells in each hemisphere create northerly and southerly winds. When the Coriolis effect acts on the winds, they blow to the east or the west, creating relatively steady, predictable winds. Locate the trade winds in **Figure 16.** *The* **trade winds** *are steady winds that flow from east to west between 30°N latitude and 30°S latitude.*

At about 30°N and 30°S air cools and sinks. This creates areas of high pressure and light, calm winds, called the doldrums. Sailboats without engines can be stranded in the doldrums.

The prevailing **westerlies** *are steady winds that flow from west to east between latitudes 30°N and 60°N, and 30°S and 60°S.* This region is also shown in **Figure 15.** *The* **polar easterlies** *are cold winds that blow from the east to the west near the North Pole and the South Pole.*

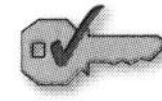

Key Concept Check What are the main wind belts on Earth?

Jet Streams

Near the top of the troposphere is a narrow band of high winds called the **jet stream**. Shown in **Figure 17,** jet streams flow around Earth from west to east, often making large loops to the north or the south. Jet streams influence weather as they move cold air from the poles toward the tropics and warm air from the tropics toward the poles. Jet streams are more erratic than prevailing winds as they move at speeds up to 300 km/h.

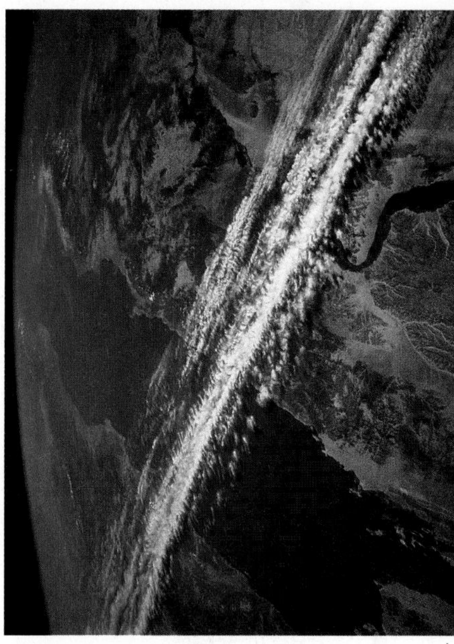

Figure 17 Jet streams are thin bands of high wind speed. The clouds seen here have condensed within a cooler jet stream.

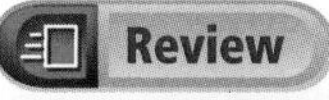

Review **Personal Tutor**

Inquiry MiniLab

20 minutes

Can you model the Coriolis effect?

Earth's rotation causes the Coriolis effect. It affects the movement of water and air on Earth.

1. Read and complete a lab safety form.
2. Draw dot A in the center of a piece of **foamboard.** Draw dot B along the outer edge of the foamboard.
3. Roll a **table-tennis ball** from dot A to dot B. Record your observations in your Science Journal.
4. Center the foamboard on a **turntable**. Have your partner rotate the foamboard at a medium speed. Roll the ball along the same path. Record your observations.

Analyze and Conclude

1. **Contrast** the path of the ball when the foamboard was not moving to when it was spinning.
2. **Key Concept** How might air moving from the North Pole to the equator travel due to Earth's rotation?

Local Winds

You have just read that global winds occur because of pressure differences around the globe. In the same way, local winds occur whenever air pressure is different from one location to another.

Sea and Land Breezes

Anyone who has spent time near a lake or an ocean shore as probably experienced the connection between temperature, air pressure, and wind. *A* **sea breeze** *is wind that blows from the sea to the land due to local temperature and pressure differences.* **Figure 18** shows how sea breezes form. On sunny days, land warms up faster than water does. The air over the land warms by conduction and rises, creating an area of low pressure. The air over the water sinks, creating an area of high pressure because it is cooler. The differences in pressure over the warm land and the cooler water result in a cool wind that blows from the sea onto land.

A **land breeze** *is a wind that blows from the land to the sea due to local temperature and pressure differences.* **Figure 18** shows how land breezes form. At night, the land cools more quickly than the water. Therefore, the air above the land cools more quickly than the air over the water. As a result, an area of lower pressure forms over the warmer water. A land breeze then blows from the land toward the water.

Reading Check Compare and contrast sea breezes and land breezes.

Figure 18 Sea breezes and land breezes are created as part of a large reversible convection current.

Local Winds

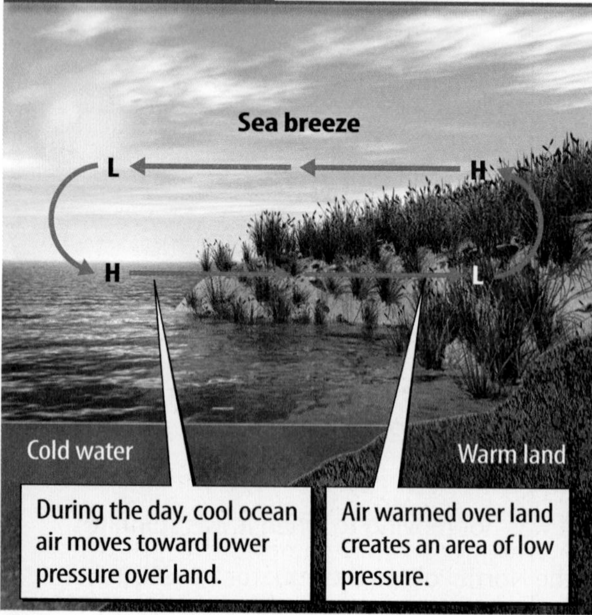
Sea breeze
L
H
H
L
Cold water
Warm land
During the day, cool ocean air moves toward lower pressure over land.
Air warmed over land creates an area of low pressure.

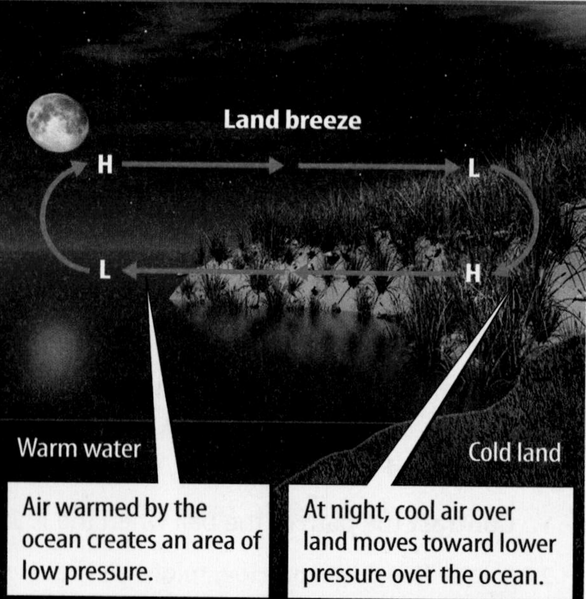
Land breeze
H
L
L
H
Warm water
Cold land
Air warmed by the ocean creates an area of low pressure.
At night, cool air over land moves toward lower pressure over the ocean.

Visual Check Sequence the steps involved in the formation of a land breeze.

Lesson 3 Review

Assessment Online Quiz

Visual Summary

Wind is created by pressure differences between one location and another.

Prevailing winds in the global wind belts are the trade winds, the westerlies, and the polar easterlies.

Sea breezes and land breezes are examples of local winds.

FOLDABLES®

Use your lesson Foldable to review the lesson. Save your Foldable for the project at the end of the chapter.

What do you think NOW?

You first read the statements below at the beginning of the chapter.

5. Uneven heating in different parts of the atmosphere creates air circulation patterns.

6. Warm air sinks and cold air rises.

Did you change your mind about whether you agree or disagree with the statements? Rewrite any false statements to make them true.

Use Vocabulary

1. The movement of air from areas of high pressure to areas of low pressure is ________.
2. A(n) ________ is wind that blows from the sea to the land due to local temperature and pressure differences.
3. **Distinguish** between westerlies and trade winds.

Understand Key Concepts 

4. Which does NOT affect global wind belts?
   - **A.** air pressure
   - **B.** land breezes
   - **C.** the Coriolis effect
   - **D.** the Sun
5. **Relate** Earth's spinning motion to the Coriolis effect.

Interpret Graphics

Use the image below to answer question 6.

6. **Explain** a land breeze.
7. **Organize** Copy and fill in the graphic organizer below to summarize Earth's global wind belts.

Wind Belt	Description
Trade winds	
Westerlies	
Polar easterlies	

Critical Thinking

8. **Infer** what would happen without the Coriolis effect.
9. **Explain** why the wind direction is often the same in Hawaii as it is in Greenland.

Launch Lab

20 minutes

How does acid rain form?

Vehicles, factories, and power plants release chemicals into the atmosphere. When these chemicals combine with water vapor, they can form acid rain.

1. Read and complete a lab safety form.
2. Half-fill a **plastic cup** with **distilled water.**
3. Dip a strip of **pH paper** into the water. Use a **pH color chart** to determine the pH of the distilled water. Record the pH in your Science Journal.
4. Use a **dropper** to add **lemon juice** to the water until the pH equals that of acid rain. Swirl and test the pH each time you add 5 drops of the lemon juice to the mixture.

Substances	pH
Hydrochloric acid	0.0
Lemon juice	2.3
Vinegar	2.9
Tomato juice	4.1
Coffee (black)	5.0
Acid rain	5.6
Rainwater	6.5
Milk	6.6
Distilled water	7.0
Blood	7.4
Baking soda solution	8.4
Toothpaste	9.9
Household ammonia	11.9
Sodium hydroxide	14.0

Think About This

1. A strong acid has a pH between 0 and 2. How does the pH of lemon juice compare to the pH of other substances? Is acid rain a strong acid?
2. **Key Concept** Why might scientists monitor the pH of rain?

Sources of Air Pollution

The contamination of air by harmful substances including gases and smoke is called **air pollution**. Air pollution is harmful to humans and other living things. Years of exposure to polluted air can weaken a human's immune system. Respiratory diseases such as asthma can be caused by air pollution.

Air pollution comes from many sources. Point-source pollution is pollution that comes from an identifiable source. Examples of point sources include smokestacks of large factories, such as the one shown in **Figure 19,** and electric power plants that burn fossil fuels. They release tons of polluting gases and particles into the air each day. An example of natural point-source pollution is an erupting volcano.

Figure 19 One example of point-source pollution is a factory smoke stack.

Nonpoint-source pollution is pollution that comes from a widespread area. One example of pollution from a nonpoint-source is air pollution in a large city. This is considered nonpoint-source pollution because it cannot be traced back to one source. Some bacteria found in swamps and marshes are examples of natural sources of nonpoint-source pollution.

Key Concept Check Compare point-source and nonpoint-source pollution.

Causes and Effects of Air Pollution

The harmful effects of air pollution are not limited to human health. Some pollutants, including ground-level ozone, can damage plants. Air pollution can also cause serious damage to human-made structures. Sulfur dioxide pollution can discolor stone, corrode metal, and damage paint on cars.

Acid Precipitation

When sulfur dioxide and nitrogen oxides combine with moisture in the atmosphere and form precipitation that has a pH lower than that of normal rainwater, it is called **acid precipitation**. Acid precipitation includes acid rain, snow, and fog. It affects the chemistry of water in lakes and rivers. This can harm the organisms living in the water. Acid precipitation damages buildings and other structures made of stone. Natural sources of sulfur dioxide include volcanoes and marshes. However, the most common sources of sulfur dioxide and nitrogen oxides are automobile exhausts and factory and power plant smoke.

Smog

Photochemical smog *is air pollution that forms from the interaction between chemicals in the air and sunlight.* Smog forms when nitrogen dioxide, released in gasoline engine exhaust, reacts with sunlight. A series of chemical reactions produces ozone and other compounds that form smog. Recall that ozone in the stratosphere helps protect organisms from the Sun's harmful rays. However, ground-level ozone can damage the tissues of plants and animals. Ground-level ozone is the main component of smog. Smog in urban areas reduces visibility and makes air difficult to breathe. **Figure 20** shows New York City on a clear day and on a smoggy day.

 **Key Concept Check** How do humans impact air quality?

FOLDABLES®

Make a horizontal three-tab Foldable and label it as shown. Use it to organize your notes about the formation of air pollution and its effects. Fold the right and left thirds over the center and label the outside *Air Pollution.*

Acid Precipitation | Smog | Particulate Pollution
Types of Air Pollution

Smog

Figure 20 Smog can be observed as haze or a brown tint in the atmosphere.

Particulate Pollution

Although you can't see them, over 10,000 solid or liquid particles are in every cubic centimeter of air. A cubic centimeter is about the size of a sugar cube. This type of pollution is called particulate matter. **Particulate** (par TIH kyuh lut) **matter** *is a mixture of dust, acids, and other chemicals that can be hazardous to human health.* The smallest particles are the most harmful. These particles can be inhaled and can enter your lungs. They can cause asthma, bronchitis, and lead to heart attacks. Children and older adults are most likely to experience health problems due to particulate matter.

WORD ORIGIN
particulate
from Latin *particula,* means "small part"

Particulate matter in the atmosphere absorbs and scatters sunlight. This can create haze. Haze particles scatter light, make things blurry, and reduce visibility.

Movement of Air Pollution

Wind can influence the effects of air pollution. Because air carries pollution with it, some wind patterns cause more pollution problems than others. Weak winds or no wind prevents pollution from mixing with the surrounding air. During weak wind conditions, pollution levels can become dangerous.

For example, the conditions in which temperature inversions form are weak winds, clear skies, and longer winter nights. As land cools at night, the air above it also cools. Calm winds, however, prevent cool air from mixing with warm air above it. **Figure 21** shows how cities located in valleys experience a temperature inversion. Cool air, along with the pollution it contains, is trapped in valleys. More cool air sinks down the sides of the mountain, further preventing layers from mixing. The pollution in the photo at the beginning of the lesson was trapped due to a temperature inversion.

Figure 21 At night, cool air sinks down the mountain sides, trapping pollution in the valley below.

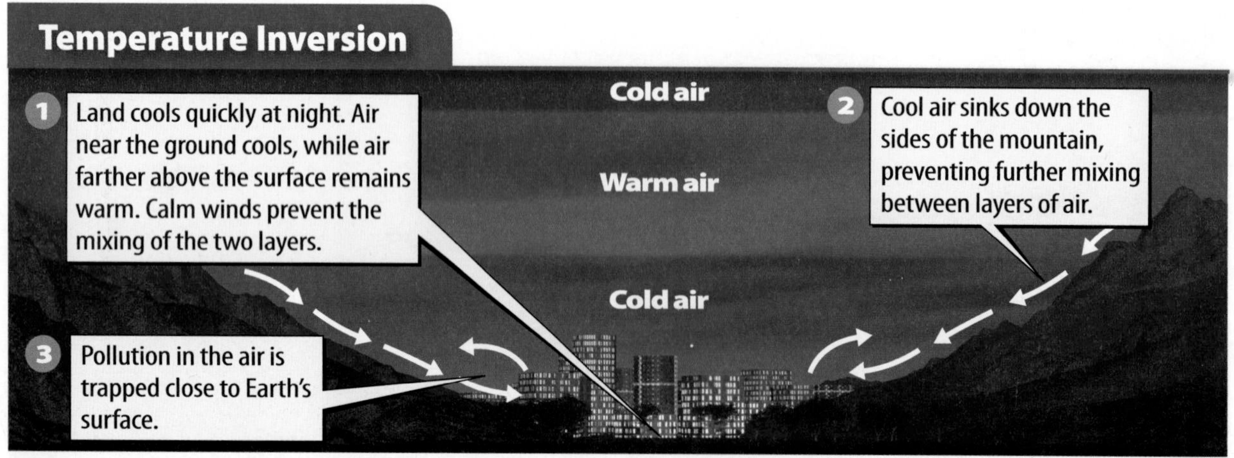

Temperature Inversion
Cold air
Warm air
Cold air
1 Land cools quickly at night. Air near the ground cools, while air farther above the surface remains warm. Calm winds prevent the mixing of the two layers.
2 Cool air sinks down the sides of the mountain, preventing further mixing between layers of air.
3 Pollution in the air is trapped close to Earth's surface.

Visual Check How is pollution trapped by a temperature inversion?

Maintaining Healthful Air Quality

Preserving the quality of Earth's atmosphere requires the cooperation of government officials, scientists, and the public. The Clean Air Act is an example of how government can help fight pollution. Since the Clean Air Act became law in 1970, steps have been taken to reduce automobile emissions. Pollutant levels have decreased significantly in the United States. Despite these advances, serious problems still remain. The amount of ground-level ozone is still too high in many large cities. Also, acid precipitation produced by air pollutants continues to harm organisms in lakes, streams, and forests.

Air Quality Standards

The Clean Air Act gives the U.S. government the power to set air quality standards. The standards protect humans, animals, plants, and buildings from the harmful effects of air pollution. All states are required to make sure that pollutants, such as carbon monoxide, nitrogen oxides, particulate matter, ozone, and sulfur dioxide, do not exceed harmful levels.

 **Reading Check** What is the Clean Air Act?

Monitoring Air Pollution

Pollution levels are continuously monitored by hundreds of instruments in all major U.S. cities. If the levels are too high, authorities may advise people to limit outdoor activities.

Inquiry MiniLab

15 minutes

Can being out in fresh air be harmful to your health?

Are you going to be affected if you play tennis for a couple hours, go biking with your friends, or even just lie on the beach? Even if you have no health problems related to your respiratory system, you still need to be aware of the quality of air in your area of activity for the day.

Analyze and Conclude

1. Which values on the AQI indicate that the air quality is good?
2. At what value is the air quality unhealthful for anyone who may have allergies and respiratory disorders?
3. Which values would be considered as warnings of emergency conditions?
4. **Key Concept** The quality of air in different areas changes throughout the day. Explain how you can use the AQI to help you know when you should limit your outdoor activity.

Air Quality Index (AQI) Values	Levels of Health Concern
0 to 50	Good
51 to 100	Moderate
101 to 150	Unhealthful for Sensitive Groups
151 to 200	Unhealthful
201 to 300	Very Unhealthful
301 to 500	Hazardous

Air Quality Trends

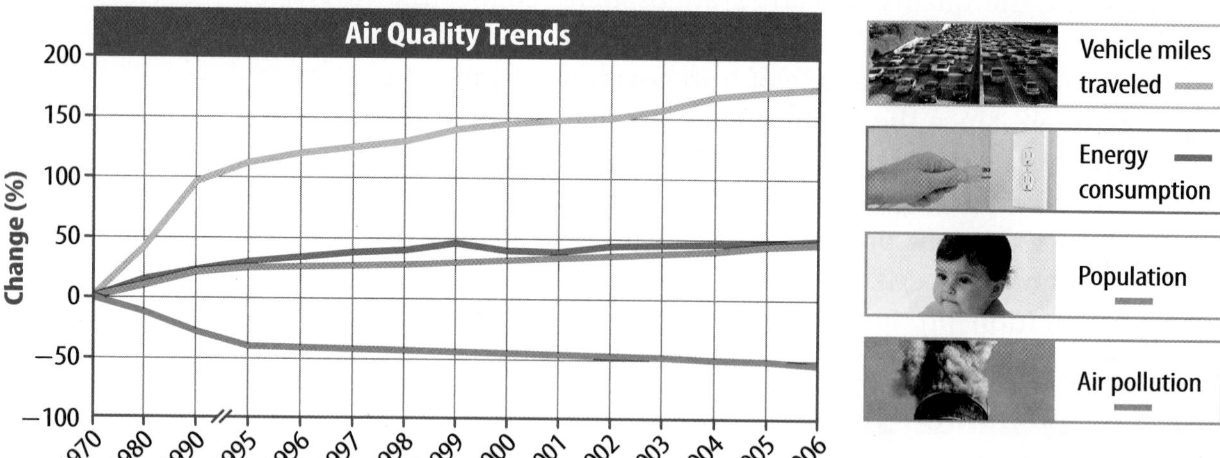

Figure 22 Pollution emissions have declined, even though the population is increasing.

Air Quality Trends

Over the last several decades, air quality in U.S. cities has improved, as shown in **Figure 22.** Even though some pollution-producing processes have increased, such as burning fossil fuels and traveling in automobiles, levels of certain air pollutants have decreased. Airborne levels of lead and carbon monoxide have decreased the most. Levels of sulfur dioxide, nitrogen oxide, and particulate matter have also decreased.

However, ground-level ozone has not decreased much. Why do ground-level ozone trends lag behind those of other pollutants? Recall that ozone can be created from chemical reactions involving automobile exhaust. As the number of cars on the road increases, air quality standards have not kept up with all pollutant levels.

Key Concept Check Why do humans monitor air quality standards?

Indoor Air Pollution

Not all air pollution is outdoors. The air inside homes and other buildings can be as much as 50 times more polluted than outdoor air! The quality of indoor air can impact human health much more than outdoor air quality.

Indoor air pollution comes from many sources. Tobacco smoke, cleaning products, pesticides, and fireplaces are some common sources. Furniture upholstery, carpets, and foam insulation also add pollutants to the air. Another indoor air pollutant is radon, an odorless gas given off by some soil and rocks. Radon leaks through cracks in a building's foundation and sometimes builds up to harmful levels inside homes. Harmful effects of radon come from breathing its particles.

Math Skills 

Use Graphs

The graph above shows the percent change in four different pollution factors from 1970 through 2006. All values are based on the 0 percent amount in 1970. For example, from 1970 to 1990, the number of vehicle miles driven increased by 100 percent, or the vehicle miles doubled. Use the graph to infer which factors might be related.

Practice

1. What was the percent change in population between 1970 and 2006?
2. What other factor changed by about the same amount during that period?

- Math Practice
- Personal Tutor

Lesson 4 Review

Assessment Online Quiz

Visual Summary

Air pollution comes from point sources, such as factories, and nonpoint sources, such as automobiles.

Photochemical smog contains ozone, which can damage tissues in plants and animals.

FOLDABLES®

Use your lesson Foldable to review the lesson. Save your Foldable for the project at the end of the chapter.

What do you think NOW?

You first read the statements below at the beginning of the chapter.

7. If no humans lived on Earth, there would be no air pollution.

8. Pollution levels in the air are not measured or monitored.

Did you change your mind about whether you agree or disagree with the statements? Rewrite any false statements to make them true.

Use Vocabulary

1. **Define** *acid precipitation* in your own words.
2. _________ forms when chemical reactions combine pollution with sunlight.
3. The contamination of air by harmful substances, including gases and smoke, is _________.

Understand Key Concepts 

4. Which is NOT true about smog?
   - **A.** It contains nitrogen oxide.
   - **B.** It contains ozone.
   - **C.** It reduces visibility.
   - **D.** It is produced only by cars.
5. **Describe** two ways humans add pollution to the atmosphere.
6. **Assess** whether urban or rural areas are more likely to have high levels of smog.
7. **Identify** and describe the law designed to reduce air pollution.

Interpret Graphics

8. **Compare and Contrast** Copy and fill in the graphic organizer below to compare and contrast details of smog and acid precipitation.

	Similarities	Differences
Smog		
Acid Precipitation		

Critical Thinking

9. **Describe** how conduction and convection are affected by paving over a grass field.

Math Skills

Math Practice

10. Based on the graph on the opposite page, what was the total percent change in air pollution between 1970 and 2006?

40 minutes

Radiant Energy Absorption

Materials

thermometer

sand

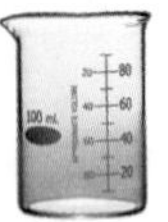

500-mL beaker

lamp

stopwatch

paper towels

spoon

potting soil

clay

Safety

Ultimately, the Sun is the source of energy for Earth. Energy from the Sun moves through the atmosphere and is absorbed and reflected from different surfaces on Earth. Light surfaces reflect energy, and dark surfaces absorb energy. Both land and sea surfaces absorb energy from the Sun, and air in contact with these surfaces is warmed through conduction.

Ask a Question

Which surfaces on Earth absorb the most energy from the Sun?

Make Observations

1. Read and complete a lab safety form.
2. Make a data table in your Science Journal to record your observations of energy transfer. Include columns for Type of Surface, Temperature Before Heating, and Temperature After Heating.
3. Half-fill a 500-mL beaker with sand. Place a thermometer in the sand and carefully add enough sand to cover the thermometer bulb—about 2 cm deep. Keep the bulb under the sand for 1 minute. Record the temperature in the data table.
4. Place the beaker under the light source. Record the temperature after 10 minutes.
5. Repeat steps 3 and 4 using soil and water.

Form a Hypothesis

6. Use the data in your table to form a hypothesis stating which surfaces on Earth, such as forests, wheat fields, lakes, snowy mountain tops, and deserts, will absorb the most radiant energy.

Test Your Hypothesis

7. Decide what materials could be used to mimic the surfaces on Earth from your hypothesis.
8. Repeat the experiment with materials approved by the teacher to test your hypothesis.
9. Examine your data. Was your hypothesis supported? Why or why not?

Analyze and Conclude

10. **Infer** which types of areas on Earth absorb the most energy from the Sun.
11. **Think Critically** When areas of Earth are changed so they become more likely to reflect or absorb energy from the Sun, how might these changes affect conduction and convection in the atmosphere?
12. **The Big Idea** Explain how thermal energy from the Sun being received by and reflected from Earth's surface is related to the role of the atmosphere in maintaining conditions suitable for life.

Communicate Your Results

Display data from your initial observations to compare your findings with your classmates' findings. Explain your hypothesis, experiment results, and conclusions to the class.

Inquiry Extension

What could you add to this investigation to show how cloud cover changes the amount of radiation that will reach Earth's surfaces? Design a study that could test the effect of cloud cover on radiation passing through Earth's atmosphere. How could you include a way to show that clouds also reflect radiant energy from the Sun?

6

Lab Tips

☑ If possible, use leaves, straw, shaved ice, and other natural materials to test your hypothesis.

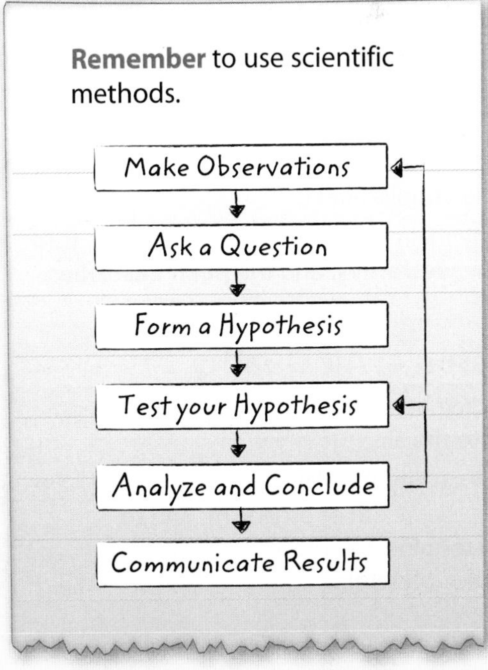

Chapter 6 Study Guide

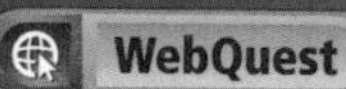

The gases in Earth's atmosphere, some of which are needed by organisms to survive, affect Earth's temperature and the transfer of thermal energy to the atmosphere.

Key Concepts Summary	Vocabulary
Lesson 1: Describing Earth's Atmosphere • Earth's **atmosphere** formed as Earth cooled and chemical and biological processes took place. • Earth's atmosphere consists of nitrogen, oxygen, and a small amount of other gases, such as CO_2 and **water vapor.** • The atmospheric layers are the **troposphere,** the **stratosphere,** the mesosphere, the thermosphere, and the exosphere. • Air pressure decreases as altitude increases. Temperature either increases or decreases as altitude increases, depending on the layer of the atmosphere. 21% Oxygen 78% Nitrogen	**atmosphere** p. 189 **water vapor** p. 190 **troposphere** p. 192 **stratosphere** p. 192 **ozone layer** p. 192 **ionosphere** p. 193
Lesson 2: Energy Transfer in the Atmosphere 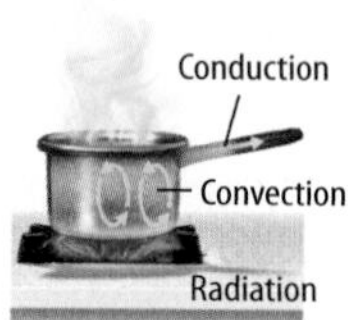 • The Sun's energy is transferred to Earth's surface and the atmosphere through **radiation, conduction, convection,** and latent heat. • Air circulation patterns are created by convection currents.	**radiation** p. 198 **conduction** p. 201 **convection** p. 201 **stability** p. 202 **temperature inversion** p. 203
Lesson 3: Air Currents • Uneven heating of Earth's surface creates pressure differences. **Wind** is the movement of air from areas of high pressure to areas of low pressure. • Air currents curve to the right or to the left due to the Coriolis effect. • The main wind belts on Earth are the **trade winds,** the **westerlies,** and the **polar easterlies.** 	**wind** p. 207 **trade winds** p. 209 **westerlies** p. 209 **polar easterlies** p. 209 **jet stream** p. 209 **sea breeze** p. 210 **land breeze** p. 210
Lesson 4: Air Quality • Some human activities release pollution into the air. • Air quality standards are monitored for the health of organisms and to determine if anti-pollution efforts are successful. 	**air pollution** p. 214 **acid precipitation** p. 215 **photochemical smog** p. 215 **particulate matter** p. 216

Study Guide

Review
- Personal Tutor
- Vocabulary eGames
- Vocabulary eFlashcards

FOLDABLES® Chapter Project

Assemble your lesson Foldables® as shown to make a Chapter Project. Use the project to review what you have learned in this chapter.

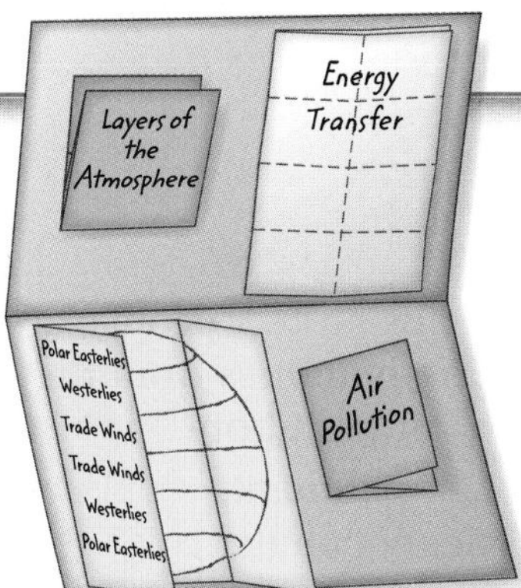

Use Vocabulary

1. Radio waves travel long distances by bouncing off electrically charged particles in the ________.
2. The Sun's thermal energy is transferred to Earth through space by ________.
3. Rising currents of warm air transfer energy from Earth to the atmosphere through ________.
4. A narrow band of winds located near the top of the troposphere is a(n) ________.
5. ________ are steady winds that flow from east to west between 30°N latitude and 30°S latitude.
6. In large urban areas, ________ forms when pollutants in the air interact with sunlight.
7. A mixture of dust, acids, and other chemicals that can be hazardous to human health is called ________.

Link Vocabulary and Key Concepts

Concepts in Motion Interactive Concept Map

Copy this concept map, and then use vocabulary terms from the previous page to complete the concept map.

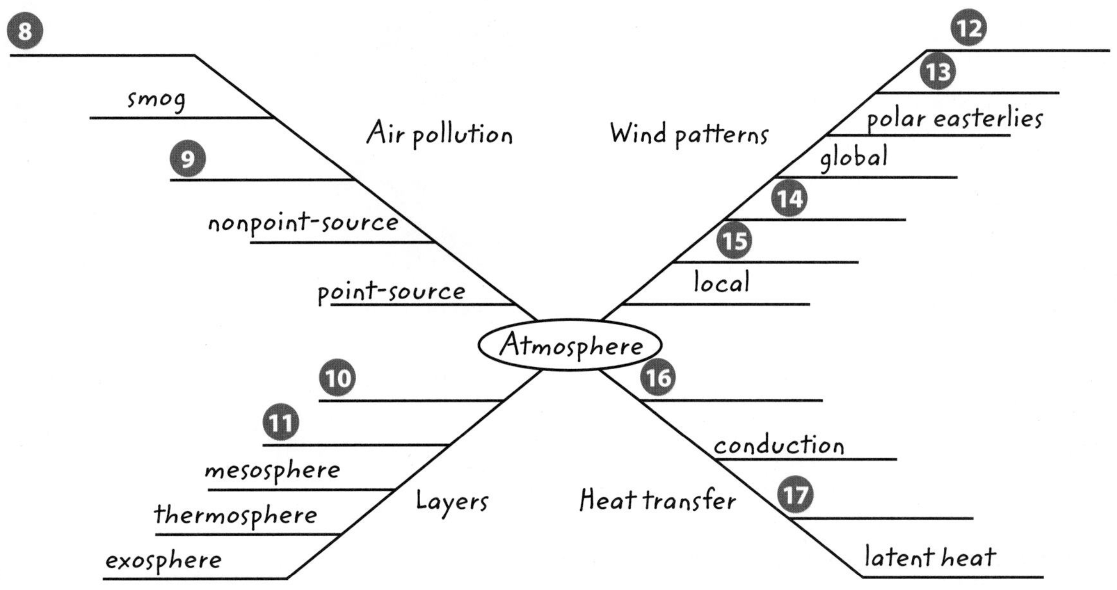

Chapter 6 Review

Understand Key Concepts 

1. Air pressure is greatest
   A. at a mountain base.
   B. on a mountain top.
   C. in the stratosphere.
   D. in the ionosphere.

2. In which layer of the atmosphere is the ozone layer found?
   A. troposphere
   B. stratosphere
   C. mesosphere
   D. thermosphere

Use the image below to answer question 3.

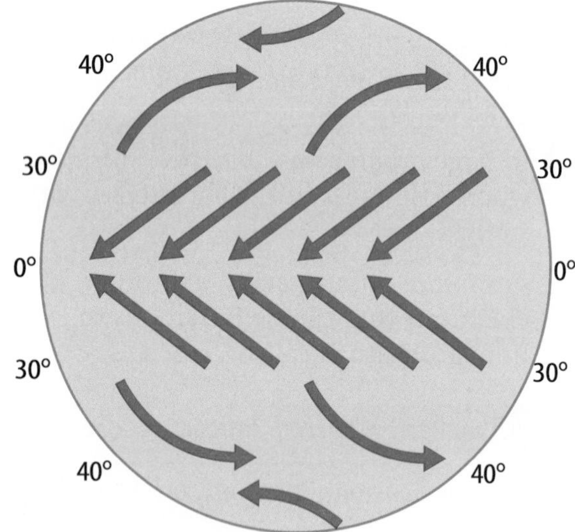

3. This diagram represents the atmosphere's
   A. air masses.
   B. global wind belts.
   C. inversions.
   D. particulate motion.

4. The Sun's energy
   A. is completely absorbed by the atmosphere.
   B. is completely reflected by the atmosphere.
   C. is in the form of latent heat.
   D. is transferred to the atmosphere after warming Earth.

5. Which type of energy is emitted from Earth to the atmosphere?
   A. ultraviolet radiation
   B. visible radiation
   C. infrared radiation
   D. aurora borealis

6. Which is a narrow band of high winds located near the top of the troposphere?
   A. polar easterly
   B. a jet stream
   C. a sea breeze
   D. a trade wind

7. Which helps protect people, animals, plants, and buildings from the harmful effects of air pollution?
   A. primary pollutants
   B. secondary pollutants
   C. ozone layer
   D. air quality standards

Use the photo below to answer question 8.

8. This photo shows a potential source of
   A. ultraviolet radiation.
   B. indoor air pollution.
   C. radon.
   D. smog.

Assessment

Online Test Practice

Critical Thinking

9 **Predict** how atmospheric carbon dioxide levels might change if more trees were planted on Earth. Explain your prediction.

10 **Compare** visible and infrared radiation.

11 **Assess** whether your home is heated by conduction or convection.

12 **Sequence** how the unequal heating of Earth's surface leads to the formation of wind.

13 **Evaluate** whether a sea breeze could occur at night.

14 **Interpret Graphics** What are the top three sources of particulate matter in the atmosphere? What could you do to reduce particulate matter from any of the sources shown here?

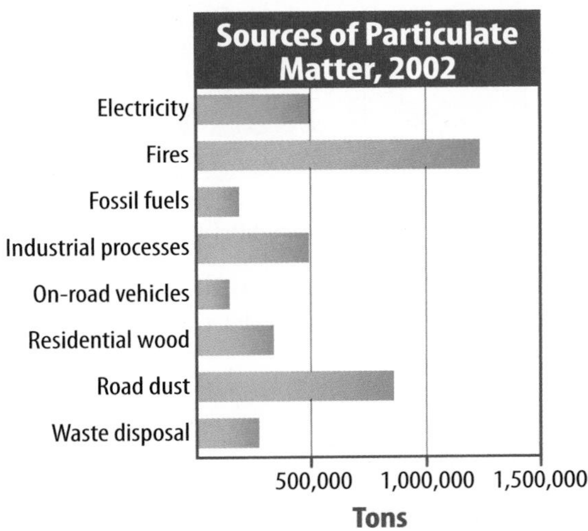

15 **Diagram** how acid precipitation forms. Include possible sources of sulfur dioxide and nitrogen oxide and organisms that can be affected by acid precipitation.

Writing in Science

16 **Write** a paragraph explaining whether you think it would be possible to permanently pollute the atmosphere with particulate matter.

REVIEW THE BIG IDEA

17 Review the title of each lesson in the chapter. List all of the characteristics and components of the troposphere and the stratosphere that affect life on Earth. Describe how life is impacted by each one.

18 Discuss how energy is transferred from the Sun throughout Earth's atmosphere.

Math Skills

Review

Math Practice

Use Graphs

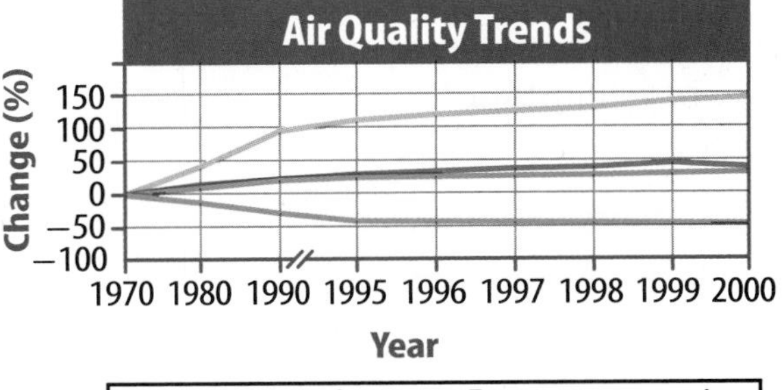

19 What was the percent change in energy usage between 1996 and 1999?

20 What happened to energy usage between 1999 and 2000?

21 What was the total percentage change between vehicle miles traveled and air pollution from 1970 to 2000?

Standardized Test Practice

Record your answers on the answer sheet provided by your teacher or on a sheet of paper.

Multiple Choice

1 What causes the phenomenon known as a mountain wave?

A radiation imbalance

B rising and sinking air

C temperature inversion

D the greenhouse effect

Use the diagram below to answer question 2.

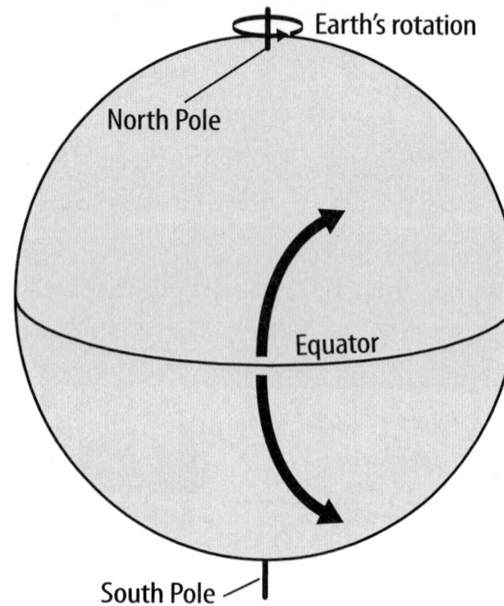

2 What phenomenon does the diagram above illustrate?

A radiation balance

B temperature inversion

C the Coriolis effect

D the greenhouse effect

3 Which do scientists call greenhouse gases?

A carbon dioxide, hydrogen, nitrogen

B carbon dioxide, methane gas, water vapor

C carbon monoxide, oxygen, argon

D carbon monoxide, ozone, radon

4 In which direction does moving air appear to turn in the Northern Hemisphere?

A down

B up

C right

D left

Use the diagram below to answer question 5.

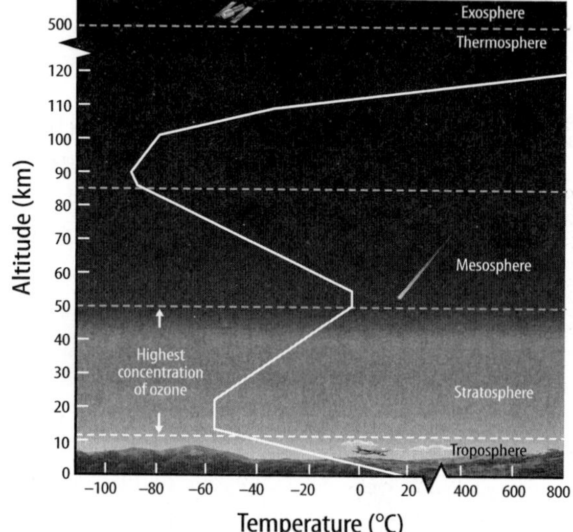

5 Which layer of the atmosphere has the widest range of temperatures?

A mesosphere

B stratosphere

C thermosphere

D troposphere

6 Which was the main component of Earth's original atmosphere?

A carbon dioxide

B nitrogen

C oxygen

D water vapor

7 Which is the primary cause of the global wind patterns on Earth?

A ice cap melting

B uneven heating

C weather changing

D waves breaking

Use the diagram below to answer question 8.

Energy Transfer Methods

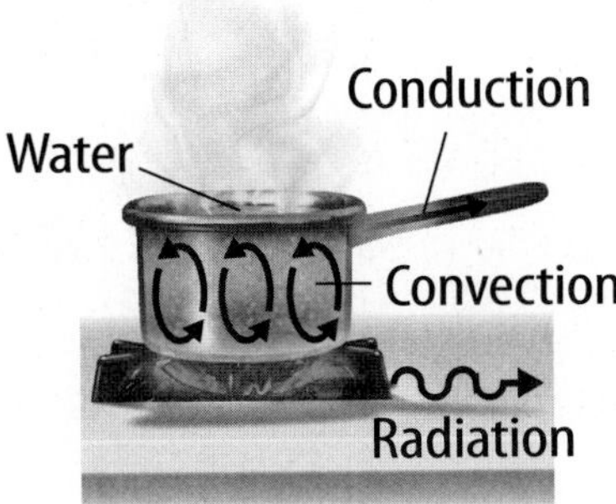

8 In the diagram above, which transfers thermal energy in the same way the Sun's energy is transferred to Earth?

A the boiling water

B the burner flame

C the hot handle

D the rising steam

9 Which substance in the air of U.S. cities has decreased least since the Clean Air Act began?

A carbon monoxide

B ground-level ozone

C particulate matter

D sulfur dioxide

Constructed Response

Use the table below to answer questions 10 and 11.

Layer	Significant Fact

10 In the table above, list in order the layers of Earth's atmosphere from lowest to highest. Provide one significant fact about each layer.

11 Explain how the first four atmospheric layers are important to life on Earth.

Use the table below to answer question 12.

Heat Transfer	Explanation
Conduction	
Convection	
Latent heat	
Radiation	

12 Complete the table to explain how heat energy transfers from the Sun to Earth and its atmosphere.

13 What are temperature inversions? How do they form? What is the relationship between temperature inversions and air pollution?

NEED EXTRA HELP?													
If You Missed Question...	1	2	3	4	5	6	7	8	9	10	11	12	13
Go to Lesson...	2	3	2	3	1	1	3	2	4	1	1	2	2, 4

Chapter 7

Weather

THE BIG IDEA **How do scientists describe and predict weather?**

Inquiry Is this a record snowfall?

Buffalo, New York, is famous for its snowstorms, averaging 3 m of snow each year. Other areas of the world might only get a few centimeters of snow a year. In some parts of the world, it never snows.

- Why do some areas get less snow than others?
- How do scientists describe and predict weather?

Get Ready to Read

What do you think?

Before you read, decide if you agree or disagree with each of these statements. As you read this chapter, see if you change your mind about any of the statements.

1. Weather is the long-term average of atmospheric patterns of an area.
2. All clouds are at the same altitude within the atmosphere.
3. Precipitation often occurs at the boundaries of large air masses.
4. There are no safety precautions for severe weather, such as tornadoes and hurricanes.
5. Weather variables are measured every day at locations around the world.
6. Modern weather forecasts are done using computers.

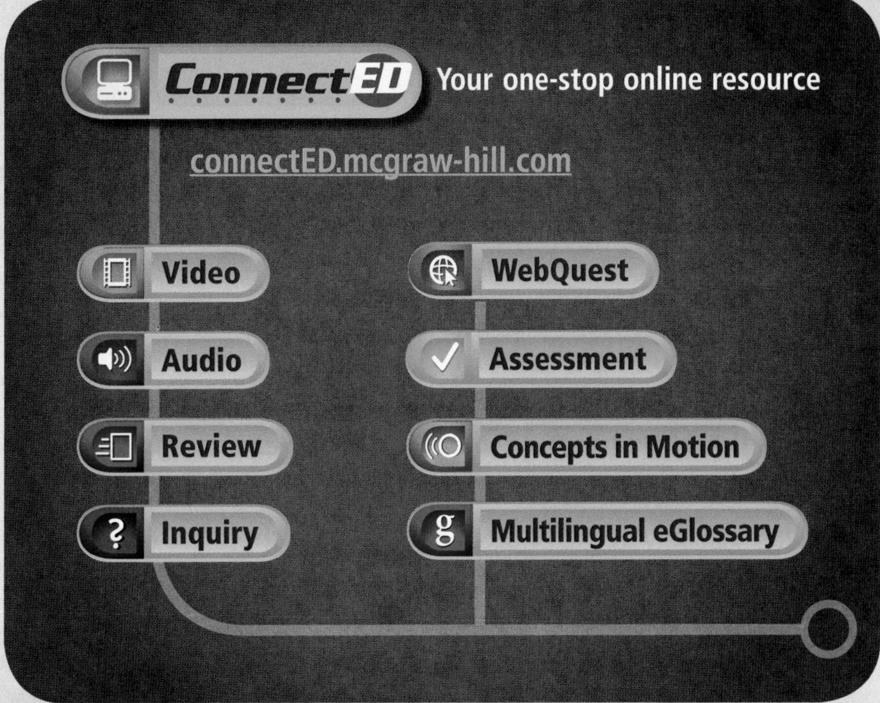

Lesson 1

Describing Weather

Reading Guide

Key Concepts

ESSENTIAL QUESTIONS

- What is weather?
- What variables are used to describe weather?
- How is weather related to the water cycle?

Vocabulary

weather p. 231
air pressure p. 232
humidity p. 232
relative humidity p. 233
dew point p. 233
precipitation p. 235
water cycle p. 235

g Multilingual eGlossary

Video

- BrainPOP®
- Science Video

Academic Standards for Science

8.2.2 Describe and model how water moves through the earth's crust, atmosphere, and oceans in a cyclic way, as liquid, vapor, and solid.

Also covers: 8.NS.4, 8.NS.7

Inquiry Why are clouds different?

If you look closely at the photo, you'll see that there are different types of clouds in the sky. How do clouds form? If all clouds consist of water droplets and ice crystals, why do they look different? Are clouds weather?

15 minutes

Can you make clouds in a bag?

When water vapor in the atmosphere cools, it condenses. The resulting water droplets make up clouds.

1. Read and complete a lab safety form.
2. Half-fill a **500-mL beaker** with **ice** and **cold water.**
3. Pour 125 mL of **warm water** into a **resealable plastic bag** and seal the bag.
4. Carefully lower the bag into the ice water. Record your observations in your Science Journal.

Think About This

1. What did you observe when the warm water in the bag was put into the beaker?
2. What explanation can you give for what happened?
3. **Key Concept** What could you see in the natural world that results from the same process?

What is weather?

Everybody talks about the weather. "Nice day, isn't it?" "How was the weather during your vacation?" Talking about weather is so common that we even use weather terms to describe unrelated topics. "That homework assignment was a breeze." Or "I'll take a rain check."

Weather *is the atmospheric conditions, along with short-term changes, of a certain place at a certain time.* If you have ever been caught in a rainstorm on what began as a sunny day, you know the weather can change quickly. Sometimes it changes in just a few hours. But other times your area might have the same sunny weather for several days in a row.

Weather Variables

Perhaps some of the first things that come to mind when you think about weather are temperature and rainfall. As you dress in the morning, you need to know what the temperature will be throughout the day to help you decide what to wear. If it is raining, you might cancel your picnic.

Temperature and rainfall are just two of the **variables** used to describe weather. Meteorologists, scientists who study and predict weather, use several specific variables that describe a variety of atmospheric conditions. These include air temperature, air pressure, wind speed and direction, humidity, cloud coverage, and precipitation.

Review Vocabulary
variable
a quantity that can change

Key Concept Check What is weather?

REVIEW VOCABULARY
kinetic energy
energy an object has due to its motion

Air Temperature

The measure of the average **kinetic energy** of molecules in the air is air temperature. When the temperature is high, molecules have a high kinetic energy. Therefore, molecules in warm air move faster than molecules in cold air. Air temperatures vary with time of day, season, location, and altitude.

Air Pressure

The pressure that a column of air exerts on the air, or surface, below it is **air pressure.** Study **Figure 1.** Is air pressure at Earth's surface more or less than air pressure at the top of the atmosphere? Air pressure decreases as altitude increases. Therefore, air pressure is greater at low altitudes than at high altitudes.

When you hear the term *barometric pressure* during a weather forecast, the meteorologist is referring to air pressure. Air pressure is measured with an instrument called a barometer, shown in **Figure 2.** Air pressure is typically measured in millibars (mb). Knowing the barometric pressure of different areas helps meteorologists predict the weather.

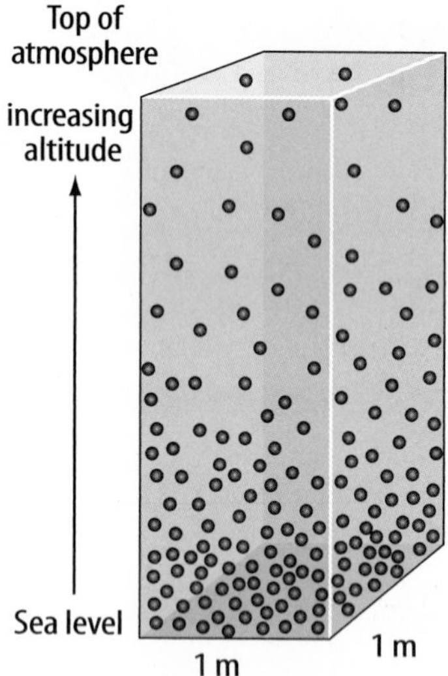

Figure 1 Increasing air pressure comes from having more molecules overhead.

Visual Check What happens to air pressure as altitude decreases?

Reading Check What instrument measures air pressure?

Wind

As air moves from areas of high pressure to areas of low pressure, it creates wind. Wind direction is the direction from which the wind is blowing. For example, the westerlies blow from west to east. Meteorologists measure wind speed using an instrument called an anemometer (a nuh MAH muh tur). An anemometer is shown in **Figure 2.**

Humidity

The amount of water vapor in the air is called **humidity** (hyew MIH duh tee). Humidity can be measured in grams of water per cubic meter of air (g/m^3). When the humidity is high, there is more water vapor in the air. On a day with high humidity, your skin might feel sticky, and sweat might not evaporate from your skin as quickly.

Figure 2 Barometers, left, and anemometers, right, are used to measure weather variables.

Relative Humidity

Think about how a sponge can absorb water. At some point, it becomes full and cannot absorb any more water. In the same way, air can only contain a certain amount of gaseous water vapor. When air is saturated, it contains as much water vapor as possible. Temperature determines the maximum amount of water vapor air can contain. Warm air can contain more water vapor than cold air. *The amount of water vapor present in the air compared to the maximum amount of water vapor the air could contain at that temperature is called* **relative humidity.**

Relative humidity is measured using an instrument called a psychrometer and is given as a percent. For example, a relative humidity of 100 percent means that the air cannot hold any more moisture and it will begin raining or form dew. If it has half it can hold, the relative humidity is 50 percent.

Reading Check Compare and contrast humidity and relative humidity.

Dew Point

When a sponge becomes saturated with water, the water starts to drip from the sponge. Similarly, when air becomes saturated with water vapor, the water vapor will condense and form water droplets. When air near the ground becomes saturated, the water vapor in air will condense to a liquid. If the temperature is above 0°C, dew forms. If the temperature is below 0°C, ice crystals, or frost, form. Higher in the atmosphere clouds form. The graph in **Figure 3** shows the total amount of water vapor that air can contain at different temperatures.

When the temperature decreases, the air can hold less moisture. As you just read, the air becomes saturated and dew forms. *The* **dew point** *is the temperature at which air is fully saturated because of decreasing temperatures while holding the amount of moisture constant.*

Inquiry MiniLab 20 minutes

When will dew form?

The relative humidity on a summer day is 80 percent. The temperature is 35°C. You want to find out if the dew point will be reached if the temperature drops to 25°C later that evening. Use **Figure 3** below to find the amount of water vapor needed for saturation at each temperature.

1. Calculate the amount of water vapor in air that is 35°C and has 80 percent relative humidity. (Hint: multiply the amount of water vapor air can contain at 35°C by the percent of relative humidity.)
2. At 25°C, air can hold 2.2 g/cm^3 of water vapor. If your answer from step 1 is less than 2.2 g/cm^3, the dew point is not reached and dew will not form. If the number is greater, dew will form.

Analyze and Conclude

Key Concept After the Sun rises in the morning the air's temperature increases. How does the relative humidity change after sunrise? What does the line represent?

Figure 3 The graph shows that as air temperature increases, more water vapor can be present.

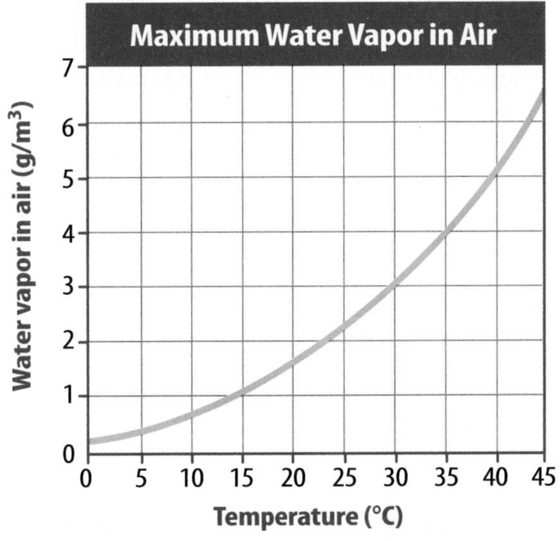

Figure 4 Clouds have different shapes and can be found at different altitudes.

Stratus clouds
- flat, white, and layered
- altitude up to 2,000 m

Cumulus clouds
- fluffy, heaped, or piled up
- 2,000 to 6,000 m altitude

Cirrus clouds
- wispy
- above 6,000 m

Clouds and Fog

When you exhale outside on a cold winter day, you can see the water vapor in your breath condense into a foggy cloud in front of your face. This also happens when warm air containing water vapor cools as it rises in the atmosphere. When the cooling air reaches its dew point, water vapor condenses on small particles in the air and forms droplets. Surrounded by thousands of other droplets, these small droplets block and reflect light. This makes them visible as clouds.

Clouds are water droplets or ice crystals suspended in the atmosphere. Clouds can have different shapes and be present at different altitudes within the atmosphere. Different types of clouds are shown in **Figure 4.** Because we observe that clouds move, we recognize that water and thermal energy are transported from one location to another. Recall that clouds are also important in reflecting some of the Sun's incoming radiation.

A cloud that forms near Earth's surface is called fog. Fog is a suspension of water droplets or ice crystals close to or at Earth's surface. Fog reduces visibility, the distance a person can see into the atmosphere.

Reading Check What is fog?

WORD ORIGIN

precipitation
from Latin *praecipitationem*, means "act or fact of falling headlong"

FOLDABLES®

Make a horizontal two-tab book and label the tabs as illustrated. Use it to collect information on clouds and fog. Find similarities and differences.

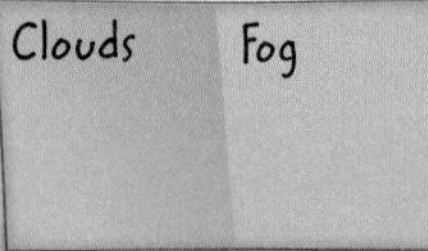

Precipitation

Recall that droplets in clouds form around small solid particles in the atmosphere. These particles might be dust, salt, or smoke. Precipitation occurs when cloud droplets combine and become large enough to fall back to Earth's surface. **Precipitation** *is water, in liquid or solid form, that falls from the atmosphere.* Examples of precipitation—rain, snow, sleet, and hail—are shown in **Figure 5.**

Rain is precipitation that reaches Earth's surface as droplets of water. Snow is precipitation that reaches Earth's surface as solid, frozen crystals of water. Sleet may originate as snow. The snow melts as it falls through a layer of warm air and refreezes when it passes through a layer of below-freezing air. Other times it is just freezing rain. Hail reaches Earth's surface as large pellets of ice. Hail starts as a small piece of ice that is repeatedly lifted and dropped by an updraft within a cloud. A layer of ice is added with each lifting. When it finally becomes too heavy for the updraft to lift, it falls to Earth.

Key Concept Check What variables are used to describe weather?

The Water Cycle

Precipitation is an important process in the water cycle. Evaporation and condensation are phase changes that are also important to the water cycle. *The* **water cycle** *is the series of natural processes in which water continually moves among oceans, land, and the atmosphere.* As illustrated in **Figure 6,** most water vapor enters the atmosphere when water is heated and evaporates at the ocean's surface. Water vapor cools as it rises in the atmosphere and condenses back into a liquid. Eventually, clouds form from droplets of liquid and solid water. Clouds produce precipitation, which falls to Earth's surface and later evaporates, continuing the cycle.

Key Concept Check How is weather related to the water cycle?

Types of Precipitation

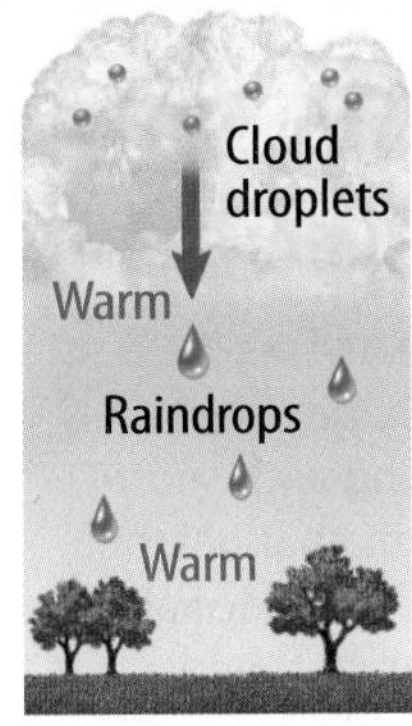

Rain

Snow

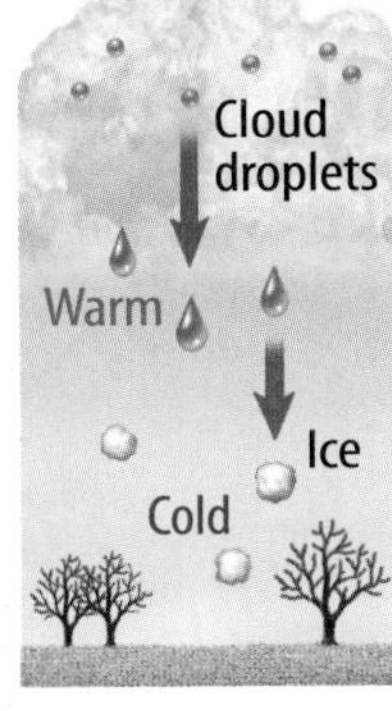

Sleet

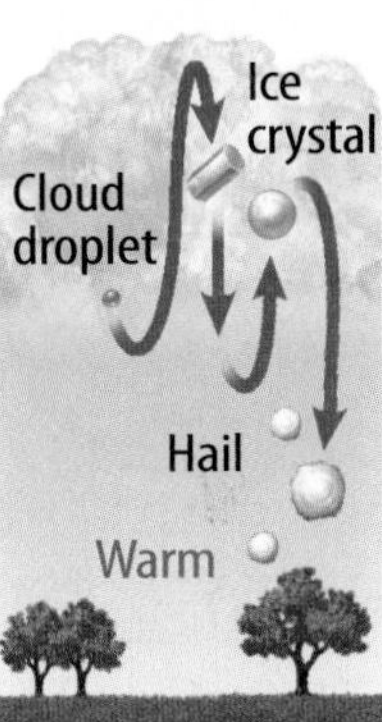

Hail

▲ **Figure 5** Rain, snow, sleet, and hail are forms of precipitation.

Visual Check What is the difference between snow and sleet?

The Water Cycle

Figure 6 The Sun's energy powers the water cycle, which is the continual movement of water between the ocean, the land, and the atmosphere.

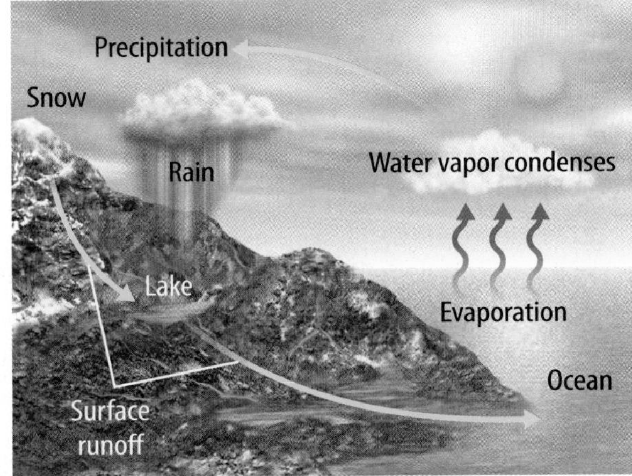

Lesson 1 Review

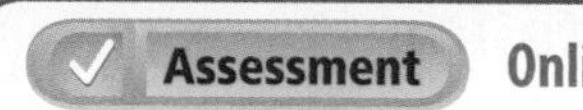

Visual Summary

Weather is the atmospheric conditions, along with short-term changes, of a certain place at a certain time.

Weather variables include air temperature, air pressure, wind, humidity, and relative humidity.

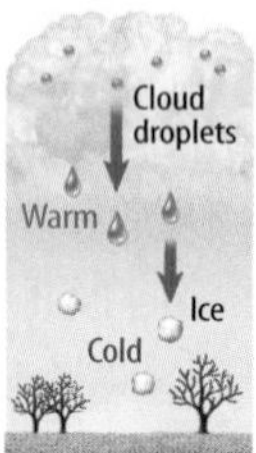

Forms of precipitation include rain, sleet, snow, and hail.

FOLDABLES®

Use your lesson Foldable to review the lesson. Save your Foldable for the project at the end of the chapter.

What do you think NOW?

You first read the statements below at the beginning of the chapter.

1. Weather is the long-term average of atmospheric patterns of an area.
2. All clouds are at the same altitude within the atmosphere.

Did you change your mind about whether you agree or disagree with the statements? Rewrite any false statements to make them true.

Use Vocabulary

1. **Define** *humidity* in your own words.
2. **Use the term** *precipitation* in a sentence.
3. ________ is the pressure that a column of air exerts on the surface below it.

Understand Key Concepts

4. Which is NOT a standard weather variable?
   A. air pressure
   B. moon phase
   C. temperature
   D. wind speed
5. **Identify** and describe the different variables used to describe weather.
6. **Relate** humidity to cloud formation.
7. **Describe** how processes in the water cycle are related to weather.

Interpret Graphics

8. **Identify** Which type of precipitation is shown in the diagram below? How does this precipitation form?

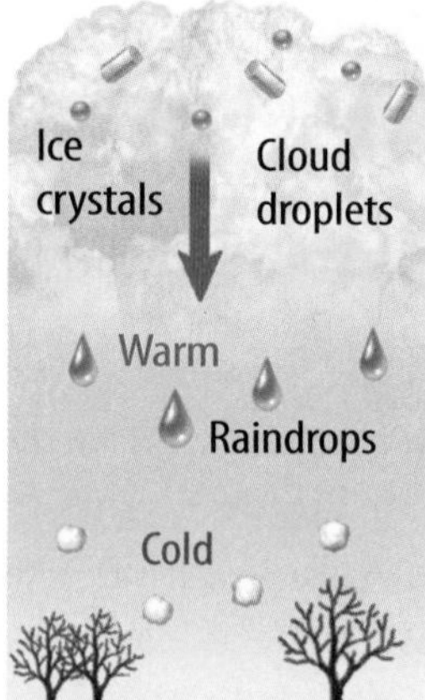

Critical Thinking

9. **Analyze** Why would your ears pop if you climbed a tall mountain?
10. **Differentiate** among cloud formation, fog formation, and dew point.

SCIENCE & SOCIETY

AMERICAN MUSEUM OF NATURAL HISTORY

Flooding caused widespread devastation in New Orleans, a city that lies below sea level. The storm surge broke through levees that had protected the city.

Is there a link between hurricanes and global warming?

Scientists worry that hurricanes might be getting bigger and happening more often.

On August 29, 2005, Hurricane Katrina roared through New Orleans, Louisiana. The storm destroyed homes and broke through levees, flooding most of the low-lying city. In the wake of the disaster, many wondered whether global warming was responsible. If warm oceans are the fuel for hurricanes, could rising temperatures cause stronger or more frequent hurricanes?

Climate scientists have several ways to investigate this question. They examine past hurricane activity, sea surface temperature, and other climate data. They compare these different types of data and look for patterns. Based on the laws of physics, they put climate and hurricane data into equations. A computer solves these equations and makes computer models. Scientists analyze the models to see whether there is a connection between hurricane activity and different climate variables.

What have scientists learned? So far they have not found a link between warming oceans and the frequency of hurricanes. However, they have found a connection between warming oceans and hurricane strength. Models suggest that rising ocean temperatures might create more destructive hurricanes with stronger winds and more rainfall.

The warm waters of the Gulf of Mexico fueled Hurricane Katrina as it spun toward Louisiana.

But global warming is not the only cause of warming oceans. As the ocean circulates, it goes through cycles of warming and cooling. Data show that the Atlantic Ocean has been in a warming phase for the past few decades.

Whether due to global warming or natural cycles, ocean temperatures are expected to rise even more in coming years. While rising ocean temperatures might not produce more hurricanes, climate research shows they could produce more powerful hurricanes. Perhaps the better question is not what caused Hurricane Katrina, but how we can prepare for equal-strength or more destructive hurricanes in the future.

It's Your Turn

DIAGRAM With a partner, create a storyboard with each frame showing one step in hurricane formation. Label your drawings. Share your storyboard with the class.

Lesson 2

Weather Patterns

Reading Guide

Key Concepts
ESSENTIAL QUESTIONS

- What are two types of pressure systems?
- What drives weather patterns?
- Why is it useful to understand weather patterns?
- What are some examples of severe weather?

Vocabulary

high-pressure system p. 239
low-pressure system p. 239
air mass p. 240
front p. 242
tornado p. 245
hurricane p. 246
blizzard p. 247

Academic Standards for Science

8.2.1 Recognize and demonstrate how the sun's energy drives convection in the atmosphere and in bodies of water, which results in ocean currents and weather patterns.

8.2.5 Describe the conditions that cause Indiana weather and weather-related events such as tornadoes, lake effect snow, blizzards, thunderstorms, and flooding.

Also covers: 8.NS.1, 8.NS.4, 8.NS.6, 8.NS.7, 8.NS.9

Inquiry What caused this flooding?

Surging waves and rain from Hurricane Katrina caused flooding in New Orleans, Louisiana. Why are flooding and other types of severe weather dangerous? How does severe weather form?

Launch Lab

10 minutes

How can temperature affect pressure?

Air molecules that have low energy can be packed closely together. As energy is added to the molecules they begin to move and bump into one another.

1. Read and complete a lab safety form.
2. Close a **resealable plastic bag** except for a small opening. Insert a **straw** through the opening and blow air into the bag until it is as firm as possible. Remove the straw and quickly seal the bag.
3. Submerge the bag in a **container** of **ice water** and hold it there for 2 minutes. Record your observations in your Science Journal.
4. Remove the bag from the ice water and submerge it in **warm water** for 2 minutes. Record your observations.

Think About This

1. What do the results tell you about the movement of air molecules in cold air and in warm air?
2. **Key Concept** What property of the air is demonstrated in this activity?

Pressure Systems

Weather is often associated with pressure systems. Recall that air pressure is the weight of the molecules in a large mass of air. When air molecules are cool, they are closer together than when they are warm. Cool air masses have high pressure, or more weight. Warm air masses have low pressure.

A **high-pressure system,** shown in **Figure 7,** *is a large body of circulating air with high pressure at its center and lower pressure outside of the system.* Because air moves from high pressure to low pressure, the air inside the system moves away from the center. Dense air sinks, bringing clear skies and fair weather.

A **low-pressure system,** also shown in **Figure 7,** *is a large body of circulating air with low pressure at its center and higher pressure outside of the system.* This causes air inside the low pressure system to rise. The rising air cools and the water vapor condenses, forming clouds and sometimes precipitation—rain or snow.

Key Concept Check Compare and contrast two types of pressure systems.

Figure 7 Air moving from areas of high pressure to areas of low pressure is called wind.

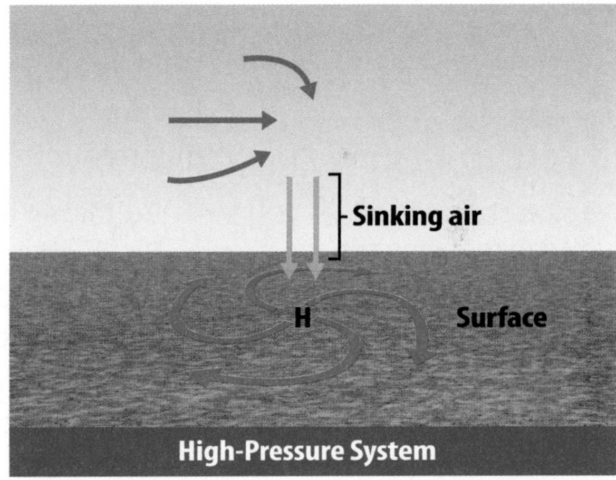

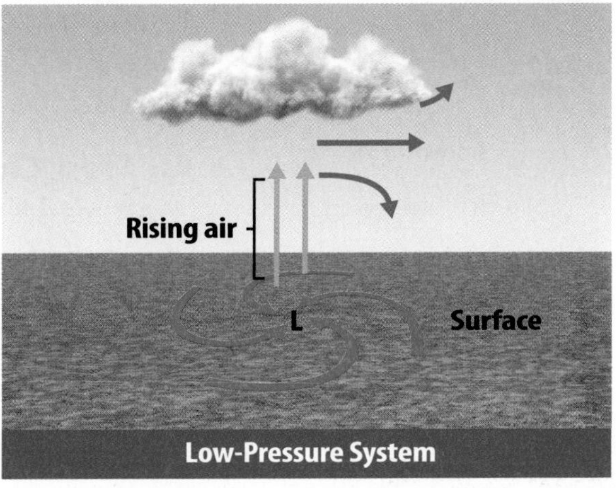

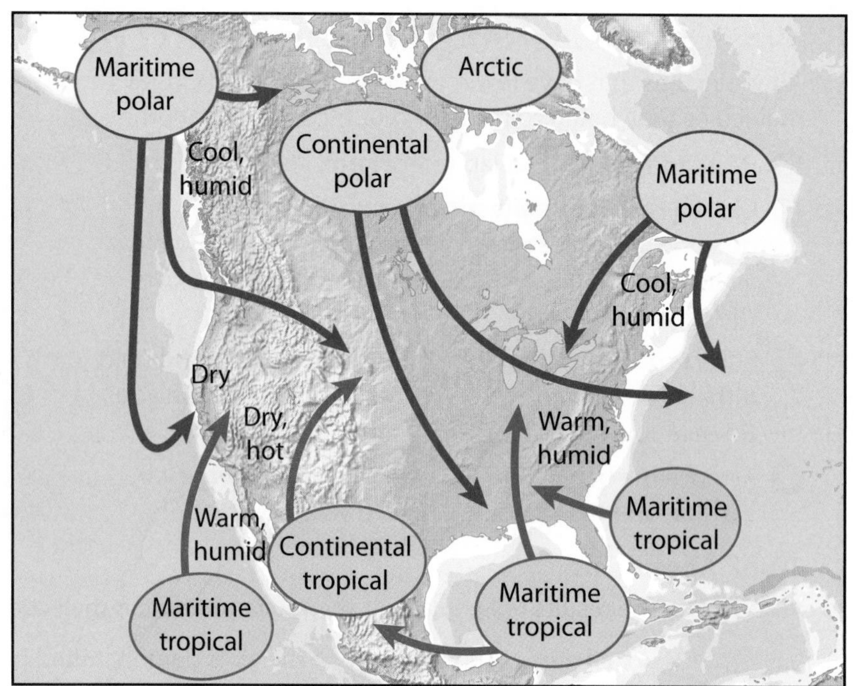

Figure 8 Five main air masses impact climate across North America.

Visual Check Where does continental polar air come from?

Air Masses

Have you ever noticed that the weather sometimes stays the same for several days in a row? For example, during winter in the northern United States, extremely cold temperatures often last for three or four days in a row. Afterward, several days might follow with warmer temperatures and snow showers.

Air masses are responsible for this pattern. **Air masses** *are large bodies of air with distinct temperature and moisture characteristics.* An air mass forms when a large high pressure system lingers over an area for several days. As a high pressure system comes in contact with Earth, the air in the system takes on the temperature and moisture characteristics of the surface below it.

Like high- and low-pressure systems, air masses can extend for a thousand kilometers or more. Sometimes one air mass covers most of the United States. Examples of the main air masses that affect weather in the United States are shown in **Figure 8.**

Air Mass Classification

Air masses are classified by their temperature and moisture characteristics. Air masses that form over land are referred to as continental air masses. Those that form over water are referred to as maritime masses. Warm air masses that form in the equatorial regions are called tropical. Those that form in cold regions are called polar. Air masses near the poles, over the coldest regions of the globe, are called arctic and antarctic air masses.

Fold a sheet of paper into thirds along the long axis. Label the outside *Air Masses.* Make another fold about 2 inches from the long edge of the paper to make a three-column chart. Label as shown.

Arctic Air Masses Forming over Siberia and the Arctic are arctic air masses. They contain bitterly cold, dry air. During winter, an arctic air mass can bring temperatures down to −40°C.

Continental Polar Air Masses Because land cannot transfer as much moisture to the air as oceans can, air masses that form over land are drier than air masses that form over oceans. Continental polar air masses are fast-moving and bring cold temperatures in winter and cool weather in summer. Find the continental polar air masses over Canada in **Figure 8.**

Maritime Polar Air Masses Forming over the northern Atlantic and Pacific Oceans, maritime polar air masses are cold and humid. They often bring cloudy, rainy weather.

Continental Tropical Air Masses Because they form in the tropics over dry, desert land, continental tropical air masses are hot and dry. They bring clear skies and high temperatures. Continental tropical air masses usually form only during summer.

Maritime Tropical Air Masses As shown in **Figure 8,** maritime tropical air masses form over the Gulf of Mexico, the Caribbean Sea, and the eastern Pacific Ocean. These moist air masses bring hot, humid air to the southeastern United States during summer. In winter, they can bring heavy snowfall.

Air masses can change as they move over the land and ocean. Warm, moist air can lose its moisture and become cool. Cold, dry air can move over water and become moist and warm.

 **Key Concept Check** What drives weather patterns?

Math Skills 

Conversions

To convert Fahrenheit (°F) units to Celsius (°C) units, use this equation:

$$°C = \frac{(°F - 32)}{1.8}$$

Convert **76°F** to °C

1. Always perform the operation in parentheses first.
   (**76°F** − 32 = **44°F**)
2. Divide the answer from Step 1 by 1.8.
   $$\frac{44°F}{1.8} = 24°C$$

To convert °C to **°F**, follow the same steps using the following equation:

$$°F = (°C \times 1.8) + 32$$

Practice

1. Convert 86°F to °C.
2. Convert 37°C to °F.

- **Math Practice**
- **Personal Tutor**

Inquiry MiniLab

20 minutes

How can you observe air pressure?

Although air seems very light, air molecules do exert pressure. You can observe air pressure in action in this activity.

1. Read and complete a lab safety form.
2. Seal an empty **plastic bottle.**
3. Place the bottle in a **bucket of ice** for 10 minutes. Record your observations in your Science Journal.

Analyze and Conclude

1. **Interpret** how air pressure affected the bottle.
2. **Key Concept** Discuss how changing air pressure in Earth's atmosphere affects other things on Earth, such as weather.

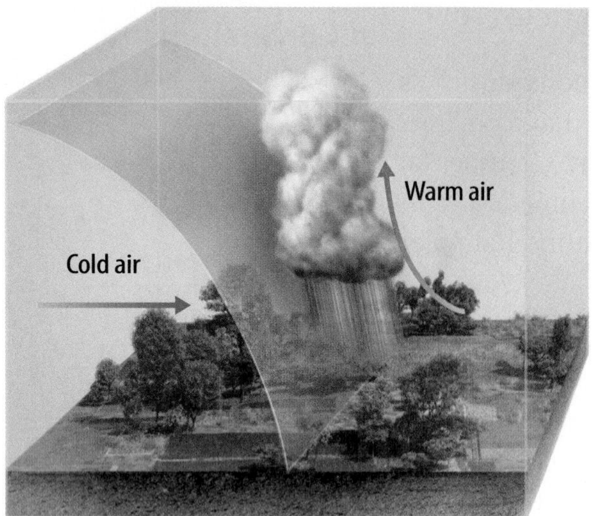

Cold

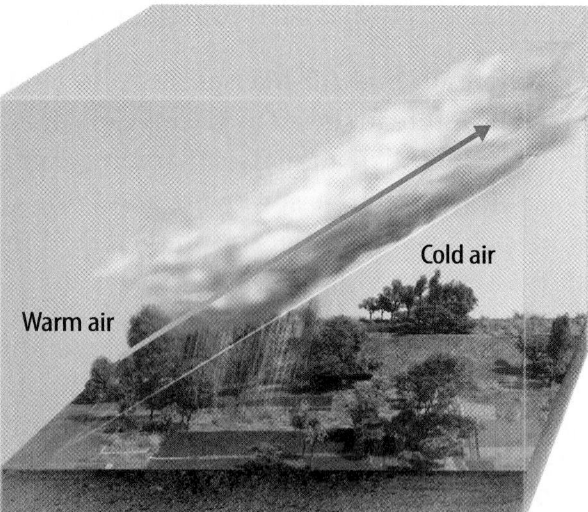

Warm

Figure 9 Certain types of fronts are associated with specific weather.

Visual Check Describe the difference between a cold front and a warm front.

Fronts

In 1918, Norwegian meteorologist Jacob Bjerknes (BYURK nehs) and his coworkers were busy developing a new method for forecasting the weather. Bjerknes noticed that specific types of weather occur at the boundaries between different air masses. Because he was trained in the army, Bjerknes used a military term to describe this boundary—front.

A military front is the boundary between opposing armies in a battle. *A weather* **front**, *however, is a boundary between two air masses.* As wind carries an air mass away from the area where it formed, it will eventually bump into another air mass. Drastic weather changes often occur at these boundaries, called fronts. Changes in temperature, humidity, clouds, wind, and precipitation are common at fronts.

SCIENCE USE V. COMMON USE
front
Science Use a boundary between two air masses

Common Use the foremost part or surface of something

Cold Fronts

When a colder air mass moves toward a warmer air mass, a cold front forms, as shown in **Figure 9.** The cold air, which is denser than the warm air, pushes underneath the warm air mass. The warm air rises. The warm air cools as it rises. Water vapor in the air condenses and clouds form. Showers and thunderstorms often form along cold fronts. It is common for temperatures to decrease as much as 10°C when a cold front passes through. The wind becomes gusty and changes direction. In many cases, cold fronts give rise to severe storms.

Reading Check What types of weather are associated with cold fronts?

Stationary

Occluded

Warm Fronts

As shown in **Figure 9,** a warm front forms when less dense, warmer air moves toward colder, denser air. The warm air rises as it glides above the cold air mass. When water vapor in the warm air condenses, it creates a wide blanket of clouds. These clouds often bring steady rain or snow for several hours or even days. A warm front not only brings warmer temperatures, but it also causes the wind to shift directions.

Both a cold front and a warm front form at the edge of an approaching air mass. Because air masses are large, the movement of fronts is used to make weather forecasts. When a cold front passes through your area, temperatures will remain low for the next few days. When a warm front arrives, you can look forward to a few days of warmer, more humid weather.

Stationary and Occluded Fronts

Sometimes an approaching front will stall for several days with warm air on one side of it and cold air on the other side. When the boundary between two air masses stalls, the front is called a stationary front. Study the stationary front shown in **Figure 9.** You might guess that cloudy skies and light rain are found along stationary fronts.

Cold fronts move faster than warm fronts. When a fast-moving cold front catches up with a slow-moving warm front, an occluded or blocked front forms. Occluded fronts, shown in **Figure 9,** usually bring precipitation.

 **Key Concept Check** Why is it useful to understand weather patterns associated with fronts?

Severe Weather

Weather that is capable of causing major damage, injuries, and death is called severe weather. Examples of severe weather include thunderstorms, tornadoes, hurricanes, and blizzards.

Thunderstorms

Also known as electrical storms because of their lightning, thunderstorms have warm temperatures, moisture, and rising air, which may be supplied by a low-pressure system. When these conditions occur, a cumulus cloud can grow into a 10-km-tall thundercloud in as little as 30 minutes.

A typical thunderstorm has a three-stage life cycle, shown in **Figure 10.** The cumulus stage is dominated by cloud formation and updrafts. Updrafts are air currents moving vertically away from the ground. After the cumulus cloud has been created, downdrafts begin to appear. Downdrafts are air currents moving vertically toward the ground. In the mature stage, heavy winds, rain, and lightning dominate the area. Within 30 minutes of reaching the mature stage, the thunderstorm begins to fade, or dissipate. In the dissipation stage, updrafts stop, winds die down, lightning ceases, and precipitation weakens.

Strong updrafts and downdrafts within a thunderstorm cause millions of tiny ice crystals to rise and sink crashing into each other. This creates positively and negatively charged particles in the cloud. The difference in the charges of particles between the cloud and the charges of particles on the ground eventually creates electricity. This is seen as a bolt of lightning. Lightning can move from cloud to cloud, cloud to ground, or ground to cloud. It can heat the nearby air to more than 27,000°C. Air molecules near the bolt rapidly expand and then contract, creating the sound identified as thunder.

Floods

Some thunderstorms can produce extended periods of heavy rain. Large snow packs also produce a lot of water as they melt. It can take time for all of the water to reach streams, rivers, lakes, and oceans. As water enters a stream, the water level continues to rise and might reach its highest point, called a crest, days after the rain or snow melt ends. If the crest occurs at a depth that is higher than the stream's banks, excess water spills over a stream's banks causing a flood. The large amounts of water involved in a flood can produce extensive damage.

Figure 10 Thunderstorms have distinct stages characterized by the direction in which air is moving.

Cumulus Stage

Mature Stage

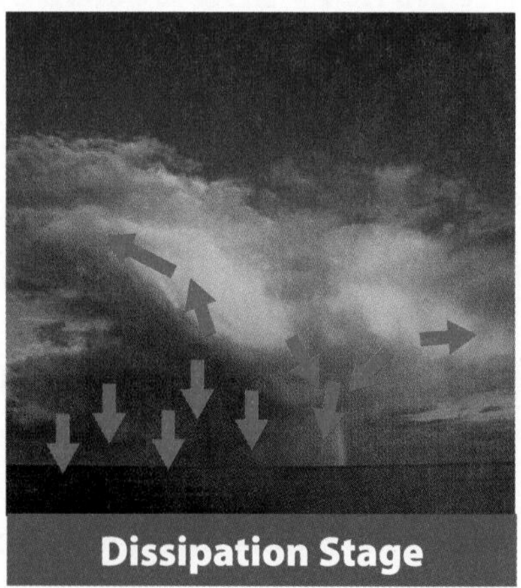

Dissipation Stage

Visual Check Describe what happens during each stage of a thunderstorm.

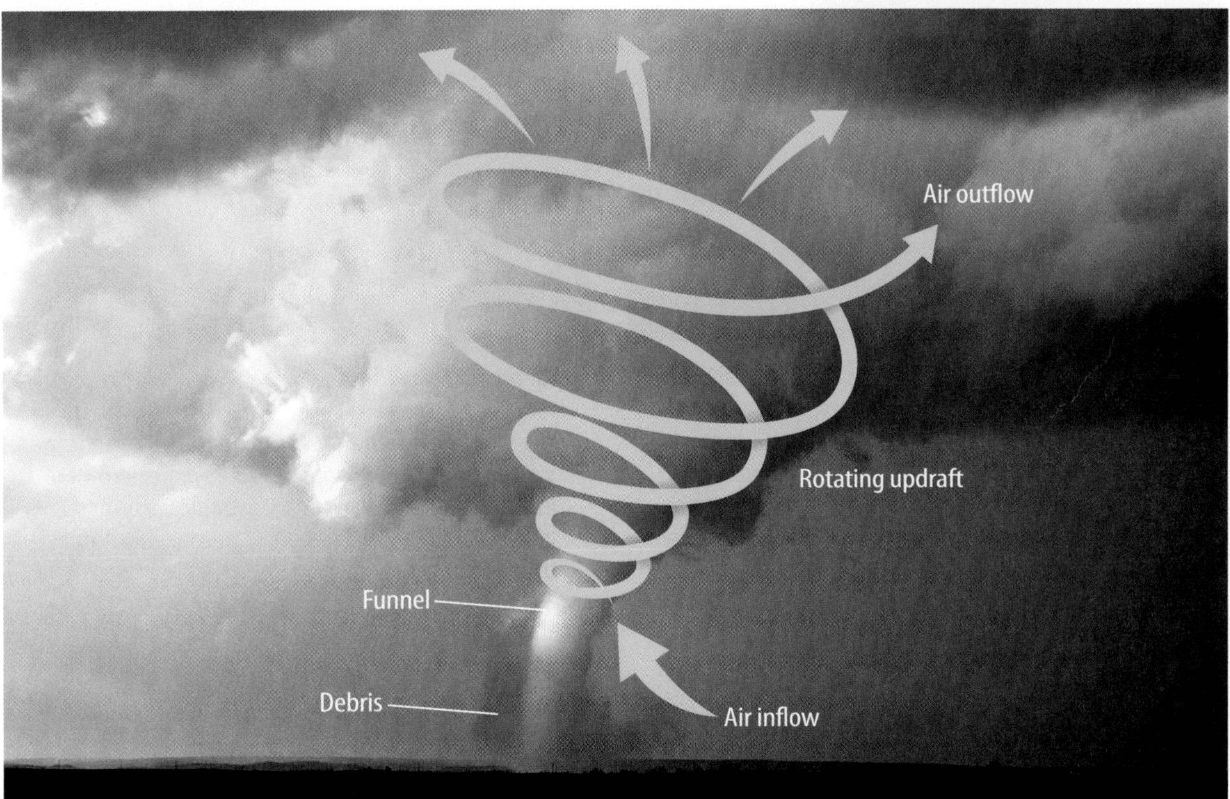

Figure 11 A funnel cloud forms when updrafts within a thunderstorm begin rotating.

Tornadoes

Perhaps you have seen photos of the damage from a tornado. *A* **tornado** *is a violent, whirling column of air in contact with the ground.* Most tornadoes have a diameter of several hundred meters. The largest tornadoes exceed 1,500 m in diameter. The intense, swirling winds within tornadoes can reach speeds of more than 400 km/h. These winds are strong enough to send cars, trees, and even entire houses flying through the air. Tornadoes usually last only a few minutes. More destructive tornadoes, however, can last for several hours.

Formation of Tornadoes When thunderstorm updrafts begin to rotate, as shown in **Figure 11,** tornadoes can form. Swirling winds spiral downward from the thunderstorm's base, creating a funnel cloud. When the funnel reaches the ground, it becomes a tornado. Although the swirling air is invisible, you can easily see the debris lifted by the tornado.

Reading Check How do tornadoes form?

Tornado Alley More tornadoes occur in the United States than anywhere else on Earth. Tornado Alley is the name given to the area of the central United States, from Nebraska to Texas, that experiences the most tornadoes. In this area, cold air blowing southward from Canada frequently collides with warm, moist air moving northward from the Gulf of Mexico. These conditions are ideal for severe thunderstorms and tornadoes.

Classifying Tornadoes Dr. Ted Fujita designed a method for classifying the strength of tornadoes. On the modified Fujita intensity scale, F0 tornadoes cause light damage, breaking tree branches and damaging billboards. F1 though F4 tornadoes cause moderate to devastating damage, including tearing roofs from homes, derailing trains, and throwing vehicles in the air. F5 tornadoes cause incredible damage, such as demolishing concrete and steel buildings and pulling the bark from trees.

Hurricane Formation

Figure 12 Hurricanes consist of alternating bands of heavy precipitation and sinking air.

Hurricane Formation

1 As warm, moist air rises into the atmosphere, it cools, water vapor condenses, and clouds form. As more air rises, it creates an area of low pressure over the ocean.

2 As air continues to rise, a tropical depression forms. Tropical depressions bring thunderstorms with winds between 37–62 km/h.

3 Air continues to rise, rotating counterclockwise. The storm builds to a tropical storm with winds in excess of 63 km/h. It produces strong thunderstorms.

4 When winds exceed 119 km/h, the storm becomes a hurricane. Only one percent of tropical storms become hurricanes.

Inside a Hurricane

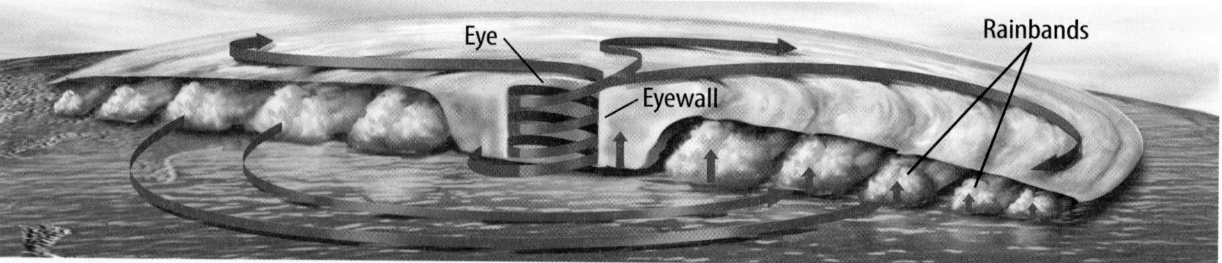

Visual Check How do hurricanes form?

WORD ORIGIN

hurricane
from Spanish *huracan,* means "tempest"

Hurricanes

An intense tropical storm with winds exceeding 119 km/h is a **hurricane.** Hurricanes are the most destructive storms on Earth. Like tornadoes, hurricanes have a circular shape with intense, swirling winds. Hurricanes do not form over land, however. Hurricanes typically form in late summer over warm, tropical ocean water. **Figure 12** sequences the steps in hurricane formation. A typical hurricane is 480 km across, more than 150 thousand times larger than a tornado. At the center of a hurricane is the eye, an area of clear skies and light winds.

Damage from hurricanes occurs as a result of strong winds and flooding. While still out at sea, hurricanes create high waves that can flood coastal areas. As a hurricane crosses the coastline, strong rains intensify and can flood and devastate entire areas. Once a hurricane moves over land or colder water, however, it loses its energy and dissipates.

In other parts of the world, these intense tropical storms have other names. In Asia, the same type of storm is called a typhoon. In Australia it is called a tropical cyclone.

Figure 13 The weight of ice from freezing rain can cause trees, power lines, and other structures to break.

Winter Storms

Not all severe weather occurs when temperatures are warm. Winter weather can also be severe. Snow and ice can make driving difficult and dangerous. When temperatures are close to freezing (0°C), rain can freeze when it hits the ground. Ice storms coat the ground, trees, and buildings with a layer of ice, as shown in **Figure 13.**

A **blizzard** *is a violent winter storm characterized by freezing temperatures, strong winds, and blowing snow.* During blizzards, swirling snow often reduces visibility to a few meters or even less. If you are outside during a blizzard, strong winds and very cold temperatures can rapidly cool exposed skin. Windchill, the combined cooling effect of cold temperature and wind on exposed skin, can cause frostbite and hypothermia (hi poh THER mee uh).

 **Key Concept Check** What are examples of severe weather?

Lake-Effect Snow

Coastlines and lakeshores can affect climate. For example, lake-effect snow often occurs around the Great Lakes in the winter.

As cold Arctic air travels over warm lake water, the air mass absorbs both heat and moisture. When the air mass once again travels over cold land to the south and east of a lake, heavy snow falls. Lake-effect snow can cause power outages and make traveling dangerous.

Severe Weather Safety

The U.S. National Weather Service issues watches and warnings for different types of severe weather. A watch means that severe weather is possible. A warning means that severe weather is already occurring. Paying close attention to severe weather watches and warnings is important and could save your life.

It is also important to know how to protect yourself during dangerous weather. During thunderstorms, you should stay inside if possible, and stay away from metal objects and electrical cords. If you are outside, stay away from water, high places and isolated trees. Dressing properly is important in all kinds of weather. When windchill temperatures are below −20°C you should dress in layers, keep your head and fingers covered, and limit your time outdoors.

Lesson 2 Review

Assessment Online Quiz

Visual Summary

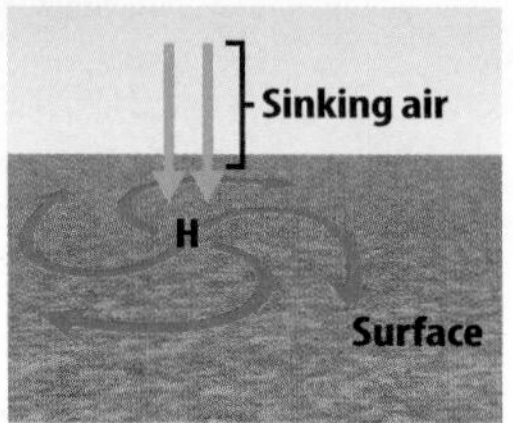

Low-pressure systems, high-pressure systems, and air masses all influence weather.

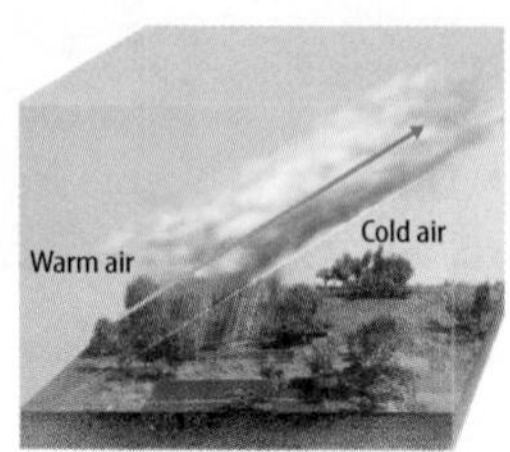

Weather often changes as a front passes through an area.

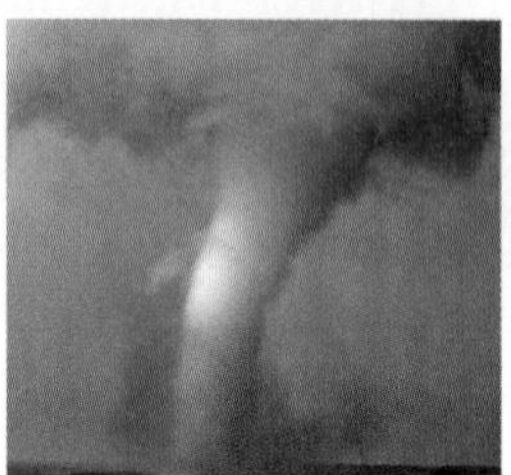

The National Weather Service issues warnings about severe weather such as thunderstorms, tornadoes, hurricanes, and blizzards.

FOLDABLES®

Use your lesson Foldable to review the lesson. Save your Foldable for the project at the end of the chapter.

What do you think NOW?

You first read the statements below at the beginning of the chapter.

3. Precipitation often occurs at the boundaries of large air masses.

4. There are no safety precautions for severe weather, such as tornadoes and hurricanes.

Did you change your mind about whether you agree or disagree with the statements? Rewrite any false statements to make them true.

Use Vocabulary

1. **Distinguish** between air mass and front.
2. **Define** *low-pressure system* using your own words.
3. **Use the term** *high-pressure system* in a sentence.

Understand Key Concepts 

4. Which air mass is humid and warm?
   A. continental polar
   B. continental tropical
   C. maritime polar
   D. maritime tropical
5. **Give an example** of cold-front weather.
6. **Compare and contrast** hurricanes and tornadoes.
7. **Explain** how thunderstorms form.

Interpret Graphics

8. **Compare and Contrast** Copy and fill in the graphic organizer below to compare and contrast high-pressure and low-pressure systems.

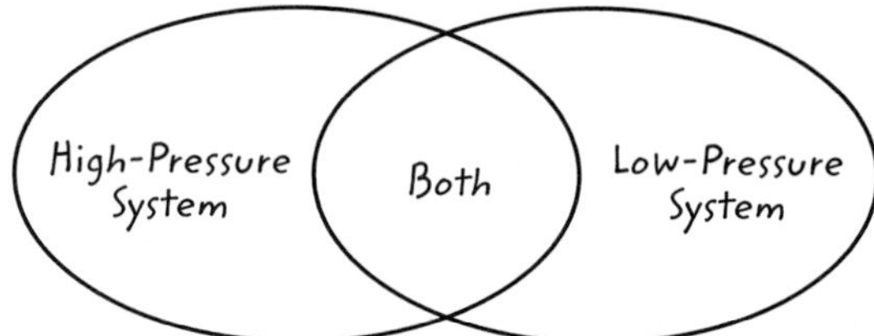

Critical Thinking

9. **Suggest** a reason that low-pressure systems are cloudy and rainy or snowy.
10. **Design** a pamphlet that contains tips on how to stay safe during different types of severe weather, such as thunderstorms and blizzards.

Math Skills

Math Practice

11. Convert 212°F to °C.
12. Convert 20°C to °F.

Why does the weather change?

One day it is sunny, the next day it is pouring rain. If you only look at one spot, the patterns that cause the weather to change are difficult to see. However, when you look on the large scale, the patterns become apparent.

Learn It

Recognizing cause and effect is an important part of science and conducting experiments. Scientists look for cause-and-effect relationships between variables. The maps below show the movement of fronts and pressure systems over a two-day period. What effect will these systems have on the weather as they move across the United States?

Try It

1. Examine the weather maps below. The thin black lines on each map represent areas where the barometric pressure is the same. The pressure is indicated by the number on the line. The center of a low- or high-pressure system is indicated by the word LOW or HIGH. Identify the location of low- and high- pressure systems on each map. Use the key below the maps to the identify the location of warm and cold fronts.
2. Find locations A, B, C, and where you live on the map. For each location, describe how the systems change positions over the two days.
3. What is the cause of and effect on precipitation and temperature at each location?

Apply It

4. The low pressure system spawned several tornadoes. Which location did they occur closest to? Explain.
5. The weather patterns generally move from west to east. Predict the weather on the third day for each location.
6. One day it is clear and sunny, but you notice that the pressure is less than it was the day before. What weather might be coming? Why?
7. **Key Concept** How does understanding weather patterns help make predicting the weather more accurate?

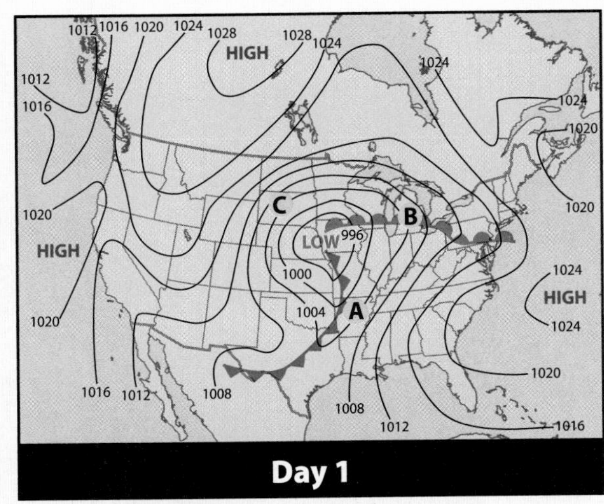

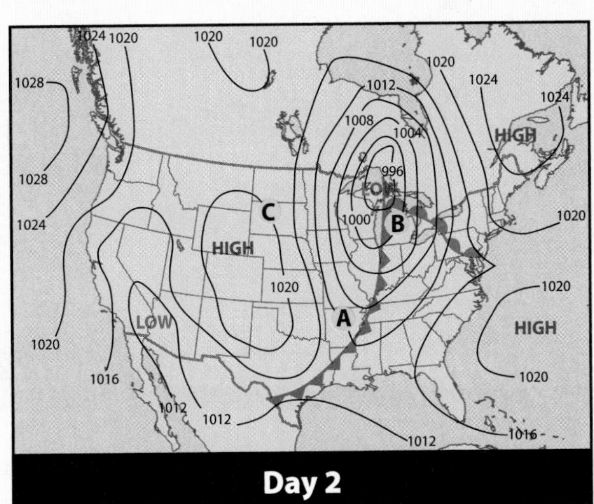

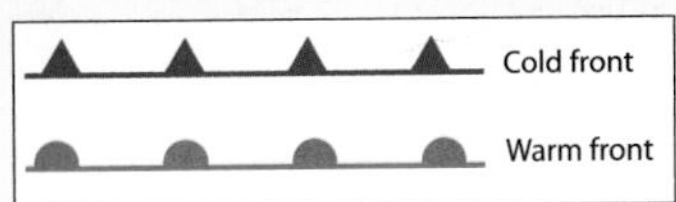

Lesson 3

Reading Guide

Key Concepts 
ESSENTIAL QUESTIONS

- What instruments are used to measure weather variables?
- How are computer models used to predict the weather?

Vocabulary

surface report p. 251
upper-air report p. 251
Doppler radar p. 252
isobar p. 253
computer model p. 254

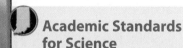

Multilingual eGlossary

Academic Standards for Science

8.2.4 Describe the physical and chemical composition of the atmosphere at different elevations.

Also covers: 8.NS.1, 8.NS.2, 8.NS.3, 8.NS.5, 8.NS.7, 8.NS.8, 8.NS.10, 8.NS.11

Weather Forecasts

Inquiry What's inside?

Information about weather variables is collected by the weather radar station shown here. Data, such as the amount of rain falling in a weather system, help meteorologists make accurate predictions about severe weather. What other instruments do meteorologists use to forecast weather? How do they collect and use data?

10 minutes

Can you understand the weather report?

Weather reports use numbers and certain vocabulary terms to help you understand the weather conditions in a given area for a given time period. Listen to a weather report for your area. Can you record all the information reported?

1. In your Science Journal, make a list of data you would expect to hear in a weather report.
2. Listen carefully to a **recording of a weather report** and jot down numbers and measurements you hear next to those on your list.
3. Listen a second time and make adjustments to your original notes, such as adding more data, if necessary.
4. Listen a third time, then share the weather forecast as you heard it.

Think About This

1. What measurements were difficult for you to apply to understanding the weather report?
2. Why are so many different types of data needed to give a complete weather report?
3. List the instruments that might be used to collect each kind of data.
4. **Key Concept** Where do meteorologists obtain the data they use to make a weather forecast?

Measuring the Weather

Weather forecasting is a lot like being a doctor. Using specialized instruments and visual observations, the doctor first measures the condition of your body. The doctor later combines these measurements with his or her knowledge of medical science. The result is a forecast of your future health, such as "You'll feel better in a few days if you rest and drink plenty of fluids."

In a similar way, the first step in making a weather forecast is to measure the conditions of the atmosphere. As you read in Lesson 1, a variety of instruments are used to measure different weather variables. These include thermometers to measure temperature, barometers to measure air pressure, psychrometers to measure relative humidity, and anemometers to measure wind speed.

Surface and Upper-Air Reports

A **surface report** *describes a set of weather measurements made on Earth's surface.* Weather variables are measured by a weather station—a collection of instruments that report temperature, air pressure, humidity, precipitation, and wind speed and direction. Cloud amounts and visibility are often measured by human observers.

An **upper-air report** *describes wind, temperature, and humidity conditions above Earth's surface.* These atmospheric conditions are measured by a radiosonde (RAY dee oh sahnd), a package of weather instruments carried many kilometers above the ground by a weather balloon. Radiosonde reports are made twice a day simultaneously at hundreds of locations around the world.

Satellite and Radar Images

Images taken from satellites orbiting about 35,000 km above Earth provide information about weather conditions on Earth. A visible light image, such as the one shown in **Figure 14,** shows white clouds over Earth. The infrared image, also shown in **Figure 14,** shows infrared energy in false color. The infrared energy comes from Earth and is stored in the atmosphere as latent heat. Monitoring infrared energy provides information about cloud height and atmospheric temperature.

Figure 14 Meteorologists use visible light and infrared satellite images to identify fronts and air masses.

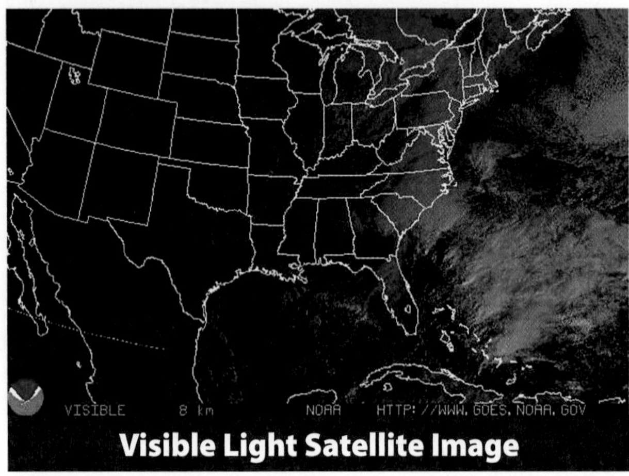

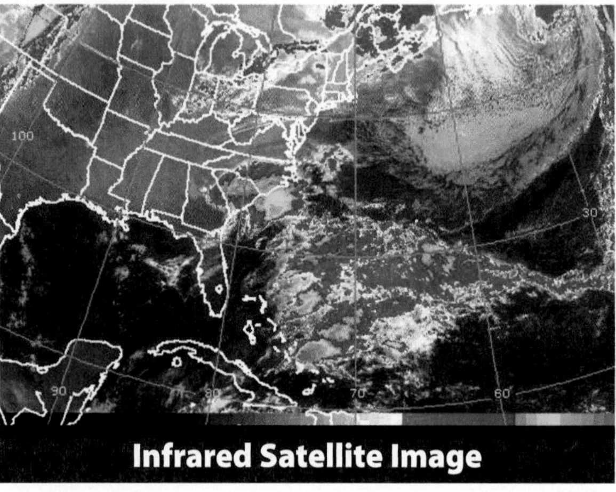

Visual Check How is an infrared satellite image different from a visible light satellite image?

Radar measures precipitation when radio waves bounce off raindrops and snowflakes. **Doppler radar** *is a specialized type of radar that can detect precipitation as well as the movement of small particles, which can be used to approximate wind speed.* Since the movement of precipitation is caused by wind, Doppler radar can be used to estimate wind speed. This can be especially important during severe weather, such as tornadoes or thunderstorms.

Key Concept Check Identify the weather variables that radiosondes, infrared satellites, and Doppler radar measure.

FOLDABLES®

Make a horizontal two-tab book and label the tabs as illustrated. Use it to collect information on satellite and radar images. Compare and contrast these information tools.

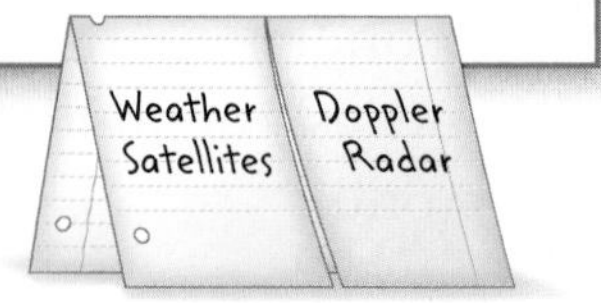

Weather Maps

Every day, thousands of surface reports, upper-air reports, and satellite and radar observations are made around the world. Meteorologists have developed tools that help them simplify and understand this enormous amount of weather data.

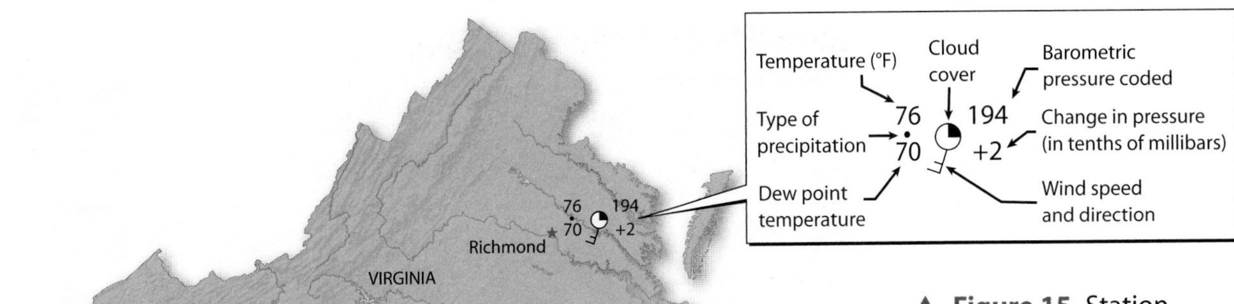

▲ **Figure 15** Station models contain information about weather variables.

The Station Model

As shown in **Figure 15,** the station model diagram displays data from many different weather measurements for a particular location. It uses numbers and symbols and displays all observations from surface reports and upper-air reports.

Mapping Temperature and Pressure

In addition to station models, weather maps also have other symbols. For example, **isobars** *are lines that connect all places on a map where pressure has the same value.* Locate an isobar on the map in **Figure 16.** Isobars show the location of high- and low-pressure systems. Isobars also provide information about wind speed. Winds are strong when isobars are close together. Winds are weaker when isobars are farther apart.

In a similar way, isotherms (not shown) are lines that connect places with the same temperature. Isotherms show which areas are warm and which are cold. Fronts are represented as lines with symbols on them, as indicated in **Figure 16.**

Reading Check Compare isobars and isotherms.

WORD ORIGIN

isobar
from Greek *isos,* means "equal"; and *baros,* means "heavy"

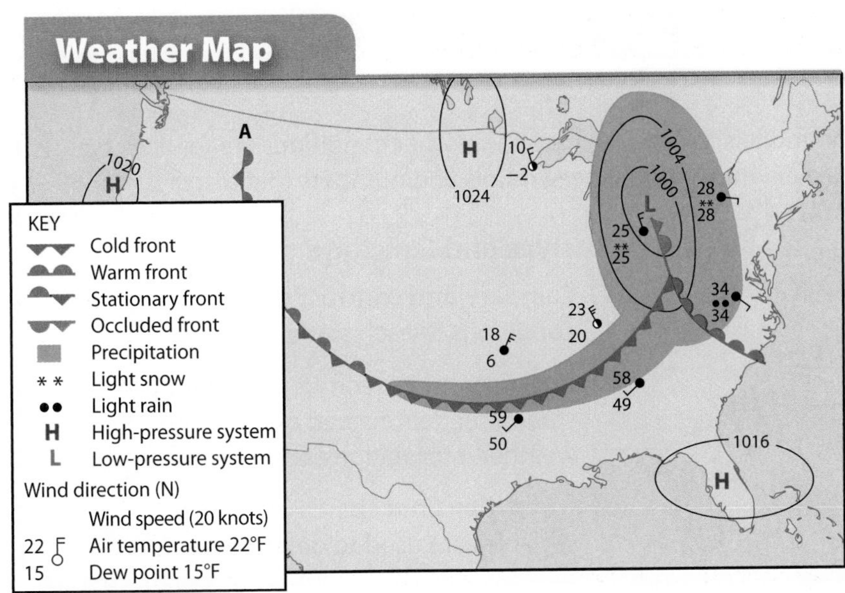

◀ **Figure 16** Weather maps contain symbols that provide information about the weather.

Visual Check Which symbols represent high-pressure and low-pressure systems?

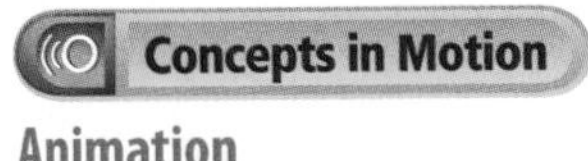

Animation

Figure 17 Meteorologists analyze data from various sources—such as radar and computer models—in order to prepare weather forecasts.

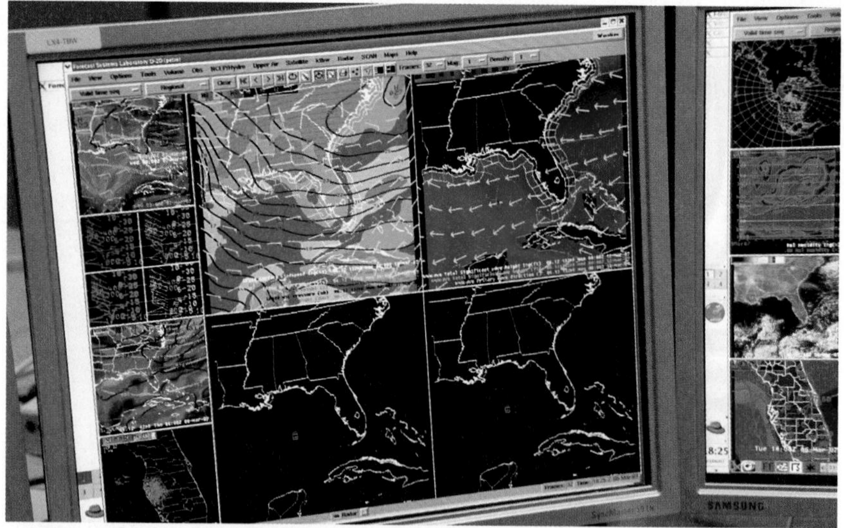

Predicting the Weather

Modern weather forecasts are made with the help of computer models, such as the ones shown in **Figure 17.** **Computer models** *are detailed computer programs that solve a set of complex mathematical formulas.* The formulas predict what temperatures and winds might occur, when and where it will rain and snow, and what types of clouds will form.

Government meteorological offices also use computers and the Internet to exchange weather measurements continuously throughout the day. Weather maps are drawn and forecasts are made using computer models. Then, through television, radio, newspapers, and the Internet, the maps and forecasts are made available to the public.

 **Key Concept Check** How are computers used to predict the weather?

Inquiry MiniLab

20 minutes

How is weather represented on a map?

Meteorologists often use station models to record what the weather conditions are for a particular location. A station model is a diagram containing symbols and numbers that displays many different weather measurements.

Use the **station model legend** provided by your teacher to interpret the data in each station model shown here.

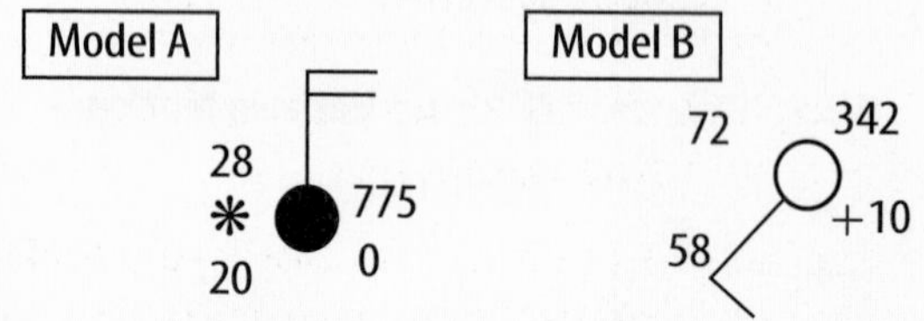

Analyze and Conclude

1. **Compare and contrast** the weather conditions at each station model.
2. **Explain** why meteorologists might use station models instead of reporting weather information another way.
3. **Key Concept** Discuss what variables are used to describe weather.

Lesson 3 Review

Assessment Online Quiz

Inquiry Virtual Lab

Visual Summary

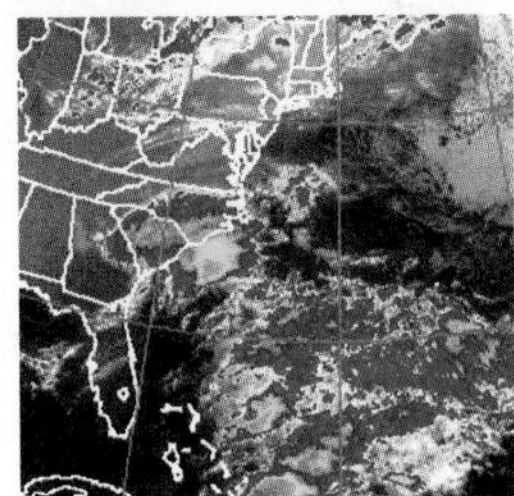

Weather variables are measured by weather stations, radiosondes, satellites, and Doppler radar.

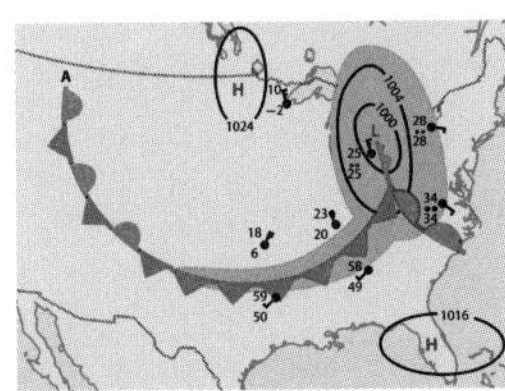

Weather maps contain information in the form of a station model, isobars and isotherms, and symbols for fronts and pressure systems.

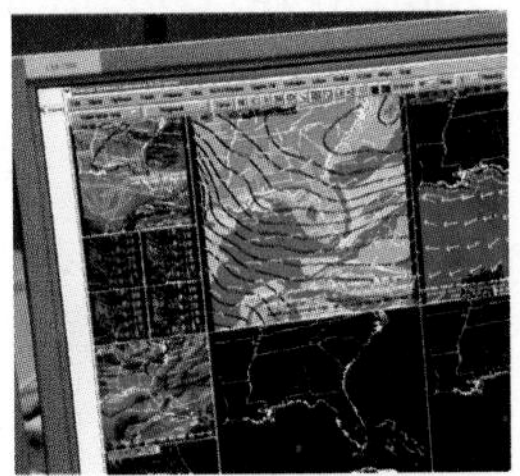

Meteorologists use computer models to help forecast the weather.

FOLDABLES®

Use your lesson Foldable to review the lesson. Save your Foldable for the project at the end of the chapter.

What do you think NOW?

You first read the statements below at the beginning of the chapter.

5. Weather variables are measured every day at locations around the world.

6. Modern weather forecasts are done using computers.

Did you change your mind about whether you agree or disagree with the statements? Rewrite any false statements to make them true.

Use Vocabulary

1. **Define** *computer model* in your own words.
2. A line connecting places with the same pressure is called a(n) ________.
3. **Use the term** *surface report* in a sentence.

Understand Key Concepts 

4. Which diagram shows surface weather measurements?
   - **A.** an infrared satellite image
   - **B.** an upper air chart
   - **C.** a station model
   - **D.** a visible satellite image
5. **List** two ways that upper-air weather conditions are measured.
6. **Describe** how computers are used in weather forecasting.
7. **Distinguish** between isobars and isotherms.

Interpret Graphics

8. **Identify** Copy and fill in the graphic organizer below to identify the components of a surface map.

Symbol	Meaning
H	

Critical Thinking

9. **Suggest** ways to forecast the weather without using computers.
10. **Explain** why isobars and isotherms make it easier to understand a weather map.

40 minutes

Materials

graph paper

local weather maps

outdoor thermometer

barometer

Can you predict the weather?

Weather forecasts are important—not just so you are dressed right when you leave the house, but also to help farmers know when to plant and harvest, to help cities know when to call in the snow plows, and to help officials know when and where to evacuate in advance of severe weather.

Ask a Question

Can you predict the weather?

Make Observations

1. Read and complete a lab safety form.
2. Collect weather data daily for a period of one week. Temperature and pressure should be recorded as a number, but precipitation, wind conditions, and cloud cover can be described in words. Make your observations at the same time each day.

3. Graph temperature in degrees and air pressure in millibars on the same sheet of paper, placing the graphs side by side, as shown on the next page. Beneath the graphs, for each day, add notes that describe precipitation, wind conditions, and cloud cover.

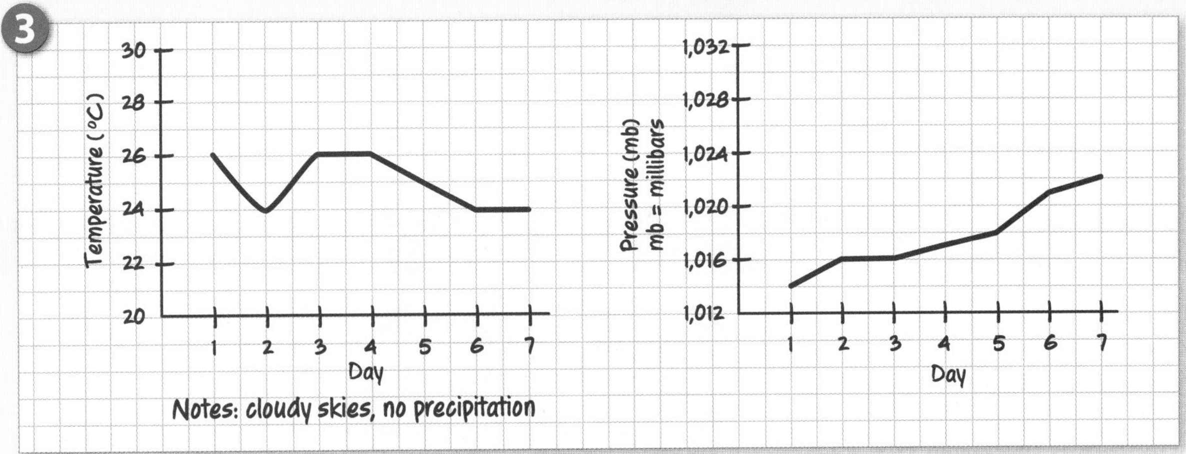

Form a Hypothesis

4. Examine your data and the weather maps. Look for factors that appear to be related. For example, your data might suggest that when the pressure decreases, clouds follow.
5. Find three sets of data pairs that seem to be related. Form three hypotheses, one for each set of data pairs.

Test Your Hypothesis

6. Look at your last day of data. Using your hypotheses, predict the weather for the next day.
7. Collect weather data the next day and evaluate your predictions.
8. Repeat steps 6 and 7 for at least two more days.

Analyze and Conclude

9. **Analyze** Compare your hypotheses with the results of your predictions. How successful were you? What additional information might have improved your predictions?
10. **The Big Idea** Scientists have more complex and sophisticated tools to help them predict their weather, but with fairly simple tools, you can make an educated guess. Write a one-paragraph summary of the data you collected and how you interpreted it to predict the weather.

Communicate Your Results

For each hypothesis you generated, make a small poster that states the hypothesis, shows a graph that supports it, and shows the results of your predictions. Write a concluding statement about the reliability of your hypothesis. Share your results with the class.

Extension

Investigate other forms of data you might collect and find out how they would help you to make a forecast. Try them out for a week and see if your ability to make predictions improves.

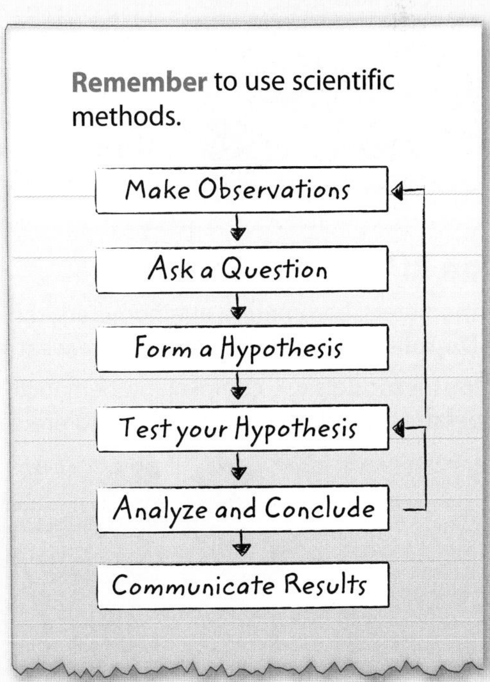

Chapter 7 Study Guide

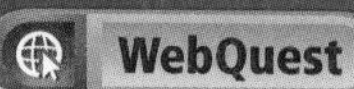

Scientists use weather variables to describe weather and study weather systems. Scientists use computers to predict the weather.

Key Concepts Summary

Lesson 1: Describing Weather

- **Weather** is the atmospheric conditions, along with short-term changes, of a certain place at a certain time.
- Variables used to describe weather are air temperature, **air pressure,** wind, **humidity,** and **relative humidity.**
- The processes in the water cycle—evaporation, condensation, and **precipitation**—are all involved in the formation of different types of weather.

Vocabulary

weather p. 231
air pressure p. 232
humidity p. 232
relative humidity p. 233
dew point p. 233
precipitation p. 235
water cycle p. 235

Lesson 2: Weather Patterns

- **Low-pressure systems** and **high-pressure systems** are two systems that influence weather.
- Weather patterns are driven by the movement of **air masses.**
- Understanding weather patterns helps make weather forecasts more accurate.
- Severe weather includes thunderstorms, **tornadoes, hurricanes,** and **blizzards.**

Vocabulary

high-pressure system p. 239
low-pressure system p. 239
air mass p. 240
front p. 242
tornado p. 245
hurricane p. 246
blizzard p. 247

Lesson 3: Weather Forecasts

- Thermometers, barometers, anemometers, radiosondes, satellites, and **Doppler radar** are used to measure weather variables.
- **Computer models** use complex mathematical formulas to predict temperature, wind, cloud formation, and precipitation.

Vocabulary

surface report p. 251
upper-air report p. 251
Doppler radar p. 252
isobar p. 253
computer model p. 254

Review
- Personal Tutor
- Vocabulary eGames
- Vocabulary eFlashcards

FOLDABLES® Chapter Project

Assemble your lesson Foldables as shown to make a Chapter Project. Use the project to review what you have learned in this chapter.

Use Vocabulary

1. The pressure that a column of air exerts on the area below it is called ________.
2. The amount of water vapor in the air is called ________.
3. The natural process in which water constantly moves among oceans, land, and the atmosphere is called the ________.
4. A(n) ________ is a boundary between two air masses.
5. At the center of a(n) ________, air rises and forms clouds and precipitation.
6. A continental polar ________ brings cold temperatures during winter.
7. When the same ________ passes through two locations on a weather map, both locations have the same pressure.
8. The humidity in the air compared to the amount air can hold is the ________.

Link Vocabulary and Key Concepts

Concepts in Motion Interactive Concept Map

Copy this concept map, and then use vocabulary terms from the previous page to complete the concept map.

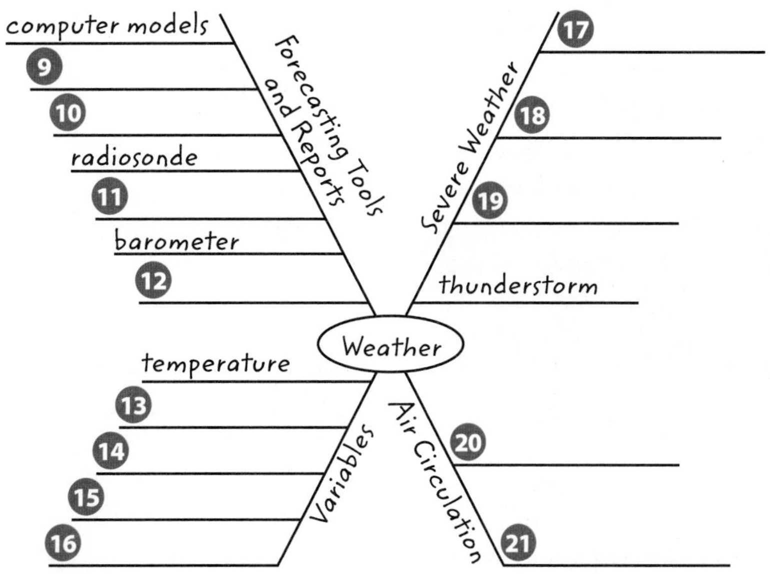

Chapter 7 Review

Understand Key Concepts 

1. Clouds form when water changes from
   A. gas to liquid.
   B. liquid to gas.
   C. solid to gas.
   D. solid to liquid.

2. Which type of precipitation reaches Earth's surface as large pellets of ice?
   A. hail
   B. rain
   C. sleet
   D. snow

3. Which of these sinking-air situations usually brings fair weather?
   A. air mass
   B. cold front
   C. high-pressure system
   D. low-pressure system

4. Which air mass contains cold, dry air?
   A. continental polar
   B. continental tropical
   C. maritime tropical
   D. maritime polar

5. Study the front below.

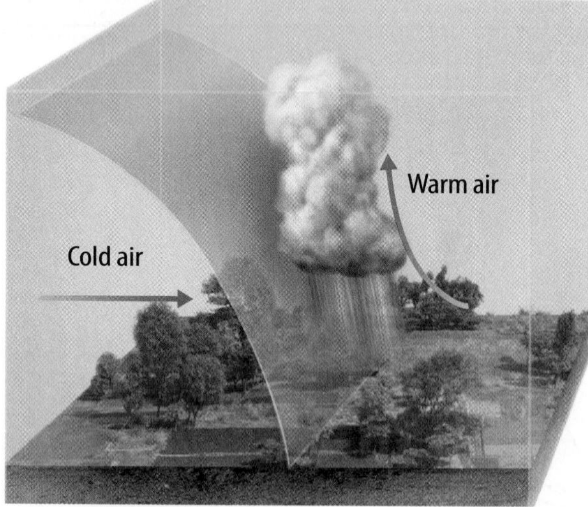

   How does this type of front form?
   A. A cold front overtakes a warm front.
   B. Cold air moves toward warmer air.
   C. The boundary between two fronts stalls.
   D. Warm air moves toward colder air.

6. Which is an intense tropical storm with winds exceeding 119 km/h?
   A. blizzard
   B. hurricane
   C. thunderstorm
   D. tornado

7. Which contains measurements of temperature, air pressure, humidity, precipitation, and wind speed and direction?
   A. a radar image
   B. a satellite image
   C. a surface report
   D. a weather station

8. What does Doppler radar measure?
   A. air pressure
   B. air temperature
   C. the rate at which air pressure changes
   D. the speed at which precipitation travels the rate at which air pressure changes

9. Study the station model below.

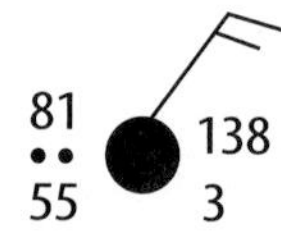

   What is the temperature according to the station model?
   A. 3°F
   B. 55°F
   C. 81°F
   D. 138°F

10. Which describes cirrus clouds?
   A. flat, white, and layered
   B. fluffy, at middle altitudes
   C. heaped or piled up
   D. wispy, at high altitudes

11. Which instrument measures wind speed?
   A. anemometer
   B. barometer
   C. psychrometer
   D. thermometer

Chapter Review

Assessment
Online Test Practice

Critical Thinking

12 **Predict** Suppose you are on a ship near the equator in the Atlantic Ocean. You notice that the barometric pressure is dropping. Predict what type of weather you might experience.

13 **Compare** a continental polar air mass with a maritime tropical air mass.

14 **Assess** why clouds usually form in the center of a low-pressure system.

15 **Predict** how maritime air masses would change if the oceans froze.

16 **Compare** two types of severe weather.

17 **Interpret Graphics** Identify the front on the weather map below. Predict the weather for areas along the front.

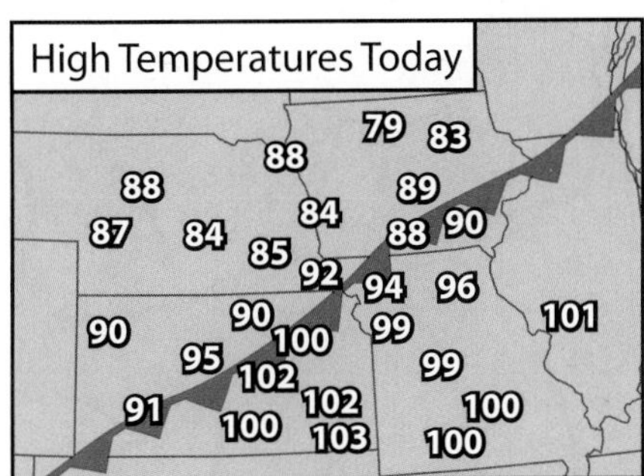

18 **Assess** the validity of the weather forecast: "Tomorrow's weather will be similar to today's weather."

19 **Compare and contrast** surface weather reports and upper-air reports. Why is it important for meterologists to monitor weather variables high above Earth's surface?

Writing in Science

20 **Write** a paragraph about the ways computers have improved weather forecasts. Be sure to include a topic sentence and a concluding sentence.

REVIEW THE BIG IDEA

21 Identify the instruments used to measure weather variables.

22 How do scientists use weather variables to describe and predict weather?

23 Describe the factors that influence weather.

24 Use the factors listed in question 23 to describe how a continental polar air mass can change to a maritime polar air mass.

Math Skills

Math Practice

Use Conversions

25 Convert from Fahrenheit to Celsius.
- **a.** Convert 0°F to °C.
- **b.** Convert 104°F to °C.

26 Convert from Celsius to Fahrenheit.
- **a.** Convert 0°C to °F.
- **b.** Convert −40°C to °F.

27 The Kelvin scale of temperature measurement starts at zero and has the same unit size as Celsius degrees. Zero degrees Celsius is equal to 273 kelvin.

Convert 295 K to Fahrenheit.

Standardized Test Practice

Record your answers on the answer sheet provided by your teacher or on a sheet of paper.

Multiple Choice

1 Which measures the average kinetic energy of air molecules?

A humidity

B pressure

C speed

D temperature

Use the diagram below to answer question 2.

2 Which weather system does the above diagram illustrate?

A high pressure

B hurricane

C low pressure

D tornado

3 What causes weather to remain the same several days in a row?

A air front

B air mass

C air pollution

D air resistance

4 Which lists the stages of a thunderstorm in order?

A cumulus, dissipation, mature

B cumulus, mature, dissipation

C dissipation, cumulus, mature

D dissipation, mature, cumulus

5 What causes air to reach its dew point?

A decreasing air currents

B decreasing humidity

C dropping air pressure

D dropping temperatures

6 Which measures air pressure?

A anemometer

B barometer

C psychrometer

D thermometer

Use the diagram below to answer question 7.

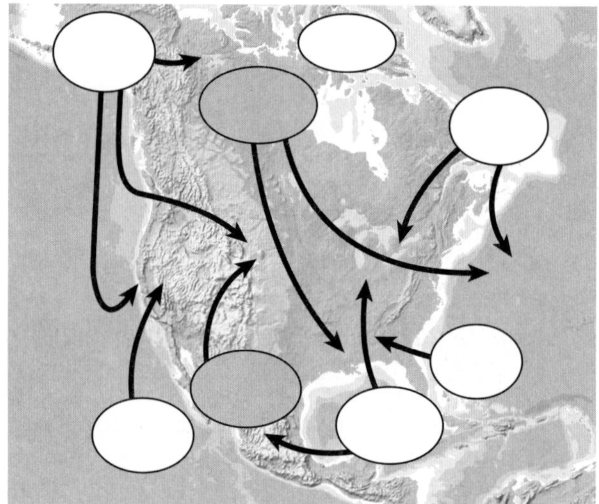

7 Which type of air masses do the shaded ovals in the diagram depict?

A antarctic

B arctic

C continental

D maritime

8 Which BEST expresses moisture saturation?

A barometric pressure

B relative humidity

C weather front

D wind direction

Assessment
Online Standardized Test Practice

Use the diagram below to answer question 9.

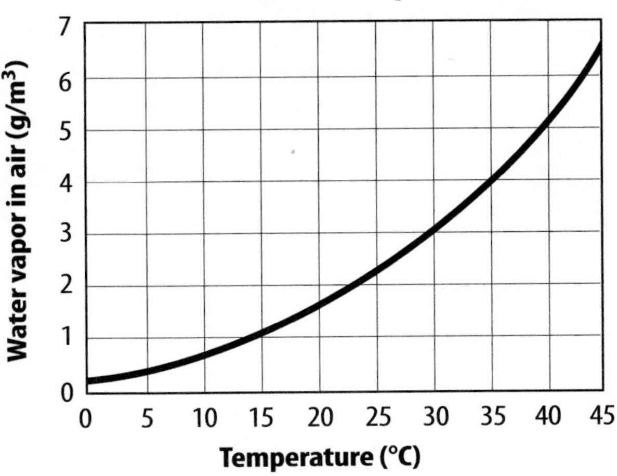

9 What happens to maximum moisture content when air temperatures increase from 15°C to 30°C?

A increases from 1 to 2 g/m^3

B increases from 1 to 3 g/m^3

C increases from 2 to 3 g/m^3

D increases from 2 to 4 g/m^3

10 When isobars are close together on a weather map,

A cloud cover is extensive.

B temperatures are high.

C warm fronts prevail.

D winds are strong.

11 Which provides energy for the water cycle?

A air currents

B Earth's core

C ocean currents

D the Sun

Constructed Response

Use the table below to answer question 12.

Weather Variable	Measurement

12 In the table above, list the variables weather scientists use to describe weather. Then describe the unit of measurement for each variable.

Use the diagram below to answer questions 13 and 14.

13 What does the diagram above depict?

14 Describe the weather conditions associated with the diagram.

15 How do weather fronts form?

NEED EXTRA HELP?															
If You Missed Question...	1	2	3	4	5	6	7	8	9	10	11	12	13	14	15
Go to Lesson...	1	2	2	2	1	1,3	2	1	1	3	1	1	2	2	2

Oceans

THE BIG IDEA **What are characteristics of oceans, and why are oceans important?**

Inquiry What makes waves so powerful?

Have you ever felt the power of an ocean wave? Oceans are large and powerful, and they can be dangerous. They are also important. Oceans contain valuable resources, and they affect Earth's climate and weather.

- What causes ocean waves and currents? How do oceans affect weather and climate? How are oceans threatened?
- What are the characteristics of oceans, and why are oceans important?

Get Ready to Read

What do you think?

Before you read, decide if you agree or disagree with each of these statements. As you read this chapter, see if you change your mind about any of the statements.

1. Oceans formed about 4 billion years ago.
2. The seafloor is flat.
3. Waves move water particles from one location to another.
4. The wind causes tides.
5. Ocean currents occur on the surface and below the surface.
6. Ocean currents affect climate and weather.
7. Most pollution in the oceans originates on land.
8. Global climate change has no effect on marine organisms.

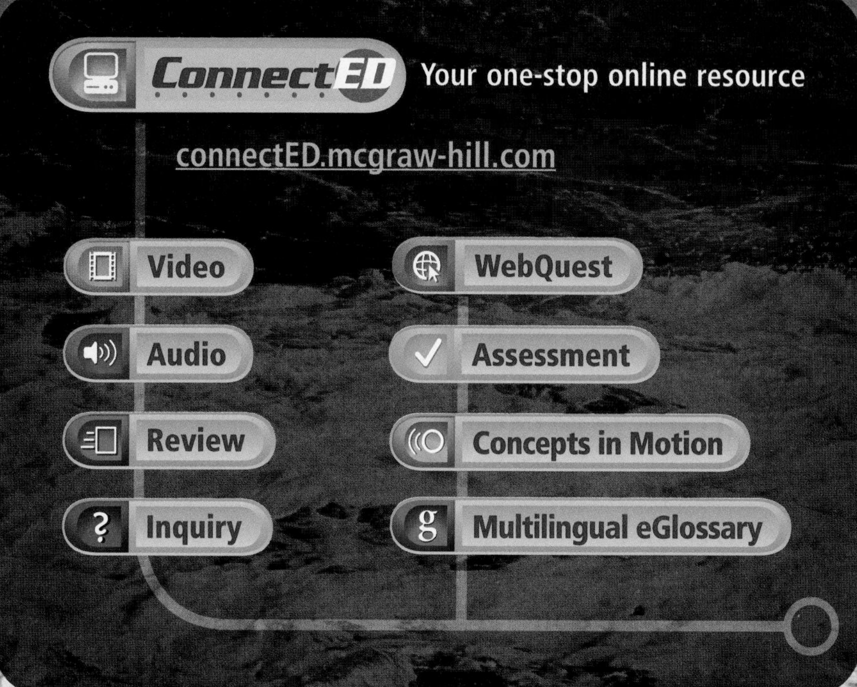

Lesson 1

Reading Guide

Key Concepts
ESSENTIAL QUESTIONS

- Why are the oceans salty?
- What does the seafloor look like?
- How do temperature, salinity, and density affect ocean structure?

Vocabulary

salinity p. 269
seawater p. 269
brackish p. 269
abyssal plain p. 270

 Multilingual eGlossary

 Video BrainPOP®

Academic Standards for Science

8.2.2 Describe and model how water moves through the earth's crust, atmosphere, and oceans in a cyclic way, as liquid, vapor, and solid.

Also covers: 8.NS.3, 8.NS.5, 8.NS.7, 8.NS.10

Composition and Structure of Earth's Oceans

Inquiry What's down there?

Conditions change with depth in the ocean. Scientists study different layers of the ocean by diving in submersibles—tiny submarines capable of withstanding extreme pressure at great depths. How does the ocean change with depth?

Launch Lab

15 minutes

How are salt and density related?

Bodies of water form layers based on differences in density. How does salt affect density?

1. Read and complete a lab safety form.
2. Half-fill a **glass** with **water.**
3. Carefully place a **hard-cooked egg** in the water. Observe what happens. Remove the egg.
4. Add 5–10 tablespoons of **salt** and stir until all the salt is dissolved.
5. Place a **ladle** or a **spoon** inside the glass and slowly pour tap water over it until the glass is three-fourths full. Gently remove the ladle or the spoon. Be careful not to disturb the layer of salt water.
6. Gently place the egg in the glass and observe.

Think About This

1. Explain any differences that you observed.
2. **Key Concept** Do you think it is easier to float in the ocean or in a freshwater lake?

Earth's Oceans

Aside from being called the water planet, did you know that sometimes Earth is also called the blue planet? If you have ever seen a photograph of Earth taken from space, such as the one in **Figure 1,** you know that Earth appears mostly blue. Earth appears blue because water covers 70 percent of its surface. Most of Earth's water—97 percent—is salt water in the oceans.

Earth's oceans are all connected. However, scientists separate the oceans into five main bodies:

- The Pacific Ocean is the largest and deepest ocean. It is larger than all of Earth's combined land area.
- The Atlantic Ocean is half the size of the Pacific. It occupies about 20 percent of Earth's surface.
- The Indian Ocean is between Africa, India, and the Indonesian Islands. It is the third largest ocean.
- The Southern Ocean surrounds Antarctica. It is Earth's fourth largest ocean. Ice covers some of its surface all year.
- The Arctic Ocean is near the North Pole. It is the smallest and shallowest ocean. Ice covers some of its surface all year.

In this lesson, you will read about the formation of the oceans, their physical and chemical characteristics, and the importance of the oceans' natural resources.

Figure 1 Earth appears blue from space because its water reflects blue wavelengths of light.

Figure 2 Volcanic eruptions on Earth today add water vapor to the atmosphere, just as they did billions of years ago.

Formation of the Oceans

Evidence indicates that Earth's oceans began to form as early as 4.2 billion years ago (bya). That is only a few hundred million years after Earth formed. Earth was very hot and active when it was young. Many volcanoes covered its surface. Like the volcano shown in **Figure 2,** these ancient volcanoes erupted huge amounts of gas. Much of the gas was made of water vapor, with small amounts of carbon dioxide and other gases. Over time, these gases formed early Earth's atmosphere.

Condensation As water moves through the water cycle, illustrated in **Figure 3,** water vapor in the atmosphere cools and condenses into a liquid. Tiny droplets of liquid combine and form clouds. As early Earth cooled, the water vapor in its atmosphere condensed and precipitated. Rain fell for tens of thousands of years, collecting on Earth's surface in low-lying basins. Eventually, these basins became the oceans.

Asteroids and Comets Evidence suggests a second source of water for Earth's oceans. During the time when oceans formed, many icy comets and asteroids from space collided with Earth. The melted ice from these objects added to the water filling Earth's ocean basins.

 **Reading Check** What are the sources of Earth's oceans?

Tectonic Changes Earth's oceans change over time. As tectonic plates move, new oceans form and old oceans disappear. However, the volume of water in the oceans has remained fairly constant since the first oceans formed.

Figure 3 Earth's water continually evaporates from the ocean and returns to the ocean through the water cycle.

Composition of Seawater

The rain that fell to Earth's surface billions of years ago washed over rocks and dissolved minerals. The minerals contained substances that form salts. Rivers and streams carried these substances to ocean basins. Some substances also came from gases released by underwater volcanoes. Together, these substances made the water salty, as shown in **Figure 4.**

Key Concept Check Why is seawater salty?

Salinity *is a measure of the mass of dissolved solids in a mass of water.* Salinity is usually expressed in parts per thousand (ppt). For example, **seawater** *is water from a sea or ocean that has an average salinity of 35 ppt.* This means that if you measured 1,000 g of seawater, 35 g would be salts and 965 g would be pure water.

The salinity of seawater changes in areas where rivers enter the ocean, such as in an estuary. There, seawater becomes brackish. **Brackish** *water, or brack water, is freshwater mixed with seawater.* The salinity of brackish water is often between 1 ppt and 17 ppt.

Substances in Seawater

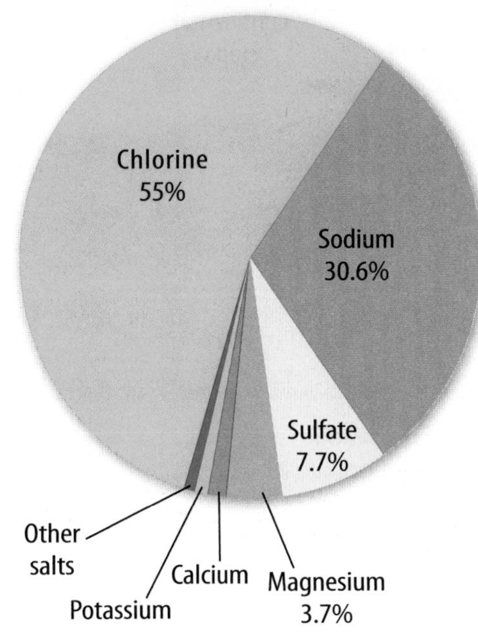

Figure 4 Five elements and one compound account for 99 percent of the dissolved substances in seawater. Evidence suggests that the proportions shown in this circle graph have been fairly constant for millions of years.

Visual Check Sodium makes up what percentage of the dissolved substances in seawater?

Inquiry MiniLab

20 minutes

How does salinity affect the density of water?

Salt water is more dense than freshwater. How much salt do you need to add to freshwater to make it dense enough to float an egg?

1. Read and complete a lab safety form.
2. Fill a **jar** with 1,000 mL of **water.** Carefully add a **hard-cooked egg** to the water. Observe the egg's position.
3. Use a **stirring rod** to stir 20 g of **salt** into the water. Again observe the egg's position.
4. Add salt in increments of 10 g. After each addition, stir the salt into the water and observe the egg. Continue to add salt in 10-g increments until the egg floats.

Analyze and Conclude

1. **Calculate** the salinity of the water in which the egg floated.
2. **Key Concept** How does salinity affect the density of water?

Seafloor Topography

Concepts in Motion Animation

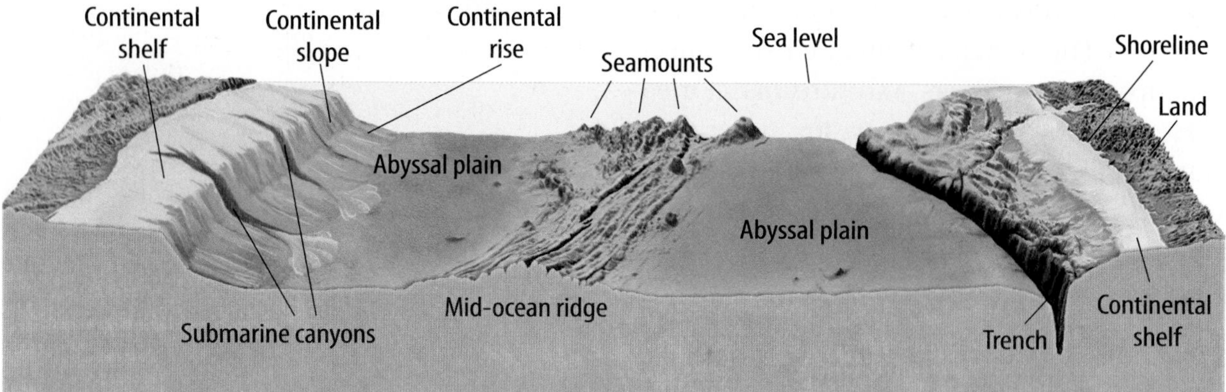

Figure 5 An ocean's seafloor is shaped like a basin. Some features of ocean basins are continental shelves, continental slopes, continental rises, abyssal plains, mid-ocean ridges, seamounts, and trenches.

Visual Check Where is new seafloor created?

The Seafloor

What do you think the ocean bottom looks like? You might be surprised to learn that the seafloor has features similar to features on land, such as plains, plateaus, canyons, and mountains.

Continental Margins

The part of an ocean basin next to a continent is called a continental margin. A continental margin extends from a continent's shoreline to the deep ocean. It is divided into three regions, which are illustrated in **Figure 5.** The continental shelf is the shallow part of a continent nearest the shore. The continental slope is the steep slope that extends from the continental shelf to the deep ocean. The continental rise is at the base of the slope. It is where sediments accumulate that fall from the continental slope.

WORD ORIGIN

abyssal
from Greek *abyssos,* means "bottomless"

Abyssal Plains

Examine **Figure 5** again. Notice the abyssal plains. **Abyssal plains** *are large, flat areas of the seafloor that extend across the deepest parts of the ocean basins.* Thick layers of sediment cover abyssal plains. In some areas, underwater volcanoes rise from the abyssal plains and form islands that extend above the ocean's surface.

FOLDABLES®

Make a top-tab book from four half-sheets of paper. Use your book to illustrate and organize information about the seafloor.

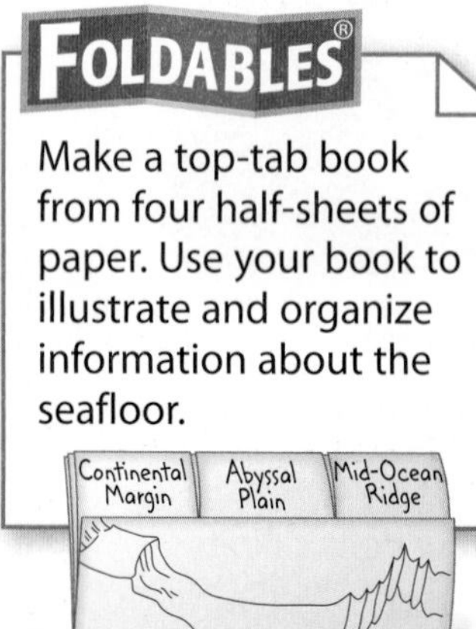

Mid-Ocean Ridges

At places on the seafloor where tectonic plates pull apart, volcanic mountains form. These underwater mountains are called mid-ocean ridges. Mid-ocean ridges form a continuous mountain range that extends through all of Earth's ocean basins. It is Earth's tallest and longest mountain range, measuring more than 65,000 km in length. As the plates slowly move apart at mid-ocean ridges, lava erupts and then cools forming new seafloor.

Ocean Trenches

Earth's oceans have an average depth of about 4,000 m. However, in areas where an oceanic tectonic plate collides with a continental plate, a deep canyon, or trench, forms along the edge of the abyssal plain. A trench is shown in **Figure 5.** Trenches are the deepest parts of the ocean. The Mariana Trench, in the western Pacific Ocean, is more than 11,000 m deep. The bottom of the Mariana Trench extends farther below sea level than Mount Everest is above sea level.

Key Concept Check Describe some features of the seafloor.

Deep Ocean Technology

Today, scientists use submersibles and other technologies to explore the seafloor. A submersible is an underwater vessel which can withstand extreme pressure at great depths. One famous submersible, DSV Alvin, set a deep-ocean record by diving to the bottom of the Mariana Trench.

In the future, remotely operated vehicles (ROVs) are likely to be used more frequently. These unmanned submersibles can be operated from a control center on a ship. Operators can see video images sent back from the ROVs and can control their propellers and **manipulator** arms. ROVs are safer, cheaper, and can generally provide more research data than manned submersibles.

Resources from the Seafloor

The seafloor contains valuable resources. **Table 1** illustrates some of the resources on or beneath the seafloor. There are two main categories of seafloor resources—energy resources and minerals. Energy resources, such as oil, natural gas, and methane hydrates, are beneath the ocean floor on continental margins. Most mineral deposits, such as the manganese nodules shown in **Table 1,** are on abyssal plains. Some minerals, including gold and zinc, have also been discovered at mid-ocean ridges.

Table 1 Resources from the Ocean Floor

Oil and Natural Gas These deposits are beneath the seafloor on continental margins. Many platforms for oil extraction have been built in the Gulf of Mexico.	
Methane Hydrates Deposits of methane gas in deep-sea sediments are called methane hydrates. They are a potential but as yet unrealized source of energy similar to fossil fuels.	
Mineral Deposits Minerals on the seafloor include manganese nodules. These nodules form when metals precipitate out of seawater. They are potentially valuable, but no large-scale mining exists.	

Table 1 Resources found on or below the seafloor include oil, methane hydrates, and manganese nodules.

ACADEMIC VOCABULARY

manipulate
(verb) to operate with hands or by mechanical means in a skillful manner

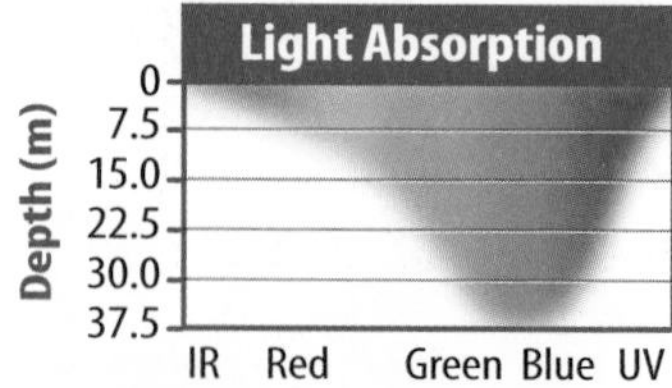

Figure 6 Wavelengths of blue and green light reach deeper into the ocean than those of red, orange, and yellow light.

Zones in the Oceans

Scientists divide oceans into distinct regions, or zones, based on physical characteristics. These characteristics include the amount of sunlight, temperature, salinity, and density.

Amount of Sunlight

If you have ever swum in a lake or an ocean, you might have noticed that the deeper the water, the darker it was. Light from the Sun penetrates below the ocean's surface. However, as depth increases, the wavelengths of light are not absorbed equally. Because of this, some colors penetrate deeper than others, as illustrated by the graph in **Figure 6.**

Surface Zone The area of shallow seawater that receives the greatest amount of sunlight is the surface zone, or sunlit zone. This zone is located above the dashed line shown in **Figure 7.** Most organisms that perform **photosynthesis** live here.

REVIEW VOCABULARY

photosynthesis
a chemical process in which light energy, water, and carbon dioxide are converted into sugar

Middle Zone By the time sunlight reaches the middle zone, or twilight zone, most of light's wavelengths have been absorbed. This zone receives only faint blue-green light. The area between the two dashed lines in **Figure 7** represents the middle zone.

Deep Zone Plants do not grow in the deep zone, or midnight zone, where there is no light. Most deep-sea animals, such as the squid shown in **Figure 7,** make their own light in chemical process called bioluminescence (BI oh LEW mah NE cents).

Reading Check Why don't plants grow in the deep zone?

Figure 7 The surface zone begins at the ocean surface and reaches a depth of about 200 m. The middle zone begins below the surface zone and reaches a depth of about 1,000 m. The deep zone is below the middle zone.

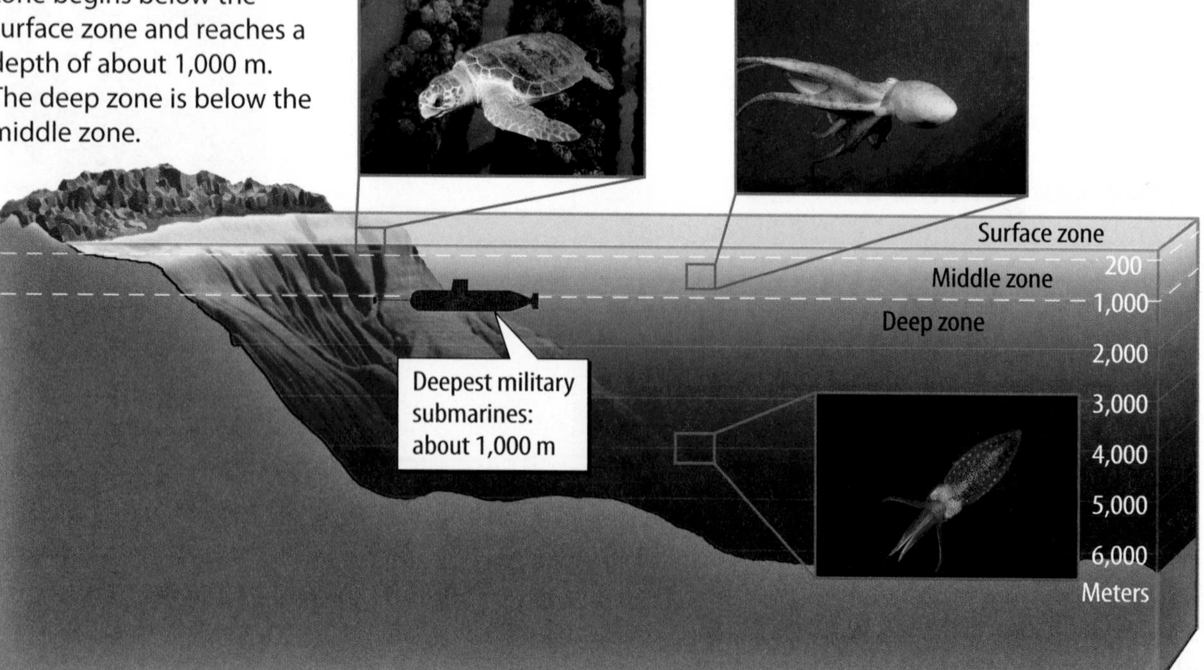

Ocean Layers

Just as oceans have zones of light, they also have zones of temperature, salinity, and density. Notice in **Figure 8** that temperature, salinity, and density vary with depth. Sometimes these characteristics can change abruptly within a relatively short change of depth. Abrupt changes in these characteristics can create distinctive layers of seawater.

Key Concept Check Why does seawater form layers?

Figure 8 Temperature, salinity, and density vary in the top 1,000 m of Earth's oceans.

Visual Check Below what depth does all ocean water have approximately the same temperature?

Changes in Temperature, Salinity, and Density

Changes in Temperature As shown in the graph to the right, temperature changes abruptly between 250 m and 900 m in temperate and tropical regions (solid line). As depth increases, water in these regions cools rapidly. That is because there is less sunlight to warm water as depth increases.

In contrast, the temperature of polar water (dotted line) remains fairly constant. This is because sunlight intensity at Earth's poles is weaker than it is in temperate and tropical regions. Polar water at all depths is cold.

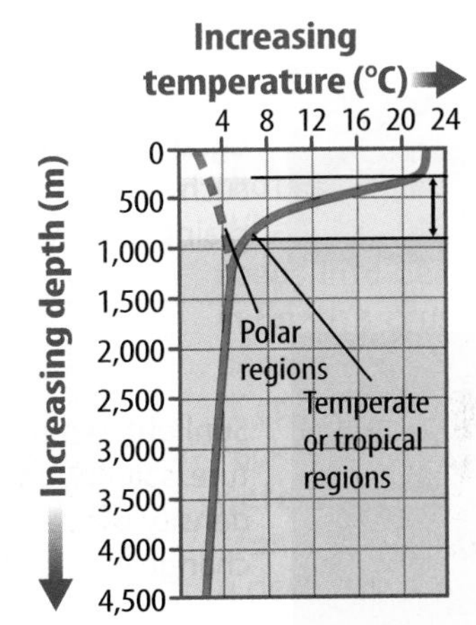

Changes in Salinity The top 500 m of warm water in temperate and tropical regions is saltier than polar water. Warm water evaporates more rapidly than cold water. When water evaporates, salt is left behind; this increases salinity at the surface.

In polar regions, freshwater from melting glaciers decreases the salinity at the surface. However, when ice forms, salt is left behind in the water. The remaining cold, salty water becomes denser and sinks to a deeper layer.

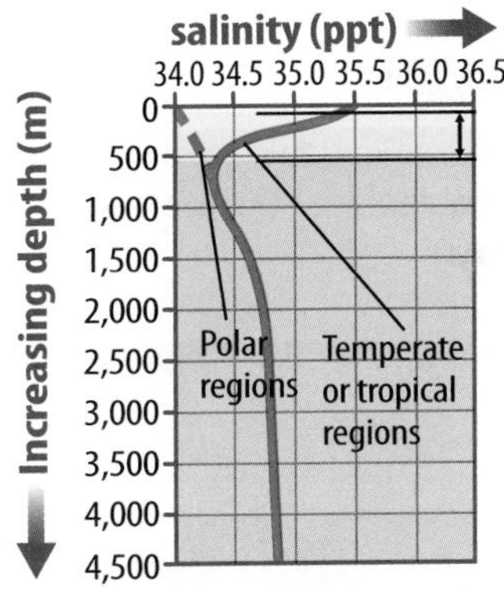

Changes in Density Seawater density is related to temperature and salinity. Cold water is denser than warm water. Salt water is denser than freshwater. Because of density differences, ocean water is layered. The densest layers are on the bottom; the least dense layers are on top.

Notice in the graph to the right that water density in polar regions remains fairly constant. Keep this in mind when you read about density currents in Lesson 3.

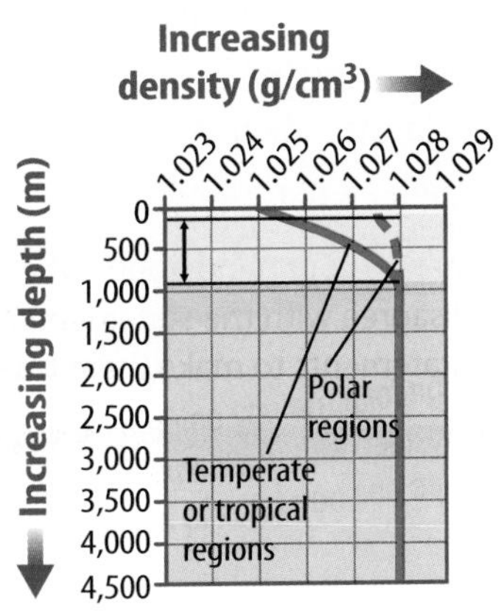

Lesson 2

Ocean Waves and Tides

Reading Guide

Key Concepts
ESSENTIAL QUESTIONS

- What causes ocean waves?
- What causes tides?

Vocabulary
tsunami p. 279
sea level p. 280
tide p. 280
tidal range p. 280
spring tide p. 281
neap tide p. 281

Multilingual eGlossary

Video BrainPOP®

Academic Standards for Science
8.2.2 Describe and model how water moves through the earth's crust, atmosphere, and oceans in a cyclic way, as liquid, vapor, and solid.

Also covers: 8.NS.7, 8.NS.8, 8.NS.11

Inquiry Surfing Under a Wave?

Is this surfer confused? Why is he under the wave? What do you think happens to a wave's energy below the surface?

Launch Lab

10 minutes

How is sea level measured?

The ocean surface is changing constantly as a result of waves, tides, and currents. In a matter of seconds, a wave can cause the ocean surface to rise and fall by several meters. In a matter of hours, a tide can also raise or lower the level of the sea by several meters.

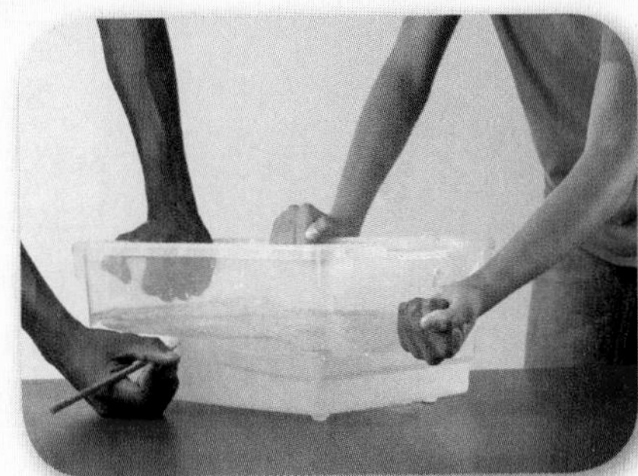

1. Read and complete a lab safety form.
2. Half-fill a **clear container** with **water.**
3. Slowly and steadily rock the container back and forth to produce waves.
4. While you gently rock the container, another student should look through the side of the container and mark the peaks and valleys of the waves with a **wax pencil.**
5. Using a **ruler,** measure the difference between the two marks. The midpoint of this measurement is equivalent to sea level.

Think About This

1. How do you think sea level changes when wind speed changes?
2. **Key Concept** How do you think oceanographers determine sea level?

Parts of a Wave

Have you ever been caught in a crashing wave? It might have been hard to catch your breath. Even if you dive deep below a wave, you can still feel some of the wave's energy. The surfer shown on the opposite page is duck diving—ducking beneath a wave to avoid the wave's full power.

There are different kinds and sizes of waves in the oceans, but all waves have the same basic parts. As shown in **Figure 9,** the crest is the highest part of a wave. The trough is the lowest part of a wave. The wave height is the vertical distance between the crest and the trough. The wavelength is the horizontal distance from crest to crest or from trough to trough.

 **Reading Check** How is wavelength measured?

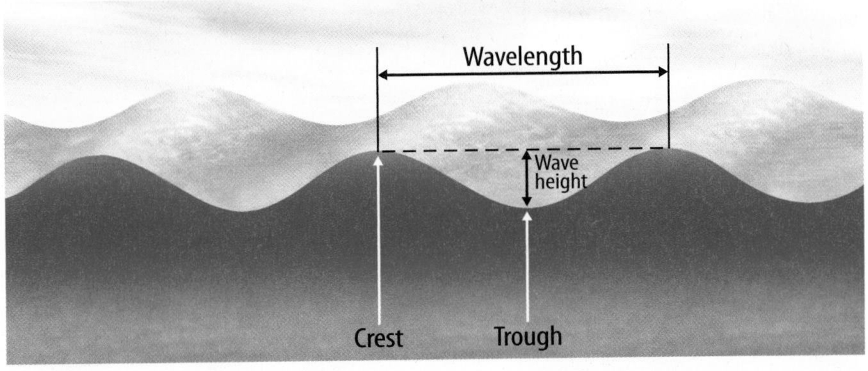

Figure 9 Ocean waves have crests and troughs.

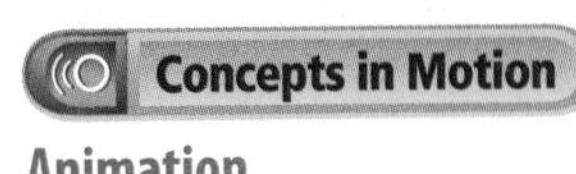

Animation

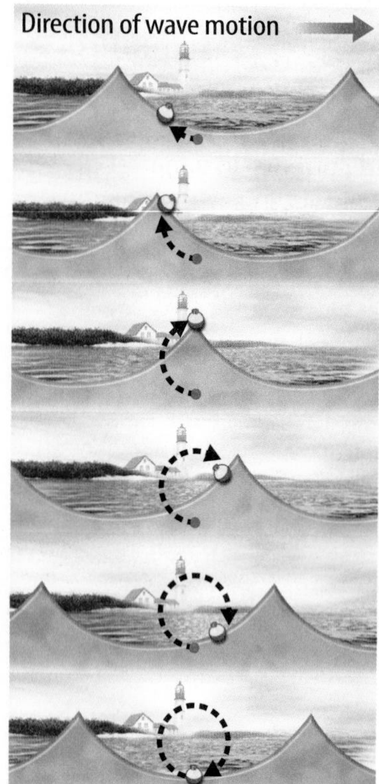

Figure 10 Just like a fishing bobber, a water particle moves in a circle as a wave passes.

Surface Waves

Wind causes the waves that roll onto a beach. They are often called surface waves. Friction from wind drags across the water's surface, causing it to ripple. The small ripples eventually become larger waves.

Key Concept Check What causes ocean surface waves?

Surface waves range in size from tiny ripples to huge waves several meters high. Three factors affect the size of surface waves—wind speed, time, and distance. The faster, longer, and farther the wind blows, the larger the resulting waves. For example, some of the largest wind-driven waves form in the Southern Ocean. It experiences fast and continuous winds that blow all the way around Antarctica.

Wave Motion

If you watch a wave wash onto a beach, you might think that a wave transports water from one location to another. However, the motion of a water particle in a wave is circular. After a wave passes, the water particle returns approximately to its original position, as shown in **Figure 10.**

The circular motion of water particles extends below the surface. However, as depth increases, the circular motion decreases. At a certain depth, called the wave base, wave motion stops. This depth is equal to a distance of one-half the wavelength of the wave above it, as illustrated in **Figure 11.**

Wave Motion at Depth

Figure 11 The circular motion of water particles becomes smaller and smaller with depth.

Visual Check If the wavelength of a surface wave is 40 m, how deep would a scuba diver have to go before feeling no wave motion?

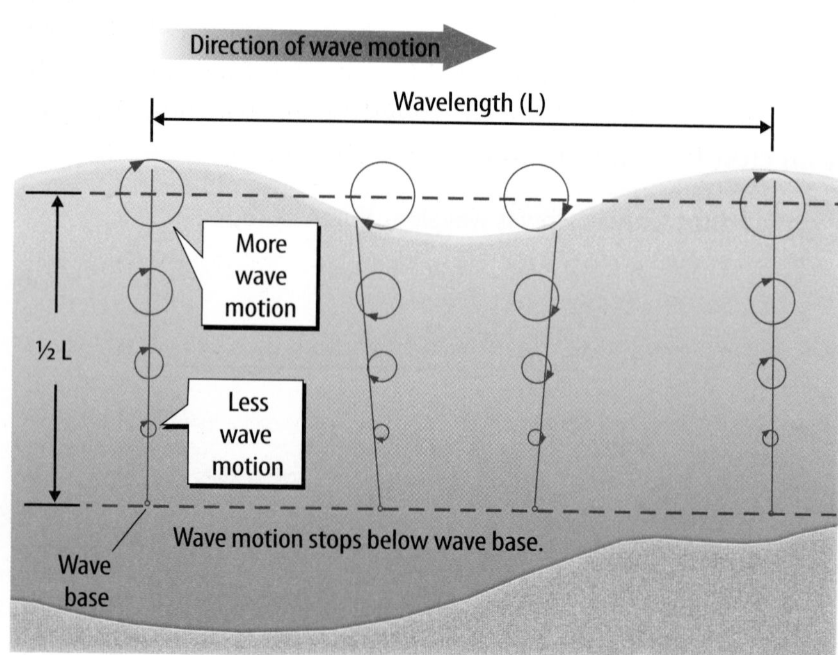

When Surface Waves Reach Shore

As a wave moves into shallow water, it changes shape and size. The change begins when the base of the wave comes in contact with the sloping seafloor, as shown in **Figure 12.** As the base of the wave drags on the seafloor, the wave's speed decreases. At the same time, the wavelength shortens and the wave height increases. When the wave reaches a certain height, the wave base can no longer support the crest, and the wave collapses, or breaks. This type of wave is called a breaker. After a wave breaks, the water surges forward onto shore.

FOLDABLES®
Make a shutter-fold book and use it to organize your notes about surface waves and tides.
Surface Waves
Tides

Breakers

Figure 12 A wave changes shape when its base comes in contact with the seafloor.

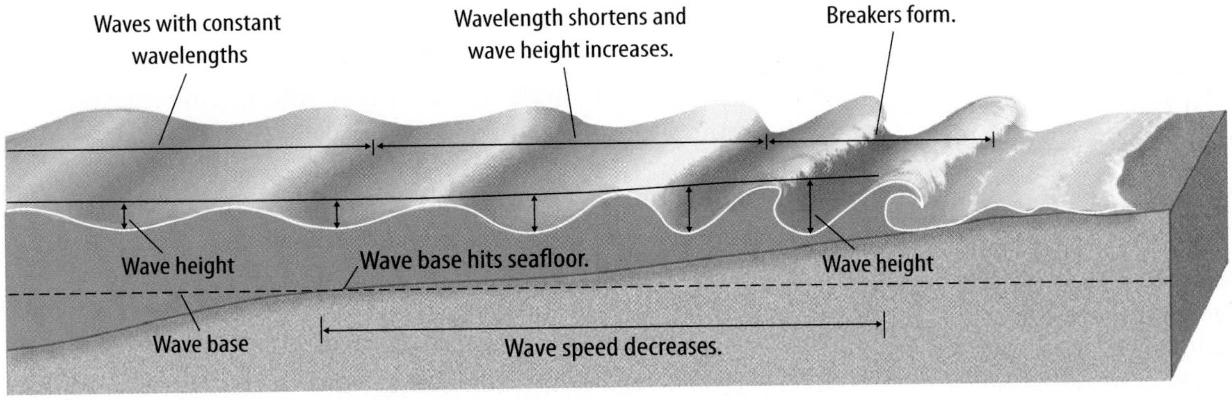

Wave base hits seafloor.

Tsunamis

You might have heard of another type of ocean wave called a tsunami. *A* **tsunami** (soo NAH mee) *is a wave that forms when an ocean disturbance suddenly moves a large volume of water.* It can be caused by an underwater earthquake or landslide, a volcanic eruption, or even ice breaking away from a glacier.

 **Key Concept Check** What can cause a tsunami?

Far from shore, a tsunami has a short wave height, often less than 30 cm high. However, the wavelength can be hundreds of kilometers long. As a tsunami approaches shore, it slows down and grows higher. Many tsunamis grow only a few meters high as they move onto shore, but some can rise as high as 30 m.

Unlike a common wind-driven wave, the water from a tsunami just keeps coming. As a result, tsunamis can cause much damage. In 2004, a series of tsunamis caused by an underwater earthquake in the Indian Ocean killed more than 225,000 people in 11 countries and destroyed entire villages.

WORD ORIGIN

tsunami
from Japanese *tsu*, means "harbor"; and *nami*, means "wave"

Math Skills 

Use Statistics

Find the **mean** by adding the numbers in a data set and dividing by the number of items in the set. The **range** is the difference between the largest and smallest numbers in a set of data.

Example: In a 48-hour period, high tides were measured at 0.701 m, 0.649 m, 0.716 m, and 0.661 m above sea level. What is the range and mean of the high tides?

Range = 0.716 m − 0.649 m = 0.067 m

Mean = (0.701 m + 0.649 m + 0.716 m + 0.661 m) ÷ 4 = 2.73 m ÷ 4 = 0.682 m

Practice

During the same 48-hour period, the low tides were measured at 0.018 m, 0.103 m, 0.048 m, and 0.091 m below sea level.

a. What is the range of the low tides?

b. What is the mean of the low tides?

- Math Practice
- Personal Tutor

Tides

When measuring sea level, scientists take into account changes to the ocean's surface caused by waves. **Sea level** *is the average level of the ocean's surface at any given time.* Scientists who measure sea level also take into account changes to the ocean's surface caused by tides. **Tides** *are the periodic rise and fall of the ocean's surface caused by the gravitational force between Earth and the Moon, and between Earth and the Sun.*

The Moon and Tides

The gravitational force that causes the largest tides is between Earth and the Moon. The attraction between them produces two bulges on ocean surfaces—one bulge on the side of Earth facing the Moon and one bulge on the side of Earth facing away from the Moon. The bulges represent high tides. High tide is the highest level of an ocean's surface. Low tide, the lowest level of an ocean, occurs between the two bulges. The difference between high tide and low tide in one coastal area is shown in **Figure 13.**

 **Key Concept Check** What causes the largest tides?

Topography and Tides

The coastlines of continents, the shape and size of ocean basins, and the depth of the oceans affect tides. The Atlantic coast experiences two alternating high and low tides almost daily. In contrast, the Gulf of Mexico experiences one high tide and one low tide each day.

The size of tides also varies on different areas of Earth's surface. In some areas, the difference between low tide and high tide is as small as 1 m. In other areas, the difference is as great as 15 m. As shown in **Figure 13,** *the difference in water level between a high tide and a low tide is the* **tidal range.**

Figure 13 Tides change the level of the ocean's surface.

High tide
Tidal range
Low tide

Tidal Forces

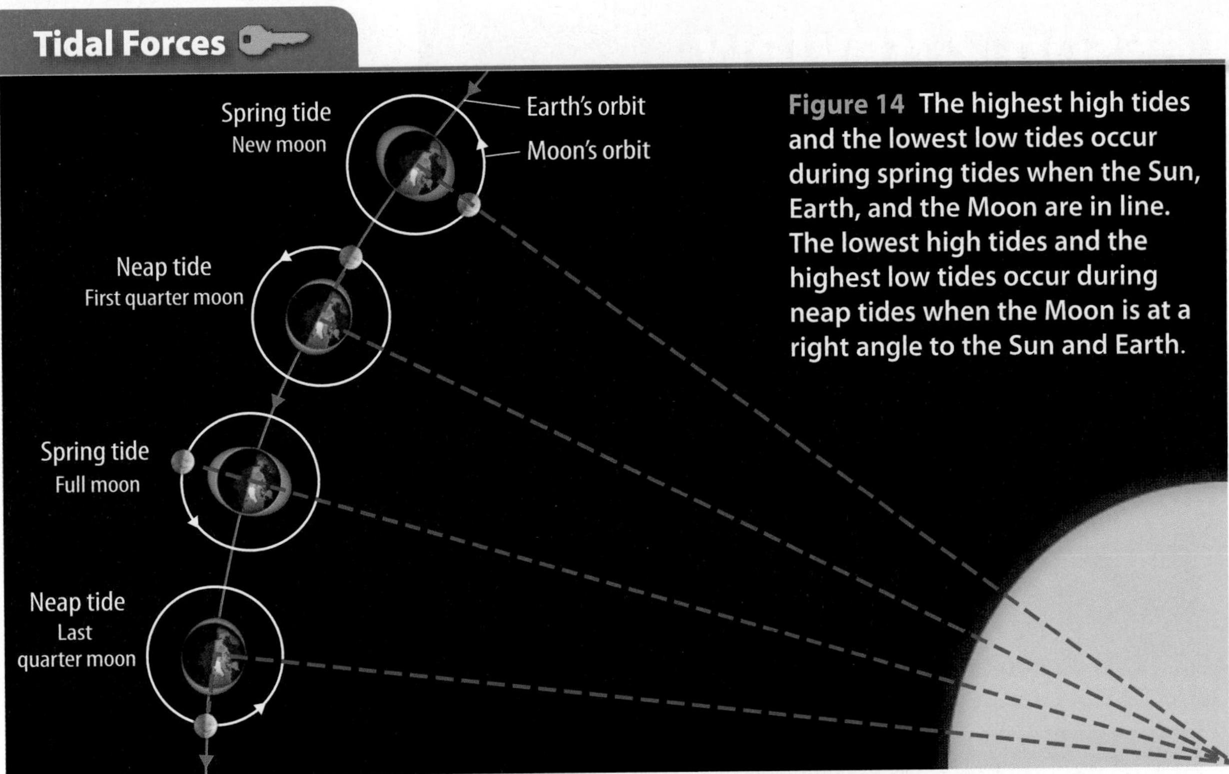

Figure 14 The highest high tides and the lowest low tides occur during spring tides when the Sun, Earth, and the Moon are in line. The lowest high tides and the highest low tides occur during neap tides when the Moon is at a right angle to the Sun and Earth.

Spring Tides

Tidal ranges are not constant. They vary depending on the positions of the Sun and the Moon with respect to Earth. Notice in **Figure 14** that when Earth, the Moon, and the Sun are aligned, the Moon is new or full. The gravitational pull on the oceans is strongest when the two forces act together. As a result, the tidal range is larger than normal. High tides are higher and low tides are lower. *A* **spring tide** *has the largest tidal range and occurs when Earth, the Moon, and the Sun form a straight line.*

Neap Tides

Look at **Figure 14** again. During a first quarter moon and a last quarter moon, the Moon is at a right angle to Earth and the Sun. The gravitational forces between Earth and the Moon and between Earth and the Sun act against each other. This means that high tides are lower than normal while low tides are higher than normal. *A* **neap tide** *has the lowest tidal range and occurs when Earth, the Moon, and the Sun form a right angle.*

Reading Check What is a neap tide?

20 minutes

Can you analyze tidal data?

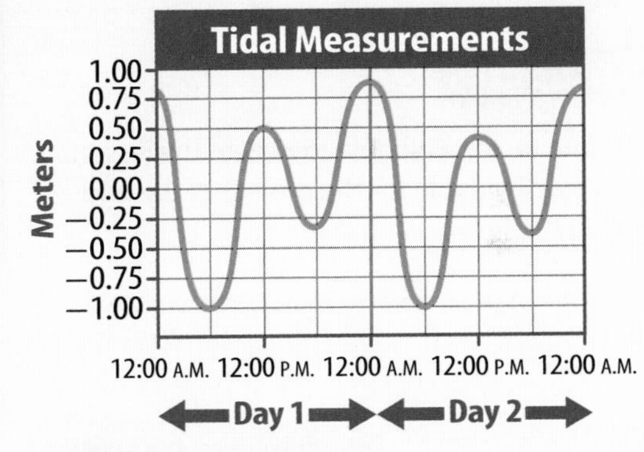

Analyze and Conclude

1. **Determine** how many high tides and low tides there are in a 24-hour period.
2. **Compare** Is the height of the high tides the same within a 24-hour period? What about the height of the low tides?
3. **Calculate** the tidal range between 12 A.M. and 6 A.M. on Day 1.
4. **Key Concept** Suppose the data represent spring tides. How would the tidal data collected during a neap tide be different?

Lesson 2 Review

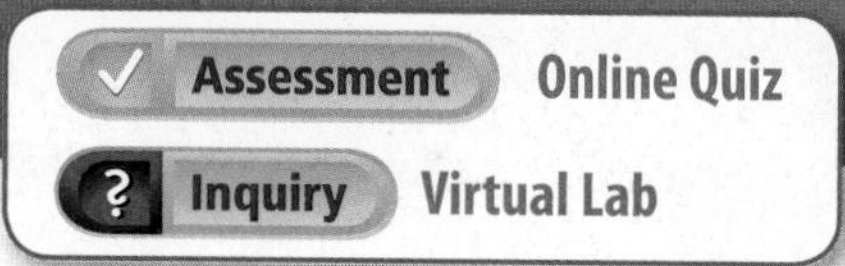

Visual Summary

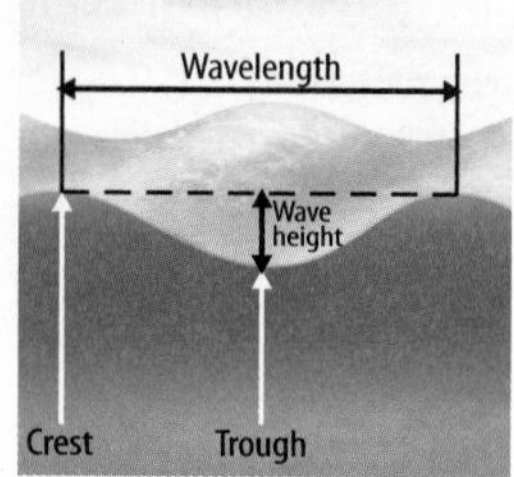

All waves have the same basic features.

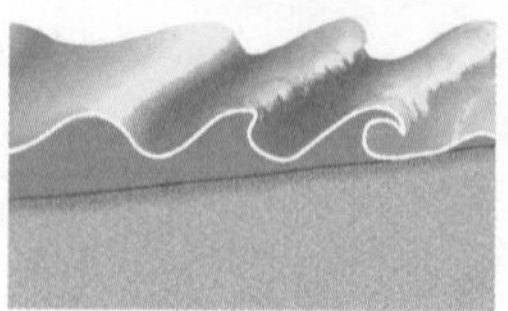

Wavelength shortens and wave height increases as a wave nears the shoreline.

The gravitational attraction between Earth and the Moon, and between Earth and the Sun causes tides.

FOLDABLES®

Use your lesson Foldable to review the lesson. Save your Foldable for the project at the end of the chapter.

What do you think NOW?

You first read the statements below at the beginning of the chapter.

3. Waves move water particles from one location to another.

4. The wind causes tides.

Did you change your mind about whether you agree or disagree with the statements? Rewrite any false statements to make them true.

Use Vocabulary

1. **Use the term** *tsunami* in a complete sentence.
2. **Define** *tide* in your own words.

Understand Key Concepts 

3. **Explain** how the Moon causes tides.
4. **Compare and contrast** the causes of surface waves and tsunamis.

Interpret Graphics

5. **Organize Information** Copy and fill in the graphic organizer below to describe spring tides and neap tides.

	Positions of Earth, Moon, and Sun
Spring tides	
Neap tides	

6. **Explain** how the figure below represents the movement of water in a wave.

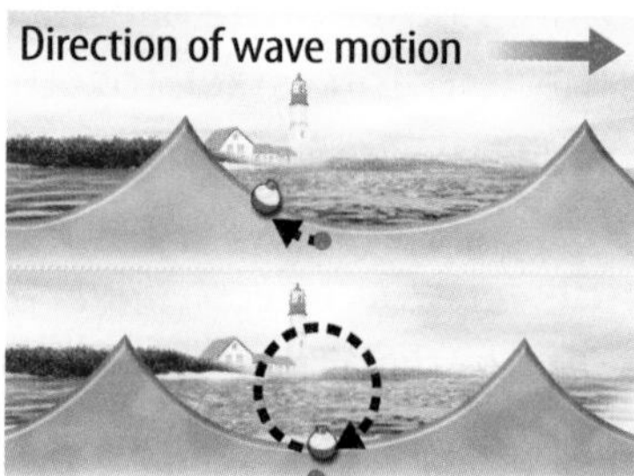

Critical Thinking

7. **Design** an experiment to measure the average tidal range in a coastal area during one month.

Math Skills

Math Practice

8. In a certain location, high tides for one day measure 8.30 m and 8.00 m. The low tides measure 0.500 m and 0.220 m.
   A. What is the range of the tides?
   B. What is the mean low tide?

Inquiry **Skill Practice** **Analyze Data** **20 minutes**

High Tides in the Bay of Fundy

The tides in the Bay of Fundy in Eastern Canada have the greatest tidal ranges of any tides on Earth. As a tide enters the Bay of Fundy, it is channeled into an increasingly narrower space. Topography of the land directly affects the tidal range.

The lines on the map of the Bay of Fundy below are similar to contour lines on a topographic map. Tidal height data has been collected along each line and then averaged to determine the mean height of the highest tide at that location across the width of the bay.

Learn It

Analyze the data on the map, to make a graph showing the change in tidal heights from the mouth of the bay to the town of Truro.

Try It

1. Make a data table with three columns in your Science Journal. Label the columns: High Tide (m), Distance from the Mouth of the Bay (cm), Distance from the Mouth of the Bay (m).
2. Use the map scale of the Bay of Fundy below and a metric ruler to determine the distance each high tide is from the mouth of the bay. Convert centimeters on your ruler to meters on the map. Record your information in your data table.
3. Using your data, graph the distance from the mouth of the bay along the x-axis (in m), and tidal height along the y-axis. Give your graph a title.

Apply It

4. **Describe** how the highest tides changed with distance.
5. **Infer** how the tides in the Bay of Fundy might change when Earth, the Moon, and the Sun are in a straight line. How might the tides change when Earth, the Moon, and the Sun are at an angle?
6. **Key Concept** Identify factors that affect tides in the Bay of Fundy.

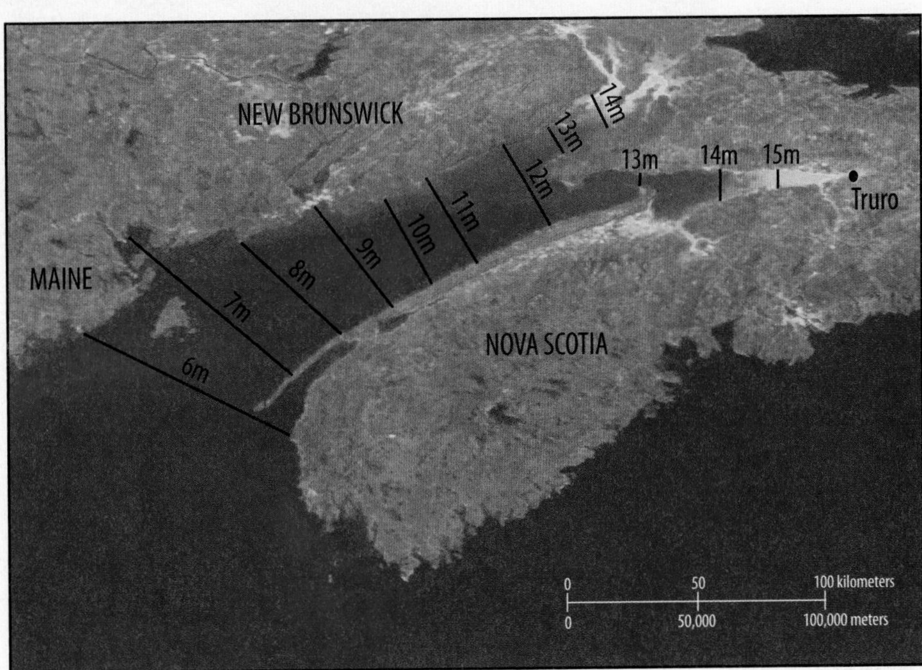

Lesson 3

Reading Guide

Key Concepts
ESSENTIAL QUESTIONS

- What are the major types of ocean currents?
- How do ocean currents affect weather and climate?

Vocabulary
ocean current p. 285
gyre p. 286
Coriolis effect p. 286
upwelling p. 287

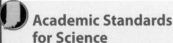

Multilingual eGlossary

Video BrainPOP®

Academic Standards for Science

8.2.1 Recognize and demonstrate how the sun's energy drives convection in the atmosphere and in bodies of water, which results in ocean currents and weather patterns.

8.2.2 Describe and model how water moves through the earth's crust, atmosphere, and oceans in a cyclic way, as liquid, vapor, and solid.

8.2.3 Describe the characteristics of ocean currents and identify their effects on weather patterns.

Also covers: 8.NS.7, 8.NS.8, 8.NS.11

Ocean Currents

Inquiry Clouds on a Mission?

Can you find the Florida Current in this satellite photo? The curve of the clouds gives it away. As the clouds move between Florida and Cuba, they follow the same path as the current. Why do you think clouds and currents sometimes follow the same path?

10 minutes

How does wind move water?

If you released a rubber ball in the waves along an ocean shoreline, the ball would go around and around in the waves. What would happen if you released a ball farther out in the ocean?

1. Read and complete a lab safety form.
2. Half fill a **container** with water.
3. Position a **fan** so it can blow across the water's surface.
4. Put two drops of **food coloring** on the surface of the water closest to the fan. Turn the fan to a low setting to produce waves.
5. Observe what happens to the food coloring.

Think About This

1. Explain the movement of the food coloring in your Science Journal.
2. What types of objects do you think the wind can move in the ocean?
3. **Key Concept** If you were on a boat about 3 km from shore and threw a rubber ball into the water, what do you think would happen?

Major Ocean Currents

During a storm in 1990, 40,000 pairs of shoes fell off a cargo ship in the middle of the Pacific Ocean. Months later, beachcombers began finding the shoes on the coasts of Oregon and Washington. How did the shoes get there? An ocean current carried them. *An* **ocean current** *is a large volume of water flowing in a certain direction.*

Surface Currents

Recall that energy from the Sun creates air currents. Energy in air currents then transfers to water and forms waves. As wind blows over water, the moving air particles drag on the surface and cause the water to move, just as they drag the wind surfer in **Figure 15.** Wind-driven currents are called surface currents.

Surface currents carry warm or cold water horizontally across the ocean's surface. They extend to about 400 m below the surface and can move as fast as 100 km/day. Earth's major wind belts, driven by energy from the Sun, influence the formation of ocean currents and their movement. For example, the trade winds that blow from Africa move warm, equatorial water toward North America and South America.

Key Concept Check How do surface currents form?

Figure 15 Just as wind drags this wind surfer across the ocean's surface, the wind also drags the top layer of water across the ocean's surface.

Major Ocean Gyres

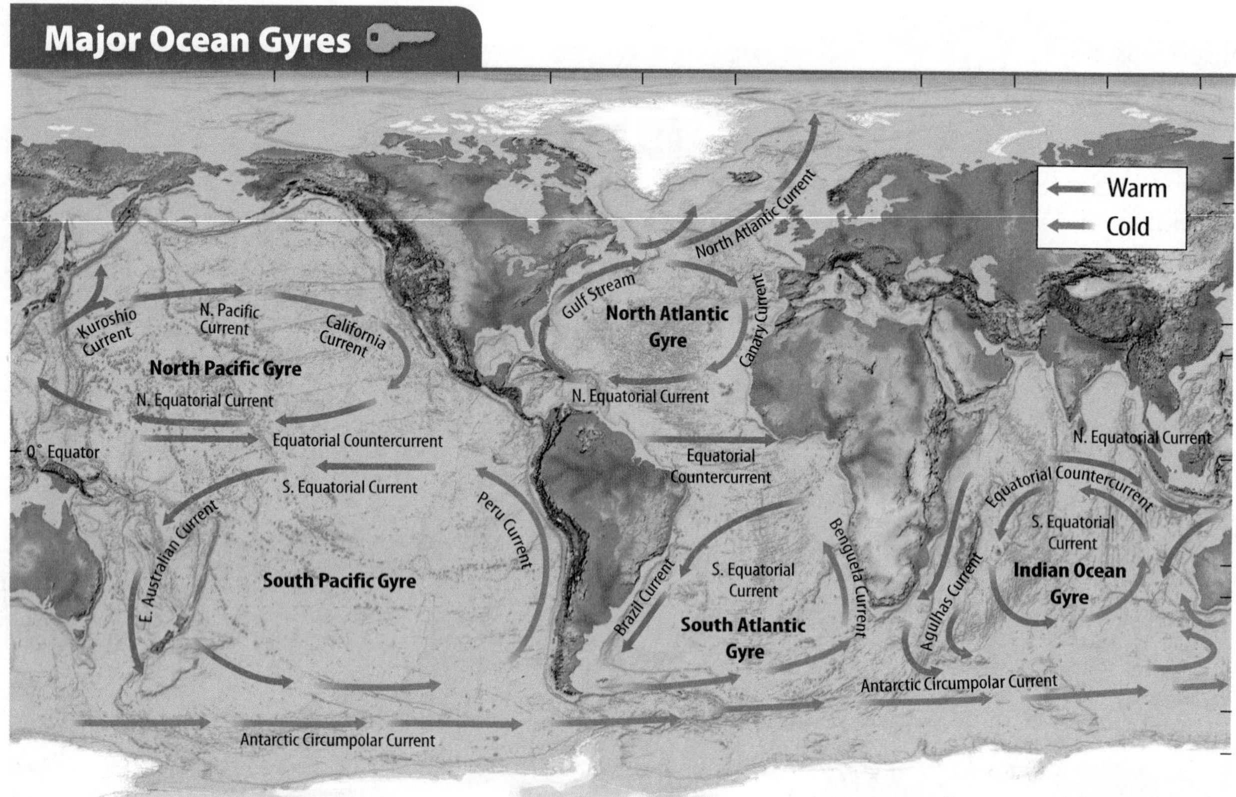

▲ **Figure 16** Gyres form on the surface of Earth's oceans.

Word Origin

gyre
from Latin *gyrus,* means "circle"

Figure 17 The Coriolis effect causes fluids to move clockwise in the Northern Hemisphere and counter-clockwise in the Southern Hemisphere. ▼

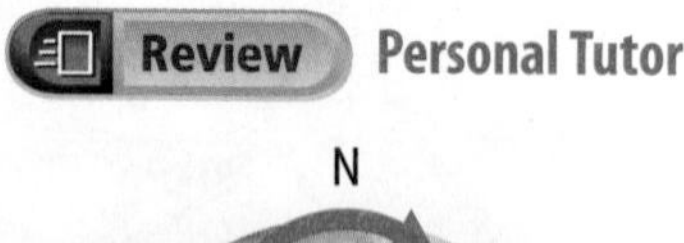

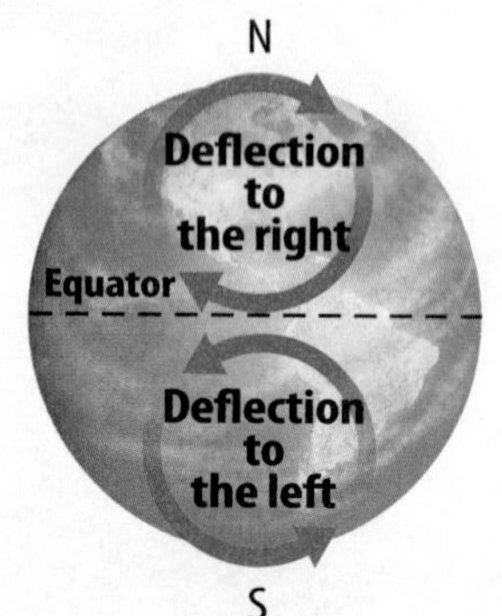

Gyres Earth's oceans contain large, looped systems of surface currents called gyres (JI urz). *A* **gyre** *is a circular system of currents.* As shown in **Figure 16,** the currents within each gyre move in the same direction. However, if you look closely, you can see that the direction of current movement in a gyre is different in each hemisphere. Gyres in the northern hemisphere circle clockwise. Gyres in the southern hemisphere circle counterclockwise.

Coriolis Effect Why do gyres move in different directions? Directions differ because of the Coriolis effect. *The* **Coriolis effect** *is the movement of wind and water to the right or left that is caused by Earth's rotation.* As shown in **Figure 17,** the Coriolis effect causes fluids such as air and water to curve to the right in the Northern Hemisphere, in a clockwise direction. In the Southern Hemisphere, the Coriolis effect causes fluids to curve to the left, in a counterclockwise direction.

Reading Check What is the Coriolis effect?

Topography The shapes of continents and other landmasses affect the direction and speed of currents. For example, gyres form small or large loops and move at different speeds depending on the land masses they contact. The Florida Current, shown in the photo at the beginning of this lesson, narrows and increases in speed as it passes through the straits of Florida.

Upwelling

Surface currents move water horizontally across the ocean's surface. Not all currents move in a horizontal direction. Some currents move water vertically. **Upwelling** *is the vertical movement of water toward the ocean's surface.* Upwelling occurs when wind blows across the ocean's surface and pushes water away from an area. Deeper, colder water is then forced to the surface. Upwelling often occurs along coastlines. **Figure 18** illustrates how upwelling occurs along the South American coast.

Upwelling brings cold, nutrient-rich water from deep in the ocean to the ocean's surface. This water supports large populations of algae, fish, and other ocean organisms.

 **Key Concept Check** How does upwelling occur?

Density Currents

Another type of vertical current is a density current. Density currents move water downward. They carry water from the surface to deeper parts of the ocean. Density currents are not caused by wind. They are caused by changes in density.

As you read in Lesson 1, cold water is denser than warm water, and salty water is denser than freshwater. As a surface current moves toward a polar area, the water cools. When seawater freezes, salt is left behind in the surrounding water. Eventually, the cold, salty water becomes so dense that it sinks, as shown in **Figure 19.** Upwelling later brings the current back to the surface. Density currents are important components of ocean circulation. They circulate thermal energy, nutrients, and gases.

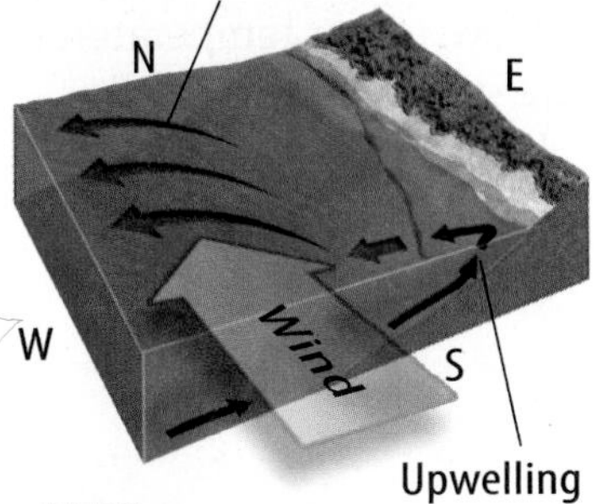

▲ **Figure 18** Upwelling off the South American coast causes cold, deep water to replace warmer water on the surface.

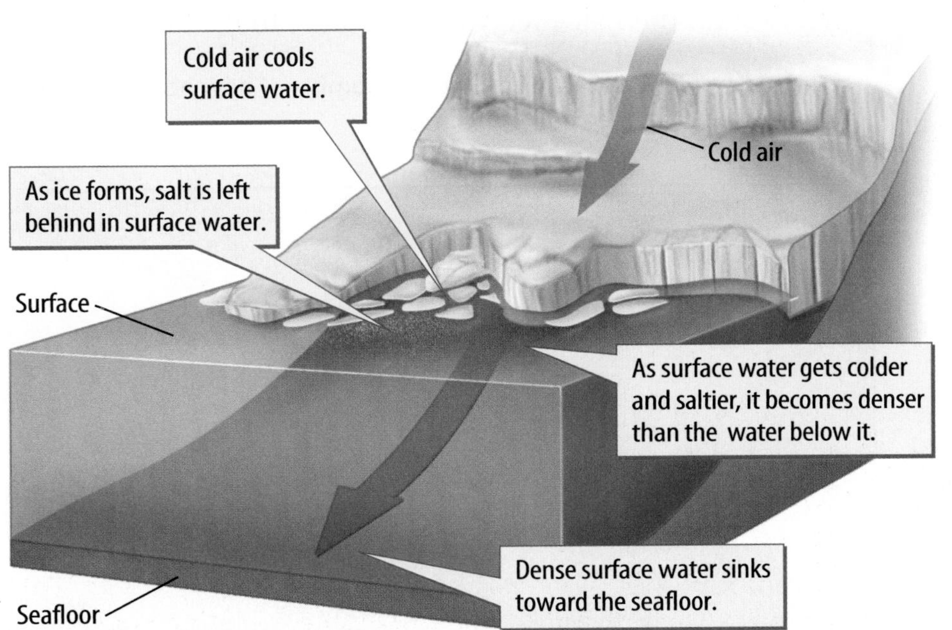

Cold air cools surface water.
Cold air
As ice forms, salt is left behind in surface water.
Surface
As surface water gets colder and saltier, it becomes denser than the water below it.
Dense surface water sinks toward the seafloor.
Seafloor

◀ **Figure 19** Cold, salty water sinks, producing a density current.

Figure 20 Higher temperatures are shown in red and yellow. Lower temperatures are shown in green and blue. ▶

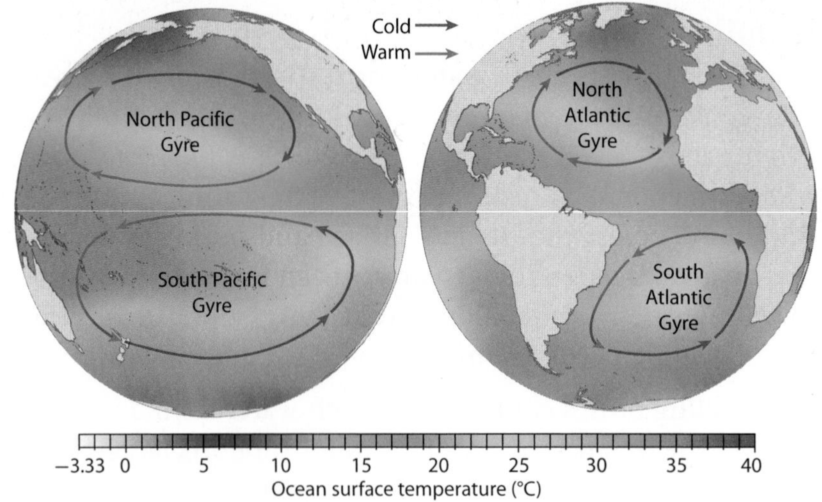

FOLDABLES®

Make a shutter-fold book. Use it to record the location of major warm-water currents and cold-water currents and to summarize how they affect weather and climate.

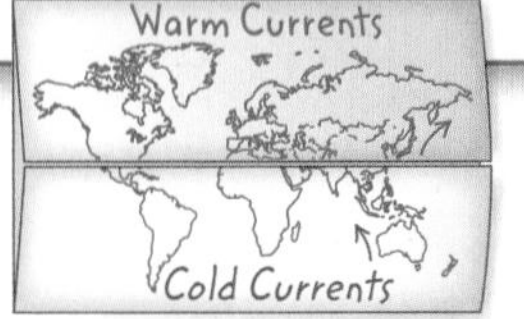

Impacts on Weather and Climate

Solar energy drives convection in the oceans causing warm- and cold-water currents in the gyres shown in **Figure 20.** These two types of surface currents affect weather and climate in different ways. Regions near warm-water currents are often warmer and wetter than regions near cold-water currents.

Surface Currents Affecting the United States

Several warm-water currents affect coastal areas of the southeastern United States. For example, the Gulf Stream, shown in **Figure 21,** transfers lots of thermal energy and moisture to the surrounding air. As a result, summer evenings are often warm and humid. An evening rain is common in these areas.

The cold California Current, also shown in **Figure 21,** affects coastal areas of the southwestern United States. A summer evening along the California coast is often cooler and drier than a summer evening in Florida. Why? This cold-water current releases less thermal energy and moisture to the air.

Key Concept Check Give an example of how ocean currents can affect weather and climate.

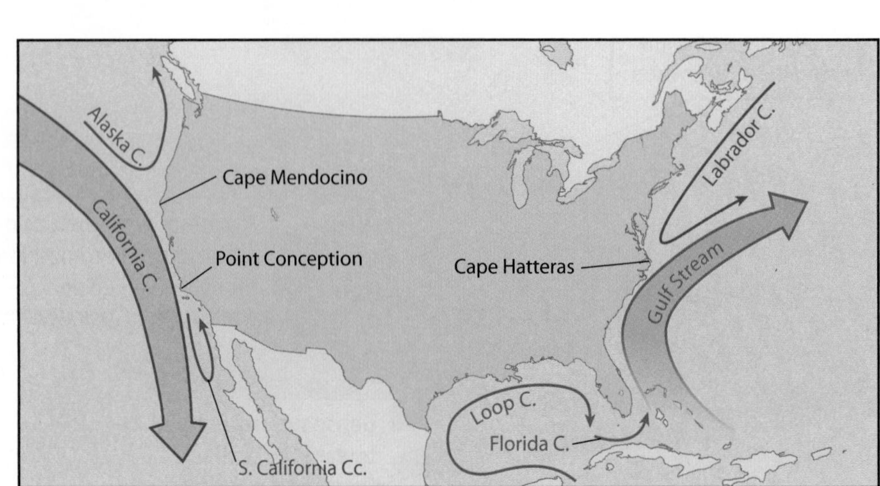

Figure 21 The Gulf Stream is a warm-water current. The California Current is a cold-water current.

Visual Check Hypothesize why hurricanes might be more common in the eastern US than in the western US. ▶

Global Conveyor Belt

Figure 22 A global belt of surface currents and density currents distributes thermal energy on Earth.

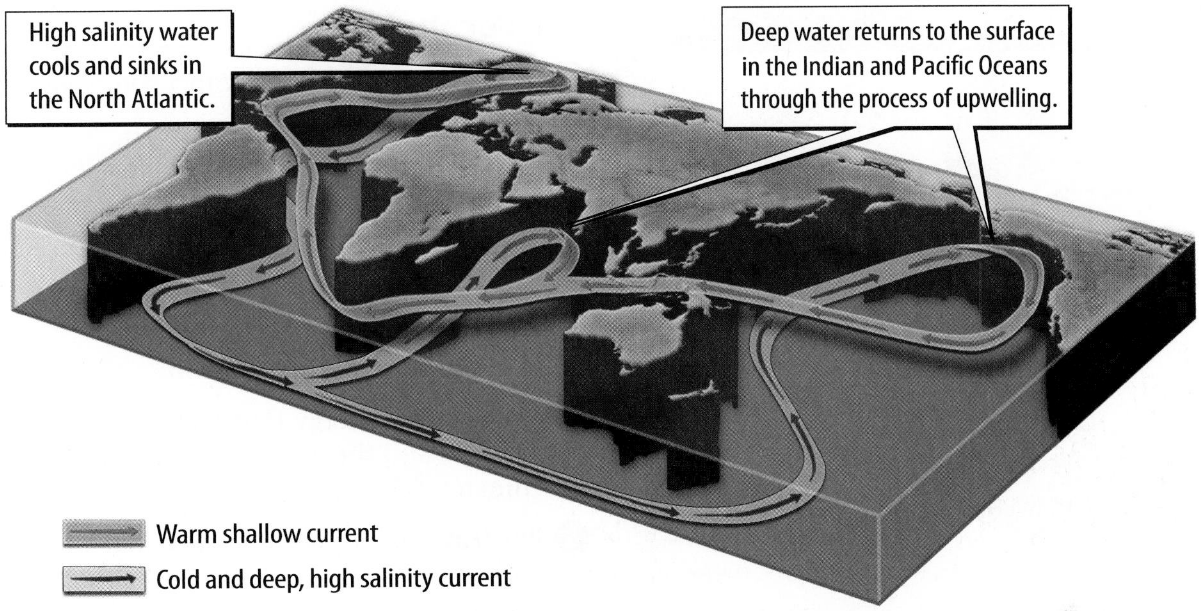

High salinity water cools and sinks in the North Atlantic.
Deep water returns to the surface in the Indian and Pacific Oceans through the process of upwelling.
Warm shallow current
Cold and deep, high salinity current

The Great Ocean Conveyor Belt

Aside from gyres, there is another large system of ocean currents that affects weather and climate. This current system is called the Great Ocean Conveyor Belt, illustrated in **Figure 22.** Scientists use this model to explain how ocean currents circulate thermal energy around Earth.

In this model, density currents in the North Atlantic Ocean and the Southern Ocean "run" the conveyor belt. Water in those regions is so cold and dense that it sinks to the ocean bottom and travels along the seafloor. Upwellings in the Pacific and Indian Oceans eventually bring this deep, cold water to the surface where it is warmed by the Sun through convection.

As warm, surface water travels from the equator toward the poles, it releases thermal energy to the atmosphere, which warms the surrounding region. Then, the cold water sinks until it is upwelled at a different location and the cycle repeats. Scientists estimate that it takes about 1,000 years to complete a cycle.

 **Key Concept Check** How does the Great Ocean Conveyor Belt affect climate?

Inquiry MiniLab — 15 minutes

How does temperature affect ocean currents?

1. Read and complete a lab safety form.
2. Fill one **foam cup** with **hot water** and one cup with **ice water.**
3. Place a **glass dish** on top of the cups. Use two other cups for balance, as shown. Half fill the dish with **room-temperature water.**
4. Put two drops of **food coloring** in the dish, one above each water-filled cup. Use one color for cold water, another for hot water. Observe for 10 min.

Analyze and Conclude

1. **Draw** a diagram of your observations in your Science Journal. Label the hot and cold areas in your drawing.
2.  **Key Concept Explain** how your observations of the colored water resemble ocean currents.

Lesson 3 Review

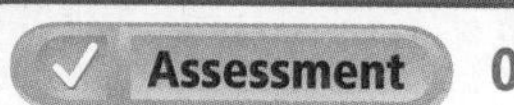

Visual Summary

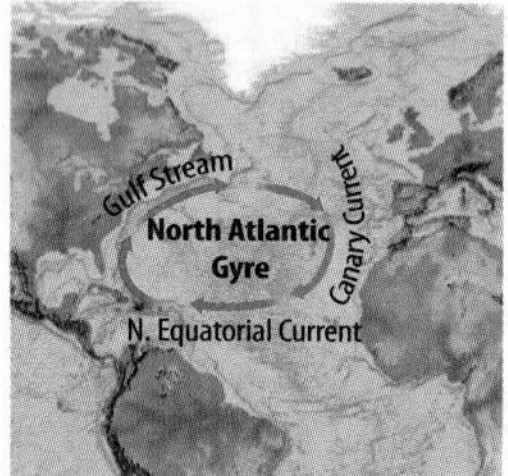

A gyre is a circular system of surface currents.

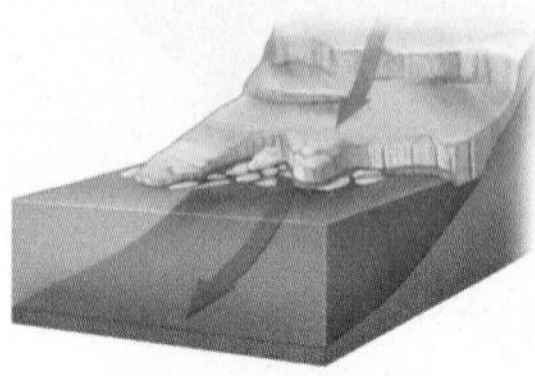

Density currents move cold water from the ocean surface to deeper parts of the ocean.

A system of surface currents and density currents distributes thermal energy around Earth.

FOLDABLES®

Use your lesson Foldable to review the lesson. Save your Foldable for the project at the end of the chapter.

What do you think NOW?

You first read the statements below at the beginning of the chapter.

5. Ocean currents occur on the surface and below the surface.

6. Ocean currents affect climate and weather.

Did you change your mind about whether you agree or disagree with the statements? Rewrite any false statements to make them true.

Use Vocabulary

1. **Use the term** *Coriolis effect* in a complete sentence.
2. A(n) ________ moves water vertically.

Understand Key Concepts 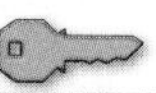

3. What causes a surface current?
   - **A.** Earth's orbit
   - **B.** Earth's rotation
   - **C.** temperature
   - **D.** wind
4. **Explain** how energy transfers between currents and the atmosphere affect climate.
5. **Illustrate** how upwelling occurs off the coast of California as wind blows from north to south.

Interpret Graphics

6. **Explain** how the surface currents in the figure below affect the western and eastern coasts of the United States.

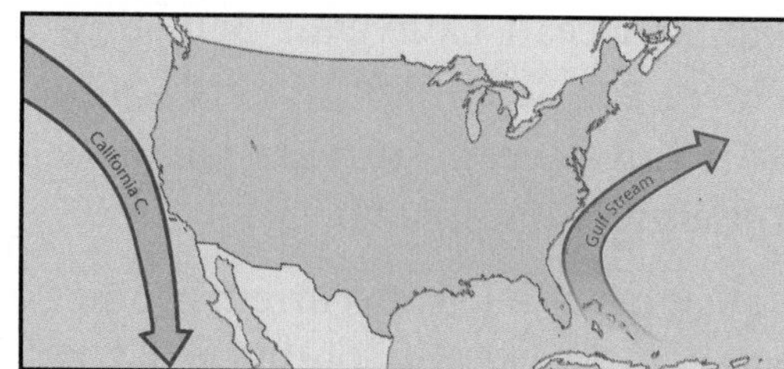

7. **Compare and Contrast** Copy and fill in the graphic organizer below to compare and contrast surface currents and density currents.

	Similarities	Differences
Surface currents		
Density currents		

Critical Thinking

8. **Design** an experiment to show how waves and currents move water in different ways.
9. **Infer** why major fishing grounds are along coastlines.

Inquiry **Skill Practice** **Interpret Data** 30 minutes

How do oceanographers study ocean currents?

Materials

world map

Cargo spills can help oceanographers study ocean currents. The longitude and latitude positions of items from spills that wash ashore contain clues about the direction and speed of currents. Interpret the data below to find out what happened to a cargo of rubber bath toys lost in a January 1992 storm in the North Pacific.

Learn It

Can you make sense of the data in the table at right? You need to **interpret data** before you can draw conclusions about them. Interpret the longitude and latitude positions of toys that washed ashore by marking them on a map.

Date	Latitude	Longitude
January 1992	45°N	178°E
March 1992	44°N	165°W
July 1992	49°N	155°W
October 1992	52°N	135°W
January 1993	59°N	149°W
March 1993	56°N	157°W
July 1993	57°N	170°W
October 1993	59°N	180°E
January 1994	56°N	166°E
March 1994	45°N	155°E
July 1994	47°N	172°E
October 1994	50°N	165°W
January 1995	47°N	140°W
October 2000	46°N	50°W
December 2003	57°N	07°W

Try It

1. Mark the longitude and latitude positions on a world map. The other data represent locations where individual bath toys were found. The first data point represents the location of the cargo spill. Label each point with a date.
2. Connect the dots in order of time. Ocean currents don't follow straight lines, so use curved lines. The toys could not float over land, so all the lines you draw should only cross water.
3. Compare the path of the toys to a world map of ocean currents and gyres.

Apply It

4. **Describe** how this data could help oceanographers chart ocean currents.
5. **Hypothesize** how toys traveled to the Atlantic Ocean.
6. **Key Concept** What types of ocean currents carry cargo debris around the world?

Lesson 4

Environmental Impacts on Oceans

Reading Guide

Key Concepts
ESSENTIAL QUESTIONS

- How does pollution affect marine organisms?
- How does global climate change affect marine ecosystems?
- Why is it important to keep oceans healthy?

Vocabulary

marine p. 294
harmful algal bloom p. 295
coral bleaching p. 296

Multilingual eGlossary

Video
What's Science Got to do With It?

Academic Standards for Science

8.2.6 Identify, explain, and discuss some effects human activities have on the biosphere, such as air, soil, light, noise and water pollution.

8.2.8 Explain that human activities, beginning with the earliest herding and agricultural activities, have drastically changed the environment and have affected the capacity of the environment to support native species. Explain current efforts to reduce and eliminate these impacts and encourage sustainability.

Also covers: 8.NS.1, 8.NS.7, 8.NS.8, 8.DP.1, 8.DP.2, 8.DP.3, 8.DP.4, 8.DP.6, 8.DP.8, 8.DP.9, 8.DP.10

Inquiry Orange Ocean?

The orange-red color of the water in this photograph comes from algae. The algae have formed a huge mat, called an algal bloom, on the ocean's surface. Algal blooms can be beautiful, but some algal blooms harm ocean ecosystems.

15 minutes

What happens to litter in the oceans?

Imagine you are on a boat hundreds of kilometers from shore. You look down at the water and see a sea turtle entangled in plastic. How did this happen?

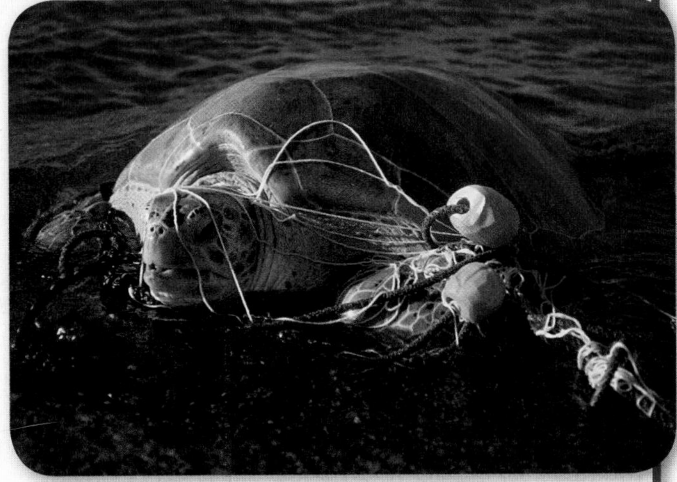

1. Read and complete a lab safety form.
2. Half-fill a large **bowl** with **water.**
3. Sprinkle **objects** your teacher has supplied into the water.
4. Gently swirl the water in the bowl until the water moves at a constant speed. Try not to create a whirlpool.

Think About This

1. What happened to the objects you sprinkled into the bowl?
2. What do you think happens to litter that is dumped into the ocean?
3. **Key Concept** What do you think you can do to prevent ocean pollution?

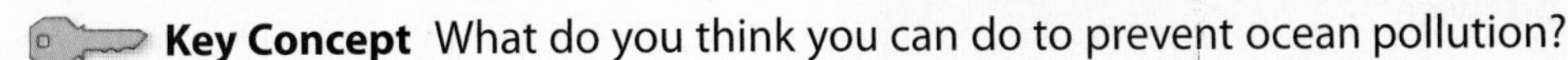

Ocean Pollution

Have you ever seen a photograph of a shorebird or seal covered in oil? Spills from oil tankers harm wildlife. They also harm the ocean. Any harm to the physical, chemical, or biological health of the ocean ecosystem is ocean pollution. Sometimes ocean pollution comes from a natural source, such as a volcanic eruption. More often, human activities cause ocean pollution.

Sources of Ocean Pollution

Like pollution on land, ocean pollution comes from both point sources and nonpoint sources. Point-source pollution can be traced to a specific source, such as a drainpipe or an oil spill. Nonpoint-source pollution cannot be traced to a specific source. Sewage runoff from land is an example.

Figure 23 shows the proportion of different sources of ocean pollution caused by humans. Notice that only 13 percent of this pollution comes from shipping or offshore mining activity. The rest comes from land. Land-based pollution includes garbage, hazardous chemicals, and fertilizers. Airborne pollution that originates on land, such as emissions from power plants or cars, is also included in this category. So is trash dumped directly into the oceans.

Figure 23 Most ocean pollution caused by humans originates on land.

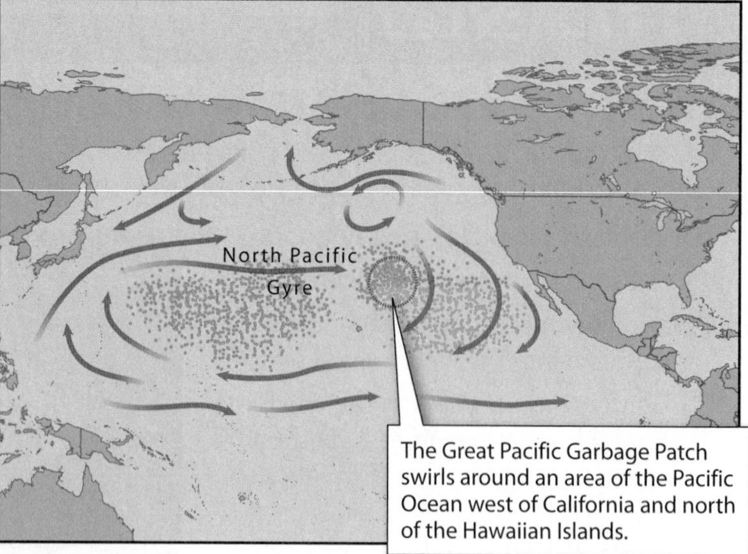

North Pacific Gyre
The Great Pacific Garbage Patch swirls around an area of the Pacific Ocean west of California and north of the Hawaiian Islands.

▲ **Figure 24** The North Pacific Gyre traps garbage in areas colored orange on the map. The *Great Pacific Garbage Patch* within this area is thought to be twice the size of Texas.

Effects of Ocean Pollution

Ocean pollution has both immediate effects and long-term effects on **marine** ecosystems. **Marine** *refers to anything related to the oceans.* Chemical waste can be poisonous to marine organisms. Fish and other organisms absorb the poison and pass it up the food chain. A large oil spill can harm marine life. So can solid waste, excess sediments, and excess nutrients.

WORD ORIGIN
marine
from Latin *marinus,* means "of the sea"

Solid Waste Trash, including plastic bottles and bags, glass, and foam containers, cause problems for marine organisms. Many birds, fish, and other animals become entangled in plastic or mistake it for food. Plastic breaks up into small pieces but it does not degrade easily. Some of it becomes trapped in the circular currents of gyres. The North Pacific Gyre has collected so much plastic and other debris that some people have named a portion of it "the Great Pacific Garbage Patch." A sample of polluted water from this patch and a map showing its location are shown in **Figure 24.**

Figure 25 This satellite image shows sediment from orange-colored soil washing into the ocean. ▼

Excess Sediments Large amounts of land-based sediment wash into oceans, as shown in **Figure 25.** Erosion often occurs on steep coastal slopes after heavy rains. Some of this erosion is natural. But some is caused by humans, who cut down trees near rivers and ocean shorelines. Without the roots of trees and other vegetation to hold sediments in place, the sediments more readily erode. Excess sediments can clog the filtering structures of marine filter feeders, such as clams and sponges. Excess sediments can also block light from reaching its normal depth. Organisms that use light for photosynthesis die.

Key Concept Check How can excess sediments in oceans affect marine organisms?

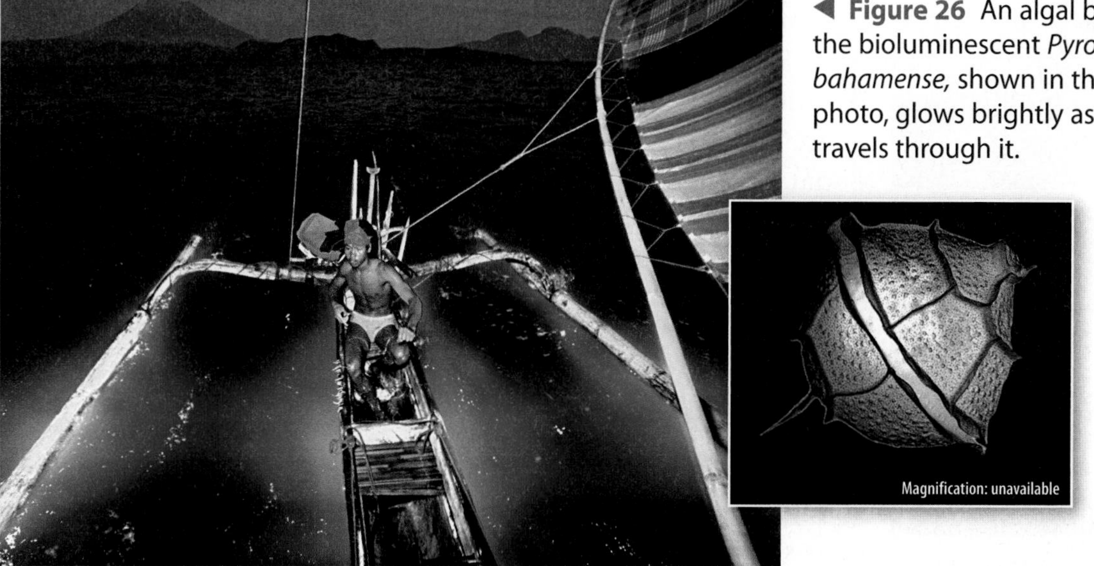

Figure 26 An algal bloom of the bioluminescent *Pyrodinium bahamense,* shown in the inset photo, glows brightly as this boat travels through it.

Excess Nutrients Algae need nutrients such as nitrogen and phosphorus to survive and grow. However, too many nutrients can cause an explosion in algal populations. An algal **bloom** occurs when algae grow and reproduce in large numbers. The photo at the beginning of this lesson shows how an algal bloom can cause water to turn orange. Algal blooms can also cause water to appear red, green, brown, or even glow at night, as shown in **Figure 26.**

SCIENCE USE V. COMMON USE

bloom

Science Use a large growth of algae

Common Use a flower

Nitrates and phosphates can be abundant in agricultural runoff as well as coastal upwelling zones. Many scientists suspect that a major source of excess nitrates and phosphates is from land-based fertilizers that wash into oceans.

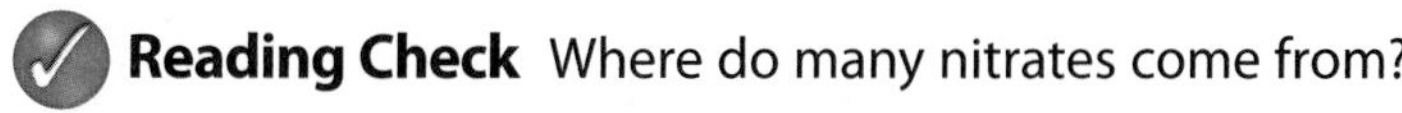

Reading Check Where do many nitrates come from?

Many algal blooms are harmless, but others can disrupt marine ecosystems and harm organisms. *A* **harmful algal bloom** *is an explosive growth of algae that harms organisms.* Harmful algal blooms have become more common in recent decades.

Why are some algal blooms harmful? The algae in some algal blooms produce poisonous substances that can kill organisms that eat them. Other algal blooms are so large that they they use up oxygen (O_2) in the water. This can happen when large numbers of algae die and decompose. Decomposition requires O_2. When many algae decompose at the same time, O_2 levels in the water drop. Fish and other marine organisms cannot get enough O_2 to survive. A fish kill resulting from a harmful algal bloom is shown in **Figure 27.**

Figure 27 Excess nitrates that wash into oceans can cause harmful algal blooms which kill fish. ▼

 **Key Concept Check** How can excess nutrients in seawater harm fish?

Figure 28 Corals contain colorful algae, which provide food for the coral. Without algae, the corals die and appear bleached.

Oceans and Global Climate Change

Solid waste, excess sediments, and algal blooms can cause immediate harm to ocean ecosystems. Other threats to oceans are related to long-term changes in Earth's climate. Climate data indicates that Earth's average surface temperature has increased over the past century. The amount of carbon dioxide (CO_2) in Earth's atmosphere has also increased.

Effects of Increasing Temperature

The increase in Earth's surface temperature has affected oceans in many ways.

Coral Bleaching Some marine organisms, such as coral, are very sensitive to temperature changes. A temperature increase as small as 1°C can cause corals to die, as shown in **Figure 28.** **Coral bleaching** *is the loss of color in corals that occurs when stressed corals expel the algae that live in them.* Coral bleaching harms corals around the world, as shown in **Figure 29.** Coral reefs provide habitat for fish and many other organisms.

 **Key Concept Check** How does water temperature affect corals?

Sea Level As Earth warms, its glaciers and ice sheets melt. This adds water to the oceans and increases sea level. Rising sea levels threaten coastal communities and marine habitats.

Dissolved O_2 The temperature of seawater affects the amount of O_2 dissolved in it. The warmer the water, the less O_2 it contains. Marine organisms need O_2 to survive. As water warms, less O_2 is available, and organisms can die.

Coral Bleaching

Figure 29 Coral bleaching occurs in many locations around the world.

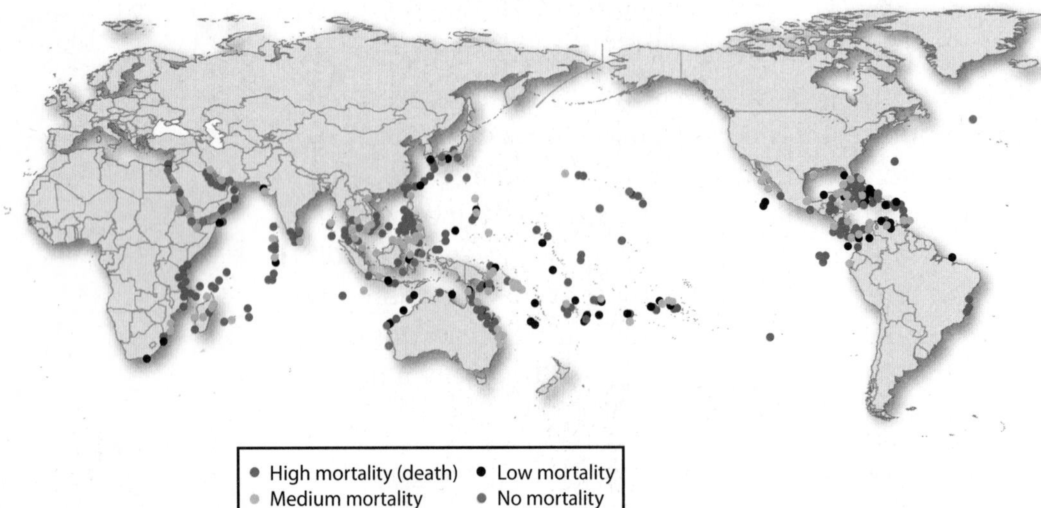

Figure 30 CO_2 and O_2 are exchanged at the ocean's surface. Waves and currents mix the gases into deeper water.

Effects of Increasing Carbon Dioxide

As illustrated in **Figure 30,** O_2 and CO_2 gases move freely between the atmosphere and seawater. As the amount of CO_2 increases in the atmosphere, the amount of CO_2 dissolved in seawater also increases. This is because of gas exchange at the ocean's surface. These gases dissolve in seawater. Wave action helps mix these gases deeper below the water surface.

CO_2 and pH When CO_2 mixes with seawater, a weak acid called carbonic acid forms. Carbonic acid lowers the pH of the water, making it slightly acidic. Data from recent studies show that the acidity of seawater has increased over the past 300 years. Scientists predict that by 2100, the oceans will become even more acidic, as illustrated in **Figure 31.**

 **Reading Check** Why are oceans becoming more acidic?

FOLDABLES®

Make a chart with three columns and three rows. Label it as shown. Use it to organize information about common gases found in seawater.

Common Gases Exchanged	How and Why	Human Concerns
Oxygen (O_2)		
Carbon Dioxide (CO_2)		

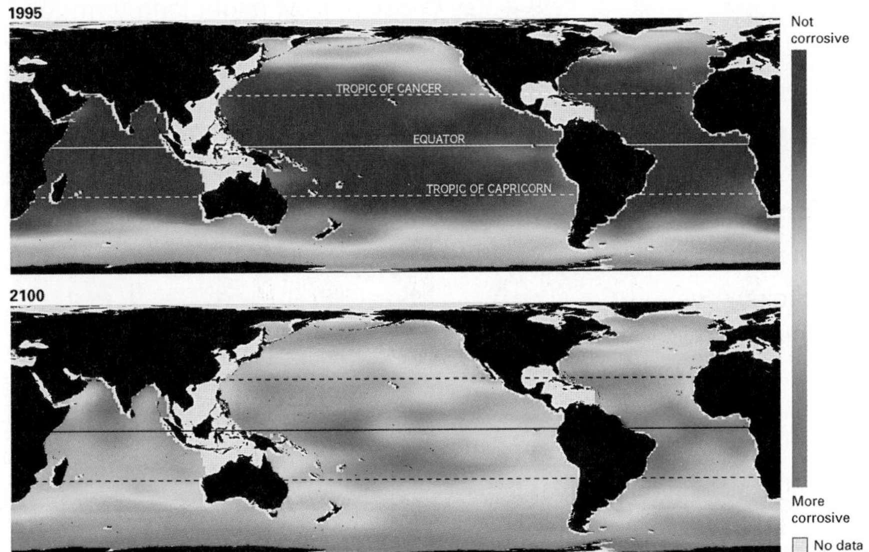

Figure 31 Scientists predict that oceans in the future will be much more acidic than they are today.

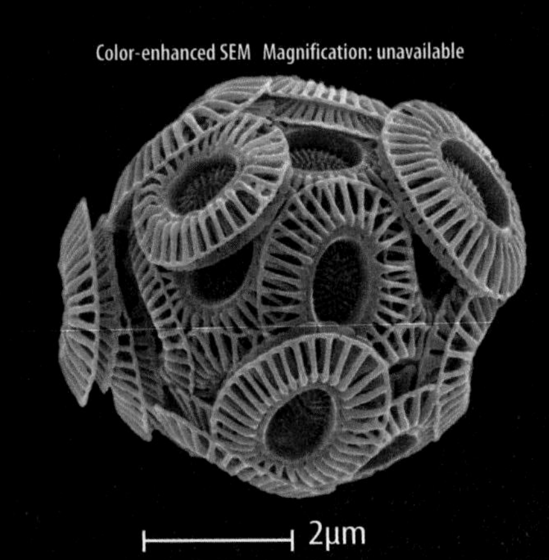

Figure 32 This tiny organism is surrounded by calcium carbonate plates.

Acidity and Marine Life Many marine organisms build shells and skeletons from calcium absorbed from seawater. Snails absorb calcium and make shells. Corals absorb calcium and build reefs. Some algae, like the one shown in **Figure 32,** make protective plates from calcium. As seawater becomes more acidic, it is harder for these organisms to absorb calcium. Increased acidity can cause shells and skeletons to weaken or dissolve. Over time, this could affect food webs. For example, if algae were unable to make protective plates, they would die. Algae form the base of food chains in many marine ecosystems.

Keeping Oceans Healthy

Earth's oceans affect Earth in many ways. As part of the water cycle, they distribute moisture. Ocean currents distribute thermal energy. Oceans provide habitat for algae and other marine organisms. Marine algae release during photosynthesis as much as 50 percent of the O_2 in Earth's atmosphere. Oceans also provide mineral and energy resources. They are a major source of food and income for humans. Keeping oceans healthy is important for the well-being of humans and other organisms on Earth.

 **Key Concept Check** Why is it important to keep oceans healthy?

Inquiry MiniLab — 20 minutes

How does the pH of seawater affect marine organisms?

How does increasing acidity affect calcium-containing shells?

1. Read and complete a lab safety form.
2. Copy the table below into your Science Journal.
3. Examine a piece of **brown eggshell** and describe its properties.
4. Place the eggshell in a **plastic cup.**
5. Half fill the cup with **white vinegar.**
6. After 15 minutes, use **forceps** to remove the eggshell. Describe its properties in your Science Journal.

Analyze and Conclude

1. **Describe** how the eggshell changed.
2. **Key Concept** How might long-term effects of increased CO_2 in seawater affect calcium-containing shells and skeletons of marine organisms?

Calcium-containing shells		
Property	Description Before Treatment	Description After Treatment
Hardness		
Thickness		
Appearance		

Lesson 4 Review

Visual Summary

A harmful algal bloom can cause fish kills.

Increased ocean temperature causes corals to bleach.

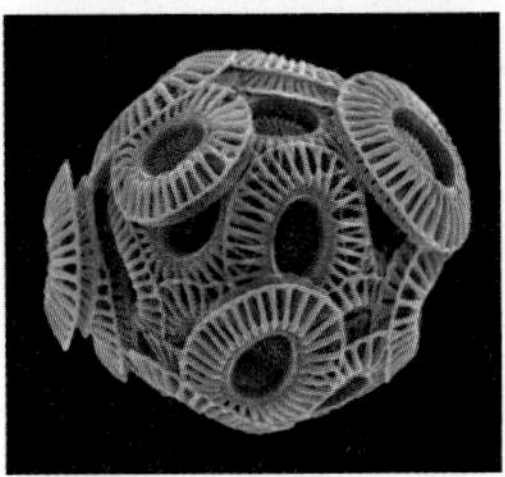

Global climate change affects the ocean's chemistry.

FOLDABLES®

Use your lesson Foldable to review the lesson. Save your Foldable for the project at the end of the chapter.

What do you think NOW?

You first read the statements below at the beginning of the chapter.

7. Most pollution in the oceans originates on land.

8. Global climate change has no effect on marine organisms.

Did you change your mind about whether you agree or disagree with the statements? Rewrite any false statements to make them true.

Use Vocabulary

1. **Define** *harmful algal bloom* in your own words.
2. **Use the term** *marine* in a complete sentence.

Understand Key Concepts 

3. How can an increase in CO_2 in the atmosphere affect seawater?
   - **A.** O_2 levels rise
   - **B.** O_2 levels decrease
   - **C.** pH rises
   - **D.** pH decreases
4. **Identify** how excess sediments affect filter feeders.
5. **Construct** a flow chart that shows the steps leading to an algal-bloom fish kill.

Interpret Graphics

6. **Determine Cause and Effect** Copy and fill in the graphic organizer below to list the causes and effects of a decreased pH of seawater.

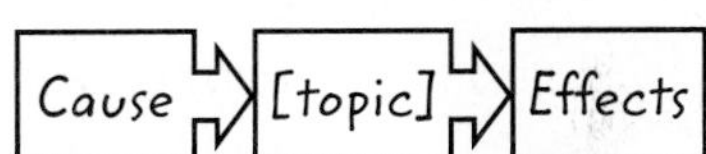

7. **Explain** how environmental conditions can affect the exchange of gases shown in the figure below.

Critical Thinking

8. **Design an experiment** to test the hypothesis that coral bleaching is caused by an increase in water temperature.
9. **Predict** the effect that increased carbon dioxide in the atmosphere could have on food webs in the ocean.

Lab

45 minutes

Predicting Whale Sightings Based on Upwelling

Materials

colored pencils

You are a guide on a blue whale tour departing from Monterey, CA. You have read that upwelling is the vertical movement of cold, nutrient-rich water from the deep ocean to the surface of the ocean. You know upwelling fertilizes the surface of the ocean and creates feeding grounds for fish and plankton-eating whales. Use oceanographic data from satellites and moorings to plan a tour to best view blue whales.

Ask a Question

Where and when can you best observe blue whales near Monterey, CA?

Make Observations

1. Analyze a map of sea surface temperatures (SST) around Monterey Bay.
2. Convert your map to a color contour map. First, construct a legend using colors. Assign warmer pencil colors to warmer temperatures and cooler pencil colors to colder temperatures. Then, outline areas that have the same temperatures in pencil. Finally, color in the sections of the map according to your legend.
3. Study your map noting the position of the upwelling in your Science Journal.
4. Examine the mooring data to the right. Plot both sea surface temperature and wind speed versus day on the same graph. Be sure to label the two vertical axes to reflect the different measurements. Note that northern winds

Data of Wind Direction and Speed

Date	SST (°C)	Wind Direction	Wind Speed (m/s)
23-May	10	N	3
25-May	10	N	8
27-May	9	N	10
29-May	9	N	8
31-May	9	N	4
2-Jun	10	S	–1
4-Jun	12	S	–4
6-Jun	13	S	–3
8-Jun	12	N	7
10-Jun	11	N	5
12-Jun	10	N	8
14-Jun	10	N	7
16-Jun	10	N	7
18-Jun	9	N	9
20-Jun	9	N	11
22-Jun	11	N	4
24-Jun	12	S	–4
26-Jun	13	S	–6
28-Jun	13	-	0
30-Jun	14	S	–1
2-Jul	13	N	6
4-Jul	11	N	9
6-Jul	9	N	10
8-Jul	9	N	10

blow from the north and have positive wind speeds and that southern winds blow from the south and have negative wind speeds.

5 Analyze your graph and determine under what wind conditions upwelling occurs.

Form a Hypothesis

6 Use your observations of the upwelling to form a hypothesis that gives the location (latitude and longitude) and wind conditions where you could best observe blue whales if you leave on a tour from Monterey, CA.

Test your Hypotheses

7 Use a map showing sightings of blue whales in Monterey Bay to compare your hypothesis to the actual locations where blue whales have been frequently observed. If your hypothesis was not supported, repeat steps 2–3.

8 Compare your prediction of wind conditions for which you could best observe blue whales with another student in your class. If you do not agree, repeat steps 5–6.

Analyze and Conclude

9 **Describe** the location and shape of the upwelling in Monterey Bay.

10 **Analyze** in which direction the wind was blowing when the satellite measurement of sea surface temperature was taken. Explain why this is important to your hypothesis.

11 **Design** a graphic organizer to show the effects of currents, sea surface temperatures, and wind direction on whale feeding areas.

12 THE BIG IDEA **The Big Idea** Explain how currents affect sea life in Monterey Bay.

Communicate Your Results

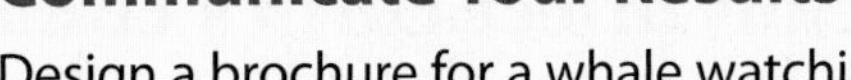

Design a brochure for a whale watching company based in Monterey, CA. Describe the technology and oceanography that you will use to ensure that your clients observe blue whales.

Inquiry Extension

During the Great Depression, Monterey Bay was one of the largest sardine fisheries in the world. John Steinbeck wrote about the time period in his book *Cannery Row.* Investigate what happened to the sardine fisheries in Monterey Bay during the nineteenth century. Write a Moment in History news report explaining the environmental factors that impacted the growth and decline of the fishery.

Lab TIPS

- ☑ When plotting your data, be sure to use the vertical axis that goes with the data you are plotting.
- ☑ Draw a line to connect your plot points.
- ☑ Use two different colors for wind speed and sea surface temperature.

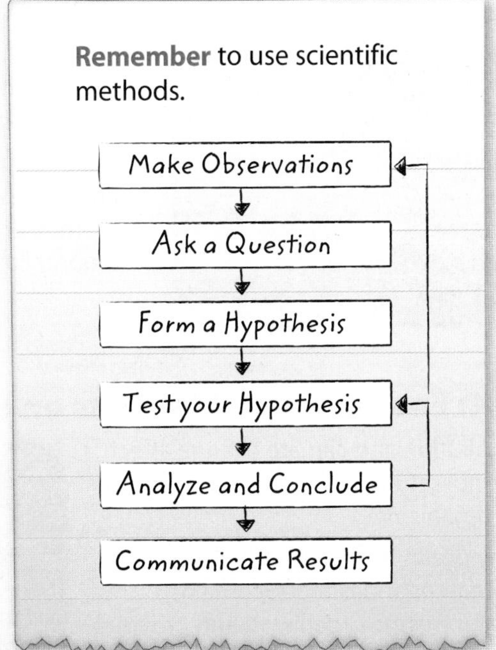

Chapter 8 Study Guide

Oceans affect Earth's climate and weather. They provide resources and habitats. But oceans are threatened by pollution and global climate change.

Key Concepts Summary	Vocabulary
Lesson 1: Composition and Structure of Earth's Oceans  • The salt in the oceans comes mostly from the erosion of rocks and soil. • The seafloor has mountains, deep trenches, and flat plains. • The oceans have zones based on light, temperature, salinity, and density.	**salinity** p. 269 **seawater** p. 269 **brackish** p. 269 **abyssal plain** p. 270
Lesson 2: Ocean Waves and Tides • The motion of water particles in a wave is circular. • Wind causes most ocean waves, but underwater disturbances cause most **tsunamis.** • The gravitational attraction between Earth and the Moon, and between Earth and the Sun causes **tides.** 	**tsunami** p. 279 **sea level** p. 280 **tide** p. 280 **tidal range** p. 280 **spring tide** p. 281 **neap tide** p. 281
Lesson 3: Ocean Currents  • Surface currents, **upwelling,** and density currents are the major **ocean currents.** • Ocean currents affect climate and weather by distributing thermal energy and moisture around Earth.	**ocean current** p. 285 **gyre** p. 286 **Coriolis effect** p. 286 **upwelling** p. 287
Lesson 4: Environmental Impacts on Oceans • Ocean pollution and climate change affect water temperature and ocean pH, harming **marine** organisms. • A healthy ocean is important because it affects weather and climate, contains habitats for marine organisms, and provides energy resources and food for humans. 	**marine** p. 294 **harmful algal bloom** p. 295 **coral bleaching** p. 296

Review
- Personal Tutor
- Vocabulary eGames
- Vocabulary eFlashcards

FOLDABLES® Chapter Project

Assemble your lesson Foldables as shown to make a Chapter Project. Use the project to review what you have learned in this chapter.

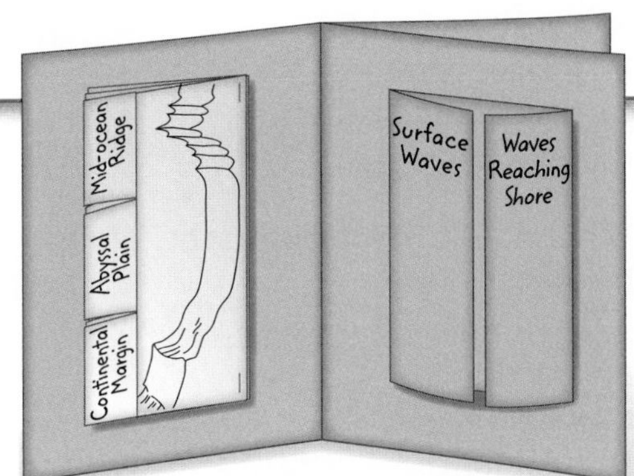

Use Vocabulary

1. Water that has lower salinity than average is ________.
2. Scientists use the term ________ to describe the amount of salt in water.
3. The average height of the ocean's surface is ________.
4. A(n) ________ occurs when Earth, the Moon, and the Sun are in a straight line.
5. A(n) ________ is a large volume of water flowing in a certain direction.
6. A(n) ________ carries warm and cold water in a circular system.
7. A(n) ________ is a vertical movement of water toward the surface.
8. A(n) ________ can occur when increased nutrients cause explosive algal growth.

Link Vocabulary and Key Concepts

Concepts in Motion Interactive Concept Map

Copy this concept map, and then use vocabulary terms from the previous page to complete the concept map.

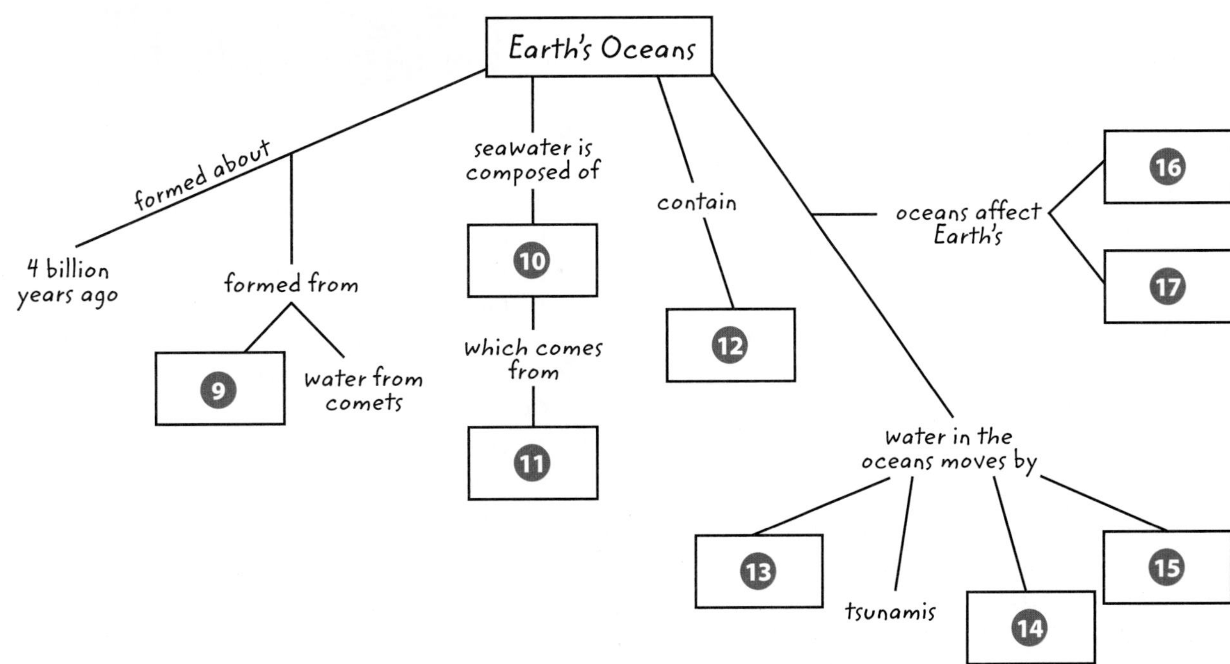

Chapter 8 Review

Understand Key Concepts 

1. Based on the circle graph below, which element is most common in seawater?

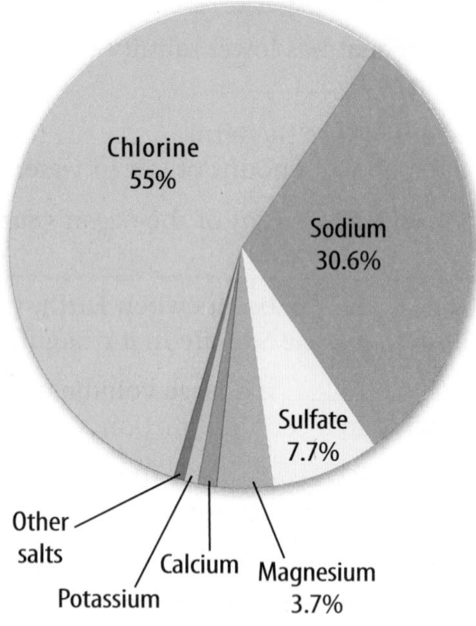

A. calcium
B. chlorine
C. sodium
D. sulfur

2. Which resource is on abyssal plains?
A. gravel
B. manganese nodules
C. methane hydrates
D. natural gas

3. Which is NOT a cause of tsunamis?
A. earthquake
B. hurricane
C. landslide
D. volcanic eruption

4. Which best describes the movement of water in a wave?
A. circular
B. horizontal
C. spiral
D. vertical

5. Where does an ocean current become most dense?
A. in polar regions
B. in temperate regions
C. near continents
D. near the equator

6. Which moves water horizontally?
A. density current
B. surface current
C. temperature current
D. upwelling

7. What does C represent in the figure below?
A. high tide
B. low tide
C. sea level
D. tidal range

A
B
C
D

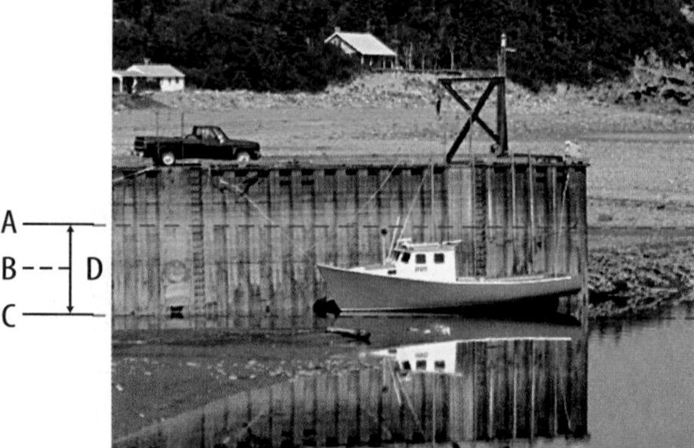

8. Which is one possible effect of an increase in carbon dioxide in the oceans?
A. Algae grow in excessive amounts.
B. Corals can't make reefs.
C. High tides occur more often.
D. Ocean sedimentation increases.

9. Which is NOT a consequence of rising ocean temperature?
A. coral bleaching
B. glacier melting
C. rising sea level
D. shells dissolving

Assessment
Online Test Practice

Critical Thinking

10 **Summarize** the sources of salt in seawater.

11 **Compare** the topography of the ocean floor with the topography of land.

12 **Illustrate** what happens to water particles when a wave passes.

13 **Explain** how a density current might form in the Arctic Ocean.

14 **Design** a model that shows how surface currents form.

15 **Relate** How can cutting trees on land affect life in the ocean?

16 **Assess** the long-term effects of a harmful algal bloom on a marine ecosystem.

17 **Hypothesize** As shown in the figure below, Earth's major warm water currents are on the western boundaries of oceans. Major cold water currents are on the eastern boundaries of oceans. Why are these major currents in these different locations?

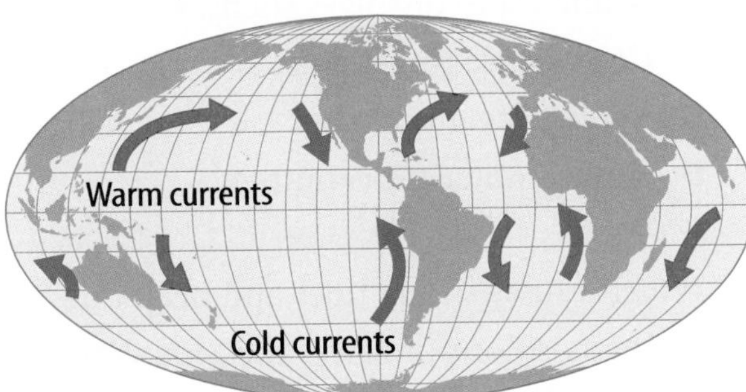

Writing in Science

18 **Compose** a letter to the editor of a newspaper or magazine with ideas of how to reduce human impacts on oceans. Include a main idea, supporting details, examples, and a concluding sentence.

REVIEW THE BIG IDEA

19 Why are oceans important? In what ways are they threatened?

20 How are waves powered? How does movement differ in waves and currents?

Math Skills

Math Practice

Use Statistics

Time (Day 1)	Height (m)	Time (Day 2)	Height (m)
00:44	13.1	01:33	13.0
07:13	0.8	08:02	0.9
13:04	13.6	13:54	13.5
19:42	0.3	20:32	0.4

The table above shows the high and low tides during a 48-hour period at the Bay of Fundy. Use the table to answer the questions.

21 What is the range of tides during the 48-hour period.

22 What is the mean of the tides during the 48-hour period?

23 What is the range of the four high tides during the 48-hour period?

24 What is the mean of the four low tides?

Standardized Test Practice

Record your answers on the answer sheet provided by your teacher or on a sheet of paper.

Multiple Choice

1 Which is a result of increasing acidity of seawater?

A Algae populations increase dramatically.

B Corals expel algae living within them.

C Oxygen is less available to marine organisms.

D Shells and skeletons of marine organisms weaken.

2 Which did NOT contribute to the formation of Earth's early oceans?

A asteroids

B condensation

C comets

D glaciers

3 What percentage of Earth's water is salt water?

A 3%

B 55%

C 70%

D 97%

Use the diagram below to answer question 4.

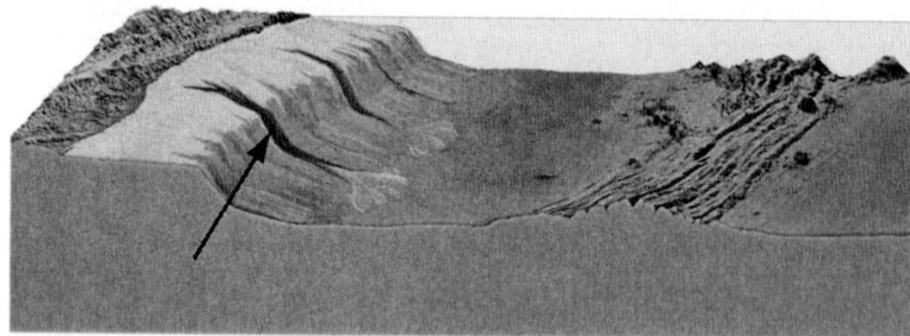

4 Which seafloor feature does the arrow in the diagram above indicate?

A abyssal plain

B continental slope

C ocean trench

D submarine canyon

Use the diagram below to answer question 5.

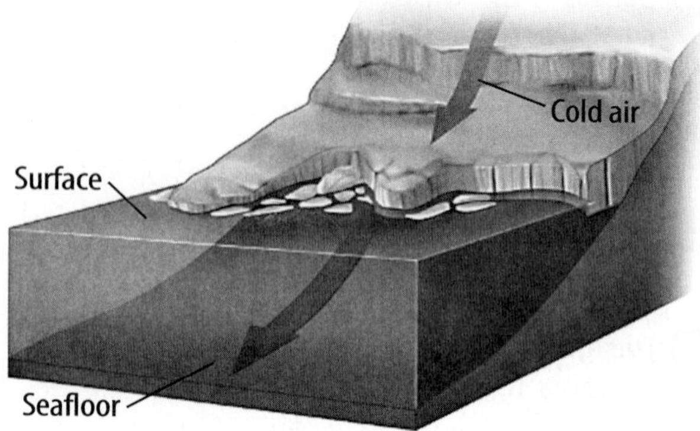

5 Which is formed by the process shown in the diagram above?

A gyres

B tsunami

C density current

D surface waves

6 Which results from upwelling in the oceans?

A Acidic water dissolves shells.

B Cold, dense water sinks.

C Marine organisms die.

D Surface water gains nutrients.

7 Which causes spring tides and neap tides?

A the positions of Earth, the Moon, and the Sun

B the rotation of Earth on its axis

C the shape of the continental margin

D the size and shape of ocean basins

8 As seawater temperature rises, the water contains

A less dissolved minerals.

B less oxygen.

C more coral.

D more nutrients.

Assessment
Online Standardized Test Practice

Use the diagram below to answer question 9.

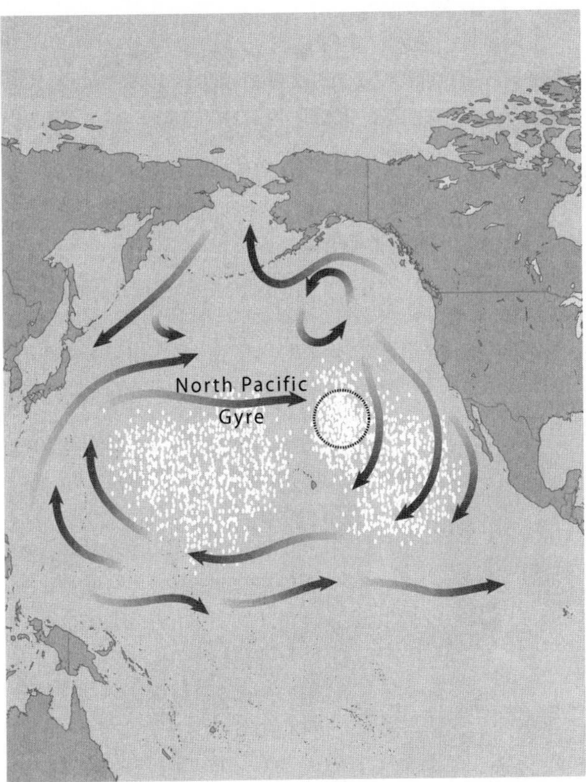

9 The circle on the diagram above indicates a region affected by

A coral bleaching.

B frequent tsunamis.

C excess nitrates and phosphates.

D pollution from solid waste.

10 Fertilizer runoff from agricultural areas into seawater can cause an excess of

A acid.

B carbon dioxide.

C nutrients.

D salts.

Constructed Response

Use the diagram below to answer questions 11–13.

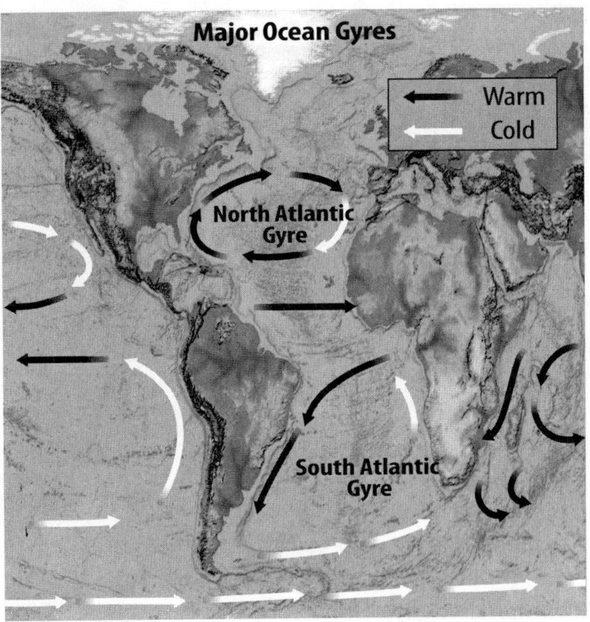

11 What type of current is marked with arrows on the map? How do these currents form? What do they do?

12 Why do these currents move in opposite directions around the North Atlantic and South Atlantic gyres?

13 How do these currents affect the climates of the surrounding continents?

14 What are two ways in which algae benefit other organisms?

15 Why are healthy oceans important to ALL life on Earth?

NEED EXTRA HELP?															
If You Missed Question...	1	2	3	4	5	6	7	8	9	10	11	12	13	14	15
Go to Lesson...	4	1	1	1	3	3	2	4	4	4	3	3	3	4	4

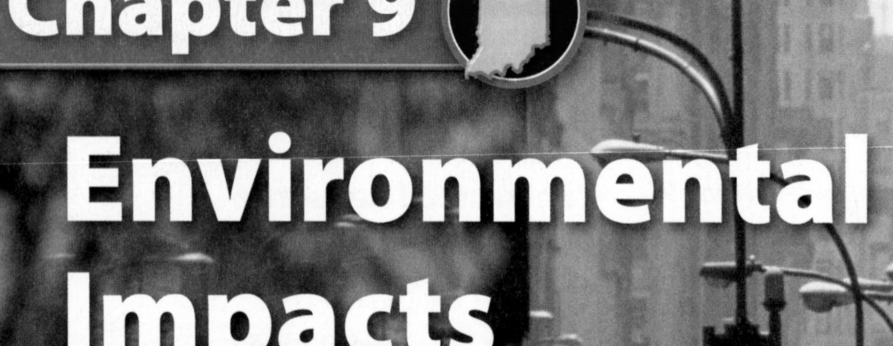

Chapter 9

Environmental Impacts

THE BIG IDEA **How do human activities impact the environment?**

Inquiry How many people are there?

More than 6 billion people live on Earth. Every day, people all over the world travel, eat, use water, and participate in recreational activities.

- What resources do people need and use?
- What might happen if any resources run out?
- How do human activities impact the environment?

Get Ready to Read

What do you think?

Before you read, decide if you agree or disagree with each of these statements. As you read this chapter, see if you change your mind about any of the statements.

1. Earth can support an unlimited number of people.
2. Humans can have both positive and negative impacts on the environment.
3. Deforestation does not affect soil quality.
4. Most trash is recycled.
5. Sources of water pollution are always easy to identify.
6. The proper method of disposal for used motor oil is to pour it down the drain.
7. The greenhouse effect is harmful to life on Earth.
8. Air pollution can affect human health.

Your one-stop online resource

connectED.mcgraw-hill.com

- Video
- Audio
- Review
- Inquiry
- WebQuest
- Assessment
- Concepts in Motion
- Multilingual eGlossary

Lesson 1

Reading Guide

Key Concepts
ESSENTIAL QUESTIONS

- What is the relationship between resource availability and human population growth?
- How do daily activities impact the environment?

Vocabulary

population p. 311

carrying capacity p. 312

Academic Standards for Science

8.2.6 Identify, explain, and discuss some effects human activities have on the biosphere, such as air, soil, light, noise and water pollution.

8.2.7 Recognize that some of Earth's resources are finite and describe how recycling, reducing consumption and the development of alternatives can reduce the rate of their depletion.

8.2.8 Explain that human activities, beginning with the earliest herding and agricultural activities, have drastically changed the environment and have affected the capacity of the environment to support native species. Explain current efforts to reduce and eliminate these impacts and encourage sustainability.

Also covers: 8.NS.1, 8.NS.2, 8.NS.3, 8.NS.7, 8.NS.8, 8.NS.9, 8.NS.10, 8.NS.11, 8.DP.1, 8.DP.2, 8.DP.3, 8.DP.4, 8.DP.5, 8.DP.6, 8.DP.7, 8.DP.8, 8.DP.9, 8.DP.10, 8.DP.11

People and the Environment

Inquiry What's the impact?

This satellite image shows light coming from Europe and Africa at night. You can see where large cities are located. What do you think the dark areas represent? When you turn on the lights at night, where does the energy to power the lights come from? How might this daily activity impact the environment?

Launch Lab

20 minutes

What happens as populations increase in size?

In the year 200, the human population consisted of about a quarter of a billion people. By the year 2000, it had increased to more than 6 billion, and by 2050, it is projected to be more than 9 billion. However, the amount of space available on Earth will remain the same.

1. Read and complete a lab safety form.
2. Place 10 **dried beans** in a **100-mL beaker.**
3. At the start signal, double the number of beans in the beaker. There should now be 20 beans.

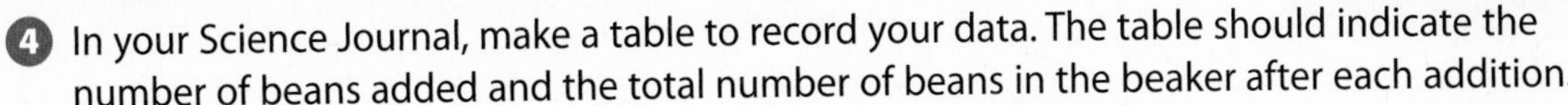

4. In your Science Journal, make a table to record your data. The table should indicate the number of beans added and the total number of beans in the beaker after each addition.

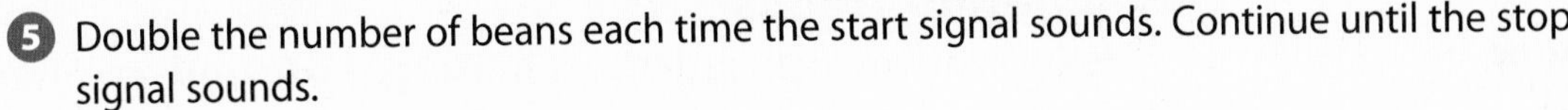

5. Double the number of beans each time the start signal sounds. Continue until the stop signal sounds.

Think About This

1. Can you add any more beans to the beaker? Why or why not?
2. How many times did you have to double the beans to fill the beaker?
3. **Key Concept** How might the growth of a population affect the availability of resources, such as space?

Population and Carrying Capacity

Have you ever seen a sign such as the one shown in **Figure 1**? The sign shows the population of a city. In this case, population means how many people live in the city. Scientists use the term *population,* too, but in a slightly different way. For scientists, *a* **population** *is all the members of a species living in a given area.* You are part of a population of humans. The other species in your area, such as birds or trees, each make up a separate population.

The Human Population

When the first American towns were settled, most had low populations. Today, some of those towns are large cities, crowded with people. In a similar way, Earth was once home to relatively few humans. Today, about 6.7 billion people live on Earth. The greatest increase in human population occurred during the last few centuries.

Figure 1 This sign shows the population of the city. Scientists use the word *population* to describe all the members of a species in an area.

Figure 2 Human population stayed fairly steady for most of history and then "exploded" in the last few hundred years.

Visual Check How does the rate of human population growth from the years 200 to 1800 compare to the rate of growth from 1800 to 2000?

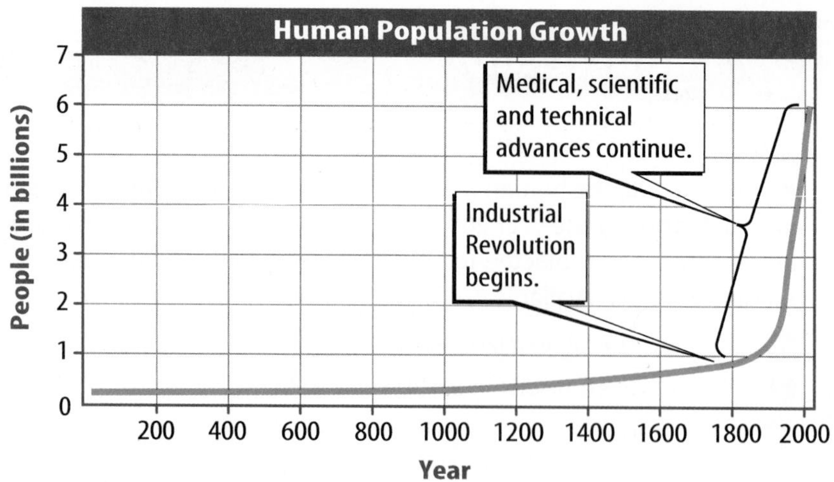

WORD ORIGIN

population
from Latin *populus*, means "people"

Population Trends

Have you ever heard the phrase ***population*** *explosion?* Population explosion describes the sudden rise in human population that has happened in recent history. The graph in **Figure 2** shows how the human population has changed. The population increased at a fairly steady rate for most of human history. In the 1800s, the population began to rise sharply.

What caused this sharp increase? Improved health care, clean water, and other technological advancements mean that more people are living longer and reproducing. In the hour or so it might take you to read this chapter, about 15,000 babies will be born worldwide.

Reading Check What factors contributed to the increase in human population?

FOLDABLES®

Use a sheet of paper to make a small vertical shutterfold. Draw the arrows on each tab and label as illustrated. Use the Foldable to discuss how human population growth is related to resources.

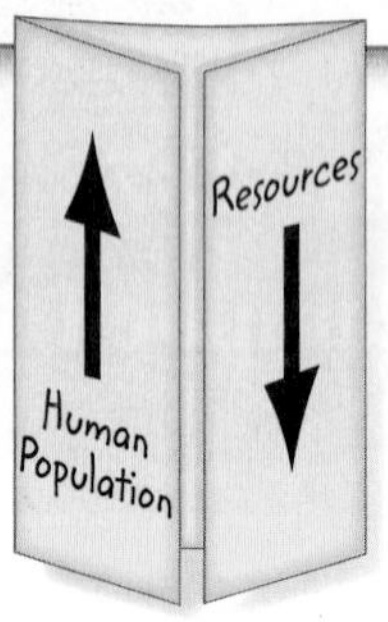

Population Limits

Every human being needs certain things, such as food, clean water, and shelter, to survive. People also need clothes, transportation, and other items. All the items used by people come from resources found on Earth. Does Earth have enough resources to support an unlimited number of humans?

Earth has limited resources. It cannot support a population of any species in a given environment beyond its carrying capacity. **Carrying capacity** *is the largest number of individuals of a given species that Earth's resources can support and maintain for a long period of time.* If the human population continues to grow beyond Earth's carrying capacity, eventually Earth will not have enough resources to support humans.

Key Concept Check What is the relationship between the availability of resources and human population growth?

Impact of Daily Actions

Each of the 6.7 billion people on Earth uses **resources** in some way. The use of these resources affects the environment. Consider the impact of one activity—a shower.

Science Use v. Common Use

resource

Science Use a natural source of supply or support

Common Use a source of information or expertise

Consuming Resources

Like many people, you might take a shower each day. The metal in the water pipes comes from resources mined from the ground. Mining can destroy habitats and pollute soil and water. Your towel might be made of cotton, a resource obtained from plants. Growing plants often involves the use of fertilizers and other chemicals that run off into water and affect its quality.

The water itself also is a resource—one that is scarce in some areas of the world. Most likely, fossil fuels are used to heat the water. Recall that fossil fuels are nonrenewable resources, which means they are used up faster than they can be replaced by natural processes. Burning fossil fuels also releases pollution into the atmosphere.

Now, think about all the activities that you do in one day, such as going to school, eating meals, or playing computer games. All of these activities use resources. Over the course of your lifetime, your potential impact on the environment is great. Multiply this impact by 6.7 billion, and you can understand why it is important to use resources wisely.

Key Concept Check What are three things you did today that impacted the environment?

Positive and Negative Impacts

As shown in **Figure 3,** not all human activities have a negative impact on the environment. In the following lessons, you will learn how human activities affect soil, water, and air quality. You will also learn things you can do to help reduce the impact of your actions on the environment.

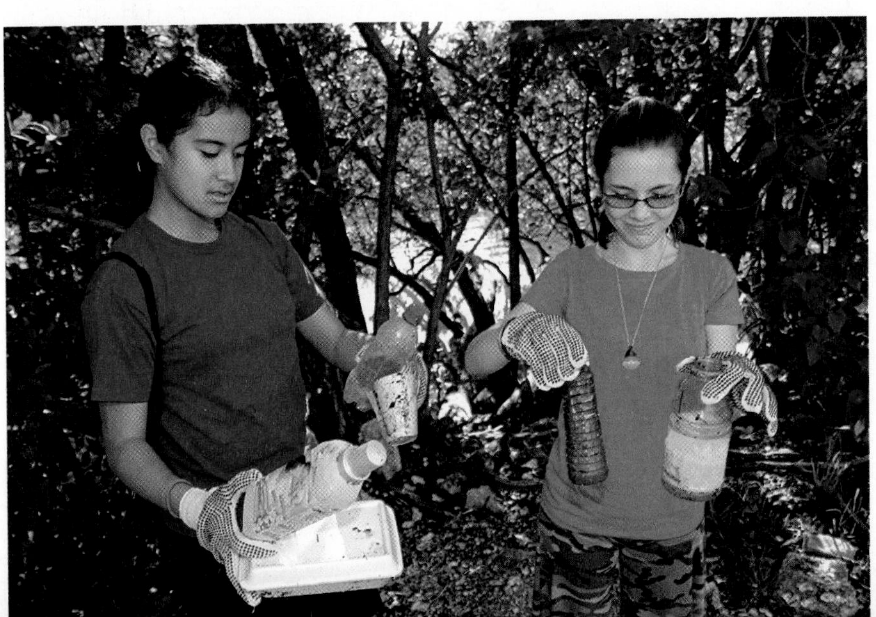

Figure 3 Cleaning up streams and picking up litter are ways people can positively impact the environment.

Lesson 1 Review

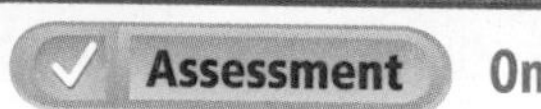

Visual Summary

Human population has exploded since the 1800s. Every day billions of people use Earth's resources. The human population will eventually reach its carrying capacity.

When humans use resources, they can have both negative and positive impacts on the environment. It is important for humans to use resources wisely.

FOLDABLES®

Use your lesson Foldable to review the lesson. Save your Foldable for the project at the end of the chapter.

What do you think NOW?

You first read the statements below at the beginning of the chapter.

1. Earth can support an unlimited number of people.
2. Humans can have both positive and negative impacts on the environment.

Did you change your mind about whether you agree or disagree with the statements? Rewrite any false statements to make them true.

Use Vocabulary

1. **Define** *carrying capacity* in your own words.
2. All the members of a certain species living in a given area is a(n) ________.

Understand Key Concepts

3. Approximately how many people live on Earth?
   A. 2.4 million
   B. 6.7 million
   C. 7.6 billion
   D. 12.1 billion
4. **Identify** something you could do to reduce your impact on the environment.
5. **Reason** Why do carrying capacities exist for all species on Earth?

Interpret Graphics

6. **Take Notes** Copy the graphic organizer below. List two human activities and the effect of each activity on the environment.

Activity	Effect on the Environment

7. **Summarize** how human population growth has changed over time, using the graph below.

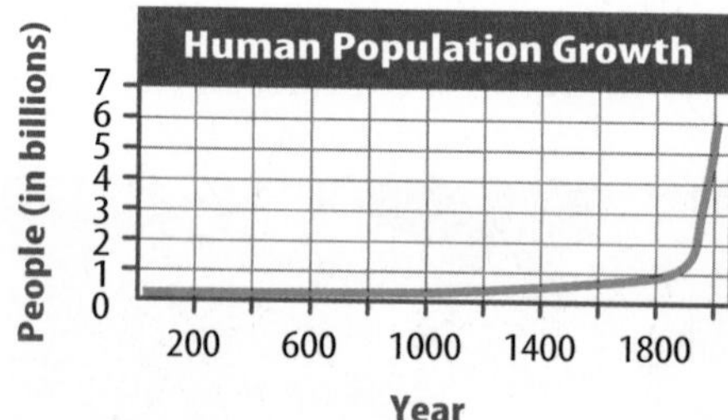

Critical Thinking

8. **Predict** What might happen if a species reaches Earth's carrying capacity?
9. **Reflect** Technological advances allow farmers to grow more crops. Do you think these advances affect the carrying capacity for humans? Explain.

What amount of Earth's resources do you use in a day?

Many of the practices we engage in today became habits long before we realized the negative effects that they have on the environment. By analyzing your daily resource use, you might identify some different practices that can help protect Earth's resources.

Learn It

In science, **data** are **collected** as accurate numbers and descriptions and organized in specific ways. The meaning of your observations can be determined by **analyzing** the data you collected.

Try It

1. With your group, design a data collection form for recording each group member's resource use for one 24-h period.
2. You should include space to collect data on water use, fossil fuel use (which may include electricity use and transportation), how much meat and dairy products you eat, how much trash you discard, and any other resources you might use in a typical 24-h period. Indicate the units in which you will record the data.
3. Share your form with the other groups, and complete a final draft using the best features from each group's design.
4. Distribute copies of the form to each group member. Record each instance and quantity of resource use during a 24-h period.
5. For each resource, calculate how much you would use in 1 year, based on your usage in the 24-h period.

Apply It

6. Consider whether a single 24-h period is representative of each of the 365 days of your year. Explain your answer.
7. How would you modify your data collection design to reflect a more realistic measure of your resource use over a year?
8. **Key Concept** Explain how two of the activities that you recorded deplete resources or pollute the soil, the water, or the air. How can you change your activities to reduce your impact or have a positive impact?

Lesson 2

Impacts on the Land

Reading Guide

Key Concepts
ESSENTIAL QUESTIONS

- What are the consequences of using land as a resource?
- How does proper waste management help prevent pollution?
- What actions help protect the land?

Vocabulary

deforestation p. 317
desertification p. 318
urban sprawl p. 320
reforestation p. 322
reclamation p. 322

Academic Standards for Science

8.2.6 Identify, explain, and discuss some effects human activities have on the biosphere, such as air, soil, light, noise and water pollution.

8.2.7 Recognize that some of Earth's resources are finite and describe how recycling, reducing consumption and the development of alternatives can reduce the rate of their depletion.

8.2.8 Explain that human activities, beginning with the earliest herding and agricultural activities, have drastically changed the environment and have affected the capacity of the environment to support native species. Explain current efforts to reduce and eliminate these impacts and encourage sustainability.

Also covers: 8.NS.7, 8.NS.8, 8.DP.1, 8.DP.10

Inquiry How do people use land?

Study this photo of an area in England, and list three ways people use land. What other possible land uses are not shown in the photo? What impact do humans have on land resources?

Inquiry Launch Lab

20 minutes

How can items be reused?

As an individual, you can have an effect on the use and the protection of Earth's resources by reducing, reusing, and recycling the materials you use every day.

1. Read and complete a lab safety form.
2. Have one member of your group pull an item from the **item bag.**
3. Discuss the item with your group and take turns describing as many different ways to reuse it as possible.
4. List the different uses in your Science Journal.
5. Repeat steps 2–4.
6. Share your lists with the other groups. What uses did other groups think of that were different from your group's ideas for the same item?

Think About This

1. Describe your group's items and three different ways that you thought to reuse each item.
2. How does reusing these items help to reduce the use of Earth's resources?
3. **Key Concept** How do you think the action of reusing items helps to protect the land?

Using Land Resources

What do the metal in staples and the paper in your notebook have in common? Both come from resources found in or on land. People use land for timber production, agriculture, and mining. All of these activities impact the environment.

Forest Resources

Trees are cut down to make wood and paper products, such as your notebook. Trees are also cut for fuel and to clear land for agriculture, grazing, or building houses or highways.

Sometimes forests are cleared, as shown in **Figure 4.** **Deforestation** *is the removal of large areas of forests for human purposes.* Approximately 130,000 km^2 of tropical rain forests are cut down each year, an area equal in size to the state of Louisiana. Tropical rain forests are home to an estimated 50 percent of all the species on Earth. Deforestation destroys habitats, which can lead to species' extinction.

Deforestation also can affect soil quality. Plant roots hold soil in place. Without these natural anchors, soil erodes away. In addition, deforestation affects air quality. Recall that trees remove carbon dioxide from the air when they undergo photosynthesis. When there are fewer trees on Earth, more carbon dioxide remains in the atmosphere. You will learn more about carbon dioxide in Lesson 4.

Figure 4 Deforestation occurs when forests are cleared for agriculture, grazing, or other purposes.

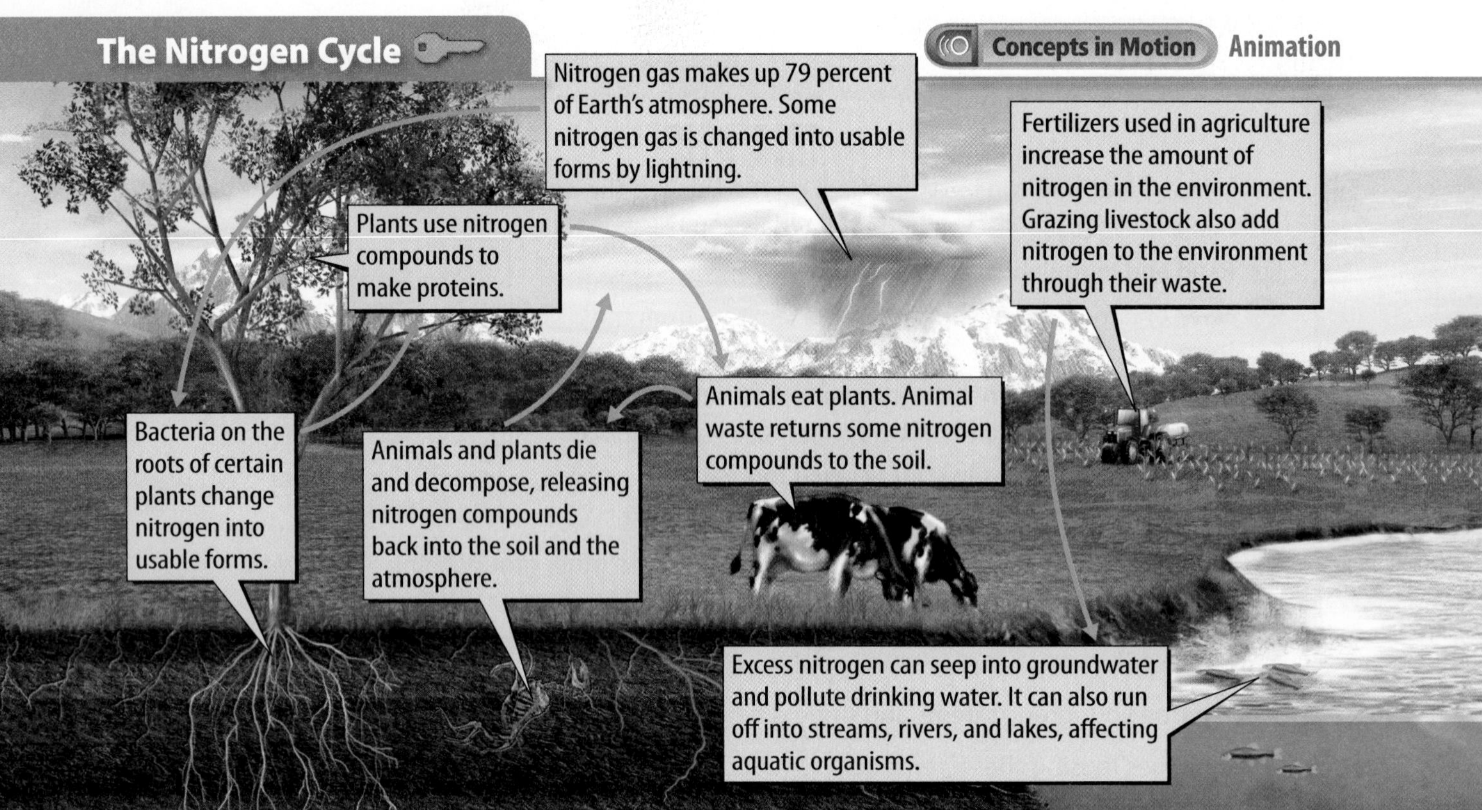

The Nitrogen Cycle
Concepts in Motion Animation
Nitrogen gas makes up 79 percent of Earth's atmosphere. Some nitrogen gas is changed into usable forms by lightning.
Fertilizers used in agriculture increase the amount of nitrogen in the environment. Grazing livestock also add nitrogen to the environment through their waste.
Plants use nitrogen compounds to make proteins.
Bacteria on the roots of certain plants change nitrogen into usable forms.
Animals and plants die and decompose, releasing nitrogen compounds back into the soil and the atmosphere.
Animals eat plants. Animal waste returns some nitrogen compounds to the soil.
Excess nitrogen can seep into groundwater and pollute drinking water. It can also run off into streams, rivers, and lakes, affecting aquatic organisms.

Figure 5 Agricultural practices can increase the amount of nitrogen that cycles through ecosystems.

Visual Check How does the use of fertilizers affect the environment?

Agriculture and the Nitrogen Cycle

It takes a lot of food to feed 6.7 billion people. To meet the food demands of the world's population, farmers often add fertilizers that contain nitrogen to soil to increase crop yields.

As shown in **Figure 5,** nitrogen is an element that naturally cycles through ecosystems. Living things use nitrogen to make proteins. And when these living things die and decompose or produce waste, they release nitrogen into the soil or the atmosphere.

Although nitrogen gas makes up about 79 percent of Earth's atmosphere, most living things cannot use nitrogen in its gaseous form. Nitrogen must be converted into a usable form. Bacteria that live on the roots of certain plants convert atmospheric nitrogen to a form that is usable by plants. Modern agricultural practices include adding fertilizer that contains a usable form of nitrogen to soil.

Scientists estimate that human activities such as manufacturing and applying fertilizers to crops have doubled the amount of nitrogen cycling through ecosystems. Excess nitrogen can kill plants adapted to low nitrogen levels and affect organisms that depend on those plants for food. Fertilizers can seep into groundwater supplies, polluting drinking water. They can also run off into streams and rivers, affecting aquatic organisms.

Other Effects of Agriculture

Agriculture can impact soil quality in other ways, too. Soil erosion can occur when land is overfarmed or overgrazed. High rates of soil erosion can lead to desertification. **Desertification** *is the development of desert-like conditions due to human activities and/or climate change.* A region of land that undergoes desertification is no longer useful for food production.

Reading Check What causes desertification?

Figure 6 Some resources must be mined from the ground.

Mining

Many useful rocks and minerals are removed from the ground by mining. For example, copper is removed from the surface by digging a strip mine, such as the one shown in **Figure 6.** Coal and other in-ground resources also can be removed by digging underground mines.

Mines are essential for obtaining much-needed resources. However, digging mines disturbs habitats and changes the landscape. If proper regulations are not followed, water can be polluted by **runoff** that contains heavy metals from mines.

Review Vocabulary

runoff
the portion of precipitation that moves over land and eventually reaches streams, rivers, lakes, and oceans

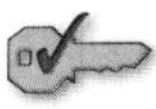 **Key Concept Check** What are some consequences of using land as a resource?

Construction and Development

You have read about important resources that are found on or in land. But did you know that land itself is a resource? People use land for living space. Your home, your school, your favorite stores, and your neighborhood streets are all built on land.

Inquiry MiniLab — 20 minutes

What happens when you mine?

Coal is a fossil fuel that provides energy for many activities. People obtain coal by mining, or digging, into Earth's surface.

1. Read and complete a lab safety form.
2. Research the difference between strip-mining and underground mining.
3. Use **salt dough** and **other materials** to build a model hill that contains coal deposits. Follow the instructions provided on how to build the model.
4. Sketch the profile of the hill. Use a **ruler** to measure the dimensions of the hill.
5. Decide which mining method to use to remove the coal. Mine the coal.
6. Try to restore the hill to its original size, shape, and forest cover.

Analyze and Conclude

1. **Compare** the appearance of your restored hill to the drawing of the original hill.
2. **Key Concept** Describe two consequences of the lost forest cover and loose soil on the mined hill.

Figure 7 Urban sprawl can lead to habitat destruction as forests are cut down to make room for housing developments.

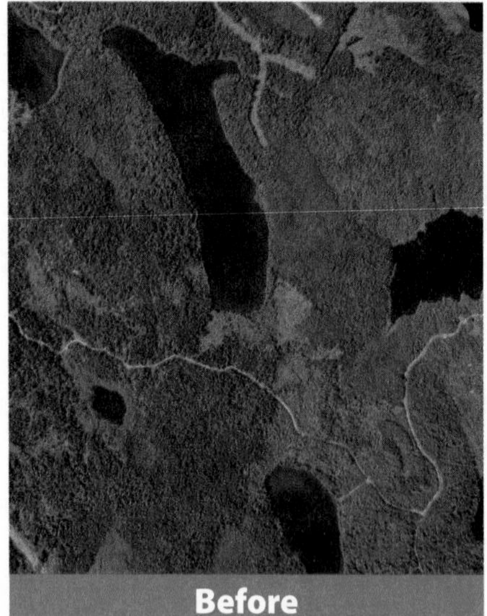
Before

After

Math Skills

Use Percentages

Between 1960 and today, interstate highways increased from a total of 16,000 km to 47,000 km. What percent increase does this represent?

1. Subtract the starting value from the final value.
   47,000 km − 16,000 km = 31,000 km
2. Divide the difference by the starting value.
   $\frac{31{,}000 \text{ km}}{16{,}000 \text{ km}} = 1.94$
3. Multiply by 100 and add a % sign.
   1.94 × 100 = 194%

Practice

In 1950, the U.S. population was about 150,000,000. By 2007, it was nearly 300,000,000. What was the percent increase?

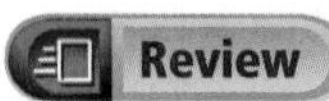
Review

- Math Practice
- Personal Tutor

Urban Sprawl

In the 1950s, large tracts of rural land in the United States were developed as suburbs, residential areas on the outside edges of a city. When the suburbs became crowded, people moved farther out into the country. More open land was cleared for still more development. *The development of land for houses and other buildings near a city is called* **urban sprawl.** The impacts of urban sprawl include habitat destruction, shown in **Figure 7**, loss of farmland, and light and noise pollution. Increased runoff also occurs, as large areas are paved for sidewalks and streets. An increase in runoff, especially if it contains sediments or chemical pollutants, can reduce the water quality of streams, rivers, and groundwater.

The picture at the beginning of Lesson 1 of this chapter shows how light from cities can be seen from outer space. On Earth, light pollution is the artificial illumination of the sky that limits the ability to see stars. Light pollution causes problems for astronomers and telescopes conducting investigations about the universe. People living in cities also are familiar with noise pollution. Noise pollution is the unwanted or excessive noise from people, transportation, or machinery. Excessive noise can cause hearing damage and disrupt wildlife.

Roadways

As urban sprawl increased, so did motor vehicle use. In 2005, there were 240 million vehicles for 295 million people, greatly increasing the need for roadways. Today, the interstate highway system includes 47,000 km of paved roadways. Like urban sprawl, roadways increase runoff and disturb habitats.

Reading Check What two trends triggered the need for more highways?

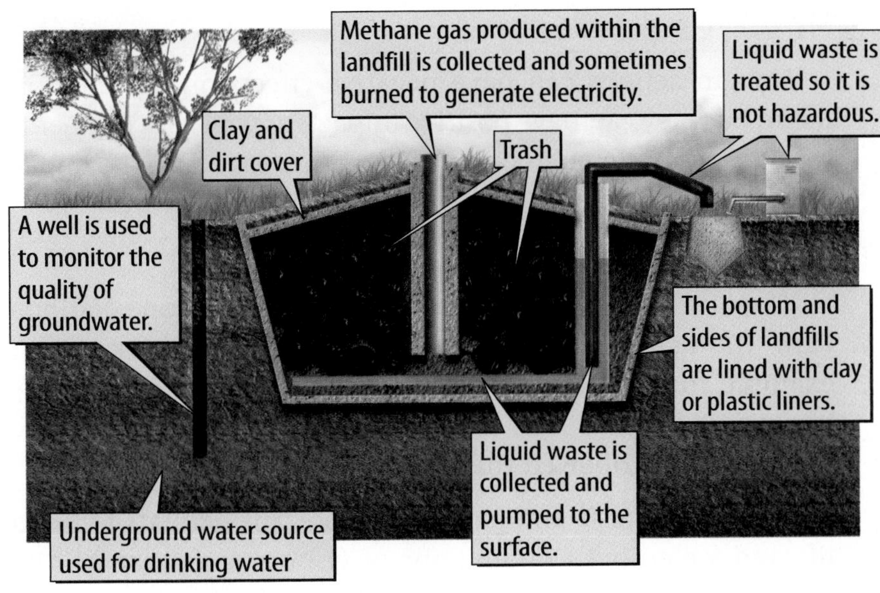

Methane gas produced within the landfill is collected and sometimes burned to generate electricity.
Liquid waste is treated so it is not hazardous.
Clay and dirt cover
Trash
A well is used to monitor the quality of groundwater.
The bottom and sides of landfills are lined with clay or plastic liners.
Liquid waste is collected and pumped to the surface.
Underground water source used for drinking water

Figure 8 About 54 percent of the trash in the United States is disposed of in landfills.

Visual Check How can the methane gas produced within a landfill be used?

Waste Management

On a typical day, each person in the United States generates about 2.1 kg of trash. That adds up to about 230 million metric tons per year! Where does all that trash go?

Landfills

About 31 percent of the trash is recycled and composted. About 14 percent is burned, and the remaining 55 percent is placed in landfills, such as the one shown in **Figure 8.** Landfills are areas where trash is buried. Landfills are another way that people use land.

A landfill is carefully designed to meet government regulations. Trash is covered by soil to keep it from blowing away. Special liners help prevent pollutants from leaking into soil and groundwater supplies.

 **Key Concept Check** What is done to prevent the trash in landfills from polluting air, soil, and water?

Hazardous Waste

Some trash cannot be placed in landfills because it contains harmful substances that can affect soil, air, and water quality. This trash is called hazardous waste. The substances in hazardous waste also can affect the health of humans and other living things.

Both industries and households generate hazardous waste. For example, hazardous waste from the medical industry includes used needles and bandages. Household hazardous waste includes used motor oil and batteries. The U.S. Environmental Protection Agency (EPA) works with state and local agencies to help people safely **dispose** of hazardous waste.

FOLDABLES®

Use a sheet of notebook paper to make a horizontal two-tab concept map. Label and draw arrows as illustrated. Use the Foldable to identify positive and negative factors that have an impact on land.

ACADEMIC VOCABULARY

dispose
(verb) to throw away

Figure 9 Yellowstone Falls are in Yellowstone National Park, which was created in 1872.

Positive Actions

Human actions can have negative effects on the environment, but they can have positive impacts as well. Governments, society, and individuals can work together to reduce the impact of human activities on land resources.

Protecting the Land

The area shown in **Figure 9** is part of Yellowstone National Park, the first national park in the world. The park was an example for the United States and other countries as they began setting aside land for preservation. State and local governments also followed this example.

Protected forests and parks are important habitats for wildlife and are enjoyed by millions of visitors each year. Mining and logging are allowed on some of these lands. However, the removal of resources must meet environmental regulations.

Reforestation and Reclamation

A forest is a complex ecosystem. With careful planning, it can be managed as a renewable resource. For example, trees can be select-cut. That means that only some trees in one area are cut down, rather than the entire forest. In addition, people can practice reforestation. **Reforestation** *involves planting trees to replace trees that have been cut or burned down.* Reforestation can keep a forest healthy or help reestablish a deforested area.

WORD ORIGIN

reclamation
from Latin *reclamare,* means "to call back"

Mined land also can be made environmentally healthy through reclamation. **Reclamation** *is the process of restoring land disturbed by mining.* The before and after photos in **Figure 10** show that the mined area has been reshaped, covered with soil, and then replanted with trees and other vegetation.

Reading Check How do reforestation and reclamation positively impact land?

Figure 10 As part of reclamation, grasses and trees were planted on this coal mine in Indiana.

Before

After

Green Spaces

In urban areas, much of the land is covered with parking lots, streets, buildings, and sidewalks. Many cities use green spaces to create natural environments in urban settings. Green spaces are areas that are left undeveloped or lightly developed. They include parks within cities and forests around suburbs. Green spaces, such as the park shown in **Figure 11,** provide recreational opportunities for people and shelter for wildlife. Green spaces also reduce runoff and improve air quality as plants remove excess carbon dioxide from the air.

How can you help?

Individuals can have a big impact on land-use issues by practicing the three Rs—reusing, reducing, and recycling. Reusing is using an item for a new purpose. For example, you might have made a bird feeder from a used plastic milk jug. Reducing is using fewer resources. You can turn off the lights when you leave a room to reduce your use of electricity.

Recycling is making a new product from a used product. Plastic containers can be recycled into new plastic products. Recycled aluminum cans are used to make new aluminum cans. Paper, shown in **Figure 11,** also can be recycled.

Figure 11 shows another way people can lessen their environmental impact on the land. The student in the bottom photo is composting food scraps into a material that is added to soil to increase its fertility. Compost is a mixture of decaying organic matter, such as leaves, food scraps, and grass clippings. It is used to improve soil quality by adding nutrients to soil. Composting and reusing, reducing, and recycling all help reduce the amount of trash that ends up in landfills.

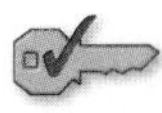

Key Concept Check What can you do to help lessen your impact on the land?

Figure 11 Green spaces, recycling, and composting are three things that can have positive impacts on land resources.

Parks provide recreational opportunities for people and habitats for wildlife, such as birds.

Using recycled paper to make new paper reduces deforestation as well as water use during paper production.

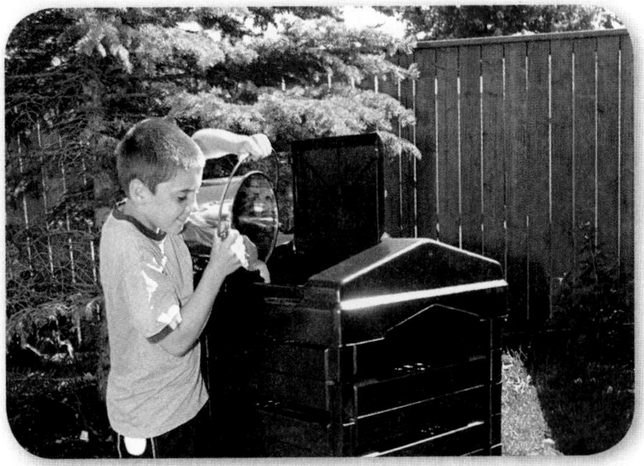

Composting speeds up the rate of decomposition for vegetable scraps, leaving a rich material that can be used as natural fertilizer.

Lesson 2 Review

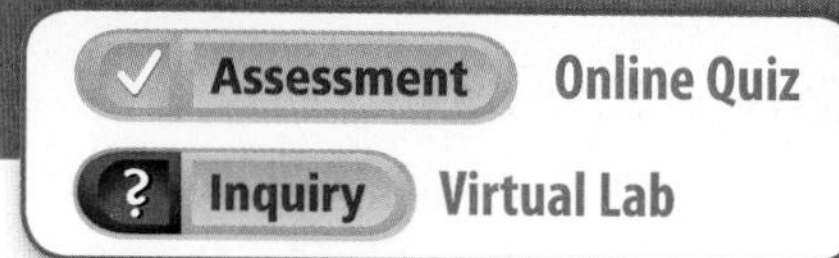

Visual Summary

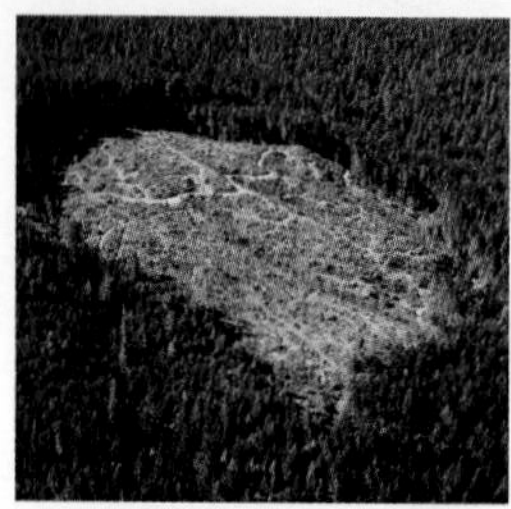

Deforestation, agriculture, and mining for useful rocks and minerals all can affect land resources negatively.

People use land for living space, which can lead to urban sprawl, an increase in roadways, and the need for proper waste disposal.

Creating national parks, preserves and local green spaces, reforestation, and practicing the three Rs are all ways people can positively impact land resources.

FOLDABLES®

Use your lesson Foldable to review the lesson. Save your Foldable for the project at the end of the chapter.

What do you think NOW?

You first read the statements below at the beginning of the chapter.

3. Deforestation does not affect soil quality.

4. Most trash is recycled.

Did you change your mind about whether you agree or disagree with the statements? Rewrite any false statements to make them true.

Use Vocabulary

1 **Distinguish** between deforestation and reforestation.

2 **Use the term** *urban sprawl* in a sentence.

3 **Define** *desertification.*

Understand Key Concepts 

4 Which has a positive impact on land?

A. composting
B. deforestation
C. mining
D. urban sprawl

5 **Apply** How can the addition of fertilizers to crops affect the nitrogen cycle?

6 **Analyze** Why must waste disposal be carefully managed?

Interpret Graphics

7 **Organize** Copy and fill in the graphic organizer below. In each oval, list one way that people use land.

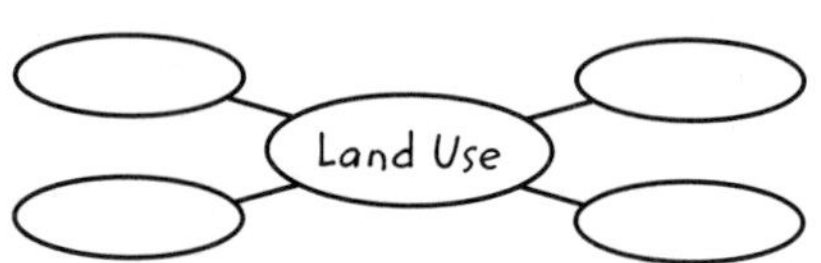

8 **Describe** the function of the liner in the diagram below.

Math Skills

Math Practice

9 In 1950, 35.1 million people lived in suburban areas. By 1990, the number had increased to 120 million people. What was the percent increase in suburban population?

Inquiry **Skill Practice** **Design an Experiment** 45 minutes

How will you design an environmentally safe landfill?

Your city is planning to build an environmentally safe landfill and is accepting design proposals. Your task is to develop and test a design to submit to city officials.

Materials

creative construction materials

paper towels

scissors

masking tape

Safety

Learn It

When you **design an experiment,** you consider the variables you want to test and how you will measure the results.

Try It

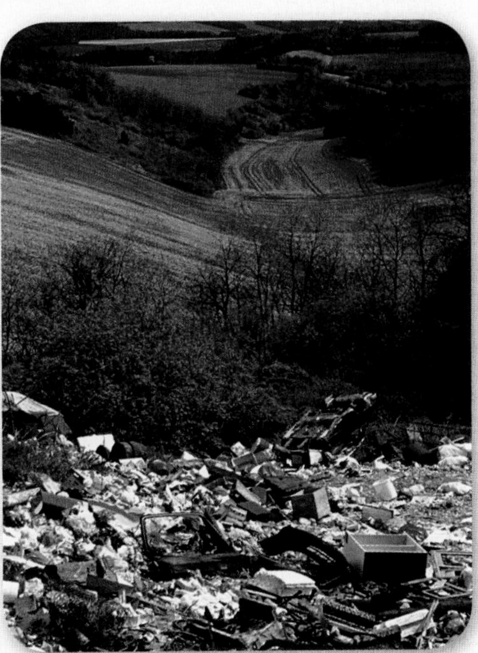

1. Read and complete a lab safety form.
2. Read the information provided about landfill requirements as set by the Environmental Protection Agency.
3. Plan and diagram your landfill design.
4. Use the materials to build your landfill model. Add waste materials.
5. Pour 350 mL of water on your landfill to simulate rain. Observe the path the water takes.
6. Collect the leachate and compare its volume with that of the other groups. Leachate is the liquid that seeps out of your landfill.
7. Compare your landfill design to that of other groups.

Apply It

8. Explain how you designed your landfill to meet requirements and function efficiently.
9. How did your landfill design compare to those of other groups? How much leachate did your group collect compared to other groups?
10. What changes would you make to the design of your landfill? What changes would you make to your procedure to test the effectiveness of your landfill?
11. **Key Concept** Explain how your landfill helped to prevent the pollution of soil and water.

Lesson 3

Impacts on Water

Reading Guide

Key Concepts

ESSENTIAL QUESTIONS

- How do humans use water as a resource?
- How can pollution affect water quality?
- What actions help prevent water pollution?

Vocabulary

point-source pollution p. 328

nonpoint-source pollution p. 329

Academic Standards for Science

8.2.6 Identify, explain, and discuss some effects human activities have on the biosphere, such as air, soil, light, noise and water pollution.

8.2.7 Recognize that some of Earth's resources are finite and describe how recycling, reducing consumption and the development of alternatives can reduce the rate of their depletion.

8.2.8 Explain that human activities, beginning with the earliest herding and agricultural activities, have drastically changed the environment and have affected the capacity of the environment to support native species. Explain current efforts to reduce and eliminate these impacts and encourage sustainability.

Also covers: 8.NS.1, 8.NS.3, 8.NS.4, 8.NS.6, 8.NS.7, 8.NS.9, 8.NS.10, 8.DP.1, 8.DP.2, 8.DP.3, 8.DP.4, 8.DP.5, 8.DP.6, 8.DP.7, 8.DP.8, 8.DP.9, 8.DP.10, 8.DP.11

Inquiry How Much Water?

About 34 percent of all water used in the United States is used to irrigate crops. Where does all this water come from? What other ways do humans use water? What happens when water is polluted or runs out?

20 minutes

Which water filter is the most effective?

Suppose you have been hired by the Super-Clean Water Treatment Plant to test new water filters. Their old filters do not remove all of the particles from the treated water. Your job is to design an effective water filter.

1. Read and complete a lab safety form.
2. Obtain a **water sample,** a **funnel,** and two **500-mL beakers.**
3. Use **coffee filters, paper towels, cotton,** and **gravel** to make a filter in the funnel. Hold the funnel over the first beaker. Pour half of your water sample into the funnel and collect the water in the beaker. Record your results in your Science Journal.
4. Remove the filter and rinse the funnel. Based on your results, make a second, more efficient filter. Repeat step 3 using the second beaker.
5. Draw a diagram of both filtering methods in your Science Journal.

Think About This

1. Were either of your filters successful in removing the particles from the water? Why or why not?
2. What changes would you make to your filter to make it work more efficiently?
3. **Key Concept** How do water treatment plants make more water available for human use?

Water as a Resource

Most of Earth's surface is covered with water, and living things on Earth are made mostly of water. Neither the largest whale nor the smallest algae can live without this important resource. Like other organisms, humans need water to survive. Humans also use water in ways that other organisms do not. People wash cars, do laundry, and use water for recreation and transportation.

Household activities, however, make up only a small part of human water use. As shown in **Figure 12,** most water in the United States is used by power plants. The water is used to generate electricity and to cool equipment. Like the land uses you learned about earlier, the use of water as a resource also impacts the environment.

Key Concept Check How do humans use water as a resource?

Water Use

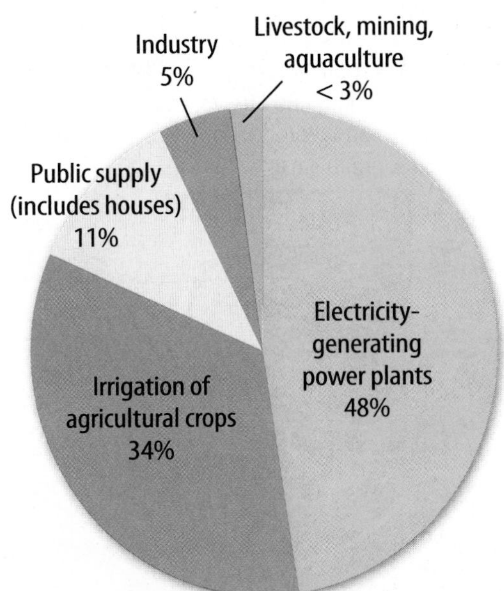

Figure 12 Power plants, industries, farms, and households all use water.

Sources of Water Pollution

Water moves from Earth's surface to the atmosphere and back again in the water cycle. Thermal energy from the Sun causes water at Earth's surface to evaporate into the atmosphere. Water vapor in the air cools as it rises, then condenses and forms clouds. Water returns to Earth's surface as precipitation. Runoff reenters oceans and rivers or it can seep into the ground. Pollution from a variety of sources can impact the quality of water as it moves through the water cycle.

Point-Source Pollution

Point-source pollution *is pollution from a single source that can be identified.* The discharge pipe in **Figure 13** that is releasing industrial waste directly into a river is an example of point-source pollution. Other examples of point-source pollution in **Figure 13** are the oil spilling from the tanker and the runoff from the mining operation.

WORD ORIGIN
pollution
from Latin *polluere,* means "to contaminate"

Sources of Water Pollution

Review Personal Tutor

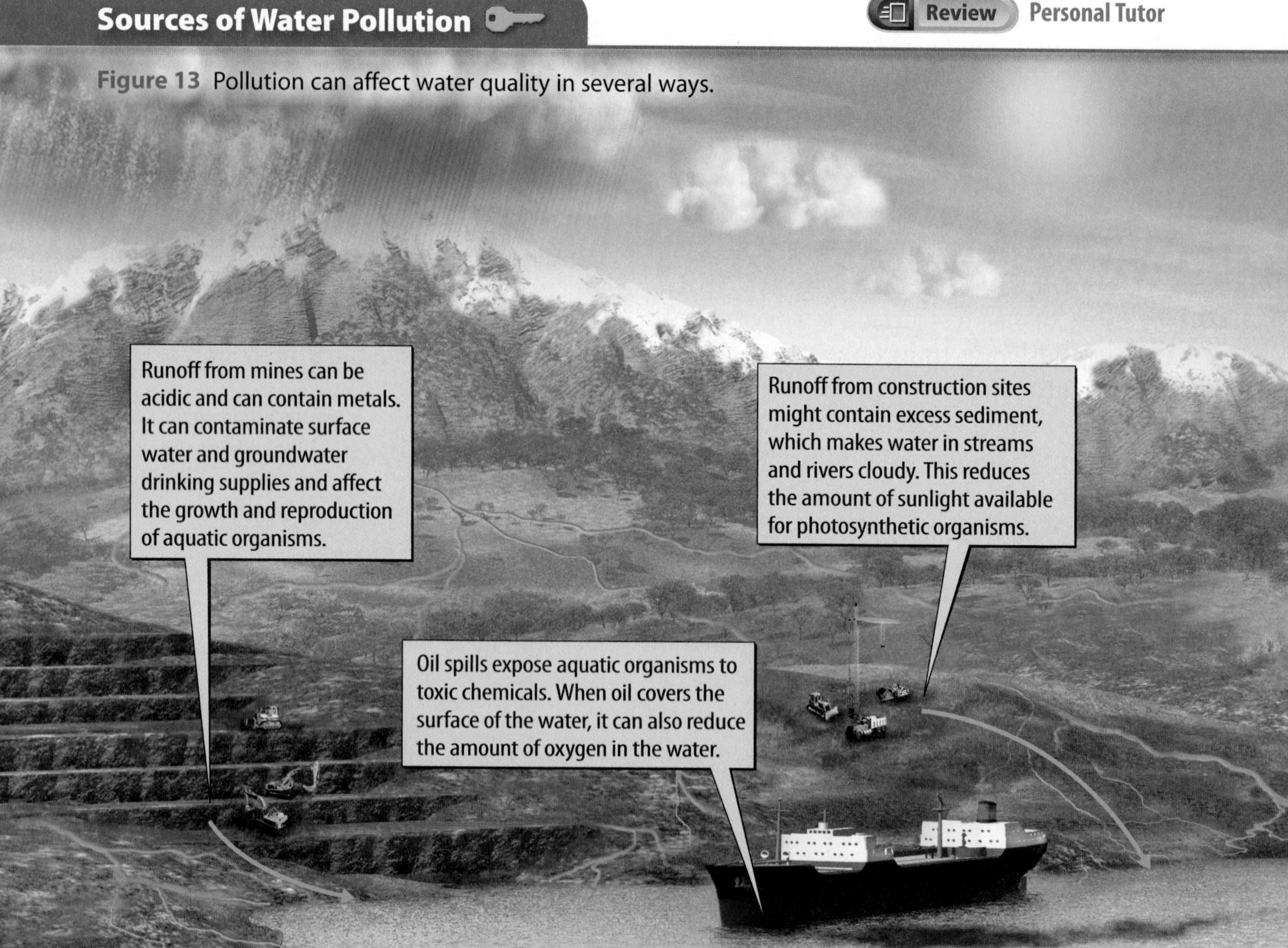

Runoff from mines can be acidic and can contain metals. It can contaminate surface water and groundwater drinking supplies and affect the growth and reproduction of aquatic organisms.
Runoff from construction sites might contain excess sediment, which makes water in streams and rivers cloudy. This reduces the amount of sunlight available for photosynthetic organisms.
Oil spills expose aquatic organisms to toxic chemicals. When oil covers the surface of the water, it can also reduce the amount of oxygen in the water.

Figure 13 Pollution can affect water quality in several ways.

Nonpoint-Source Pollution

Pollution from several widespread sources that cannot be traced back to a single location is called **nonpoint-source pollution.** As precipitation runs over Earth's surface, the water picks up materials and substances from farms and urban developments, such as the ones shown in **Figure 13.** These different sources might be several kilometers apart. This makes it difficult to trace the pollution in the water back to one specific source. Runoff from farms and urban developments are examples of nonpoint-source pollution. Runoff from construction sites, which can contain excess amounts of sediment, is another example of nonpoint-source pollution.

Most of the water pollution in the United States comes from nonpoint sources. This kind of pollution is harder to pinpoint and therefore harder to control.

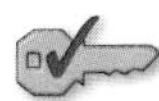

Key Concept Check How can pollution affect water quality?

FOLDABLES®

Make a vertical three-tab book. Draw a Venn diagram on the front. Cut the folds to form three tabs. Label as illustrated. Use the Foldable to compare and contrast sources of pollution.

Point-Source Pollution
Both
Nonpoint-Source Pollution

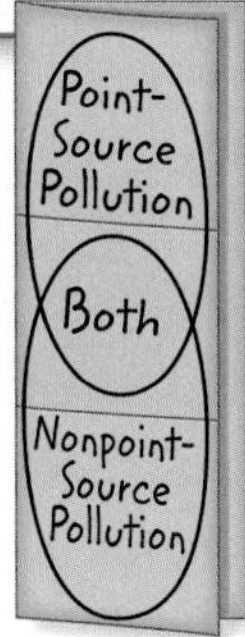

Visual Check What are the point sources and nonpoint sources of pollution in this illustration?

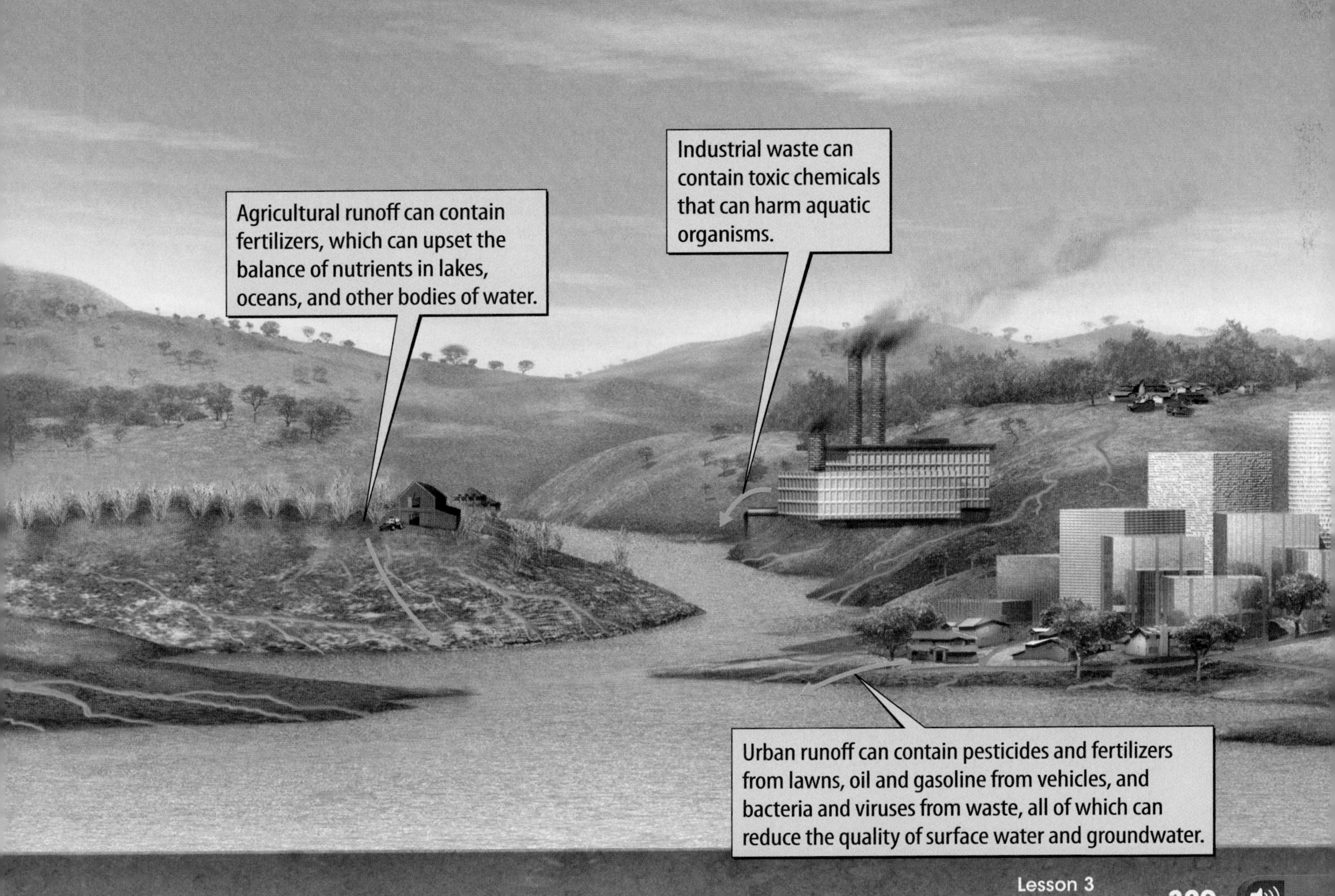

Agricultural runoff can contain fertilizers, which can upset the balance of nutrients in lakes, oceans, and other bodies of water.
Industrial waste can contain toxic chemicals that can harm aquatic organisms.
Urban runoff can contain pesticides and fertilizers from lawns, oil and gasoline from vehicles, and bacteria and viruses from waste, all of which can reduce the quality of surface water and groundwater.

Figure 14 In 1969, burning litter and chemical pollution floating on the Cuyahoga River in northeastern Ohio inspired international efforts to clean up the Great Lakes.

Positive Actions

Once pollution enters water, it is difficult to remove. In fact, it can take decades to clean polluted groundwater! That is why most efforts to reduce water pollution focus on preventing it from entering the environment, rather than cleaning it up.

International Cooperation

In the 1960s, Lake Erie, one of the Great Lakes, was heavily polluted by runoff from fertilized fields and industrial wastes. Rivers that flowed into the lake were polluted, too. Litter soaked with chemicals floated on the surface of one of these rivers—the Cuyahoga River. As shown in **Figure 14,** the litter caught fire. The fire spurred Canada and the United States—the two countries that border the Great Lakes—into action.

The countries formed several agreements to clean up the Great Lakes. The goals of the countries are pollution prevention, as well as cleanup and research. Although, the Great Lakes still face challenges from aquatic species that are not native to the lakes and from the impact of excess sediments, pollution from toxic chemicals has decreased.

Reading Check Why is it important to focus on preventing water pollution before it happens?

Inquiry MiniLab

20 minutes

What's in well water?

The graph shows the level of nitrates in well water in Spanish Springs Valley, Nevada, over a 10-year period. Nitrate is a form of nitrogen that can contaminate groundwater when it leaches out of septic systems.

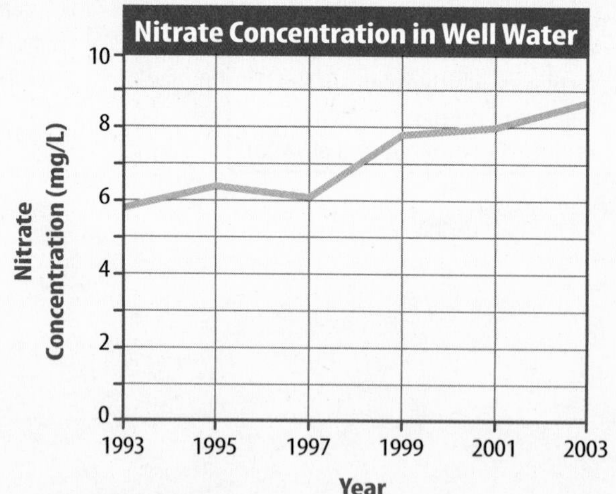

Analyze and Conclude

1. **Describe** what happened to the average level of nitrate in the well water of Spanish Springs Valley between 1993 and 2003.
2. **Analyze** Excess nitrate in drinking water can cause serious illness, especially in infants. The maximum allowable level in public drinking water is 10 mg/L. How close did the highest level of nitrate concentration come to the maximum level allowed?
3. **Key Concept** An article in the newspaper described a Spanish Springs Valley project to connect all houses to the sewer system. Predict how this will affect nitrate levels in the well water.

National Initiatives

In addition to working with other governments, the United States has laws to help maintain water quality within its borders. The Clean Water Act, for example, regulates sources of water pollution, including sewage systems. The Safe Drinking Water Act protects supplies of drinking water throughout the country.

How can you help?

Laws are effective ways to reduce water pollution. But simple actions taken by individuals can have positive impacts, too.

Reduce Use of Harmful Chemicals Many household products, such as paints and cleaners, contain harmful chemicals. People can use alternative products that do not contain toxins. For example, baking soda and white vinegar are safe, inexpensive cleaning products. In addition, people can reduce their use of artificial fertilizers on gardens and lawns. As you read earlier, compost can enrich soils without harming water quality.

Dispose of Waste Safely Sometimes using products that contain pollutants is necessary. Vehicles, for example, cannot run without motor oil. This motor oil has to be replaced regularly. People should never pour motor oil or other hazardous substances into drains, onto the ground, or directly into streams or lakes. These substances must be disposed of safely. Your local waste management agency has tips for safe disposal of hazardous waste.

Conserve Water Water pollution can be reduced simply by reducing water use. Easy ways to conserve water include taking shorter showers and turning off the water when you brush your teeth. **Figure 15** shows other ways to reduce water use.

Key Concept Check How can individuals help prevent water pollution?

Figure 15 People can help reduce water pollution by conserving water.

Visual Check How does sweeping a deck help reduce water pollution?

Keeping water in the refrigerator instead of running water from a faucet until the water is cold helps conserve water.

Sweeping leaves and branches from a deck instead of spraying them off using water from a hose helps conserve water.

Lesson 3 Review

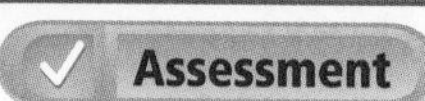

Visual Summary

Water is an important resource; all living things need water to survive. Water is used for agriculture, for electricity production, and in homes and businesses every day.

Water pollution can come from many sources, including chemicals from agriculture and industry and oil spills.

International cooperation and national laws help prevent water pollution. Individuals can help conserve water by reducing water use and disposing of wastes properly.

FOLDABLES®

Use your lesson Foldable to review the lesson. Save your Foldable for the project at the end of the chapter.

What do you think NOW?

You first read the statements below at the beginning of the chapter.

5. Sources of water pollution are always easy to identify.

6. The proper method of disposal for used motor oil is to pour it down the drain.

Did you change your mind about whether you agree or disagree with the statements? Rewrite any false statements to make them true.

Use Vocabulary

1 **Define** *nonpoint-source pollution* and *point-source pollution* in your own words.

2 **Use the term** *nonpoint-source pollution* in a sentence.

Understand Key Concepts

3 Which uses the most water in the United States?

A. factories
B. farms
C. households
D. power plants

4 **Survey** three classmates to find out how they conserve water at home.

5 **Diagram** Make a diagram showing how runoff from lawns can impact water quality.

Interpret Graphics

6 **Sequence** Draw a graphic organizer such as the one below to illustrate the cleanup of Lake Erie, beginning with the pollution of the lake.

7 **Classify** the pollution source shown below as point-source or nonpoint-source. Explain your reasoning.

Critical Thinking

8 **Visualize** a map of a river that flows through several countries. Explain why international cooperation is needed to reduce water pollution.

9 **Identify** a human activity that impacts water quality negatively. Then describe a positive action that can help reduce the pollution caused by the activity.

Dead Zones

GREEN SCIENCE

What causes lifeless areas in the ocean?

For thousands of years, people have lived on coasts, making a living by shipping goods or by fishing. Today, fisheries in the Gulf of Mexico provide jobs for thousands of people and food for millions more. Although humans and other organisms depend on the ocean, human activities can harm marine ecosystems. Scientists have been tracking dead zones in the ocean for several decades. They believe that these zones are a result of human activities on land.

A large dead zone in the Gulf of Mexico forms every year when runoff from spring and summer rain in the Midwest drains into the Mississippi River. The runoff contains nitrogen and phosphorous from fertilizer, animal waste, and sewage from farms and cities. This nutrient-rich water flows into the gulf. Algae feed on excess nutrients and multiply rapidly, creating an algal bloom. The results of the algal bloom are shown below.

Some simple changes in human activity can help prevent dead zones. People upstream from the Gulf can decrease the use of fertilizer and apply it at times when it is less likely to be carried away by runoff. Picking up or containing animal waste can help, too. Also, people can modernize and improve septic and sewage systems. How do we know these steps would work? Using them has already restored life to dead zones in the Great Lakes!

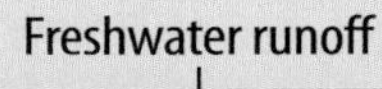

1 River water containing nitrogen and phosphorous flows into the Gulf of Mexico.

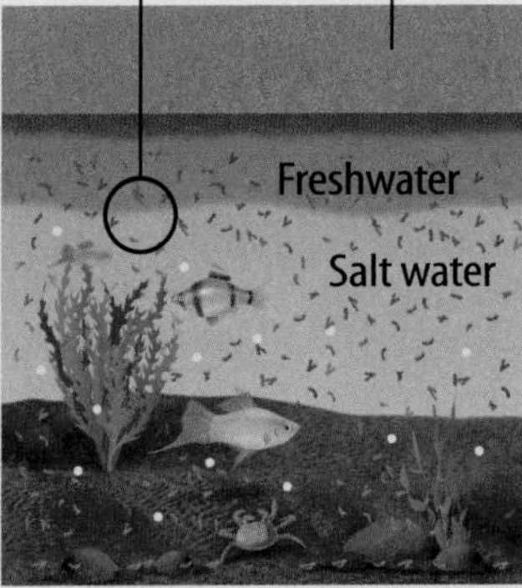

2 After the algal bloom, dead algae sink to the ocean floor.

3 Decomposing algae deplete the water's oxygen, killing other organisms.

It's Your Turn

RESEARCH AND REPORT Earth's oceans contain about 150 dead zones. Choose three. Plot them on a map and write a report about what causes each dead zone.

Lesson 4

Impacts on the Atmosphere

Reading Guide

Key Concepts
ESSENTIAL QUESTIONS

- What are some types of air pollution?
- How are global warming and the carbon cycle related?
- How does air pollution affect human health?
- What actions help prevent air pollution?

Vocabulary

photochemical smog p. 335
acid precipitation p. 336
particulate matter p. 336
global warming p. 337
greenhouse effect p. 338
Air Quality Index p. 339

Multilingual eGlossary

Video BrainPOP®

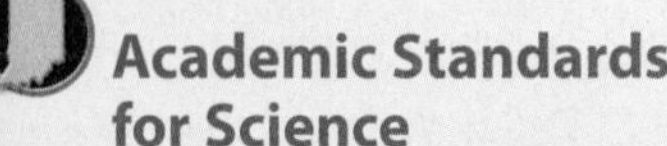

Academic Standards for Science

Covers: 8.2.6, 8.2.7, 8.2.8, 8.NS.2, 8.NS.7, 8.NS.11, 8.DP.1, 8.DP.2, 8.DP.3, 8.DP.4, 8.DP.5, 8.DP.6, 8.DP.7, 8.DP.8, 8.DP.9, 8.DP.10, 8.DP.11

Inquiry Why wear a mask?

In some areas of the world, people wear masks to help protect themselves against high levels of air pollution. Where does this pollution come from? How do you think air pollution affects human health and the environment?

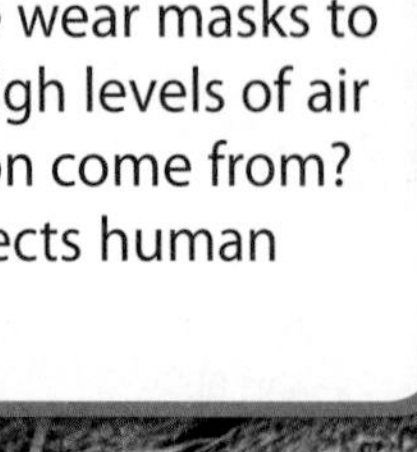

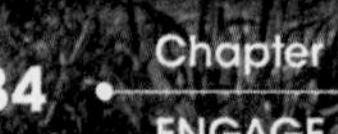

Launch Lab

20 minutes

Where's the air?

In 1986, an explosion at a nuclear power plant in Chernobyl, Russia, sent radioactive pollution 6 km into the atmosphere. Within three weeks, the radioactive cloud had reached Italy, Finland, Iceland, and North America.

1. Read and complete a lab safety form.
2. With your group, move to your assigned area of the room.
3. Lay out **sheets of paper** to cover the table.
4. When the **fan** starts blowing, observe whether water droplets appear on the paper. Record your observations in your Science Journal.
5. Lay out another set of paper sheets and record your observations when the fan blows in a different direction.

Think About This

1. Did the water droplets reach your location? Why or why not?
2. How is the movement of air and particles by the fan similar to the movement of the pollution from Chernobyl? How does the movement differ?
3. **Key Concept** How do you think the health of a person in Iceland could be affected by the explosion in Chernobyl?

Importance of Clean Air

Your body, and the bodies of other animals, uses oxygen in air to produce some of the energy it needs. Many organisms can survive for only a few minutes without air. But the air you breathe must be clean or it can harm your body.

Types of Air Pollution

Human activities can produce pollution that enters the air and affects air quality. Types of air pollution include smog, acid precipitation, particulate matter, chlorofluorocarbons (CFCs), and carbon monoxide.

Smog

The brownish haze in the sky in **Figure 16** is photochemical smog. **Photochemical smog** *is caused when nitrogen and carbon compounds in the air react in sunlight.* Nitrogen and carbon compounds are released when fossil fuels are burned to provide energy for vehicles and power plants. These compounds react in sunlight and form other substances. One of these substances is ozone. Ozone high in the atmosphere helps protect living things from the Sun's ultraviolet radiation. However, ozone close to Earth's surface is a major component of smog.

Figure 16 Burning fossil fuels releases compounds that can react in sunlight and form smog.

Acid Precipitation

Another form of pollution that occurs as a result of burning fossil fuels is acid precipitation. **Acid precipitation** *is rain or snow that has a lower pH than that of normal rainwater.* The pH of normal rainwater is about 5.6. Acid precipitation forms when gases containing nitrogen and sulfur react with water, oxygen, and other chemicals in the atmosphere. Acid precipitation falls into lakes and ponds or onto the ground. It makes the water and the soil more acidic. Many living things cannot survive if the pH of water or soil becomes too low. The trees shown in **Figure 17** have been affected by acid precipitation.

Figure 17  Acid precipitation can make the soil acidic and kill trees and other plant life.

Review

Personal Tutor

Particulate Matter

The mix of both solid and liquid particles in the air is called **particulate matter.** Solid particles include smoke, dust, and dirt. These particles enter the air from natural processes, such as volcanic eruptions and forest fires. Human activities, such as burning fossil fuels at power plants and in vehicles, also release particulate matter. Inhaling particulate matter can cause coughing, difficulty breathing, and other respiratory problems.

WORD ORIGIN

particulate
from Latin *particula*, means "small part"

CFCs

Ozone in the upper atmosphere absorbs harmful ultraviolet (UV) rays from the Sun. Using products that contain CFCs, such as air conditioners and refrigerators made before 1996, affects the ozone layer. CFCs react with sunlight and destroy ozone molecules. As a result, the ozone layer thins and more UV rays reach Earth's surface. Increased skin cancer rates have been linked with an increase in UV rays.

FOLDABLES®

Make a two-tab book. Label the tabs as illustrated. Use your Foldable to record factors that increase or decrease air pollution.

Carbon Monoxide

Carbon monoxide is a gas released from vehicles and industrial processes. Forest fires also release carbon monoxide into the air. Wood-burning and gas stoves are sources of carbon monoxide indoors. Breathing carbon monoxide reduces the amount of oxygen that reaches the body's tissues and organs.

Key Concept Check What are some types of air pollution?

The Carbon Cycle

Concepts in Motion Animation

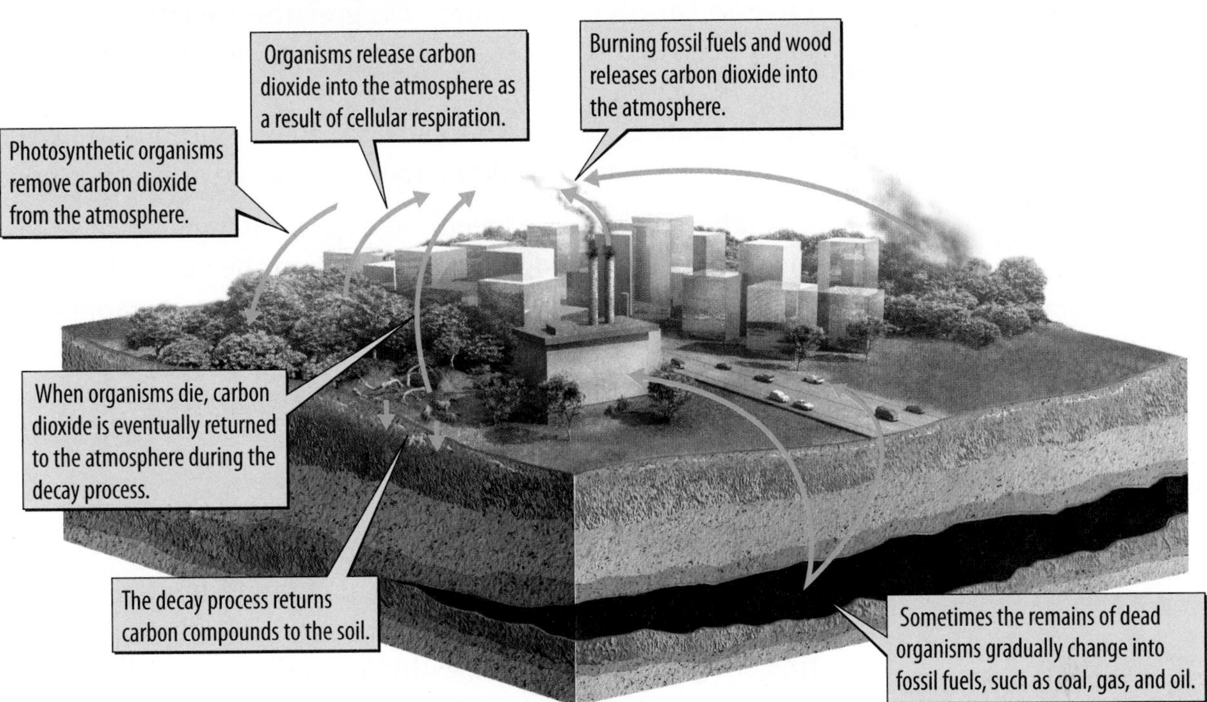

Organisms release carbon dioxide into the atmosphere as a result of cellular respiration.
Burning fossil fuels and wood releases carbon dioxide into the atmosphere.
Photosynthetic organisms remove carbon dioxide from the atmosphere.
When organisms die, carbon dioxide is eventually returned to the atmosphere during the decay process.
The decay process returns carbon compounds to the soil.
Sometimes the remains of dead organisms gradually change into fossil fuels, such as coal, gas, and oil.

Figure 18 Some human activities can increase the amount of carbon dioxide in the atmosphere.

Visual Check Which processes add carbon to the atmosphere?

Global Warming and the Carbon Cycle

Air pollution affects natural cycles on Earth. For example, burning fossil fuels for electricity, heating, and transportation releases substances that cause acid precipitation. Burning fossil fuels also releases carbon dioxide into the atmosphere, as shown in **Figure 18.** An increased concentration of carbon dioxide in the atmosphere can lead to **global warming,** *an increase in Earth's average surface temperature.* Earth's temperature has increased about 0.7°C over the past 100 years. Scientists estimate it will rise an additional 1.8 to 4.0°C over the next 100 years. Even a small increase in Earth's average surface temperature can cause widespread problems.

Effects of Global Warming

Warmer temperatures can cause ice to melt, making sea levels rise. Higher sea levels can cause flooding along coastal areas. In addition, warmer ocean waters might lead to an increase in the intensity and frequency of storms.

Global warming also can affect the kinds of living things found in ecosystems. Some hardwood trees, for example, do not thrive in warm environments. These trees will no longer be found in some areas if temperatures continue to rise.

Key Concept Check How are global warming and the carbon cycle related?

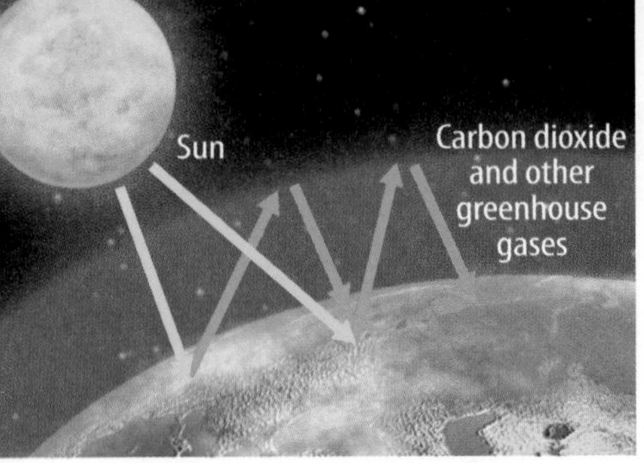

Figure 19 Greenhouse gases absorb and reradiate thermal energy from the Sun and warm Earth's surface.

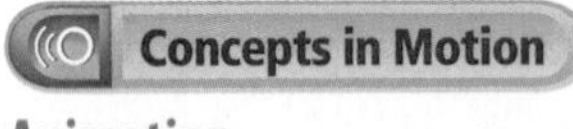
Concepts in Motion
Animation

The Greenhouse Effect

Why does too much carbon dioxide in the atmosphere increase Earth's temperature? *The* **greenhouse effect** *is the natural process that occurs when certain gases in the atmosphere absorb and reradiate thermal energy from the Sun.* As shown in **Figure 19,** this thermal energy warms Earth's surface. Without the greenhouse effect, Earth would be too cold for life as it exists now.

Carbon dioxide is a greenhouse gas. Other greenhouse gases include methane and water vapor. When the amount of greenhouse gases increases, more thermal energy is trapped and Earth's surface temperature rises. Global warming occurs.

Reading Check How are the greenhouse effect and global warming related?

Health Disorders

Air pollution affects the environment and human health as well. Air pollution can cause respiratory problems, including triggering asthma attacks. Asthma is a disorder of the respiratory system in which breathing passageways narrow during an attack, making it hard for a person to breathe. **Figure 20** shows some health disorders caused by pollutants in the air.

Key Concept Check How can air pollution affect human health?

Figure 20 Air pollution can harm the environment and your health.

Health Effects of Air Pollution

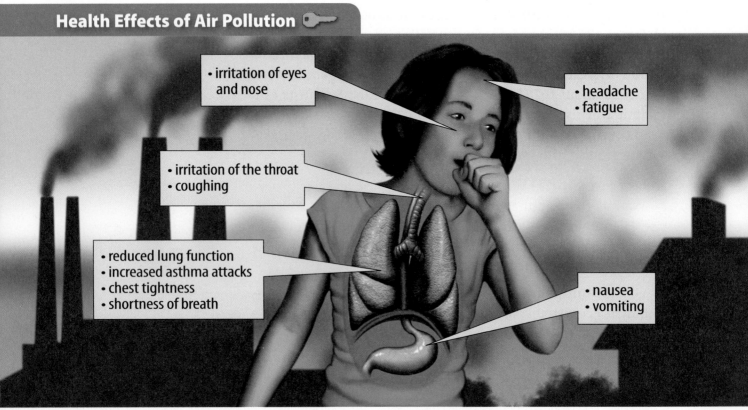

- irritation of eyes and nose
- headache
- fatigue
- irritation of the throat
- coughing
- reduced lung function
- increased asthma attacks
- chest tightness
- shortness of breath
- nausea
- vomiting

Table 1 Air Quality Index

Ozone Concentration (parts per million)	Air Quality Index Values	Air Quality Description	Preventative Actions
0.0 to 0.064	0 to 50	good	No preventative actions needed.
0.065 to 0.084	51 to 100	moderate	Highly sensitive people should limit prolonged outdoor activity.
0.085 to 0.104	101 to 150	unhealthy for sensitive groups	Sensitive people should limit prolonged outdoor activity.
0.105 to 0.124	151 to 200	unhealthy	All groups should limit prolonged outdoor activity.
0.125 to 0.404	201 to 300	very unhealthy	Sensitive people should avoid outdoor activity. All other groups should limit outdoor activity.

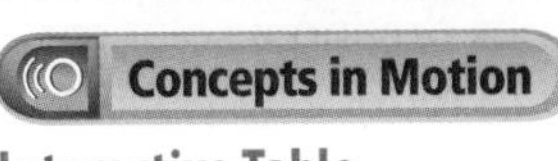

Interactive Table

Measuring Air Quality

Some pollutants, such as smoke from forest fires, are easily seen. Other pollutants, such as carbon monoxide, are invisible. How can people know when levels of air pollution are high?

The EPA works with state and local agencies to measure and report air quality. *The* **Air Quality Index** (AQI) *is a scale that ranks levels of ozone and other air pollutants.* Study the AQI for ozone in **Table 1.** It uses color codes to rank ozone levels on a scale of 0 to 300. Although ozone in the upper atmosphere blocks harmful rays from the Sun, ozone that is close to Earth's surface can cause health problems, including throat irritation, coughing, and chest pain. The EPA cautions that no one should do physical activities outside when AQI values reach 300.

Inquiry MiniLab

10 minutes

What's in the air?

Suppose your friend suffers from asthma. People with respiratory problems such as asthma are usually more sensitive to air pollution. *Sensitive* is a term used on the AQI. Use the AQI in **Table 1** to answer the questions below.

Analyze and Conclude

1. **Identify** Today's AQI value is 130. What is the concentration of ozone in the air?
2. **Decide** Is today a good day for you and your friend to go to the park to play basketball for a few hours? Why or why not?
3. **Key Concept** Predict how you and your friend might be affected by the air if you played basketball today.

Hybrid car

Solar car

Figure 21 Energy-efficient and renewable-energy vehicles help reduce air pollution.

Visual Check How does driving a solar car help reduce air pollution?

Positive Actions

Countries around the world are working together to reduce air pollution. For example, 190 countries, including the United States, have signed the Montreal Protocol to phase out the use of CFCs. Levels of CFCs have since decreased. The Kyoto Protocol aims to reduce emissions of greenhouse gases. Currently, 184 countries have accepted the agreement.

National Initiatives

In the United States, the Clean Air Act sets limits on the amount of certain pollutants that can be released into the air. Since the law was passed in 1970, amounts of carbon monoxide, ozone near Earth's surface, and acid precipitation-producing substances have decreased by more than 50 percent. Toxins from industrial factories have gone down by 90 percent.

Cleaner Energy

Using renewable energy resources such as solar power, wind power, and geothermal energy to heat homes helps reduce air pollution. Recall that renewable resources are resources that can be replaced by natural processes in a relatively short amount of time. People also can invest in more energy-efficient appliances and vehicles. The hybrid car shown in **Figure 21** uses both a battery and fossil fuels for power. It is more energy efficient and emits less pollution than vehicles that are powered by fossil fuels alone. The solar car shown in **Figure 21** uses only the Sun's energy for power.

How can you help?

Reducing energy use means that fewer pollutants are released into the air. You can turn the thermostat down in the winter and up in the summer to save energy. You can walk to the store or use public transportation. Each small step you take to conserve energy helps improve air, water, and soil quality.

 **Key Concept Check** How can people help prevent air pollution?

Lesson 4 Review

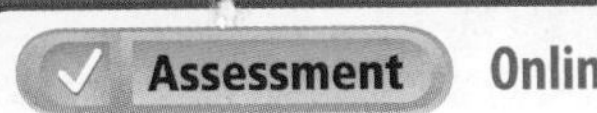

Visual Summary

Burning fossil fuels releases nitrogen and carbon compounds and particulate matter into the air.

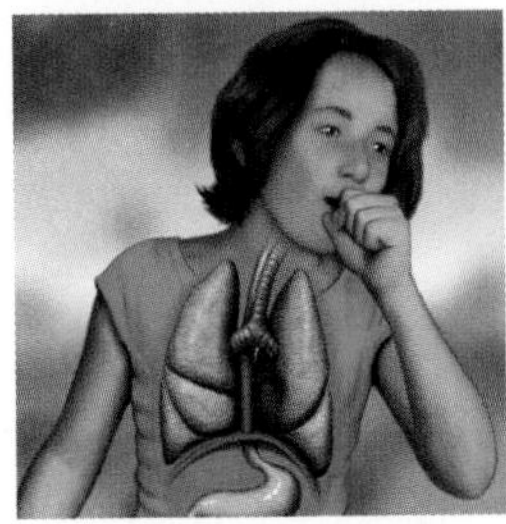

Air pollution can affect human health, causing eye, nose, and throat irritation, increased asthma, and headaches.

Certain laws and international agreements require people to reduce air pollution. Individuals can reduce air pollution by using alternative forms of energy to heat homes and power vehicles.

FOLDABLES®

Use your lesson Foldable to review the lesson. Save your Foldable for the project at the end of the chapter.

What do you think NOW?

You first read the statements below at the beginning of the chapter.

7. The greenhouse effect is harmful to life on Earth.

8. Air pollution can affect human health.

Did you change your mind about whether you agree or disagree with the statements? Rewrite any false statements to make them true.

Use Vocabulary

1. **Use the term** *air quality index* in a sentence.
2. The natural heating of Earth's surface that occurs when certain gases absorb and reradiate thermal energy from the Sun is ________.
3. **Define** *global warming* in your own words.

Understand Key Concepts

4. Which is NOT a possible heath effect of exposure to air pollution?
   - **A.** chest tightness
   - **B.** eye irritation
   - **C.** increased lung function
   - **D.** shortness of breath
5. **Relate** What happens in the carbon cycle when fossil fuels are burned for energy?
6. **Compare** the goals of the Montreal Protocol and the Kyoto Protocol.

Interpret Graphics

7. **Sequence** Copy and fill in the graphic organizer below to identify types of air pollution.

8. **Describe** air quality when the ozone concentration is 0.112 ppm using the table below.

Ozone Concentration (ppm)	Air Quality Index Values	Air Quality Description
0.105 to 0.124	151 to 200	unhealthy
0.125 to 0.404	201 to 300	very unhealthy

Critical Thinking

9. **Predict** Some carbon is stored in frozen soils in the Arctic. What might happen to Earth's climate if these soils thawed?

Lab

3 class periods

Materials

office supplies

magazines

computer with Internet access

Safety

Design a Green City

City planners have asked the architectural firms in town to design an eco-friendly city that will be based on an environmentally responsible use of land, water, and energy. The city should include homes, businesses, schools, green spaces, industry, waste management, and transportation options.

Question

What are the most environmentally friendly materials and practices to use when designing a green city?

Procedure

1. Make a list of the things you will include in your city.
2. Research environmentally responsible structures and practices for the elements of your city. Your research may include using the library or talking with owners, employees, or patrons of businesses to identify existing environmental problems. Use the questions below to help guide your research.

- What materials can you use for building the structures?
- What building practices and designs can you use to minimize environmental impact?
- How will you address energy use by homeowners, businesses, and industry?
- How will you address water use for homes, businesses, and industry?
- How will you address energy use and pollution issues related to public transportation?
- What is the most environmentally friendly system of waste management?

3. Analyze the information you gathered in step 2. Discuss how you will use what you have learned as you design your city.
4. Design your city. Use the colored pencils and markers to draw a map of the city, including all of the elements of the city. Add captions, other graphics, and/or a key to explain any elements or actions and their intended results.
5. Copy and complete the *Required Elements and Actions* chart on the following page. For each element in your city, explain the environmental issue associated with the element and what action you took in your city to address the issue. Does your design include an action for each element?

Required Elements and Actions		
Element	**Environmental Issue**	**Action Taken**
Waste management	All waste goes into landfills.	designed a curbside recycling program

6 If needed, modify your design to include any other actions you need to take.

Analyze and Conclude

7 Describe one identified environmental issue, the action taken, and the intended outcome in your design plans.

8 Compare your design to the designs of other groups. What did they do differently?

9 **The Big Idea** Predict whether there will be any changes in the quality of your city's water resources after years of use of your design. Explain your answer.

Communicate Your Results

Suppose your classmates are members of the city planning board. Present your design to the board. Explain the structures and practices that are intended to make the city environmentally responsible.

Extension

Make a 3-D model of your city. Try to use recycled or environmentally friendly materials to represent the structures in your city.

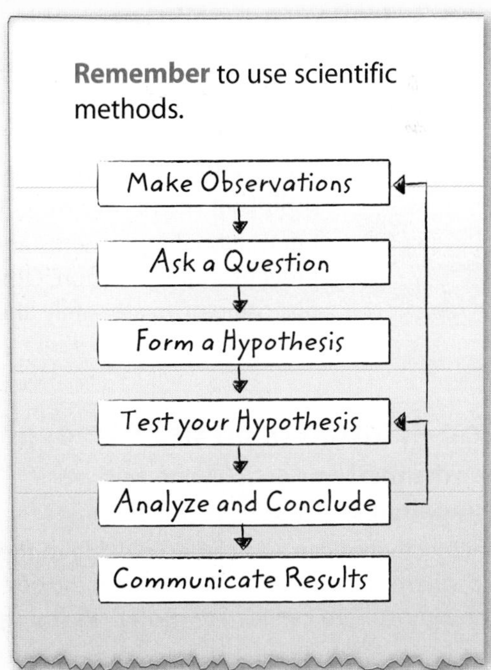

Chapter 9 Study Guide

Human activities can impact the environment negatively, including deforestation, water pollution, and global warming, and positively, such as through reforestation, reclamation, and water conservation.

Key Concepts Summary

Lesson 1: People and the Environment

- Earth has limited resources and cannot support unlimited human **population** growth.
- Daily actions can deplete resources and pollute soil, water, and air.

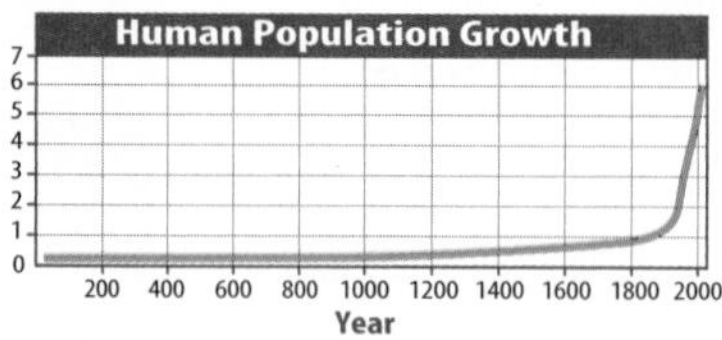

Vocabulary

population p. 311
carrying capacity p. 312

Lesson 2: Impacts on the Land

- **Deforestation, desertification,** habitat destruction, and increased rates of extinction are associated with using land as a resource.
- Landfills are constructed to prevent contamination of soil and water by pollutants from waste. Hazardous waste must be disposed of in a safe manner.
- Positive impacts on land include preservation, **reforestation,** and **reclamation.**

Vocabulary

deforestation p. 317
desertification p. 318
urban sprawl p. 320
reforestation p. 322
reclamation p. 322

Lesson 3: Impacts on Water

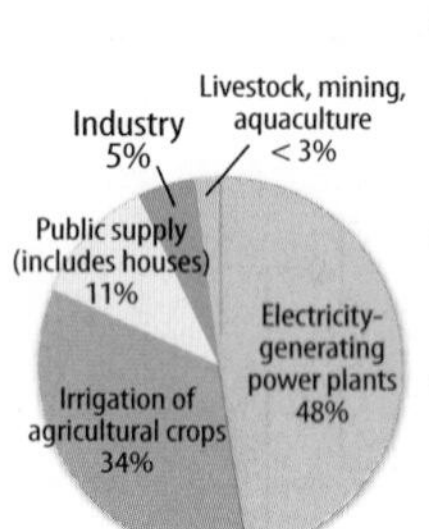

- Humans use water in electricity production, industry, and agriculture, as well as for recreation and transportation.
- **Point-source pollution** and **nonpoint-source pollution** can reduce water quality.
- International agreements and national laws help prevent water pollution. Other positive actions include disposing of waste safely and conserving water.

Vocabulary

point-source pollution p. 328
nonpoint-source pollution p. 329

Lesson 4: Impacts on the Atmosphere

- **Photochemical smog,** CFCs, and **acid precipitation** are types of air pollution.
- Human activities can add carbon dioxide to the atmosphere. Increased levels of carbon dioxide in the atmosphere can lead to **global warming.**
- Air pollutants such as ozone can irritate the respiratory system, reduce lung function, and cause asthma attacks.
- International agreements, laws, and individual actions such as conserving energy help decrease air pollution.

Vocabulary

photochemical smog p. 335
acid precipitation p. 336
particulate matter p. 336
global warming p. 337
greenhouse effect p. 338
Air Quality Index p. 339

Review
- Personal Tutor
- Vocabulary eGames
- Vocabulary eFlashcards

FOLDABLES® Chapter Project

Assemble your lesson Foldables as shown to make a Chapter Project. Use the project to review what you have learned in this chapter.

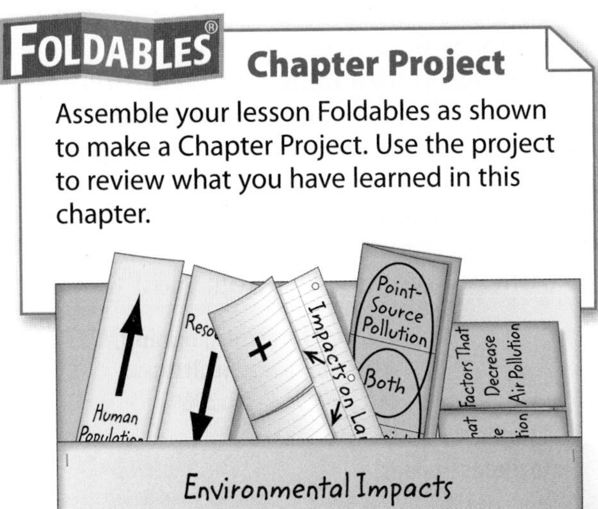

Use Vocabulary

1. Use the term *carrying capacity* in a sentence.
2. Distinguish between desertification and deforestation.
3. Planting trees to replace logged trees is called ________.
4. Distinguish between point-source and nonpoint-source pollution.
5. Define *greenhouse effect* in your own words.
6. Solid and liquid particles in the air are called ________.

Link Vocabulary and Key Concepts

Concepts in Motion Interactive Concept Map

Copy this concept map, and then use vocabulary terms from the previous page to complete the concept map.

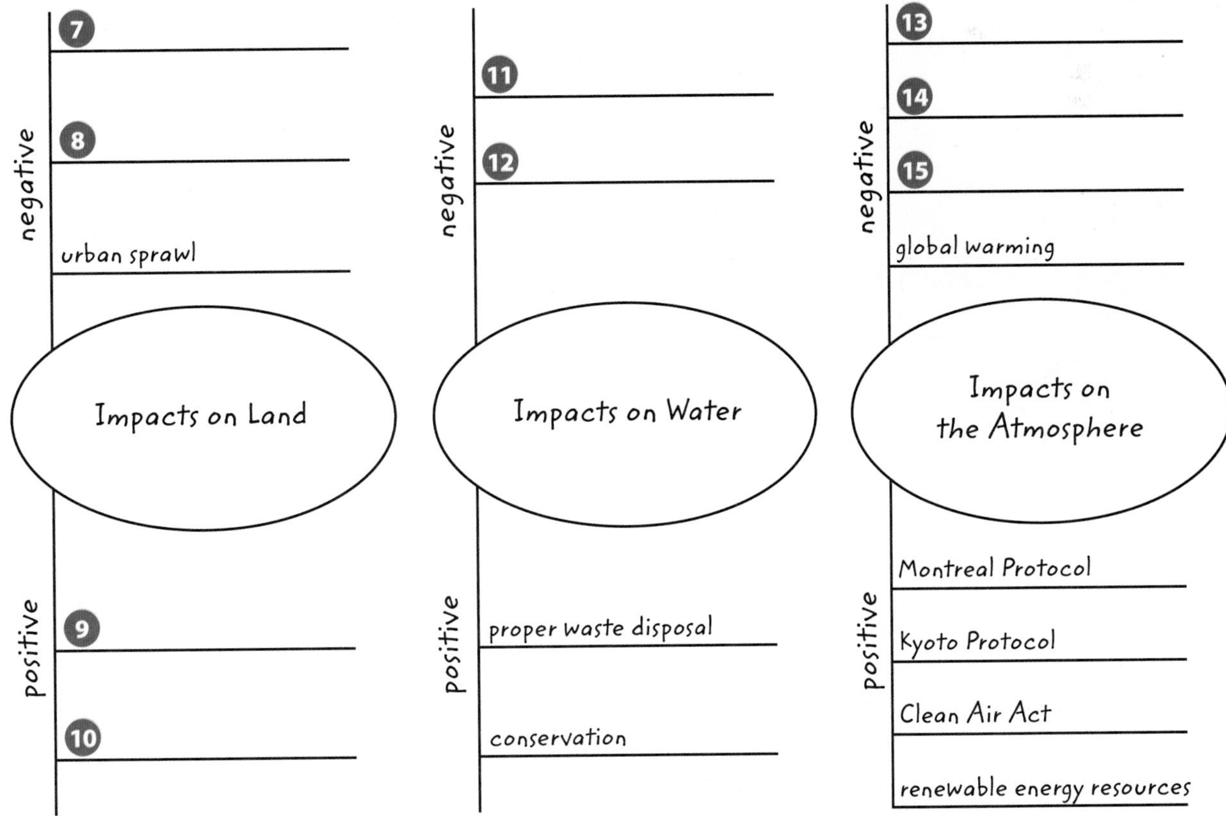

Chapter 9 Review

Understand Key Concepts 

1 Which is a population?
A. all the animals in a zoo
B. all the living things in a forest
C. all the people in a park
D. all the plants in a meadow

2 Which had the greatest influence on the growth of the human population?
A. higher death rates
B. increased marriage rates
C. medical advances
D. widespread disease

3 What percentage of species on Earth live in tropical rain forests?
A. 10 percent
B. 25 percent
C. 50 percent
D. 75 percent

4 What process is illustrated in the diagram below?

Newly planted trees

A. desertification
B. recycling
C. reforestation
D. waste management

5 Which could harm human health?
A. compost
B. hazardous waste
C. nitrogen
D. reclamation

6 Which source of pollution would be hardest to trace and control?
A. runoff from a city
B. runoff from a mine
C. an oil leak from an ocean tanker
D. water from a factory discharge pipe

7 According to the diagram below, which is the correct ranking of water use in the United States, in order from most to least?

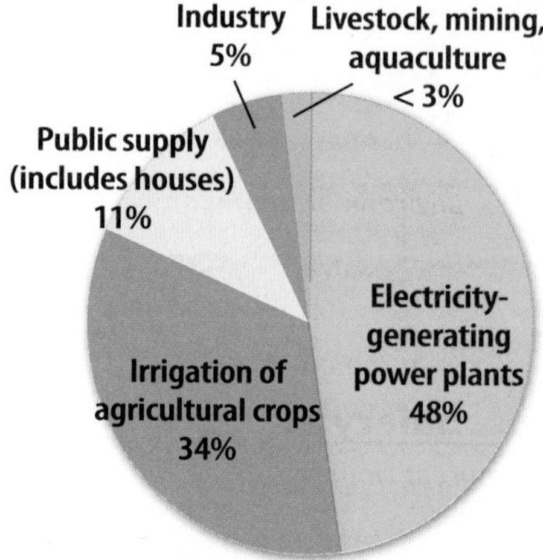

A. industrial, public supply, irrigation, power plants
B. irrigation, industrial, public supply, power plants
C. power plants, irrigation, public supply, industrial
D. public supply, power plants, industrial, irrigation

8 What is the main purpose of the Safe Drinking Water Act?
A. to ban point-source pollution
B. to clean up the Great Lakes
C. to protect drinking-water supplies
D. to regulate landfills

9 Why has the use of CFCs been phased out?
A. They cause acid rain.
B. They produce smog.
C. They destroy ozone molecules.
D. They impact the nitrogen cycle.

Assessment
Online Test Practice

Critical Thinking

10 **Decide** Rates of human population growth are higher in developing countries than in developed countries. Yet, people in developed countries use more resources than those in developing countries. Should international efforts focus on reducing population growth or reducing resource use? Explain.

11 **Relate** How does the carrying capacity for a species help regulate its population growth?

12 **Assess** your personal impact on the environment today. Include both positive and negative impacts on soil, water, and air.

13 **Infer** How does deforestation affect levels of carbon in the atmosphere?

14 **Role-Play** Suppose you are a soil expert advising a farmer on the use of fertilizers. What would you tell the farmer about the environmental impact of the fertilizers?

15 **Create** Use the data below to create a circle graph showing waste disposal methods in the United States.

Waste Disposal Methods—United States	
Method	**Percent of Waste Disposed**
Landfill	55%
Recycling/composting	31%
Incineration	14%

Writing in Science

16 **Compose** a letter to a younger student to help him or her understand air pollution. The letter should identify the different kinds of pollution and explain their causes.

REVIEW THE BIG IDEA

17 How do human activities impact the environment? Give one example each of how human activities impact land, water, and air resources.

18 What positive actions can people take to reduce or reverse negative impacts on the environment?

Math Skills

Math Practice

Use Percentages

19 Between 1960 and 1990, the number of people per square mile in the United States grew from 50.7 people to 70.3 people. What was the percent change?

20 Between 1950 and 1998, the rural population in the United States decreased from 66.2 million to 53.8 million people. What was the percent change in rural population?

21 During the twentieth century, the population of the western states increased from 4.3 million people to 61.2 million people. What was the percent change during the century?

Standardized Test Practice

Record your answers on the answer sheet provided by your teacher or on a sheet of paper.

Multiple Choice

1 Which action can help restore land that has been disturbed by mining?

A deforestation

B desertification

C preservation

D reclamation

2 Which is a consequence of deforestation?

A Animal habitats are destroyed.

B Carbon in the atmosphere is reduced.

C Soil erosion is prevented.

D The rate of extinction is slowed.

Use the graph below to answer question 3.

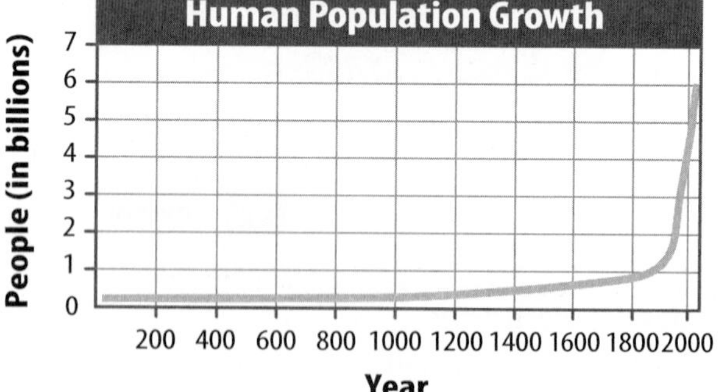

3 During which time span did the human population increase most?

A 1400–1600

B 1600–1800

C 1800–1900

D 1900–2000

4 Which accounts for the least water use in the United States?

A electricity-generating power plants

B irrigation of agricultural crops

C mines, livestock, and aquaculture

D public supply, including houses

5 Which is a point source of water pollution?

A discharge pipes

B runoff from farms

C runoff from construction sites

D runoff from urban areas

6 Which air pollutant contains ozone?

A acid precipitation

B carbon monoxide

C CFCs

D smog

Use the figure below to answer question 7.

7 What is the function of the well in the figure above?

A to generate electricity

B to monitor quality of groundwater

C to prevent pollution of nearby land

D to treat hazardous water

8 Which action helps prevent water pollution?

A pouring motor oil on the ground

B putting hazardous wastes in the trash

C using fertilizers when gardening

D using vinegar when cleaning

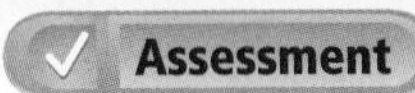

Online Standardized Test Practice

9 What effect does ozone near Earth's surface have on the human body?

A It increases lung function.

B It increases throat irritation.

C It reduces breathing problems.

D It reduces skin cancer.

Use the figure below to answer question 10.

10 Which term describes what is shown in the figure above?

A acid precipitation

B global warming

C greenhouse effect

D urban sprawl

11 Which results in habitat destruction?

A reclamation

B reforestation

C urban sprawl

D water conservation

Constructed Response

Use the figure below to answer questions 12 and 13.

12 Which events shown in the figure remove carbon dioxide from the atmosphere?

13 Relate the carbon cycle shown in the figure to global warming and the greenhouse effect.

14 List two actions that help prevent air pollution. Then explain the pros and the cons of taking each action.

15 Explain how taking a hot shower can impact the environment.

16 Create an advertisement for a solar car. Include information about the environmental impacts of the car in your ad.

NEED EXTRA HELP?																
If You Missed Question...	1	2	3	4	5	6	7	8	9	10	11	12	13	14	15	16
Go to Lesson...	2	2	1	3	3	4	2	3	4	2	2	4	4	4	1	4

Unit 4

LIFE: Changes & Interactions

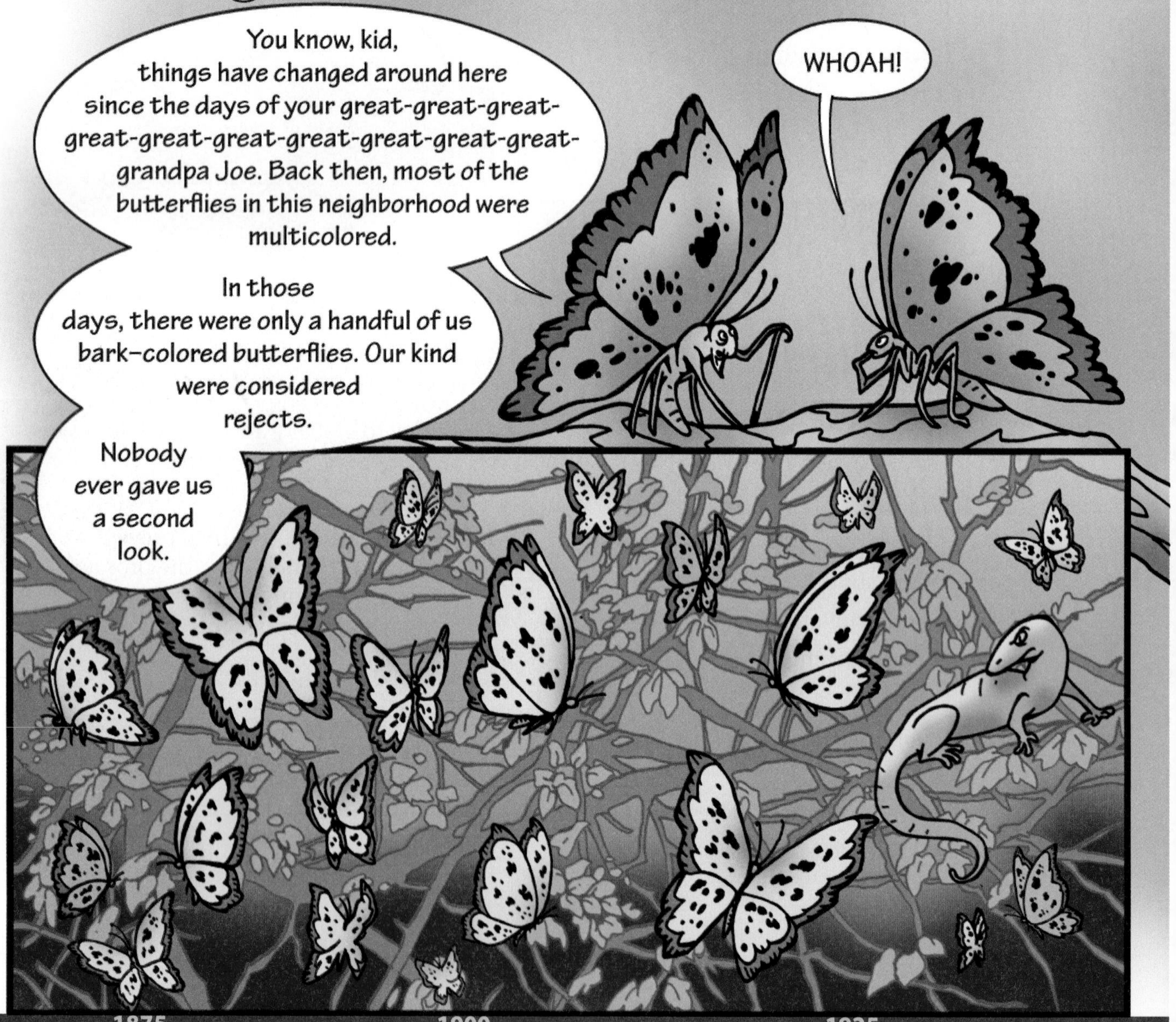

You know, kid, things have changed around here since the days of your great-great-great-great-great-great-great-great-great-great-grandpa Joe. Back then, most of the butterflies in this neighborhood were multicolored.

In those days, there were only a handful of us bark-colored butterflies. Our kind were considered rejects.

Nobody ever gave us a second look.

WHOAH!

1875 1900 1925

1859
Charles Darwin publishes *On the Origin of Species,* in which he explains his theory of natural selection.

1865
Gregor Mendel traces inheritance patterns of certain traits in pea plants and publishes *Experiments on Plant Hybridization.*

1905
Nettie Stevens and Edmund Wilson independently describe the XY sex-determination system, in which males have XY chromosomes and females have XX chromosomes.

1910
Thomas Hunt Morgan determines that genes are carried on chromosomes.

1933
Jean Brachet shows that DNA is found in chromosomes and that RNA is present in the cytoplasm of all cells.

1950 — 1975 — 2000

1953
James D. Watson and Francis Crick develop the double-helix model of DNA.

1964
Howard Temin and David Baltimore independently discover that some viruses can reverse the direction of DNA to RNA transcription.

1985
Alec Jeffreys coins the term *DNA fingerprinting* and develops the procedure later used in paternity, immigration, and murder cases.

2003
The Human Genome Project is completed with 99% of the human genome sequenced to 99.99% accuracy.

Inquiry
Visit ConnectED for this unit's STEM activity.

Graphs

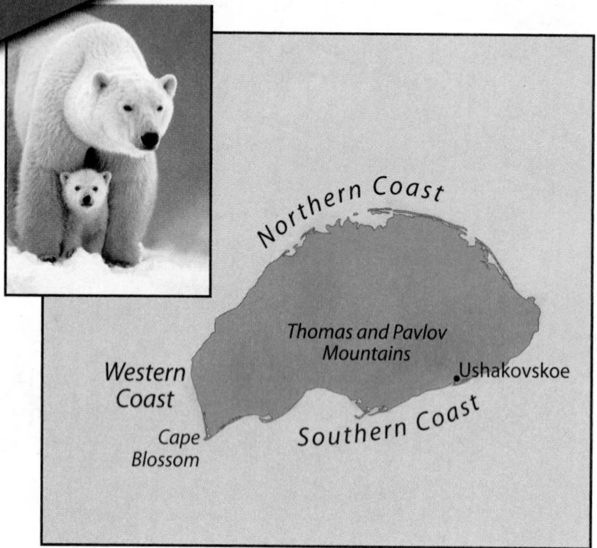

Figure 1 Scientists collect data about polar bears on Wrangel Island, Russia.

Polar bears are one of the largest land mammals. They hunt for food on ice packs that stretch across the Arctic Ocean. Recently, ice in the Arctic has not been as thick as it has been in the past. In addition, the ice does not cover as much area as it used to, making it difficult for polar bears to hunt. Scientists collect data about how these changes in the ice affect polar bear populations. One well-studied population of polar bears is on Wrangel Island, Russia, shown in **Figure 1.** Scientists collect and study data on polar bears to draw conclusions and make predictions about a possible polar bear extinction. Scientists often use graphs to better understand data. A **graph** is a type of chart that shows relationships between variables. Scientists use graphs to visually organize and summarize data. You can use different types of graphs to present different kinds of data.

Types of Graphs

Bar Graphs

The horizontal *x*-axis on a bar graph often contains categories rather than measurements. The heights of the bars show the measured quantity. For example, the *x*-axis on this bar graph contains different locations on Wrangel Island. The heights of the bars show how many bears researchers observed. The different colors show the age categories of polar bears. Where were ten adult polar bears observed?

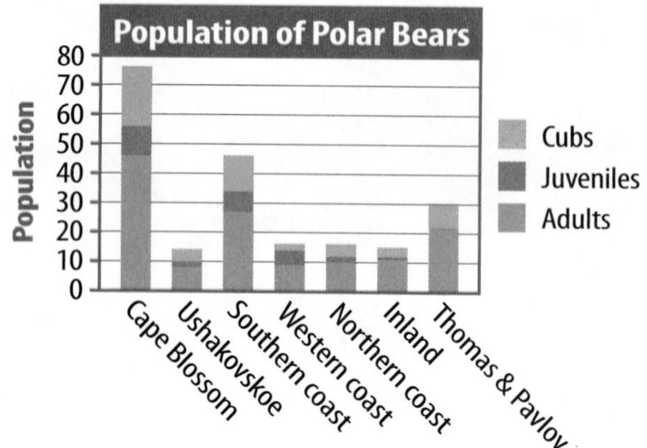

Circle Graphs

A circle graph usually illustrates the percentage of each category of data as it relates to the whole. This circle graph shows the percentage of different age categories of polar bears on Wrangel Island. Adults, shown by the blue color, make up the largest percentage of the total population. This circle graph contains similar data to the bar graph but presents it in a different way. What percentage of the total polar bear population are cubs?

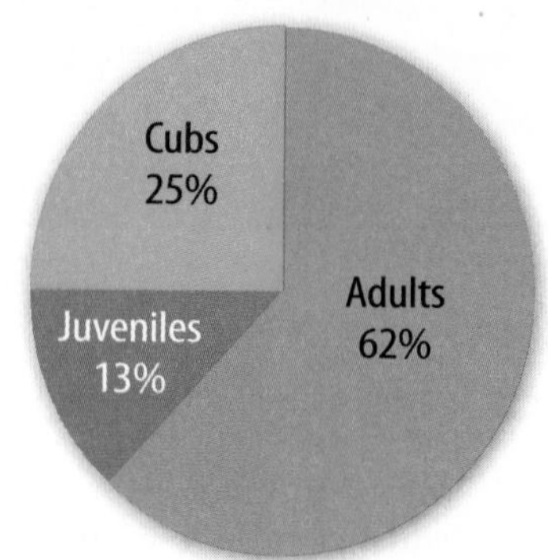

30 minutes

What can graphs tell you about polar bears?

A colleague gives you some data she collected about polar bears on Wrangel Island. She observed the condition of bears near Cape Blossom and classified the bears as starving, average, or healthy. She also recorded the age category of each bear. What can you learn by graphing these data?

1. Make a bar graph of the number of bears in each category that are starving, in average condition, or healthy.
2. Add the numbers of starving bears. Add the total number of bears. Divide the number of starving bears by the total number of bears and multiply by 100 to calculate the percentage of starving bears. Repeat the calculations to find the percentages of average-condition and healthy bears. Make a circle graph showing the different conditions of the bears. For more information on how to make circle graphs, go to the Science Skill Handbook in the back of your book.

	Starving	Average	Healthy
Adult	3	11	14
Juvenile	4	33	13
Cub	3	12	6

Analyze and Conclude

1. **Analyze** On your bar graph, indicate how you can tell which age category of bears is the healthiest.
2. **Determine** What group of bears do you think left the most walrus carcasses? Explain.

Line Graphs

A line graph helps you analyze how a change in one variable affects another variable. Scientists on Wrangel Island counted all the polar bears on the island each year for 10 years. They plotted each year of the survey on the horizontal *x*-axis and the bear population on the vertical *y*-axis. The population decreased between years 2 and 4. It increased between years 6 and 8. How did the population change during the last three years of the survey?

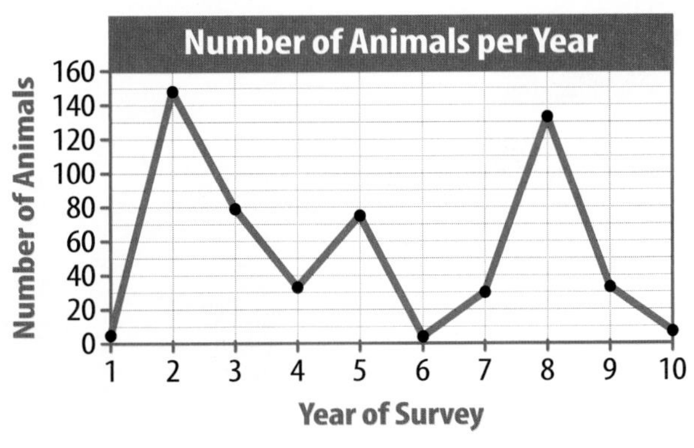

Double Line Graphs

You can use a double line graph to compare relationships of two sets of data. The blue line represents the population of polar bears. The red line represents the number of walrus carcasses found on Wrangel Island. You can see that the blue and orange lines follow a similar pattern. This tells scientists that these two sets of data are related. Walruses are an important food source for polar bears on the island.

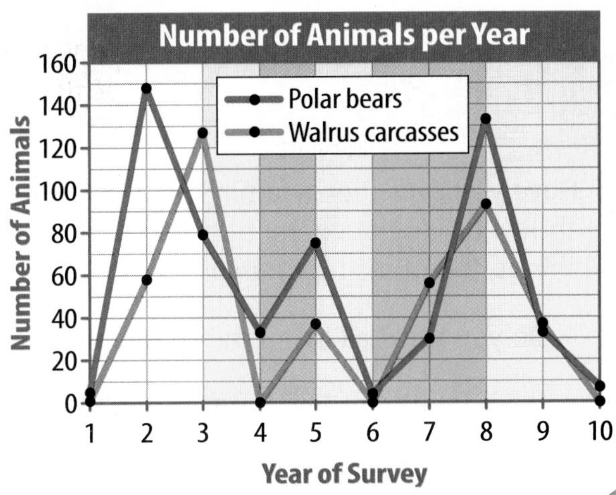

Chapter 10

Reproduction of Organisms

Why do living things reproduce?

Inquiry Time to bond?

Have you ever seen a family of animals, such as the one of penguins shown here? Notice the baby penguin beside its parents. Like all living things, penguins reproduce.

- Do you think all living things have two parents?
- What might happen if the penguins did not reproduce?
- Why do living things reproduce?

Get Ready to Read

What do you think?

Before you read, decide if you agree or disagree with each of these statements. As you read this chapter, see if you change your mind about any of the statements.

1. Humans produce two types of cells: body cells and sex cells.
2. Environmental factors can cause variation among individuals.
3. Two parents always produce the best offspring.
4. Cloning produces identical individuals from one cell.
5. All organisms have two parents.
6. Asexual reproduction occurs only in microorganisms.

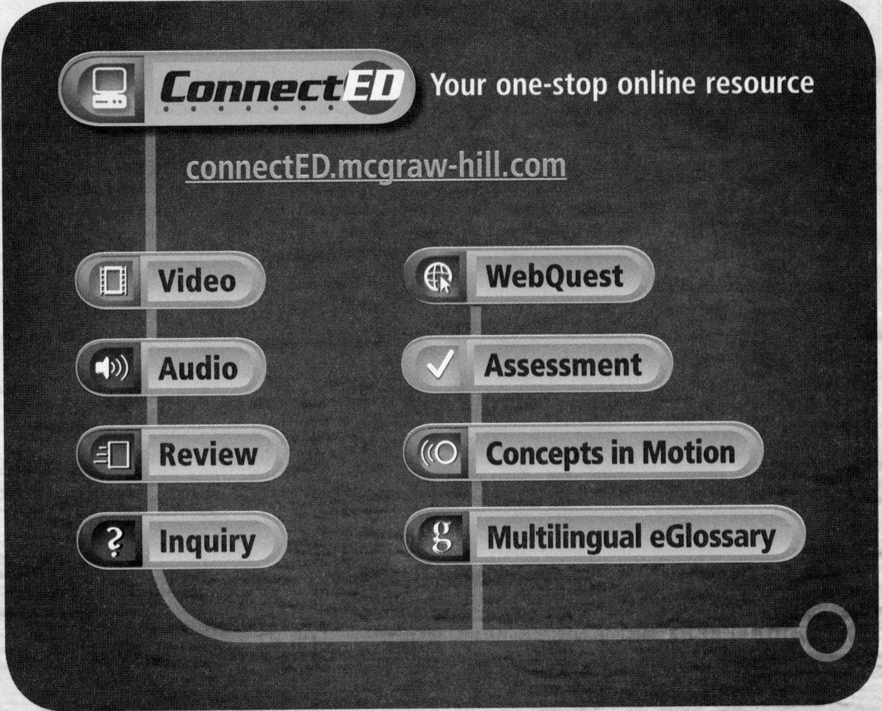

Lesson 1

Sexual Reproduction and Meiosis

Reading Guide

Key Concepts
ESSENTIAL QUESTIONS

- What is sexual reproduction, and why is it beneficial?
- What is the order of the phases of meiosis, and what happens during each phase?
- Why is meiosis important?

Vocabulary

sexual reproduction p. 357
egg p. 357
sperm p. 357
fertilization p. 357
zygote p. 357
diploid p. 358
homologous chromosomes p. 358
haploid p. 359
meiosis p. 359

Multilingual eGlossary

Video BrainPOP®

Academic Standards for Science

8.3.1 Explain that reproduction is essential for the continuation of every species and is the mechanism by which all organisms transmit genetic information.

Also covers: 8.3.2, 8.3.3, 8.3.10, 8.NS.7

Inquiry Modern Art?

This photo looks like a piece of modern art. It is actually an image of plant cells. The cells are dividing by a process that occurs during the production of sex cells.

Inquiry Launch Lab

15 minutes

Why do offspring look different?

Unless you're an identical twin, you probably don't look exactly like any siblings you might have. You might have differences in physical characteristics such as eye color, hair color, ear shape, or height. Why are there differences in the offspring from the same parents?

1. Read and complete a lab safety form.
2. Open the **paper bag** labeled *Male Parent,* and, without looking, remove three **beads.** Record the bead colors in your Science Journal, and replace the beads.
3. Open the **paper bag** labeled *Female Parent,* and remove three **beads.** Record the bead colors, and replace the beads.
4. Repeat steps 2 and 3 for each member of the group.
5. After each member has recorded his or her bead colors, study the results. Each combination of male and female beads represents an offspring.

Think About This

1. Compare your group's offspring to another group's offspring. What similarities or differences do you observe?
2. What caused any differences you observed? Explain.
3. **Key Concept** Why might this type of reproduction be beneficial to an organism?

What is sexual reproduction?

Have you ever seen a litter of kittens? One kitten might have orange fur like its mother. A second kitten might have gray fur like its father. Still another kitten might look like a combination of both parents. How is this possible?

The kittens look different because of sexual reproduction. **Sexual reproduction** *is a type of reproduction in which the genetic materials from two different cells combine, producing an offspring.* The cells that combine are called sex cells. Sex cells form in reproductive organs. *The female sex cell, an* **egg,** *forms in an ovary. The male sex cell, a* **sperm,** *forms in a testis. During a process called* **fertilization** (fur tuh luh ZAY shun), *an egg cell and a sperm cell join together.* This produces a new cell. *The new cell that forms from fertilization is called a* **zygote.** As shown in **Figure 1,** the zygote develops into a new organism.

Review Personal Tutor

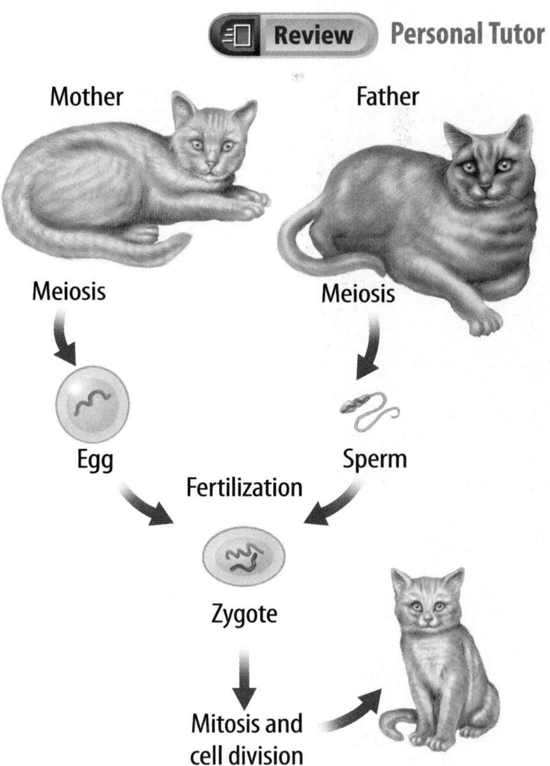

Figure 1 The zygote that forms during fertilization can become a multicellular organism.

Diploid Cells

Following fertilization, a zygote goes through mitosis and cell division. These processes produce nearly all the cells in a multicellular organism. Organisms that reproduce sexually form two kinds of cells—body cells and sex cells. In body cells of most organisms, similar chromosomes occur in pairs. **Diploid** *cells are cells that have pairs of chromosomes.*

Chromosomes

Pairs of chromosomes that have genes for the same traits arranged in the same order are called **homologous** (huh MAH luh gus) **chromosomes.** Because one chromosome is inherited from each parent, the chromosomes are not identical. For example, the kittens mentioned earlier in this lesson inherited a gene for orange fur color from their mother. They also inherited a gene for gray fur color from their father. So, some kittens might be orange, and some might be gray. Both genes for fur color are at the same place on homologous chromosomes, but they code for different colors.

Different organisms have different numbers of chromosomes. Recall that diploid cells have pairs of chromosomes. Notice in **Table 1** that human diploid cells have 23 pairs of chromosomes for a total of 46 chromosomes. A fruit fly diploid cell has 4 pairs of chromosomes, and a rice diploid cell has 12 pairs of chromosomes.

Table 1 An organism's chromosomes can be matched as pairs of chromosomes that have genes for the same traits.

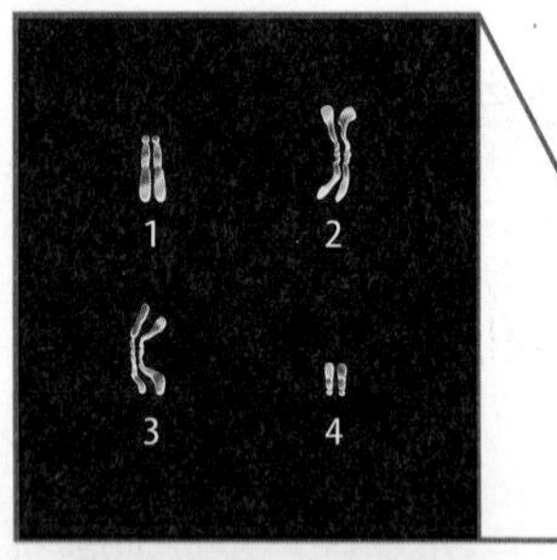

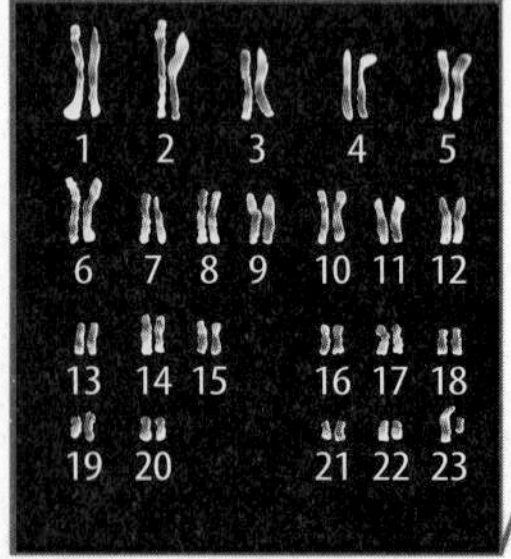

Concepts in Motion Interactive Table

Table 1 Chromosomes of Selected Organisms

Organism	Number of Chromosomes	Number of Homologous Pairs
Fruit fly	8	4
Rice	24	12
Yeast	32	16
Cat	38	19
Human	46	23
Dog	78	39
Fern	1,260	630

Having the correct number of chromosomes is very important. If a zygote has too many or too few chromosomes, it will not develop properly. For example, a genetic condition called Down syndrome occurs when a person has an extra copy of chromosome 21. A person with Down syndrome can have short stature, heart defects, or mental disabilities.

Haploid Cells

Organisms that reproduce sexually also form egg and sperm cells, or sex cells. Sex cells have only one chromosome from each pair of chromosomes. **Haploid** *cells are cells that have only one chromosome from each pair.* Organisms produce sex cells using a special type of cell division called meiosis. *In* **meiosis,** *one diploid cell divides and makes four haploid sex cells.* Meiosis occurs only during the formation of sex cells.

Reading Check How do diploid cells differ from haploid cells?

WORD ORIGIN

haploid
from Greek *haploeides,* means "single"

The Phases of Meiosis

Next, you will read about the phases of meiosis. Many of the phases might seem familiar to you because they also occur during mitosis. Recall that mitosis and cytokinesis involve one division of the nucleus and the cytoplasm. Meiosis involves two divisions of the nucleus and the cytoplasm. These divisions are called meiosis I and meiosis II. They result in four haploid cells—cells with half the number of chromosomes as the original cell. As you read about meiosis, think about how it produces sex cells with a reduced number of chromosomes.

FOLDABLES®

Make a shutter-fold book and label it as shown. Use it to describe and illustrate the phases of meiosis.

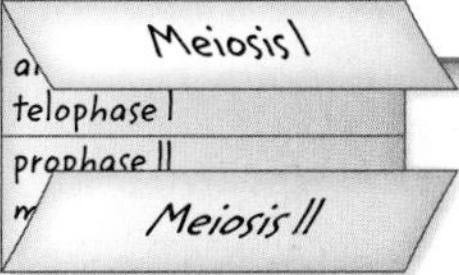

Inquiry MiniLab **20 minutes**

How does one cell produce four cells?

When a diploid cell goes through meiosis, it produces four haploid cells. How does this happen?

1. Read and complete a lab safety form.
2. Make a copy of the diagram by tracing circles around a **jar lid** on your **paper.** Label as shown.
3. Use **chenille craft wires** to make red and blue duplicated chromosomes 2.5 cm long and green and yellow duplicated chromosomes 1.5 cm long. Recall that a duplicated chromosome has two sister chromatids connected at the centromere.
4. Place the chromosomes in the diploid cell.
5. Move one long chromosome and one short chromosome into each of the middle cells.
6. Separate the two strands of the chromosomes, and place one strand into each of the haploid cells.

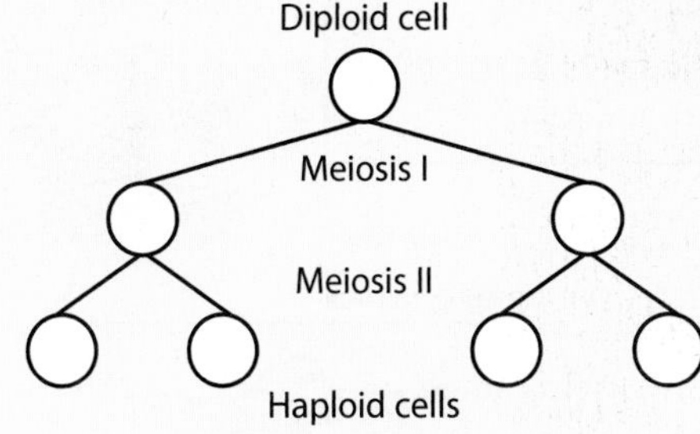

Analyze and Conclude

1. **Describe** What happened to the chromosomes during meiosis I? During meiosis II?
2. **Think Critically** Why are two haploid cells (sperm and egg) needed to form a zygote?
3. **Key Concept** How does one cell form four cells during meiosis?

Phases of Meiosis I

A reproductive cell goes through interphase before beginning meiosis I, which is shown in **Figure 2.** During interphase, the reproductive cell grows and copies, or duplicates, its chromosomes. Each duplicated chromosome consists of two sister chromatids joined together by a centromere.

1 Prophase I In the first phase of meiosis I, duplicated chromosomes condense and thicken. Homologous chromosomes come together and form pairs. The membrane surrounding the nucleus breaks apart, and the nucleolus disappears.

2 Metaphase I Homologous chromosome pairs line up along the middle of the cell. A spindle fiber attaches to each chromosome.

3 Anaphase I Chromosome pairs separate and are pulled toward the opposite ends of the cell. Notice that the sister chromatids stay together.

4 Telophase I A nuclear membrane forms around each group of duplicated chromosomes. The cytoplasm divides through cytokinesis and two daughter cells form. Sister chromatids remain together.

Meiosis Concepts in Motion Animation

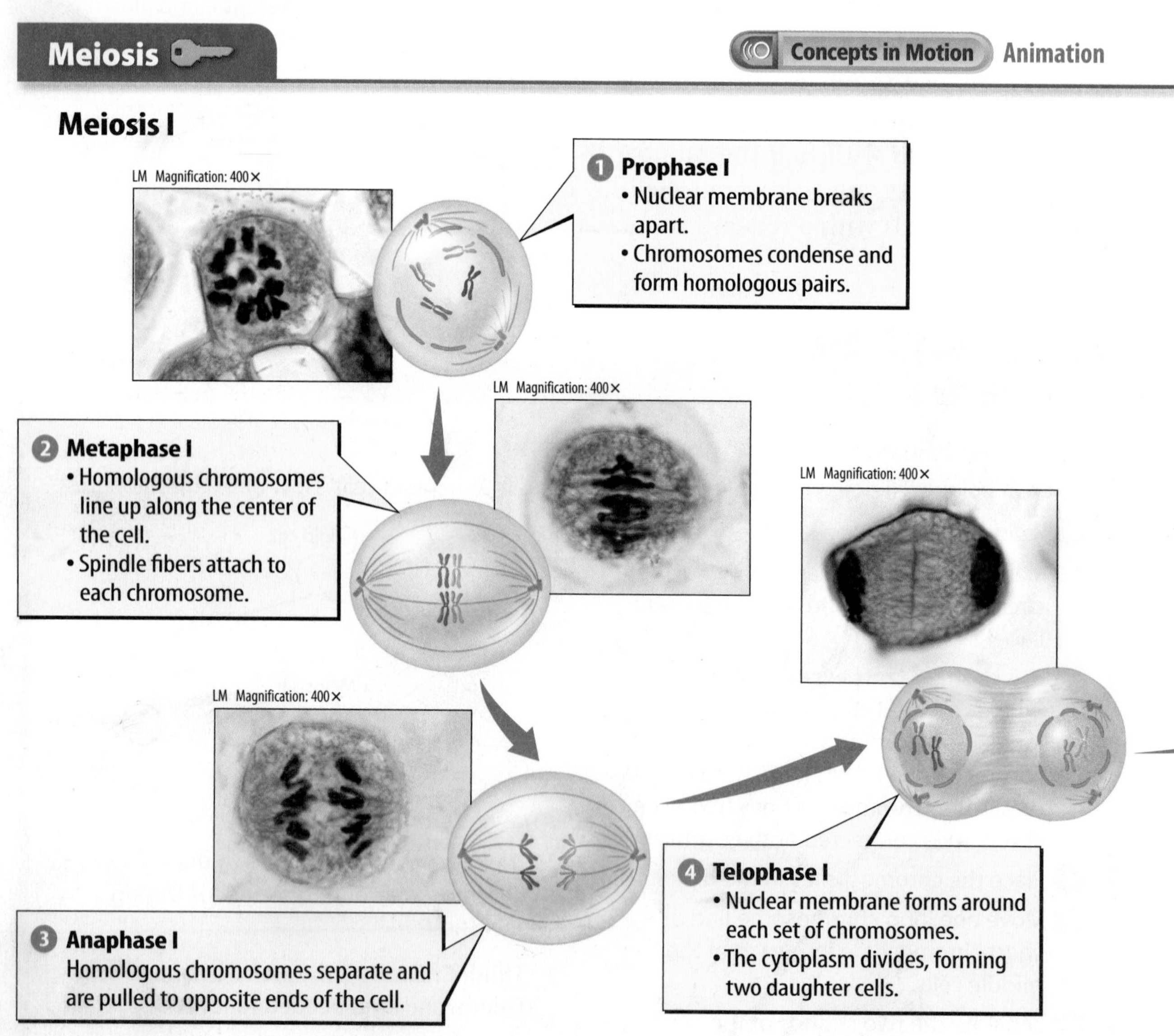

Meiosis I
LM Magnification: 400×
1 Prophase I
• Nuclear membrane breaks apart.
• Chromosomes condense and form homologous pairs.
2 Metaphase I
• Homologous chromosomes line up along the center of the cell.
• Spindle fibers attach to each chromosome.
LM Magnification: 400×
LM Magnification: 400×
LM Magnification: 400×
3 Anaphase I
Homologous chromosomes separate and are pulled to opposite ends of the cell.
4 Telophase I
• Nuclear membrane forms around each set of chromosomes.
• The cytoplasm divides, forming two daughter cells.

Figure 2 Unlike mitosis, meiosis involves two divisions of the nucleus and the cytoplasm.

Phases of Meiosis II

After meiosis I, the two cells formed during this stage go through a second division of the nucleus and the cytoplasm. This process, shown in **Figure 2,** is called meiosis II.

5 Prophase II Chromosomes are not copied again before prophase II. They remain as condensed, thickened sister chromatids. The nuclear membrane breaks apart, and the nucleolus disappears in each cell.

6 Metaphase II The pairs of sister chromatids line up along the middle of the cell in single file.

7 Anaphase II The sister chromatids of each duplicated chromosome are pulled away from each other and move toward opposite ends of the cells.

8 Telophase II During the final phase of meiosis—telophase II—a nuclear membrane forms around each set of chromatids, which are again called chromosomes. The cytoplasm divides through cytokinesis, and four haploid cells form.

Key Concept Check List the phases of meiosis in order.

Meiosis II

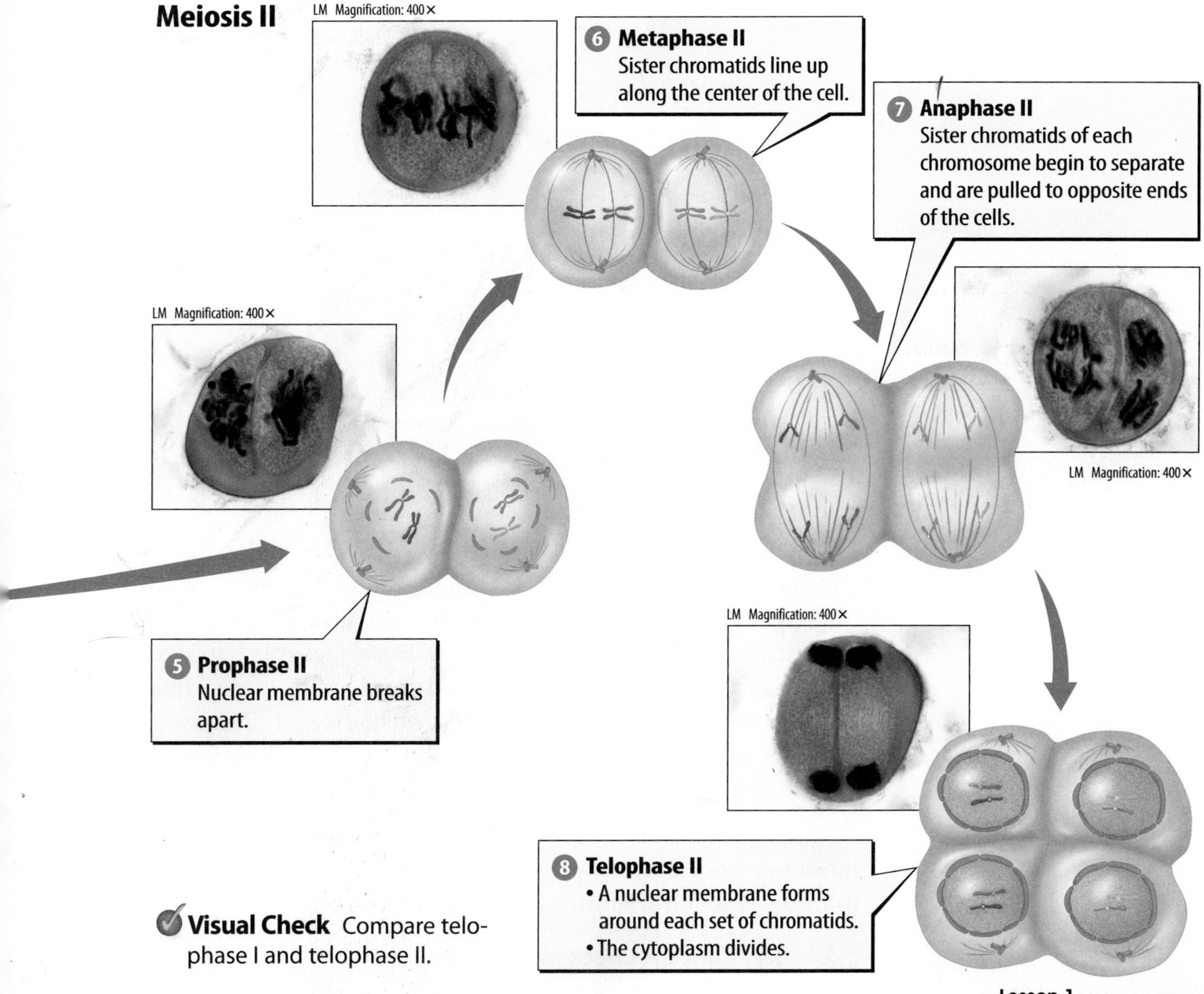

LM Magnification: 400×

6 Metaphase II
Sister chromatids line up along the center of the cell.

7 Anaphase II
Sister chromatids of each chromosome begin to separate and are pulled to opposite ends of the cells.

LM Magnification: 400×

LM Magnification: 400×

5 Prophase II
Nuclear membrane breaks apart.

LM Magnification: 400×

8 Telophase II
- A nuclear membrane forms around each set of chromatids.
- The cytoplasm divides.

Visual Check Compare telophase I and telophase II.

Why is meiosis important?

Meiosis forms sex cells with the correct haploid number of chromosomes. This maintains the correct diploid number of chromosomes in organisms when sex cells join. Meiosis also creates genetic variation by producing haploid cells.

Maintaining Diploid Cells

Recall that diploid cells have pairs of chromosomes. Meiosis helps to maintain diploid cells in offspring by making haploid sex cells. When haploid sex cells join together during fertilization, they make a diploid zygote, or fertilized egg. The zygote then divides by mitosis and cell division and creates a diploid organism. **Figure 3** illustrates how the diploid number is maintained in ducks.

Figure 3 Meiosis ensures that the chromosome number of a species stays the same from generation to generation.

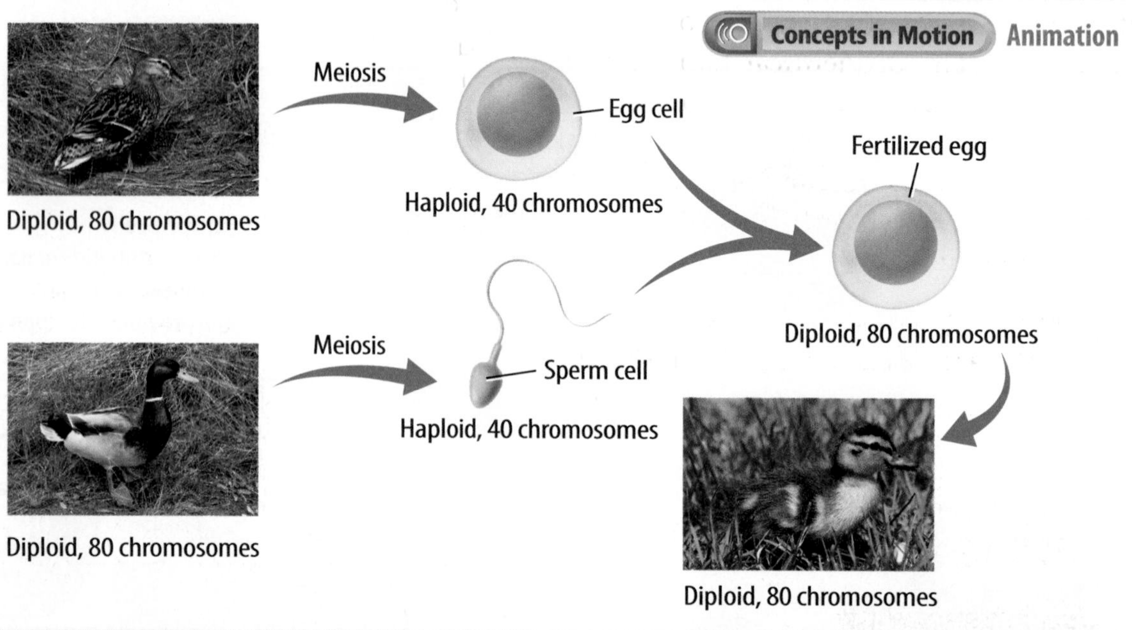

Creating Haploid Cells

The result of meiosis is haploid sex cells. This helps maintain the correct number of chromosomes in each generation of offspring. The formation of haploid cells also is important because it allows for genetic variation. How does this happen? Sex cells can have different sets of chromosomes, depending on how chromosomes line up during metaphase I. Because a cell only gets one chromosome from each pair of homologous chromosomes, the resulting sex cells can be different.

The genetic makeup of offspring is a combination of chromosomes from two sex cells. Variation in the sex cells results in more genetic variation in the next generation.

 **Key Concept Check** Why is meiosis important?

How do mitosis and meiosis differ?

Sometimes, it's hard to remember the differences between mitosis and meiosis. Use **Table 2** to review these processes.

During mitosis and cell division, a body cell and its nucleus divide once and produce two identical cells. These processes are important for growth and repair or replacement of damaged tissue. Some organisms reproduce by these processes. The two daughter cells produced by mitosis and cell division have the same genetic information.

During meiosis, a reproductive cell and its nucleus divide twice and produce four cells—two pairs of identical haploid cells. Each cell has half the number of chromosomes as the original cell. Meiosis happens in the reproductive organs of multicellular organisms. Meiosis forms sex cells used for sexual reproduction.

Reading Check How many cells are produced during mitosis? During meiosis?

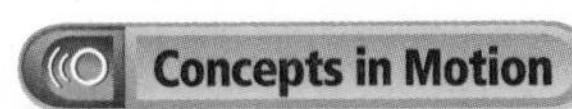

Interactive Table

Table 2 Comparison of Types of Cell Division

Characteristic	Meiosis	Mitosis and Cell Division
Number of chromosomes in parent cell	diploid	diploid
Type of parent cell	reproductive	body
Number of divisions of nucleus	2	1
Number of daughter cells produced	4	2
Chromosome number in daughter cells	haploid	diploid
Function	forms sperm and egg cells	growth, cell repair, some types of reproduction

Math Skills

Use Proportions

An equation that shows that two ratios are equivalent is a proportion. The ratios $\frac{1}{2}$ and $\frac{3}{6}$ are equivalent, so they can be written as $\frac{1}{2} = \frac{3}{6}$.

You can use proportions to figure out how many daughter cells will be produced during mitosis. If you know that one cell produces two daughter cells at the end of mitosis, you can use proportions to calculate how many daughter cells will be produced by eight cells undergoing mitosis.

Set up an equation of the two ratios. $\frac{1}{2} = \frac{8}{y}$

Cross-multiply. $1 \times y = 8 \times 2$

$1y = 16$

Divide each side by 1. $y = 16$

Practice

You know that one cell produces four daughter cells at the end of meiosis. How many daughter cells would be produced if eight sex cells undergo meiosis?

- Math Practice
- Personal Tutor

Advantages of Sexual Reproduction

Review Vocabulary
DNA
the genetic information in a cell

Did you ever wonder why a brother and a sister might not look alike? The answer is sexual reproduction. The main advantage of sexual reproduction is that offspring inherit half their DNA from each parent. Offspring are not likely to inherit the same DNA from the same parents. Different DNA means that each offspring has a different set of traits. This results in genetic variation among the offspring.

Key Concept Check Why is sexual reproduction beneficial?

Genetic Variation

As you just read, genetic variation exists among humans. You can look at your friends to see genetic variation. Genetic variation occurs in all organisms that reproduce sexually. Consider the plants shown in **Figure 4.** The plants are members of the same species, but they have different traits, such as the ability to resist disease.

Due to genetic variation, individuals within a population have slight differences. These differences might be an advantage if the environment changes. Some individuals might have traits that enable them to survive unusually harsh conditions such as a drought or severe cold. Other individuals might have traits that make them resistant to disease.

Genetic Variation

Disease-resistant cassava leaves

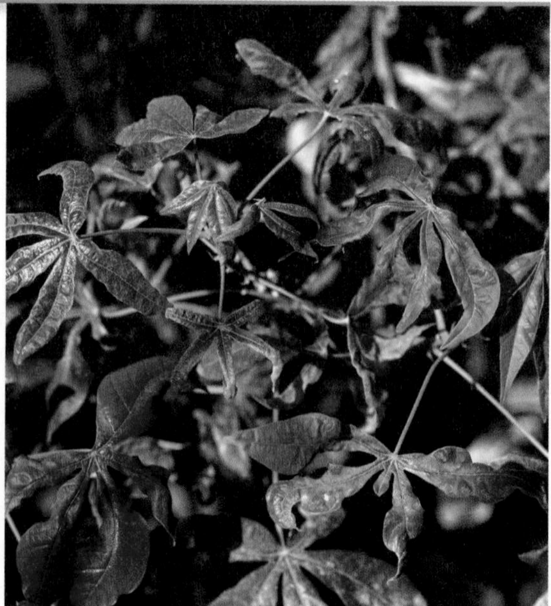
Cassava leaves with cassava mosaic disease

Figure 4 These plants belong to the same species. However, one is more disease-resistant than the other.

Visual Check How does cassava mosaic disease affect cassava leaves?

Selective Breeding

Did you know that broccoli, kohlrabi, kale, and cabbage all descended from one type of mustard plant? It's true. More than 2,000 years ago farmers noticed that some mustard plants had different traits, such as larger leaves or bigger flower buds. The farmers started to choose which traits they wanted by selecting certain plants to reproduce and grow. For example, some farmers chose only the plants with the biggest flowers and stems and planted their seeds. Over time, the offspring of these plants became what we know today as broccoli, shown in **Figure 5.** This process is called selective breeding. Selective breeding has been used to develop many types of plants and animals with desirable traits. It is another example of the benefits of sexual reproduction.

Figure 5 The wild mustard is the common ancestor to all these plants.

Selective Breeding

Disadvantages of Sexual Reproduction

Although sexual reproduction produces more genetic variation, it does have some disadvantages. Sexual reproduction takes time and energy. Organisms have to grow and develop until they are mature enough to produce sex cells. Then the organisms have to form sex cells—either eggs or sperm. Before they can reproduce, organisms usually have to find mates. Searching for a mate can take a long time and requires energy. The search for a mate might also expose individuals to predators, diseases, or harsh environmental conditions. In addition, sexual reproduction is limited by certain factors. For example, fertilization cannot take place during pregnancy, which can last as long as two years in some mammals.

Reading Check What are the disadvantages of sexual reproduction?

Lesson 1 Review

Online Quiz

Visual Summary

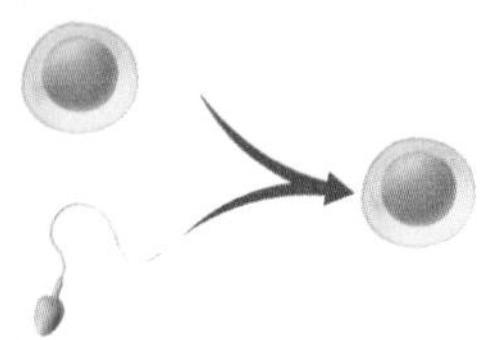

Fertilization occurs when an egg cell and a sperm cell join together.

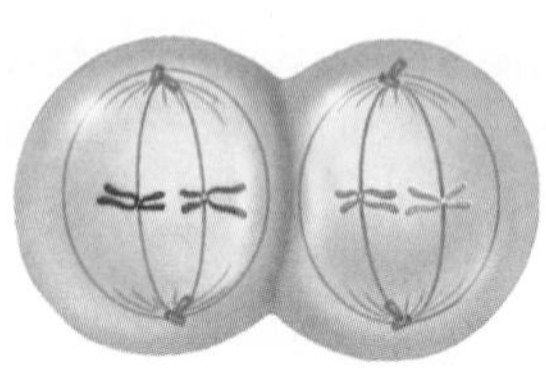

Organisms produce sex cells through meiosis.

Sexual reproduction results in genetic variation among individuals.

FOLDABLES®

Use your lesson Foldable to review the lesson. Save your Foldable for the project at the end of the chapter.

What do you think NOW?

You first read the statements below at the beginning of the chapter.

1. Humans produce two types of cells: body cells and sex cells.
2. Environmental factors can cause variation among individuals.
3. Two parents always produce the best offspring.

Did you change your mind about whether you agree or disagree with the statements? Rewrite any false statements to make them true.

Use Vocabulary

1. **Use the terms** *egg, sperm,* and *zygote* in a sentence.
2. **Distinguish** between haploid and diploid.
3. **Define** *homologous chromosomes* in your own words.

Understand Key Concepts 

4. **Define** sexual reproduction.
5. **Draw and label** the phases of meiosis.
6. Homologous chromosomes separate during which phase of meiosis?
   A. anaphase I
   B. anaphase II
   C. metaphase I
   D. metaphase II

Interpret Graphics

7. **Organize** Copy and fill in the graphic organizer below to sequence the phases of meiosis I and meiosis II.

Meiosis I [ ] → [ ] → [ ] → [ ]

Meiosis II [ ] → [ ] → [ ] → [ ]

Critical Thinking

8. **Analyze** Why is the result of the stage of meiosis shown below an advantage for organisms that reproduce sexually?

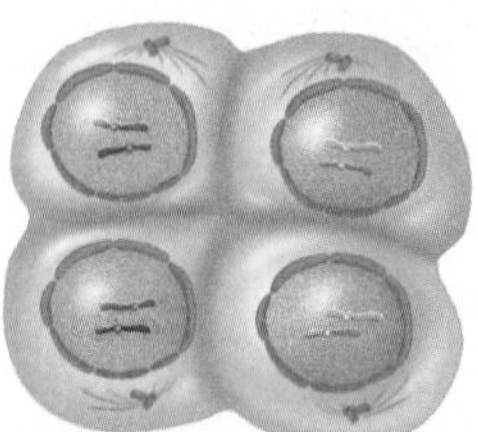

Math Skills 

Review

Math Practice

9. If 15 cells undergo meiosis, how many daughter cells would be produced?
10. If each daughter cell from question 9 undergoes meiosis, how many total daughter cells will there be?

CAREERS in SCIENCE

The Spider Mating Dance

Meet Norman Platnick, a scientist studying spiders.

Norman Platnick is fascinated by all spider species—from the dwarf tarantula-like spiders of Panama to the blind spiders of New Zealand. These are just two of the over 1,400 species he's discovered worldwide.

How does Platnick identify new species? One way is the pedipalps. Every spider has two pedipalps, but they vary in shape and size among the over 40,000 species. Pedipalps look like legs but function more like antennae and mouthparts. Male spiders use their pedipalps to aid in reproduction.

Getting Ready When a male spider is ready to mate, he places a drop of sperm onto a sheet of silk he constructs. Then he dips his pedipalps into the drop to draw up the sperm.

Finding a Mate The male finds a female of the same species by touch or by sensing certain chemicals she releases.

Courting and Mating Males of some species court a female with a special dance. For other species, a male might present a female with a gift, such as a fly wrapped in silk. During mating, the male uses his pedipalps to transfer sperm to the female.

What happens to the male after mating? That depends on the species. Some are eaten by the female, while others move on to find new mates.

▲ **Spiders reproduce sexually, so each offspring has a unique combination of genes from its parents. Over many generations, this genetic variation has led to the incredible diversity of spiders in the world today.**

◀ **Norman Platnick is an arachnologist (uh rak NAH luh just) at the American Museum of Natural History. Arachnologists are scientists who study spiders.**

It's Your Turn

RESEARCH Select a species of spider and research its mating rituals. What does a male do to court a female? What is the role of the female? What happens to the spiderlings after they hatch? Use images to illustrate a report on your research.

Lesson 2

Asexual Reproduction

Reading Guide

Key Concepts
ESSENTIAL QUESTIONS

- What is asexual reproduction, and why is it beneficial?
- How do the types of asexual reproduction differ?

Vocabulary

asexual reproduction p. 369
fission p. 370
budding p. 371
regeneration p. 372
vegetative reproduction p. 373
cloning p. 374

g Multilingual eGlossary

Academic Standards for Science

8.3.1 Explain that reproduction is essential for the continuation of every species and is the mechanism by which all organisms transmit genetic information.

8.3.2 Compare and contrast the transmission of genetic information in sexual and asexual reproduction.

Also covers: 8.NS.1, 8.NS.7, 8.NS.11

Inquiry Plants on Plants?

Look closely at the edges of this plant's leaves. Tiny plants are growing there. This type of plant can reproduce without meiosis and fertilization.

Inquiry Launch Lab

20 minutes

How do yeast reproduce?

Some organisms can produce offspring without meiosis or fertilization. You can observe this process when you add sugar and warm water to dried yeast.

1. Read and complete a lab safety form.
2. Pour 125 mL of water into a **beaker.** The water should be at a temperature of 34°C.
3. Add 5 g of **sugar** and 5 g of **yeast** to the water. Stir slightly. Record your observations after 5 minutes in your Science Journal.
4. Using a **dropper,** put a drop of the yeast solution on a **microscope slide.** Place a **coverslip** over the drop.
5. View the yeast solution under a **microscope.** Draw what you see in your Science Journal.

Think About This

1. What evidence did you observe that yeast reproduce?
2. **Key Concept** How do you think this process differs from sexual reproduction?

What is asexual reproduction?

Lunch is over and you are in a rush to get to class. You wrap up your half-eaten sandwich and toss it into your locker. A week goes by before you spot the sandwich in the corner of your locker. The surface of the bread is now covered with fuzzy mold—not very appetizing. How did that happen?

The mold on the sandwich is a type of fungus (FUN gus). A fungus releases enzymes that break down organic matter, such as food. It has structures that penetrate and anchor to food, much like roots anchor plants to soil. A fungus can multiply quickly in part because generally a fungus can reproduce either sexually or asexually. Recall that sexual reproduction involves two parent organisms and the processes of meiosis and fertilization. Offspring inherit half their DNA from each parent, resulting in genetic variation among the offspring.

In **asexual reproduction,** *one parent organism produces offspring without meiosis and fertilization.* Because the offspring inherit all their DNA from one parent, they are genetically identical to each other and to their parent.

Key Concept Check Describe asexual reproduction in your own words.

FOLDABLES®

Fold a sheet of paper into a six-celled chart. Label the front "Asexual Reproduction," and label the chart inside as shown. Use it to compare types of asexual reproduction.

Fission	Mitotic cell division	Budding
Animal regeneration	Vegetative reproduction	Cloning

Types of Asexual Reproduction

There are many different types of organisms that reproduce by asexual reproduction. In addition to fungi, bacteria, protists, plants, and animals can reproduce asexually. In this lesson, you will learn how organisms reproduce asexually.

Fission

Recall that prokaryotes have a simpler cell structure than eukaryotes. A prokaryote's DNA is not contained in a nucleus. For this reason, mitosis does not occur and cell division in a prokaryote is a simpler process than in a eukaryote. *Cell division in prokaryotes that forms two genetically identical cells is known as* **fission.**

WORD ORIGIN
fission
from Latin *fissionem,* means "a breaking up, cleaving"

Fission begins when a prokaryote's DNA molecule is copied. Each copy attaches to the cell membrane. Then the cell begins to grow longer, pulling the two copies of DNA apart. At the same time, the cell membrane begins to pinch inward along the middle of the cell. Finally the cell splits and forms two new identical offspring. The original cell no longer exists.

As shown in **Figure 6,** *E. coli,* a common bacterium, divides through fission. Some bacteria can divide every 20 minutes. At that rate, 512 bacteria can be produced from one original bacterium in about three hours.

Reading Check What advantage might asexual reproduction by fission have over sexual reproduction?

Fission

Figure 6 Bacteria can divide very rapidly through fission.

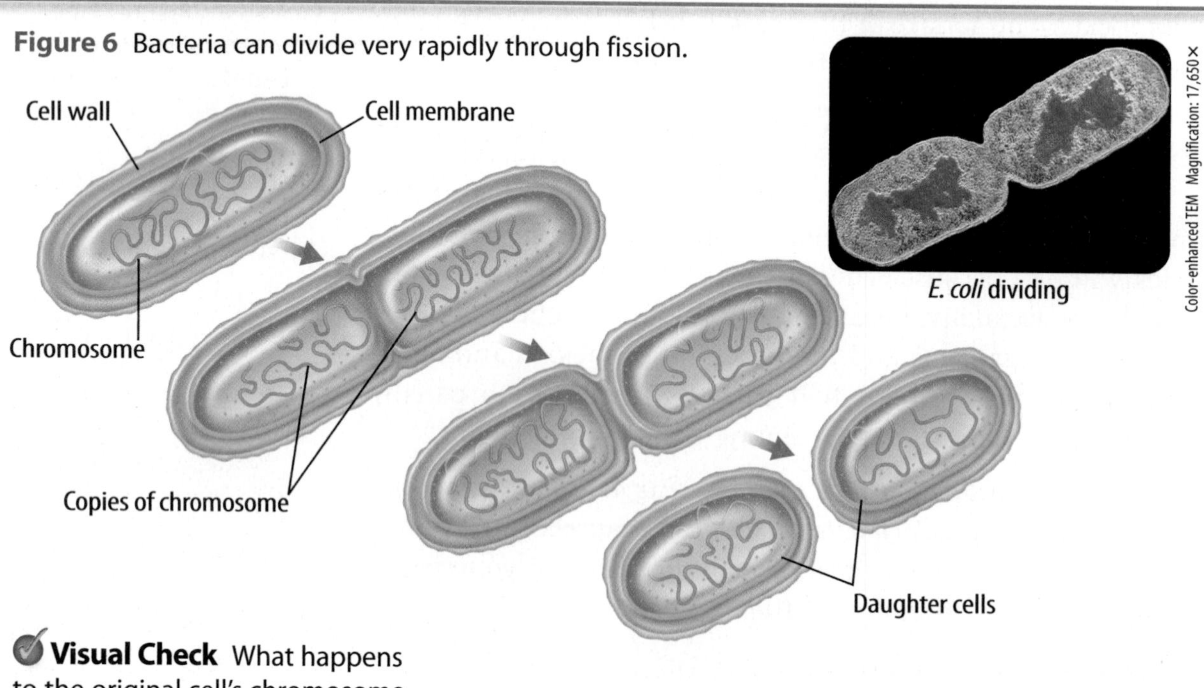

Visual Check What happens to the original cell's chromosome during fission?

Mitotic Cell Division

Many unicellular eukaryotes reproduce by mitotic cell division. In this type of asexual reproduction, an organism forms two offspring through mitosis and cell division. In **Figure 7,** an amoeba's nucleus has divided by mitosis. Next, the cytoplasm and its contents divide through cytokinesis and two new amoebas form.

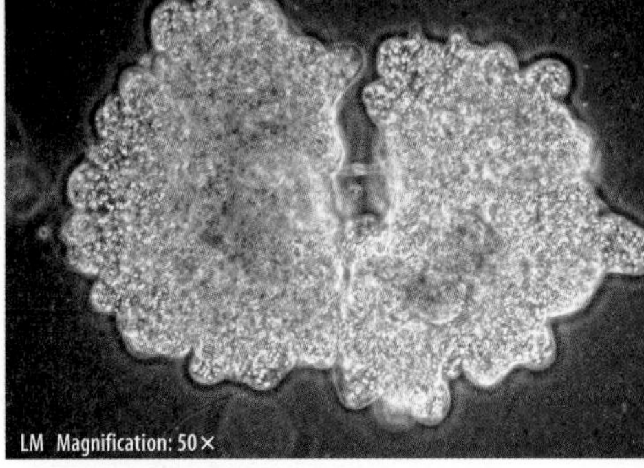

▲ **Figure 7** During mitotic cell division, an amoeba divides its chromosomes and cell contents evenly between the daughter cells.

Budding

In **budding,** *a new organism grows by mitosis and cell division on the body of its parent.* The bud, or offspring, is genetically identical to its parent. When the bud becomes large enough, it can break from the parent and live on its own. In some cases, an offspring remains attached to its parent and starts to form a colony. **Figure 8** shows a hydra in the process of budding. The hydra is an example of a multicellular organism that can reproduce asexually. Unicellular eukaryotes, such as yeast, can also reproduce through budding, as you saw in the Launch Lab.

Budding

Figure 8 The hydra bud has the same genetic makeup as its parent.

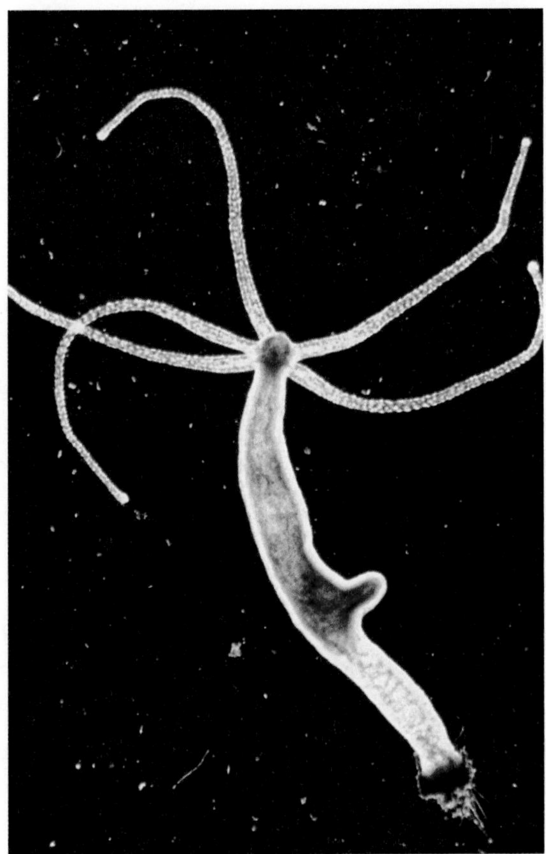

Bud forms.

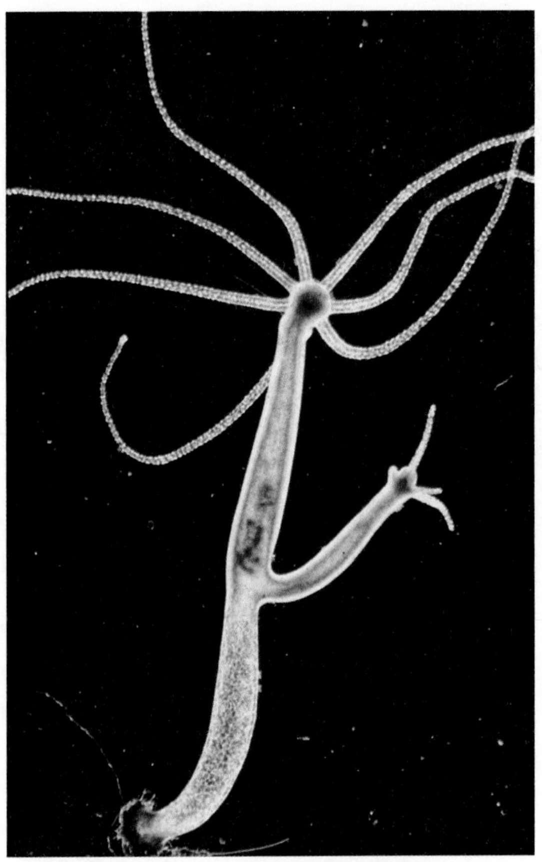

Bud develops a mouth and tentacles.

Animal Regeneration

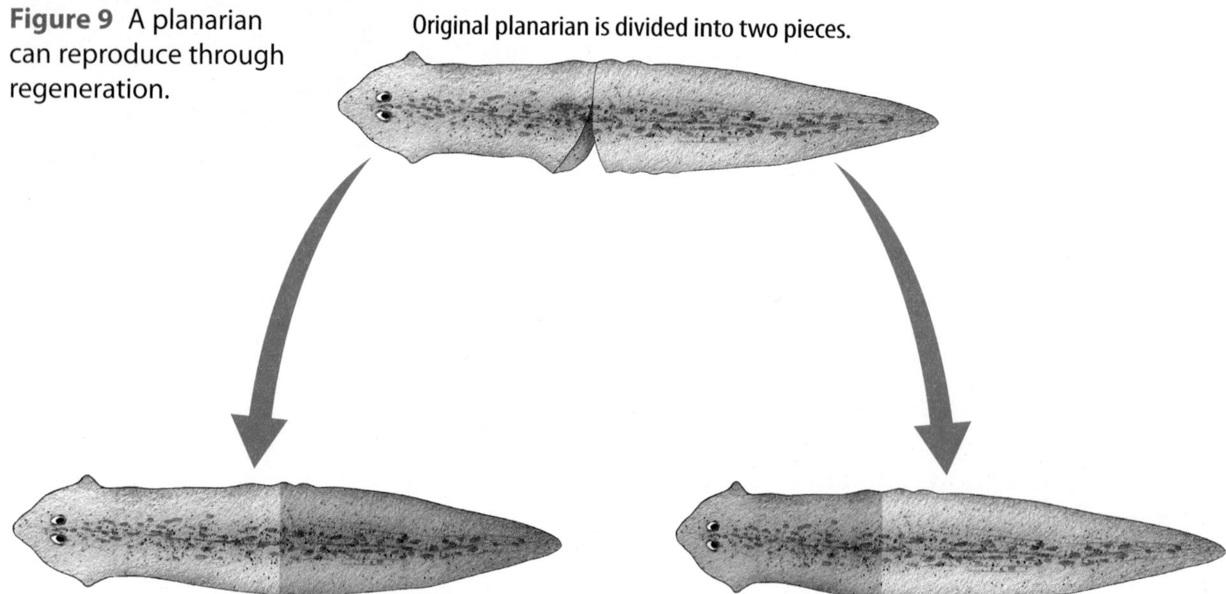

Original planarian is divided into two pieces.
The head end regenerates a new tail.
The tail end regenerates a new head.

Figure 9 A planarian can reproduce through regeneration.

Animal Regeneration

Another type of asexual reproduction, **regeneration**, *occurs when an offspring grows from a piece of its parent.* The ability to regenerate a new organism varies greatly among animals.

Academic Vocabulary
potential
(noun) possibility

Producing New Organisms Some sea stars have five arms. If separated from the parent sea star, each arm has the **potential** to grow into a new organism. To regenerate a new sea star, the arm must contain a part of the central disk of the parent. If conditions are right, one five-armed sea star can produce as many as five new organisms.

Sea urchins, sea cucumbers, sponges, and planarians, such as the one shown in **Figure 9,** can also reproduce through regeneration. Notice that each piece of the original planarian becomes a new organism. As with all types of asexual reproduction, the offspring is genetically identical to the parent.

Reading Check What is true of all cases of asexual reproduction?

Producing New Parts When you hear the term *regeneration,* you might think about a salamander regrowing a lost tail or leg. Regeneration of damaged or lost body parts is common in many animals. Newts, tadpoles, crabs, hydra, and zebra fish are all able to regenerate body parts. Even humans are able to regenerate some damaged body parts, such as the skin and the liver. This type of regeneration, however, is not considered asexual reproduction. It does not produce a new organism.

Vegetative Reproduction

Plants can also reproduce asexually in a process similar to regeneration. **Vegetative reproduction** *is a form of asexual reproduction in which offspring grow from a part of a parent plant.* For example, the strawberry plants shown in **Figure 10** send out long horizontal stems called stolons. Wherever a stolon touches the ground, it can produce roots. Once the stolons have grown roots, a new plant can grow—even if the stolons have broken off the parent plant. Each new plant grown from a stolon is genetically identical to the parent plant.

Vegetative reproduction usually involves structures such as the roots, the stems, and the leaves of plants. In addition to strawberries, many other plants can reproduce by this method, including raspberries, potatoes, and geraniums.

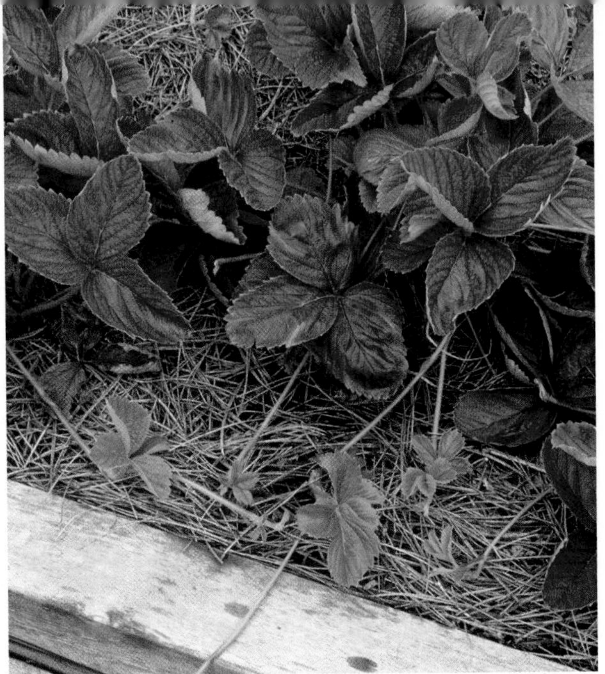

Figure 10 The smaller plants were grown from stolons produced by the parent plant.

Visual Check Which plants in the figure are the parent plants?

Inquiry MiniLab — 15 minutes

What parts of plants can grow?

You probably know that plants can grow from seeds. But you might be surprised to learn that other parts of plants can grow and produce a new plant.

1. Carefully examine the photos of vegetative reproduction.
2. Create a data chart in your Science Journal to record your observations. Identify which part of the plant (leaf, stem, etc.) would be used to grow a new plant.

Analyze and Conclude

1. **Explain** How is the vegetative reproduction you observed a kind of asexual reproduction?
2. **Infer** how farmers or gardeners might use vegetative reproduction.
3. **Key Concept** Describe a method you might use to produce a new plant using vegetative reproduction.

Cloning

Fission, budding, and regeneration are all types of asexual reproduction that can produce genetically identical offspring in nature. In the past, the term *cloning* described any process that produced genetically identical offspring. Today, however, the word usually refers to a technique developed by scientists and performed in laboratories. **Cloning** *is a type of asexual reproduction performed in a laboratory that produces identical individuals from a cell or from a cluster of cells taken from a multicellular organism.* Farmers and scientists often use cloning to make copies of organisms or cells that have desirable traits, such as large flowers.

Science Use v. Common Use

culture

Science Use the process of growing living tissue in a laboratory

Common Use the social customs of a group of people

Plant Cloning Some plants can be cloned using a method called tissue **culture,** as shown in **Figure 11.** Tissue culture enables plant growers and scientists to make many copies of a plant with desirable traits, such as sweet fruit. Also, a greater number of plants can be produced more quickly than by vegetative reproduction.

Tissue culture also enables plant growers to reproduce plants that might have become infected with a disease. To clone such a plant, a scientist can use cells from a part of a plant where they are rapidly undergoing mitosis and cell division. This part of a plant is called a meristem. Cells in meristems are disease-free. Therefore, if a plant becomes infected with a disease, it can be cloned using meristem cells.

Figure 11 New carrot plants can be produced from cells of a carrot root using tissue culture techniques.

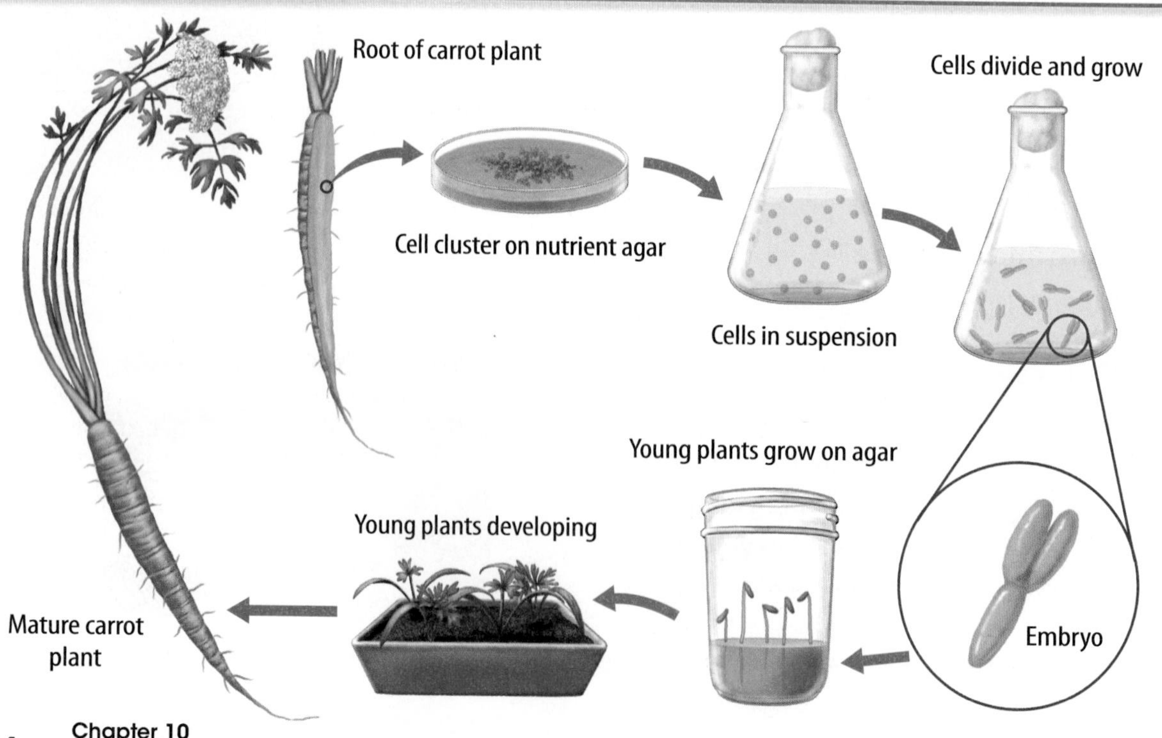

Animal Cloning In addition to cloning plants, scientists have been able to clone many animals. Because all of a clone's chromosomes come from one parent (the donor of the nucleus), the clone is a genetic copy of its parent. The first mammal cloned was a sheep named Dolly. **Figure 12** illustrates how this was done.

Scientists are currently working to save some endangered species from extinction by cloning. Although cloning is an exciting advancement in science, some people are concerned about the high cost and the ethics of this technique. Ethical issues include the possibility of human cloning. You might be asked to consider issues like this during your lifetime.

Key Concept Check Compare and contrast the different types of asexual reproduction.

Figure 12 Scientists used two different sheep to produce the cloned sheep known as Dolly.

Animal Cloning

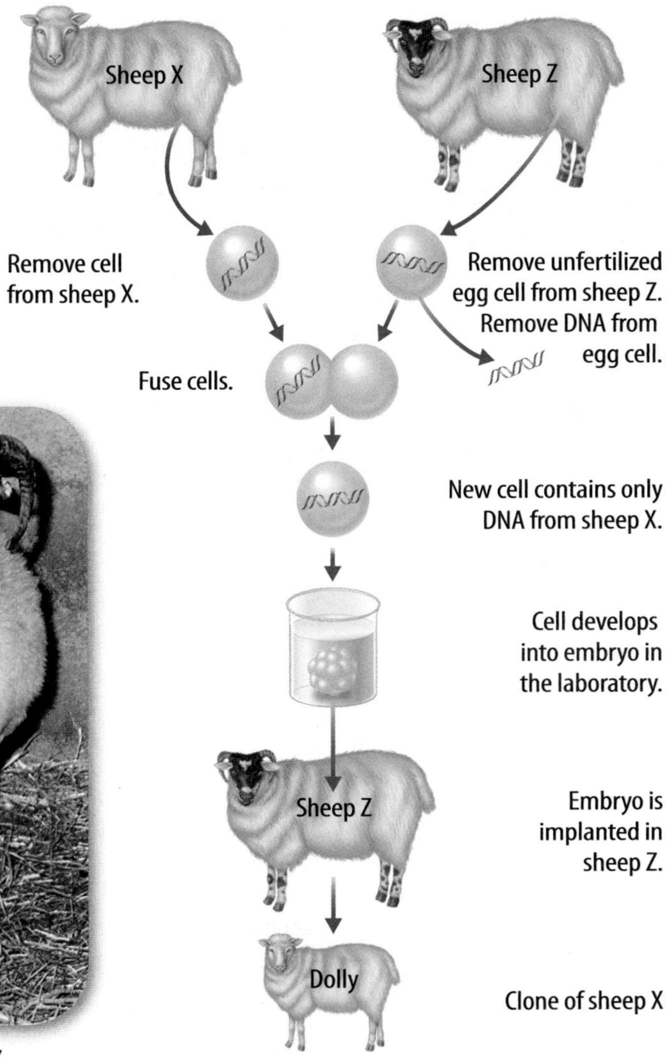

Sheep X

Sheep Z

Remove cell from sheep X.

Remove unfertilized egg cell from sheep Z. Remove DNA from egg cell.

Fuse cells.

New cell contains only DNA from sheep X.

Cell develops into embryo in the laboratory.

Sheep Z

Embryo is implanted in sheep Z.

Dolly

Clone of sheep X

Dolly

Sheep Z

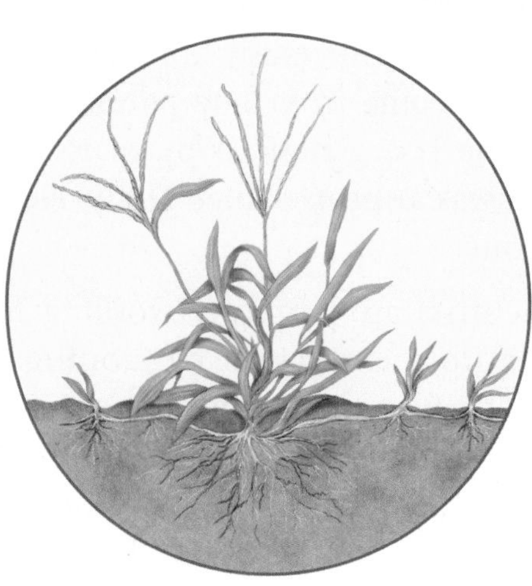

Figure 13 Crabgrass can spread quickly because it reproduces asexually.

Advantages of Asexual Reproduction

What are the advantages to organisms of reproducing asexually? Asexual reproduction enables organisms to reproduce without a mate. Recall that searching for a mate takes time and energy. Asexual reproduction also enables some organisms to rapidly produce a large number of offspring. For example, the crabgrass shown in **Figure 13** reproduces asexually by underground stems called stolons. This enables one plant to spread and colonize an area in a short period of time.

 **Key Concept Check** How is asexual reproduction beneficial?

Disadvantages of Asexual Reproduction

Although asexual reproduction usually enables organisms to reproduce quickly, it does have some disadvantages. Asexual reproduction produces offspring that are genetically identical to their parent. This results in little genetic variation within a population. Why is genetic variation important? Recall from Lesson 1 that genetic variation can give organisms a better chance of surviving if the environment changes. Think of the crabgrass. Imagine that all the crabgrass plants in a lawn are genetically identical to their parent plant. If a certain weed killer can kill the parent plant, then it can kill all the crabgrass plants in the lawn. This might be good for your lawn, but it is a disadvantage for the crabgrass.

Another disadvantage of asexual reproduction involves genetic changes, called mutations, that can occur. If an organism has a harmful mutation in its cells, the mutation will be passed to asexually reproduced offspring. This could affect the offspring's ability to survive.

Lesson 2 Review

Assessment Online Quiz
Inquiry Virtual Lab

Visual Summary

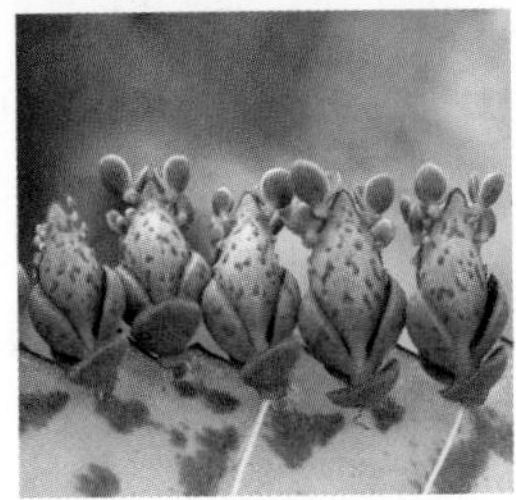

In asexual reproduction, offspring are produced without meiosis and fertilization.

Cloning is one type of asexual reproduction.

Asexual reproduction enables organisms to reproduce quickly.

FOLDABLES®

Use your lesson Foldable to review the lesson. Save your Foldable for the project at the end of the chapter.

What do you think NOW?

You first read the statements below at the beginning of the chapter.

4. Cloning produces identical individuals from one cell.

5. All organisms have two parents.

6. Asexual reproduction occurs only in microorganisms.

Did you change your mind about whether you agree or disagree with the statements? Rewrite any false statements to make them true.

Use Vocabulary

1. In ________ _________, only one parent organism produces offspring.
2. **Define** the term *cloning* in your own words.
3. **Use the term** *regeneration* in a sentence.

Understand Key Concepts 

4. **State** two reasons why asexual reproduction is beneficial.
5. Which is an example of asexual reproduction by regeneration?
   - **A.** cloning sheep
   - **B.** lizard regrowing a tail
   - **C.** sea star arm producing a new organism
   - **D.** strawberry plant producing stolons
6. **Construct** a chart that includes an example of each type of asexual reproduction.

Interpret Graphics

7. **Examine** the diagram below and write a short paragraph describing the process of tissue culture.

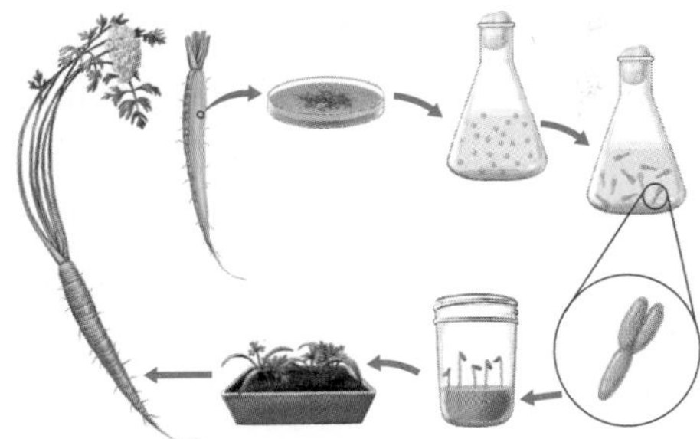

8. **Organize** Copy and fill in the graphic organizer below to list the different types of asexual reproduction that occur in multicellular organisms.

Critical Thinking

9. **Justify** the use of cloning to save endangered animals.

40 minutes

Mitosis and Meiosis

Materials

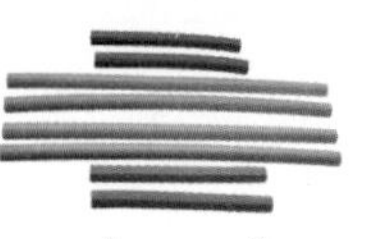

pool noodles

Safety

During cellular reproduction, many changes occur in the nucleus of cells involving the chromosomes. You could think about these changes as a set of choreographed moves like you would see in a dance. In this lab you will act out the moves that chromosomes make during mitosis and meiosis in order to understand the steps that occur when cells reproduce.

Ask a Question

How do chromosomes change and move during mitosis and meiosis?

Make Observations

1. Read and complete a lab safety form.
2. Form a cell nucleus with four chromosomes represented by students holding four different colors of pool noodles. Other students play the part of the nuclear membrane and form a circle around the chromosomes.

3. The chromosomes duplicate during interphase. Each chromosome is copied, creating a chromosome with two sister chromatids.
4. Perform mitosis.
   - **a.** During prophase, the nuclear membrane breaks apart, and the nucleolus disappears.
   - **b.** In metaphase, duplicated chromosomes align in the middle of the cell.
   - **c.** The sister chromatids separate in anaphase.
   - **d.** In telophase, the nuclear membrane reforms around two daughter cells.
5. Repeat steps 2 and 3. Perform meiosis.
   - **a.** In prophase I, the nuclear membrane breaks apart, the nucleolus disappears, and homologous chromosomes pair up.
   - **b.** In metaphase I, homologous chromosomes line up along the center of the cell.
   - **c.** During anaphase I, the pairs of homologous chromosomes separate.
   - **d.** In telophase I, the nuclear membrane reforms.
   - **e.** Each daughter cell now performs meiosis II independently. In prophase II, the nuclear membrane breaks down, and the nucleolus disappears.
   - **f.** During metaphase II, duplicated chromosomes align in the middle of the cell.

g. Sister chromatids separate in anaphase II.

h. In telophase II, the nuclear membrane reforms.

Form a Hypothesis

6 Use your observations to form a hypothesis about the results of an error in meiosis. For example, you might explain the results of an error during anaphase I.

Test your Hypothesis

7 Perform meiosis, incorporating the error you chose in step 6.

8 Compare the outcome to your hypothesis. Does your data support your hypothesis? If not, revise your hypothesis and repeat steps 6–8.

Analyze and Conclude

9 **Compare and Contrast** How are mitosis and meiosis I similar? How are they different?

10 **The Big Idea** What is the difference between the chromosomes in cells at the beginning and the end of mitosis? At the beginning and end of meiosis?

11 **Critique** How did performing cellular replications using pool noodles help you understand mitosis and meiosis?

Communicate Your Results

Create a chart of the changes and movements of chromosomes in each of the steps in meiosis and mitosis. Include colored drawings of chromosomes and remember to draw the cell membranes.

Extension

Investigate some abnormalities that occur when mistakes are made during mitosis or meiosis. Draw a chart of the steps of reproduction showing how the mistake is made. Write a short description of the problems that result from the mistake.

Lab Tips

- Figure out where the boundaries of your cell are before you start.
- Review the phases of mitosis and meiosis before beginning to act out how the chromosomes move during each process.

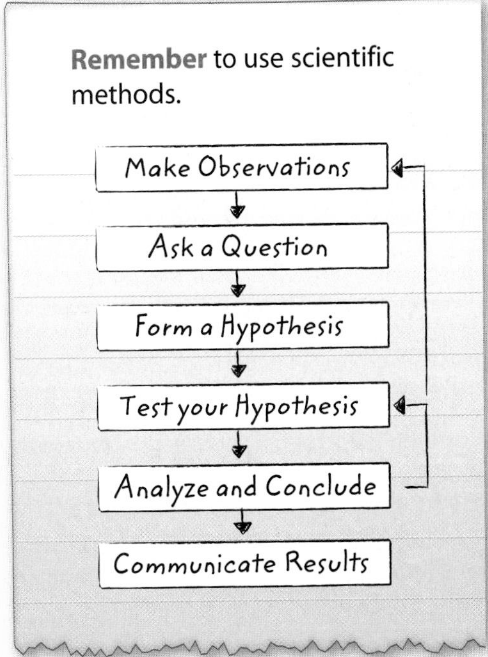

Chapter 10 Study Guide

Reproduction ensures the survival of species.

Key Concepts Summary

Lesson 1: Sexual Reproduction and Meiosis

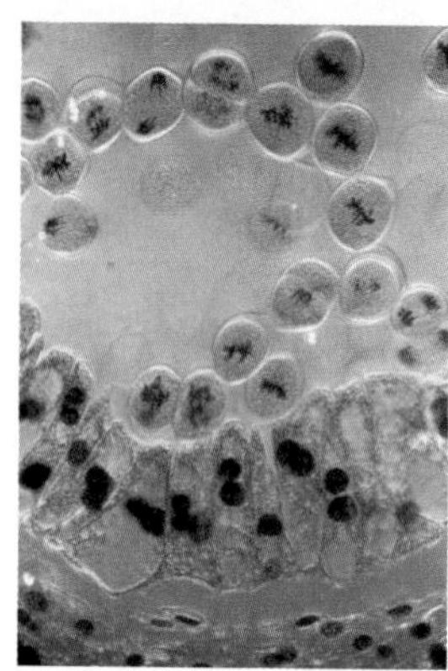

- **Sexual reproduction** is the production of an offspring from the joining of a **sperm** and an **egg.**
- Division of the nucleus and cytokinesis happens twice in **meiosis.** Meiosis I separates homologous chromosomes. Meiosis II separates sister chromatids.
- Meiosis maintains the chromosome number of a species from one generation to the next.

Vocabulary

sexual reproduction p. 357
egg p. 357
sperm p. 357
fertilization p. 357
zygote p. 357
diploid p. 358
homologous chromosomes p. 358
haploid p. 359
meiosis p. 359

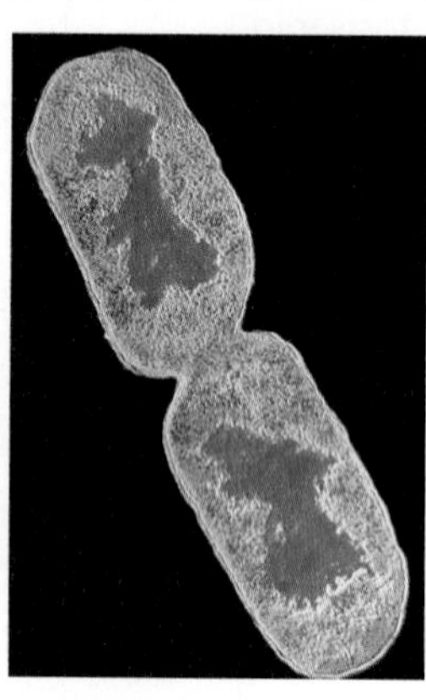

Lesson 2: Asexual Reproduction

- **Asexual reproduction** is the production of offspring by one parent, which results in offspring that are genetically identical to the parent.
- Types of asexual reproduction include **fission,** mitotic cell division, **budding, regeneration, vegetative reproduction,** and **cloning.**
- Asexual reproduction can produce a large number of offspring in a short amount of time.

asexual reproduction p. 369
fission p. 370
budding p. 371
regeneration p. 372
vegetative reproduction p. 373
cloning p. 374

Study Guide

Review

- Personal Tutor
- Vocabulary eGames
- Vocabulary eFlashcards

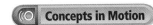

FOLDABLES® Chapter Project

Assemble your lesson Foldables as shown to make a Chapter Project. Use the project to review what you have learned in this chapter.

Use Vocabulary

1. Define meiosis in your own words.
2. Distinguish between an egg and a zygote.
3. Use the vocabulary words *haploid* and *diploid* in a sentence.
4. Cell division in prokaryotes is called ________.
5. Define the term *vegetative reproduction* in your own words.
6. Distinguish between regeneration and budding.
7. A type of reproduction in which the genetic materials from two different cells combine, producing an offspring, is called ________ ________.

Concepts in Motion Interactive Concept Map

Link Vocabulary and Key Concepts

Copy this concept map, and then use vocabulary terms from the previous page to complete the concept map.

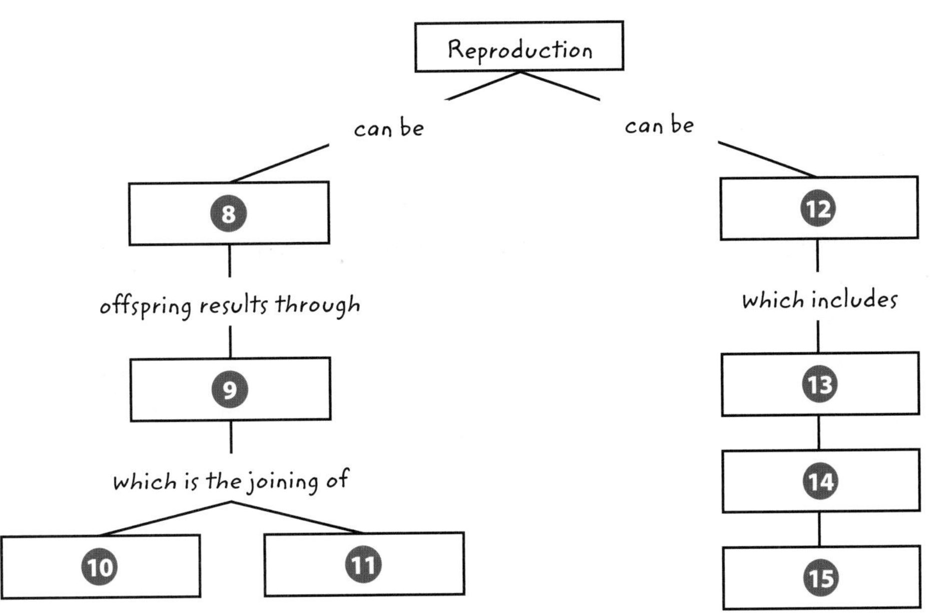

Chapter 10 Review

Understand Key Concepts 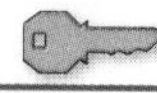

1. Which is an advantage of sexual reproduction?
   A. Offspring are identical to the parents.
   B. Offspring with genetic variation are produced.
   C. Organisms don't have to search for a mate.
   D. Reproduction is rapid.

2. Which describes cells that have only one copy of each chromosome?
   A. diploid
   B. haploid
   C. homologous
   D. zygote

Use the figure below to answer questions 3 and 4.

3. Which phase of meiosis I is shown in the diagram?
   A. anaphase I
   B. metaphase I
   C. prophase I
   D. telophase I

4. Which phase of meiosis I comes after the phase in the diagram?
   A. anaphase I
   B. metaphase I
   C. prophase I
   D. telophase I

5. Tissue culture is an example of which type of reproduction?
   A. budding
   B. cloning
   C. fission
   D. regeneration

6. Which type of asexual reproduction is shown in the figure below?

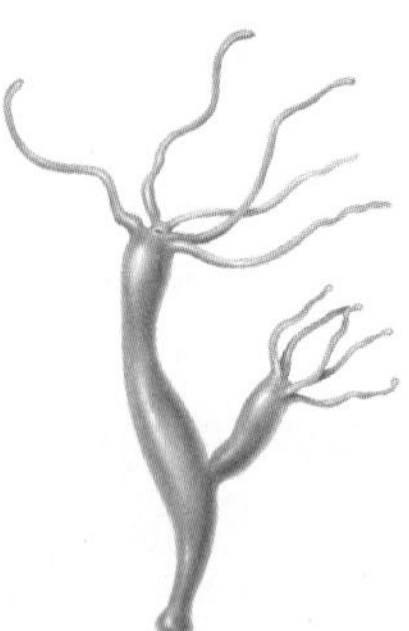

   A. budding
   B. cloning
   C. fission
   D. regeneration

7. A bacterium can reproduce by which method?
   A. budding
   B. cloning
   C. fission
   D. regeneration

8. Which statement best describes why genetic variation is beneficial to populations of organisms?
   A. Individuals look different from one another.
   B. Only one parent is needed to produce offspring.
   C. Populations of the organism increase more rapidly.
   D. Species can better survive environmental changes.

9. In which phase of meiosis II do sister chromatids line up along the center of the cell?
   A. anaphase II
   B. metaphase II
   C. prophase II
   D. telophase II

Critical Thinking

10 **Contrast** haploid cells and diploid cells.

11 **Model** Make a model of homologous chromosomes using materials of your choice.

12 **Form a hypothesis** about the effect of a mistake in separating homologous chromosomes during meiosis.

13 **Analyze** Crabgrass reproduces asexually by vegetative reproduction. Use the figure below to explain why this form of reproduction is an advantage for the crabgrass.

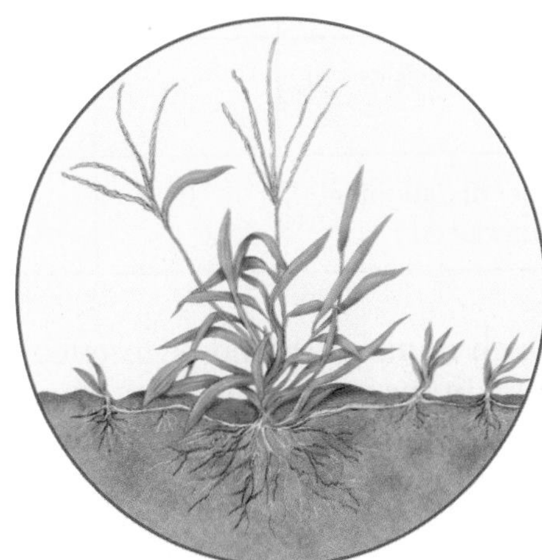

14 **Compare** budding and cloning.

15 **Create** a table showing the advantages and disadvantages of asexual reproduction.

16 **Compare and contrast** sexual reproduction and asexual reproduction.

Writing in Science

17 **Create** a plot for a short story that describes an environmental change and the importance of genetic variation in helping a species survive that change. Include characters, a setting, a climax, and an ending for your plot.

REVIEW THE BIG IDEA

18 Think of all the advantages of sexual and asexual reproduction. Use these ideas to summarize why organisms reproduce.

19 The baby penguin below has a mother and a father. Do all living things have two parents? Explain.

Math Skills

Math Practice

Use Proportions

20 During mitosis, the original cell produces two daughter cells. How many daughter cells will be produced if 250 mouse cells undergo mitosis?

21 During meiosis, the original reproductive cell produces four daughter cells. How many daughter cells will be produced if 250 mouse reproductive cells undergo meiosis?

22 Two reproductive cells undergo meiosis. Each daughter cell also undergoes meiosis. How many cells are produced when the daughter cells divide?

Standardized Test Practice

Record your answers on the answer sheet provided by your teacher or on a sheet of paper.

Multiple Choice

1 How do sea stars reproduce?

A cloning

B fission

C animal regeneration

D vegetative reproduction

Use the diagram below to answer questions 2 and 3.

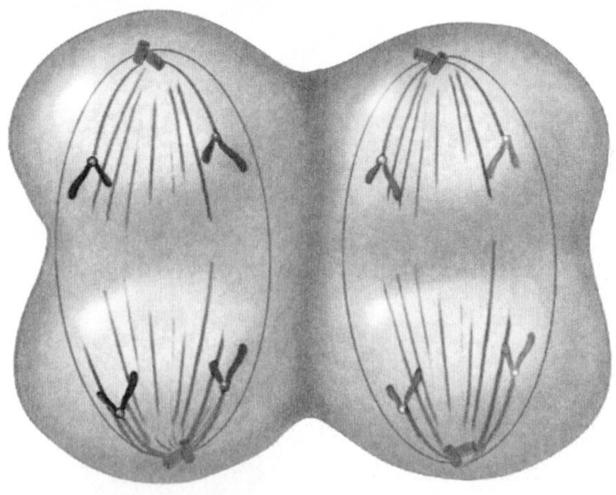

2 What stage of meiosis does the drawing illustrate?

A anaphase I

B anaphase II

C prophase I

D prophase II

3 Which stage takes place *before* the one in the diagram above?

A metaphase I

B metaphase II

C telophase I

D telophase II

4 What type of asexual reproduction includes stolons?

A budding

B cloning

C animal regeneration

D vegetative reproduction

Use the table below to answer question 5.

Comparison of Types of Cell Division		
Characteristic	**Meiosis**	**Mitosis**
Number of divisions of nucleus	2	A
Number of daughter cells produced	B	2

5 Which numbers should be inserted for A and B in the chart?

A A=1 and B=2

B A=1 and B=4

C A=2 and B=2

D A=2 and B=4

6 Which results in genetic variation?

A cloning

B fission

C sexual reproduction

D vegetative reproduction

7 Which is NOT true of homologous chromosomes?

A The are identical.

B They are in pairs.

C They have genes for the same traits.

D They have genes that are in the same order.

Assessment

Online Standardized Test Practice

Use the figure below to answer question 8.

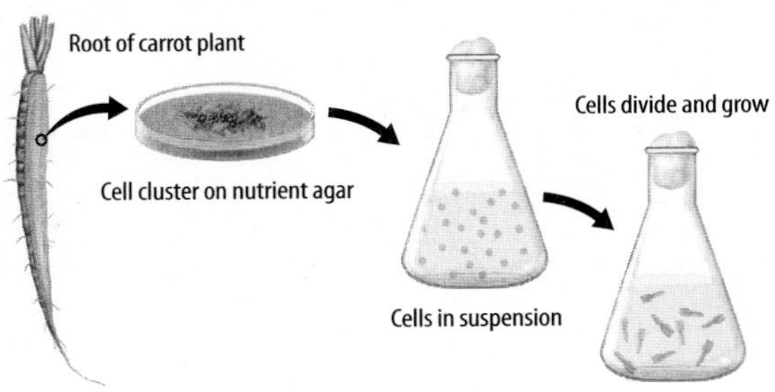

8 The figure illustrates the first four steps of which reproductive process?

A animal cloning

B regeneration

C tissue culture

D vegetative reproduction

9 If 12 reproductive cells undergo meiosis, how many daughter cells will result?

A 12

B 24

C 48

D 60

10 Which is NOT true of asexual reproduction?

A Many offspring can be produced rapidly.

B Offspring are different from the parents.

C Offspring have no genetic variation.

D Organisms can reproduce without a mate.

Constructed Response

Use the figure below to answer questions 11 and 12.

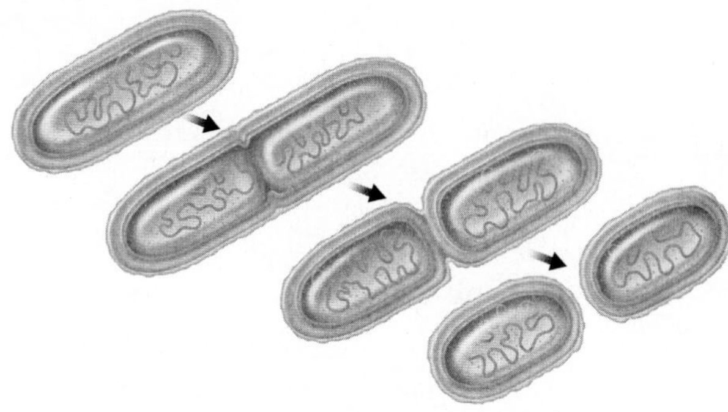

11 Identify the type of asexual reproduction shown in the figure above. How does it differ from sexual reproduction?

12 Compare and contrast budding with the type of asexual reproduction shown in the figure above.

13 What are some differences between the results of selectively breeding plants and cloning them?

14 Use the example of the wild mustard plant to describe the benefits of selective breeding.

15 What are the advantages and disadvantages of cloning animals?

NEED EXTRA HELP?															
If You Missed Question...	1	2	3	4	5	6	7	8	9	10	11	12	13	14	15
Go to Lesson...	2	1	1	2	1	1	1	2	1	2	1,2	2	1,2	1	2

Chapter 11

Genetics

THE BIG IDEA

How are traits passed from parents to offspring?

Inquiry How did this happen?

The color of this fawn is caused by a genetic trait called albinism. Albinism is the absence of body pigment. Notice that the fawn's mother has brown hair, the normal fur color of an adult whitetail deer.

- Why do you think the fawn looks so different from its mother?
- What do you think determines the color of the offspring?
- How do you think traits are passed from generation to generation?

Get Ready to Read

What do you think?

Before you read, decide if you agree or disagree with each of these statements. As you read this chapter, see if you change your mind about any of the statements.

1. Like mixing paints, parents' traits always blend in their offspring.
2. If you look more like your mother than you look like your father, then you received more traits from your mother.
3. All inherited traits follow Mendel's patterns of inheritance.
4. Scientists have tools to predict the form of a trait an offspring might inherit.
5. Any condition present at birth is genetic.
6. A change in the sequence of an organism's DNA always changes the organism's traits.

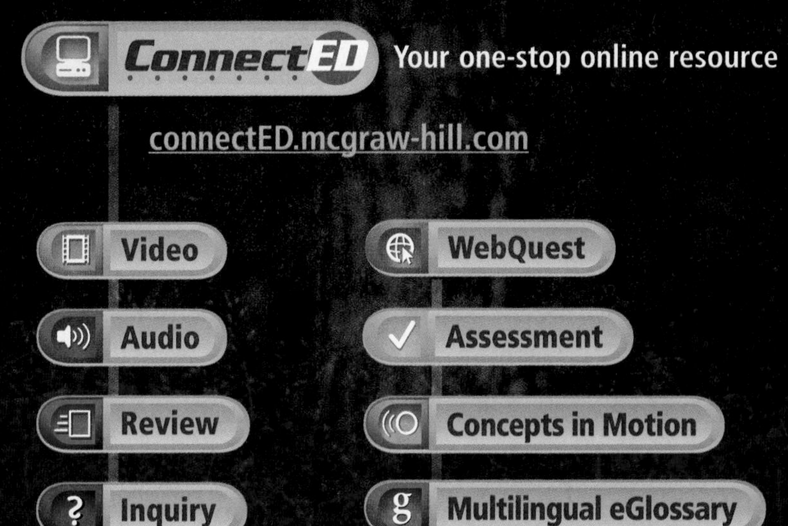

Lesson 1

Mendel and His Peas

Reading Guide

Key Concepts

ESSENTIAL QUESTIONS

- Why did Mendel perform cross-pollination experiments?
- What did Mendel conclude about inherited traits?
- How do dominant and recessive factors interact?

Vocabulary

heredity p. 389

genetics p. 389

dominant trait p. 395

recessive trait p. 395

Multilingual eGlossary

Video BrainPOP®

Academic Standards for Science

8.3.1 Explain that reproduction is essential for the continuation of every species and is the mechanism by which all organisms transmit genetic information.

Also covers: 8.NS.7, 8.NS.8, 8.NS.11

Inquiry Same Species?

Have you ever seen a black ladybug? It is less common than the orange variety you might know, but both are the same species of beetle. So why do they look different? Believe it or not, a study of pea plants helped scientists explain these differences.

Inquiry Launch Lab

10 minutes

What makes you unique?

Traits such as eye color have many different types, but some traits have only two types. By a show of hands, determine how many students in your class have each type of trait below.

Student Traits		
Trait	Type 1	Type 2
Earlobes	Unattached	Attached
Thumbs	Curved	Straight
Interlacing fingers	Left thumb over right thumb	Right thumb over left thumb

Think About This

1. Why might some students have types of traits that others do not have?
2. If a person has dimples, do you think his or her offspring will have dimples? Explain.
3. **Key Concept** What do you think determines the types of traits you inherit?

Early Ideas About Heredity

Have you ever mixed two paint colors to make a new color? Long ago, people thought an organism's characteristics, or traits, mixed like colors of paint because offspring resembled both parents. This is known as blending inheritance.

Today, scientists know that **heredity** (huh REH duh tee)—*the passing of traits from parents to offspring*—is more complex. For example, you might have blue eyes but both of your parents have brown eyes. How does this happen? More than 150 years ago, Gregor Mendel, an Austrian monk, performed experiments that helped answer these questions and disprove the idea of blending inheritance. Because of his research, Mendel is known as the father of **genetics** (juh NEH tihks)—*the study of how traits are passed from parents to offspring.*

Word Origin

genetics
from Greek *genesis,* means "origin"

Mendel's Experimental Methods

During the 1850s, Mendel studied genetics by doing controlled breeding experiments with pea plants. Pea plants were ideal for genetic studies because

- they reproduce quickly. This enabled Mendel to grow many plants and collect a lot of data.
- they have easily observed traits, such as flower color and pea shape. This enabled Mendel to observe whether or not a trait was passed from one generation to the next.
- Mendel could control which pairs of plants reproduced. This enabled him to determine which traits came from which plant pairs.

Pollination in Pea Plants

To observe how a trait was inherited, Mendel controlled which plants pollinated other plants. Pollination occurs when pollen lands on the pistil of a flower. **Sperm** cells from the pollen then can fertilize **egg** cells in the pistil. Pollination in pea plants can occur in two ways. Self-pollination occurs when pollen from one plant lands on the pistil of a flower on the same plant, as shown in **Figure 1.** Cross-pollination occurs when pollen from one plant reaches the pistil of a flower on a different plant. Cross-pollination occurs naturally when wind, water, or animals such as bees carry pollen from one flower to another. Mendel allowed one group of flowers to self-pollinate. With another group, he cross-pollinated the plants himself.

REVIEW VOCABULARY

sperm
a haploid sex cell formed in the male reproductive organs

egg
a haploid sex cell formed in the female reproductive organs

Self-Pollination

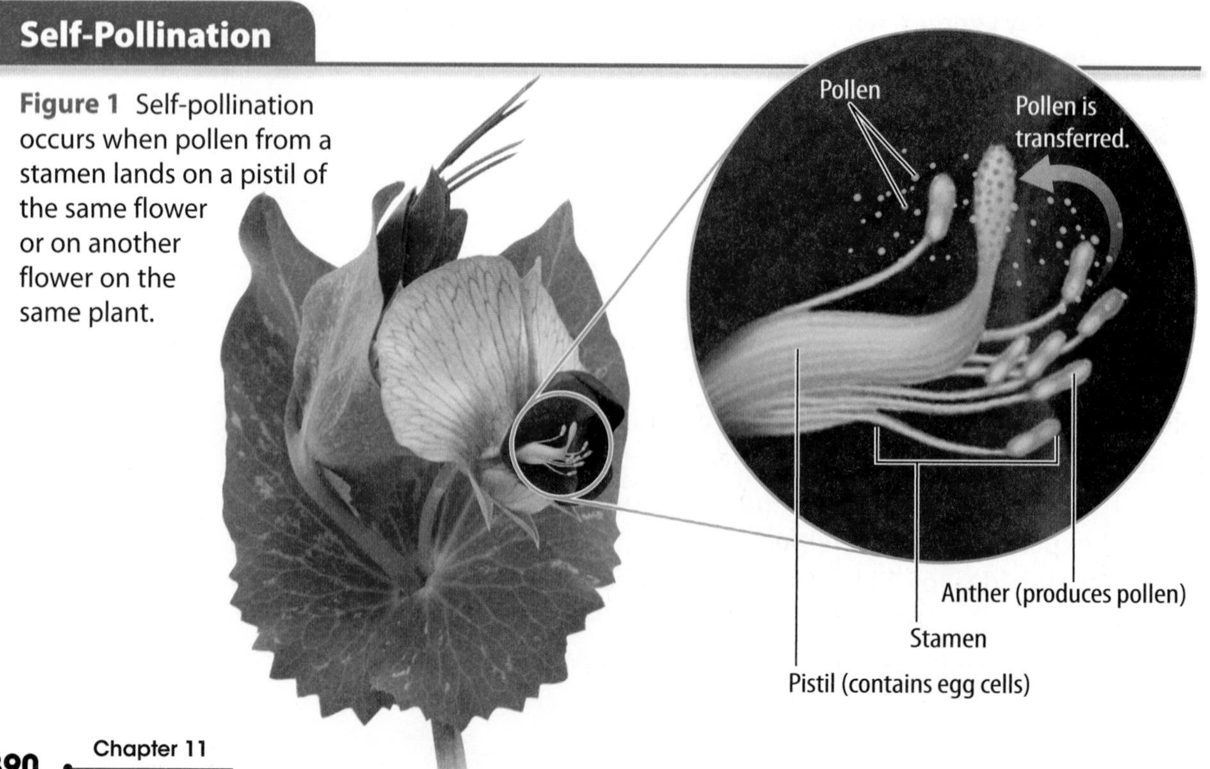

Figure 1 Self-pollination occurs when pollen from a stamen lands on a pistil of the same flower or on another flower on the same plant.

True-Breeding Plants

Mendel began his experiments with plants that were true-breeding for the trait he would test. When a true-breeding plant self-pollinates, it always produces offspring with traits that match the parent. For example, when a true-breeding pea plant with wrinkled seeds self-pollinates, it produces only plants with wrinkled seeds. In fact, plants with wrinkled seeds appear generation after generation.

Mendel's Cross-Pollination

By cross-pollinating plants himself, Mendel was able to select which plants pollinated other plants. **Figure 2** shows an example of a manual cross between a plant with white flowers and one with purple flowers.

Figure 2 Mendel removed the stamens of one flower and pollinated that flower with pollen from a flower of a different plant. In this way, he controlled pollination.

Cross-Pollination

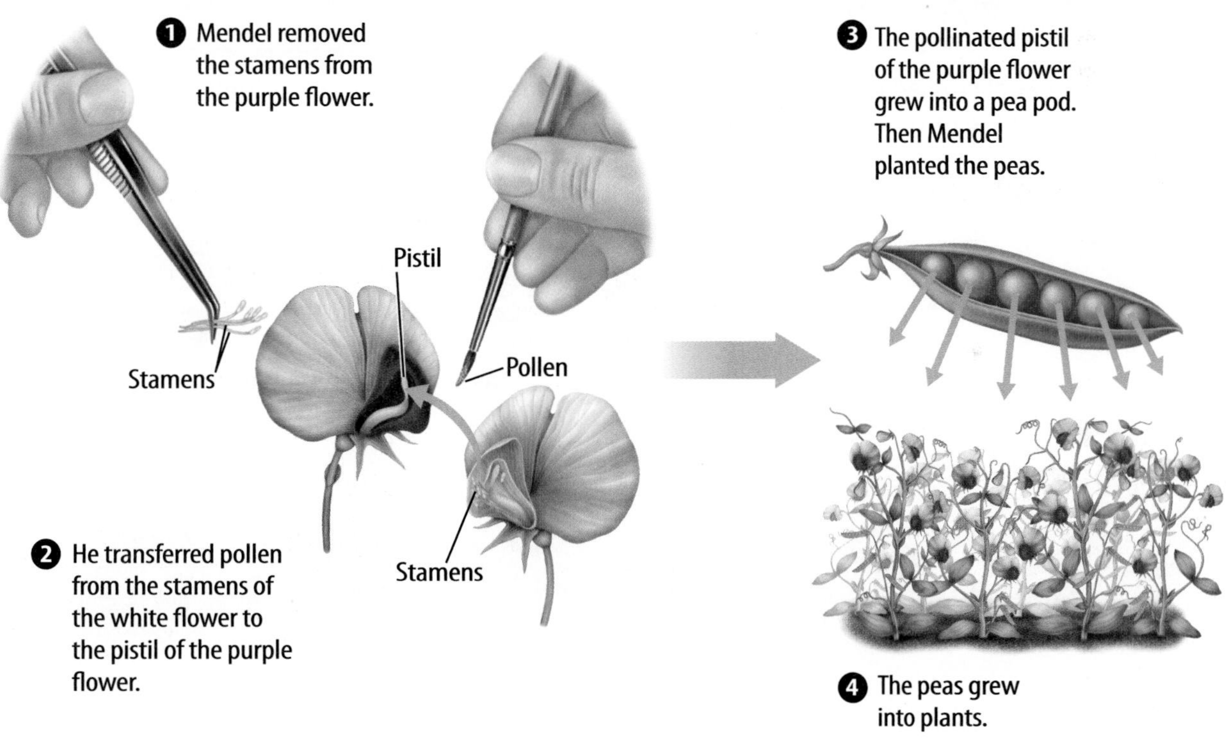

1 Mendel removed the stamens from the purple flower.
Stamens
Pistil
Pollen
Stamens
2 He transferred pollen from the stamens of the white flower to the pistil of the purple flower.
3 The pollinated pistil of the purple flower grew into a pea pod. Then Mendel planted the peas.
4 The peas grew into plants.

Mendel cross-pollinated hundreds of plants for each set of traits, such as flower color—purple or white; seed color—green or yellow; and seed shape—round or wrinkled. With each cross-pollination, Mendel recorded the traits that appeared in the offspring. By testing such a large number of plants, Mendel was able to predict which crosses would produce which traits.

Key Concept Check Why did Mendel perform cross-pollination experiments?

Mendel's Results

Once Mendel had enough true-breeding plants for a trait that he wanted to test, he cross-pollinated selected plants. His results are shown in **Figure 3**.

First-Generation Crosses

A cross between true-breeding plants with purple flowers produced plants with only purple flowers. A cross between true-breeding plants with white flowers produced plants with only white flowers. But something unexpected happened when Mendel crossed true-breeding plants with purple flowers and true-breeding plants with white flowers—all the offspring had purple flowers.

New Questions Raised

The results of the crosses between true-breeding plants with purple flowers and true-breeding plants with white flowers led to more questions for Mendel. Why did all the offspring always have purple flowers? Why were there no white flowers? Why didn't the cross produce offspring with pink flowers—a combination of the white and purple flower colors? Mendel carried out more experiments with pea plants to answer these questions.

Reading Check Predict the offspring of a cross between two true-breeding pea plants with smooth seeds.

First-Generation Crosses

Figure 3 Mendel crossed three combinations of true-breeding plants and recorded the flower colors of the offspring.

Purple × Purple

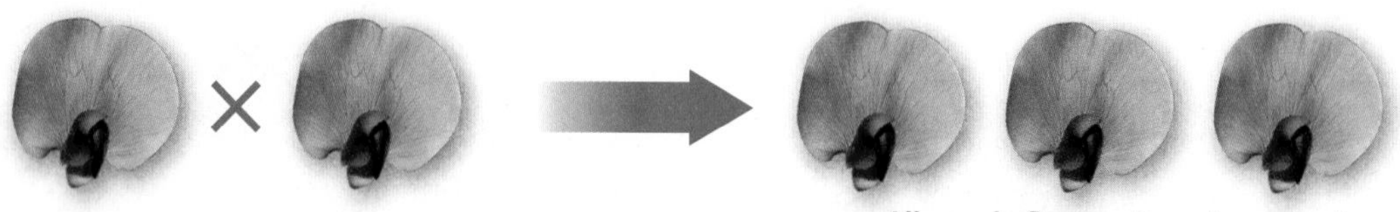

All purple flowers (true-breeding)

White × White

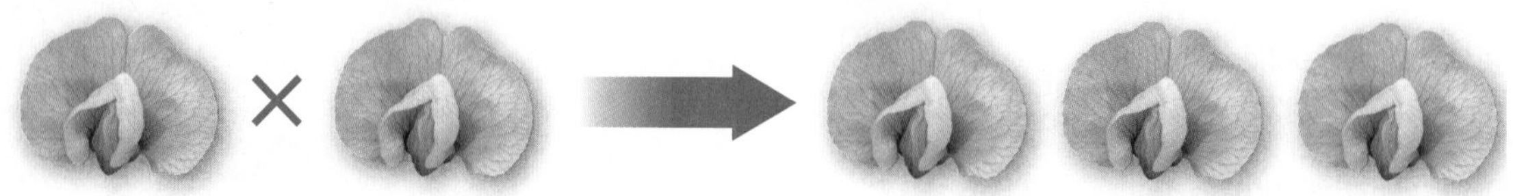

All white flowers (true-breeding)

Purple (true-breeding) × White (true-breeding)

All purple flowers (hybrids)

Visual Check Suppose you cross hundreds of true-breeding plants with purple flowers with hundreds of true-breeding plants with white flowers. Based on the results of this cross in the figure above, would any offspring produce white flowers? Explain.

Second-Generation (Hybrid) Crosses

The first-generation purple-flowering plants are called **hybrid** plants. This means they came from true-breeding parent plants with different forms of the same trait. Mendel wondered what would happen if he cross-pollinated two purple-flowering hybrid plants.

As shown in **Figure 4,** some of the offspring had white flowers, even though both parents had purple flowers. The results were similar each time Mendel cross-pollinated two hybrid plants. The trait that had disappeared in the first generation always reappeared in the second generation.

The same result happened when Mendel cross-pollinated pea plants for other traits. For example, he found that cross-pollinating a true-breeding yellow-seeded pea plant with a true-breeding green-seeded pea plant always produced yellow-seeded hybrids. A second-generation cross of two yellow-seeded hybrids always yielded plants with yellow seeds and plants with green seeds.

Reading Check What is a hybrid plant?

SCIENCE USE V. COMMON USE

hybrid

Science Use the offspring of two animals or plants with different forms of the same trait

Common Use having two types of components that perform the same function, such as a vehicle powered by both a gas engine and an electric motor

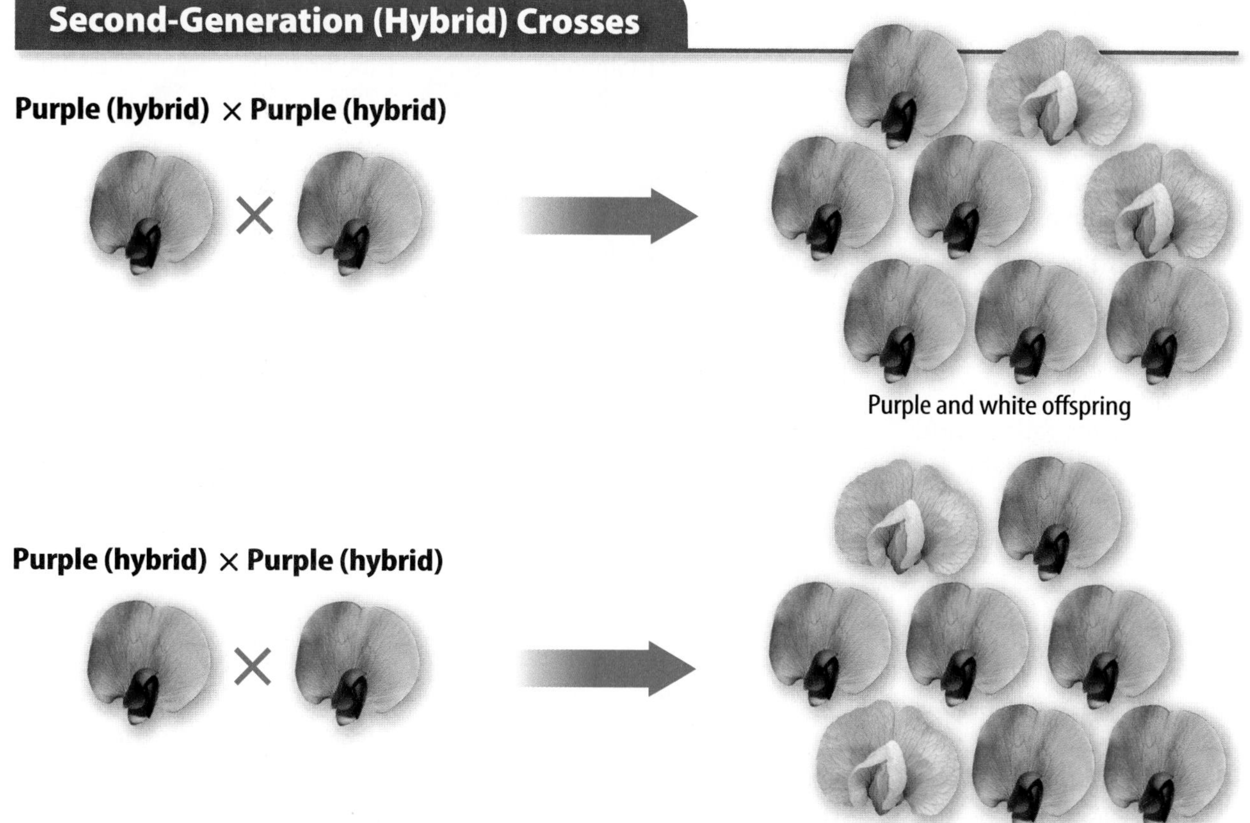

Figure 4 Mendel cross-pollinated first-generation hybrid offspring to produce second-generation offspring. In each case, the trait that had disappeared from the first generation reappeared in the second generation.

Concepts in Motion Interactive Table

Table 1 When Mendel crossed two hybrids for a given trait, the trait that had disappeared then reappeared in a ratio of about 3:1.

Table 1 Results of Hybrid Crosses

Characteristic	Trait and Number of Offspring	Trait and Number of Offspring	Ratio
Flower color	Purple 705	White 224	3.15:1
Flower position	Axial (Side of stem) 651	Terminal (End of stem) 207	3.14:1
Seed color	Yellow 6,022	Green 2,001	3.01:1
Seed shape	Round 5,474	Wrinkled 1,850	2.96:1
Pod shape	Inflated (Smooth) 882	Constricted (Bumpy) 299	2.95:1
Pod color	Green 428	Yellow 152	2.82:1
Stem length	Long 787	Short 277	2.84:1

Math Skills

Use Ratios

A ratio is a comparison of two numbers or quantities by division. For example, the ratio comparing 6,022 yellow seeds to **2,001** green seeds can be written as follows:

6,022 to **2,001** or

6,022 : **2,001** or

$\frac{6,022}{2,001}$

To simplify the ratio, divide the first number by the second number.

$\frac{6,022}{2,001} = \frac{3}{1}$ or 3:1

Practice

There are 14 girls and 7 boys in a science class. Simplify the ratio.

- Math Practice
- Personal Tutor

More Hybrid Crosses

Mendel counted and recorded the traits of offspring from many experiments in which he cross-pollinated hybrid plants. Data from these experiments are shown in **Table 1.** He analyzed these data and noticed patterns. For example, from the data of crosses between hybrid plants with purple flowers, he found that the ratio of purple flowers to white flowers was about 3:1. This means purple-flowering pea plants grew from this cross three times more often than white-flowering pea plants grew from the cross. He calculated similar ratios for all seven traits he tested.

Mendel's Conclusions

After analyzing the results of his experiments, Mendel concluded that two genetic factors control each inherited trait. He also proposed that when organisms reproduce, each reproductive cell—sperm or egg—contributes one factor for each trait.

Key Concept Check What did Mendel conclude about inherited traits?

Dominant and Recessive Traits

Recall that when Mendel cross-pollinated a true-breeding plant with purple flowers and a true-breeding plant with white flowers, the hybrid offspring had only purple flowers. Mendel hypothesized that the hybrid offspring had one genetic factor for purple flowers and one genetic factor for white flowers. But why were there no white flowers?

Mendel also hypothesized that the purple factor is the only factor seen or expressed because it blocks the white factor. *A genetic factor that blocks another genetic factor is called a* **dominant** (DAH muh nunt) **trait.** A dominant trait, such as purple pea flowers, is observed when offspring have either one or two dominant factors. *A genetic factor that is blocked by the presence of a dominant factor is called a* **recessive** (rih SE sihv) **trait.** A recessive trait, such as white pea flowers, is observed only when two recessive genetic factors are present in offspring.

From Parents to Second Generation

For the second generation, Mendel cross-pollinated two hybrids with purple flowers. About 75 percent of the second-generation plants had purple flowers. These plants had at least one dominant factor. Twenty-five percent of the second-generation plants had white flowers. These plants had the same two recessive factors.

Key Concept Check How do dominant and recessive factors interact?

FOLDABLES®

Make a vertical two-tab book and label it as shown. Use it to organize your notes on dominant and recessive factors.

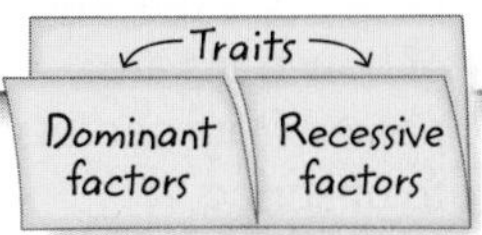

Inquiry MiniLab 20 minutes

Which is the dominant trait?

Imagine you are Gregor Mendel's lab assistant studying pea plant heredity. Mendel has crossed true-breeding plants with axial flowers and true-breeding plants with terminal flowers. Use the data below to determine which trait is dominant.

Pea Flower Location Results		
Generation	Axial (Number of Offspring)	Terminal (Number of Offspring)
First	794	0
Second	651	207

Analyze and Conclude

1. **Determine** which trait is dominant and which trait is recessive. Support your answer with data.
2. **Key Concept** Analyze the first-generation data. What evidence do you have that one trait is dominant over the other?

Lesson 1 Review

Assessment Online Quiz

Visual Summary

Genetics is the study of how traits are passed from parents to offspring.

Mendel studied genetics by doing cross-breeding experiments with pea plants.

Purple 705

White 224

Mendel's experiments with pea plants showed that some traits are dominant and others are recessive.

Use your lesson Foldable to review the lesson. Save your Foldable for the project at the end of the chapter.

What do you think NOW?

You first read the statements below at the beginning of the chapter.

1. Like mixing paints, parents' traits always blend in their offspring.
2. If you look more like your mother than you look like your father, then you received more traits from your mother.

Did you change your mind about whether you agree or disagree with the statements? Rewrite any false statements to make them true.

Use Vocabulary

1. **Distinguish** between heredity and genetics.
2. **Define** the terms *dominant* and *recessive.*
3. **Use the term** *recessive* in a complete sentence.

Understand Key Concepts 

4. A recessive trait is observed when an organism has ________ recessive genetic factor(s).

   A. 0 **B.** 1 **C.** 2 **D.** 3

5. **Summarize** Mendel's conclusions about how traits pass from parents to offspring.
6. **Describe** how Mendel cross-pollinated pea plants.

Interpret Graphics

7. **Suppose** the two true-breeding plants shown below were crossed.

What color would the flowers of the offspring be? Explain.

Critical Thinking

8. **Design an experiment** to test for true-breeding plants.
9. **Examine** how Mendel's conclusions disprove blending inheritance.

Math Skills

Math Practice

10. A cross between two pink camellia plants produced the following offspring: 7 plants with red flowers, 7 with white flowers, and 14 with pink flowers. What is the ratio of red to white to pink?

SCIENCE & SOCIETY

Pioneering the Science of Genetics

One man's curiosity leads to a branch of science.

Gregor Mendel—monk, scientist, gardener, and beekeeper—was a keen observer of the world around him. Curious about how traits pass from one generation to the next, he grew and tested almost 30,000 pea plants. Today, Mendel is called the father of genetics. After Mendel published his findings, however, his "laws of heredity" were overlooked for several decades.

In 1900, three European scientists, working independently of one another, rediscovered Mendel's work and replicated his results. Then, other biologists quickly began to recognize the importance of Mendel's work.

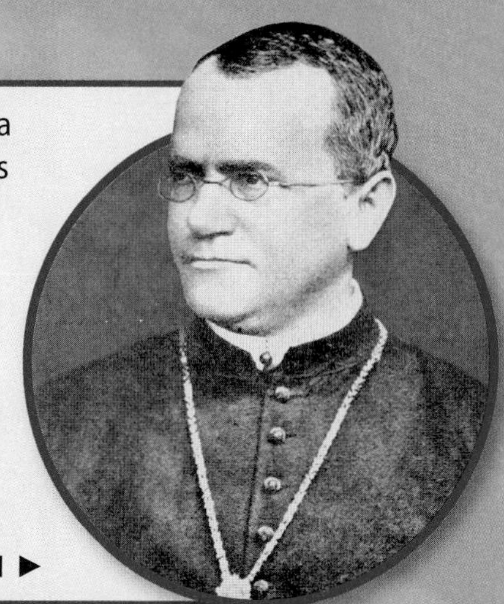

Gregor Mendel ▶

1902: American physician Walter Sutton demonstrates that Mendel's laws of inheritance can be applied to chromosomes. He concludes that chromosomes contain a cell's hereditary material on genes.

1906: William Bateson, a United Kingdom scientist, coins the term *genetics*. He uses it to describe the study of inheritance and the science of biological inheritance.

1952: American geneticists Martha Chase and Alfred Hershey prove that DNA transmits inherited traits from one generation to the next.

1953: Francis Crick and James Watson determine the structure of the DNA molecule. Their work begins the field of molecular biology and leads to important scientific and medical research in genetics.

2003: The National Human Genome Research Institute (NHGRI) completes mapping and sequencing human DNA. Researchers and scientists are now trying to discover the genetic basis for human health and disease.

It's Your Turn

RESEARCH What are some genetic diseases? Report on how genome-based research might help cure these diseases in the future.

Lesson 2

Understanding Inheritance

Reading Guide

Key Concepts
ESSENTIAL QUESTIONS

- What determines the expression of traits?
- How can inheritance be modeled?
- How do some patterns of inheritance differ from Mendel's model?

Vocabulary

gene p. 400
allele p. 400
phenotype p. 400
genotype p. 400
homozygous p. 401
heterozygous p. 401
Punnett square p. 402
incomplete dominance p. 404
codominance p. 404
polygenic inheritance p. 405

Academic Standards for Science

8.3.3 Explain that genetic information is transmitted from parents to offspring mostly by chromosomes.

8.3.5 Identify and describe the difference between inherited traits and physical and behavioral traits that are acquired or learned.

Also covers: 8.NS.3, 8.NS.5, 8.NS.7

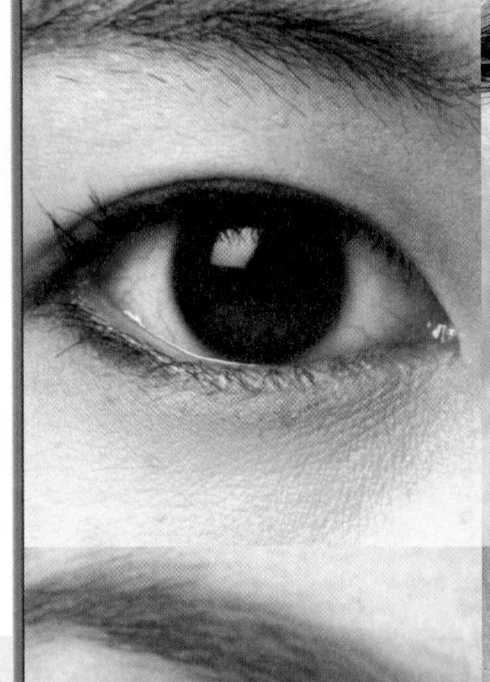

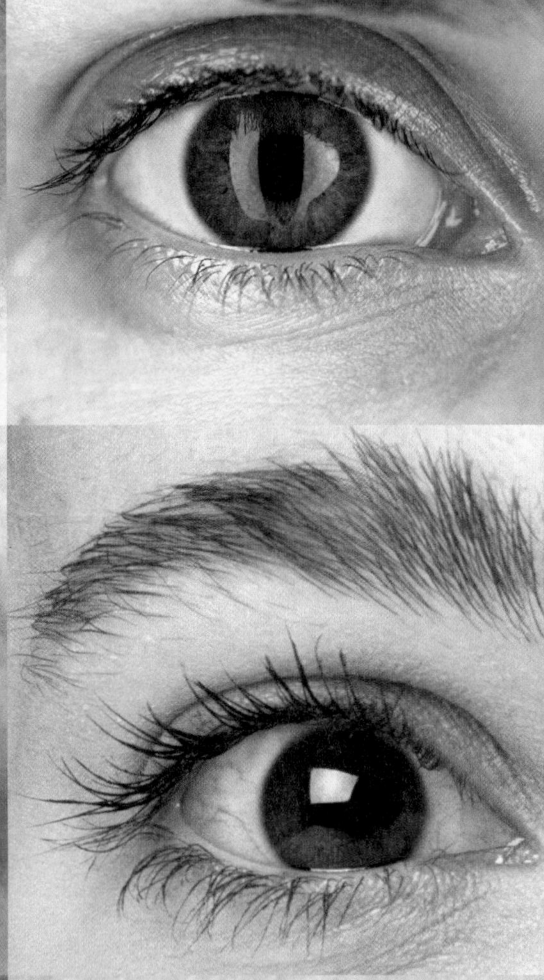

Inquiry Make the Connection

Physical traits, such as those shown in these eyes, can vary widely from person to person. Take a closer look at the eyes on this page. What traits can you identify among them? How do they differ?

Inquiry Launch Lab

15 minutes

What is the span of your hand?

Mendel discovered some traits have a simple pattern of inheritance—dominant or recessive. However, some traits, such as eye color, have more variation. Is human hand span a Mendelian trait?

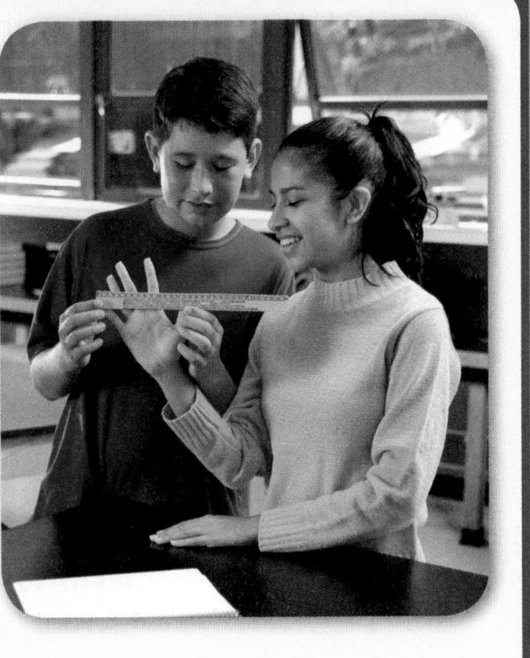

1. Read and complete a lab safety form.
2. Use a **metric ruler** to measure the distance (in cm) between the tips of your thumb and little finger with your hand stretched out.
3. As a class, record everyone's name and hand span in a data table.

Think About This

1. What range of hand span measurements did you observe?
2. **Key Concept** Do you think hand span is a simple Mendelian trait like pea plant flower color?

What controls traits?

Mendel concluded that two factors—one from each parent—control each trait. Mendel hypothesized that one factor came from the egg cell and one factor came from the sperm cell. What are these factors? How are they passed from parents to offspring?

Chromosomes

When other scientists studied the parts of a cell and combined Mendel's work with their work, these factors were more clearly understood. Scientists discovered that inside each cell is a nucleus that contains thread-like structures called chromosomes. Over time, scientists learned that chromosomes contain genetic information that controls traits. We now know that Mendel's "factors" are part of chromosomes and that each cell in offspring contains chromosomes from both parents. As shown in **Figure 5**, these chromosomes exist as pairs—one chromosome from each parent.

Figure 5 Humans have 23 pairs of chromosomes. Each pair has one chromosome from the father and one chromosome from the mother.

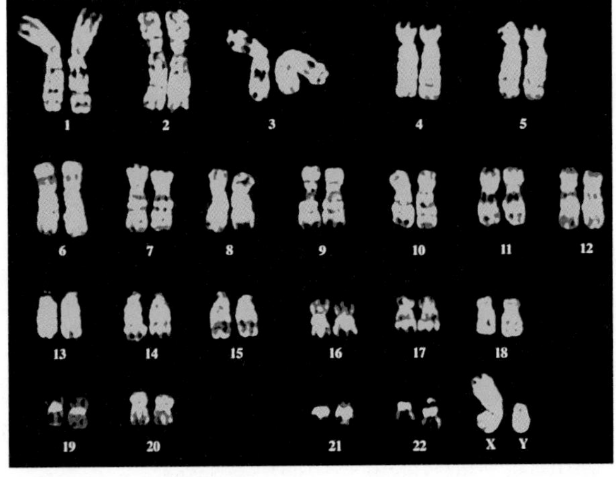

Genes and Alleles

Scientists have discovered that each chromosome can have information about hundreds or even thousands of traits. *A* **gene** (JEEN) *is a section on a chromosome that has genetic information for one trait.* For example, a gene of a pea plant might have information about flower color. Recall that an offspring inherits two genes (factors) for each trait—one from each parent. The genes can be the same or different, such as purple or white for pea flower color. *The different forms of a gene are called* **alleles** (uh LEELs). Pea plants can have two purple alleles, two white alleles, or one of each allele. In **Figure 6,** the chromosome pair has information about three traits—flower position, pod shape, and stem length.

 **Reading Check** How many alleles controlled flower color in Mendel's experiments?

Genotype and Phenotype

Look again at the photo at the beginning of this lesson. What trait can you observe? You might observe that eye color can be shades of blue or brown. *Geneticists call how a trait appears, or is expressed, the trait's* **phenotype** (FEE nuh tipe).

Word Origin
phenotype
from Greek *phainein,* means "to show"

Mendel concluded that two alleles control the expression or phenotype of each trait. *The two alleles that control the phenotype of a trait are called the trait's* **genotype** (JEE nuh tipe). Although you cannot see an organism's genotype, you can make inferences about a genotype based on its phenotype. For example, a pea plant with a phenotype of white flowers has two recessive alleles for that trait. These two alleles are its genotype. Not all traits are inherited, however. Certain traits, such as the ability to tie your shoes, are acquired, or learned.

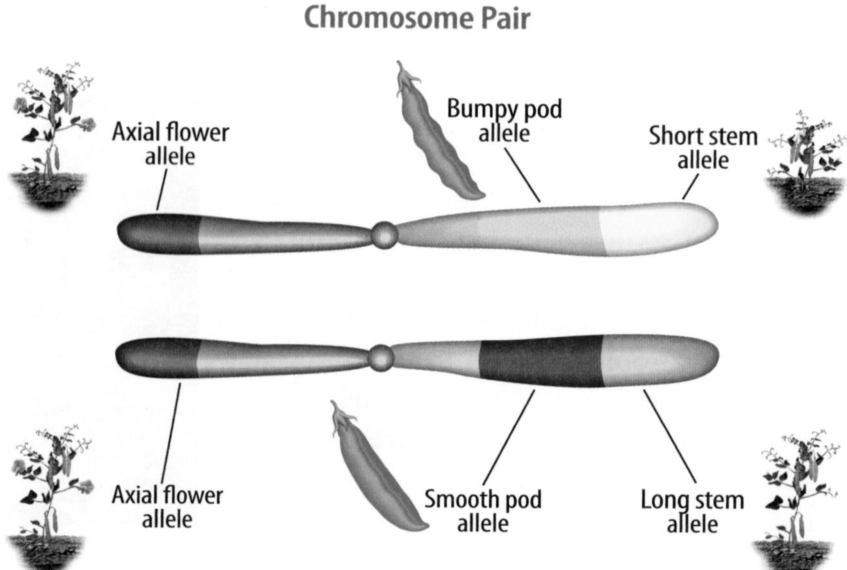

Figure 6 The alleles for flower position are the same on both chromosomes. However, the chromosome pair has different alleles for pod shape and stem length.

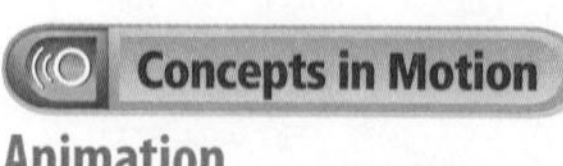

Animation

Symbols for Genotypes Scientists use symbols to represent the alleles in a genotype. In genetics, uppercase letters represent dominant alleles and lowercase letters represent recessive alleles. **Table 2** shows the possible genotypes for both round and wrinkled seed phenotypes. Notice that the dominant allele, if present, is written first.

Table 2 Phenotype and Genotype

Phenotypes (observed traits)	Genotypes (alleles of a gene)
Round	Homozygous dominant *(RR)*
	Heterozygous *(Rr)*
Wrinkled	Homozygous recessive *(rr)*

A round seed can have two genotypes—*RR* and *Rr*. Both genotypes have a round phenotype. Why does *Rr* result in round seeds? This is because the round allele *(R)* is dominant to the wrinkled allele *(r)*.

A wrinkled seed has the recessive genotype, *rr*. The wrinkled-seed phenotype is possible only when the same two recessive alleles *(rr)* are present in the genotype.

Homozygous and Heterozygous *When the two alleles of a gene are the same, its genotype is* **homozygous** (hoh muh ZI gus). Both *RR* and *rr* are homozygous genotypes, as shown in **Table 2.**

If the two alleles of a gene are different, its genotype is **heterozygous** (he tuh roh ZI gus). *Rr* is a heterozygous genotype.

Key Concept Check How do alleles determine the expression of traits?

Inquiry MiniLab — 20 minutes

Can you infer genotype?

If you know that dragon traits are either dominant or recessive, can you use phenotypes of traits to infer genotypes?

1. Select one **trait card** from each of three **dragon trait bags.** Record the data in your Science Journal.
2. Draw a picture of your dragon based on your data. Label each trait *homozygous* or *heterozygous.*
3. Copy the table below in your Science Journal. For each of the three traits, place one check mark in the appropriate box.

Dragon Traits

Phenotype	Homozygous	Heterozygous
Green body		
Red body		
Four legs		
Two legs		
Long wings		
Short wings		

4. Combine your data with your classmates' data.

Analyze and Conclude

1. **Describe** any patterns you find in the data table.
2. **Determine** which trait is dominant and which is recessive. Support your reasoning.
3. **Determine** the genotype(s) for each phenotype. Support your reasoning.
4. **Key Concept** Decide whether you could have correctly determined your dragon's genotype without data from other dragons. Support your reasoning.

Punnett Square

Review Personal Tutor

Figure 7 A Punnett square can be used to predict the possible genotypes of the offspring. Offspring from a cross between two heterozygous parents can have one of three genotypes.

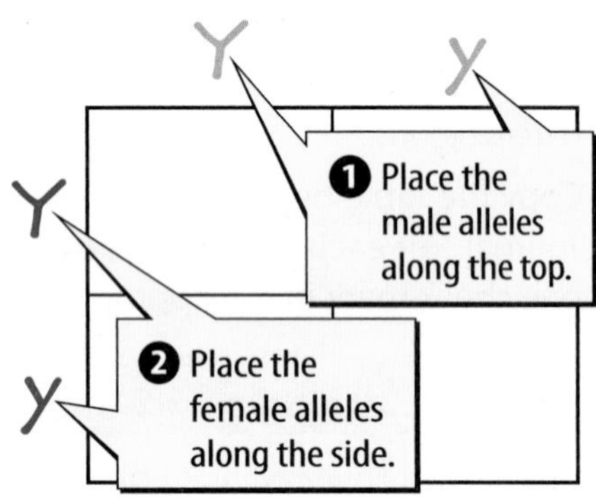

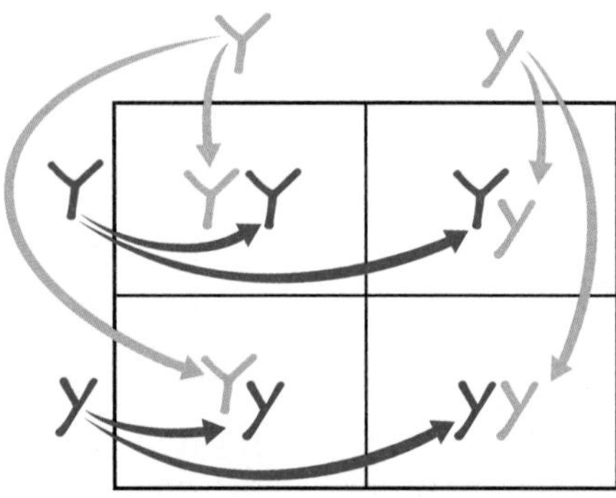

3 Copy female alleles across each row. Copy male alleles down each column. Always list the dominant trait first.

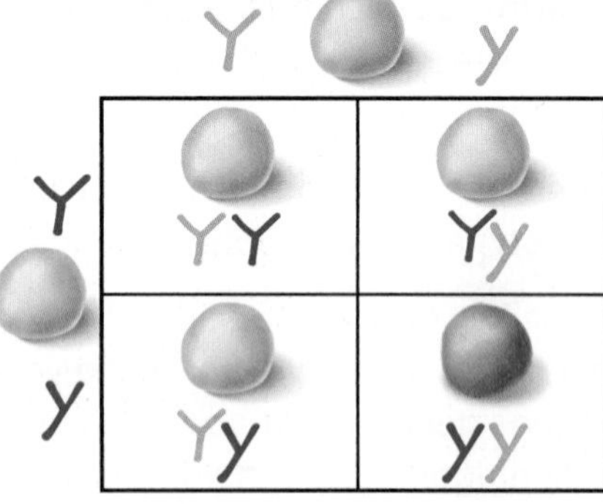

Visual Check What phenotypes are possible for pea offspring of this cross?

Modeling Inheritance

Have you ever flipped a coin and guessed heads or tails? Because a coin has two sides, there are only two possible outcomes—heads or tails. You have a 50 percent chance of getting heads and a 50 percent chance of getting tails. The chance of getting an outcome can be represented by a ratio. The ratio of heads to tails is 50:50 or 1:1.

Reading Check What does a ratio of 2:1 mean?

Plant breeders and animal breeders use a method for predicting how often traits will appear in offspring that does not require performing the crosses thousands of times. Two tools—a Punnett square and a pedigree—can be used to predict and identify traits among genetically related individuals.

Punnett Squares

If the genotypes of the parents are known, then the different genotypes and phenotypes of the offspring can be predicted. *A* **Punnett square** *is a model used to predict possible genotypes and phenotypes of offspring.* Follow the steps in **Figure 7** to learn how to make a Punnett square.

Analyzing a Punnett Square

Figure 7 shows an example of a cross between two pea plants that are heterozygous for pea seed color—*Yy* and *Yy*. Yellow is the dominant allele—*Y*. Green is the recessive allele—*y*. The offspring can have one of three genotypes—*YY*, *Yy*, or *yy*. The ratio of genotypes is written as 1:2:1.

Because *YY* and *Yy* represent the same phenotype—yellow—the offspring can have one of only two phenotypes—yellow or green. The ratio of phenotypes is written 3:1. Therefore, about 75 percent of the offspring of the cross between two heterozygous pea plants will produce yellow seeds. About 25 percent of the plants will produce green seeds.

Using Ratios to Predict

Given a 3:1 ratio, you can expect that an offspring from heterozygous parents has a 3:1 chance of having yellow seeds. But you cannot expect that a group of four seeds will have three yellow seeds and one green seed. This is because one offspring does not affect the phenotype of another offspring. In a similar way, the outcome of one coin toss does not affect the outcome of other coin tosses.

However, if you counted large numbers of offspring from a particular cross, the overall ratio would be close to the ratio predicted by a Punnett square. Mendel did not use Punnett squares. However, by studying nearly 30,000 pea plants, his ratios nearly matched those that would have been predicted by a Punnett square for each cross.

Pedigrees

Another tool that can show inherited traits is a pedigree. A pedigree shows phenotypes of genetically related family members. It can also help determine genotypes. In the pedigree in **Figure 8,** three offspring have a trait—attached earlobes—that the parents do not have. If these offspring received one allele for this trait from each parent, but neither parent displays the trait, the offspring must have received two recessive alleles.

 **Key Concept Check** How can inheritance be modeled?

Pedigree

Figure 8 In this pedigree, the parents and two offspring have unattached ear lobes—the dominant phenotype. Three offspring have attached ear lobes—the recessive phenotype.

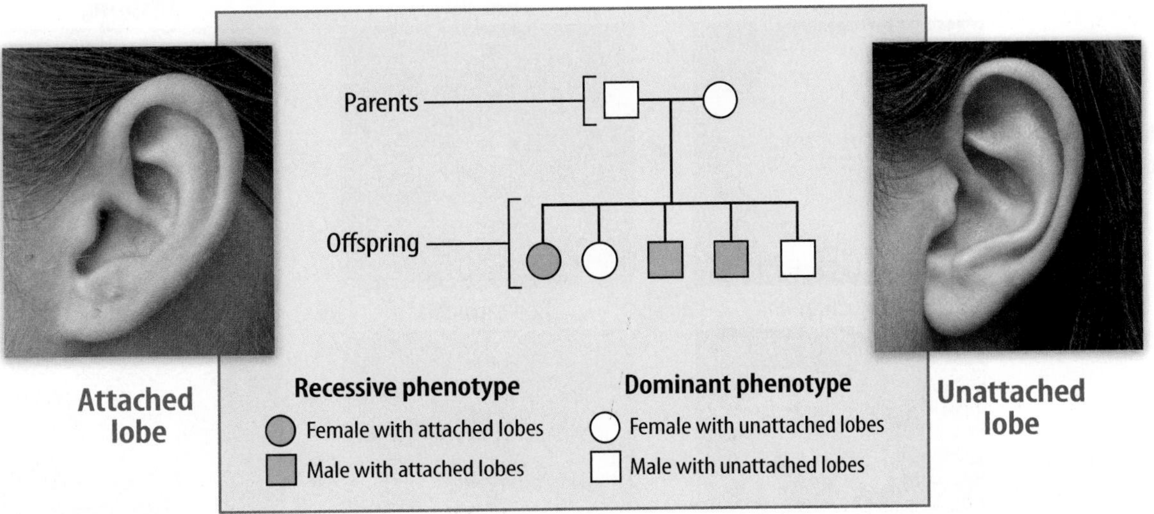

Visual Check If the genotype of the offspring with attached lobes is *uu,* what is the genotype of the parents? How can you tell?

Complex Patterns of Inheritance

By chance, Mendel studied traits only influenced by one gene with two alleles. However, we know now that some inherited traits have complex patterns of inheritance.

FOLDABLES®

Use two sheets of paper to make a layered book. Label it as shown. Use it to organize your notes on inheritance patterns.

Inheritance Patterns
Incomplete dominance
Multiple alleles
Polygenic inheritance

Types of Dominance

Recall that for pea plants, the presence of one dominant allele produces a dominant phenotype. However, not all allele pairs have a dominant-recessive interaction.

Incomplete Dominance Sometimes traits appear to be combinations of alleles. *Alleles show* **incomplete dominance** *when the offspring's phenotype is a combination of the parents' phenotypes.* For example, a pink camellia, as shown in **Figure 9,** results from incomplete dominance. A cross between a camellia plant with white flowers and a camellia plant with red flowers produces only camellia plants with pink flowers.

Codominance The coat color of some cows is an example of another type of interaction between two alleles. *When both alleles can be observed in a phenotype, this type of interaction is called* **codominance.** If a cow inherits the allele for white coat color from one parent and the allele for red coat color from the other parent, the cow will have both red and white hairs.

Types of Dominance

Figure 9 In incomplete dominance, neither parent's phenotype is visible in the offspring's phenotype. In codominance, both parents' phenotypes are visible separately in the offspring's phenotype.

Table 3 Human ABO Blood Types

Phenotype	Possible Genotypes
Type A	I^AI^A or I^Ai
Type B	I^BI^B or I^Bi
Type O	ii
Type AB	I^AI^B

Multiple Alleles

Unlike the genes in Mendel's pea plants, some genes have more than two alleles, or multiple alleles. Human ABO blood type is an example of a trait that is determined by multiple alleles. There are three different alleles for the ABO blood type—I^A, I^B, and i. The way the alleles combine results in one of four blood types—A, B, AB, or O. The I^A and I^B alleles are codominant to each other, but they both are dominant to the i allele. Even though there are multiple alleles, a person can inherit only two of these alleles—one from each parent, as shown in **Table 3.**

Polygenic Inheritance

Mendel **concluded** that each trait was determined by only one gene. However, we now know that a trait can be affected by more than one gene. **Polygenic inheritance** *occurs when multiple genes determine the phenotype of a trait.* Because several genes determine a trait, many alleles affect the phenotype even though each gene has only two alleles. Therefore, polygenic inheritance has many possible phenotypes.

ACADEMIC VOCABULARY
conclude
(verb) to reach a logically necessary end by reasoning

Look again at the photo at the beginning of this lesson. Eye color in humans is an example of polygenic inheritance. There are also many phenotypes for height in humans, as shown in **Figure 10.** Other human characteristics determined by polygenic inheritance are weight and skin color.

Key Concept Check How does polygenic inheritance differ from Mendel's model?

Figure 10 The eighth graders in this class have different heights.

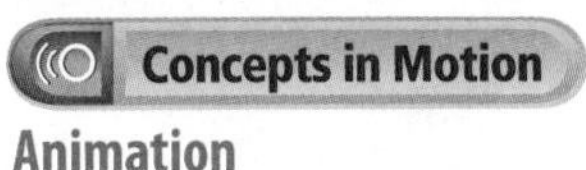

Animation

Genes and the Environment

You read earlier in this lesson that an organism's genotype determines its phenotype. Scientists have learned that genes are not the only factors that can affect phenotypes. An organism's environment can also affect its phenotype. For example, the flower color of one type of hydrangea is determined by the soil in which the hydrangea plant grows. **Figure 11** shows that acidic soil produces blue flowers and basic, or alkaline, soil produces pink flowers. Other examples of environmental effects on phenotype are also shown in **Figure 11.**

For humans, healthful choices can also affect phenotype. Many genes affect a person's chances of having heart disease. However, what a person eats and the amount of exercise he or she gets can influence whether heart disease will develop.

Reading Check What environmental factors affect phenotype?

Figure 11 Environmental factors, such as temperature and sunlight, can affect phenotype.

◀ These hydrangea plants are genetically identical. The plant grown in acidic soil produced blue flowers. The plant grown in alkaline soil produced pink flowers.

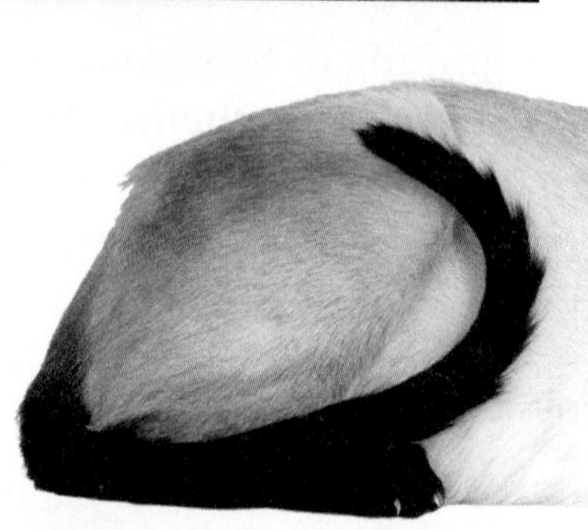

Siamese cats have alleles that produce a dark pigment only in cooler areas of the body. That's why a Siamese cat's ear tips, nose, paws, and tail are darker than other areas of its body. ▶

◀ The wing patterns of the map butterfly, *Araschnia levana,* depend on what time of year the adult develops. Adults that developed in the spring have more orange in their wings than those that developed in the summer.

Lesson 2 Review

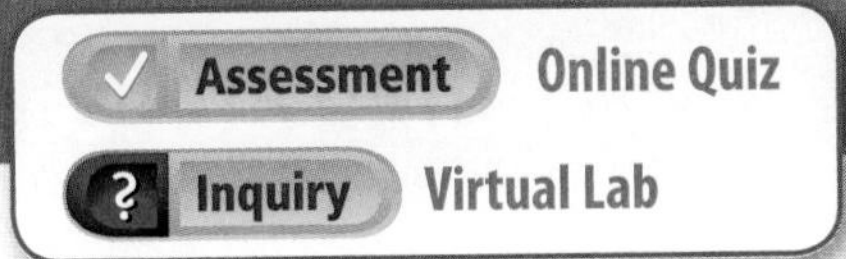

Visual Summary

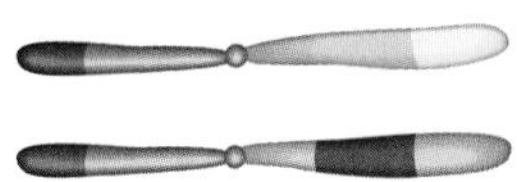

The genes for traits are located on chromosomes.

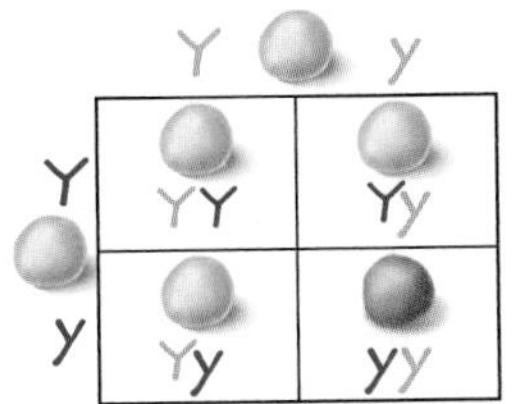

Geneticists use Punnett squares to predict the possible genotypes and phenotypes of offspring.

In polygenic inheritance, traits are determined by more than one gene and have many possible phenotypes.

FOLDABLES®

Use your lesson Foldable to review the lesson. Save your Foldable for the project at the end of the chapter.

What do you think NOW?

You first read the statements below at the beginning of the chapter.

3. All inherited traits follow Mendel's patterns of inheritance.

4. Scientists have tools to predict the form of a trait an offspring might inherit.

Did you change your mind about whether you agree or disagree with the statements? Rewrite any false statements to make them true.

Use Vocabulary

1. **Use the terms** *phenotype* and *genotype* in a complete sentence.
2. **Contrast** homozygous and heterozygous.
3. **Define** *incomplete dominance* in your own words.

Understand Key Concepts 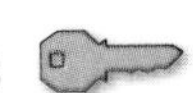

4. How many alleles control a Mendelian trait, such as pea seed color?
   A. one
   B. two
   C. three
   D. four
5. **Explain** where the alleles for a given trait are inherited from.
6. **Describe** how the genotypes *RR* and *Rr* result in the same phenotype.
7. **Summarize** how polygenic inheritance differs from Mendelian inheritance.

Interpret Graphics

8. **Analyze** this pedigree. If ■ represents a male with the homozygous recessive genotype (*aa*), what is the mother's genotype?

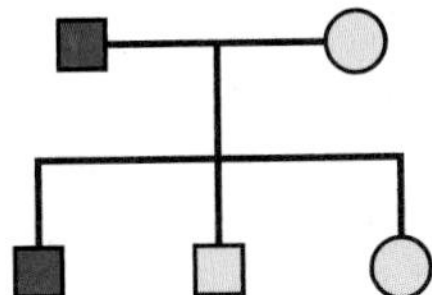

Critical Thinking

9. **Predict** the possible blood genotypes of a child, using the table below, if one parent is type O and the other parent is type A.

Phenotype	Genotype
Blood Type O	*ii*
Blood Type A	I^AI^A or I^Ai

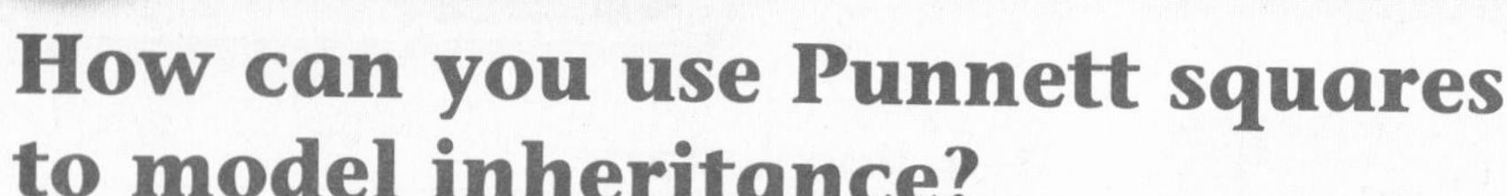

25 minutes

How can you use Punnett squares to model inheritance?

Geneticists use models to explain how traits are inherited from one generation to the next. A simple model of Mendelian inheritance is a Punnett square. A Punnett square is a model of reproduction between two parents and the possible genotypes and phenotypes of the resulting offspring. It also models the probability that each genotype will occur.

Learn It

In science, a **model** is a representation of how something in the natural world works. A model is used to explain or predict a natural process. Maps, diagrams, three-dimensional representations, and mathematical formulas can all be used to help model nature.

Try It

1. Copy the Punnett square on this page in your Science Journal. Use it to complete a cross between a fruit fly with straight wings *(cc)* and a fruit fly with curly wings *(CC)*.
2. According to your Punnett square, which genotypes are possible in the offspring?
3. Using the information in your Punnett square, calculate the ratio of the dominant phenotype to the recessive phenotype in the offspring.

Apply It

4. Based on the information in your Punnett square, how many offspring will have curly wings? Straight wings?
5. If you switch the locations of the parent genotypes around the Punnett square, does it affect the potential genotypes of their offspring? Explain.
6. **Key Concept** Design and complete a Punnett square to model a cross between two fruit flies that are heterozygous for the curly wings *(Cc)*. What are the phenotypic ratios of the offspring?

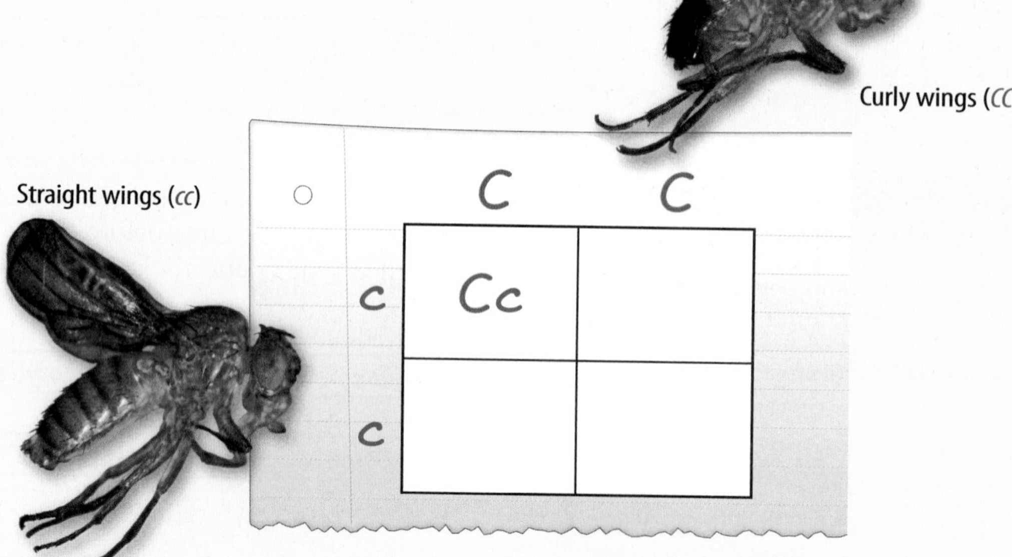

Lesson 3

Reading Guide

Key Concepts
ESSENTIAL QUESTIONS

- What is DNA?
- What is the role of RNA in protein production?
- How do changes in the sequence of DNA affect traits?

Vocabulary

DNA p. 410
nucleotide p. 411
replication p. 412
RNA p. 413
transcription p. 413
translation p. 414
mutation p. 415

Multilingual eGlossary

Academic Standards for Science

8.3.4 Understand the relationship between deoxyribonucleic acid (DNA), genes, and chromosomes.

Also covers: 8.NS.1, 8.NS.7, 8.NS.11

DNA and Genetics

Inquiry What are these coils?

What color are your eyes? How tall are you? Traits are controlled by genes. But genes never leave the nucleus of the cell. How does a gene control a trait? These stringy coils hold the answer to that question.

Launch Lab

20 minutes

How are codes used to determine traits?

Interpret this code to learn more about how an organism's body cells use codes to determine genetic traits.

1. Analyze the pattern of the simple code shown to the right. For example, >< L = DOG
2. In your Science Journal, record the correct letters for the symbols in the code below.

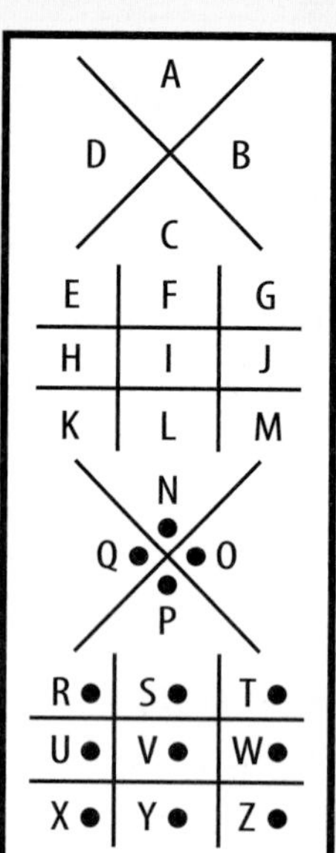

Think About This

1. What do all codes, such as Morse code and Braille, have in common?
2. What do you think might happen if there is a mistake in the code?
3. **Key Concept** How do you think an organism's cells might use code to determine its traits?

The Structure of DNA

Have you ever put together a toy or a game for a child? If so, it probably came with directions. Cells put molecules together in much the same way you might assemble a toy. They follow a set of directions.

Genes provide directions for a cell to assemble molecules that express traits such as eye color or seed shape. Recall from Lesson 2 that a gene is a section of a chromosome. Chromosomes are made of proteins and deoxyribonucleic (dee AHK sih ri boh noo klee ihk) acid, or **DNA**—*an organism's genetic material.* A gene is a segment of DNA on a chromosome.

Cells and organisms contain millions of different molecules. Countless numbers of directions are needed to make all those molecules. How do all these directions fit on a few chromosomes? The information, or directions, needed for an organism to grow, maintain itself, and reproduce is contained in DNA. As shown in **Figure 12**, strands of DNA in a chromosome are tightly coiled, like a telephone cord or a coiled spring. This coiling allows more genes to fit in a small space.

Key Concept Check What is DNA?

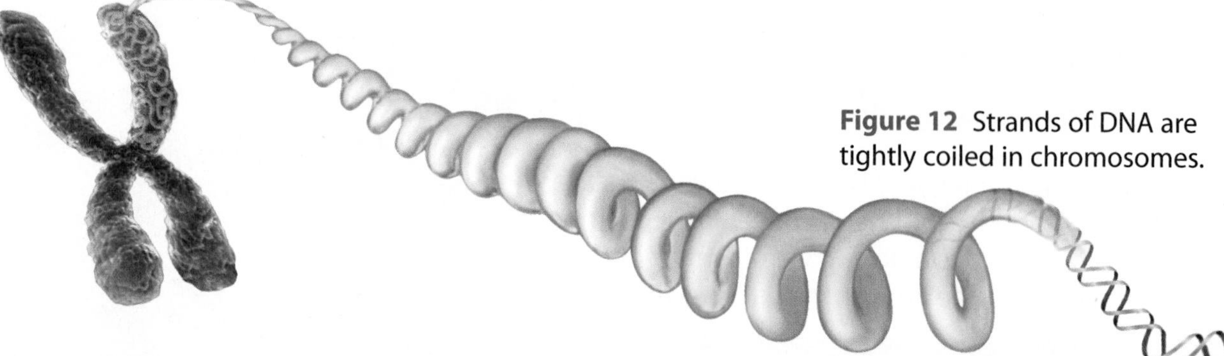

Figure 12 Strands of DNA are tightly coiled in chromosomes.

A Complex Molecule

What's the best way to fold clothes so they will fit into a drawer or a suitcase? Scientists asked a similar question about DNA. What is the shape of the DNA molecule, and how does it fit into a chromosome? The work of several scientists revealed that DNA is like a twisted zipper. This twisted zipper shape is called a double helix. A model of DNA's double helix structure is shown in **Figure 13.**

How did scientists make this discovery? Rosalind Franklin and Maurice Wilkins were two scientists in London who used X-rays to study DNA. Some of the X-ray data indicated that DNA has a helix shape.

American scientist James Watson visited Franklin and Wilkins and saw one of the DNA X-rays. Watson realized that the X-ray gave valuable clues about DNA's structure. Watson worked with an English scientist, Francis Crick, to build a model of DNA.

Watson and Crick based their work on information from Franklin's and Wilkins's X-rays. They also used chemical information about DNA discovered by another scientist, Erwin Chargaff. After several tries, Watson and Crick built a model that showed how the smaller molecules of DNA bond together and form a double helix.

Four Nucleotides Shape DNA

DNA's twisted-zipper shape is because of molecules called nucleotides. *A* **nucleotide** *is a molecule made of a nitrogen base, a sugar, and a phosphate group.* Sugar-phosphate groups form the sides of the DNA zipper. The nitrogen bases bond and form the teeth of the zipper. As shown in **Figure 13,** there are four nitrogen bases: adenine (A), cytosine (C), thymine (T), and guanine (G). A and T always bond together, and C and G always bond together.

Reading Check What is a nucleotide?

Figure 13 A DNA double helix is made of two strands of DNA. Each strand is a chain of nucleotides.

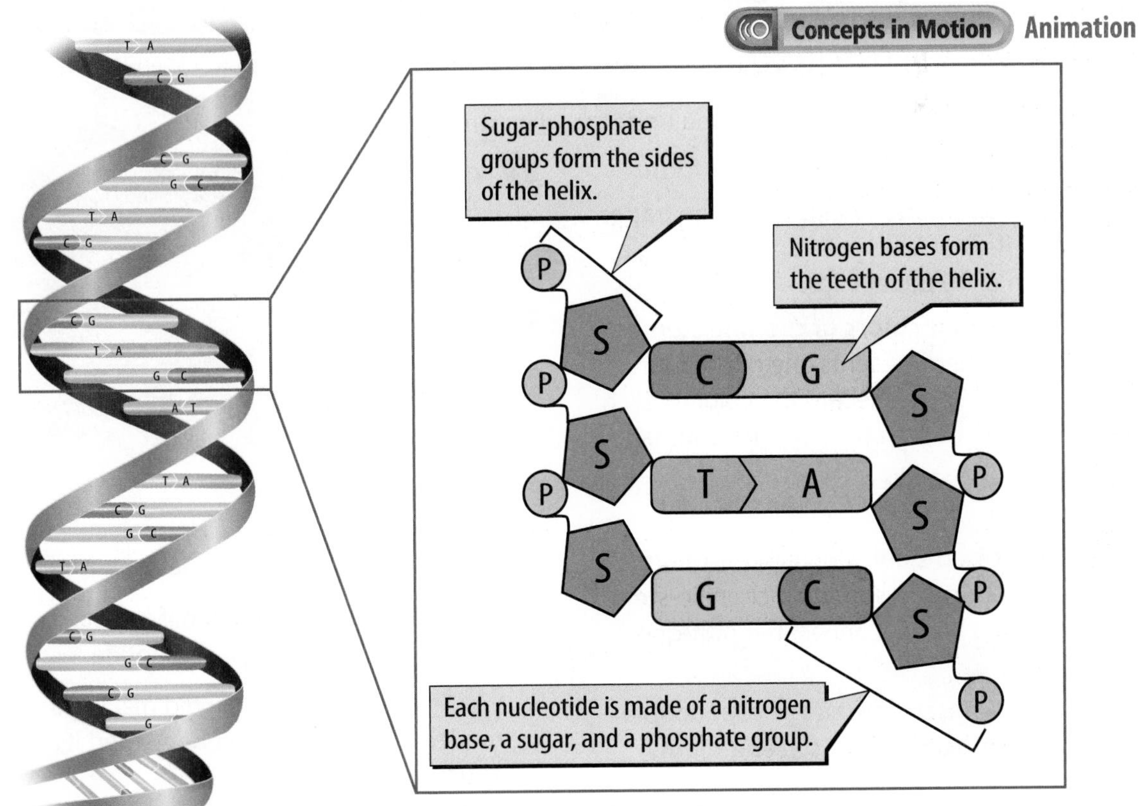
Concepts in Motion
Animation
Sugar-phosphate groups form the sides of the helix.
Nitrogen bases form the teeth of the helix.
Each nucleotide is made of a nitrogen base, a sugar, and a phosphate group.
P
S
C
G
T
A

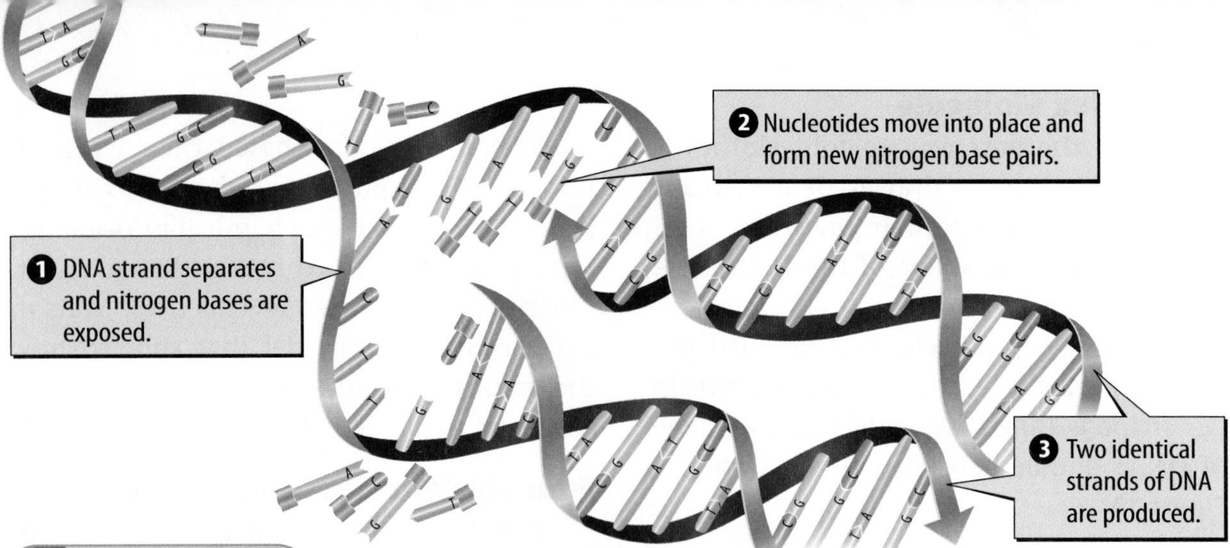
1 DNA strand separates and nitrogen bases are exposed.
2 Nucleotides move into place and form new nitrogen base pairs.
3 Two identical strands of DNA are produced.

Concepts in Motion

Animation

Figure 14 Before a cell divides, its DNA is replicated.

How DNA Replicates

Cells contain DNA in chromosomes. So, every time a cell divides, all chromosomes must be copied for the new cell. The new DNA is identical to existing DNA. *The process of copying a DNA molecule to make another DNA molecule is called* **replication.** You can follow the steps of DNA replication in **Figure 14.** First, the strands separate in many places, exposing individual bases. Then nucleotides are added to each exposed base. This produces two identical strands of DNA.

Reading Check What is replication?

Inquiry MiniLab

25 minutes

How can you model DNA?

Making a model of DNA can help you understand its structure.

1. Read and complete a lab safety form.
2. Link a **small paper clip** to a **large paper clip.** Repeat four more times, making a chain of 10 paper clips.
3. Choose **four colors of chenille stems.** Each color represents one of the four nitrogen bases. Record the color of each nitrogen base in your Science Journal.
4. Attach a chenille stem to each large paper clip.
5. Repeat step 2 and step 4, but this time attach the corresponding chenille-stem nitrogen bases. Connect the nitrogen bases.
6. Securely insert one end of your double chain into a **block of styrene foam.**
7. Repeat step 6 with the other end of your chain.
8. Gently turn the blocks to form a double helix.

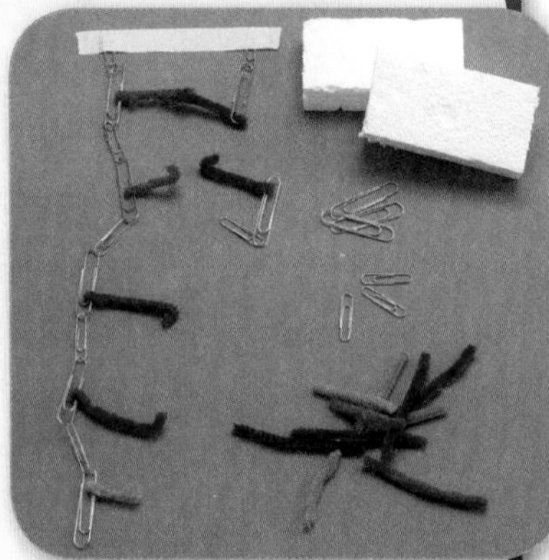

Analyze and Conclude

1. **Explain** which part of a DNA molecule is represented by each material you used.
2. **Predict** what might happen if a mistake were made in creating a nucleotide.
3. **Key Concept** How did making a model of DNA help you understand its structure?

Making Proteins

Recall that proteins are important for every cellular process. The DNA of each cell carries a complete set of genes that provides instructions for making all the proteins a cell requires. Most genes contain instructions for making proteins. Some genes contain instructions for when and how quickly proteins are made.

Junk DNA

As you have learned, all genes are segments of DNA on a chromosome. However, you might be surprised to learn that most of your DNA is not part of any gene. For example, about 97 percent of the DNA on human chromosomes does not form genes. Segments of DNA that are not parts of genes are often called junk DNA. It is not yet known whether junk DNA segments have functions that are important to cells.

The Role of RNA in Making Proteins

How does a cell use the instructions in a gene to make proteins? Proteins are made with the help of ribonucleic acid **(RNA)**—*a type of nucleic acid that carries the code for making proteins from the nucleus to the cytoplasm.* RNA also carries amino acids around inside a cell and forms a part of ribosomes.

RNA, like DNA, is made of nucleotides. However, there are key differences between DNA and RNA. DNA is double-stranded, but RNA is single-stranded. RNA has the nitrogen base uracil (U) instead of thymine (T) and the sugar ribose instead of deoxyribose.

The first step in making a protein is to make mRNA from DNA. *The process of making mRNA from DNA is called* **transcription.** **Figure 15** shows how mRNA is transcribed from DNA.

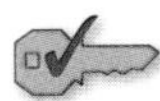

Key Concept Check What is the role of RNA in protein production?

Transcription

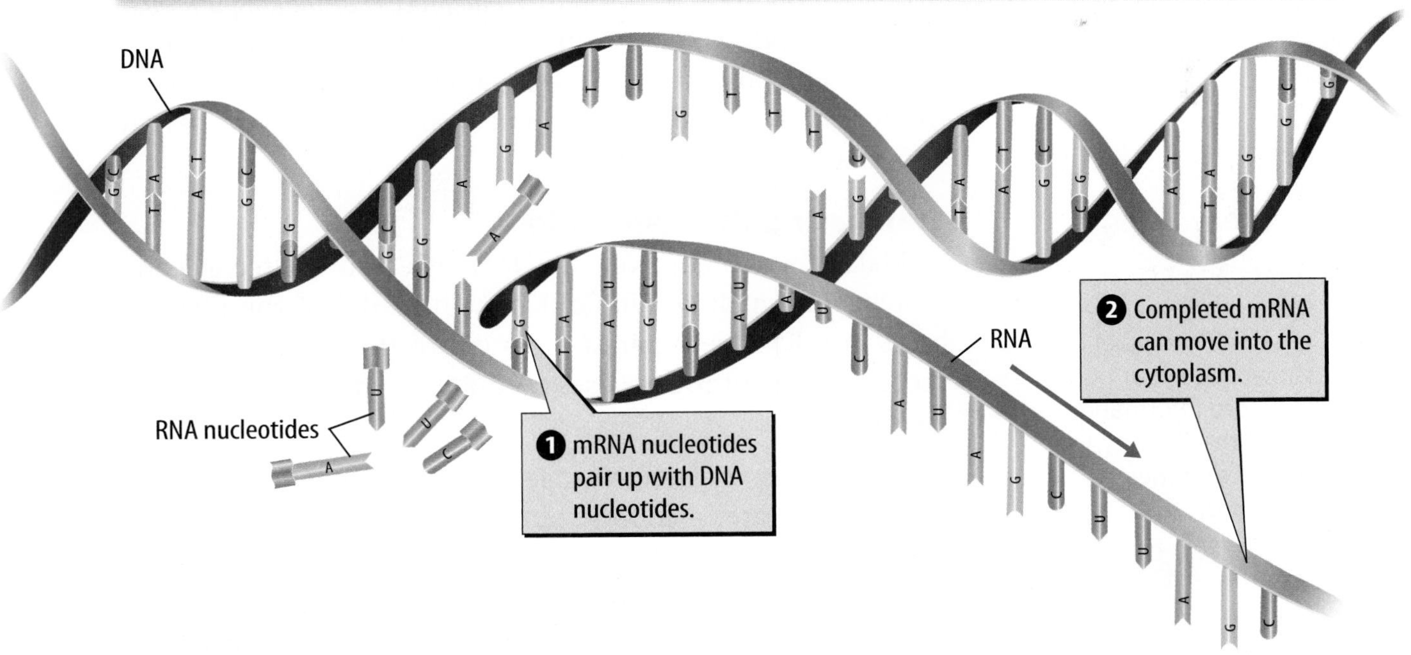

❶ mRNA nucleotides pair up with DNA nucleotides.

❷ Completed mRNA can move into the cytoplasm.

Figure 15 Transcription is the first step in making a protein. During transcription, the sequence of nitrogen bases on a gene determines the sequence of bases on mRNA.

Translation

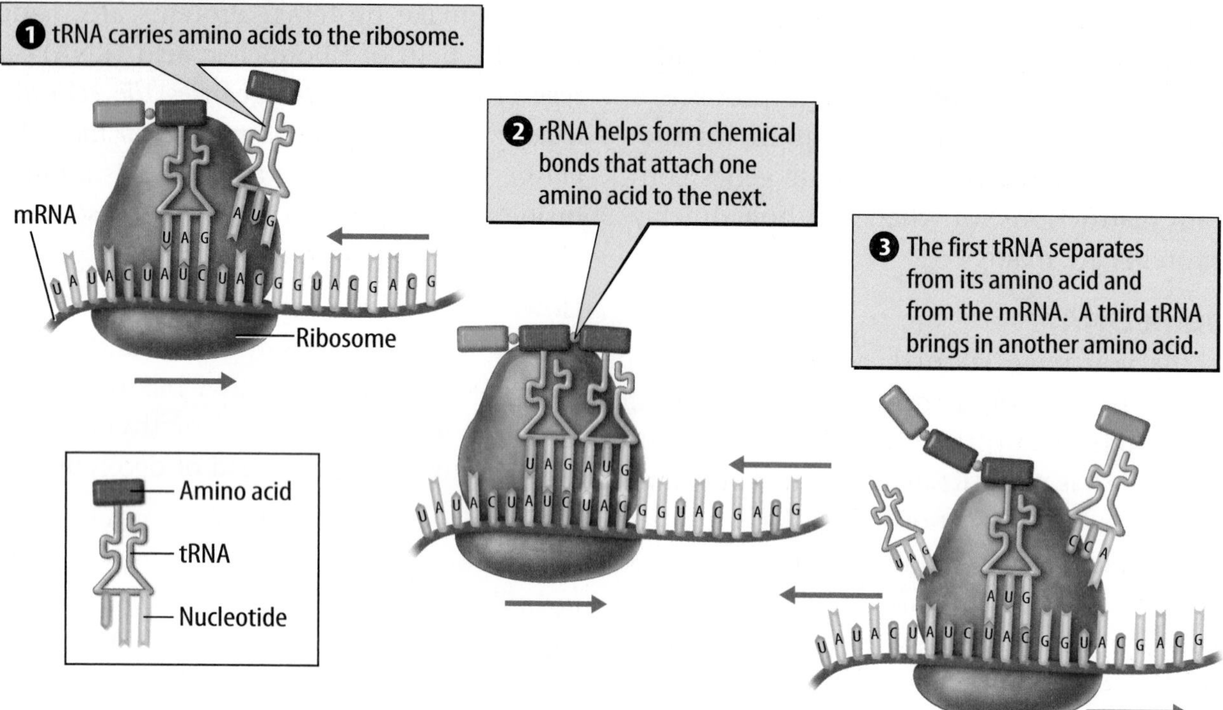

1 tRNA carries amino acids to the ribosome.
mRNA
Ribosome
2 rRNA helps form chemical bonds that attach one amino acid to the next.
3 The first tRNA separates from its amino acid and from the mRNA. A third tRNA brings in another amino acid.
Amino acid
tRNA
Nucleotide

Figure 16 A protein forms as mRNA moves through a ribosome. Different amino acid sequences make different proteins. A complete protein is a folded chain of amino acids.

Three Types of RNA

On the previous page, you read about messenger RNA (mRNA). There are two other types of RNA, transfer RNA (tRNA) and ribosomal RNA (rRNA). **Figure 16** illustrates how the three work together to make proteins. *The process of making a protein from RNA is called* **translation.** Translation occurs in ribosomes. Recall that ribosomes are cell organelles that are attached to the rough endoplasmic reticulum (rough ER). Ribosomes are also in a cell's cytoplasm.

Translating the RNA Code

Making a protein from mRNA is like using a secret code. Proteins are made of amino acids. The order of the nitrogen bases in mRNA determines the order of the amino acids in a protein. Three nitrogen bases on mRNA form the code for one amino acid.

Each series of three nitrogen bases on mRNA is called a codon. There are 64 codons, but only 20 amino acids. Some of the codons code for the same amino acid. One of the codons codes for an amino acid that is the beginning of a protein. This codon signals that translation should start. Three of the codons do not code for any amino acid. Instead, they code for the end of the protein. They signal that translation should stop.

Reading Check What is a codon?

FOLDABLES®

Make a vertical three-tab book and label it as shown. Use your book to record information about the three types of RNA and their functions.

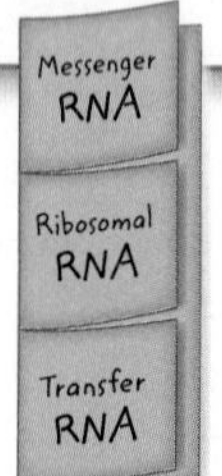

Mutations

You have read that the sequence of nitrogen bases in DNA determines the sequence of nitrogen bases in mRNA, and that the mRNA sequence determines the sequence of amino acids in a protein. You might think these sequences always stay the same, but they can change. *A change in the nucleotide sequence of a gene is called a* **mutation.**

The 46 human chromosomes contain between 20,000 and 25,000 genes that are copied during DNA replication. Sometimes, mistakes can happen during replication. Most mistakes are corrected before replication is completed. A mistake that is not corrected can result in a mutation. Mutations can be triggered by exposure to X-rays, ultraviolet light, radioactive materials, and some kinds of chemicals.

WORD ORIGIN
mutation
from Latin *mutare*, means "to change"

Types of Mutations

There are several types of DNA mutations. Three types are shown in **Figure 17.** In a deletion mutation, one or more nitrogen bases are left out of the DNA sequence. In an insertion mutation, one or more nitrogen bases are added to the DNA. In a substitution mutation, one nitrogen base is replaced by a different nitrogen base.

Each type of mutation changes the sequence of nitrogen base pairs. This can cause a mutated gene to code for a different protein than a normal gene. Some mutated genes do not code for any protein. For example, a cell might lose the ability to make one of the proteins it needs.

Figure 17 Three types of mutations are substitution, insertion, and deletion.

Visual Check Which base pairs were omitted during replication in the deletion mutation?

Mutations

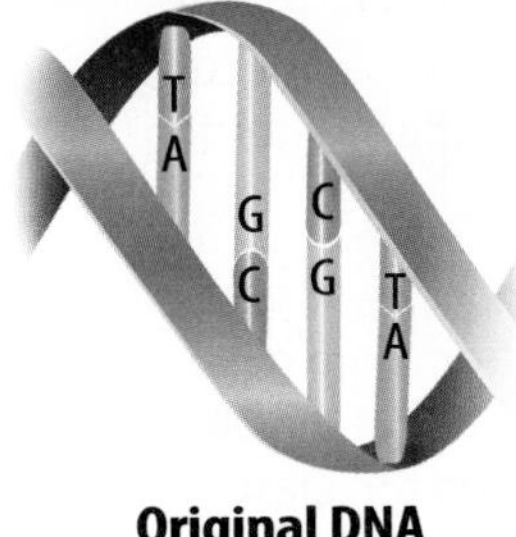

Original DNA sequence

Substitution
The C-G base pair has been replaced with a T-A pair.

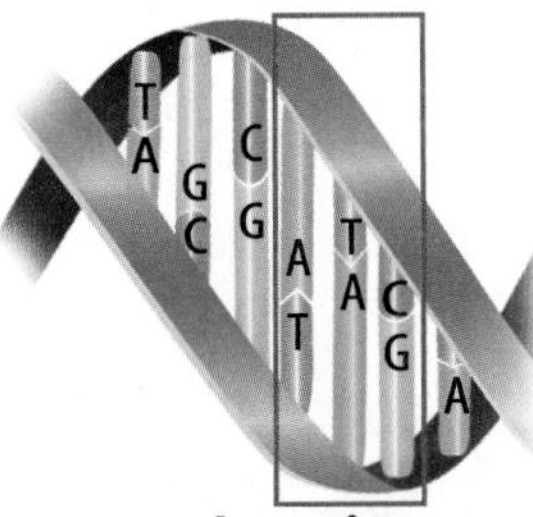

Insertion
Three base pairs have been added.

Deletion
Three base pairs have been removed. Other base pairs will move in to take their place.

Results of a Mutation

The effects of a mutation depend on where in the DNA sequence the mutation happens and the type of mutation. Proteins express traits. Because mutations can change proteins, they can cause traits to change. Some mutations in human DNA cause genetic disorders, such as those described in **Table 4.**

However, not all mutations have negative effects. Some mutations don't cause changes in proteins, so they don't affect traits. Other mutations might cause a trait to change in a way that benefits the organism.

Key Concept Check How do changes in the sequence of DNA affect traits?

Scientists still have much to learn about genes and how they determine an organism's traits. Scientists are researching and experimenting to identify all genes that cause specific traits. With this knowledge, we might be one step closer to finding cures and treatments for genetic disorders.

Table 4 Genetic Disorders

Defective Gene or Chromosome	Disorder	Description
Chromosome 12, PAH gene	Phenylketonuria (PKU)	People with defective PAH genes cannot break down the amino acid phenylalanine. If phenylalanine builds up in the blood, it poisons nerve cells.
Chromosome 7, CFTR gene	Cystic fibrosis	In people with defective CFTR genes, salt cannot move in and out of cells normally. Mucus builds up outside cells. The mucus can block airways in lungs and affect digestion.
Chromosome 7, elastin gene	Williams syndrome	People with Williams syndrome are missing part of chromosome 7, including the elastin gene. The protein made from the elastin gene makes blood vessels strong and stretchy.
Chromosome 17, BRCA 1; Chromosome 13, BRCA 2	Breast cancer and ovarian cancer	A defect in BRCA1 and/or BRCA2 does not mean the person will have breast cancer or ovarian cancer. People with defective BRCA1 or BRCA2 genes have an increased risk of developing breast cancer and ovarian cancer.

Lesson 3 Review

✓ Assessment Online Quiz

Visual Summary

DNA is a complex molecule that contains the code for an organism's genetic information.

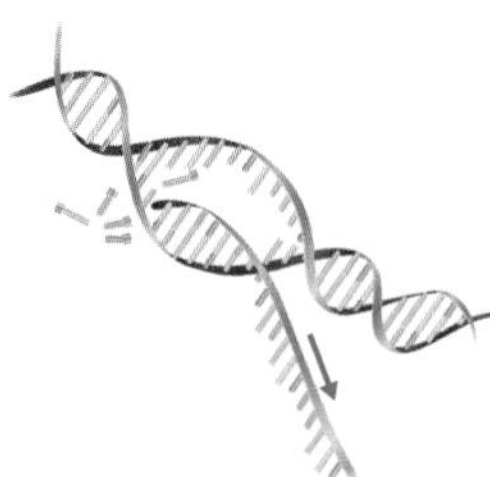

RNA carries the codes for making proteins.

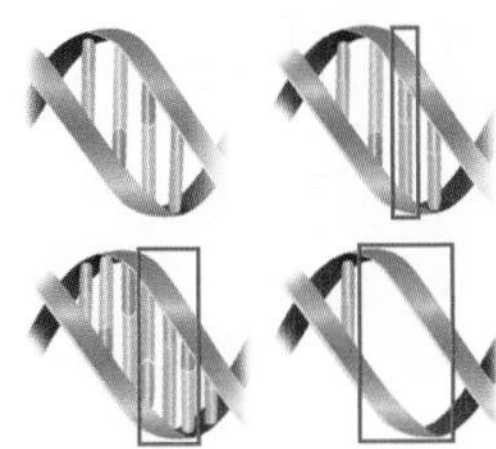

An organism's nucleotide sequence can change through the deletion, insertion, or substitution of nitrogen bases.

FOLDABLES®

Use your lesson Foldable to review the lesson. Save your Foldable for the project at the end of the chapter.

What do you think NOW?

You first read the statements below at the beginning of the chapter.

5. Any condition present at birth is genetic.

6. A change in the sequence of an organism's DNA always changes the organism's traits.

Did you change your mind about whether you agree or disagree with the statements? Rewrite any false statements to make them true.

Use Vocabulary

1. **Distinguish** between transcription and translation.
2. **Use the terms** *DNA* and *nucleotide* in a sentence.
3. A change in the sequence of nitrogen bases in a gene is called a(n) ________.

Understand Key Concepts 

4. Where does the process of transcription occur?
   - **A.** cytoplasm
   - **B.** ribosomes
   - **C.** cell nucleus
   - **D.** outside the cell
5. **Illustrate** Make a drawing that illustrates the process of translation.
6. **Distinguish** between the sides of the DNA double helix and the teeth of the DNA double helix.

Interpret Graphics

7. **Identify** The products of what process are shown in the figure below?

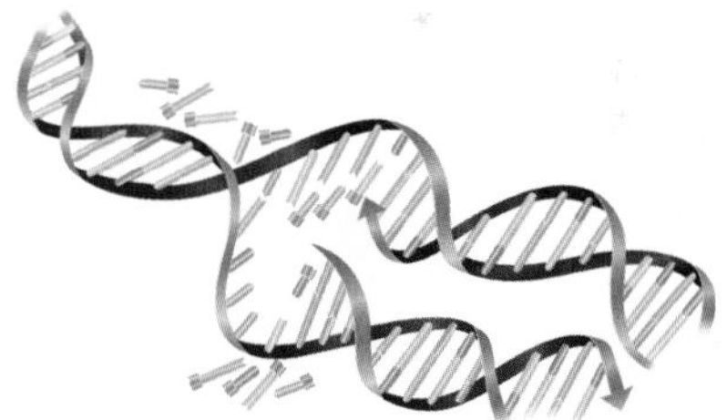

8. **Sequence** Draw a graphic organizer like the one below about important steps in making a protein, beginning with DNA and ending with protein.

Critical Thinking

9. **Hypothesize** What would happen if a cell were unable to make mRNA?
10. **Assess** What is the importance of DNA replication occurring without any mistakes?

Lab **40 minutes**

Gummy Bear Genetics

Materials

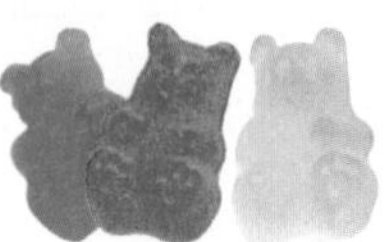

gummy bears

calculator

paper bag

Safety

Imagine you are on a team of geneticists that is doing "cross-breeding experiments" with gummy bears. Unfortunately, the computer containing your data has crashed. All you have left are six gummy-bear litters that resulted from six sets of parents. But no one can remember which parents produced which litter. You know that gummy-bear traits have either Mendelian inheritance or incomplete dominance. Can you determine which parents produced each set of offspring and how gummy bear traits are inherited?

Ask a Question

What are the genotypes and phenotypes of the parents for each litter?

Make Observations

1. Obtain a bag of gummy bears. Sort the bears by color (phenotype).

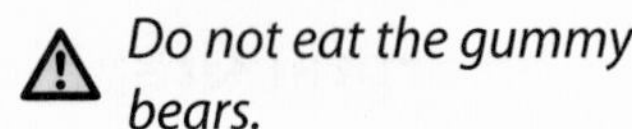

⚠ *Do not eat the gummy bears.*

2. Count the number (frequency) of bears for each phenotype. Then, calculate the ratio of phenotypes for each litter.
3. Combine data from your litter with those of your classmates using a data table like the one below.
4. As a class, select a letter to represent the alleles for color. Record the possible genotypes for your bears in the class data table.

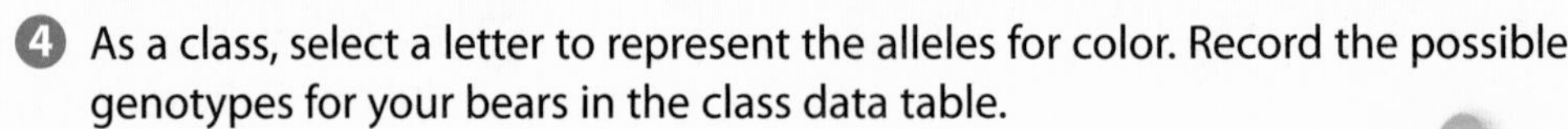

Gummy Bear Cross Data for Lab Group

Cross #	Phenotype Frequencies	Ratio	Possible Genotypes	Mode of Inheritance	Predicted Parental Genotypes
EXAMPLE	15 green/5 pink	3:1	GG or Gg/gg	Mendelian	Gg x Gg
1.					
2.					
3.					
4.					

Form a Hypothesis

5. Use the data to form a hypothesis about the probable genotypes and phenotypes of the parents of your litter and the probable type of inheritance.

Test Your Hypothesis

6. Design and complete a Punnett square using the predicted parental genotypes in your hypothesis.
7. Compare your litter's phenotype ratio with the ratio predicted by the Punnett square. Do your data support your hypothesis? If not, revise your hypothesis and repeat steps 5–7.

Analyze and Conclude

8. **Infer** What were the genotypes of the parents? The phenotypes? How do you know?
9. **The Big Idea** Determine the probable modes of inheritance for each phenotype. Explain your reasoning.
10. **Graph** Using the data you collected, draw a bar graph that compares the phenotype frequency for each gummy bear phenotype.

Communicate Your Results

Create a video presentation of the results of your lab. Describe the question you investigated, the steps you took to answer the question, and the data that support your conclusions. Share your video with your classmates.

Inquiry Extension

Think of a question you have about genetics. For example, can you design a pedigree to trace a Mendelian trait in your family? To investigate your question, design a controlled experiment or an observational study.

6

Reminder

Using Ratios

- ☑ A ratio is a comparison of two numbers.
- ☑ A ratio of 15:5 can be reduced to 3:1.

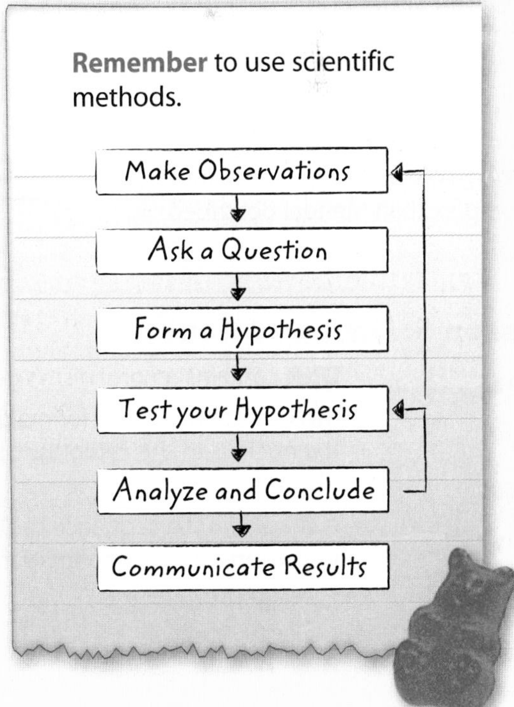

Chapter 11 Study Guide

Inherited genes are the basis of an organism's traits.

Key Concepts Summary

Lesson 1: Mendel and His Peas

- Mendel performed cross-pollination experiments to track which traits were produced by specific parental crosses.
- Mendel found that two genetic factors—one from a sperm cell and one from an egg cell—control each trait.
- **Dominant** traits block the expression of **recessive** traits. Recessive traits are expressed only when two recessive factors are present.

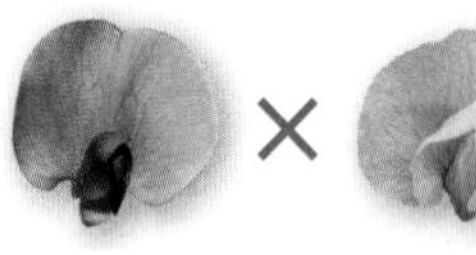
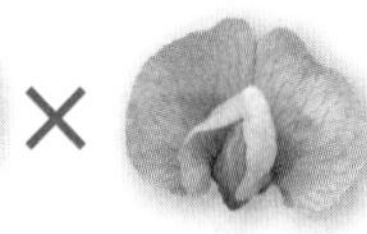

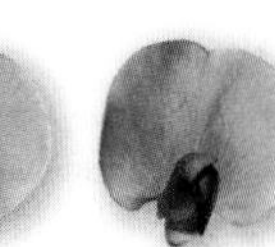

Vocabulary

heredity p. 389
genetics p. 389
dominant p. 395
recessive p. 395

Lesson 2: Understanding Inheritance

- **Phenotype** describes how a trait appears.
- **Genotype** describes alleles that control a trait.
- **Punnett squares** and pedigrees are tools to model patterns of inheritance.
- Many patterns of inheritance, such as **codominance** and **polygenic inheritance**, are more complex than Mendel described.

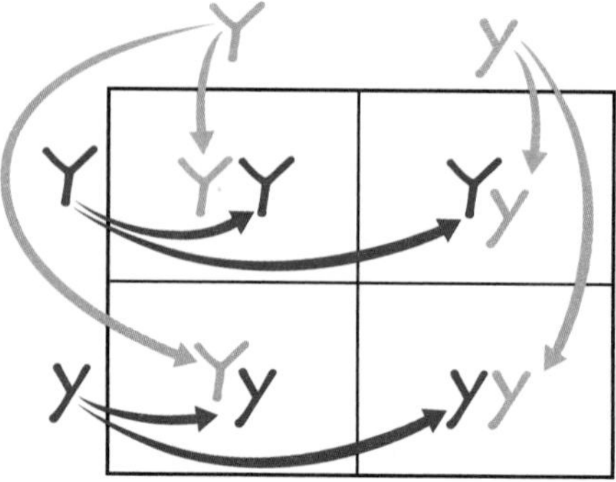

Vocabulary

gene p. 400
allele p. 400
phenotype p. 400
genotype p. 400
homozygous p. 401
heterozygous p. 401
Punnett square p. 402
incomplete dominance p. 404
codominance p. 404
polygenic inheritance p. 405

Lesson 3: DNA and Genetics

- **DNA** contains an organism's genetic information.
- **RNA** carries the codes for making proteins from the nucleus to the cytoplasm. RNA also forms part of ribosomes.
- A change in the sequence of DNA, called a **mutation**, can change the traits of an organism.

Vocabulary

DNA p. 410
nucleotide p. 411
replication p. 412
RNA p. 413
transcription p. 413
translation p. 414
mutation p. 415

Study Guide

Review

- Personal Tutor
- Vocabulary eGames
- Vocabulary eFlashcards

FOLDABLES® Chapter Project

Assemble your lesson Foldables as shown to make a Chapter Project. Use the project to review what you have learned in this chapter.

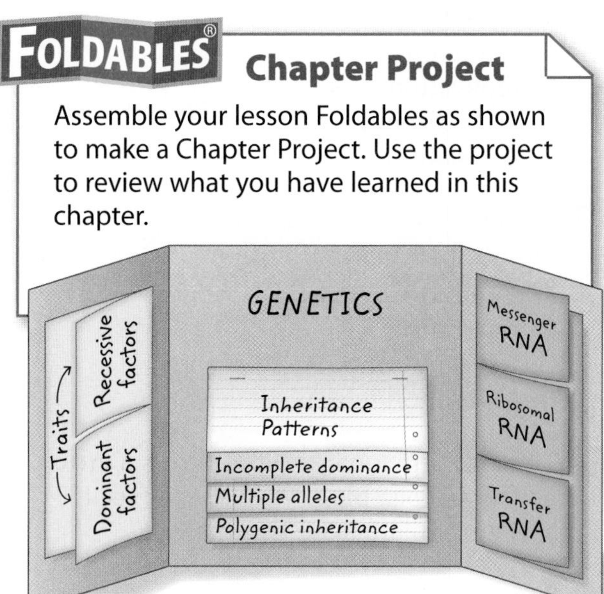

Use Vocabulary

1. The study of how traits are passed from parents to offspring is called ________.
2. The passing of traits from parents to offspring is ________.
3. Human height, weight, and skin color are examples of characteristics determined by ________.
4. A helpful device for predicting the ratios of possible genotypes is a(n) ________.
5. The code for a protein is called a(n) ________.
6. An error made during the copying of DNA is called a(n) ________.

Link Vocabulary and Key Concepts

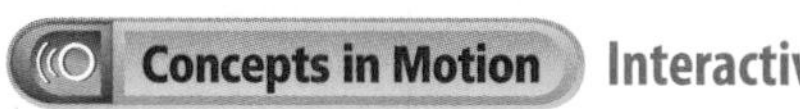

Interactive Concept Map

Copy this concept map, and then use vocabulary terms from the previous page to complete the concept map.

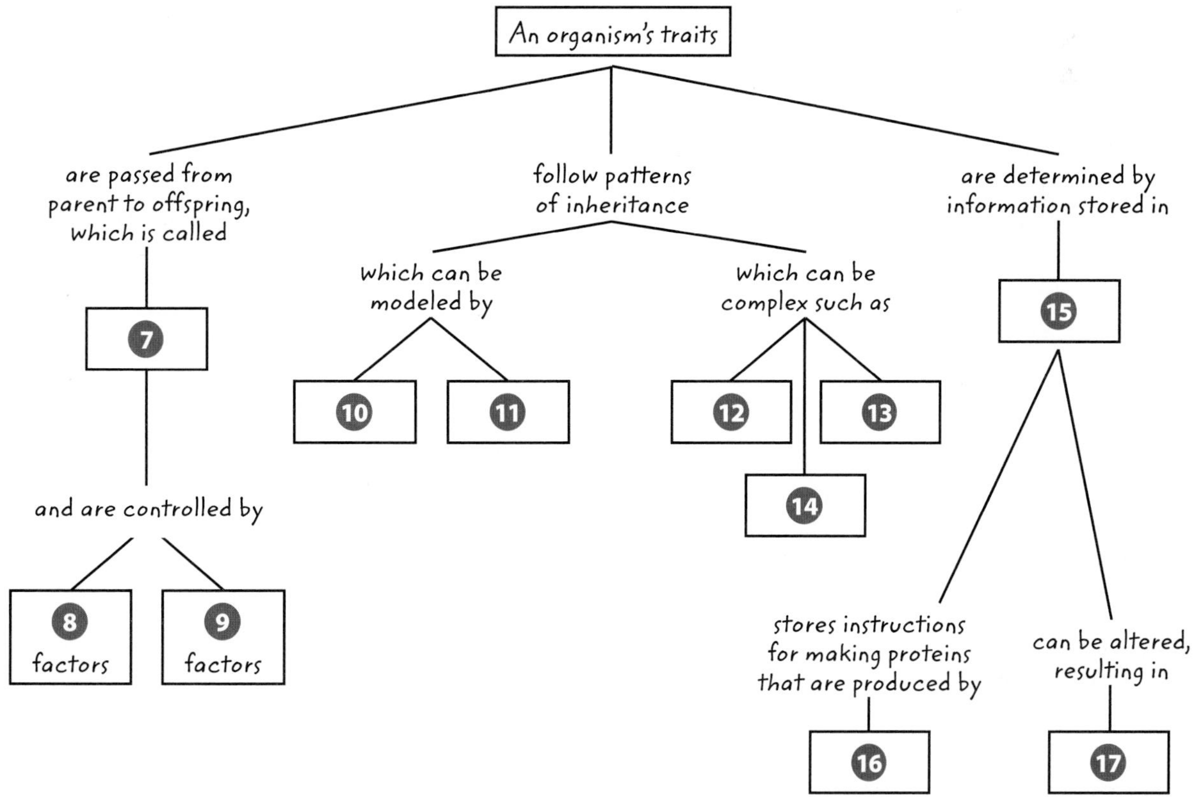

Chapter 11 Review

Understand Key Concepts 

1. The process shown below was used by Mendel during his experiments.

What is the process called?
A. cross-pollination
B. segregation
C. asexual reproduction
D. blending inheritance

2. Which statement best describes Mendel's experiments?
A. He began with hybrid plants.
B. He controlled pollination.
C. He observed only one generation.
D. He used plants that reproduce slowly.

3. Before Mendel's discoveries, which statement describes how people believed traits were inherited?
A. Parental traits blend like colors of paint to produce offspring.
B. Parental traits have no effect on their offspring.
C. Traits from only the female parent are inherited by offspring.
D. Traits from only the male parent are inherited by offspring.

4. Which term describes the offspring of a first-generation cross between parents with different forms of a trait?
A. genotype
B. hybrid
C. phenotype
D. true-breeding

5. Which process makes a copy of a DNA molecule?
A. mutation
B. replication
C. transcription
D. translation

6. Which process uses the code on an RNA molecule to make a protein?
A. mutation
B. replication
C. transcription
D. translation

7. The Punnett square below shows a cross between a pea plant with yellow seeds and a pea plant with green seeds.

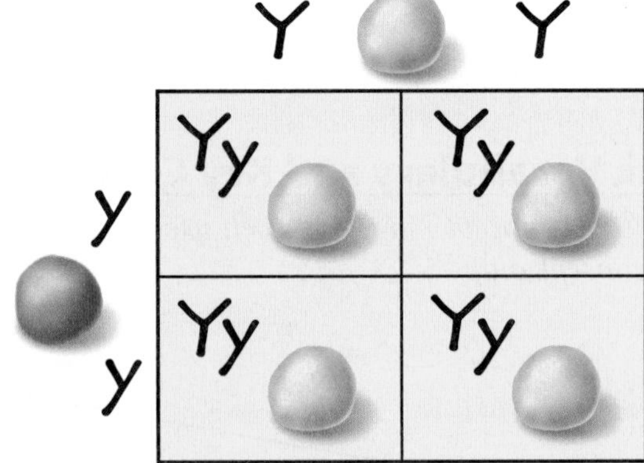

If mating produces 100 offspring, about how many will have yellow seeds?
A. 25
B. 50
C. 75
D. 100

8. Which term describes multiple genes affecting the phenotype of one trait?
A. codominance
B. blending inheritance
C. incomplete dominance
D. polygenic inheritance

Assessment
Online Test Practice

Critical Thinking

9 **Compare** heterozygous genotype and homozygous genotype.

10 **Distinguish** between multiple alleles and polygenic inheritance.

11 **Give an example** of how the environment can affect an organism's phenotype.

12 **Predict** In pea plants, the allele for smooth pods is dominant to the allele for bumpy pods. Predict the genotype of a plant with bumpy pods. Can you predict the genotype of a plant with smooth pods? Explain.

13 **Interpret Graphics** In tomato plants, red fruit *(R)* is dominant to yellow fruit *(r)*. Interpret the Punnett square below, which shows a cross between a heterozygous red plant and a yellow plant. Include the possible genotypes and corresponding phenotypes.

	R	r
r	Rr	rr
r	Rr	rr

14 **Compare and contrast** characteristics of replication, transcription, translation, and mutation. Which of these processes takes place only in the nucleus of a cell? Which can take place in both the nucleus and the cytoplasm? How do you know?

Writing in Science

15 **Write** a paragraph contrasting the blending theory of inheritance with the current theory of inheritance. Include a main idea, supporting details, and a concluding sentence.

REVIEW THE BIG IDEA

16 How are traits passed from generation to generation? Explain how dominant and recessive alleles interact to determine the expression of traits.

17 The photo below shows an albino offspring from a non-albino mother. If albinism is a recessive trait, what are the possible genotypes of the mother, the father, and the offspring?

Math Skills

Math Practice

Use Ratios

18 A cross between two heterozygous pea plants with yellow seeds produced 1,719 yellow seeds and 573 green seeds. What is the ratio of yellow to green seeds?

19 A cross between two heterozygous pea plants with smooth green pea pods produced 87 bumpy yellow pea pods, 261 smooth yellow pea pods, 261 bumpy green pea pods, and 783 smooth green pea pods. What is the ratio of bumpy yellow to smooth yellow to bumpy green to smooth green pea pods?

20 A jar contains three red, five green, two blue, and six yellow marbles. What is the ratio of red to green to blue to yellow marbles?

Standardized Test Practice

Record your answers on the answer sheet provided by your teacher or on a sheet of paper.

Multiple Choice

Use the diagram below to answer questions 1 and 2.

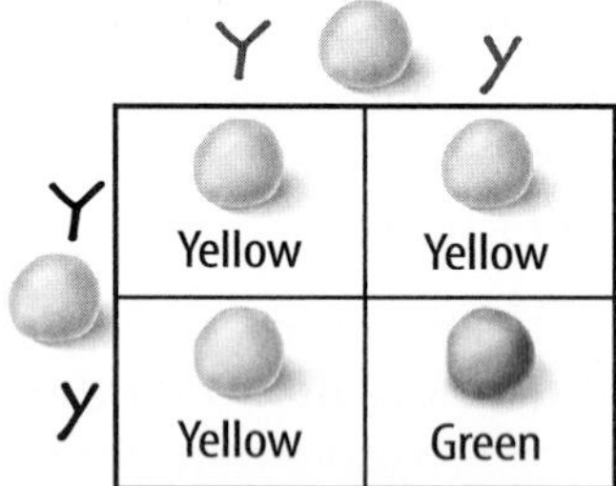

1 Which genotype belongs in the lower right square?

A YY

B Yy

C yY

D yy

2 What percentage of plants from this cross will produce yellow seeds?

A 25 percent

B 50 percent

C 75 percent

D 100 percent

3 When Mendel crossed a true-breeding plant with purple flowers and a true-breeding plant with white flowers, ALL offspring had purple flowers. This is because white flowers are

A dominant.

B heterozygous.

C polygenic.

D recessive.

4 Which process copies an organism's DNA?

A mutation

B replication

C transcription

D translation

Use the chart below to answer question 5.

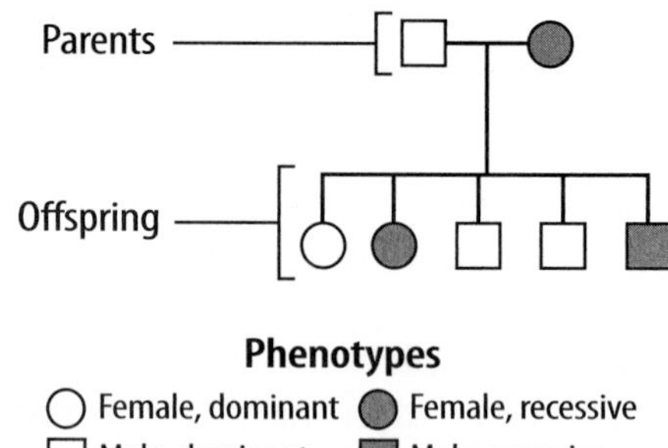

5 Based on the pedigree above, how many offspring from this cross had the recessive phenotype?

A 1

B 2

C 3

D 5

6 Which is NOT true of a hybrid?

A It has one recessive allele.

B It has pairs of chromosomes.

C Its genotype is homozygous.

D Its phenotype is dominant.

7 Alleles are different forms of a

A chromosome.

B gene.

C nucleotide.

D protein.

8 Which is true of an offspring with incomplete dominance?

A Both alleles can be observed in its phenotype.

B Every offspring shows the dominant phenotype.

C Multiple genes determine its phenotype.

D Offspring phenotype is a combination of the parents' phenotypes.

Use the diagrams below to answer question 9.

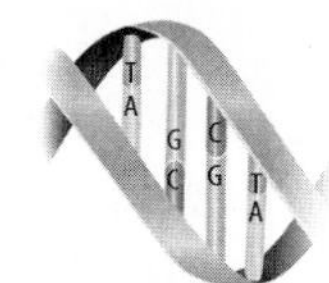

Before Replication

After Replication

9 The diagrams above show a segment of DNA before and after replication. Which occurred during replication?

A deletion

B insertion

C substitution

D translation

10 Which human characteristic is controlled by polygenic inheritance?

A blood type

B earlobe position

C eye color

D thumb shape

11 Mendel crossed a true-breeding plant with round seeds and a true-breeding plant with wrinkled seeds. Which was true of every offspring of this cross?

A They had the recessive phenotype.

B They showed a combination of traits.

C They were homozygous.

D They were hybrid plants.

Constructed Response

Use the diagram below to answer questions 12 and 13.

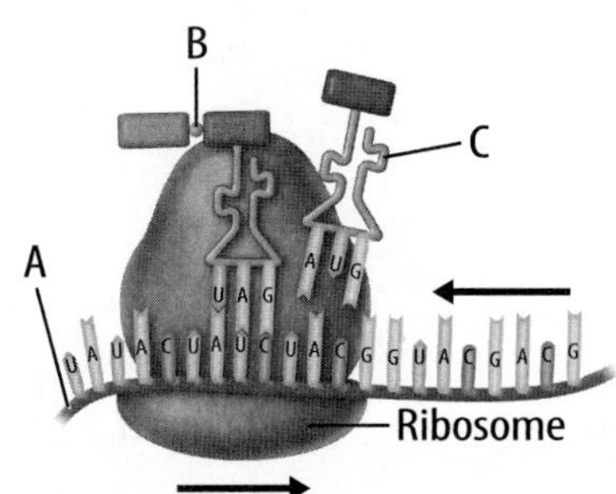

12 Describe what is happening in the phase of translation shown in the diagram.

13 What are the three types of RNA in the diagram? How do these types work together during translation?

14 What is the importance of translation in your body?

15 Mendel began his experiments with true-breeding plants. Why was this important?

16 How did Mendel's experimental methods help him develop his hypotheses on inheritance?

17 What environmental factors affect the phenotypes of organisms other than humans? Provide three examples from nature. What factor, other than genes, affects human phenotype? Give two examples. Why is knowledge of this non-genetic factor helpful?

NEED EXTRA HELP?																	
If You Missed Question...	1	2	3	4	5	6	7	8	9	10	11	12	13	14	15	16	17
Go to Lesson...	2	2	1	3	2	1,2	2	2	3	2	1	3	3	3	1	1	2

Chapter 12

The Environment and Change Over Time

THE BIG IDEA

How do species adapt to changing environments over time?

Swarm of Bees?

A type of orchid plant, called a bee orchid, produces this flower. You might have noticed that the flower looks like a bee.

- What is the advantage to the plant to have flowers that look like bees?
- How did the appearance of the flower develop over time?
- How do species adapt to changing environments over time?

Get Ready to Read

What do you think?

Before you read, decide if you agree or disagree with each of these statements. As you read this chapter, see if you change your mind about any of the statements.

1. Original tissues can be preserved as fossils.
2. Organisms become extinct only in mass extinction events.
3. Environmental change causes variations in populations.
4. Variations can lead to adaptations.
5. Living species contain no evidence that they are related to each other.
6. Plants and animals share similar genes.

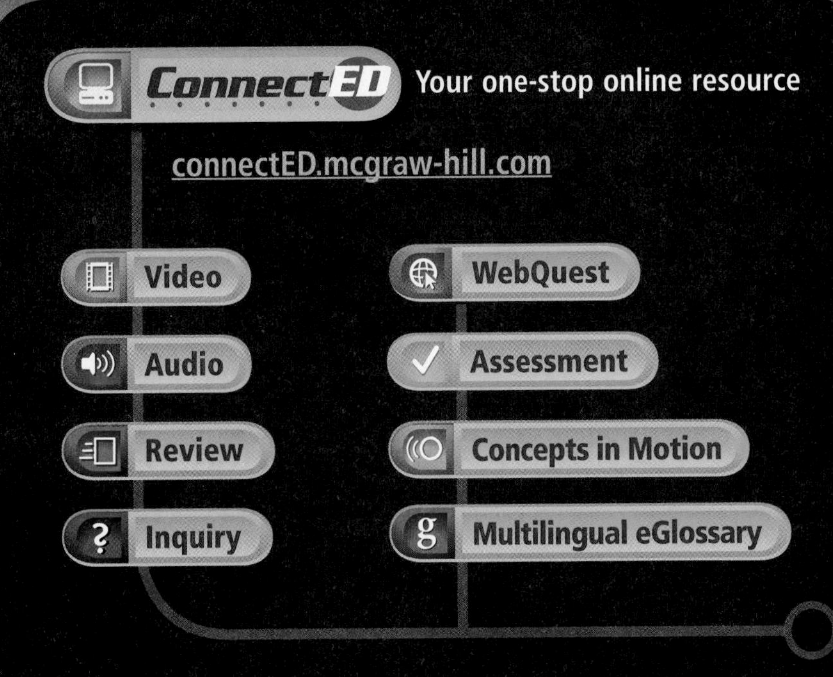

Lesson 1

Reading Guide

Key Concepts
ESSENTIAL QUESTIONS

- How do fossils form?
- How do scientists date fossils?
- How are fossils evidence of biological evolution?

Vocabulary

fossil record p. 429
mold p. 431
cast p. 431
trace fossil p. 431
geologic time scale p. 433
extinction p. 434
biological evolution p. 435

Multilingual eGlossary

Video BrainPOP®

Academic Standards for Science

8.3.9 Describe the effect of environmental changes on populations of organisms when their adaptive characteristics put them at a disadvantage for survival. Describe how extinction of a species can ultimately result.

Also covers: 8.NS.7, 8.NS.8, 8.NS.9, 8.NS.11

Fossil Evidence of Evolution

Inquiry What can be learned from fossils?

When scientists find fossils, they use them as evidence to try to answer questions about past life on Earth. When did this organism live? What did this organism eat? How did it move or grow? How did this organism die? To what other organisms is this one related?

Launch Lab

20 minutes

How do fossils form?

Evidence from fossils helps scientists understand how organisms have changed over time. Some fossils form when impressions left by organisms in sand or mud are filled in by sediments that harden.

1. Read and complete a lab safety form.
2. Place a **container of moist sand** on top of **newspaper.** Press a **shell** into the moist sand. Carefully remove the shell. Brush any sand on the shell onto the newspaper.
3. Observe the impression, and record your observations in your Science Journal.
4. Pour **plaster of paris** into the impression. Wait for it to harden. ⚠ *The mix gets hot as it sets—do not touch it until it has hardened.*
5. Remove the shell fossil from the sand, and brush it off.
6. Observe the structure of the fossil, and record your observations.

Think About This

1. What effect did the shell have on the sand?
2. **Key Concept** What information do you think someone could learn about the shell and the organism that lived inside it by examining the fossil?

The Fossil Record

On your way to school, you might have seen an oak tree or heard a robin. Although these organisms shed leaves or feathers, their characteristics remain the same from day to day. It might seem as if they have been on Earth forever. However, if you were to travel a few million years back in time, you would not see oak trees or robins. You would see different species of trees and birds. That is because species change over time.

You might already know that fossils are the remains or evidence of once-living organisms. *The* **fossil record** *is made up of all the fossils ever discovered on Earth.* It contains millions of fossils that represent many thousands of species. Most of these species are no longer alive on Earth. The fossil record provides evidence that species have changed over time. Fossils help scientists picture what these species looked like. **Figure 1** shows how scientists think the giant bird *Titanus* might have looked when it was alive. The image is based on fossils that have been discovered and are represented in the photo on the previous page.

The fossil record is enormous, but it is still incomplete. Scientists think it represents only a small fraction of all the organisms that have ever lived on Earth.

Figure 1 Based on fossil evidence, scientists can recreate the physical appearance of species that are no longer alive on Earth.

Fossil Formation

If you have ever seen vultures or other animals eating a dead animal, you know they leave little behind. Any soft **tissues** animals do not eat, bacteria break down. Only the dead animal's hard parts, such as bones, shells, and teeth, remain. In most instances, these hard parts also break down over time. However, under rare conditions, some become fossils. The soft tissues of animals and plants, such as skin, muscles, or leaves, can also become fossils, but these are even more rare. Some of the ways that fossils can form are shown in **Table 1.**

SCIENCE USE V. COMMON USE
tissue
Science Use similar cells that work together and perform a function

Common Use a piece of soft, absorbent paper

 **Reading Check** Why is it rare for soft tissue to become a fossil?

Mineralization

After an organism dies, its body could be buried under mud, sand, or other sediments in a stream or river. If minerals in the water replace the organism's original material and harden into rock, a fossil forms. This process is called mineralization. Minerals in water also can filter into the small spaces of a dead organism's tissues and become rock. Most mineralized fossils are of shell or bone, but wood can also become a mineralized fossil, as shown in **Table 1.**

Carbonization

In carbonization, a fossil forms when a dead organism is compressed over time and pressure drives off the organism's liquids and gases. As shown in **Table 1,** only the carbon outline, or film, of the organism remains.

Table 1 Fossils form in several ways.

Visual Check What types of organisms or tissues are often preserved as carbon films?

Table 1 How Fossils Form

	Mineralization	Carbonization
Description	Rock-forming minerals in water filled in the small spaces in the tissue of these pieces of petrified wood. Water also replaced some of the wood's tissue. Mineralization can preserve the internal structures of an organism.	Fossil films made by carbonization are usually black or dark brown. Fish, insects, and plant leaves, such as this fern frond, are often preserved as carbon films.
Example		

Molds and Casts

Sometimes when an organism dies, its shell or bone might make an impression in mud or sand. When the sediment hardens, so does the impression. *The impression of an organism in a rock is called a* **mold.** Sediments can later fill in the mold and harden to form a cast. *A* **cast** *is a fossil copy of an organism in a rock.* A single organism can form both a mold and a cast, as shown in **Table 1.** Molds and casts show only external features of organisms.

Trace Fossils

Evidence of an organism's movement or behavior—not just its physical structure—also can be preserved in rock. *A* **trace fossil** *is the preserved evidence of the activity of an organism.* For example, an organism might walk across mud. The tracks, such as the ones shown in **Table 1,** can fossilize if they are filled with sediment that hardens.

WORD ORIGIN

fossil
from Latin *fossilis,* means "to obtain by digging"

Original Material

In rare cases, the original tissues of an organism can be preserved. Examples of original-material fossils include mammoths frozen in ice and saber-toothed cats preserved in tar pits. Fossilized remains of ancient humans have been found in bogs. Most of these fossils are younger than 10,000 years old. However, the insect encased in amber in **Table 1** is millions of years old. Scientists also have found original tissue preserved in the bone of a dinosaur that lived 70 million years ago (mya).

Key Concept Check List the different ways fossils can form.

Molds and Casts	Trace Fossils	Original Material
When sediments hardened around this buried trilobite, a mold formed. Molds are usually of hard parts, such as shells or bone. If a mold is later filled with more sediments that harden, the mold can form a cast. 	These footprints were made when a dinosaur walked across mud that later hardened. This trace fossil might provide evidence of the speed and weight of the dinosaur. 	If original tissues of organisms are buried in the absence of oxygen for long periods of time, they can fossilize. The insect in this amber became stuck in tree sap that later hardened. 

Dating Fossils

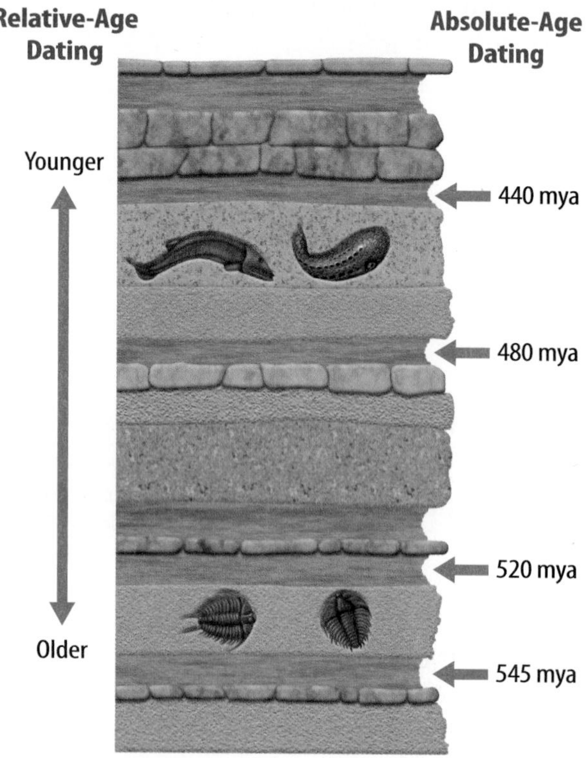

Figure 2 If the age of the igneous layers is known, as shown above, it is possible to estimate the age of the sedimentary layers—and the fossils they contain—between them.

Visual Check What is the estimated age of the trilobite fossils (bottom layer of fossils)?

REVIEW VOCABULARY

isotopes
atoms of the same element that have different numbers of neutrons

Make a small shutter-fold book. Label it as shown. Under the left tab describe relative-age dating. Under the right tab describe absolute-age dating.

Relative-Age Dating | Absolute-Age Dating

Determining a Fossil's Age

Scientists cannot date most fossils directly. Instead, they date the rocks the fossils are embedded inside. Rocks erode or are recycled over time. However, scientists can determine ages for most of Earth's rocks.

Relative-Age Dating

How does your age compare to the ages of those around you? You might be younger than a brother but older than a sister. This is your relative age. Similarly, a rock is either older or younger than rocks nearby. In relative-age dating, scientists determine the relative order in which rock layers were deposited. In an undisturbed rock formation, they know that the bottom layers are oldest and the top layers are youngest, as shown in **Figure 2.** Relative-age dating helps scientists determine the relative order in which species have appeared on Earth over time.

Key Concept Check How does relative-age dating help scientists learn about fossils?

Absolute-Age Dating

Absolute-age dating is more precise than relative-age dating. Scientists take advantage of radioactive decay, a natural clocklike process in rocks, to learn a rock's absolute age, or its age in years. In radioactive decay, unstable **isotopes** in rocks change into stable isotopes over time. Scientists measure the ratio of unstable isotopes to stable isotopes to find the age of a rock. This ratio is best measured in igneous rocks.

Igneous rocks form from volcanic magma. Magma is so hot that it is rare for parts of organisms in it to remain and form fossils. Most fossils form in sediments, which become sedimentary rock. To measure the age of sedimentary rock layers, scientists calculate the ages of igneous layers above and below them. In this way, they can estimate the ages of the fossils embedded within the sedimentary layers, as shown in **Figure 2.**

Fossils over Time

How old do you think Earth's oldest fossils are? You might be surprised to learn that evidence of microscopic, unicellular organisms has been found in rocks 3.4 billion years old. The oldest fossils visible to the unaided eye are about 565 million years old.

The Geologic Time Scale

It is hard to keep track of time that is millions and billions of years long. Scientists organize Earth's history into a time line called the geologic time scale. *The* **geologic time scale** *is a chart that divides Earth's history into different time units.* The longest time units in the geological time scale are eons. As shown in **Figure 3,** Earth's history is divided into four eons. Earth's most recent eon—the Phanerozoic (fa nuh ruh ZOH ihk) eon—is subdivided into three eras, also shown in **Figure 3.**

Reading Check What is the geologic time scale?

Dividing Time

You might have noticed in **Figure 3** that neither eons nor eras are equal in length. When scientists began developing the geologic time scale in the 1800s, they did not have absolute-age dating methods. To mark time boundaries, they used fossils. Fossils provided an easy way to mark time. Scientists knew that different rock layers contained different types of fossils. Some of the fossils scientists use to mark the time boundaries are shown in **Figure 3.**

Often, a type of fossil found in one rock layer did not appear in layers above it. Even more surprising, entire collections of fossils in one layer were sometimes absent from layers above them. It seemed as if whole communities of organisms had suddenly disappeared.

Reading Check What do scientists use to mark boundaries in the geologic time scale?

Review Personal Tutor

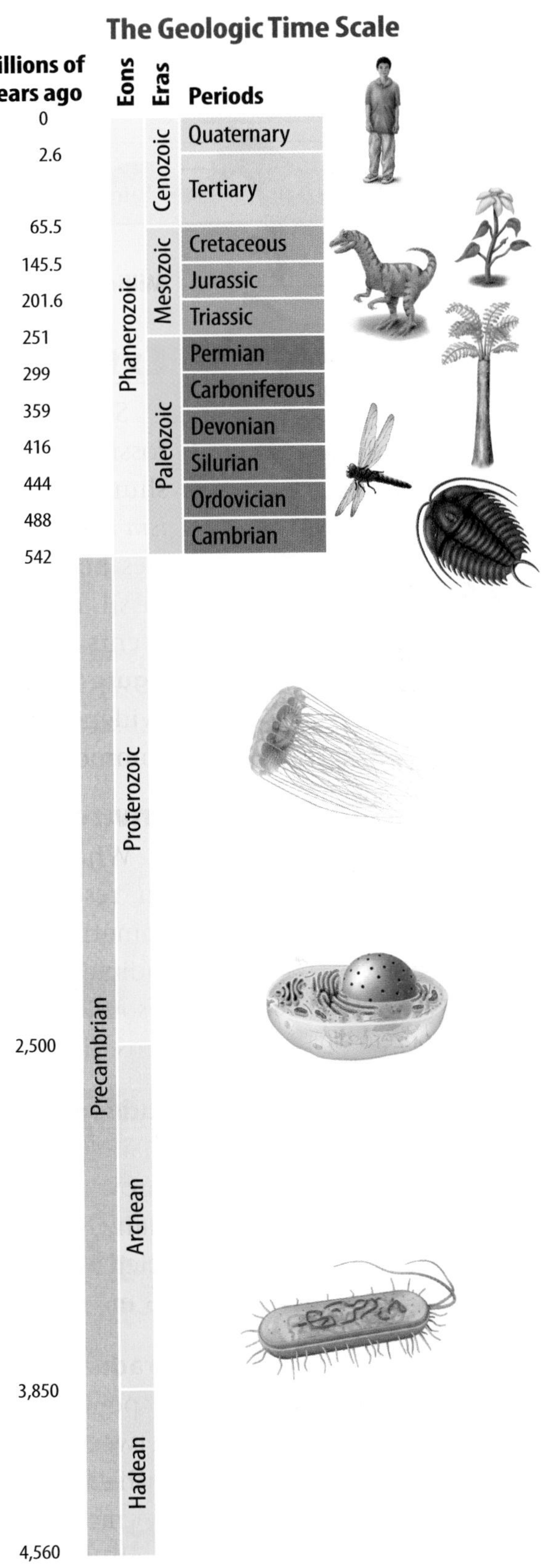

Figure 3 The Phanerozoic eon began about 540 million years ago and continues to the present day. It contains most of Earth's fossil record.

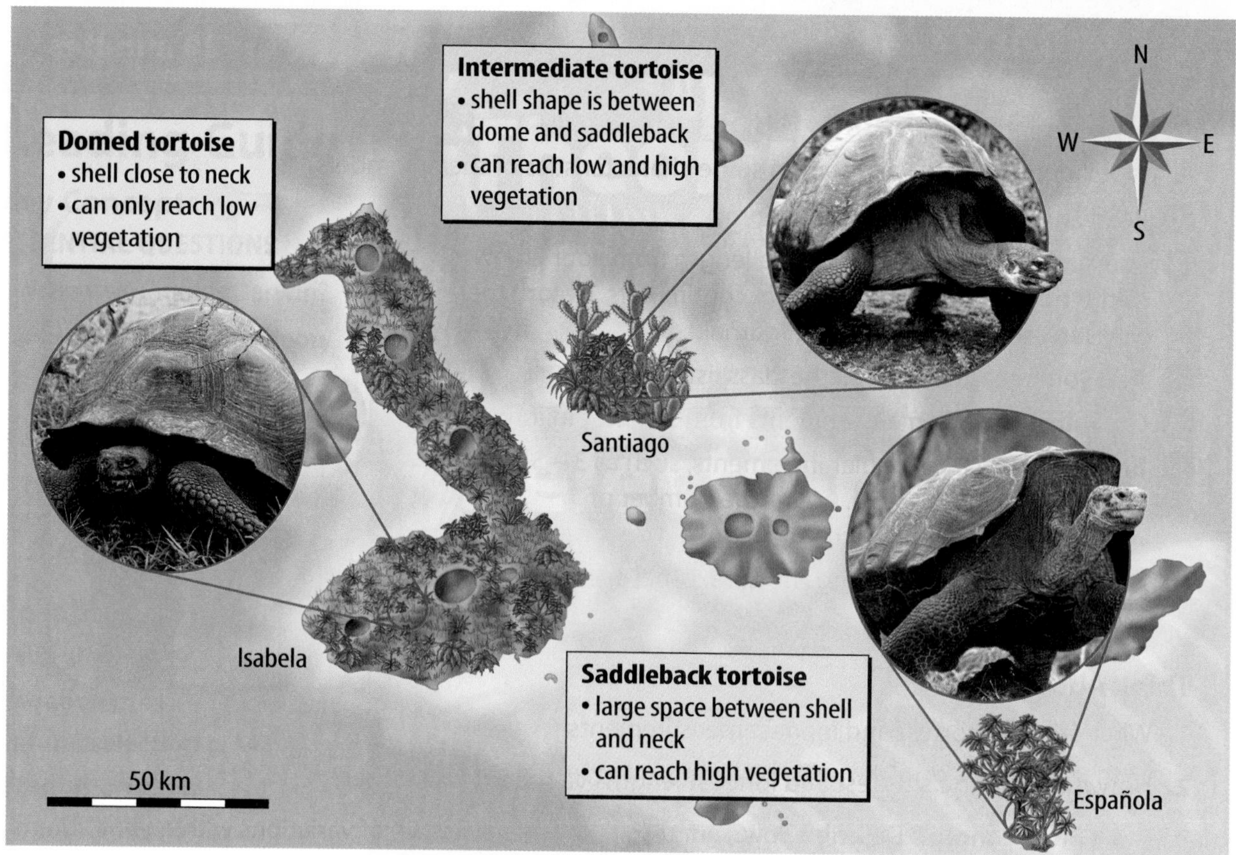

Figure 6 Each island in the Galápagos has a different environment. Tortoises look different depending on which island environment they inhabit.

Visual Check What type of vegetation do domed tortoises eat?

Voyage of the *Beagle*

Darwin served as a naturalist on the HMS *Beagle,* a survey ship of the British navy. During his voyage around the world, Darwin observed and collected many plants and animals.

The Galápagos Islands

Darwin was especially interested in the organisms he saw on the Galápagos (guh LAH puh gus) Islands. The islands, shown in **Figure 6,** are located 1,000 km off the South American coast in the Pacific Ocean. Darwin saw that each island had a slightly different environment. Some were dry. Some were more humid. Others had mixed environments.

Tortoises Giant tortoises lived on many of the islands. When a resident told him that the tortoises on each island looked different, as shown in **Figure 6,** Darwin became curious.

Mockingbirds and Finches Darwin also became curious about the variety of mockingbirds and finches he saw and collected on the islands. Like the tortoises, different types of mockingbirds and finches lived in different island environments. Later, he was surprised to learn that many of these varieties were different enough to be separate species.

Reading Check What made Darwin become curious about the organisms that lived on the Galápagos Islands?

Darwin's Theory

Darwin realized there was a relationship between each species and the food sources of the island it lived on. Look again at **Figure 6.** You can see that tortoises with long necks lived on islands that had tall cacti. Their long necks enabled them to reach high to eat the cacti. The tortoises with short necks lived on islands that had plenty of short grass.

Common Ancestors

Darwin became **convinced** that all the tortoise species were related. He thought they all shared a common ancestor. He suspected that a storm had carried a small ancestral tortoise population to one of the islands from South America millions of years before. Eventually, the tortoises spread to the other islands. Their neck lengths and shell shapes changed to match their islands' food sources. How did this happen?

ACADEMIC VOCABULARY

convince
(verb) to overcome by argument

Variations

Darwin knew that individual members of a species exhibit slight differences, or variations. *A* **variation** *is a slight difference in an inherited trait of individual members of a species.* Even though the snail shells in **Figure 7** are not all exactly the same, they are all from snails of the same species. You can also see variations in the zebras in the photo at the beginning of this lesson. Variations arise naturally in populations. They occur in the offspring as a result of sexual reproduction. You might recall that variations are caused by random mutations, or changes, in genes. Mutations can lead to changes in phenotype. Recall that an organism's phenotype is all of the observable traits and characteristics of the organism. Genetic changes to phenotype can be passed on to future generations.

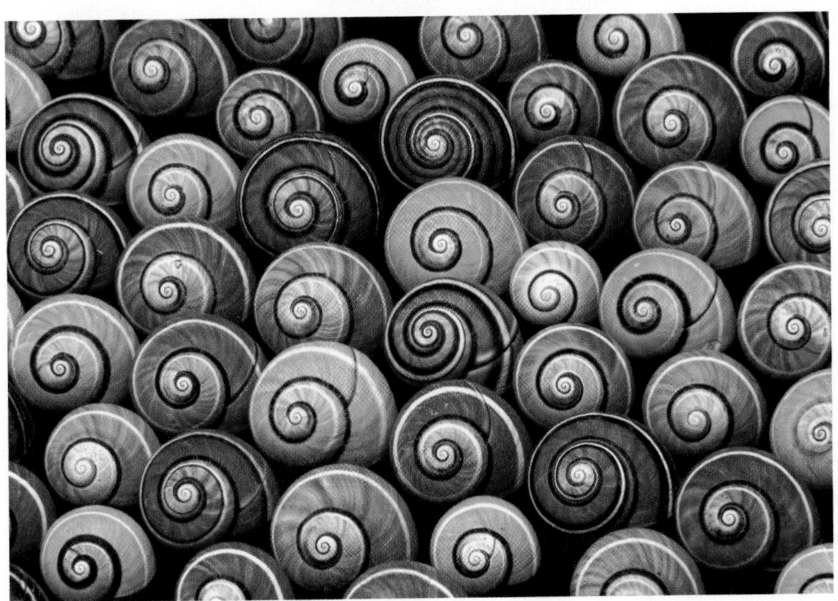

Figure 7 The variations among the shells of a species of tree snail occur naturally within the population.

Visual Check Describe three variations among these snail shells.

Natural Selection

Darwin did not know about genes. But he realized that variations were the key to the puzzle of how populations of tortoises and other organisms evolved. Darwin understood that food is a limiting resource, which means that the food in each island environment could not support every tortoise that was born. Tortoises had to compete with each other for food. As the tortoises spread to the various islands, some were born with random variations in neck length. If a variation benefited a tortoise, allowing it to compete for food better than other tortoises, the tortoise lived longer. Because it lived longer, it reproduced more. It passed on its variations to its offspring.

This is Darwin's theory of evolution by natural selection. **Natural selection** *is the process by which populations of organisms with variations that help them survive in their environments live longer, compete better, and reproduce more than those that do not have the variations.* Natural selection explains how populations change as their environments change. It explains the process by which Galápagos tortoises became matched to their food sources, as illustrated in **Figure 8.** It also explains the diversity of the Galápagos finches and mockingbirds. Birds with beak variations that help them compete for food live longer and reproduce more.

Key Concept Check What role do variations have in the theory of evolution by natural selection?

Natural Selection

1 Reproduction A population of tortoises produces many offspring that inherit its characteristics.

2 Variation A tortoise is born with a variation that makes its neck slightly longer.

3 Competition Due to limited resources, not all offspring will survive. An offspring with a longer neck can eat more cacti than other tortoises. It lives longer and produces more offspring.

4 Selection Over time, the variation is inherited by more and more offspring. Eventually, all tortoises have longer necks.

Figure 8 A beneficial variation in neck length spreads through a tortoise population by natural selection.

Adaptations

Natural selection explains how all species change over time as their environments change. Through natural selection, a helpful variation in one individual can be passed on to future members of a population. As time passes, more variations arise. The accumulation of many similar variations can lead to an adaptation (a dap TAY shun). *An* **adaptation** *is an inherited trait that increases an organism's chance of surviving and reproducing in its environment.* The long neck of certain species of tortoises is an adaptation to an environment with tall cacti.

WORD ORIGIN

adaptation
from Latin *adaptare,* means "to fit"

Key Concept Check How do variations lead to adaptations?

Types of Adaptations

Every species has many adaptations. Scientists classify adaptations into three categories: structural, behavioral, and functional. Structural adaptations involve color, shape, and other physical characteristics. The shape of a tortoise's neck is a structural adaptation. Behavioral adaptations involve the way an organism behaves or acts. Hunting at night and moving in herds are examples of behavioral adaptations. Functional adaptations involve internal body systems that affect biochemistry. A drop in body temperature during hibernation is an example of a functional adaptation. **Figure 9** illustrates examples of all three types of adaptations in the desert jackrabbit.

Figure 9 The desert jackrabbit has structural, behavioral, and functional adaptations. These adaptations enable it to survive in its desert environment.

Structural adaptation The jackrabbit's powerful legs help it run fast to escape from predators.

Behavioral adaptation The jackrabbit stays still during the hottest part of the day, helping it conserve energy.

Functional adaptation The blood vessels in the jackrabbit's ears expand to enable the blood to cool before re-entering the body.

Seahorse

Caterpillar

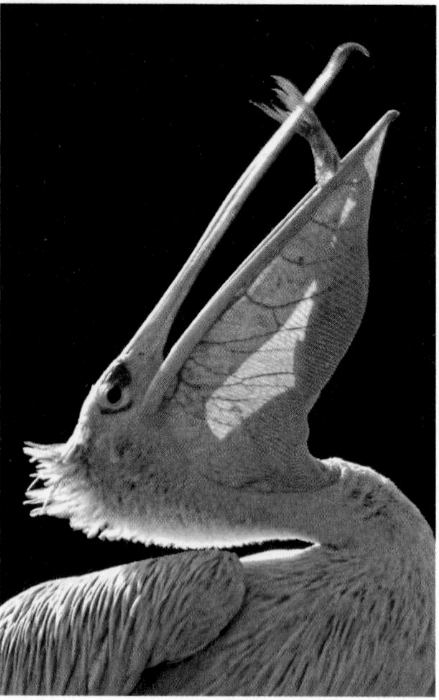

Pelican

▲ **Figure 10**  Species evolve adaptations as they interact with their environments, which include other species.

Environmental Interactions

Have you ever wanted to be invisible? Many species have evolved adaptations that make them nearly invisible. The seahorse in **Figure 10** is the same color and has a texture similar to the coral it is resting on. This is a structural adaptation called camouflage (KAM uh flahj). **Camouflage** *is an adaptation that enables a species to blend in with its environment.*

Some species have adaptations that draw attention to them. The caterpillar in **Figure 10** resembles a snake. Predators see it and are scared away. *The resemblance of one species to another species is* **mimicry** (MIH mih kree). Camouflage and mimicry are adaptations that help species avoid being eaten. Many other adaptations help species eat. The pelican in **Figure 10** has a beak and mouth uniquely adapted to its food source—fish.

Reading Check How do camouflage and mimicry differ?

Environments are complex. Species must adapt to an environment's living parts as well as to an environment's nonliving parts. Nonliving things include temperature, water, nutrients in soil, and climate. Deciduous trees shed their leaves due to changes in climate. Camouflage, mimicry, and mouth shape are adaptations mostly to an environment's living parts. An extreme example of two species adapting to each other is shown in **Figure 11.**

Living and nonliving factors are always changing. Even slight environmental changes affect how species adapt. If a species is unable to adapt, it becomes extinct. The fossil record contains many fossils of species unable to adapt to change.

Figure 11 This orchid and its moth pollinator have evolved so closely together that one cannot exist without the other. ▼

Artificial Selection

Adaptations provide evidence of how closely Earth's species match their environments. This is exactly what Darwin's theory of evolution by natural selection predicted. Darwin provided many examples of adaptation in *On the Origin of Species,* the book he wrote to explain his theory. Darwin did not write this book until 20 years after he developed his theory. He spent those years collecting more evidence for his theory by studying barnacles, orchids, corals, and earthworms.

Darwin also had a hobby of breeding domestic pigeons. He selectively bred pigeons of different colors and shapes to produce new, fancy varieties. *The breeding of organisms for desired characteristics is called* **selective breeding.** Like many domestic plants and animals produced from selective breeding, pigeons look different from their ancestors, as shown in **Figure 12.** Darwin realized that changes caused by selective breeding were much like changes caused by natural selection. Instead of nature selecting variations, humans selected them. Darwin called this process artificial selection.

Figure 12 The pouter pigeon (bottom left) and the fantail pigeon (bottom right) were derived from the wild rock pigeon (top).

Artificial selection explains and supports Darwin's theory. As you will read in Lesson 3, other evidence also supports the idea that species evolve from other species.

Inquiry MiniLab — 20 minutes

Who survives?

Camouflage helps organisms blend in. This can help them avoid predators or sneak up on prey. Camouflage helps organisms survive in their environments.

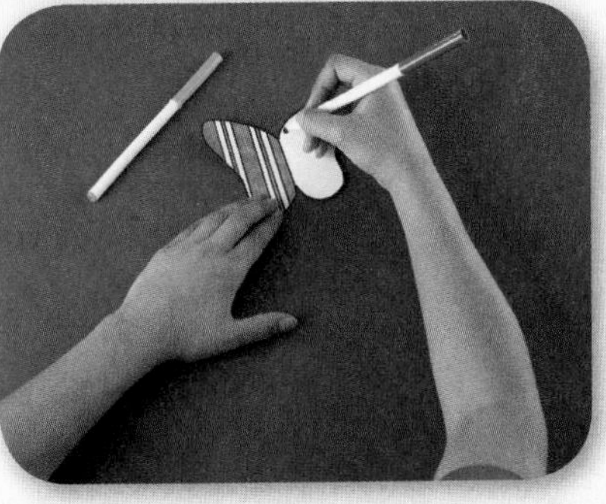

1. Read and complete a lab safety form.
2. Choose an area of your classroom where your moth will rest with open wings during the day.
3. Use **scissors, paper, markers,** and a **ruler** to design a moth that measures 2–5 cm in width with open wings and will be camouflaged where it is placed. Write the location where the moth is to be placed. Give the location and your completed moth to your teacher.
4. On the following day, you will have 1 minute to spot as many moths in the room as you can.
5. In your Science Journal, record the location of moths spotted by your team.
6. Find the remaining moths that were not spotted. Observe their appearance.

Analyze and Conclude

1. **Compare** the appearances and resting places of the moths that were spotted with those that were not spotted.
2. **Key Concept** Explain how camouflage enables an organism to survive in its environment.

Lesson 2 Review

Assessment Online Quiz

Visual Summary

Charles Darwin developed his theory of evolution partly by observing organisms in their natural environments.

Natural selection occurs when organisms with certain variations live longer, compete better, and reproduce more often than organisms that do not have the variations.

Adaptations occur when a beneficial variation is eventually inherited by all members of a population.

FOLDABLES®

Use your lesson Foldable to review the lesson. Save your Foldable for the project at the end of the chapter.

What do you think NOW?

You first read the statements below at the beginning of the chapter.

3. Environmental change causes variations in populations.

4. Variations can lead to adaptations.

Did you change your mind about whether you agree or disagree with the statements? Rewrite any false statements to make them true.

Use Vocabulary

1. A person who studies plants and animals by observing them is a(n) ________.
2. Through ________, populations of organisms adapt to their environments.
3. Some species blend in to their environments through ________.

Understand Key Concepts 

4. The observation that the Galápagos tortoises did not all live in the same environment helped Darwin
   - **A.** develop his theory of adaptation.
   - **B.** develop his theory of evolution.
   - **C.** observe mimicry in nature.
   - **D.** practice artificial selection.
5. **Assess** the importance of variations to natural selection.
6. **Compare and contrast** natural selection and artificial selection.

Interpret Graphics

7. **Explain** how the shape of the walking stick at right helps the insect survive in its environment.

8. **Sequence** Copy the graphic organizer below and sequence the steps by which a population of organisms changes by natural selection.

Critical Thinking

9. **Conclude** how Earth's birds developed their diversity through natural selection.

Peter and Rosemary Grant

CAREERS in SCIENCE

Observing Natural Selection

Charles Darwin was a naturalist during the mid-1800s. Based on his observations of nature, he developed the theory of evolution by natural selection. Do scientists still work this way—drawing conclusions from observations? Is there information still to be learned about natural selection? The answer to both questions is yes.

Peter and Rosemary Grant are naturalists who have observed finches in the Galápagos Islands for more than 30 years. They have found that variations in the finches' food supply determine which birds will survive and reproduce. They have observed natural selection in action.

The Grants live on Daphne Major, an island in the Galápagos, for part of each year. They observe and take measurements to compare the size and shape of finches' beaks from year to year. They also examine the kinds of seeds and nuts available for the birds to eat. They use this information to relate changes in the birds' food supply to changes in the finch species' beaks.

The island's ecosystem is fragile, so the Grants take great care not to change the environment of Daphne Major as they observe the finches. They carefully plan their diet to avoid introducing new plant species to the island. They bring all the freshwater they need to drink, and they wash in the ocean. For the Grants, it's just part of the job. As naturalists, they try to observe without interfering with the habitat in which they are living.

▲ **Peter and Rosemary Grant make observations and collect data in the field.**

▲ **This large ground finch is one of the kinds of birds studied by the Grants.**

It's Your Turn

RESEARCH AND REPORT Find out more about careers in evolution, ecology, or population biology. What kind of work is done in the laboratory? What kind of work is done in the field? Write a report to explain your findings.

Lesson 3

Biological Evidence of Evolution

Reading Guide

Key Concepts
ESSENTIAL QUESTIONS

- What evidence from living species supports the theory that species descended from other species over time?
- How are Earth's organisms related?

Vocabulary

comparative anatomy p. 450
homologous structure p. 450
analogous structure p. 451
vestigial structure p. 451
embryology p. 452

Academic Standards for Science

8.3.6 Observe anatomical structures of a variety of organisms and describe their similarities and differences. Use the data collected to organize the organisms into groups and predict their relatedness.

8.3.8 Examine traits of individuals within a population of organisms that may give them an advantage in survival and reproduction in a given environment or when the environment changes.

8.3.9 Describe the effect of environmental changes on populations of organisms when their adaptive characteristics put them at a disadvantage for survival. Describe how extinction of a species can ultimately result.

Also covers: 8.NS.7, 8.NS.9, 8.NS.11

Inquiry Does this bird fly?

Some birds, such as the flightless cormorant above, have wings but cannot fly. Their wings are too small to support their bodies in flight. Why do they still have wings? What can scientists learn about the ancestors of present-day birds that have wings but do not fly?

Inquiry Launch Lab

15 minutes

How is the structure of a spoon related to its function?

Would you eat your morning cereal with a spoon that had holes in it? Is using a teaspoon the most efficient way to serve mashed potatoes and gravy to a large group of people? How about using an extra large spoon, or ladle, to eat soup from a small bowl?

1. Read and complete a lab safety form.
2. In a small group, examine your **set of spoons** and discuss your observations.
3. Sketch or describe the structure of each spoon in your Science Journal. Discuss the purpose that each spoon shape might serve.
4. Label the spoons in your Science Journal with their purposes.

Think About This

1. Describe the similarities and differences among the spoons.
2. If spoons were organisms, what do you think the ancestral spoon would look like?
3. **Key Concept** Explain how three of the spoons have different structures and functions, even though they are related by their similarities.

Evidence for Evolution

Recall the sequence of horse fossils from Lesson 1. The sequence might have suggested to you that horses evolved in a straight line—that one species replaced another in a series of orderly steps. Evolution does not occur this way. The diagram in **Figure 13** shows a more realistic version of horse evolution, which looks more like a bush than a straight line. Different horse species were sometimes alive at the same time. They are related to each other because each descended from a common ancestor.

Living species that are closely related share a close common ancestor. The degree to which species are related depends on how closely in time they diverged, or split, from their common ancestor. Although the fossil record is incomplete, it contains many examples of fossil sequences showing close ancestral relationships. Living species show evidence of common ancestry, too.

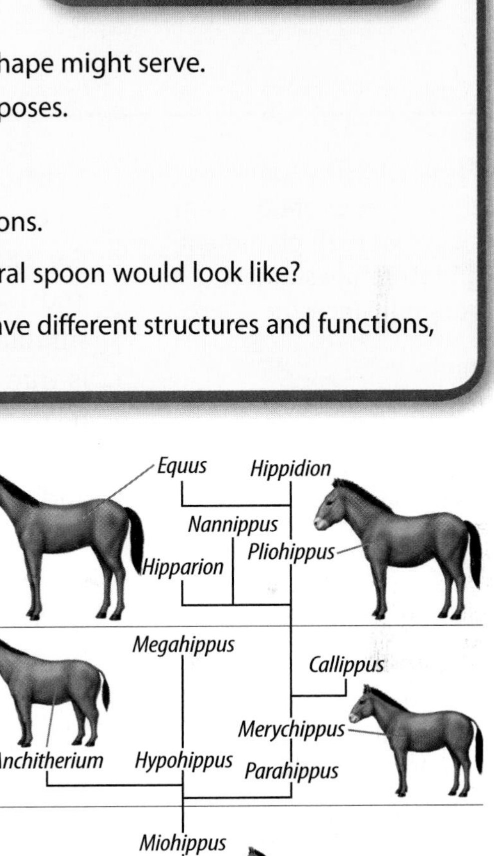

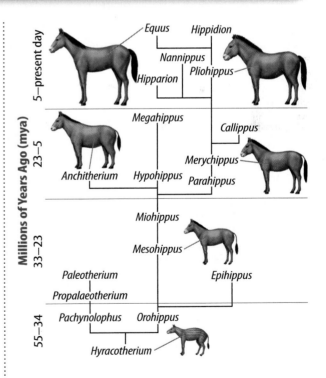

Figure 13 The fossil record indicates that different species of horses often overlapped with each other.

Visual Check Which horse is the common ancestor to all horse species in this graph?

Homologous Structures

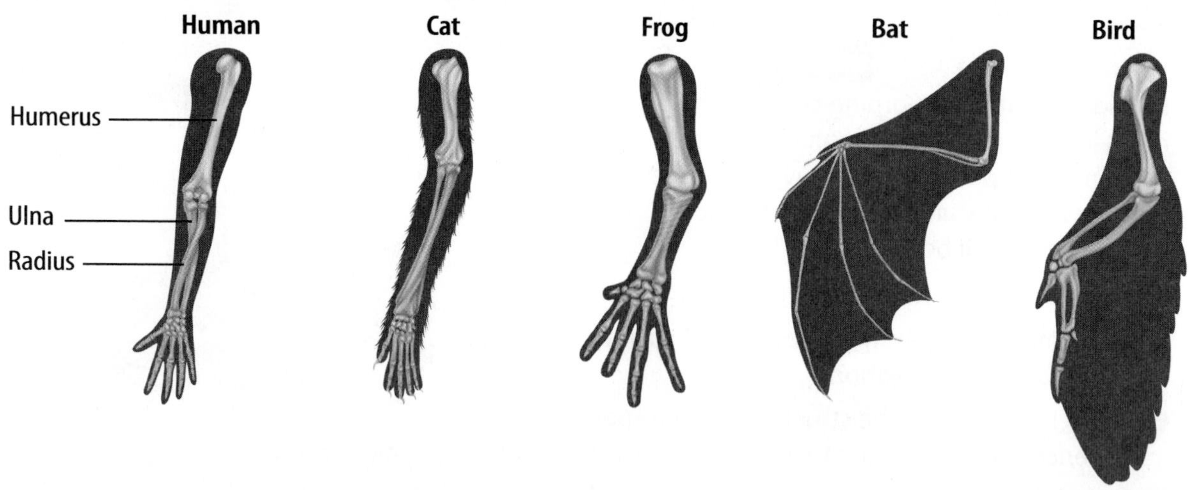

Figure 14 The forelimbs of these species are different sizes, but their placement and structure suggest common ancestry.

Comparative Anatomy

Common ancestry is not difficult to see in many species. For example, it might seem easy to tell that robins, finches, and hawks evolved from a common ancestor. They all have similar features, such as feathers, wings, and beaks. The same is true for tigers, leopards, and house cats. But how are hawks related to cats? How are both hawks and cats related to frogs and bats? Observations of structural and functional similarities and differences in species that do not look alike are possible through comparative anatomy. **Comparative anatomy** *is the study of similarities and differences among structures of living species.*

Homologous Structures Humans, cats, frogs, bats, and birds look different and move in different ways. Humans use their arms for balance and their hands to grasp objects. Cats use their forelimbs to walk, run, and jump. Frogs use their forelimbs to jump. Bats and birds use their forelimbs as wings for flying. However, the forelimb bones of these species exhibit similar patterns, as shown in **Figure 14.** **Homologous** (huh MAH luh gus) **structures** *are body parts of organisms that are similar in structure and position but different in function.*

Homologous structures, such as the forelimbs of humans, cats, frogs, bats, and birds, suggest that these species are related. The more similar two structures are to each other, the more likely it is that the species have evolved from a recent common ancestor.

Key Concept Check How do homologous structures provide evidence for evolution?

FOLDABLES®

Make a table with five rows and three columns. Label the rows and columns of the table as shown below. Give your table a title.

	Explanation	Example
Comparative Anatomy		
Vestigial Structures		
Developmental Biology		
Molecular Biology		

Analogous Structures Can you think of a body part in two species that serves the same purpose but differs in structure? How about the wings of birds and flies? Both wings in **Figure 15** are used for flight. But bird wings are covered with feathers. Fly wings are covered with tiny hairs. *Body parts that perform a similar function but differ in structure are* **analogous** (uh NAH luh gus) **structures.** Differences in the structure of bird and fly wings indicate that birds and flies are not closely related.

▲ **Figure 15** Though used for the same function—flight—the wings of birds (top) and insects (bottom) are too different in structure to suggest close common ancestry.

Vestigial Structures

The bird in the photo at the beginning of this lesson has short, stubby wings. Yet it cannot fly. The bird's wings are an example of vestigial structures. **Vestigial** (veh STIH jee ul) **structures** *are body parts that have lost their original function through evolution.* The best explanation for vestigial structures is that the species with a vestigial structure is related to an ancestral species that used the structure for a specific purpose.

The whale shown in **Figure 16** has tiny pelvic bones inside its body. The presence of pelvic bones in whales suggests that whales descended from ancestors that used legs for walking on land. The fossil evidence supports this conclusion. Many fossils of whale ancestors show a gradual loss of legs over millions of years. They also show, at the same time, that whale ancestors became better adapted to their watery environments.

Key Concept Check How are vestigial structures evidence of descent from ancestral species?

Figure 16 Present-day whales have vestigial structures in the form of small pelvic bones. ▼

Between 50–40 million years ago, this mammal breathed air and walked clumsily on land. It spent a lot of time in water, but swimming was difficult because of its rear legs. Individuals born with variations that made their rear legs smaller lived longer and reproduced more. This mammal is an ancestor of modern whales.

Pelvis

Ambulocetus natans

Vestigial pelvis

Modern toothed whale

After 10–15 million more years of evolution, the ancestors of modern whales could not walk on land. They were adapted to an aquatic environment. Modern whales have two small vestigial pelvic bones that no longer support legs.

Pharyngeal Pouches

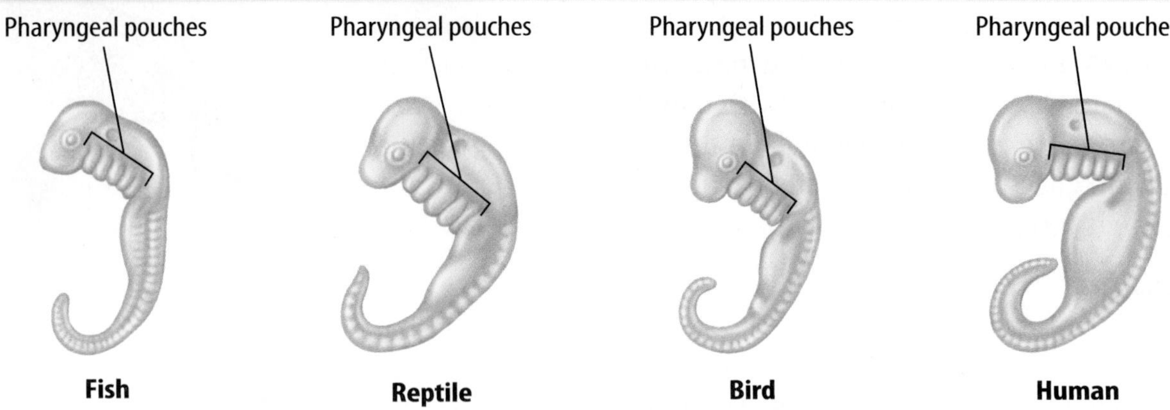

Figure 17 All vertebrate embryos exhibit pharyngeal pouches at a certain stage of their development. These features, which develop into neck and face parts, suggest relatedness.

Developmental Biology

You have just read that studying the internal structures of organisms can help scientists learn more about how organisms are related. Studying the development of embryos can also provide scientists with evidence that certain species are related. *The science of the development of embryos from fertilization to birth is called* **embryology** (em bree AH luh jee).

Word Origin

embryology
from Greek *embryon,* means "to swell" and from Greek *logia,* means "study of"

Pharyngeal Pouches Embryos of different species often resemble each other at different stages of their development. For example, all vertebrate embryos have pharyngeal (fuh rihn JEE ul) pouches at one stage, as shown in **Figure 17.** This feature develops into different body parts in each vertebrate. Yet, in all vertebrates, each part is in the face or neck. For example, in reptiles, birds, and humans, part of the pharyngeal pouch develops into a gland in the neck that regulates calcium. In fish, the same part becomes the gills. One function of gills is to regulate calcium. The similarities in function and location of gills and glands suggest a strong evolutionary relationship between fish and other vertebrates.

Key Concept Check How do pharyngeal pouches provide evidence of relationships among species?

Molecular Biology

Studies of fossils, comparative anatomy, and embryology provide support for Darwin's theory of evolution by natural selection. Molecular biology is the study of gene structure and function. Discoveries in molecular biology have confirmed and extended much of the data already collected about the theory of evolution. Darwin did not know about genes, but scientists today know that mutations in genes are the source of variations upon which natural selection acts. Genes provide powerful support for evolution.

Reading Check What is molecular biology?

Comparing Sequences All organisms on Earth have genes. All genes are made of DNA, and all genes work in similar ways. This supports the idea that all organisms are related. Scientists can study relatedness of organisms by comparing genes and proteins among living species. For example, nearly all organisms contain a gene that codes for cytochrome *c*, a protein required for cellular respiration. Some species, such as humans and rhesus monkeys, have nearly identical cytochrome *c*. The more closely related two species are, the more similar their genes and proteins are.

 **Key Concept Check** How is molecular biology used to determine relationships among species?

Divergence Scientists have found that some stretches of shared DNA mutate at regular, predictable rates. Scientists use this "molecular clock" to estimate at what time in the past living species diverged from common ancestors. For example, as shown in **Figure 18,** molecular data indicate that whales and porpoises are more closely related to hippopotamuses than they are to any other living species.

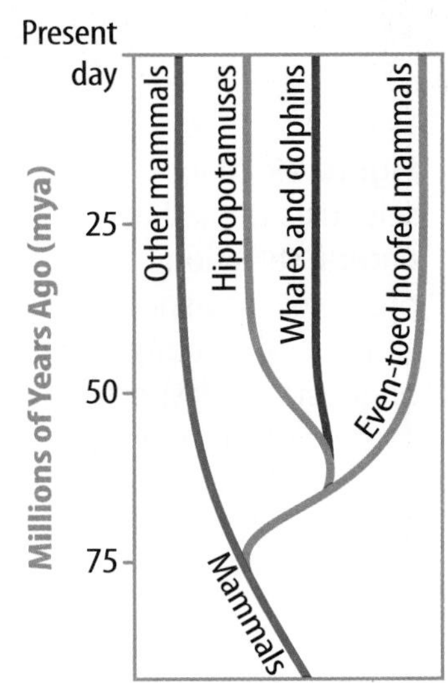

Figure 18 Whales and hippopotamuses share an ancestor that lived 50–60 mya.

Inquiry MiniLab

10 minutes

How related are organisms?

Proteins, such as cytochrome *c*, are made from combinations of just 20 amino acids. The graph below shows the number of amino acid differences in cytochrome *c* between humans and other organisms.

1. Use the graph at right to answer the questions below.

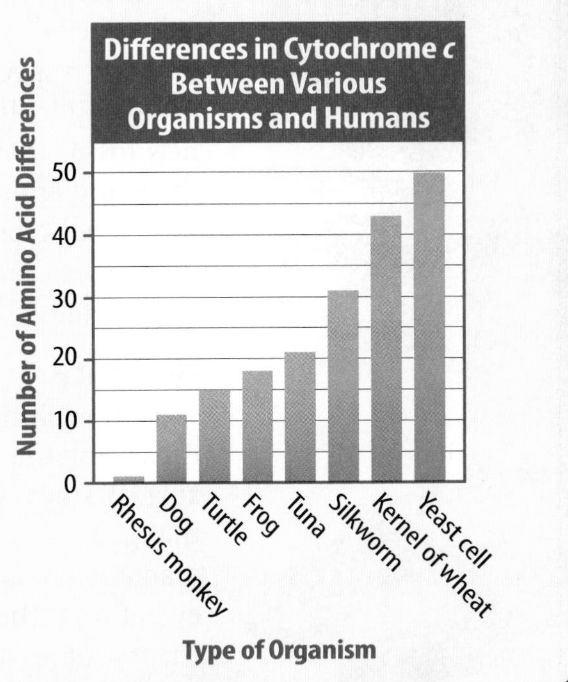

Analyze and Conclude

1. **Identify** Which organism has the least difference in the number of amino acids in cytochrome *c* compared to humans? Which organism has the most difference?
2. **Infer** Which organisms do you think might be more closely related to each other: a dog and a turtle or a dog and a silkworm? Explain your answer.
3. **Key Concept** Notice the differences in the number of amino acids in cytochrome *c* between each organism and humans. How might these differences explain the relatedness of each organism to humans?

Figure 19 Many scientists think that natural selection produces new species slowly and steadily. Other scientists think species exist stably for long periods, then change occurs in short bursts. ▶

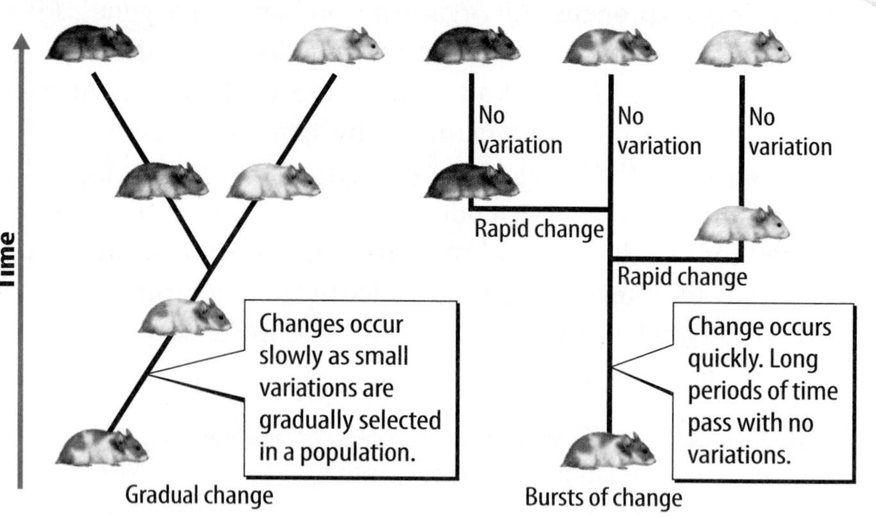

Figure 20 *Tiktaalik* lived 385–359 mya. Like amphibians, it had wrists and lungs. Like fish, it had fins, gills, and scales. Scientists think it is an intermediate species linking fish and amphibians. ▼

The Study of Evolution Today

The theory of evolution by natural selection is the cornerstone of modern biology. Since Darwin published his theory, scientists have confirmed, refined, and extended Darwin's work. They have observed natural selection in hundreds of living species. Their studies of fossils, anatomy, embryology, and molecular biology have all provided evidence of relatedness among living and extinct species.

How New Species Form

New evidence supporting the theory of evolution by natural selection is discovered nearly every day. But scientists debate some of the details. **Figure 19** shows that scientists have different ideas about the rate at which natural selection produces new species—slowly and gradually or quickly, in bursts. The origin of a species is difficult to study on human time scales. It is also difficult to study in the incomplete fossil record. Yet, new fossils that have features of species that lived both before them and after them are discovered all the time. For example, the *Tiktaalik* fossil shown in **Figure 20** has both fish and amphibian features. Further fossil discoveries will help scientists study more details about the origin of new species.

Diversity

How evolution has produced Earth's wide diversity of organisms using the same basic building blocks—genes—is an active area of study in evolutionary biology. Scientists are finding that genes can be reorganized in simple ways and give rise to dramatic changes in organisms. Though scientists now study evolution at the molecular level, the basic principles of Darwin's theory of evolution by natural selection have remained unchanged for over 150 years.

Lesson 3 Review

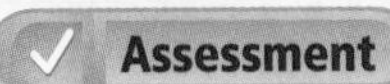

Visual Summary

By comparing the anatomy of organisms and looking for homologous or analogous structures, scientists can determine if organisms had a common ancestor.

Some organisms have vestigial structures, suggesting that they descended from a species that used the structure for a purpose.

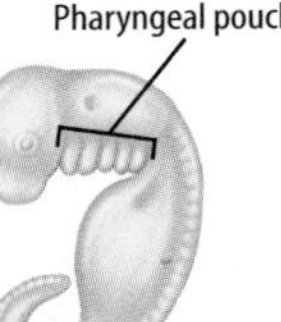

Scientists use evidence from developmental and molecular biology to help determine if organisms are related.

FOLDABLES®

Use your lesson Foldable to review the lesson. Save your Foldable for the project at the end of the chapter.

What do you think NOW?

You first read the statements below at the beginning of the chapter.

5. Living species contain no evidence that they are related to each other.

6. Plants and animals share similar genes.

Did you change your mind about whether you agree or disagree with the statements? Rewrite any false statements to make them true.

Use Vocabulary

1. **Define** *embryology* in your own words.
2. **Distinguish** between a homologous structure and an analogous structure.
3. **Use the term** *vestigial structure* in a complete sentence.

Understand Key Concepts 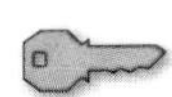

4. Scientists use molecular biology to determine how two species are related by comparing the genes in one species to genes
   - **A.** in extinct species.
   - **B.** in human species.
   - **C.** in related species.
   - **D.** in related fossils.
5. **Discuss** how pharyngeal pouches provide evidence for biological evolution.
6. **Explain** Some blind cave salamanders have eyes. How might this be evidence that cave salamanders evolved from sighted ancestors?

Interpret Graphics

7. **Interpret** The wings of a flightless cormorant are an example of which type of structure?

8. **Assess** Copy and fill in the graphic organizer below to identify four areas of study that provide evidence for evolution.

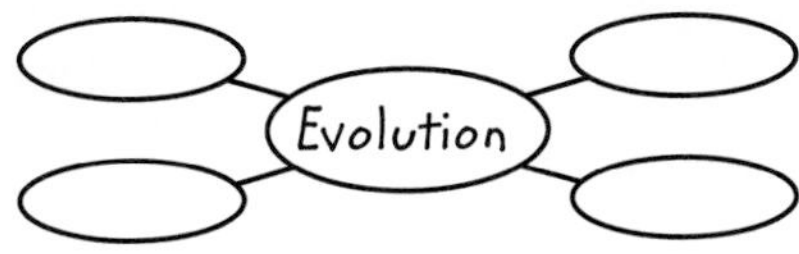

Critical Thinking

9. **Predict** what a fossil that illustrates the evolution of a bird from a reptile might look like.

2 class periods

Model Adaptations in an Organism

Materials

clay

colored pencils

colored markers

toothpicks

construction paper

Also needed: creative construction materials, glue, scissors

Safety

Conditions on our planet have changed since Earth formed over 4.5 billion years ago. Changes in the concentrations of gases in the atmosphere, temperature, and the amount of precipitation make Earth different today from when it first formed. Other events, such as volcanic eruptions, meteorite strikes, tsunamis, or wildfires, can drastically and rapidly change the conditions in certain environments. As you have read, Earth's fossil record provides evidence that, over millions of years, many organisms developed adaptations that enabled them to survive as Earth's environmental conditions changed.

Ask a Question

How do adaptations enable an organism to survive changes in the environment?

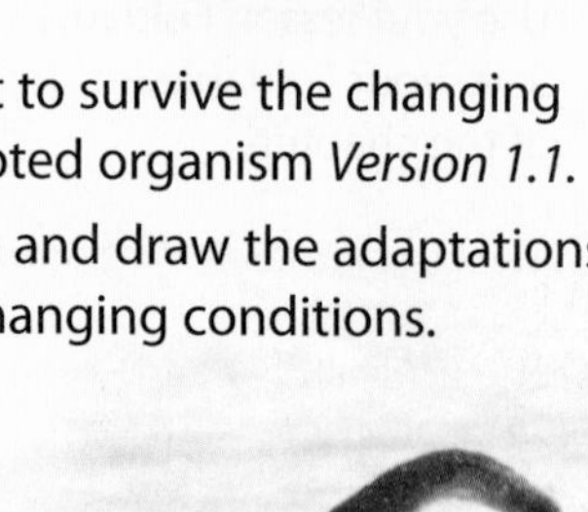

Volcanic eruption

Make Observations

1. Read and complete a lab safety form.
2. Obtain Version 1.0 of the organism you will model from your teacher.
3. Your teacher will describe Event 1 that has occurred on Earth while your organism is alive. Use markers and a piece of construction paper to design adaptations to your organism that would enable it to survive the changing conditions that result from Event 1. Label the adapted organism *Version 1.1.*
4. For each event that your teacher describes, design and draw the adaptations that would enable your organism to survive the changing conditions. Label each new organism *Version 1.X,* filling in the *X* with the appropriate version number.
5. Use the materials provided to make a model of the final version of your organism, showing all of the adaptations.

Predation

Form a Hypothesis

6. After reviewing and discussing all of the adaptations of your organism, formulate a hypothesis to explain how physical adaptations help an organism survive changes to the environment.

Test Your Hypothesis

7. Research evidence from the fossil record that shows one adaptation that developed and enabled an organism to survive over time under the conditions of one of the environmental events experienced by your model organism.
8. Record the information in your Science Journal.

Meteorite impact

Analyze and Conclude

9. **Compare** the adaptations that the different groups gave their organisms to survive each event described by your teacher. What kinds of different structures were created to help each organism survive?
10. **The Big Idea** Describe three variations in human populations that would enable some individuals to survive severe environmental changes.

Communicate Your Results

Present your completed organisms to the class and/or judges of "Ultimate Survivor." Explain the adaptations and the reasoning behind them in either an oral presentation or a demonstration, during which classmates and/or judges will review the models.

Inquiry Extension

Compare the organisms made by groups in your class to the organisms created by groups in other sections. Observe the differences in the adaptations of the organisms. In each section, the events were presented in a different order. How might this have affected the final appearance and characteristics of the different organisms?

Lab Tips

- ☑ Make sure you think of all of the implications of an environmental change event before you decide upon an adaptation.
- ☑ Decide upon your reasoning for the adaptation before putting the adaptation on your model.

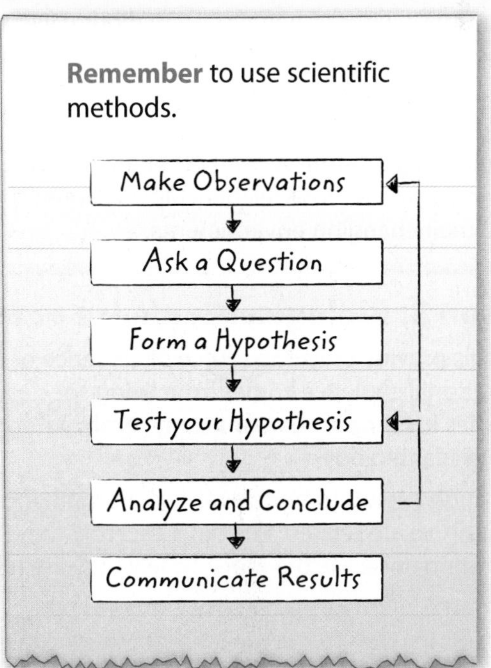

Chapter 12 Study Guide

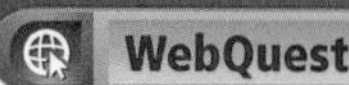

Through natural selection, species evolve as they adapt to Earth's changing environments.

Key Concepts Summary

Lesson 1: Fossil Evidence of Evolution

- Fossils form in many ways, including mineral replacement, carbonization, and impressions in sediment.
- Scientists can learn the ages of fossils by techniques of relative-age dating and absolute-age dating.
- Though incomplete, the **fossil record** contains patterns suggesting the **biological evolution** of related species.

Vocabulary

fossil record p. 429
mold p. 431
cast p. 431
trace fossil p. 431
geologic time scale p. 433
extinction p. 434
biological evolution p. 435

Lesson 2: Theory of Evolution by Natural Selection

- The 19th century **naturalist** Charles Darwin developed a theory of evolution that is still studied today.
- Darwin's theory of evolution by **natural selection** is the process by which populations with **variations** that help them survive in their environments live longer and reproduce more than those without beneficial variations. Over time, beneficial variations spread through populations, and new species that are adapted to their environments evolve.
- **Camouflage**, **mimicry**, and other **adaptations** are evidence of the close relationships between species and their changing environments.

Vocabulary

naturalist p. 439
variation p. 441
natural selection p. 442
adaptation p. 443
camouflage p. 444
mimicry p. 444
selective breeding p. 445

Lesson 3: Biological Evidence of Evolution

- Fossils provide only one source of evidence of evolution. Additional evidence comes from living species, including studies in **comparative anatomy**, **embryology**, and molecular biology.
- Through evolution by natural selection, all of Earth's organisms are related. The more recently they share a common ancestor, the more closely they are related.

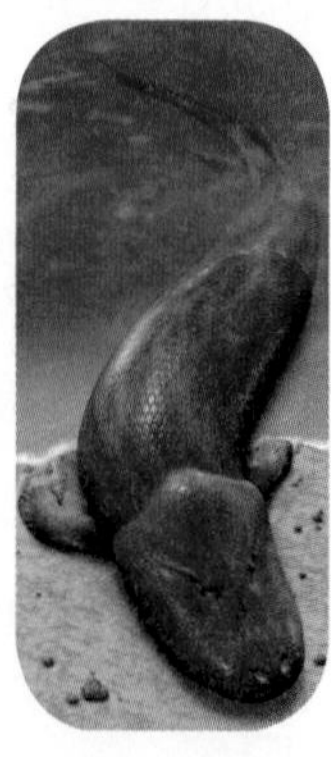

Vocabulary

comparative anatomy p. 450
homologous structure p. 450
analogous structure p. 451
vestigial structure p. 451
embryology p. 452

Study Guide

Review

- Personal Tutor
- Vocabulary eGames
- Vocabulary eFlashcards

FOLDABLES® Chapter Project

Assemble your lesson Foldables as shown to make a Chapter Project. Use the project to review what you have learned in this chapter.

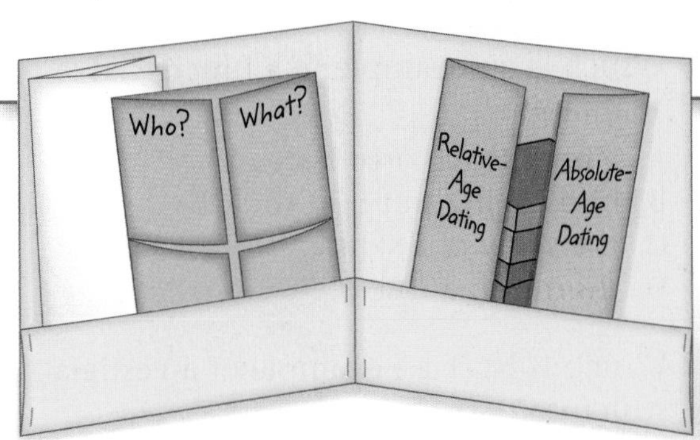

Use Vocabulary

Distinguish between the following terms.

1. *mold* and *cast*
2. *absolute-age dating* and *relative-age dating*
3. *extinction* and *biological evolution*
4. *variations* and *adaptations*
5. *camouflage* and *mimicry*
6. *natural selection* and *selective breeding*
7. *homologous structure* and *analogous structure*
8. *embryology* and *comparative anatomy*
9. *vestigial structure* and *homologous structure*

Link Vocabulary and Key Concepts

Interactive Concept Map

Copy this concept map, and then use vocabulary terms from the previous page to complete the concept map.

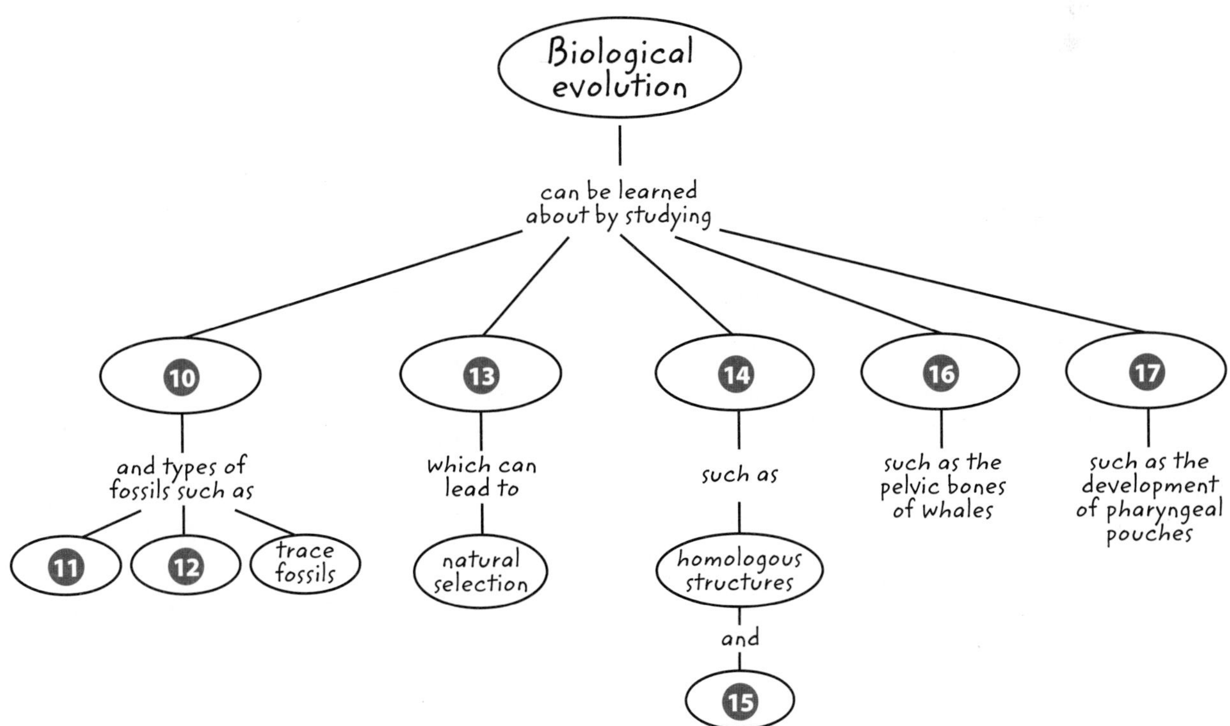

Chapter 12 Review

Understand Key Concepts

1. Why do scientists think the fossil record is incomplete?
   A. Fossils decompose over time.
   B. The formation of fossils is rare.
   C. Only organisms with hard parts become fossils.
   D. There are no fossils before the Phanerozoic eon.

2. What do the arrows on the graph below represent?

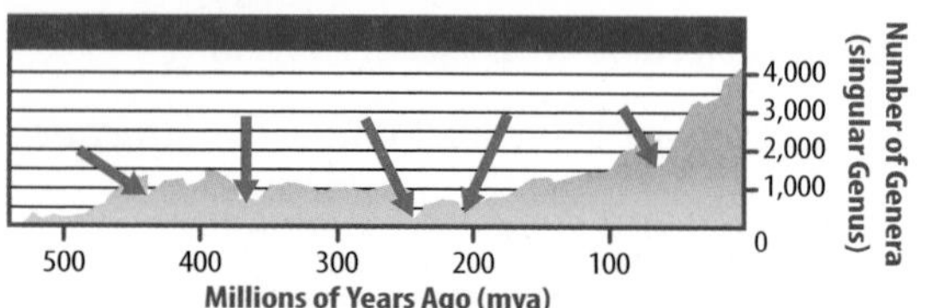

   A. extinction events
   B. meteorite impacts
   C. changes in Earth's temperature
   D. the evolution of a new species

3. What can scientists learn about fossils using techniques of absolute-age dating?
   A. estimated ages of fossils in rock layers
   B. precise ages of fossils in rock layers
   C. causes of fossil disappearances in rock layers
   D. structural similarities to other fossils in rock layers

4. Which is the sequence by which natural selection works?
   A. selection → adaptation → variation
   B. selection → variation → adaptation
   C. variation → adaptation → selection
   D. variation → selection → adaptation

5. Which type of fossil forms through carbonization?
   A. cast
   B. mold
   C. fossil film
   D. trace fossil

6. Which is the source of variations in a population of organisms?
   A. changes in environment
   B. changes in genes
   C. the interaction of genes with an environment
   D. the interaction of individuals with an environment

7. Which is an example of a functional adaptation?
   A. a brightly colored butterfly
   B. birds flying south in the fall
   C. the spray of a skunk
   D. thorns on a rose

8. Which is NOT an example of a vestigial structure?
   A. eyes of a blind salamander
   B. pelvic bones in a whale
   C. thorns on a rose bush
   D. wings on a flightless bird

9. Which do the images below represent?

Human

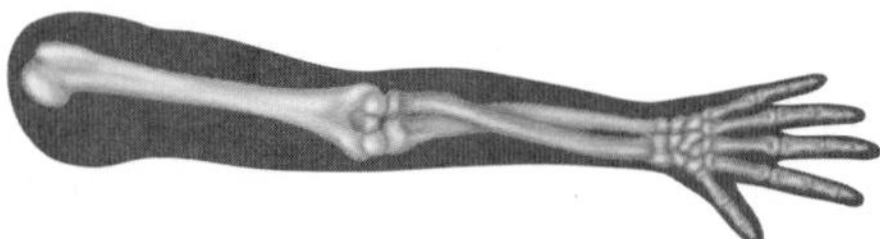

Cat

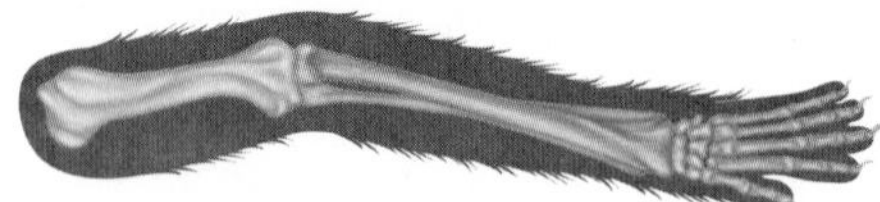

   A. analogous structures
   B. embryological structures
   C. homologous structures
   D. vestigial structures

10. Which is an example of a sudden change that could lead to the extinction of species?
    A. a mountain range isolates a species
    B. Earth's tectonic plates move
    C. a volcano erupts
    D. sea level changes

Assessment

Online Test Practice

Critical Thinking

11. **Explain** the relationship between fossils and extinction events.
12. **Infer** In 2004, a fossil of an organism that had fins and gills, but also lungs and wrists, was discovered. What might this fossil suggest about evolution?
13. **Summarize** Darwin's theory of natural selection using the Galápagos tortoises or finches as an example.
14. **Assess** how the determination that Earth is 4.6 billion years provided support for the idea that all species evolved from a common ancestor.
15. **Describe** how cytochrome *c* provides evidence of evolution.
16. **Explain** why the discovery of genes was powerful support for Darwin's theory of natural selection.
17. **Interpret Graphics** The diagram below shows two different methods by which evolution by natural selection might proceed. Discuss how these two methods differ.

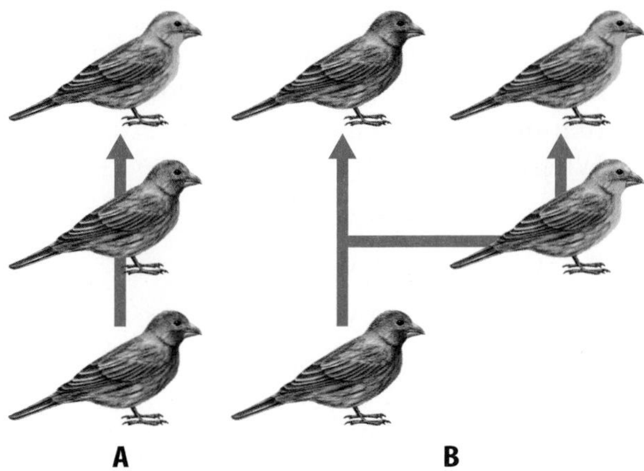

Writing in Science

18. **Write** a paragraph explaining how natural selection and selective breeding are related. Include a main idea, supporting details, and a concluding sentence.

REVIEW THE BIG IDEA

19. How do species adapt to changing environments over time? Explain how evidence from the fossil record and from living species suggests that Earth's species are related. List each type of evidence and provide an example of each.
20. The photo below shows an orchid that looks like a bee. How might this adaptation be evidence of evolution by natural selection?

Math Skills

Review

Math Practice

Use Scientific Notation

21. The earliest fossils appeared about 3,500,000,000 years ago. Express this number in scientific notation.
22. The oldest fossils visible to the unaided eye are about 565,000,000 years old. What is this time in scientific notation?
23. The oldest human fossils are about 1×10^4 years old. Express this as a whole number.

Standardized Test Practice

Record your answers on the answer sheet provided by your teacher or on a sheet of paper.

Multiple Choice

1 Which may form over time from the impression a bird feather makes in mud?

A cast

B mold

C fossil film

D trace fossil

2 Which is NOT one of the three main categories of adaptations?

A behavioral

B functional

C pharyngeal

D structural

Use the figure below to answer question 3.

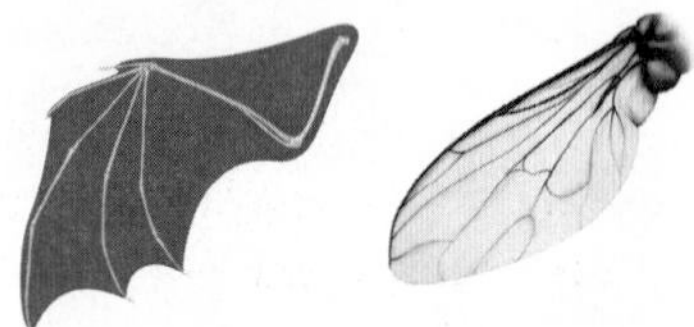

3 The figure shows the wings of a bat and an insect. Which term describes these structures?

A analogous

B developmental

C homologous

D vestigial

4 What is an adaptation?

A a body part that has lost its original function through evolution

B a characteristic that better equips an organism to survive in its environment

C a feature that appears briefly during early development

D a slight difference among the individuals in a species

5 What causes variations to arise in a population?

A changes in the environment

B competition for limited resources

C random mutations in genes

D rapid population increases

Use the image below to answer question 6.

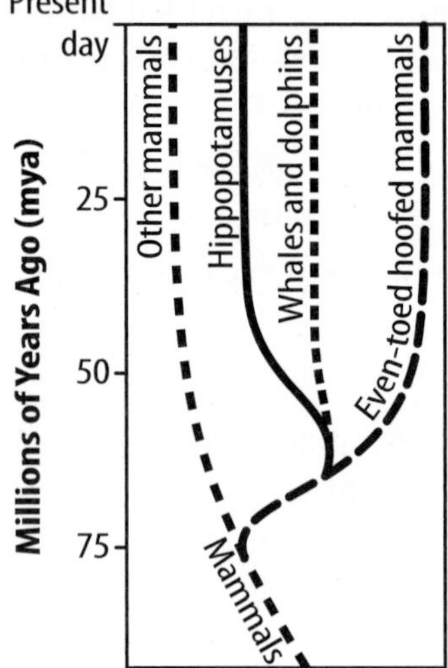

6 The molecular clock above shows that even-toed hoofed mammals and other mammals shared a common ancestor. When did this ancestor live?

A 25–35 million years ago

B 50–60 million years ago

C 60–75 million years ago

D 75 million years ago

7 Which term describes the method Darwin used that resulted in pigeons with desired traits?

A evolution

B mimicry

C natural selection

D selective breeding

Assessment
Online Standardized Test Practice

Use the figure below to answer question 8.

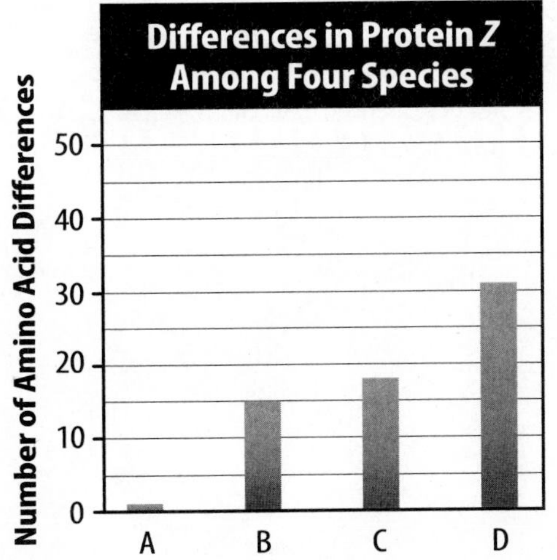

8 The chart shows that species B and C have the fewest amino acid differences for a protein among four species. What does this suggest about their evolutionary relationship?

A They are more closely related to each other than to the other species.

B They evolved at a faster rate when compared to the other species.

C They share a developmental similarity not observed in the other species.

D They do not share a common ancestor with the other species.

9 Which developmental similarity among all vertebrates is evidence that they share a common ancestor?

A analogous structures

B pharyngeal pouches

C variation rates

D vestigial structures

Constructed Response

Use the figure below to answer questions 10 and 11.

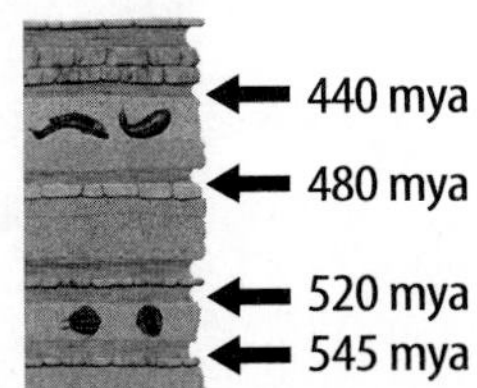

10 What is the approximate age of the fish fossils (top layer of fossils)? Express your answer as a range, and explain how you derived the answer.

11 What type of material or rock most likely forms the layer that contains the fossils? In your response, explain how these fossils formed.

12 Explain how a sudden and drastic environmental change might lead to the extinction of a species.

13 Darwin formulated his theory of evolution by natural selection based on the observation that food is a limiting resource. What did he mean by that? Use the Galápagos tortoises to explain your answer.

14 Explain how the fossil record provides evidence of biological evolution.

NEED EXTRA HELP?														
If You Missed Question...	1	2	3	4	5	6	7	8	9	10	11	12	13	14
Go to Lesson...	1	2	3	2	2	3	2	3	3	1	1	1	2	1

Chapter 13

Animal Diversity

THE BIG IDEA

What are the major groups of animals, and how do they differ?

Inquiry Are these animals?

What are the blue structures attached to these underwater rocks? Did someone spill paint on a clump of algae? This is a colony of animals called tunicates (TEW nuh kayts), also known as sea squirts. Believe it or not, they are classified in the same phylum as humans.

- What characteristics do you think tunicates have in common with other animals?
- How do tunicates differ from other animals?

Get Ready to Read

What do you think?

Before you read, decide if you agree or disagree with each of these statements. As you read this chapter, see if you change your mind about any of the statements.

1. All animals digest food.
2. Corals and jellyfish belong to the same phylum.
3. Most animals have backbones.
4. All worms belong to the same phylum.
5. All chordates have backbones.
6. Reptiles have three-chambered hearts.

connectED.mcgraw-hill.com

- Video
- Audio
- Review
- Inquiry
- WebQuest
- Assessment
- Concepts in Motion
- Multilingual eGlossary

Lesson 1

Reading Guide

Key Concepts
ESSENTIAL QUESTIONS

- What characteristics do all animals have?
- How are animals classified?

Vocabulary

vertebrate p. 468
invertebrate p. 468
radial symmetry p. 469
bilateral symmetry p. 469
asymmetry p. 469

Multilingual eGlossary

Academic Standards for Science

8.3.6 Observe anatomical structures of a variety of organisms and describe their similarities and differences. Use the data collected to organize the organisms into groups and predict their relatedness.

Also covers: 8.NS.1, 8.NS.6, 8.NS.9

What defines an animal?

Inquiry A Pair of Leaves?

What kind of organism is shown in this photo? Although they might look like leaves, they are butterflies, a type of animal. What makes leaves and butterflies different? All animals share some characteristics that leaves do not.

Launch Lab

10 minutes

What does an animal look like?

Have you ever seen an animal that looks like a vase? How about an animal that looks just like a twig? There are even some animals that look like alien spaceships. The forms that animals take are almost as varied as your imagination.

1. Look at a **photograph of an animal.** Without showing the picture to your partner, describe the animal in as much detail as possible.
2. Have your partner draw the animal using your description as a guide.
3. Compare the drawing to the photograph.

Think About This

1. Could someone looking at the drawing identify it as the same animal in the photograph? Why or why not?
2. **Key Concept** What characteristics do you think you and the animal you described have in common?

Animal Characteristics

When you look at an animal, what do you expect to see? Would you expect every animal to have legs and eyes? Ants and birds have legs, but the snake in **Figure 1** does not. Snails, spiders, and many other animals have eyes, but jellyfish do not. Although animals have many traits that make them unique, all animals have certain characteristics in common. Members of the Kingdom Animalia have the following characteristics:

- Animals are multicellular and eukaryotes.
- Animal cells are specialized for different functions, such as digestion, reproduction, vision, or taste.
- Animals have a protein, called collagen (KAHL uh juhn), that surrounds the cells and helps them keep their shape.
- Animals get energy for life processes by eating other organisms.
- Animals, such as the snake in **Figure 1,** digest their food.

In addition to the characteristics above, most animals reproduce sexually and are capable of movement at some point in their lives.

Figure 1 The snake began digesting its prey even before it finished swallowing.

Key Concept Check What characteristics do all animals have?

Animal Classification

Scientists have described and named more than 1.5 million species of animals. Every year, thousands more are added to that number. Many scientists estimate that Earth is home to millions of animal species that no one has discovered—at least, not yet. What might happen if you discovered an animal no one else had ever seen? How would you begin to classify it?

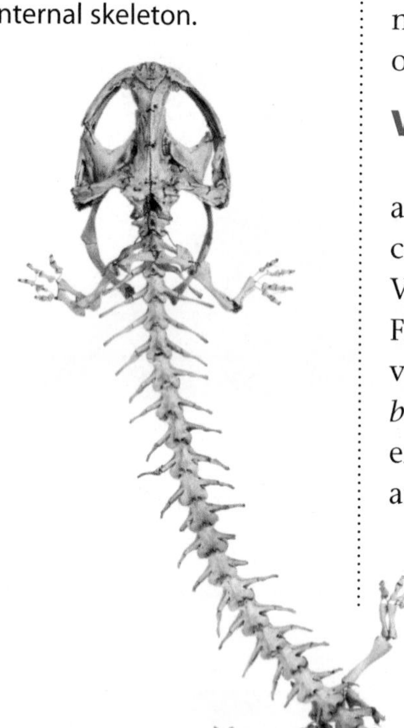

Figure 2 A backbone, or spine, is part of a vertebrate's internal skeleton.

Vertebrates and Invertebrates

You could start classifying an animal by finding out if the animal has a backbone. Animals can be grouped into two large categories: vertebrates (VUR tuh brayts) and invertebrates (ihn VUR tuh brayts). *A* **vertebrate** *is an animal with a backbone.* Fish, humans, and the lizard shown in **Figure 2** are examples of vertebrates. *An* **invertebrate** *is an animal that does not have a backbone.* Worms, spiders, snails, crayfish, and insects are examples of invertebrates. Invertebrates make up most of the animal kingdom—about 95 percent.

Reading Check What is the difference between a vertebrate and an invertebrate?

Inquiry MiniLab

15 minutes

What is this animal?

Biologists use many characteristics to classify animals. A dichotomous key helps you identify animals based on differences in characteristics. Use the dichotomous key to identify different animals.

1 Obtain a set of **animal pictures.** Follow the dichotomous key at right to identify each animal in the set.

1a. has a backbone **1b.** does not have a backbone	puffer fish go to step 2
2a. has bilateral symmetry **2b.** has radial symmetry	nudibranch go to step 3
3a. has spines **3b.** does not have spines	go to step 4 ctenophore
4a. spherical shape **4b.** cylindrical shape	sea urchin sea cucumber

Analyze and Conclude

1. **Observe** How many steps were there in the dichotomous key? How many organisms did you identify? What is the relationship between the number of steps in the dichotomous key and the number of animals identified?
2. **Explain** Were you uncertain about the identification of any animal? How did you decide on its identification?
3. **Key Concept** What characteristics did you use to classify each organism?

Animal Symmetry

Figure 3 Animals can be classified as having radial symmetry, bilateral symmetry, or asymmetry.

Visual Check What kind of symmetry does a bird have?

Radial symmetry

Bilateral symmetry

Asymmetry

Symmetry

Another step you could take to classify an animal is to determine what kind of symmetry it has. As shown in **Figure 3,** symmetry describes an organism's body plan. Symmetry can help identify the phylum to which an animal belongs.

An animal with **radial symmetry** *can be divided into two parts that are nearly mirror images of each other anywhere through its central axis.* A radial animal has a top and a bottom but no head or tail. It can be divided along more than one plane and still have two nearly identical halves. Examples include jellyfish, sea stars, and sea anemones.

An animal with **bilateral symmetry** *can be divided into two parts that are nearly mirror images of each other.* Examples include birds, mammals, reptiles, worms, and insects.

An animal with **asymmetry** *cannot be divided into any two parts that are nearly mirror images of each other.* An asymmetrical animal, such as the sponge in **Figure 3,** does not have a symmetrical body plan.

 **Reading Check** What is bilateral symmetry?

WORD ORIGIN

bilateral
from Latin *bi-*, means "two" and *latus*, means "side"

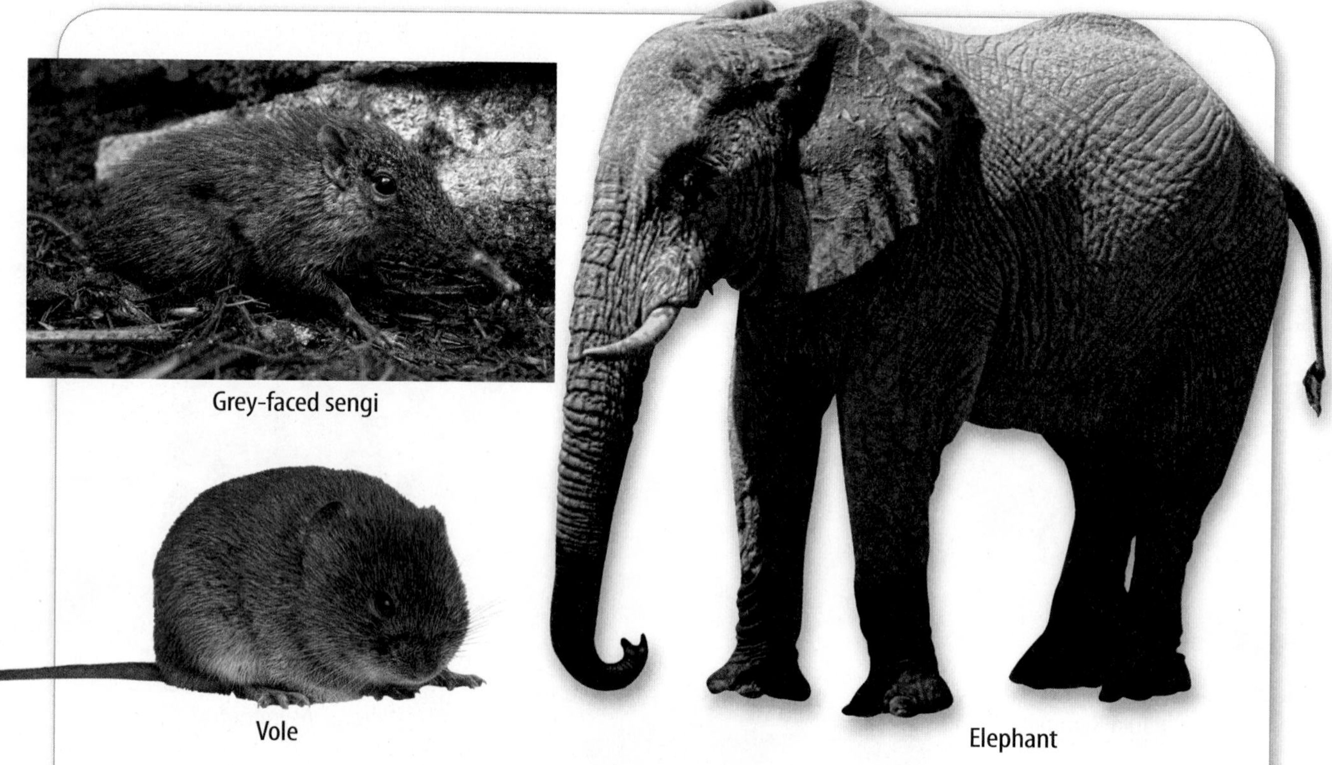

Figure 4 The grey-faced sengi was first observed in Africa in 2006. Sengis look like voles, but molecular evidence shows that they are more closely related to elephants.

Molecular Classification

Molecules such as DNA, RNA, and proteins in an animal's cells also can be used for classification. For example, scientists can compare the DNA from two animals to determine if they are related. The more similar the DNA, the more closely the animals are related.

Molecular classification has led to new discoveries about relationships among species. Scientists used to classify the grey-faced sengi shown in **Figure 4** as a close relative of shrews and voles. Recently, molecular evidence has shown that sengis are more closely related to elephants and aardvarks.

Key Concept Check How are animals classified?

FOLDABLES®

Make a small horizontal four-door book. Leave a 1-cm space between the tabs. Draw arrows and label the book as shown. Use it to record your notes about the classification of animals.

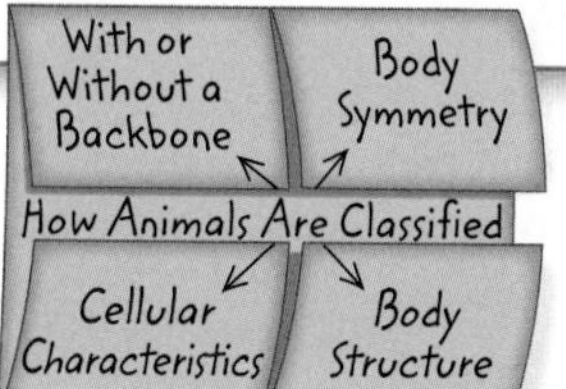

Major Phyla

Scientists classify the members of the animal kingdom into as many as 35 phyla (singular, phylum). The nine major phyla, shown in **Figure 5,** contain 95–99 percent of all animal species. Animals belonging to the same phylum have similar body structures and other characteristics. For example, all sponges (the phylum Porifera [puh RIH fuh ruh]) have asymmetry, and their cells do not form tissues. Only one animal phylum, Chordata (kor DAH tuh), contains vertebrates, also shown in **Figure 5.** The other major phyla contain only invertebrates.

Kingdom Animalia

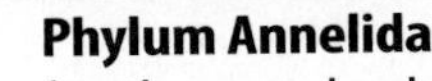

Phylum Annelida
(earthworms, leeches, marine worms)

Phylum Arthropoda
(insects, spiders, shrimp, crabs)

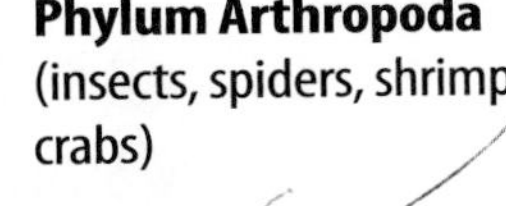

Phylum Chordata
(tunicates, lancelets, vertebrates)

Phylum Mollusca
(snails, slugs, clams, mussels, octopi, squid)

Phylum Echinodermata
(sea stars, sea urchins, sea cucumbers)

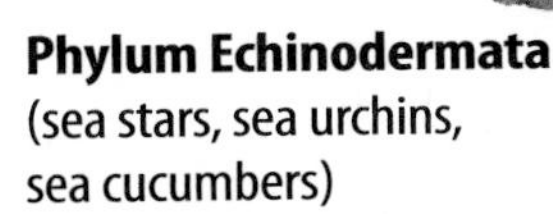

Phylum Nematoda
(roundworms)

Phylum Platyhelminthes
(flatworms)

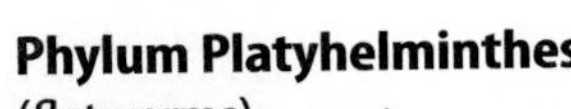

Phylum Cnidaria
(jellyfish, sea anemones, corals)

Phylum Porifera
(sponges)

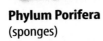

KINGDOM ANIMALIA
(classified according to body plan)

Figure 5 Most animals can be classified in one of nine major phyla.

Visual Check What are the major phyla of animals?

Lesson 1 Review

Assessment Online Quiz

Visual Summary

All animals share a series of characteristics.

Animals can be classified in several ways.

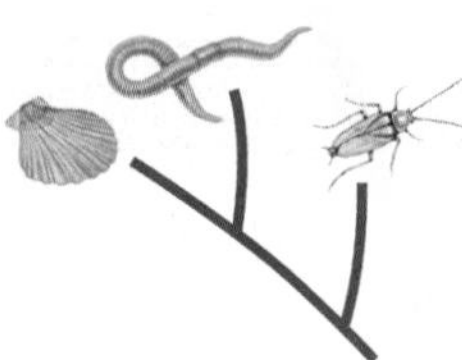

Animal classifications are always changing based on advanced technology.

FOLDABLES®

Use your lesson Foldable to review the lesson. Save your Foldable for the project at the end of the chapter.

What do you think NOW?

You first read the statements below at the beginning of the chapter.

1. All animals digest food.
2. Corals and jellyfish belong to the same phylum.

Did you change your mind about whether you agree or disagree with the statements? Rewrite any false statements to make them true.

Use Vocabulary

1. **Define** *asymmetry.*
2. **Distinguish** between vertebrate and invertebrate animals.
3. **Compare and contrast** radial symmetry and bilateral symmetry.

Understand Key Concepts 

4. **List** the characteristics that all animals have in common.
5. Which characteristic applies to a horse?
   - **A.** asymmetry
   - **B.** invertebrate
   - **C.** spherical
   - **D.** vertebrate

Interpret Graphics

6. **Classify** each object below as having bilateral symmetry, radial symmetry, or asymmetry.

7. **Summarize Information** Copy the graphic organizer below, and use it to summarize the ways animals can be separated into groups.

Critical Thinking

8. **Develop** a series of instructions that could be used to determine if an animal should be classified in the phylum Arthropoda, Echinodermata, or Chordata.
9. **Analyze** how the classification of the grey-faced sengi changed over time. How might technological advances change how other animals are classified?

CAREERS in SCIENCE

A Family Tree for Bats

Meet Nancy Simmons, a taxonomist who identifies bats.

When most people are going to bed, taxonomist Nancy Simmons is going to work. She's off to capture bats in a dense rain forest of South America. Because bats are most active at night, she and her team from the American Museum of Natural History work from dusk until dawn. They must capture, identify, and release the bats while it's dark.

Taxonomists study animals to see how they are related to each other and use that information to classify them. To classify a bat, Simmons carefully examines its body. She looks at characteristics such as wing size, fur color, and the shape of the bat's teeth. These characteristics help her classify each bat into a family or a group that shares physical features and behaviors.

In 1999 Dr. Simmons added a new member to the bat family tree. In the rain forest in Peru, her team discovered a species they named *Micronycteris matses,* the Matses' big-eared bat. Like other species in its genus, *M. matses* is small with large round ears, a long snout, and a fold of skin on its nose called a nose-leaf. *M. matses* is unique, however, because of its combination of dark brown fur, medium body size, small bottom front teeth, and short fur around its ears.

Dr. Simmons is looking for links between *M. matses* and other bat species. She compares their bodies, behavior, and even their DNA. Her goal is to create a family tree for all bats. With over a thousand species of bats worldwide, Dr. Simmons has plenty of work still to do.

All Kinds of Bats

Bats live on every continent except Antarctica, in areas ranging from tropical rain forests to chilly mountaintops. They also have an amazing variety of shapes and sizes. With over 1,100 species, bats make up one-fifth of the world's mammals.

Simmons holds a bat that she caught in her net.

▲ This species is the largest in the New World—it weighs about 150 g.

It's Your Turn

RESEARCH Investigate a species of bat in your area. Record where it lives in the environment and its characteristics, such as wingspan, fur color, and weight. With a partner, compare your bats. What do they have in common? What is different?

Lesson 2

Invertebrate Phyla

Reading Guide

Key Concepts 

ESSENTIAL QUESTIONS

- What are the characteristics of invertebrates?
- How do the invertebrate phyla differ?

Vocabulary

exoskeleton p. 479

appendage p. 479

 Multilingual eGlossary

 Video BrainPOP®

Academic Standards for Science

8.3.6 Observe anatomical structures of a variety of organisms and describe their similarities and differences. Use the data collected to organize the organisms into groups and predict their relatedness.

Also covers: 8.NS.3, 8.NS.7, 8.NS.9

Inquiry How did it get there?

This octopus is alive and got inside the bottle by slowly pushing its soft, flexible body inside. Like many invertebrates, an octopus does not have a skeleton made of bone or other hard structures.

Inquiry Launch Lab

10 minutes

What does an invertebrate look like?

Some invertebrates have features that are similar to yours, such as eyes and legs. Others have little in common with you. What do you see when you look at invertebrates close-up?

1. Read and complete a lab safety form.
2. Examine a **collection of invertebrates,** and record your observations in your Science Journal.
3. Use a **magnifying lens** to further examine the invertebrates. Record any additional observations.
4. Make a Venn diagram in your Science Journal to compare similarities and contrast differences among the invertebrates.

Think About This

1. Which two invertebrates were the most dissimilar? Why?
2. Did you see any details using a magnifying lens that you missed by looking just with your eyes?
3. **Key Concept** What characteristics do you think all the invertebrates you looked at have in common?

Characteristics of Invertebrates

Can you imagine living without a backbone? Most animals do just that. As you have read, invertebrates are animals that lack a backbone. In most cases, invertebrates have no **internal** structures to help support their bodies. They also tend to be smaller and move more slowly than vertebrates. As shown in **Figure 6,** over 95 percent of all animal species that have been recorded are invertebrates.

You probably could recognize a jellyfish or a clam if you saw one. What about an anemone or a sea cucumber? Invertebrates are a diverse group. Their physical characteristics range from the simple structures of sponges and jellyfish to the more complex bodies of worms, snails, and insects. Each invertebrate phylum contains animals with similar body plans and physical characteristics.

Key Concept Check What are the characteristics of invertebrates?

ACADEMIC VOCABULARY
internal
(adjective) existing inside something

Invertebrate and Vertebrate Species

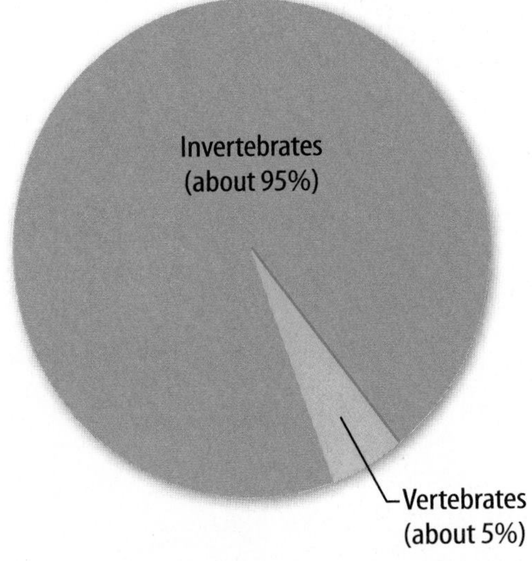

Figure 6 Invertebrates make up more than 95 percent of all living species on Earth.

FOLDABLES®

Make a horizontal three-tab book. Draw arrows and label the tabs as shown. Use the Foldable to identify differences found within the invertebrate phyla.

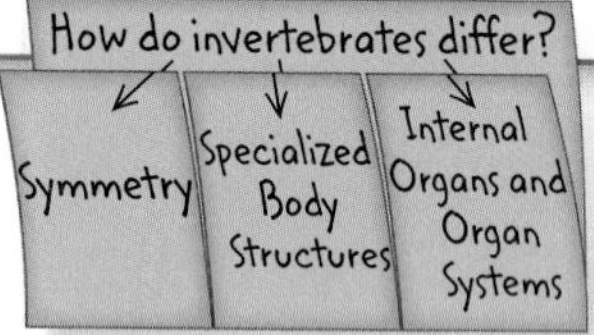
How do invertebrates differ?
Symmetry
Specialized Body Structures
Internal Organs and Organ Systems

Sponges and Cnidarians

The simplest of the invertebrates are the sponges, which belong to the phylum Porifera. All sponges share several characteristics.

All sponges are asymmetrical and have no tissues, organs, or organ systems. Their cells are specialized for capturing food, digestion, and reproduction. Other cells provide support inside the layers of the sponge. All sponges live in water, and most species live in ocean environments.

The phylum Cnidaria (ni DAR ee uh) includes jellyfish, sea anemones, hydras, and corals. Cnidarians, such as the sea anemone shown in **Figure 7,** differ from all other animals based on their unique characteristics.

Cnidarians have no organs or organ systems, but, unlike sponges, they have radial symmetry. They have a single body opening surrounded by tentacles. Simple tissues, including muscles, nerves, and digestive tissue, enable cnidarians to survive by moving, reacting to stimuli, and digesting food. They have specialized cells, called nematocysts (NE mah toh sihsts), that are used for defense and capturing food. Similar to sponges, most species of cnidarians live in ocean environments, and all live in water.

Reading Check What characteristics do poriferans and cnidarians share?

Figure 7 The tentacles of all cnidarians contain stinging structures for capturing food and defending against predators.

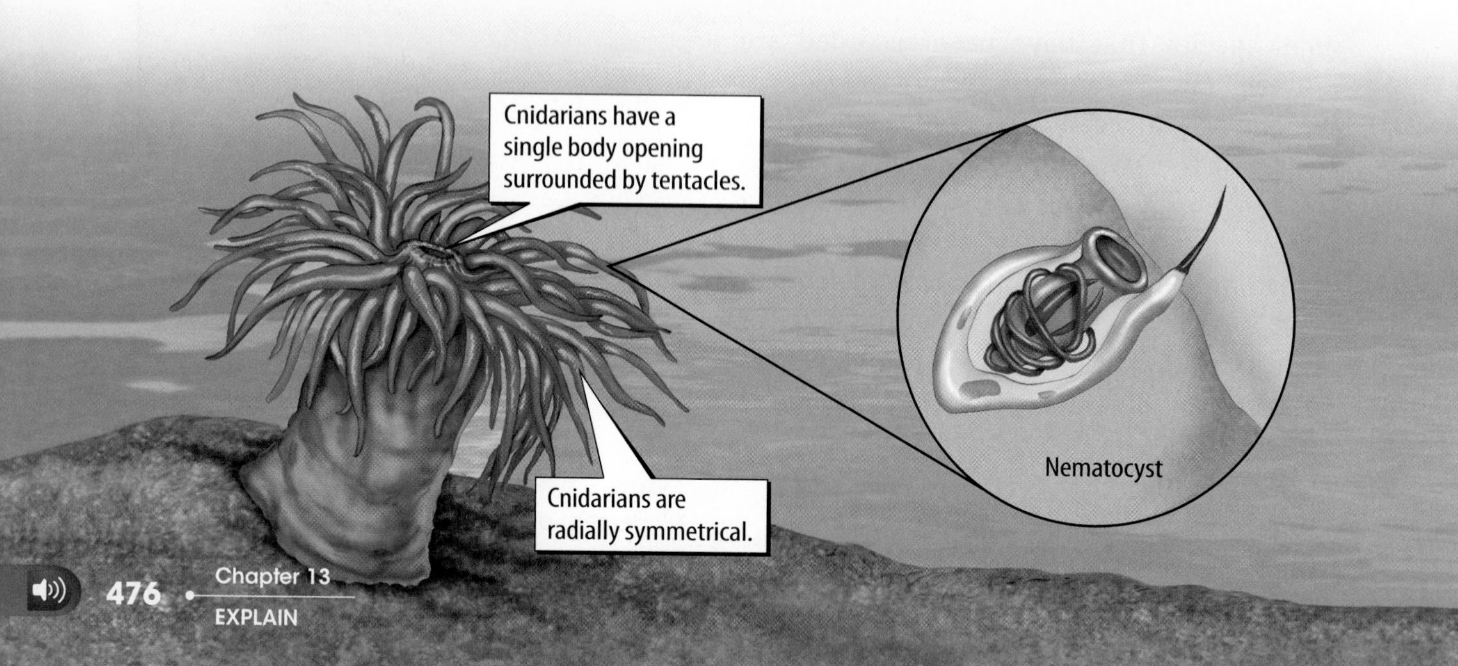
Cnidarians have a single body opening surrounded by tentacles.
Nematocyst
Cnidarians are radially symmetrical.

Flatworms and Roundworms

Flatworms are invertebrates that belong to the phylum Platyhelminthes (pla tih hel MIHN theez). All flatworms, including the tapeworm shown in **Figure 8,** have bilateral symmetry with nerve, muscle, and digestive tissues and a simple brain. They have soft and flattened bodies that are usually only a few cells thick. The digestive system of a flatworm has only one opening: a mouth.

Flatworms live in moist environments. Most, like tapeworms, are parasites that live in or on the bodies of other organisms and rely on them for food. Others are free-living, and many live in oceans or other marine environments.

 **Reading Check** What characteristics do all flatworms share?

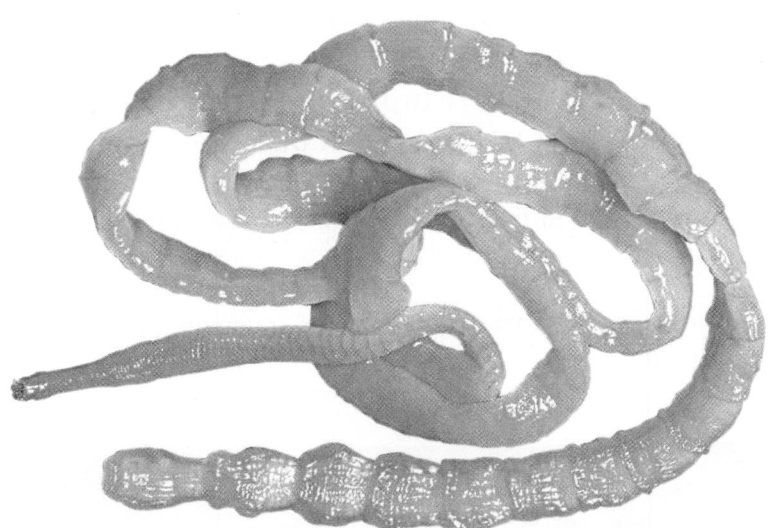

◀ **Figure 8** Most flatworm species, including this tapeworm, are parasites. They depend on other organisms for food and a place to live.

Visual Check How would you describe a flatworm's body?

Roundworms, also called nematodes, belong to the phylum Nematoda (ne muh TOH duh). Roundworms, like flatworms, have bilateral symmetry with nerve, muscle, and digestive tissues and a simple brain. However, unlike flatworms, their bodies are round and covered with a stiff outer covering called a cuticle. A roundworm's digestive system has two openings: a mouth and an anus. Food enters the mouth and is digested as it travels to the anus where wastes are excreted.

Roundworms live in moist environments. Some species are parasites that live in animals' digestive systems. Free-living roundworms such as the one pictured in **Figure 9** eat material such as fecal matter and dead organisms.

Reading Check How do flatworms and roundworms differ?

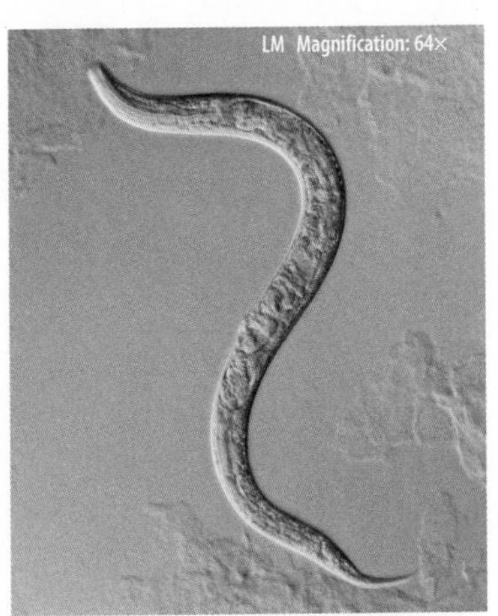

▲ **Figure 9** Roundworms are narrow and tapered at both ends. Most species are less than 1 mm long.

Mollusks and Annelids

The phylum Mollusca (mah LUS kuh) includes snails, slugs, clams, mussels, octopi, and squid. All mollusks, including the snail shown in **Figure 10,** have bilateral symmetry. Their bodies are soft, and some species have hard shells that protect their bodies. You might have seen a slug slithering along the ground after a rainstorm. Slugs are one type of mollusk without a shell.

Mollusks have digestive systems with two openings. A body cavity contains the heart, the stomach, and other organs. The mollusk circulatory system contains blood, but no blood vessels. Their nervous systems include eyes and other sensory organs as well as simple brains. Members of this phylum must remain wet and live in water or moist environments.

▲ **Figure 10** Snails have shells that protect their bodies.

The phylum Annelida includes earthworms, leeches, and marine worms. Annelid worms, including the one shown in **Figure 11,** have bilateral symmetry and soft bodies. Their bodies consist of repeating segments covered with a thin cuticle. Their digestive systems have two openings. Annelids have circulatory systems that are made up of blood vessels that carry blood throughout the body. Their nervous systems include a simple brain. Annelids live in water or moist environments such as soil.

Reading Check What do mollusks and segmented worms have in common?

Figure 11 One characteristic that distinguishes annelids from other worms is their segments. ▼

Visual Check How does this annelid differ from an earthworm?

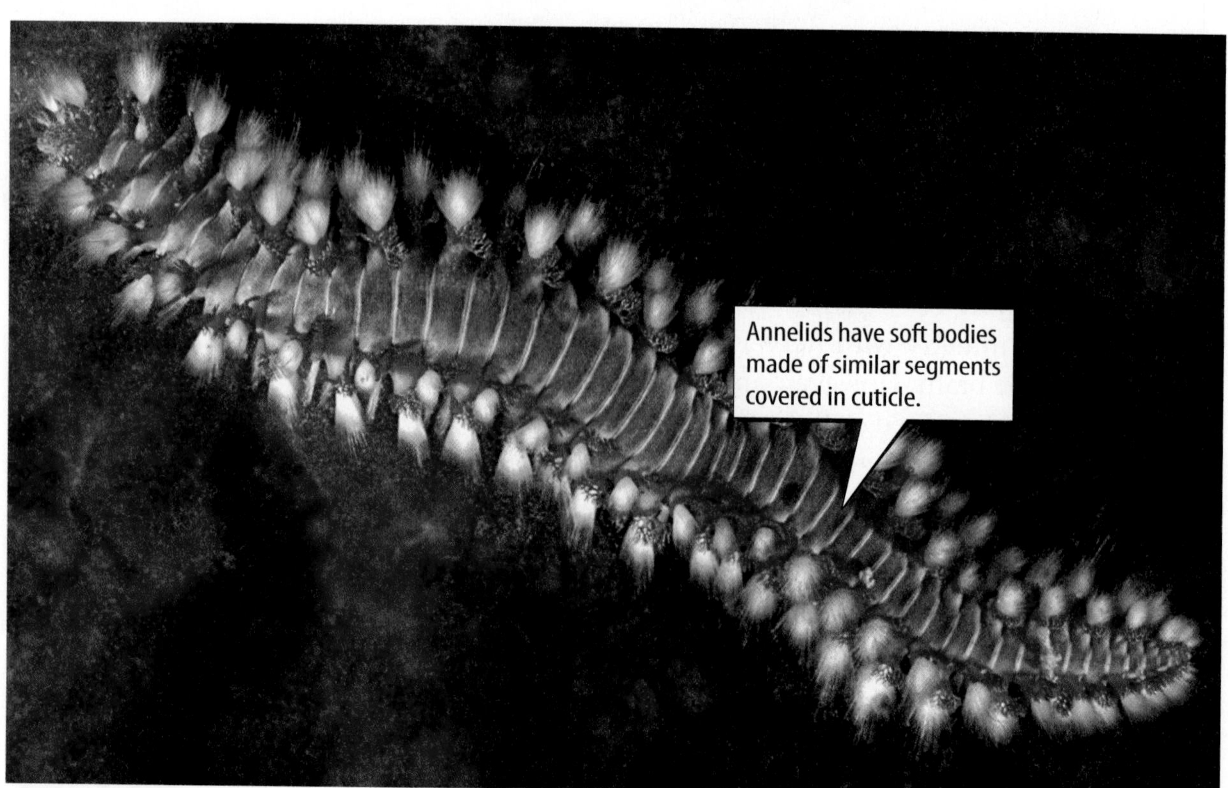

Annelids have soft bodies made of similar segments covered in cuticle.

Arthropods

The phylum Arthropoda includes insects, spiders, shrimp, crabs, and their relatives. More species belong to this phylum than all the other animal phyla combined. There are more than 1 million identified species of arthropods.

All arthropods have bilateral symmetry. They also have **exoskeletons**—*thick, hard outer coverings that protect and support animals' bodies.* Arthropods have several pairs of jointed appendages. *An* **appendage** *is a structure, such as a leg or an arm, that extends from the central part of the body.* The body parts of arthropods are segmented and specialized for different functions such as flying and eating. Unlike many of the other animals you have read about so far, arthropods live in almost every environment on Earth.

Word Origin

appendage
from Latin *appendere,* means "to cause to hang from"

Reading Check What do exoskeletons do?

Insects

The largest order of arthropods is the insects, which includes the stag beetle shown in **Figure 12.** All insect species have three pairs of jointed legs, three body segments, a pair of antennae, and a pair of compound eyes. Many species also have one or two pairs of wings.

There are 16 major groups of insects. However, most insect species belong to one of five groups. Beetles form the largest group of insects. About 40 percent of all known species of insects are beetles.

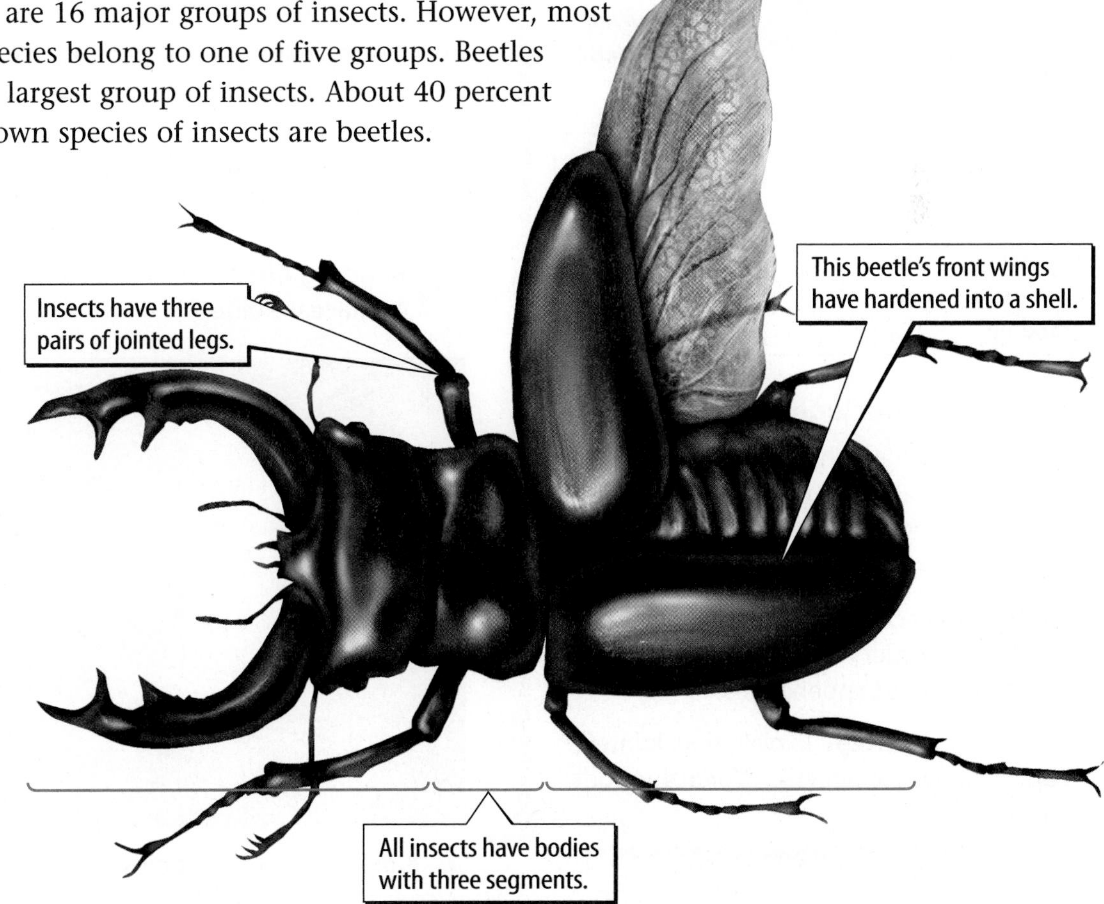
Insects have three pairs of jointed legs.
This beetle's front wings have hardened into a shell.
All insects have bodies with three segments.

Figure 12 A stag beetle has characteristics common to all insect species.

MiniLab 20 minutes

How does your arm move?

Both arthropods and mammals have jointed appendages. Try doing some simple tasks without bending your appendages to understand how useful jointed appendages are.

1. Using **newspaper** and **masking tape,** wrap your partner's arm at the elbow so he or she cannot bend it.

2. Ask your partner to perform the tasks in the data table below. Record your observations and your partner's experiences.

Task	Completed? (yes/no)	How was behavior changed?
Walk 5 m.		
Take a drink of water.		
Lay down on the ground and then stand up.		

Analyze and Conclude

1. **Summarize** Rank the tasks in order from hardest to easiest to perform without jointed appendages. What made the tasks harder to perform?
2. **Infer** What activities that you must perform in order to survive are impossible without jointed appendages?
3. **Key Concept** Explain how jointed appendages are necessary for arthropods to survive.

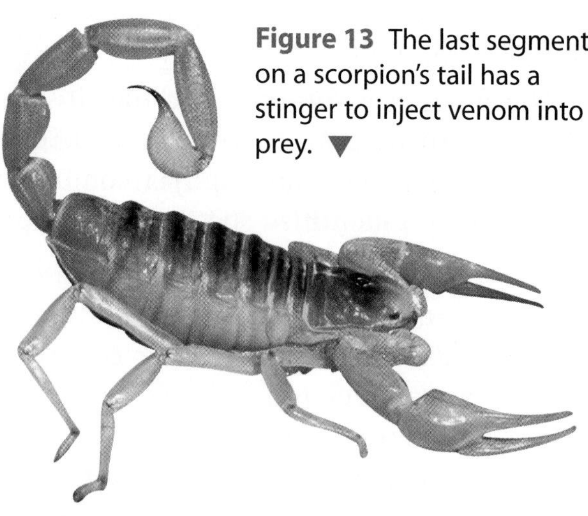

Figure 13 The last segment on a scorpion's tail has a stinger to inject venom into prey. ▼

Arachnids

Spiders, ticks, and scorpions, such as the one shown in **Figure 13,** are arachnids (uh RAK nudz). All arachnids have four pairs of jointed legs and two body segments. They do not have antennae or wings.

Crustaceans

Crabs, shrimp, lobsters, and their close relatives are crustaceans (krus TAY shunz). All crustaceans have one or two pairs of antennae. They also have jointed appendages in the mouth area that are specialized for biting and crushing food. Many people like to eat crustaceans, including lobsters and crabs, such as the one shown in **Figure 14.**

Reading Check How do arachnids and crustaceans differ?

▲ **Figure 14** Like most crustaceans, this crab's eyes are on stalks.

Echinoderms

The phylum Echinodermata (ih kin uh DUR muh tuh) includes sea stars, sea cucumbers, and sea urchins, such as the one shown in **Figure 15.** *Echinoderm* (ih KI nuh durm) means "spiny skin." Echinoderms have some unique features that are not in any of the other invertebrate phyla. They also are more closely related to vertebrates than to any other phyla.

All echinoderms have radial symmetry. Unlike any other phyla, echinoderms have hard plates embedded in the skin that support the body. Thousands of small, muscular, fluid-filled tubes, called tube feet, enable them to move and feed. They also have complete digestive systems including a mouth and an anus. Echinoderms live only in oceans. However, some can survive out of the water for short periods during low tides.

Key Concept Check How do the invertebrate phyla differ?

Math Skills

Use Percentages

More than 95 percent of animals are invertebrates. This means that 95 out of every 100 animals is some type of invertebrate. Out of every 1,000 animal species, 48 are mollusks. What percentage of animal species are mollusks?

Express the information as a fraction.

$$\frac{48}{1,000}$$

Change the fraction to a decimal.

$$\frac{48}{1,000} = 0.048$$

Multiply by 100 and add a % sign.

$$0.048 \times 100 = 4.8\%$$

Practice

Out of 900,000 species of arthropods, 304,200 are beetles. What percentage of arthropods are beetles?

- **Math Practice**
- **Personal Tutor**

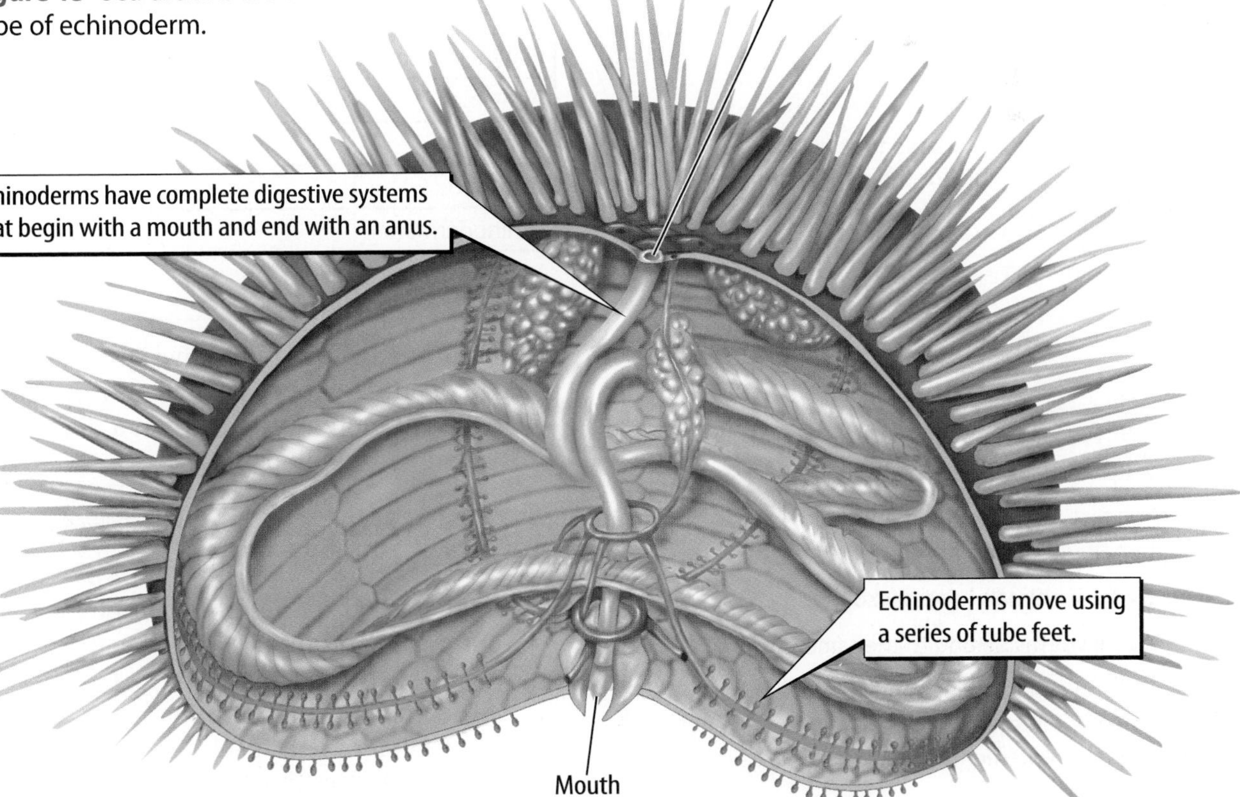

Anus
Echinoderms have complete digestive systems that begin with a mouth and end with an anus.
Echinoderms move using a series of tube feet.
Mouth

Figure 15 Sea urchins are one type of echinoderm.

Lesson 2 Review

Assessment Online Quiz

Inquiry Virtual Lab

Visual Summary

Most invertebrates have no internal structures that support their bodies.

There are more arthropods than members of any other phyla.

The largest order of arthropods is the insects.

FOLDABLES®

Use your lesson Foldable to review the lesson. Save your Foldable for the project at the end of the chapter.

What do you think NOW?

You first read the statements below at the beginning of the chapter.

3. Most animals have backbones.

4. All worms belong to the same phylum.

Did you change your mind about whether you agree or disagree with the statements? Rewrite any false statements to make them true.

Use Vocabulary

1. **Define** *exoskeleton.*
2. **Distinguish** between the phylum Platyhelminthes and the phylum Nematoda.
3. **Use the term** *appendage* in a sentence.

Understand Key Concepts 

4. Which phylum contains asymmetrical invertebrates that have no tissues?
   A. Annelida
   B. Cnidaria
   C. Echinodermata
   D. Porifera
5. **Describe** the characteristics of the phylum that contains invertebrates with wings.

Interpret Graphics

6. **Summarize Information** Copy the table below, and fill in the features common to the members of each invertebrate phylum.

Phylum	Characteristics	Example
Porifera		
Cnidaria		
Platyhelminthes		
Annelida		
Nematoda		
Arthropoda		
Echinodermata		

Critical Thinking

7. **Hypothesize** how a digestive system with two openings would enable an organism to absorb more nutrients than a digestive system with one opening.

Math Skills

Math Practice

8. About 11,000 species of Lepidoptera (butterflies and moths) have been identified in the United States. Only 679 of them are butterflies. What percentage of the Lepidoptera species in the United States are butterflies?

Inquiry **Skill Practice** **Classify** 30 minutes

How do you build a dichotomous key?

A dichotomous key helps you classify animals based on their characteristics. *Dichotomous* means "divided in two parts." Each step of the key has two choices. You choose the one that applies to the animal you are studying, and it directs you to the next set of choices. By picking the best choices for an animal's characteristics, you can classify animals in a list of possibilities.

Materials

invertebrates

magnifying lens

Safety

Learn It

Sorting objects into groups based on common features is called **classifying.** When classifying, first observe the objects being classified. Then select one feature that is shared by some, but not all, of the objects. Place all the members that share a feature into a subgroup. You can classify members into smaller and smaller subgroups based on characteristics.

Try It

1. Read and complete a lab safety form.
2. Study your invertebrate collection. You may want to use a magnifying lens. Step 1 of your dichotomous key is to divide your collection into two groups based on a characteristic. Make a table like the one shown below.

Step	Characteristic	"Go to"/ Identity
1.	legs present	step 2
	legs absent	step 3

3. Now think about the subgroup of animals that have the characteristic in step 1. Divide these animals into two smaller subgroups based on another characteristic. Enter this choice in step 2 of your dichotomous key.
4. Suppose only one animal in your collection falls into a subgroup. Place the identity of the animal in the right column of the table.

Step	Characteristic	"Go to"/ Identity
1.	legs present	step 2
	legs absent	step 3
2.	wings present	step 4
	wings absent	pavement ant *(Tetramorium caespitum)*

5. Repeat steps 3–5 until the animals are each in their own subgroup and the dichotomous key leads you to the identity of each animal.

Apply It

6. **Identify** Remove the labels from your animal collection. Trade your collection and your dichotomous key with a classmate. Identify all the animals in your classmate's collection using his or her key. Check your answers.
7. **Key Concept** What characteristics did all the animals you identified have in common?

Lesson 3

Phylum Chordata

Reading Guide

Key Concepts
ESSENTIAL QUESTIONS

- What are the characteristics of all chordates?
- What are the characteristics of all vertebrates?
- How do the classes of vertebrates differ?

Vocabulary

chordate p. 485
notochord p. 485

Multilingual eGlossary

Video BrainPOP®

Academic Standards for Science

8.3.6 Observe anatomical structures of a variety of organisms and describe their similarities and differences. Use the data collected to organize the organisms into groups and predict their relatedness.

Also covers: 8.NS.7, 8.NS.11, 8.DP.1, 8.DP.2, 8.DP.3, 8.DP.4, 8.DP.5, 8.DP.6, 8.DP.7, 8.DP.9, 8.DP.10, 8.DP.11

Inquiry One of a Kind?

Several different types of animals come to this watering hole to get a drink. These elephants, antelopes, and birds look very different, but would you guess that they were all related? All of these animals belong to the phylum Chordata and share several characteristics.

10 minutes

How can you model a backbone?

All vertebrates have backbones. Most backbones are made out of a stack of short bones called vertebrae. Some vertebrae are shaped like discs with holes in the center. The largest structure passing through the center of the stack of vertebrae is the spinal cord. Between each of the vertebrae are padlike structures, called discs, that cushion the bones. Try building a model of a backbone.

1. Read and complete a lab safety form.
2. Obtain **pasta wheels, circular gummy candies,** and a **chenille stem.** ⚠ Do not eat the lab materials.
3. Assemble the materials to make a model of a backbone.
4. Gently bend and move your model backbone. Observe how the parts move and interact with each other.

Think About This

1. When you bend your model backbone, how are the vertebrae, the discs, and the spinal cord affected?
2. When you compress your model backbone, how are the vertebrae, the discs, and the spinal cord affected?
3. **Key Concept** How do you think the structure of the backbone provides advantages to the body plan of vertebrates?

Characteristics of Chordates

Recall that one way to classify an animal is to check for a backbone and that animals with backbones are called vertebrates. Another way to classify animals is to look for the four characteristics of a chordate (KOR dat). *A* **chordate** *is an animal that has a notochord, a nerve cord, a tail, and structures called pharyngeal* (fer IN jee ul) *pouches at some point in its life.* In vertebrates, these characteristics are present only during embryonic development. *A* **notochord** *is a flexible, rod-shaped structure that supports the body of a developing chordate.* The nerve cord develops into the central nervous system. The pharyngeal pouches are between the mouth and the digestive system.

Most chordates are vertebrates, but the chordates also include two groups of invertebrates: tunicates and lancelets (LAN sluhts), shown in **Figure 16.** Invertebrate chordates are rarely more than a few centimeters long and live in salt water. In vertebrate chordates, such as humans, the notochord develops into a backbone during the growth of an embryo.

Key Concept Check What are the characteristics of chordates?

Figure 16 Lancelets can swim but spend most of their lives almost completely buried in sand.

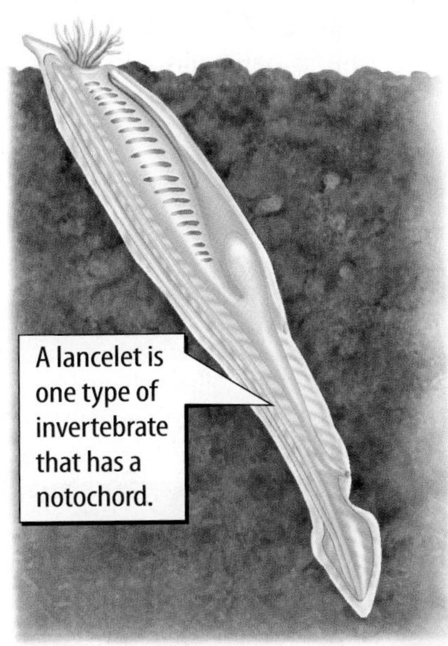

A lancelet is one type of invertebrate that has a notochord.

FOLDABLES®

Make a vertical five-tab book. Label the tabs as shown. Use the Foldable to identify specific characteristics and examples of vertebrates.

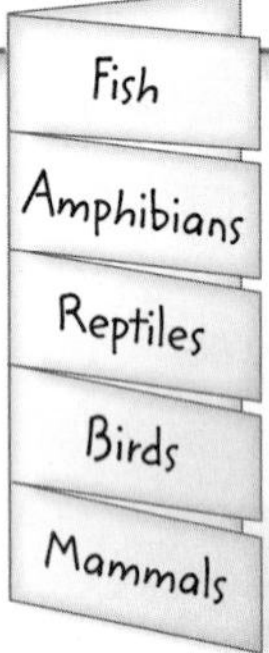

Characteristics of Vertebrates

Recall that all vertebrates have a backbone, also called a spinal column or spine. The backbone is a series of structures that surround and protect the nerve cord, or spinal cord. The spinal cord connects all the nerves in the body to the brain. Bones that form a backbone are called vertebrae (VUR tuh bray). If you gently touch the back of your neck, the bones you feel are some of your vertebrae.

Vertebrates have well-developed organ systems. All vertebrates have digestive systems with two openings, circulatory systems that move blood through the body, and nervous systems that include brains. The five major groups of vertebrates are fish, amphibians, reptiles, birds, and mammals.

Key Concept Check What are the characteristics of all vertebrates?

Fish

Most fish spend their entire lives in water. They have two important characteristics in common: gills for absorbing oxygen gas from water and paired fins for swimming. Fish are grouped into one of three classes.

Hagfish and lampreys lack jaws and are in a group called jawless fish. Sharks, such as the one shown in **Figure 17,** skates, and rays are cartilaginous fish. They have skeletons made of a tough, fibrous tissue called cartilage (KAR tuh lihj). Both jawless and cartilaginous fish have internal structures made of cartilage.

Trout, guppies, perch, tuna, mackerel, and thousands of other species do not have cartilaginous skeletons. Instead, they have bones and are grouped together as bony fish.

Figure 17 Like all fish, sharks have gills and fins.

Structures called gills enable fish to absorb oxygen from the water.

Amphibians

Frogs, toads, and salamanders belong to the class Amphibia, as shown in **Figure 18.** Most **amphibians** spend part of their lives in water and part on land. Their bodies change as they grow older. In many species, the young have different body forms than the adults do.

Amphibians have skeletons made of bone and have legs for movement. Their skin is smooth and moist, and their hearts have three chambers. Amphibians lay eggs that do not have hard protective coverings, or shells. Their eggs must be laid in moist environments, such as ponds. Young live in water and have gills; most adults develop lungs and live on land.

 **Reading Check** How do amphibians differ from fish?

WORD ORIGIN

amphibian
from Greek *amphi-*, means "of both kinds" and *bios*, means "life"

Adult amphibians have lungs and live on land.
Amphibian eggs do not have shells.
Young amphibians have gills.

Figure 18 The body forms of many amphibians change as they grow.

Visual Check How does the body form of this salamander change as it grows?

SCIENCE USE V. COMMON USE

scale

Science Use small, flat plate that forms part of an animal's external covering

Common Use an instrument for measuring the mass of an object

Reptiles

Lizards, snakes, turtles, crocodiles, and alligators belong to the class Reptilia. A leopard gecko, one example of this class, is shown in **Figure 19.**

All reptiles share several characteristics. Their skin is waterproof and covered in **scales.** Like amphibians, most reptiles have three-chambered hearts. Unlike amphibians, lizards and other reptiles have lungs throughout their lives.

Most reptiles lay fluid-filled eggs with leathery shells. Unlike amphibian eggs, reptile eggs are laid on land rather than in water. Young reptiles do not change form as they mature into adult reptiles.

Reading Check How do reptiles differ from amphibians?

Most reptile hearts have three chambers.
Some reptiles lay eggs with leathery shells.

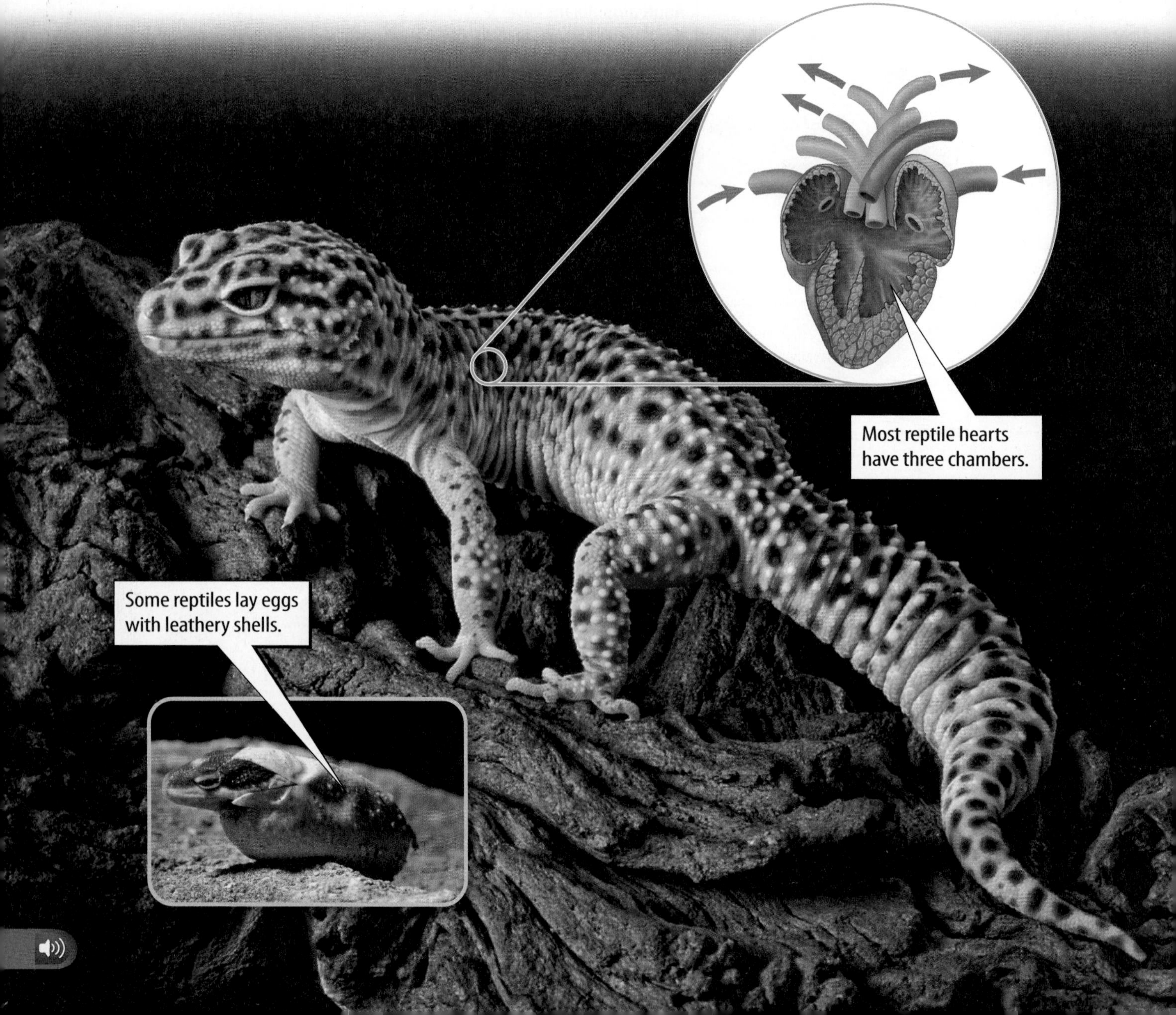

Figure 19 This lizard has a three-chambered heart and lays fluid-filled eggs.

Birds

All birds, including the owl shown in **Figure 20,** are in the class Aves. Many birds make nests to hold their **eggs,** and many have unique calls or songs.

REVIEW VOCABULARY

egg
a female sex cell that forms in an ovary

Birds have lightweight bones. Their skin is covered with feathers and scales. Birds also have two legs and two wings. Many birds can fly, and they have stiff feathers that enable them to move through the air. Birds that spend a lot of time in the water have oil glands that help water roll off their feathers.

Birds have beaks and do not chew their food. Instead, their digestive systems include gizzards, organs that help grind food into smaller pieces. Their circulatory systems include four-chambered hearts. Birds also lay fluid-filled eggs with hard shells and feed and care for their young.

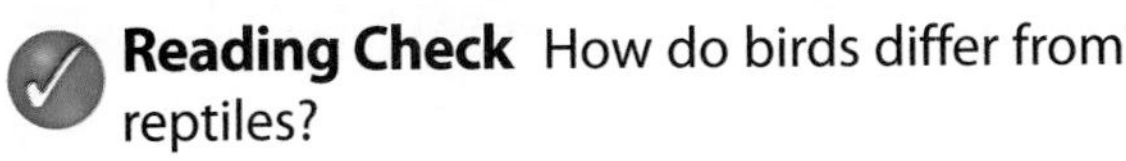

Reading Check How do birds differ from reptiles?

Figure 20 All birds have several characteristics in common, including lightweight bones and four-chambered hearts.

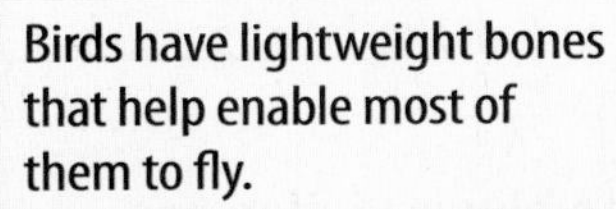

Birds have lightweight bones that help enable most of them to fly.

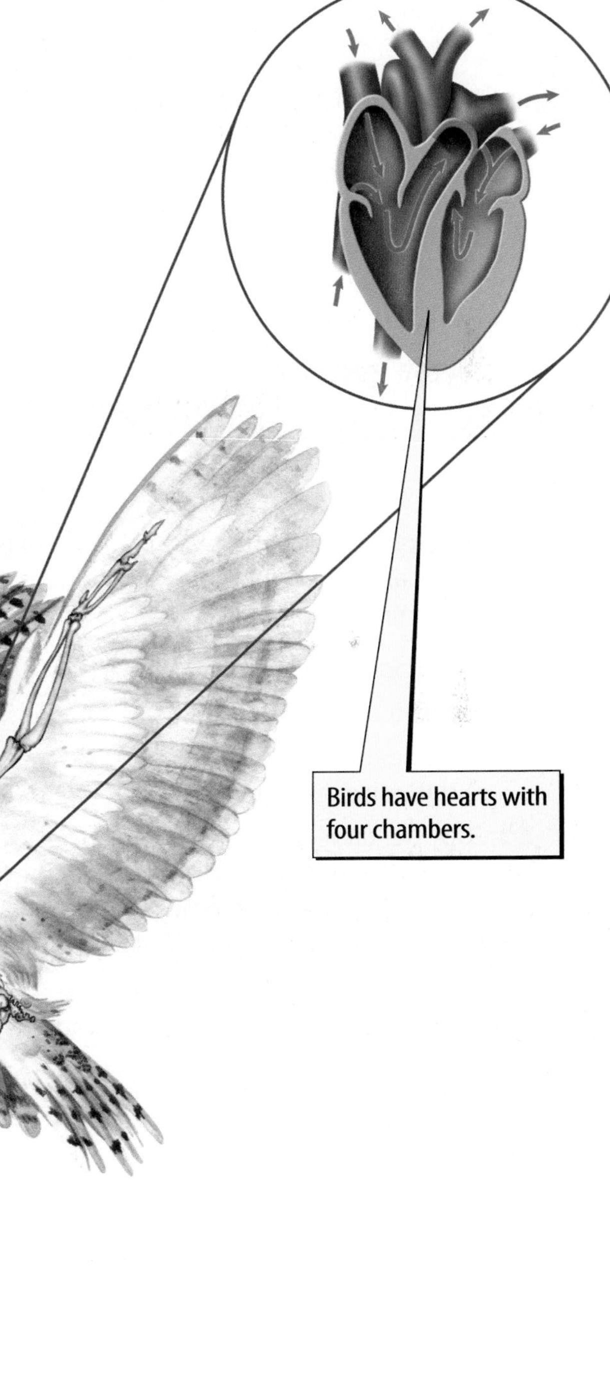

Birds have hearts with four chambers.

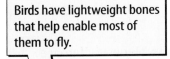

Figure 21 Mammals have hair or fur and mammary glands.

Mammals

Dogs, cats, goats, rats, seals, whales, and humans are among the many vertebrates belonging to the class Mammalia. All mammals have hair or fur covering their bodies. As shown in **Figure 21,** they tear and chew their food using teeth. Mammals have complete digestive systems, which include a mouth and an anus, and a complex nervous system including a brain.

The most notable characteristic of mammals, however, is the presence of mammary glands. These glands produce milk that feeds young mammals. Although many mammals have live young, a few species, including the duck-billed platypus, lay eggs.

 **Key Concept Check** How do the classes of vertebrates differ?

Inquiry MiniLab

15 minutes

Whose bones are these?

The skeletons of vertebrates are made up of bones. Bones have different characteristics depending on the animal in which they are found and their function in the body. Observe bones from different animals.

1. Read and complete a lab safety form.
2. Obtain a collection of **bones.**
3. Examine the shape, the texture, the mass, and the size of the bones.
4. Copy the table below in your Science Journal. Record your observations in the table. Add extra columns if you notice other characteristics you would like to record.

Analyze and Conclude

1. **Compare** What traits did all the bones you observed share?
2. **Contrast** What was the biggest difference among the bones you observed?
3.  **Key Concept** Use your observations to identify bones from two different classes of vertebrates.

Bone	Shape	Texture	Mass	Size	Other Observations
1					
2					
3					
4					

Lesson 3 Review

Assessment Online Quiz

Visual Summary

Most chordates are vertebrates.

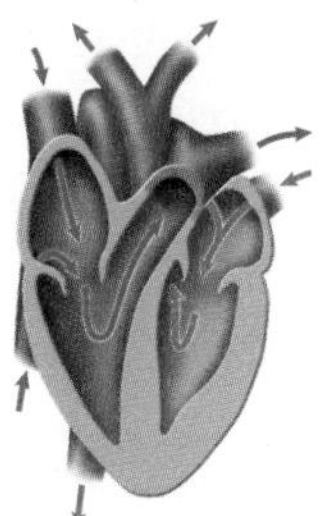

Vertebrates have well-developed organ systems including digestive systems with two openings, circulatory systems that move blood through the body, and nervous systems including brains.

Mammals produce milk to feed their young.

FOLDABLES®

Use your lesson Foldable to review the lesson. Save your Foldable for the project at the end of the chapter.

What do you think NOW?

You first read the statements below at the beginning of the chapter.

5. All chordates have backbones.

6. Reptiles have three-chambered hearts.

Did you change your mind about whether you agree or disagree with the statements? Rewrite any false statements to make them true.

Use Vocabulary

1. **Distinguish** between reptiles and amphibians.
2. **Define** *notochord.*

Understand Key Concepts

3. Which characteristic is common to all chordates?
   A. bones
   B. fur
   C. lungs
   D. notochord
4. **List** the characteristics common to all fish.
5. **Compare and contrast** birds and mammals.

Interpret Graphics

6. **Summarize Information** Copy the table below, and fill in the features of each type of chordate.

Type of Animal	Characteristics	Example Animals
Invertebrate chordates		
Vertebrate chordates		

7. **Analyze** To which class of vertebrates does the animal below belong? How do you know?

Critical Thinking

8. **Assess** Why does a backbone make vertebrates better adapted for life on land than invertebrates? Explain your answer.
9. **Infer** What is the advantage of having bones that protect the central nerve cord?

Lab

60 minutes

Design Your Own Phylum

Materials

markers

colored pencils

In this chapter, you have learned that different types of animals have different characteristics. Some animals have radial symmetry. Others have bilateral symmetry. Still others have no symmetry at all. Vertebrates have backbones. Invertebrates do not. Your task is to design a new phylum of alien animals that has never before been described. What are the characteristics of the animals in your phylum? Remember that animals must perform tasks in order to survive, such as capturing food and reproducing. What characteristics enable the animals in your phylum to survive?

Question

What characteristics enable you to identify animals in your new phylum? What different characteristics do animals in your phylum have?

Procedure

1. Read and complete a lab safety form.
2. Spend time thinking about your phylum. In your Science Journal, write down characteristics that are common to all the animals in your phylum. Try writing a list of structures animals must have and functions that animals must perform as a guide for creating your phylum's characteristics. Create a name for your phylum.
3. Create five different species of animals in your phylum. Write a list of characteristics for each of these animals that make them different from each other. Name each animal.
4. On five separate pieces of paper, draw each of your animals to the best of your ability.
5. Build a dichotomous key that someone could use to identify the animals in your phylum.

6 Trade pictures of animals and dichotomous keys with a classmate. Using your classmate's dichotomous key, identify each of the animals in the drawings.

7 **Analyze** Show your classmate your identifications. Were your answers correct? If not, make modifications to your identifications. Record your changes in your Science Journal.

Analyze and Conclude

8 **Compare** your phylum with your classmate's phylum. What characteristics did the two phyla share? Name some characteristics that were different.

9 **Evaluate** What types of characteristics were the most useful for identifying animals? What types were the hardest to use?

10 **The Big Idea** If your new phylum was included in Kingdom Animalia, where would it go? Why would it be placed in that location?

Communicate Your Results

Suppose that you are a zoologist, and you have discovered animals in your new phylum. Prepare a press release describing your phylum. Use your pictures to illustrate the characteristics of the animals you discovered. Explain where you found your animals, how they survive in the wild, and any other information that makes your phylum interesting.

Inquiry Extension

Try building physical models of the animals in your phylum. Use wood, wire, clay, paint, and other sculpting materials.

Lab Tips

- ☑ Try thinking about the environment where you would find your phylum to help you think of characteristics that enable it to live there.
- ☑ Think about the animals that might have been ancestors to phyla that exist today. What predators might the animals in your phylum have?

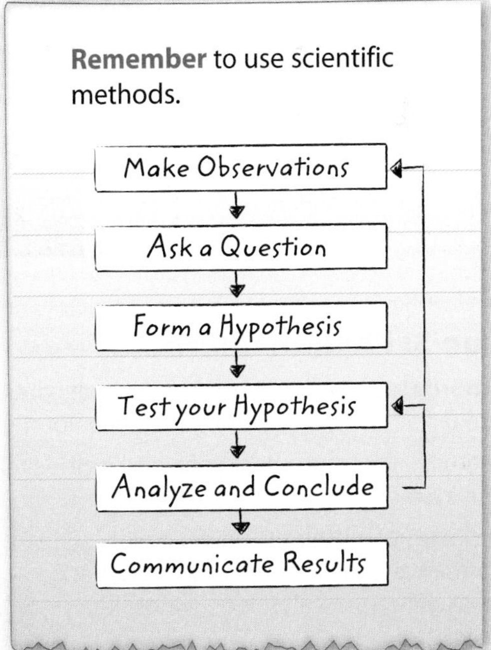

Chapter 13 Study Guide

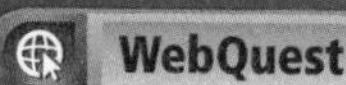

The major groups of animals include sponges, cnidarians, flatworms, roundworms, mollusks, segmented worms, arthropods, and chordates. They differ based on body structures and types of reproduction.

Key Concepts Summary

Lesson 1: What defines an animal?

- Animals are eukaryotic, multicellular organisms that eat other organisms, digest food, and have collagen to support cells. Most animals reproduce sexually and can move.
- Animals can be classified based on the presence of a backbone; body symmetry; the characteristics of proteins, DNA, and other molecules that make up their cells; and the kinds of body structures they possess.

Vocabulary

vertebrate p. 468
invertebrate p. 468
radial symmetry p. 469
bilateral symmetry p. 469
asymmetry p. 469

Lesson 2: Invertebrate Phyla

- Invertebrates have no backbone or internal skeleton, and they tend to be smaller and slower-moving than vertebrates.
- Invertebrates differ based on symmetry, presence or absence of certain types of specialized body structures, and presence or absence of specific internal organs and organ systems.

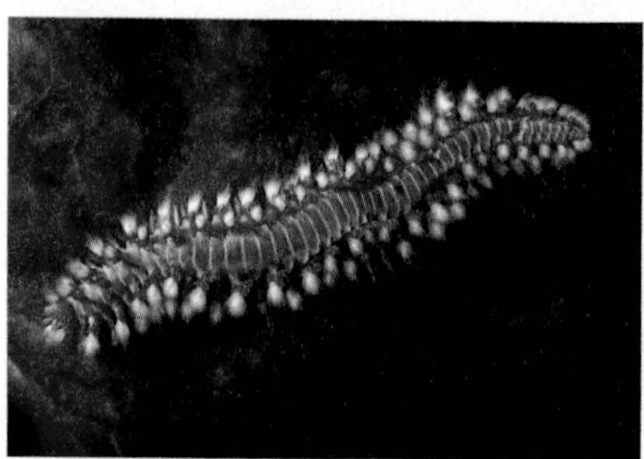

Vocabulary

exoskeleton p. 479
appendage p. 479

Lesson 3: Phylum Chordata

- All **chordates** have a **notochord**, a nerve cord, pharyngeal pouches, and a tail at some time during their development.
- All vertebrates have a backbone and well-developed organs and organ systems.
- The classes of vertebrates differ based on presence or absence of characteristics such as gills, fins, scales, legs, wings, fur, and eggs.

Vocabulary

chordate p. 485
notochord p. 485

Review
- Personal Tutor
- Vocabulary eGames
- Vocabulary eFlashcards

FOLDABLES® Chapter Project

Assemble your lesson Foldables as shown to make a Chapter Project. Use the project to review what you have learned in this chapter.

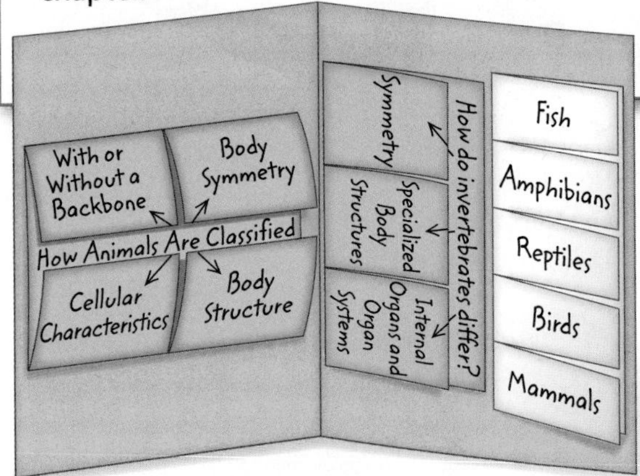

Use Vocabulary

Write the vocabulary term that best matches each phrase.

1. body plan that can be divided into two nearly equal parts anywhere through its central axis
2. body plan that cannot be divided into two nearly equal parts
3. structure that develops into a backbone in vertebrates
4. a structure such as a leg or an arm
5. two sides that are nearly mirror images of each other
6. a thick, hard covering on arthropods

Link Vocabulary and Key Concepts

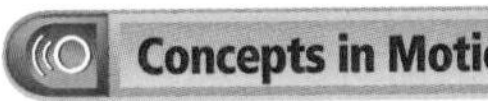

Interactive Concept Map

Copy this concept map, and then use vocabulary terms from the previous page to complete the concept map.

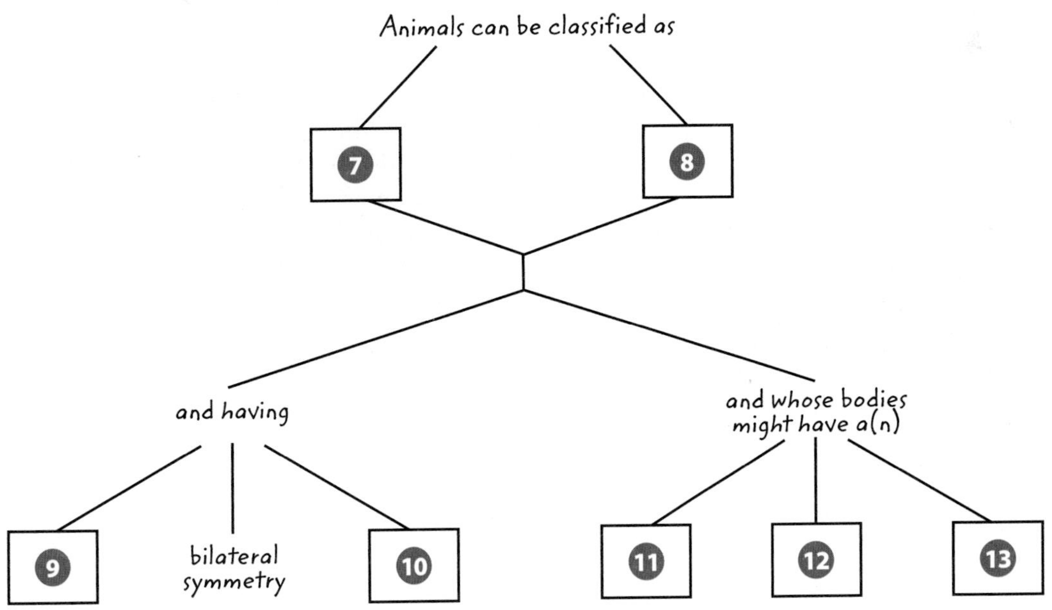

Chapter 13 Review

Understand Key Concepts

1. Which characteristic does NOT apply to animals?
   A. collagen
   B. photosynthesis
   C. digestive system
   D. eukaryotic cell

2. What characteristic applies to the animal shown below?

   A. asymmetry
   B. vertebrate
   C. bilateral symmetry
   D. radial symmetry

3. Which characteristic separates the animal kingdom into two categories?
   A. backbone
   B. DNA
   C. notochord
   D. symmetry

4. Which characteristics do all cnidarians have in common?
   A. free swimming, radial symmetry
   B. radial symmetry, attached to rocks
   C. tentacles, bilateral symmetry
   D. tentacles, stinging cells

5. Which characteristic is NOT shared by both flatworms and nematodes?
   A. bilateral symmetry
   B. a simple brain
   C. live in moist environments
   D. two openings in digestive system

6. To which phylum does the animal below belong?

   A. Annelida
   B. Mollusca
   C. Nematoda
   D. Platyhelminthes

Use the figure below to answer questions 7 and 8.

7. What characteristic distinguishes the animal shown above from a fish?
   A. bones
   B. notochord
   C. nerve cord
   D. no gills

8. To which phylum does this animal belong?
   A. Annelida
   B. Cnidaria
   C. Chordata
   D. Mollusca

Critical Thinking

9 **Create** a table that compares the three types of symmetry in the animal kingdom.

10 **Analyze** Why is digestion important to animals, but not to plants?

11 **Infer** Animals have cells specialized for different functions. Why is this feature an advantage for survival in a multicellular organism?

12 **Analyze** Explain how you could determine whether the animals shown below are from the same phylum or different phyla.

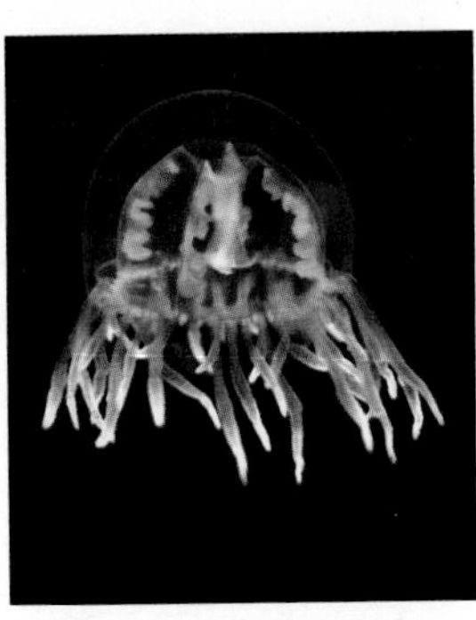

13 **Evaluate** Why are sponges, cnidarians, flatworms, and roundworms limited to life in water or moist environments?

14 **Compare** What characteristics do fish and lancelets have in common? How are they different?

15 **Infer** Why do most vertebrates have appendages such as fins, wings, and legs, whereas most invertebrates do not?

Writing in Science

16 **Write** a paragraph giving two ways a scuba diver could tell the difference between a sea anemone and a sea slug during an ocean dive.

REVIEW THE BIG IDEA

17 In what ways does a body with an internal skeleton have an advantage over a body with no internal or external support?

18 What are the major groups of animals, and how do they differ?

Math Skills

Math Practice

Use Percentages

19 Worldwide, there are about 300,000 species of Lepidoptera, of which an estimated 14,500 are butterflies. What percentage of Lepidoptera species are butterflies?

20 Of the estimated 1.2 million species of invertebrates, about 40,000 are crustaceans. What percentage of invertebrates are crustaceans?

21 Of the estimated 1.2 million species of invertebrates, about 950,000 are insects. What percentage of invertebrates are insects?

Standardized Test Practice

Record your answers on the answer sheet provided by your teacher or on a sheet of paper.

Multiple Choice

1 Which is a characteristic of all vertebrates?

A digestive system with one opening

B offspring hatch from eggs

C respiratory system with lungs

D spinal cord enclosed in bones

Use the figure below to answer question 2.

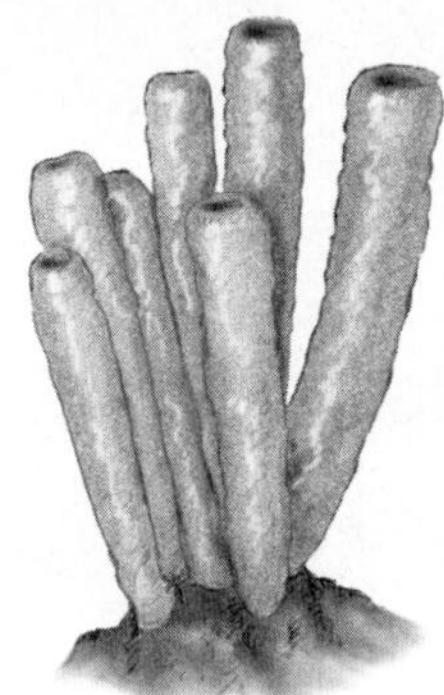

2 Which is true of the animal shown above?

A It has bilateral symmetry.

B It has radial symmetry.

C It is an invertebrate.

D It is a vertebrate.

3 Which animals make up Phylum Chordata?

A insects, spiders, and crabs

B mussels, octopuses, and squids

C snails, slugs, and clams

D vertebrates, lancelets, and tunicates

4 Which is a characteristic of all invertebrates?

A backbone absent

B exoskeleton present

C symmetry absent

D tube feet present

5 Which is NOT a characteristic of all animals?

A digesting food

B eating other organisms

C having specialized cells

D moving around

Use the figure below to answer question 6.

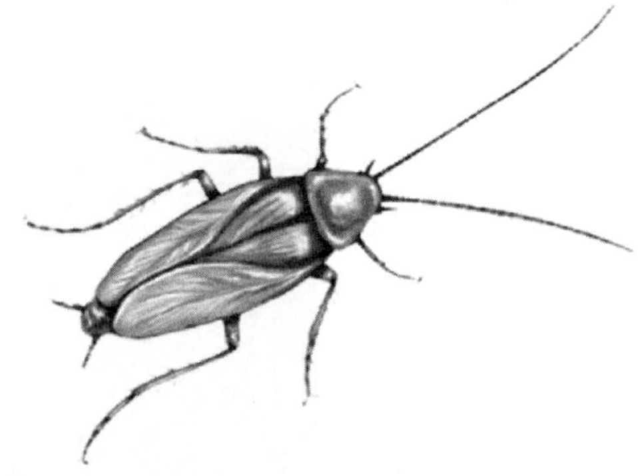

6 The animal in the figure above is classified in which phylum?

A Arthropoda

B Chordata

C Echinodermata

D Mollusca

7 Which animal has radial symmetry?

A flatworm

B jellyfish

C octopus

D sponge

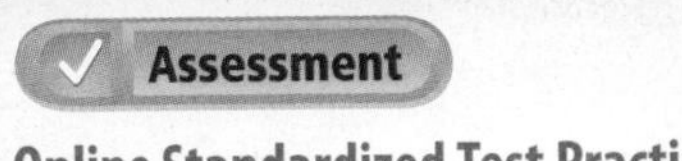

Use the figure below to answer questions 8 and 9.

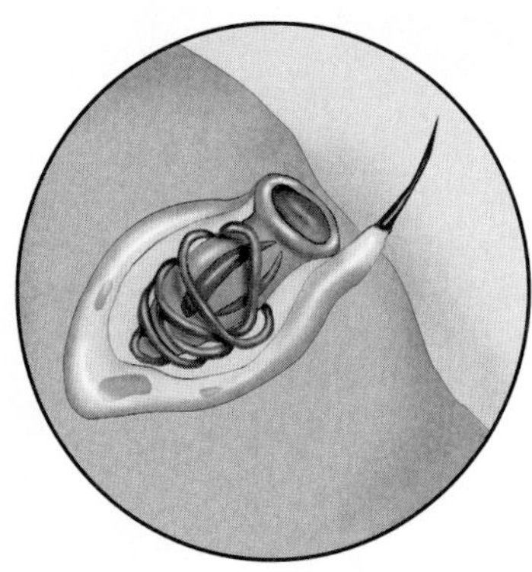

8 Which animals contain the structure shown in the figure?

A bees and wasps

B jellyfish and corals

C octopuses and squids

D sea stars and sea urchins

9 How do animals use the structure shown in the figure?

A for breathing

B for feeding

C for mating

D for seeing

10 Which class of vertebrates feeds milk to its young?

A amphibians

B fish

C mammals

D reptiles

Constructed Response

Use the figure below to answer questions 11 and 12.

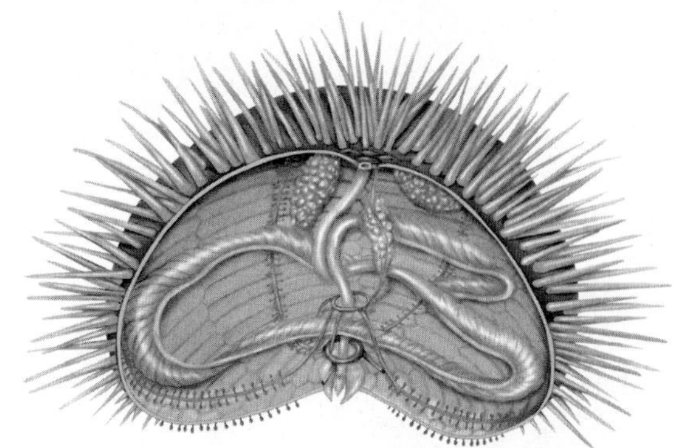

11 Identify the phylum of the animal shown in the figure. What type of animal is it? Give examples of other animals in this phylum.

12 Use the figure above to describe at least three characteristics typical of the phylum represented.

13 Which adaptations enable birds and reptiles to live on land while fish and amphibians must live in or near water for at least part of their life cycles?

14 List the four characteristics of all chordates. Explain the relationship of each characteristic to an adult human.

NEED EXTRA HELP?														
If You Missed Question...	1	2	3	4	5	6	7	8	9	10	11	12	13	14
Go to Lesson...	3	1	1	2	1	1	1	2	2	3	2	2	3	3

Student Resources

For Students and Parents/Guardians

These resources are designed to help you achieve success in science. You will find useful information on laboratory safety, math skills, and science skills. In addition, science reference materials are found in the Reference Handbook. You'll find the information you need to learn and sharpen your skills in these resources.

Table of Contents

Scientific Methods

Scientists use an orderly approach called the scientific method to solve problems. This includes organizing and recording data so others can understand them. Scientists use many variations in this method when they solve problems.

Identify a Question

The first step in a scientific investigation or experiment is to identify a question to be answered or a problem to be solved. For example, you might ask which gasoline is the most efficient.

Gather and Organize Information

After you have identified your question, begin gathering and organizing information. There are many ways to gather information, such as researching in a library, interviewing those knowledgeable about the subject, testing and working in the laboratory and field. Fieldwork is investigations and observations done outside of a laboratory.

Researching Information Before moving in a new direction, it is important to gather the information that already is known about the subject. Start by asking yourself questions to determine exactly what you need to know. Then you will look for the information in various reference sources, like the student is doing in **Figure 1.** Some sources may include textbooks, encyclopedias, government documents, professional journals, science magazines, and the Internet. Always list the sources of your information.

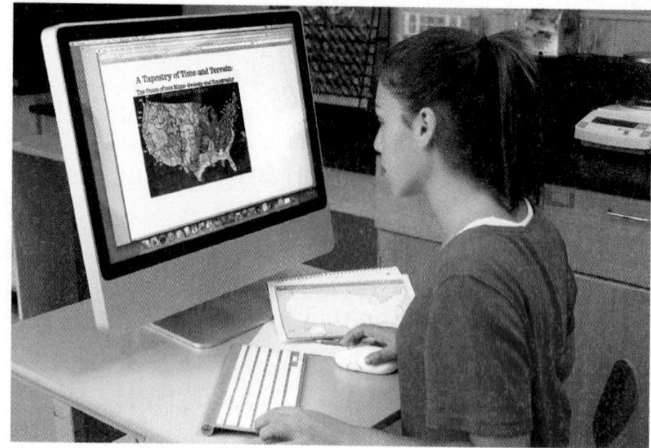

Figure 1 The Internet can be a valuable research tool.

Evaluate Sources of Information Not all sources of information are reliable. You should evaluate all of your sources of information, and use only those you know to be dependable. For example, if you are researching ways to make homes more energy efficient, a site written by the U.S. Department of Energy would be more reliable than a site written by a company that is trying to sell a new type of weatherproofing material. Also, remember that research always is changing. Consult the most current resources available to you. For example, a 1985 resource about saving energy would not reflect the most recent findings.

Sometimes scientists use data that they did not collect themselves, or conclusions drawn by other researchers. This data must be evaluated carefully. Ask questions about how the data were obtained, if the investigation was carried out properly, and if it has been duplicated exactly with the same results. Would you reach the same conclusion from the data? Only when you have confidence in the data can you believe it is true and feel comfortable using it.

Interpret Scientific Illustrations As you research a topic in science, you will see drawings, diagrams, and photographs to help you understand what you read. Some illustrations are included to help you understand an idea that you can't see easily by yourself, like the tiny particles in an atom in **Figure 2.** A drawing helps many people to remember details more easily and provides examples that clarify difficult concepts or give additional information about the topic you are studying. Most illustrations have labels or a caption to identify or to provide more information.

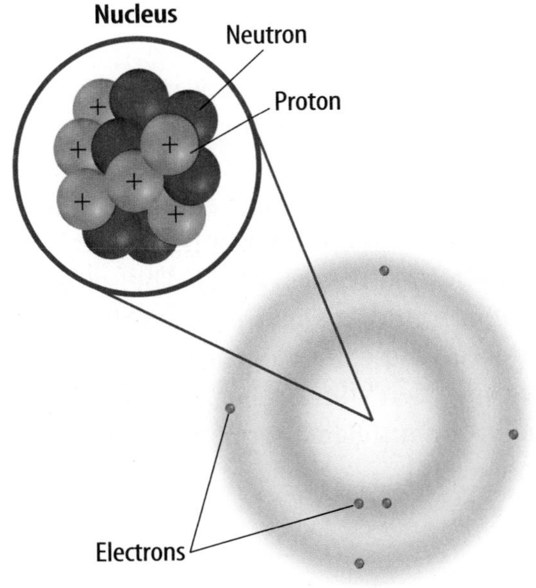

Figure 2 This drawing shows an atom of carbon with its six protons, six neutrons, and six electrons.

Concept Maps One way to organize data is to draw a diagram that shows relationships among ideas (or concepts). A concept map can help make the meanings of ideas and terms more clear, and help you understand and remember what you are studying. Concept maps are useful for breaking large concepts down into smaller parts, making learning easier.

Network Tree A type of concept map that not only shows a relationship, but how the concepts are related is a network tree, shown in **Figure 3.** In a network tree, the words are written in the ovals, while the description of the type of relationship is written across the connecting lines.

When constructing a network tree, write down the topic and all major topics on separate pieces of paper or notecards. Then arrange them in order from general to specific. Branch the related concepts from the major concept and describe the relationship on the connecting line. Continue to more specific concepts until finished.

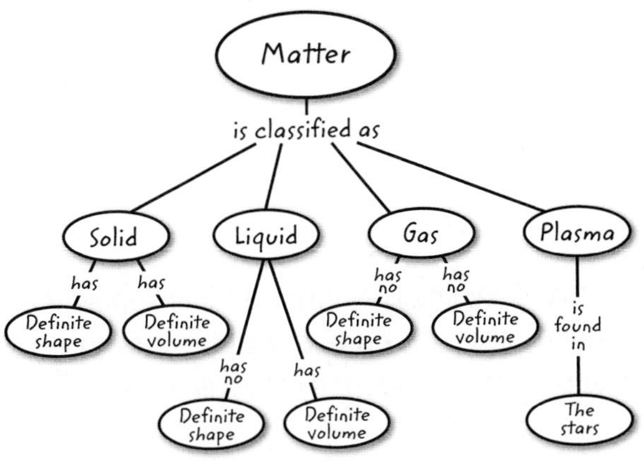

Figure 3 A network tree shows how concepts or objects are related.

Events Chain Another type of concept map is an events chain. Sometimes called a flow chart, it models the order or sequence of items. An events chain can be used to describe a sequence of events, the steps in a procedure, or the stages of a process.

When making an events chain, first find the one event that starts the chain. This event is called the initiating event. Then, find the next event and continue until the outcome is reached, as shown in **Figure 4.**

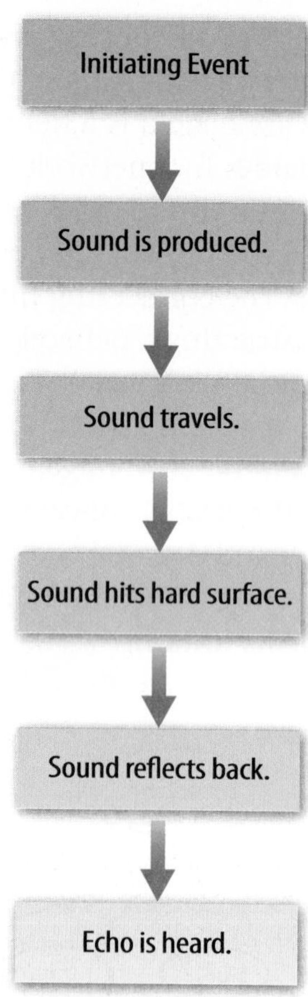

Figure 4 Events-chain concept maps show the order of steps in a process or event. This concept map shows how a sound makes an echo.

Cycle Map A specific type of events chain is a cycle map. It is used when the series of events do not produce a final outcome, but instead relate back to the beginning event, such as in **Figure 5.** Therefore, the cycle repeats itself.

To make a cycle map, first decide what event is the beginning event. This is also called the initiating event. Then list the next events in the order that they occur, with the last event relating back to the initiating event. Words can be written between the events that describe what happens from one event to the next. The number of events in a cycle map can vary, but usually contain three or more events.

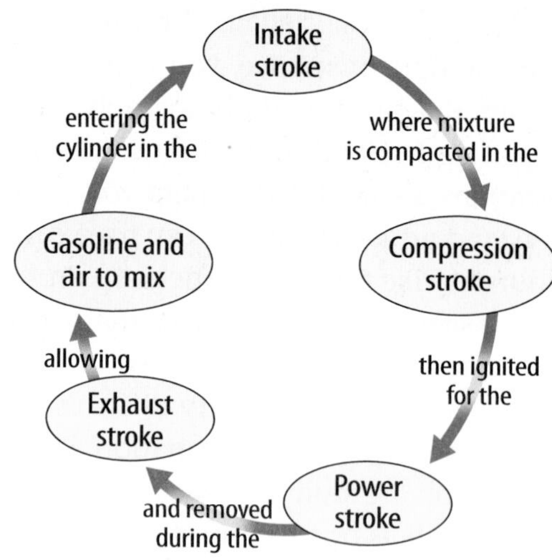

Figure 5 A cycle map shows events that occur in a cycle.

Spider Map A type of concept map that you can use for brainstorming is the spider map. When you have a central idea, you might find that you have a jumble of ideas that relate to it but are not necessarily clearly related to each other. The spider map on sound in **Figure 6** shows that if you write these ideas outside the main concept, then you can begin to separate and group unrelated terms so they become more useful.

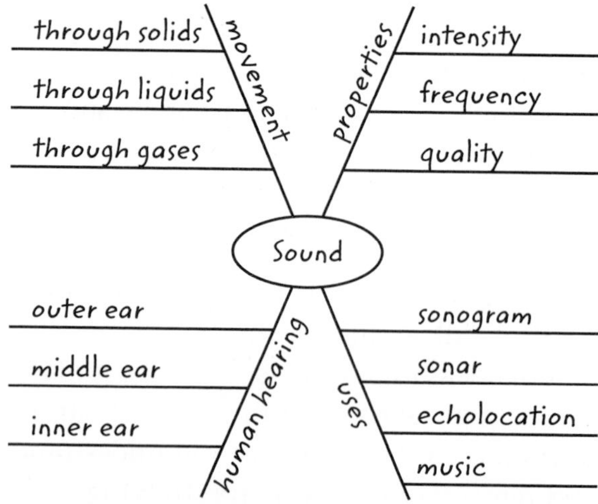

Figure 6 A spider map allows you to list ideas that relate to a central topic but not necessarily to one another.

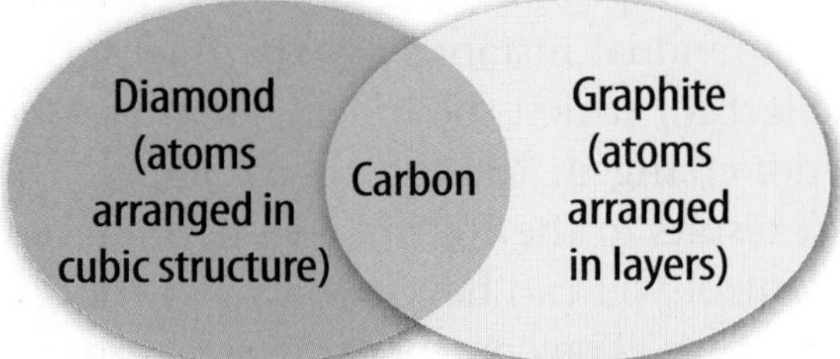

Figure 7 This Venn diagram compares and contrasts two substances made from carbon.

Venn Diagram To illustrate how two subjects compare and contrast you can use a Venn diagram. You can see the characteristics that the subjects have in common and those that they do not, shown in **Figure 7.**

To create a Venn diagram, draw two overlapping ovals that that are big enough to write in. List the characteristics unique to one subject in one oval, and the characteristics of the other subject in the other oval. The characteristics in common are listed in the overlapping section.

Make and Use Tables One way to organize information so it is easier to understand is to use a table. Tables can contain numbers, words, or both.

To make a table, list the items to be compared in the first column and the characteristics to be compared in the first row. The title should clearly indicate the content of the table, and the column or row heads should be clear. Notice that in **Table 1** the units are included.

Table 1 Recyclables Collected During Week

Day of Week	Paper (kg)	Aluminum (kg)	Glass (kg)
Monday	5.0	4.0	12.0
Wednesday	4.0	1.0	10.0
Friday	2.5	2.0	10.0

Make a Model One way to help you better understand the parts of a structure, the way a process works, or to show things too large or small for viewing is to make a model. For example, an atomic model made of a plastic-ball nucleus and pipe-cleaner electron shells can help you visualize how the parts of an atom relate to each other. Other types of models can be devised on a computer or represented by equations.

Form a Hypothesis

A possible explanation based on previous knowledge and observations is called a hypothesis. After researching gasoline types and recalling previous experiences in your family's car you form a hypothesis—our car runs more efficiently because we use premium gasoline. To be valid, a hypothesis has to be something you can test by using an investigation.

Predict When you apply a hypothesis to a specific situation, you predict something about that situation. A prediction makes a statement in advance, based on prior observation, experience, or scientific reasoning. People use predictions to make everyday decisions. Scientists test predictions by performing investigations. Based on previous observations and experiences, you might form a prediction that cars are more efficient with premium gasoline. The prediction can be tested in an investigation.

Design an Experiment A scientist needs to make many decisions before beginning an investigation. Some of these include: how to carry out the investigation, what steps to follow, how to record the data, and how the investigation will answer the question. It also is important to address any safety concerns.

Test the Hypothesis

Now that you have formed your hypothesis, you need to test it. Using an investigation, you will make observations and collect data, or information. This data might either support or not support your hypothesis. Scientists collect and organize data as numbers and descriptions.

Follow a Procedure In order to know what materials to use, as well as how and in what order to use them, you must follow a procedure. **Figure 8** shows a procedure you might follow to test your hypothesis.

Procedure

Step 1	Use regular gasoline for two weeks.
Step 2	Record the number of kilometers between fill-ups and the amount of gasoline used.
Step 3	Switch to premium gasoline for two weeks.
Step 4	Record the number of kilometers between fill-ups and the amount of gasoline used.

Figure 8 A procedure tells you what to do step by step.

Identify and Manipulate Variables and Controls In any experiment, it is important to keep everything the same except for the item you are testing. The one factor you change is called the independent variable. The change that results is the dependent variable. Make sure you have only one independent variable, to assure yourself of the cause of the changes you observe in the dependent variable. For example, in your gasoline experiment the type of fuel is the independent variable. The dependent variable is the efficiency.

Many experiments also have a control—an individual instance or experimental subject for which the independent variable is not changed. You can then compare the test results to the control results. To design a control you can have two cars of the same type. The control car uses regular gasoline for four weeks. After you are done with the test, you can compare the experimental results to the control results.

Collect Data

Whether you are carrying out an investigation or a short observational experiment, you will collect data, as shown in **Figure 9.** Scientists collect data as numbers and descriptions and organize it in specific ways.

Observe Scientists observe items and events, then record what they see. When they use only words to describe an observation, it is called qualitative data. Scientists' observations also can describe how much there is of something. These observations use numbers, as well as words, in the description and are called quantitative data. For example, if a sample of the element gold is described as being "shiny and very dense" the data are qualitative. Quantitative data on this sample of gold might include "a mass of 30 g and a density of 19.3 g/cm^3."

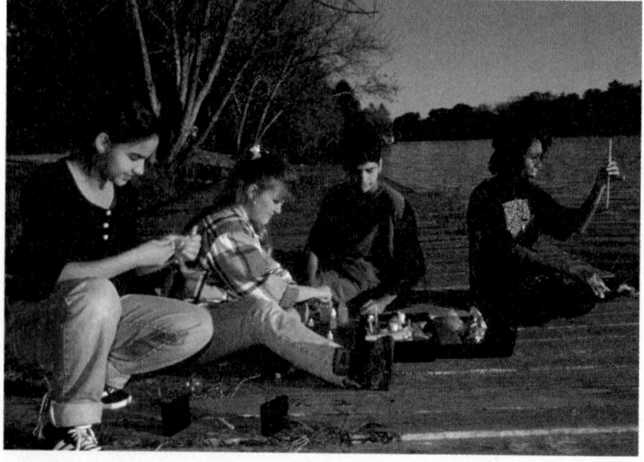

Figure 9 Collecting data is one way to gather information directly.

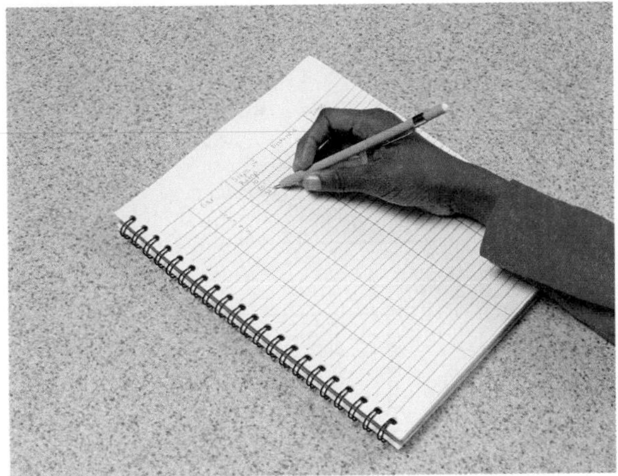

Figure 10 Record data neatly and clearly so it is easy to understand.

When you make observations you should examine the entire object or situation first, and then look carefully for details. It is important to record observations accurately and completely. Always record your notes immediately as you make them, so you do not miss details or make a mistake when recording results from memory. Never put unidentified observations on scraps of paper. Instead they should be recorded in a notebook, like the one in **Figure 10.** Write your data neatly so you can easily read it later. At each point in the experiment, record your observations and label them. That way, you will not have to determine what the figures mean when you look at your notes later. Set up any tables that you will need to use ahead of time, so you can record any observations right away. Remember to avoid bias when collecting data by not including personal thoughts when you record observations. Record only what you observe.

Estimate Scientific work also involves estimating. To estimate is to make a judgment about the size or the number of something without measuring or counting. This is important when the number or size of an object or population is too large or too difficult to accurately count or measure.

Sample Scientists may use a sample or a portion of the total number as a type of estimation. To sample is to take a small, representative portion of the objects or organisms of a population for research. By making careful observations or manipulating variables within that portion of the group, information is discovered and conclusions are drawn that might apply to the whole population. A poorly chosen sample can be unrepresentative of the whole. If you were trying to determine the rainfall in an area, it would not be best to take a rainfall sample from under a tree.

Measure You use measurements every day. Scientists also take measurements when collecting data. When taking measurements, it is important to know how to use measuring tools properly. Accuracy also is important.

Length To measure length, the distance between two points, scientists use meters. Smaller measurements might be measured in centimeters or millimeters.

Length is measured using a metric ruler or meter stick. When using a metric ruler, line up the 0-cm mark with the end of the object being measured and read the number of the unit where the object ends. Look at the metric ruler shown in **Figure 11.** The centimeter lines are the long, numbered lines, and the shorter lines are millimeter lines. In this instance, the length would be 4.50 cm.

Figure 11 This metric ruler has centimeter and millimeter divisions.

Mass The SI unit for mass is the kilogram (kg). Scientists can measure mass using units formed by adding metric prefixes to the unit gram (g), such as milligram (mg). To measure mass, you might use a triple-beam balance similar to the one shown in **Figure 12.** The balance has a pan on one side and a set of beams on the other side. Each beam has a rider that slides on the beam.

When using a triple-beam balance, place an object on the pan. Slide the largest rider along its beam until the pointer drops below zero. Then move it back one notch. Repeat the process for each rider proceeding from the larger to smaller until the pointer swings an equal distance above and below the zero point. Sum the masses on each beam to find the mass of the object. Move all riders back to zero when finished.

Instead of putting materials directly on the balance, scientists often take a tare of a container. A tare is the mass of a container into which objects or substances are placed for measuring their masses. To mass objects or substances, find the mass of a clean container. Remove the container from the pan, and place the object or substances in the container. Find the mass of the container with the materials in it. Subtract the mass of the empty container from the mass of the filled container to find the mass of the materials you are using.

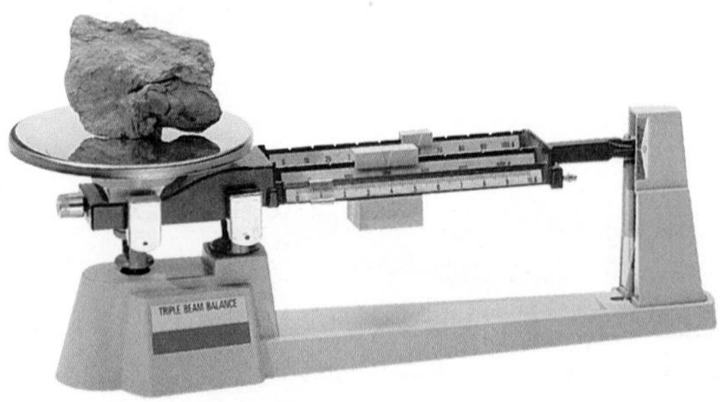

Figure 12 A triple-beam balance is used to determine the mass of an object.

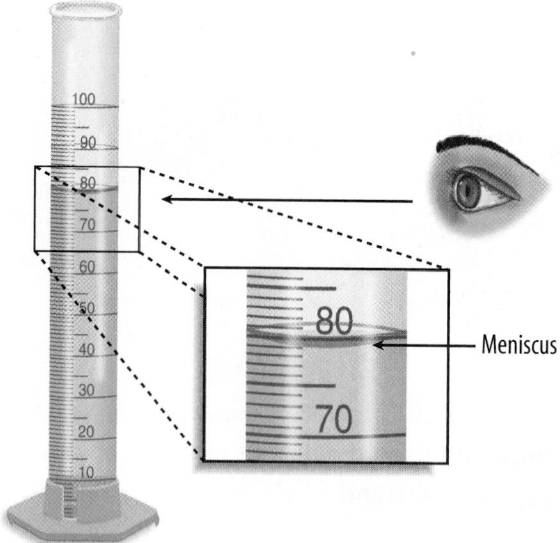

Figure 13 Graduated cylinders measure liquid volume.

Liquid Volume To measure liquids, the unit used is the liter. When a smaller unit is needed, scientists might use a milliliter. Because a milliliter takes up the volume of a cube measuring 1 cm on each side it also can be called a cubic centimeter ($cm^3 = cm \times cm \times cm$).

You can use beakers and graduated cylinders to measure liquid volume. A graduated cylinder, shown in **Figure 13,** is marked from bottom to top in milliliters. In lab, you might use a 10-mL graduated cylinder or a 100-mL graduated cylinder. When measuring liquids, notice that the liquid has a curved surface. Look at the surface at eye level, and measure the bottom of the curve. This is called the meniscus. The graduated cylinder in **Figure 13** contains 79.0 mL, or 79.0 cm^3, of a liquid.

Temperature Scientists often measure temperature using the Celsius scale. Pure water has a freezing point of 0°C and boiling point of 100°C. The unit of measurement is degrees Celsius. Two other scales often used are the Fahrenheit and Kelvin scales.

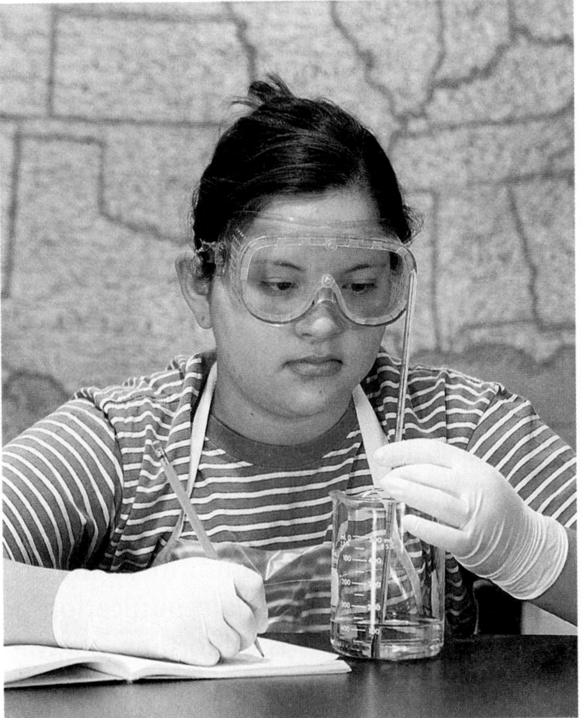

Figure 14 A thermometer measures the temperature of an object.

Scientists use a thermometer to measure temperature. Most thermometers in a laboratory are glass tubes with a bulb at the bottom end containing a liquid such as colored alcohol. The liquid rises or falls with a change in temperature. To read a glass thermometer like the thermometer in **Figure 14,** rotate it slowly until a red line appears. Read the temperature where the red line ends.

Form Operational Definitions An operational definition defines an object by how it functions, works, or behaves. For example, when you are playing hide and seek and a tree is home base, you have created an operational definition for a tree.

Objects can have more than one operational definition. For example, a ruler can be defined as a tool that measures the length of an object (how it is used). It can also be a tool with a series of marks used as a standard when measuring (how it works).

Analyze the Data

To determine the meaning of your observations and investigation results, you will need to look for patterns in the data. Then you must think critically to determine what the data mean. Scientists use several approaches when they analyze the data they have collected and recorded. Each approach is useful for identifying specific patterns.

Interpret Data The word *interpret* means "to explain the meaning of something." When analyzing data from an experiment, try to find out what the data show. Identify the control group and the test group to see whether or not changes in the independent variable have had an effect. Look for differences in the dependent variable between the control and test groups.

Classify Sorting objects or events into groups based on common features is called classifying. When classifying, first observe the objects or events to be classified. Then select one feature that is shared by some members in the group, but not by all. Place those members that share that feature in a subgroup. You can classify members into smaller and smaller subgroups based on characteristics. Remember that when you classify, you are grouping objects or events for a purpose. Keep your purpose in mind as you select the features to form groups and subgroups.

Compare and Contrast Observations can be analyzed by noting the similarities and differences between two or more objects or events that you observe. When you look at objects or events to see how they are similar, you are comparing them. Contrasting is looking for differences in objects or events.

Recognize Cause and Effect A cause is a reason for an action or condition. The effect is that action or condition. When two events happen together, it is not necessarily true that one event caused the other. Scientists must design a controlled investigation to recognize the exact cause and effect.

Draw Conclusions

When scientists have analyzed the data they collected, they proceed to draw conclusions about the data. These conclusions are sometimes stated in words similar to the hypothesis that you formed earlier. They may confirm a hypothesis, or lead you to a new hypothesis.

Infer Scientists often make inferences based on their observations. An inference is an attempt to explain observations or to indicate a cause. An inference is not a fact, but a logical conclusion that needs further investigation. For example, you may infer that a fire has caused smoke. Until you investigate, however, you do not know for sure.

Apply When you draw a conclusion, you must apply those conclusions to determine whether the data supports the hypothesis. If your data do not support your hypothesis, it does not mean that the hypothesis is wrong. It means only that the result of the investigation did not support the hypothesis. Maybe the experiment needs to be redesigned, or some of the initial observations on which the hypothesis was based were incomplete or biased. Perhaps more observation or research is needed to refine your hypothesis. A successful investigation does not always come out the way you originally predicted.

Avoid Bias Sometimes a scientific investigation involves making judgments. When you make a judgment, you form an opinion. It is important to be honest and not to allow any expectations of results to bias your judgments. This is important throughout the entire investigation, from researching to collecting data to drawing conclusions.

Communicate

The communication of ideas is an important part of the work of scientists. A discovery that is not reported will not advance the scientific community's understanding or knowledge. Communication among scientists also is important as a way of improving their investigations.

Scientists communicate in many ways, from writing articles in journals and magazines that explain their investigations and experiments, to announcing important discoveries on television and radio. Scientists also share ideas with colleagues on the Internet or present them as lectures, like the student is doing in **Figure 15.**

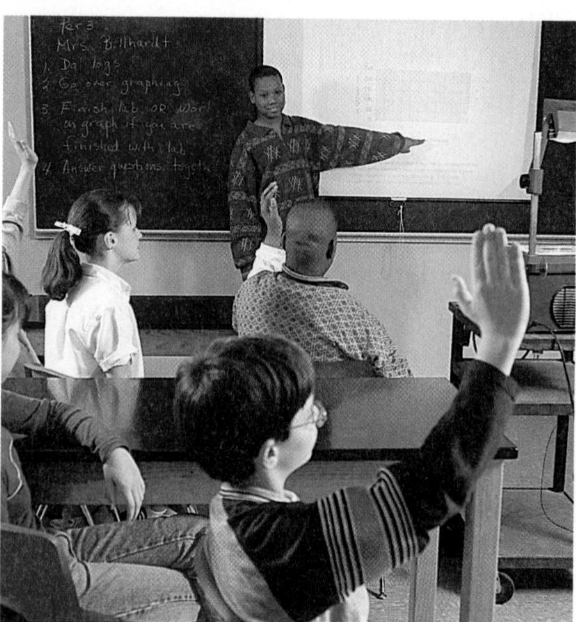

Figure 15 A student communicates to his peers about his investigation.

These safety symbols are used in laboratory and field investigations in this book to indicate possible hazards. Learn the meaning of each symbol and refer to this page often. *Remember to wash your hands thoroughly after completing lab procedures.*

PROTECTIVE EQUIPMENT

Do not begin any lab without the proper protection equipment.

GOGGLES

Proper eye protection must be worn when performing or observing science activities which involve items or conditions as listed below.

APRON

Wear an approved apron when using substances that could stain, wet, or destroy cloth.

SOAP

Wash hands with soap and water before removing goggles and after all lab activities.

GLOVES

Wear gloves when working with biological materials, chemicals, animals, or materials that can stain or irritate hands.

LABORATORY HAZARDS

Symbols	Potential Hazards	Precaution	Response
DISPOSAL	contamination of classroom or environment due to improper disposal of materials such as chemicals and live specimens	• DO NOT dispose of hazardous materials in the sink or trash can. • Dispose of wastes as directed by your teacher.	• If hazardous materials are disposed of improperly, notify your teacher immediately.
EXTREME TEMPERATURE	skin burns due to extremely hot or cold materials such as hot glass, liquids, or metals; liquid nitrogen; dry ice	• Use proper protective equipment, such as hot mitts and/or tongs, when handling objects with extreme temperatures.	• If injury occurs, notify your teacher immediately.
SHARP OBJECTS	punctures or cuts from sharp objects such as razor blades, pins, scalpels, and broken glass	• Handle glassware carefully to avoid breakage. • Walk with sharp objects pointed downward, away from you and others.	• If broken glass or injury occurs, notify your teacher immediately.
ELECTRICAL	electric shock or skin burn due to improper grounding, short circuits, liquid spills, or exposed wires	• Check condition of wires and apparatus for fraying or uninsulated wires, and broken or cracked equipment. • Use only GFCI-protected outlets	• DO NOT attempt to fix electrical problems. Notify your teacher immediately.
CHEMICAL	skin irritation or burns, breathing difficulty, and/or poisoning due to touching, swallowing, or inhalation of chemicals such as acids, bases, bleach, metal compounds, iodine, poinsettias, pollen, ammonia, acetone, nail polish remover, heated chemicals, mothballs, and any other chemicals labeled or known to be dangerous	• Wear proper protective equipment such as goggles, apron, and gloves when using chemicals. • Ensure proper room ventilation or use a fume hood when using materials that produce fumes. • NEVER smell fumes directly. • NEVER taste or eat any material in the laboratory.	• If contact occurs, immediately flush affected area with water and notify your teacher. • If a spill occurs, leave the area immediately and notify your teacher.
FLAMMABLE	unexpected fire due to liquids or gases that ignite easily such as rubbing alcohol	• Avoid open flames, sparks, or heat when flammable liquids are present.	• If a fire occurs, leave the area immediately and notify your teacher.
OPEN FLAME	burns or fire due to open flame from matches, Bunsen burners, or burning materials	• Tie back loose hair and clothing. • Keep flame away from all materials. • Follow teacher instructions when lighting and extinguishing flames. • Use proper protection, such as hot mitts or tongs, when handling hot objects.	• If a fire occurs, leave the area immediately and notify your teacher.
ANIMAL SAFETY	injury to or from laboratory animals	• Wear proper protective equipment such as gloves, apron, and goggles when working with animals. • Wash hands after handling animals.	• If injury occurs, notify your teacher immediately.
BIOLOGICAL	infection or adverse reaction due to contact with organisms such as bacteria, fungi, and biological materials such as blood, animal or plant materials	• Wear proper protective equipment such as gloves, goggles, and apron when working with biological materials. • Avoid skin contact with an organism or any part of the organism. • Wash hands after handling organisms.	• If contact occurs, wash the affected area and notify your teacher immediately.
FUME	breathing difficulties from inhalation of fumes from substances such as ammonia, acetone, nail polish remover, heated chemicals, and mothballs	• Wear goggles, apron, and gloves. • Ensure proper room ventilation or use a fume hood when using substances that produce fumes. • NEVER smell fumes directly.	• If a spill occurs, leave area and notify your teacher immediately.
IRRITANT	irritation of skin, mucous membranes, or respiratory tract due to materials such as acids, bases, bleach, pollen, mothballs, steel wool, and potassium permanganate	• Wear goggles, apron, and gloves. • Wear a dust mask to protect against fine particles.	• If skin contact occurs, immediately flush the affected area with water and notify your teacher.
RADIOACTIVE	excessive exposure from alpha, beta, and gamma particles	• Remove gloves and wash hands with soap and water before removing remainder of protective equipment.	• If cracks or holes are found in the container, notify your teacher immediately.

Safety in the Science Laboratory

Introduction to Science Safety

The science laboratory is a safe place to work if you follow standard safety procedures. Being responsible for your own safety helps to make the entire laboratory a safer place for everyone. When performing any lab, read and apply the caution statements and safety symbol listed at the beginning of the lab.

General Safety Rules

1. Complete the *Lab Safety Form* or other safety contract BEFORE starting any science lab.
2. Study the procedure. Ask your teacher any questions. Be sure you understand safety symbols shown on the page.
3. Notify your teacher about allergies or other health conditions which can affect your participation in a lab.
4. Learn and follow use and safety procedures for your equipment. If unsure, ask your teacher.
5. Never eat, drink, chew gum, apply cosmetics, or do any personal grooming in the lab. Never use lab glassware as food or drink containers. Keep your hands away from your face and mouth.
6. Know the location and proper use of the safety shower, eye wash, fire blanket, and fire alarm.

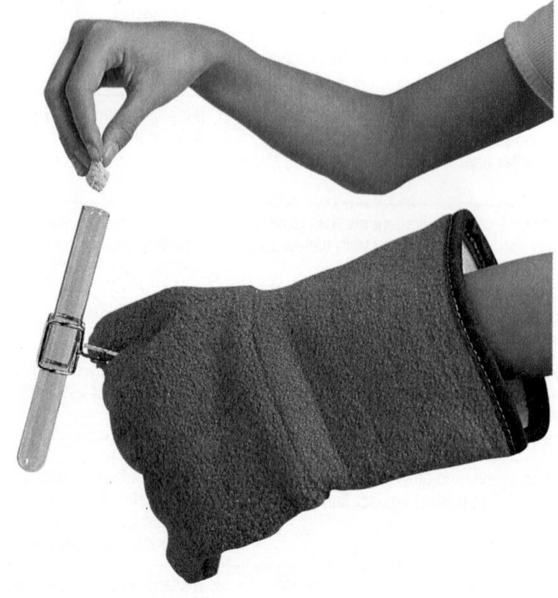

Prevent Accidents

1. Use the safety equipment provided to you. Goggles and a safety apron should be worn during investigations.
2. Do NOT use hair spray, mousse, or other flammable hair products. Tie back long hair and tie down loose clothing.
3. Do NOT wear sandals or other open-toed shoes in the lab.
4. Remove jewelry on hands and wrists. Loose jewelry, such as chains and long necklaces, should be removed to prevent them from getting caught in equipment.
5. Do not taste any substances or draw any material into a tube with your mouth.
6. Proper behavior is expected in the lab. Practical jokes and fooling around can lead to accidents and injury.
7. Keep your work area uncluttered.

Laboratory Work

1. Collect and carry all equipment and materials to your work area before beginning a lab.
2. Remain in your own work area unless given permission by your teacher to leave it.

3. Always slant test tubes away from yourself and others when heating them, adding substances to them, or rinsing them.
4. If instructed to smell a substance in a container, hold the container a short distance away and fan vapors towards your nose.
5. Do NOT substitute other chemicals/substances for those in the materials list unless instructed to do so by your teacher.
6. Do NOT take any materials or chemicals outside of the laboratory.
7. Stay out of storage areas unless instructed to be there and supervised by your teacher.

Laboratory Cleanup

1. Turn off all burners, water, and gas, and disconnect all electrical devices.
2. Clean all pieces of equipment and return all materials to their proper places.
3. Dispose of chemicals and other materials as directed by your teacher. Place broken glass and solid substances in the proper containers. Never discard materials in the sink.
4. Clean your work area.
5. Wash your hands with soap and water thoroughly BEFORE removing your goggles.

Emergencies

1. Report any fire, electrical shock, glassware breakage, spill, or injury, no matter how small, to your teacher immediately. Follow his or her instructions.
2. If your clothing should catch fire, STOP, DROP, and ROLL. If possible, smother it with the fire blanket or get under a safety shower. NEVER RUN.
3. If a fire should occur, turn off all gas and leave the room according to established procedures.
4. In most instances, your teacher will clean up spills. Do NOT attempt to clean up spills unless you are given permission and instructions to do so.
5. If chemicals come into contact with your eyes or skin, notify your teacher immediately. Use the eyewash, or flush your skin or eyes with large quantities of water.
6. The fire extinguisher and first-aid kit should only be used by your teacher unless it is an extreme emergency and you have been given permission.
7. If someone is injured or becomes ill, only a professional medical provider or someone certified in first aid should perform first-aid procedures.

Math Review

Use Fractions

A fraction compares a part to a whole. In the fraction $\frac{2}{3}$, the 2 represents the part and is the numerator. The 3 represents the whole and is the denominator.

Reduce Fractions To reduce a fraction, you must find the largest factor that is common to both the numerator and the denominator, the greatest common factor (GCF). Divide both numbers by the GCF. The fraction has then been reduced, or it is in its simplest form.

Example

Twelve of the 20 chemicals in the science lab are in powder form. What fraction of the chemicals used in the lab are in powder form?

Step 1 Write the fraction.

$$\frac{\text{part}}{\text{whole}} = \frac{12}{20}$$

Step 2 To find the GCF of the numerator and denominator, list all of the factors of each number.

Factors of 12: 1, 2, 3, 4, 6, 12 (the numbers that divide evenly into 12)

Factors of 20: 1, 2, 4, 5, 10, 20 (the numbers that divide evenly into 20)

Step 3 List the common factors.

1, 2, 4

Step 4 Choose the greatest factor in the list. The GCF of 12 and 20 is 4.

Step 5 Divide the numerator and denominator by the GCF.

$$\frac{12 \div 4}{20 \div 4} = \frac{3}{5}$$

In the lab, $\frac{3}{5}$ of the chemicals are in powder form.

Practice Problem At an amusement park, 66 of 90 rides have a height restriction. What fraction of the rides, in its simplest form, has a height restriction?

Add and Subtract Fractions with Like Denominators To add or subtract fractions with the same denominator, add or subtract the numerators and write the sum or difference over the denominator. After finding the sum or difference, find the simplest form for your fraction.

Example 1

In the forest outside your house, $\frac{1}{8}$ of the animals are rabbits, $\frac{3}{8}$ are squirrels, and the remainder are birds and insects. How many are mammals?

Step 1 Add the numerators.

$$\frac{1}{8} + \frac{3}{8} = \frac{(1 + 3)}{8} = \frac{4}{8}$$

Step 2 Find the GCF.

$\frac{4}{8}$ (GCF, 4)

Step 3 Divide the numerator and denominator by the GCF.

$$\frac{4 \div 4}{8 \div 4} = \frac{1}{2}$$

$\frac{1}{2}$ of the animals are mammals.

Example 2

If $\frac{7}{16}$ of the Earth is covered by freshwater, and $\frac{1}{16}$ of that is in glaciers, how much freshwater is not frozen?

Step 1 Subtract the numerators.

$$\frac{7}{16} - \frac{1}{16} = \frac{(7 - 1)}{16} = \frac{6}{16}$$

Step 2 Find the GCF.

$\frac{6}{16}$ (GCF, 2)

Step 3 Divide the numerator and denominator by the GCF.

$$\frac{6 \div 2}{16 \div 2} = \frac{3}{8}$$

$\frac{3}{8}$ of the freshwater is not frozen.

Practice Problem A bicycle rider is riding at a rate of 15 km/h for $\frac{4}{9}$ of his ride, 10 km/h for $\frac{2}{9}$ of his ride, and 8 km/h for the remainder of the ride. How much of his ride is he riding at a rate greater than 8 km/h?

Add and Subtract Fractions with Unlike Denominators To add or subtract fractions with unlike denominators, first find the least common denominator (LCD). This is the smallest number that is a common multiple of both denominators. Rename each fraction with the LCD, and then add or subtract. Find the simplest form if necessary.

Example 1

A chemist makes a paste that is $\frac{1}{2}$ table salt (NaCl), $\frac{1}{3}$ sugar ($C_6H_{12}O_6$), and the remainder is water (H_2O). How much of the paste is a solid?

Step 1 Find the LCD of the fractions.

$\frac{1}{2} + \frac{1}{3}$ (LCD, 6)

Step 2 Rename each numerator and each denominator with the LCD.

Step 3 Add the numerators.

$\frac{3}{6} + \frac{2}{6} = \frac{(3+2)}{6} = \frac{5}{6}$

$\frac{5}{6}$ of the paste is a solid.

Example 2

The average precipitation in Grand Junction, CO, is $\frac{7}{10}$ inch in November, and $\frac{3}{5}$ inch in December. What is the total average precipitation?

Step 1 Find the LCD of the fractions.

$\frac{7}{10} + \frac{3}{5}$ (LCD, 10)

Step 2 Rename each numerator and each denominator with the LCD.

Step 3 Add the numerators.

$\frac{7}{10} + \frac{6}{10} = \frac{(7+6)}{10} = \frac{13}{10}$

$\frac{13}{10}$ inches total precipitation, or $1\frac{3}{10}$ inches.

Practice Problem On an electric bill, about $\frac{1}{8}$ of the energy is from solar energy and about $\frac{1}{10}$ is from wind power. How much of the total bill is from solar energy and wind power combined?

Example 3

In your body, $\frac{7}{10}$ of your muscle contractions are involuntary (cardiac and smooth muscle tissue). Smooth muscle makes $\frac{3}{15}$ of your muscle contractions. How many of your muscle contractions are made by cardiac muscle?

Step 1 Find the LCD of the fractions.

$\frac{7}{10} - \frac{3}{15}$ (LCD, 30)

Step 2 Rename each numerator and each denominator with the LCD.

$\frac{7 \times 3}{10 \times 3} = \frac{21}{30}$

$\frac{3 \times 2}{15 \times 2} = \frac{6}{30}$

Step 3 Subtract the numerators.

$\frac{21}{30} - \frac{6}{30} = \frac{(21-6)}{30} = \frac{15}{30}$

Step 4 Find the GCF.

$\frac{15}{30}$ (GCF, 15)

$\frac{1}{2}$

$\frac{1}{2}$ of all muscle contractions are cardiac muscle.

Example 4

Tony wants to make cookies that call for $\frac{3}{4}$ of a cup of flour, but he only has $\frac{1}{3}$ of a cup. How much more flour does he need?

Step 1 Find the LCD of the fractions.

$\frac{3}{4} - \frac{1}{3}$ (LCD, 12)

Step 2 Rename each numerator and each denominator with the LCD.

$\frac{3 \times 3}{4 \times 3} = \frac{9}{12}$

$\frac{1 \times 4}{3 \times 4} = \frac{4}{12}$

Step 3 Subtract the numerators.

$\frac{9}{12} - \frac{4}{12} = \frac{(9-4)}{12} = \frac{5}{12}$

$\frac{5}{12}$ of a cup of flour

Practice Problem Using the information provided to you in Example 3 above, determine how many muscle contractions are voluntary (skeletal muscle).

Multiply Fractions To multiply with fractions, multiply the numerators and multiply the denominators. Find the simplest form if necessary.

Example

Multiply $\frac{3}{5}$ by $\frac{1}{3}$.

Step 1 Multiply the numerators and denominators.

$$\frac{3}{5} \times \frac{1}{3} = \frac{(3 \times 1)}{(5 \times 3)} \ \frac{3}{15}$$

Step 2 Find the GCF.

$$\frac{3}{15} \text{ (GCF, 3)}$$

Step 3 Divide the numerator and denominator by the GCF.

$$\frac{3 \div 3}{15 \div 3} = \frac{1}{5}$$

$\frac{3}{5}$ multiplied by $\frac{1}{3}$ is $\frac{1}{5}$.

Practice Problem Multiply $\frac{3}{14}$ by $\frac{5}{16}$.

Find a Reciprocal Two numbers whose product is 1 are called multiplicative inverses, or reciprocals.

Example

Find the reciprocal of $\frac{3}{8}$.

Step 1 Inverse the fraction by putting the denominator on top and the numerator on the bottom.

$$\frac{8}{3}$$

The reciprocal of $\frac{3}{8}$ is $\frac{8}{3}$.

Practice Problem Find the reciprocal of $\frac{4}{9}$.

Divide Fractions To divide one fraction by another fraction, multiply the dividend by the reciprocal of the divisor. Find the simplest form if necessary.

Example 1

Divide $\frac{1}{9}$ by $\frac{1}{3}$.

Step 1 Find the reciprocal of the divisor.

The reciprocal of $\frac{1}{3}$ is $\frac{3}{1}$.

Step 2 Multiply the dividend by the reciprocal of the divisor.

$$\frac{\frac{1}{9}}{\frac{1}{3}} = \frac{1}{9} \times \frac{3}{1} = \frac{(1 \times 3)}{(9 \times 1)} = \frac{3}{9}$$

Step 3 Find the GCF.

$$\frac{3}{9} \text{ (GCF, 3)}$$

Step 4 Divide the numerator and denominator by the GCF.

$$\frac{3 \div 3}{9 \div 3} = \frac{1}{3}$$

$\frac{1}{9}$ divided by $\frac{1}{3}$ is $\frac{1}{3}$.

Example 2

Divide $\frac{3}{5}$ by $\frac{1}{4}$.

Step 1 Find the reciprocal of the divisor.

The reciprocal of $\frac{1}{4}$ is $\frac{4}{1}$.

Step 2 Multiply the dividend by the reciprocal of the divisor.

$$\frac{\frac{3}{5}}{\frac{1}{4}} = \frac{3}{5} \times \frac{4}{1} = \frac{(3 \times 4)}{(5 \times 1)} = \frac{12}{5}$$

$\frac{3}{5}$ divided by $\frac{1}{4}$ is $\frac{12}{5}$ or $2\frac{2}{5}$.

Practice Problem Divide $\frac{3}{11}$ by $\frac{7}{10}$.

Use Ratios

When you compare two numbers by division, you are using a ratio. Ratios can be written 3 to 5, 3:5, or $\frac{3}{5}$. Ratios, like fractions, also can be written in simplest form.

Ratios can represent one type of probability, called odds. This is a ratio that compares the number of ways a certain outcome occurs to the number of possible outcomes. For example, if you flip a coin 100 times, what are the odds that it will come up heads? There are two possible outcomes, heads or tails, so the odds of coming up heads are 50:100. Another way to say this is that 50 out of 100 times the coin will come up heads. In its simplest form, the ratio is 1:2.

Example 1

A chemical solution contains 40 g of salt and 64 g of baking soda. What is the ratio of salt to baking soda as a fraction in simplest form?

Step 1 Write the ratio as a fraction.

$$\frac{\text{salt}}{\text{baking soda}} = \frac{40}{64}$$

Step 2 Express the fraction in simplest form. The GCF of 40 and 64 is 8.

$$\frac{40}{64} = \frac{40 \div 8}{64 \div 8} = \frac{5}{8}$$

The ratio of salt to baking soda in the sample is 5:8.

Example 2

Sean rolls a 6-sided die 6 times. What are the odds that the side with a 3 will show?

Step 1 Write the ratio as a fraction.

$$\frac{\text{number of sides with a 3}}{\text{number of possible sides}} = \frac{1}{6}$$

Step 2 Multiply by the number of attempts.

$\frac{1}{6} \times 6$ attempts $= \frac{6}{6}$ attempts $= 1$ attempt

1 attempt out of 6 will show a 3.

Practice Problem Two metal rods measure 100 cm and 144 cm in length. What is the ratio of their lengths in simplest form?

Use Decimals

A fraction with a denominator that is a power of ten can be written as a decimal. For example, 0.27 means $\frac{27}{100}$. The decimal point separates the ones place from the tenths place.

Any fraction can be written as a decimal using division. For example, the fraction $\frac{5}{8}$ can be written as a decimal by dividing 5 by 8. Written as a decimal, it is 0.625.

Add or Subtract Decimals When adding and subtracting decimals, line up the decimal points before carrying out the operation.

Example 1

Find the sum of 47.68 and 7.80.

Step 1 Line up the decimal places when you write the numbers.

$$\begin{array}{r} 47.68 \\ +\ 7.80 \\ \hline \end{array}$$

Step 2 Add the decimals.

$$\begin{array}{r} {}^{1\,1} \\ 47.68 \\ +\ 7.80 \\ \hline 55.48 \end{array}$$

The sum of 47.68 and 7.80 is 55.48.

Example 2

Find the difference of 42.17 and 15.85.

Step 1 Line up the decimal places when you write the number.

$$\begin{array}{r} 42.17 \\ -15.85 \\ \hline \end{array}$$

Step 2 Subtract the decimals.

$$\begin{array}{r} {}^{3\,11\,1} \\ 42.17 \\ -15.85 \\ \hline 26.32 \end{array}$$

The difference of 42.17 and 15.85 is 26.32.

Practice Problem Find the sum of 1.245 and 3.842.

Science Skill Handbook | Math Skill Handbook | Foldables Handbook | Reference Handbook | Glossary/Glosario | Index

Multiply Decimals To multiply decimals, multiply the numbers like numbers without decimal points. Count the decimal places in each factor. The product will have the same number of decimal places as the sum of the decimal places in the factors.

Example

Multiply 2.4 by 5.9.

Step 1 Multiply the factors like two whole numbers.

$24 \times 59 = 1416$

Step 2 Find the sum of the number of decimal places in the factors. Each factor has one decimal place, for a sum of two decimal places.

Step 3 The product will have two decimal places.

14.16

The product of 2.4 and 5.9 is 14.16.

Practice Problem Multiply 4.6 by 2.2.

Divide Decimals When dividing decimals, change the divisor to a whole number. To do this, multiply both the divisor and the dividend by the same power of ten. Then place the decimal point in the quotient directly above the decimal point in the dividend. Then divide as you do with whole numbers.

Example

Divide 8.84 by 3.4.

Step 1 Multiply both factors by 10.

$3.4 \times 10 = 34, 8.84 \times 10 = 88.4$

Step 2 Divide 88.4 by 34.

$$\begin{array}{r} 2.6 \\ 34\overline{)88.4} \\ -68 \\ \hline 20\,4 \\ -20\,4 \\ \hline 0 \end{array}$$

8.84 divided by 3.4 is 2.6.

Practice Problem Divide 75.6 by 3.6.

Use Proportions

An equation that shows that two ratios are equivalent is a proportion. The ratios $\frac{2}{4}$ and $\frac{5}{10}$ are equivalent, so they can be written as $\frac{2}{4} = \frac{5}{10}$. This equation is a proportion.

When two ratios form a proportion, the cross products are equal. To find the cross products in the proportion $\frac{2}{4} = \frac{5}{10}$, multiply the 2 and the 10, and the 4 and the 5. Therefore $2 \times 10 = 4 \times 5$, or $20 = 20$.

Because you know that both ratios are equal, you can use cross products to find a missing term in a proportion. This is known as solving the proportion.

Example

The heights of a tree and a pole are proportional to the lengths of their shadows. The tree casts a shadow of 24 m when a 6-m pole casts a shadow of 4 m. What is the height of the tree?

Step 1 Write a proportion.

$$\frac{\text{height of tree}}{\text{height of pole}} = \frac{\text{length of tree's shadow}}{\text{length of pole's shadow}}$$

Step 2 Substitute the known values into the proportion. Let h represent the unknown value, the height of the tree.

$\frac{h}{6} \times \frac{24}{4}$

Step 3 Find the cross products.

$h \times 4 = 6 \times 24$

Step 4 Simplify the equation.

$4h \times 144$

Step 5 Divide each side by 4.

$\frac{4h}{4} \times \frac{144}{4}$

$h = 36$

The height of the tree is 36 m.

Practice Problem The ratios of the weights of two objects on the Moon and on Earth are in proportion. A rock weighing 3 N on the Moon weighs 18 N on Earth. How much would a rock that weighs 5 N on the Moon weigh on Earth?

Use Percentages

The word *percent* means "out of one hundred." It is a ratio that compares a number to 100. Suppose you read that 77 percent of Earth's surface is covered by water. That is the same as reading that the fraction of Earth's surface covered by water is $\frac{77}{100}$. To express a fraction as a percent, first find the equivalent decimal for the fraction. Then, multiply the decimal by 100 and add the percent symbol.

Example 1

Express $\frac{13}{20}$ as a percent.

Step 1 Find the equivalent decimal for the fraction.

```
     0.65
20)13.00
   12 0
    1 00
    1 00
       0
```

Step 2 Rewrite the fraction $\frac{13}{20}$ as 0.65.

Step 3 Multiply 0.65 by 100 and add the % symbol.

$0.65 \times 100 = 65 = 65\%$

So, $\frac{13}{20} = 65\%$.

This also can be solved as a proportion.

Example 2

Express $\frac{13}{20}$ as a percent.

Step 1 Write a proportion.

$$\frac{13}{20} = \frac{x}{100}$$

Step 2 Find the cross products.

$1300 = 20x$

Step 3 Divide each side by 20.

$$\frac{1300}{20} = \frac{20x}{20}$$

$65\% = x$

Practice Problem In one year, 73 of 365 days were rainy in one city. What percent of the days in that city were rainy?

Solve One-Step Equations

A statement that two expressions are equal is an equation. For example, $A = B$ is an equation that states that A is equal to B.

An equation is solved when a variable is replaced with a value that makes both sides of the equation equal. To make both sides equal the inverse operation is used. Addition and subtraction are inverses, and multiplication and division are inverses.

Example 1

Solve the equation $x - 10 = 35$.

Step 1 Find the solution by adding 10 to each side of the equation.

$$x - 10 = 35$$
$$x - 10 + 10 = 35 - 10$$
$$x = 45$$

Step 2 Check the solution.

$$x - 10 = 35$$
$$45 - 10 = 35$$
$$35 = 35$$

Both sides of the equation are equal, so $x = 45$.

Example 2

In the formula $a = bc$, find the value of c if $a = 20$ and $b = 2$.

Step 1 Rearrange the formula so the unknown value is by itself on one side of the equation by dividing both sides by b.

$$a = bc$$
$$\frac{a}{b} = \frac{bc}{b}$$
$$\frac{a}{b} = c$$

Step 2 Replace the variables a and b with the values that are given.

$$\frac{a}{b} = c$$
$$\frac{20}{2} = c$$
$$10 = c$$

Step 3 Check the solution.

$$a = bc$$
$$20 = 2 \times 10$$
$$20 = 20$$

Both sides of the equation are equal, so $c = 10$ is the solution when $a = 20$ and $b = 2$.

Practice Problem In the formula $h = gd$, find the value of d if $g = 12.3$ and $h = 17.4$.

Use Statistics

The branch of mathematics that deals with collecting, analyzing, and presenting data is statistics. In statistics, there are three common ways to summarize data with a single number—the mean, the median, and the mode.

The **mean** of a set of data is the arithmetic average. It is found by adding the numbers in the data set and dividing by the number of items in the set.

The **median** is the middle number in a set of data when the data are arranged in numerical order. If there were an even number of data points, the median would be the mean of the two middle numbers.

The **mode** of a set of data is the number or item that appears most often.

Another number that often is used to describe a set of data is the range. The **range** is the difference between the largest number and the smallest number in a set of data.

Example

The speeds (in m/s) for a race car during five different time trials are 39, 37, 44, 36, and 44.

To find the mean:

Step 1 Find the sum of the numbers.

$39 + 37 + 44 + 36 + 44 = 200$

Step 2 Divide the sum by the number of items, which is 5.

$200 \div 5 = 40$

The mean is 40 m/s.

To find the median:

Step 1 Arrange the measures from least to greatest.

36, 37, 39, 44, 44

Step 2 Determine the middle measure.

36, 37, <u>39</u>, 44, 44

The median is 39 m/s.

To find the mode:

Step 1 Group the numbers that are the same together.

44, 44, 36, 37, 39

Step 2 Determine the number that occurs most in the set.

<u>44, 44,</u> 36, 37, 39

The mode is 44 m/s.

To find the range:

Step 1 Arrange the measures from greatest to least.

44, 44, 39, 37, 36

Step 2 Determine the greatest and least measures in the set.

<u>44,</u> 44, 39, 37, <u>36</u>

Step 3 Find the difference between the greatest and least measures.

$44 - 36 = 8$

The range is 8 m/s.

Practice Problem Find the mean, median, mode, and range for the data set 8, 4, 12, 8, 11, 14, 16.

A **frequency table** shows how many times each piece of data occurs, usually in a survey. **Table 1** below shows the results of a student survey on favorite color.

Table 1 Student Color Choice

Color	Tally	Frequency
red	IIII	4
blue	~~IIII~~	5
black	II	2
green	III	3
purple	~~IIII~~ II	7
yellow	~~IIII~~ I	6

Based on the frequency table data, which color is the favorite?

Use Geometry

The branch of mathematics that deals with the measurement, properties, and relationships of points, lines, angles, surfaces, and solids is called geometry.

Perimeter The **perimeter** (P) is the distance around a geometric figure. To find the perimeter of a rectangle, add the length and width and multiply that sum by two, or $2(l + w)$. To find perimeters of irregular figures, add the length of the sides.

Example 1

Find the perimeter of a rectangle that is 3 m long and 5 m wide.

Step 1 You know that the perimeter is 2 times the sum of the width and length.

$P = 2(3 \text{ m} + 5 \text{ m})$

Step 2 Find the sum of the width and length.

$P = 2(8 \text{ m})$

Step 3 Multiply by 2.

$P = 16 \text{ m}$

The perimeter is 16 m.

Example 2

Find the perimeter of a shape with sides measuring 2 cm, 5 cm, 6 cm, 3 cm.

Step 1 You know that the perimeter is the sum of all the sides.

$P = 2 + 5 + 6 + 3$

Step 2 Find the sum of the sides.

$P = 2 + 5 + 6 + 3$

$P = 16$

The perimeter is 16 cm.

Practice Problem Find the perimeter of a rectangle with a length of 18 m and a width of 7 m.

Practice Problem Find the perimeter of a triangle measuring 1.6 cm by 2.4 cm by 2.4 cm.

Area of a Rectangle The **area** (A) is the number of square units needed to cover a surface. To find the area of a rectangle, multiply the length times the width, or $l \times w$. When finding area, the units also are multiplied. Area is given in square units.

Example

Find the area of a rectangle with a length of 1 cm and a width of 10 cm.

Step 1 You know that the area is the length multiplied by the width.

$A = (1 \text{ cm} \times 10 \text{ cm})$

Step 2 Multiply the length by the width. Also multiply the units.

$A = 10 \text{ cm}^2$

The area is 10 cm^2.

Practice Problem Find the area of a square whose sides measure 4 m.

Area of a Triangle To find the area of a triangle, use the formula:

$A = \frac{1}{2}(\text{base} \times \text{height})$

The base of a triangle can be any of its sides. The height is the perpendicular distance from a base to the opposite endpoint, or vertex.

Example

Find the area of a triangle with a base of 18 m and a height of 7 m.

Step 1 You know that the area is $\frac{1}{2}$ the base times the height.

$A = \frac{1}{2}(18 \text{ m} \times 7 \text{ m})$

Step 2 Multiply $\frac{1}{2}$ by the product of 18×7. Multiply the units.

$A = \frac{1}{2}(126 \text{ m}^2)$

$A = 63 \text{ m}^2$

The area is 63 m^2.

Practice Problem Find the area of a triangle with a base of 27 cm and a height of 17 cm.

Circumference of a Circle The **diameter** (d) of a circle is the distance across the circle through its center, and the **radius** (r) is the distance from the center to any point on the circle. The radius is half of the diameter. The distance around the circle is called the **circumference** (C). The formula for finding the circumference is:

$C = 2\pi r$ or $C = \pi d$

The circumference divided by the diameter is always equal to 3.1415926... This nonterminating and nonrepeating number is represented by the Greek letter π (pi). An approximation often used for π is 3.14.

Example 1

Find the circumference of a circle with a radius of 3 m.

Step 1 You know the formula for the circumference is 2 times the radius times π.

$C = 2\pi(3)$

Step 2 Multiply 2 times the radius.

$C = 6\pi$

Step 3 Multiply by π.

$C \approx 19$ m

The circumference is about 19 m.

Example 2

Find the circumference of a circle with a diameter of 24.0 cm.

Step 1 You know the formula for the circumference is the diameter times π.

$C = \pi(24.0)$

Step 2 Multiply the diameter by π.

$C \approx 75.4$ cm

The circumference is about 75.4 cm.

Practice Problem Find the circumference of a circle with a radius of 19 cm.

Area of a Circle The formula for the area of a circle is: $A = \pi r^2$

Example 1

Find the area of a circle with a radius of 4.0 cm.

Step 1 $A = \pi(4.0)^2$

Step 2 Find the square of the radius.

$A = 16\pi$

Step 3 Multiply the square of the radius by π.

$A \approx 50 \text{ cm}^2$

The area of the circle is about 50 cm^2.

Example 2

Find the area of a circle with a radius of 225 m.

Step 1 $A = \pi(225)^2$

Step 2 Find the square of the radius.

$A = 50625\pi$

Step 3 Multiply the square of the radius by π.

$A \approx 159043.1$

The area of the circle is about 159043.1 m^2.

Example 3

Find the area of a circle whose diameter is 20.0 mm.

Step 1 Remember that the radius is half of the diameter.

$A = \pi\left(\frac{20.0}{2}\right)^2$

Step 2 Find the radius.

$A = \pi(10.0)^2$

Step 3 Find the square of the radius.

$A = 100\pi$

Step 4 Multiply the square of the radius by π.

$A \approx 314 \text{ mm}^2$

The area of the circle is about 314 mm^2.

Practice Problem Find the area of a circle with a radius of 16 m.

Science Skill Handbook
Math Skill Handbook
Foldables Handbook
Reference Handbook
Glossary/Glosario
Index

Volume The measure of space occupied by a solid is the **volume** (V). To find the volume of a rectangular solid multiply the length times width times height, or $V = l \times w \times h$. It is measured in cubic units, such as cubic centimeters (cm^3).

Example

Find the volume of a rectangular solid with a length of 2.0 m, a width of 4.0 m, and a height of 3.0 m.

Step 1 You know the formula for volume is the length times the width times the height.

$V = 2.0 \text{ m} \times 4.0 \text{ m} \times 3.0 \text{ m}$

Step 2 Multiply the length times the width times the height.

$V = 24 \text{ m}^3$

The volume is 24 m^3.

Practice Problem Find the volume of a rectangular solid that is 8 m long, 4 m wide, and 4 m high.

To find the volume of other solids, multiply the area of the base times the height.

Example 1

Find the volume of a solid that has a triangular base with a length of 8.0 m and a height of 7.0 m. The height of the entire solid is 15.0 m.

Step 1 You know that the base is a triangle, and the area of a triangle is $\frac{1}{2}$ the base times the height, and the volume is the area of the base times the height.

$V = \left[\frac{1}{2}(b \times h)\right] \times 15$

Step 2 Find the area of the base.

$V = \left[\frac{1}{2}(8 \times 7)\right] \times 15$

$V = \left(\frac{1}{2} \times 56\right) \times 15$

Step 3 Multiply the area of the base by the height of the solid.

$V = 28 \times 15$

$V = 420 \text{ m}^3$

The volume is 420 m^3.

Example 2

Find the volume of a cylinder that has a base with a radius of 12.0 cm, and a height of 21.0 cm.

Step 1 You know that the base is a circle, and the area of a circle is the square of the radius times π, and the volume is the area of the base times the height.

$V = (\pi r^2) \times 21$

$V = (\pi 12^2) \times 21$

Step 2 Find the area of the base.

$V = 144\pi \times 21$

$V = 452 \times 21$

Step 3 Multiply the area of the base by the height of the solid.

$V \approx 9{,}500 \text{ cm}^3$

The volume is about 9,500 cm^3.

Example 3

Find the volume of a cylinder that has a diameter of 15 mm and a height of 4.8 mm.

Step 1 You know that the base is a circle with an area equal to the square of the radius times π. The radius is one-half the diameter. The volume is the area of the base times the height.

$V = (\pi r^2) \times 4.8$

$V = \left[\pi\left(\frac{1}{2} \times 15\right)^2\right] \times 4.8$

$V = (\pi 7.5^2) \times 4.8$

Step 2 Find the area of the base.

$V = 56.25\pi \times 4.8$

$V \approx 176.71 \times 4.8$

Step 3 Multiply the area of the base by the height of the solid.

$V \approx 848.2$

The volume is about 848.2 mm^3.

Practice Problem Find the volume of a cylinder with a diameter of 7 cm in the base and a height of 16 cm.

Science Skill Handbook
Math Skill Handbook
Foldables Handbook
Reference Handbook
Glossary/Glosario
Index

Science Applications

Measure in SI

The metric system of measurement was developed in 1795. A modern form of the metric system, called the International System (SI), was adopted in 1960 and provides the standard measurements that all scientists around the world can understand.

The SI system is convenient because unit sizes vary by powers of 10. Prefixes are used to name units. Look at **Table 2** for some common SI prefixes and their meanings.

Table 2 Common SI Prefixes

Prefix	Symbol	Meaning	
kilo-	k	1,000	thousandth
hecto-	h	100	hundred
deka-	da	10	ten
deci-	d	0.1	tenth
centi-	c	0.01	hundreth
milli-	m	0.001	thousandth

Example

How many grams equal one kilogram?

Step 1 Find the prefix *kilo-* in **Table 2.**

Step 2 Using **Table 2,** determine the meaning of *kilo-*. According to the table, it means 1,000. When the prefix *kilo-* is added to a unit, it means that there are 1,000 of the units in a "kilounit."

Step 3 Apply the prefix to the units in the question. The units in the question are grams. There are 1,000 grams in a kilogram.

Practice Problem Is a milligram larger or smaller than a gram? How many of the smaller units equal one larger unit? What fraction of the larger unit does one smaller unit represent?

Dimensional Analysis

Convert SI Units In science, quantities such as length, mass, and time sometimes are measured using different units. A process called dimensional analysis can be used to change one unit of measure to another. This process involves multiplying your starting quantity and units by one or more conversion factors. A conversion factor is a ratio equal to one and can be made from any two equal quantities with different units. If 1,000 mL equal 1 L then two ratios can be made.

$$\frac{1{,}000 \text{ mL}}{1 \text{ L}} = \frac{1 \text{ L}}{1{,}000 \text{ mL}} = 1$$

One can convert between units in the SI system by using the equivalents in **Table 2** to make conversion factors.

Example

How many cm are in 4 m?

Step 1 Write conversion factors for the units given. From **Table 2,** you know that 100 cm = 1 m. The conversion factors are

$$\frac{100 \text{ cm}}{1 \text{ m}} \textit{ and } \frac{1 \text{ m}}{100 \text{ cm}}$$

Step 2 Decide which conversion factor to use. Select the factor that has the units you are converting from (m) in the denominator and the units you are converting to (cm) in the numerator.

$$\frac{100 \text{ cm}}{1 \text{ m}}$$

Step 3 Multiply the starting quantity and units by the conversion factor. Cancel the starting units with the units in the denominator. There are 400 cm in 4 m.

$$4 \cancel{\text{m}} = \frac{100 \text{ cm}}{1 \cancel{\text{m}}} = 400 \text{ cm}$$

Practice Problem How many milligrams are in one kilogram? (Hint: You will need to use two conversion factors from **Table 2.**)

Table 3 Unit System Equivalents

Type of Measurement	Equivalent
Length	1 in = 2.54 cm 1 yd = 0.91 m 1 mi = 1.61 km
Mass and weight*	1 oz = 28.35 g 1 lb = 0.45 kg 1 ton (short) = 0.91 tonnes (metric tons) 1 lb = 4.45 N
Volume	1 in^3 = 16.39 cm^3 1 qt = 0.95 L 1 gal = 3.78 L
Area	1 in^2 = 6.45 cm^2 1 yd^2 = 0.83 m^2 1 mi^2 = 2.59 km^2 1 acre = 0.40 hectares
Temperature	$°C = \frac{(°F - 32)}{1.8}$ K = °C + 273

*Weight is measured in standard Earth gravity.

Convert Between Unit Systems **Table 3** gives a list of equivalents that can be used to convert between English and SI units.

Example

If a meterstick has a length of 100 cm, how long is the meterstick in inches?

Step 1 Write the conversion factors for the units given. From **Table 3,** 1 in = 2.54 cm.

$$\frac{1 \text{ in}}{2.54 \text{ cm}} \textit{ and } \frac{2.54 \text{ cm}}{1 \text{ in}}$$

Step 2 Determine which conversion factor to use. You are converting from cm to in. Use the conversion factor with cm on the bottom.

$$\frac{1 \text{ in}}{2.54 \text{ cm}}$$

Step 3 Multiply the starting quantity and units by the conversion factor. Cancel the starting units with the units in the denominator. Round your answer to the nearest tenth.

$$100 \cancel{\text{cm}} \times \frac{1 \text{ in}}{2.54 \cancel{\text{cm}}} = 39.37 \text{ in}$$

The meterstick is about 39.4 in long.

Practice Problem 1 A book has a mass of 5 lb. What is the mass of the book in kg?

Practice Problem 2 Use the equivalent for in and cm (1 in = 2.54 cm) to show how 1 $in^3 \approx$ 16.39 cm^3.

Science Skill Handbook
Math Skill Handbook
Foldables Handbook
Reference Handbook
Glossary/Glosario
Index

Precision and Significant Digits

When you make a measurement, the value you record depends on the precision of the measuring instrument. This precision is represented by the number of significant digits recorded in the measurement. When counting the number of significant digits, all digits are counted except zeros at the end of a number with no decimal point such as 2,050, and zeros at the beginning of a decimal such as 0.03020. When adding or subtracting numbers with different precision, round the answer to the smallest number of decimal places of any number in the sum or difference. When multiplying or dividing, the answer is rounded to the smallest number of significant digits of any number being multiplied or divided.

Example

The lengths 5.28 and 5.2 are measured in meters. Find the sum of these lengths and record your answer using the correct number of significant digits.

Step 1 Find the sum.

5.28 m	2 digits after the decimal
+ 5.2 m	1 digit after the decimal
10.48 m	

Step 2 Round to one digit after the decimal because the least number of digits after the decimal of the numbers being added is 1.

The sum is 10.5 m.

Practice Problem 1 How many significant digits are in the measurement 7,071,301 m? How many significant digits are in the measurement 0.003010 g?

Practice Problem 2 Multiply 5.28 and 5.2 using the rule for multiplying and dividing. Record the answer using the correct number of significant digits.

Scientific Notation

Many times numbers used in science are very small or very large. Because these numbers are difficult to work with scientists use scientific notation. To write numbers in scientific notation, move the decimal point until only one non-zero digit remains on the left. Then count the number of places you moved the decimal point and use that number as a power of ten. For example, the average distance from the Sun to Mars is 227,800,000,000 m. In scientific notation, this distance is 2.278×10^{11} m. Because you moved the decimal point to the left, the number is a positive power of ten.

The mass of an electron is about 0.000 000 000 000 000 000 000 000 000 000 911 kg. Expressed in scientific notation, this mass is 9.11×10^{-31} kg. Because the decimal point was moved to the right, the number is a negative power of ten.

Example

Earth is 149,600,000 km from the Sun. Express this in scientific notation.

Step 1 Move the decimal point until one non-zero digit remains on the left.

1.496 000 00

Step 2 Count the number of decimal places you have moved. In this case, eight.

Step 2 Show that number as a power of ten, 10^8.

Earth is 1.496×10^8 km from the Sun.

Practice Problem 1 How many significant digits are in 149,600,000 km? How many significant digits are in 1.496×10^8 km?

Practice Problem 2 Parts used in a high performance car must be measured to 7×10^{-6} m. Express this number as a decimal.

Practice Problem 3 A CD is spinning at 539 revolutions per minute. Express this number in scientific notation.

Make and Use Graphs

Data in tables can be displayed in a graph—a visual representation of data. Common graph types include line graphs, bar graphs, and circle graphs.

Line Graph A line graph shows a relationship between two variables that change continuously. The independent variable is changed and is plotted on the x-axis. The dependent variable is observed, and is plotted on the *y*-axis.

Example

Draw a line graph of the data below from a cyclist in a long-distance race.

Table 4 Bicycle Race Data

Time (h)	Distance (km)
0	0
1	8
2	16
3	24
4	32
5	40

Step 1 Determine the *x*-axis and *y*-axis variables. Time varies independently of distance and is plotted on the *x*-axis. Distance is dependent on time and is plotted on the *y*-axis.

Step 2 Determine the scale of each axis. The *x*-axis data ranges from 0 to 5. The *y*-axis data ranges from 0 to 50.

Step 3 Using graph paper, draw and label the axes. Include units in the labels.

Step 4 Draw a point at the intersection of the time value on the *x*-axis and corresponding distance value on the *y*-axis. Connect the points and label the graph with a title, as shown in **Figure 8.**

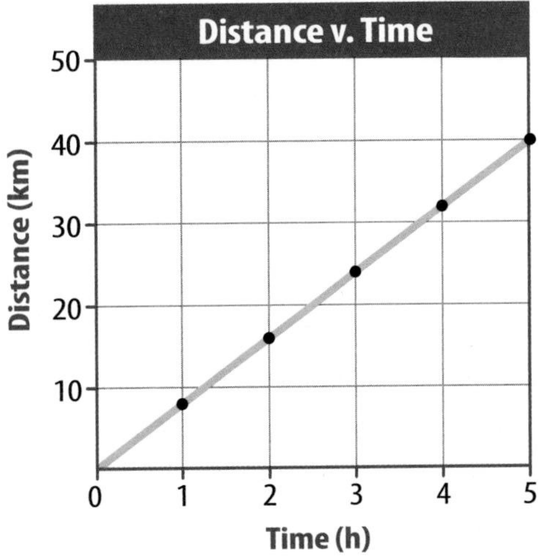

Figure 8 This line graph shows the relationship between distance and time during a bicycle ride.

Practice Problem A puppy's shoulder height is measured during the first year of her life. The following measurements were collected: (3 mo, 52 cm), (6 mo, 72 cm), (9 mo, 83 cm), (12 mo, 86 cm). Graph this data.

Find a Slope The slope of a straight line is the ratio of the vertical change, rise, to the horizontal change, run.

$$\text{Slope} = \frac{\text{vertical change (rise)}}{\text{horizontal change (run)}} = \frac{\text{change in } y}{\text{change in } x}$$

Example

Find the slope of the graph in **Figure 8**.

Step 1 You know that the slope is the change in *y* divided by the change in *x*.

$$\text{Slope} = \frac{\text{change in } y}{\text{change in } x}$$

Step 2 Determine the data points you will be using. For a straight line, choose the two sets of points that are the farthest apart.

$$\text{Slope} = \frac{(40 - 0)\text{ km}}{(5 - 0)\text{ h}}$$

Step 3 Find the change in *y* and *x*.

$$\text{Slope} = \frac{40\text{ km}}{5\text{ h}}$$

Step 4 Divide the change in *y* by the change in *x*.

$$\text{Slope} = \frac{8\text{ km}}{\text{h}}$$

The slope of the graph is 8 km/h.

Bar Graph To compare data that does not change continuously you might choose a bar graph. A bar graph uses bars to show the relationships between variables. The x-axis variable is divided into parts. The parts can be numbers such as years, or a category such as a type of animal. The y-axis is a number and increases continuously along the axis.

Example

A recycling center collects 4.0 kg of aluminum on Monday, 1.0 kg on Wednesday, and 2.0 kg on Friday. Create a bar graph of this data.

Step 1 Select the x-axis and y-axis variables. The measured numbers (the masses of aluminum) should be placed on the y-axis. The variable divided into parts (collection days) is placed on the x-axis.

Step 2 Create a graph grid like you would for a line graph. Include labels and units.

Step 3 For each measured number, draw a vertical bar above the x-axis value up to the y-axis value. For the first data point, draw a vertical bar above Monday up to 4.0 kg.

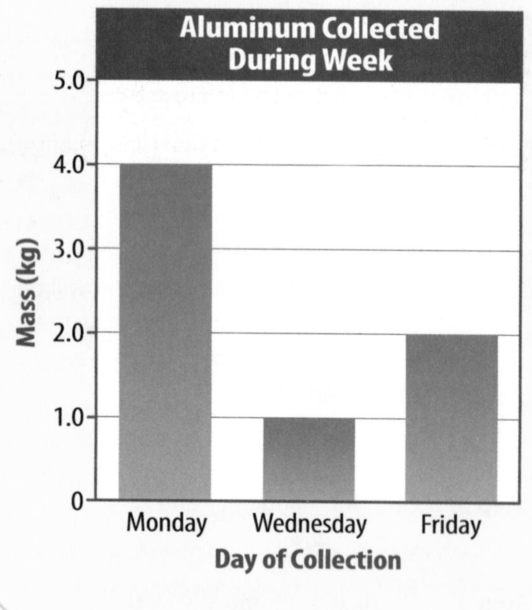

Practice Problem Draw a bar graph of the gases in air: 78% nitrogen, 21% oxygen, 1% other gases.

Circle Graph To display data as parts of a whole, you might use a circle graph. A circle graph is a circle divided into sections that represent the relative size of each piece of data. The entire circle represents 100%, half represents 50%, and so on.

Example

Air is made up of 78% nitrogen, 21% oxygen, and 1% other gases. Display the composition of air in a circle graph.

Step 1 Multiply each percent by 360° and divide by 100 to find the angle of each section in the circle.

$$78\% \times \frac{360°}{100} = 280.8°$$

$$21\% \times \frac{360°}{100} = 75.6°$$

$$1\% \times \frac{360°}{100} = 3.6°$$

Step 2 Use a compass to draw a circle and to mark the center of the circle. Draw a straight line from the center to the edge of the circle.

Step 3 Use a protractor and the angles you calculated to divide the circle into parts. Place the center of the protractor over the center of the circle and line the base of the protractor over the straight line.

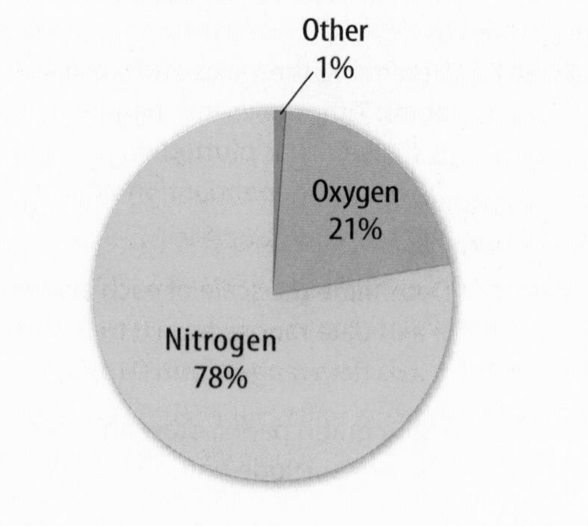

Practice Problem Draw a circle graph to represent the amount of aluminum collected during the week shown in the bar graph to the left.

Student Study Guides & Instructions

By Dinah Zike

1. You will find suggestions for Study Guides, also known as Foldables or books, in each chapter lesson and as a final project. Look at the end of the chapter to determine the project format and glue the Foldables in place as you progress through the chapter lessons.

2. Creating the Foldables or books is simple and easy to do by using copy paper, art paper, and Internet printouts. Photocopies of maps, diagrams, or your own illustrations may also be used for some of the Foldables. Notebook paper is the most common source of material for study guides and 83% of all Foldables are created from it. When folded to make books, notebook paper Foldables easily fit into 11″ × 17″ or 12″ × 18″ chapter projects with space left over. Foldables made using photocopy paper are slightly larger and they fit into Projects, but snugly. Use the least amount of glue, tape, and staples needed to assemble the Foldables.

3. Seven of the Foldables can be made using either small or large paper. When 11″ × 17″ or 12″ × 18″ paper are used, these become projects for housing smaller Foldables. Project format boxes are located within the instructions to remind you of this option.

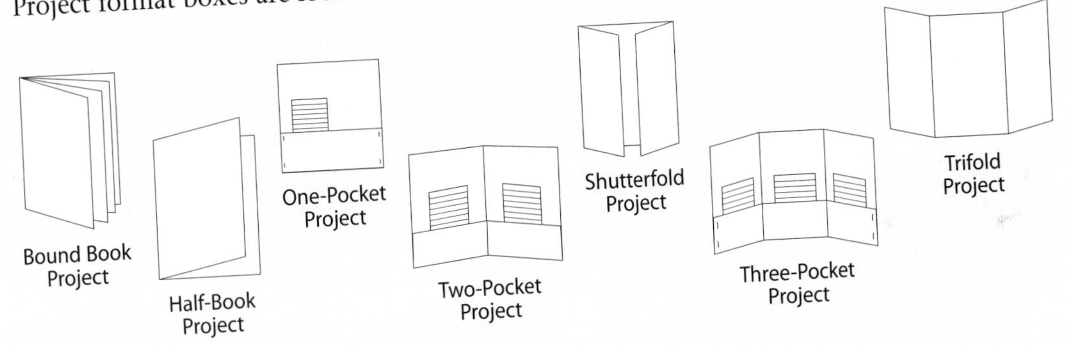

4. Use one-gallon self-locking plastic bags to store your projects. Place strips of two-inch clear tape along the left, long side of the bag and punch holes through the taped edge. Cut the bottom corners off the bag so it will not hold air. Store this Project Portfolio inside a three-hole binder. To store a large collection of project bags, use a giant laundry-soap box. Holes can be punched in some of the Foldable Projects so they can be stored in a three-hole binder without using a plastic bag. Punch holes in the pocket books before gluing or stapling the pocket.

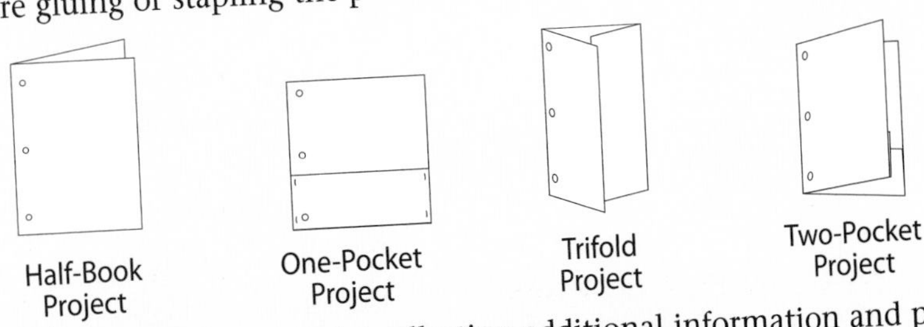

5. Maximize the use of the projects by collecting additional information and placing it on the back of the project and other unused spaces of the large Foldables.

Science Skill Handbook | Math Skill Handbook | Foldables Handbook | Reference Handbook | Glossary/Glosario | Index

Half-Book Foldable® By Dinah Zike

Step 1 Fold a sheet of notebook or copy paper in half.

Label the exterior tab and use the inside space to write information.

PROJECT FORMAT
Use 11″ × 17″ or 12″ × 18″ paper on the horizontal axis to make a large project book.

Variations

Paper can be folded vertically, like a *hamburger* or horizontally, like a *hotdog*.

A

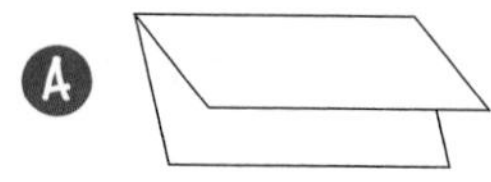

B

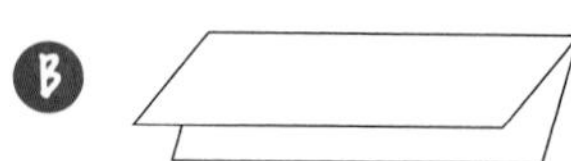

C Half-books can be folded so that one side is ½ inch longer than the other side. A title or question can be written on the extended tab.

Worksheet Foldable or Folded Book® By Dinah Zike

Step 1 Make a half-book (see above) using work sheets, Internet print-outs, diagrams, or maps.

Step 2 Fold it in half again.

Variations

A This folded sheet as a small book with two pages can be used for comparing and contrasting, cause and effect, or other skills.

B When the sheet of paper is open, the four sections can be used separately or used collectively to show sequences or steps.

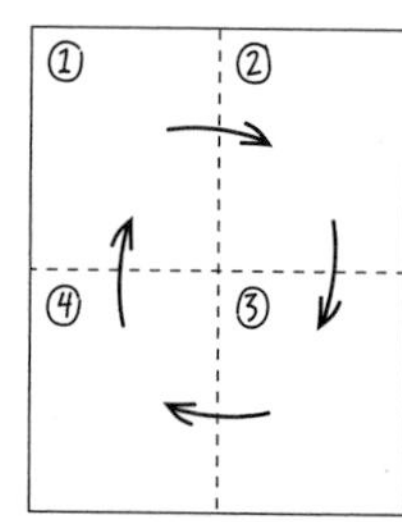

Two-Tab and Concept-Map Foldable® By Dinah Zike

Step 1 Fold a sheet of notebook or copy paper in half vertically or horizontally.

Step 2 Fold it in half again, as shown.

Step 3 Unfold once and cut along the fold line or valley of the top flap to make two flaps.

Variations

A Concept maps can be made by leaving a ½ inch tab at the top when folding the paper in half. Use arrows and labels to relate topics to the primary concept.

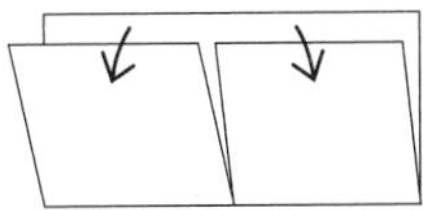

B Use two sheets of paper to make multiple page tab books. Glue or staple books together at the top fold.

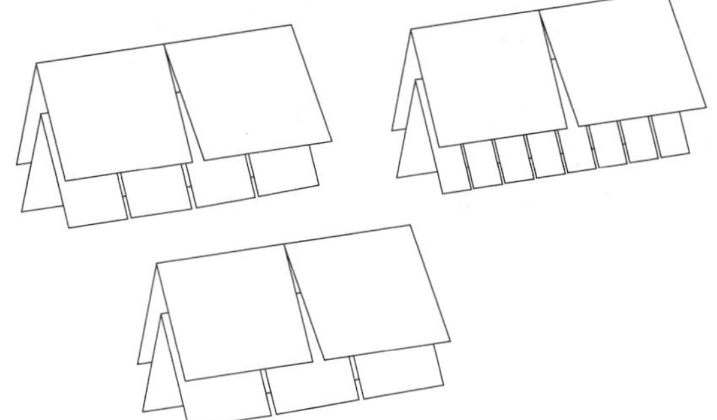

Three-Quarter Foldable® By Dinah Zike

Step 1 Make a two-tab book (see above) and cut the left tab off at the top of the fold line.

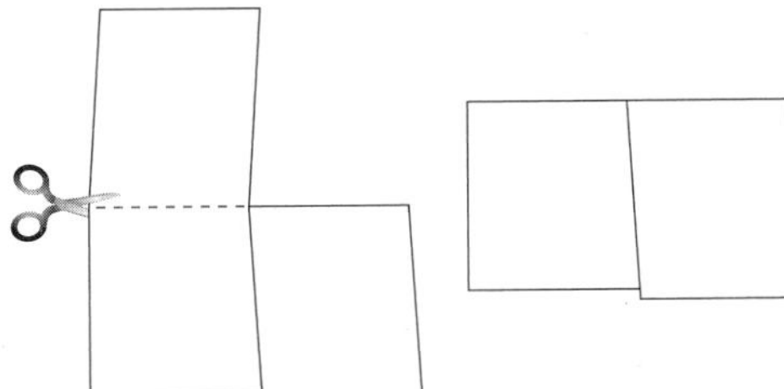

Variations

A Use this book to draw a diagram or a map on the exposed left tab. Write questions about the illustration on the top right tab and provide complete answers on the space under the tab.

B Compose a self-test using multiple choice answers for your questions. Include the correct answer with three wrong responses. The correct answers can be written on the back of the book or upside down on the bottom of the inside page.

Three-Tab Foldable® By Dinah Zike

Step 1 Fold a sheet of paper in half horizontally.

Step 2 Fold into thirds.

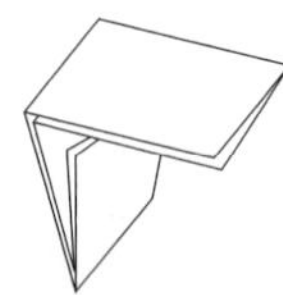

Step 3 Unfold and cut along the folds of the top flap to make three sections.

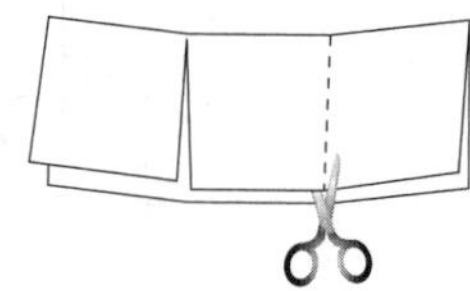

Variations

A Before cutting the three tabs draw a Venn diagram across the front of the book.

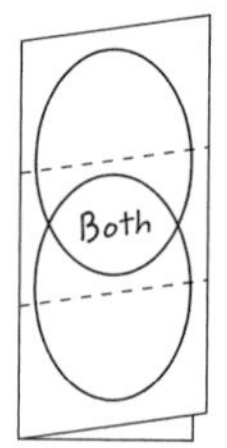

B Make a space to use for titles or concept maps by leaving a ½ inch tab at the top when folding the paper in half.

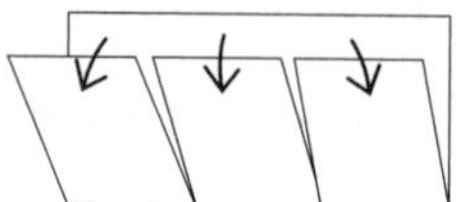

Four-Tab Foldable® By Dinah Zike

Step 1 Fold a sheet of paper in half horizontally.

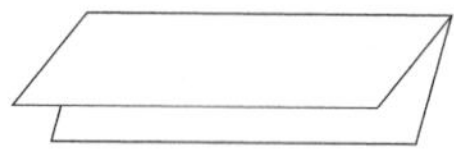

Step 2 Fold in half and then fold each half as shown below.

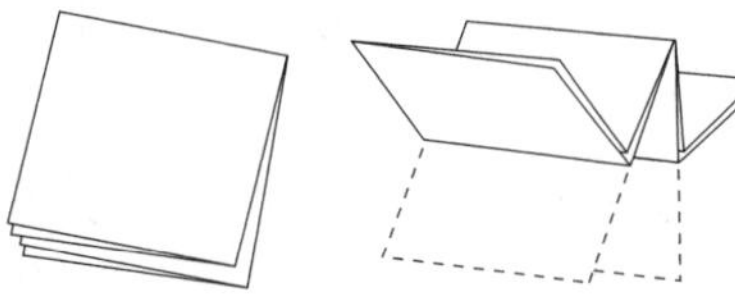

Step 3 Unfold and cut along the fold lines of the top flap to make four tabs.

Variations

A Make a space to use for titles or concept maps by leaving a ½ inch tab at the top when folding the paper in half.

B Use the book on the vertical axis, with or without an extended tab.

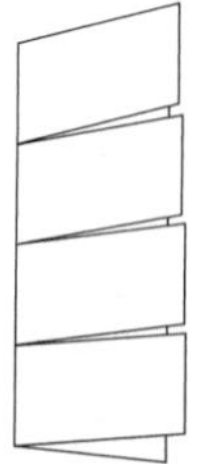

Folding Fifths for a Foldable® By Dinah Zike

Step 1 Fold a sheet of paper in half horizontally.

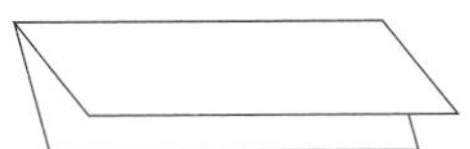

Step 2 Fold again so one-third of the paper is exposed and two-thirds are covered.

Step 3 Fold the two-thirds section in half.

Step 4 Fold the one-third section, a single thickness, backward to make a fold line.

Variations

A Unfold and cut along the fold lines to make five tabs.

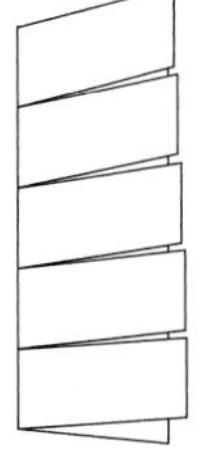

B Make a five-tab book with a ½ inch tab at the top (see two-tab instructions).

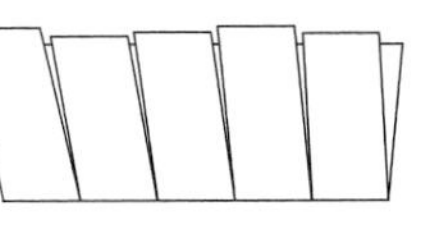

C Use 11″ × 17″ or 12″ × 18″ paper and fold into fifths for a five-column and/or row table or chart.

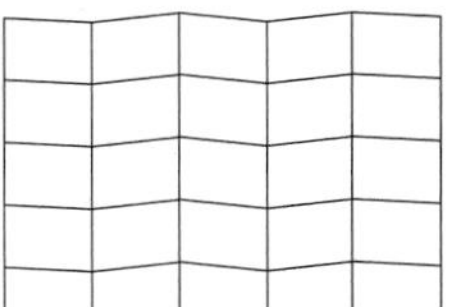

Folded Table or Chart, and Trifold Foldable® By Dinah Zike

Step 1 Fold a sheet of paper in the required number of vertical columns for the table or chart.

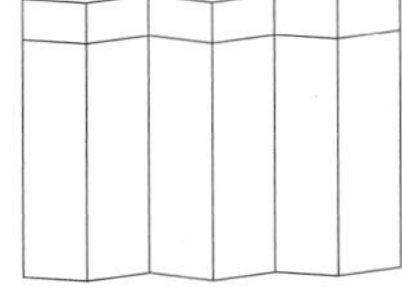

Step 2 Fold the horizontal rows needed for the table or chart.

PROJECT FORMAT
Use 11″ × 17″ or 12″ × 18″ paper and fold it to make a large trifold project book or larger tables and charts.

Variations

A Make a trifold by folding the paper into thirds vertically or horizontally.

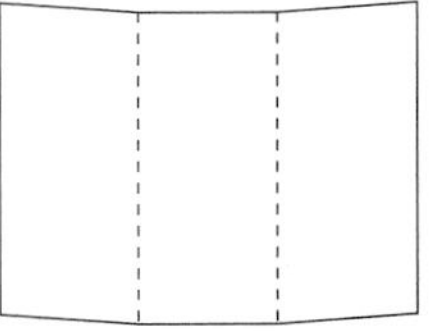

B Make a trifold book. Unfold it and draw a Venn diagram on the inside.

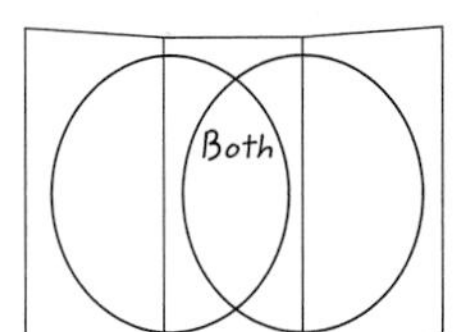

Two or Three-Pockets Foldable® By Dinah Zike

Step 1 Fold up the long side of a horizontal sheet of paper about 5 cm.

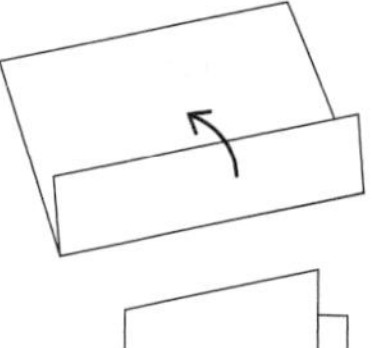

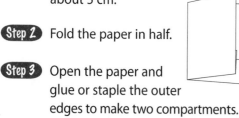

Step 2 Fold the paper in half.

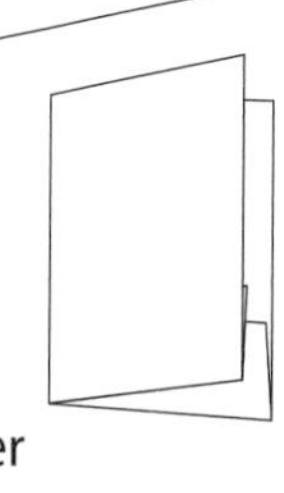

Step 3 Open the paper and glue or staple the outer edges to make two compartments.

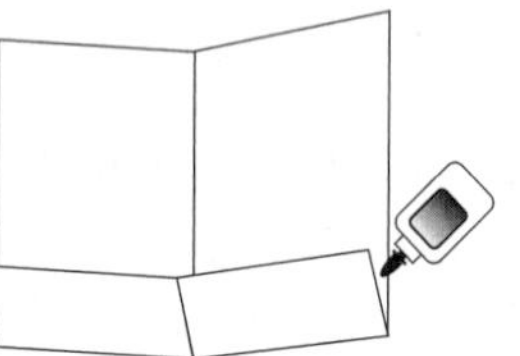

Variations

A Make a multi-page booklet by gluing several pocket books together.

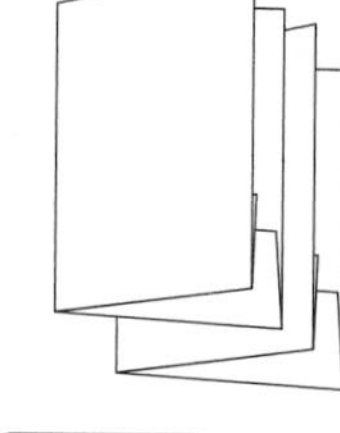

B Make a three-pocket book by using a trifold (see previous instructions).

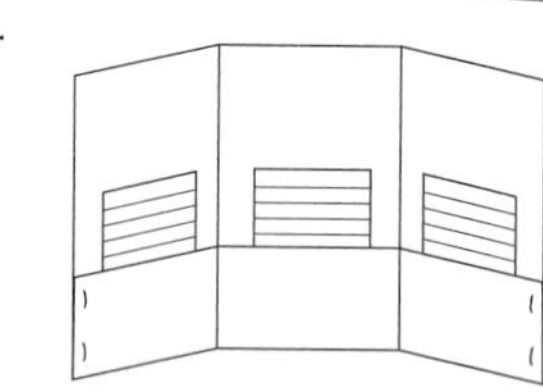

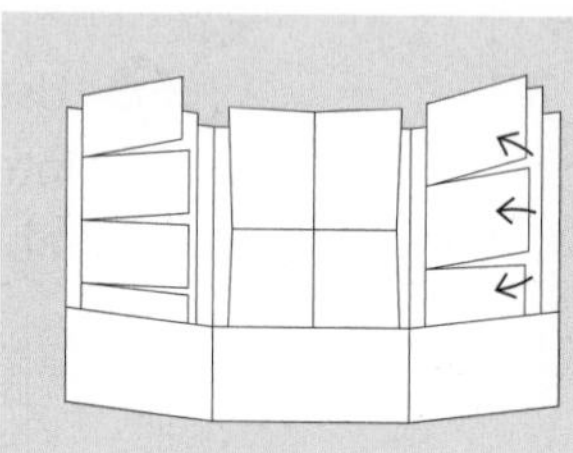

PROJECT FORMAT
Use 11″ × 17″ or 12″ × 18″ paper and fold it horizontally to make a large multi-pocket project.

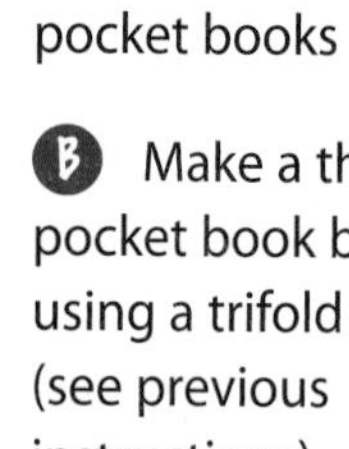

Matchbook Foldable® By Dinah Zike

Step 1 Fold a sheet of paper almost in half and make the back edge about 1–2 cm longer than the front edge.

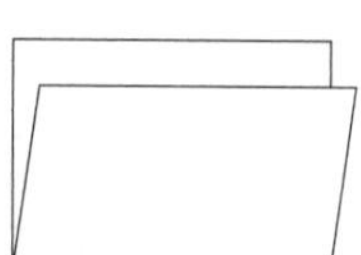

Step 2 Find the midpoint of the shorter flap.

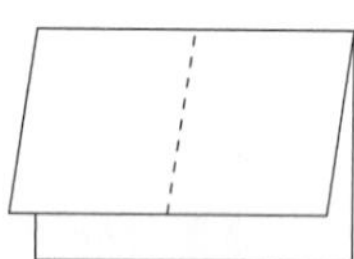

Step 3 Open the paper and cut the short side along the fold lines making two tabs.

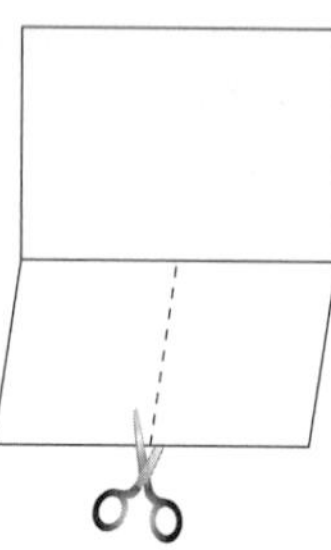

Step 4 Close the book and fold the tab over the short side.

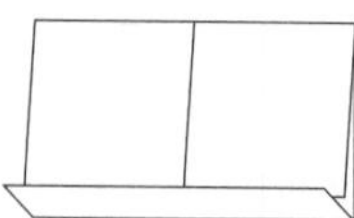

Variations

A Make a single-tab matchbook by skipping Steps 2 and 3.

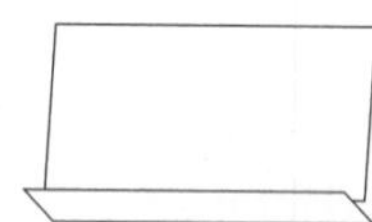

B Make two smaller matchbooks by cutting the single-tab matchbook in half.

Shutterfold Foldable® By Dinah Zike

Step 1 Begin as if you were folding a vertical sheet of paper in half, but instead of creasing the paper, pinch it to show the midpoint.

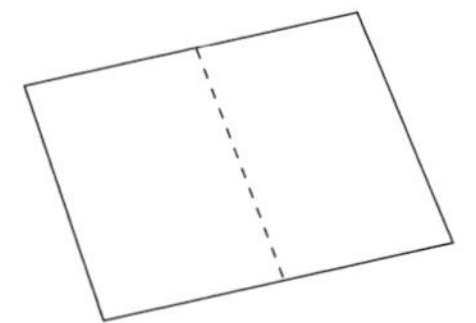

PROJECT FORMAT

Use 11″ × 17″ or 12″ × 18″ paper and fold it to make a large shutterfold project.

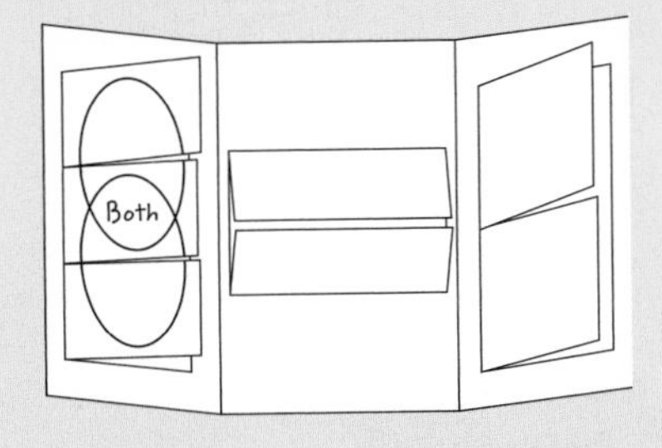

Step 2 Fold the top and bottom to the middle and crease the folds.

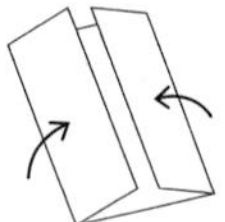

Variations

A Use the shutterfold on the horizontal axis.

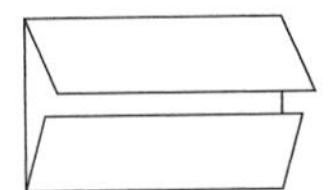

B Create a center tab by leaving .5–2 cm between the flaps in Step 2.

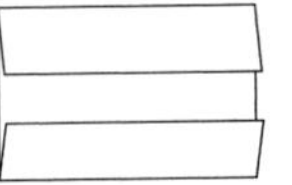

Four-Door Foldable® By Dinah Zike

Step 1 Make a shutterfold (see above).

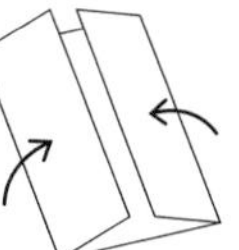

Step 2 Fold the sheet of paper in half.

Step 3 Open the last fold and cut along the inside fold lines to make four tabs.

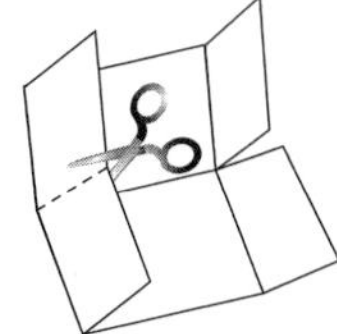
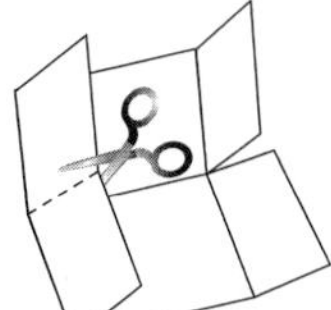

Variations

A Use the four-door book on the opposite axis.

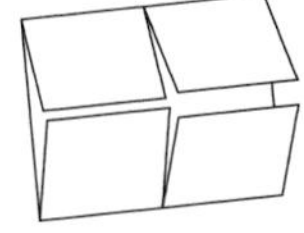

B Create a center tab by leaving .5–2 cm between the flaps in Step 1.

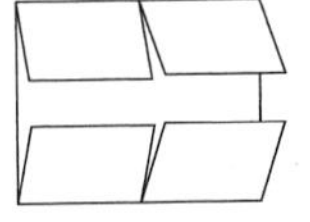

Bound Book Foldable® By Dinah Zike

Step 1 Fold three sheets of paper in half. Place the papers in a stack, leaving about .5 cm between each top fold. Mark all three sheets about 3 cm from the outer edges.

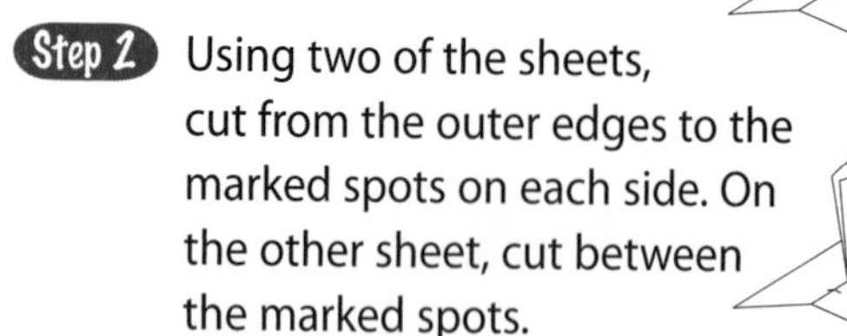

Step 2 Using two of the sheets, cut from the outer edges to the marked spots on each side. On the other sheet, cut between the marked spots.

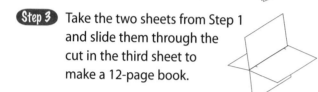

Step 3 Take the two sheets from Step 1 and slide them through the cut in the third sheet to make a 12-page book.

Step 4 Fold the bound pages in half to form a book.

Variation

A Use two sheets of paper to make an eight-page book, or increase the number of pages by using more than three sheets.

PROJECT FORMAT
Use two or more sheets of 11″ × 17″ or 12″ × 18″ paper and fold it to make a large bound book project.

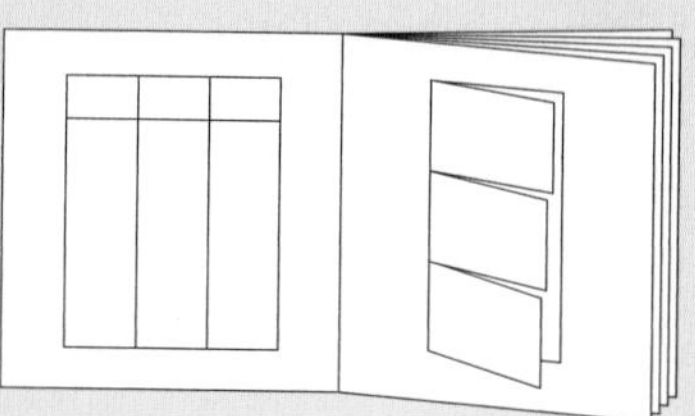

Accordian Foldable® By Dinah Zike

Step 1 Fold the selected paper in half vertically, like a *hamburger*.

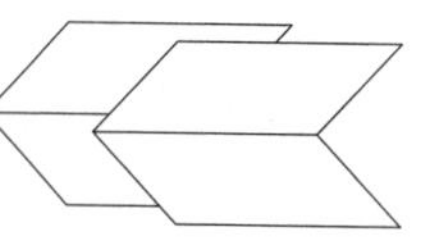

Step 2 Cut each sheet of folded paper in half along the fold lines.

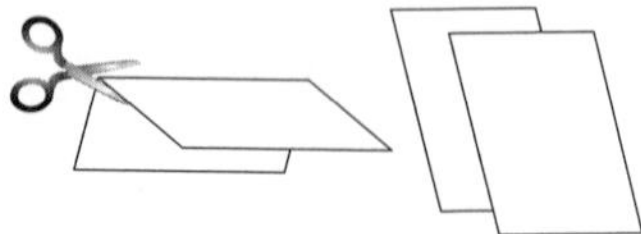

Step 3 Fold each half-sheet almost in half, leaving a 2 cm tab at the top.

Step 4 Fold the top tab over the short side, then fold it in the opposite direction.

Variations

A Glue the straight edge of one paper inside the tab of another sheet. Leave a tab at the end of the book to add more pages.

B Tape the straight edge of one paper to the tab of another sheet, or just tape the straight edges of nonfolded paper end to end to make an accordian.

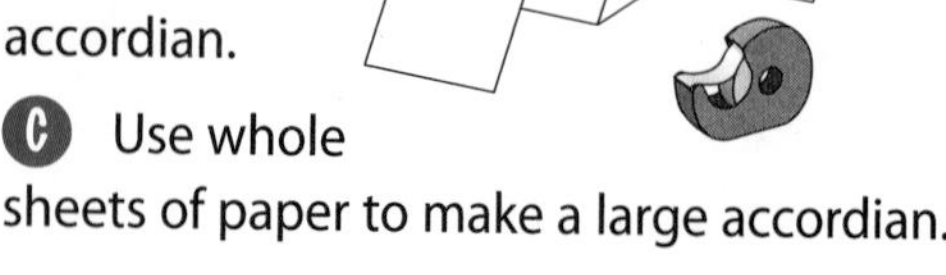

C Use whole sheets of paper to make a large accordian.

Layered Foldable® By Dinah Zike

Step 1 Stack two sheets of paper about 1–2 cm apart. Keep the right and left edges even.

Step 2 Fold up the bottom edges to to form four tabs. Crease the fold to hold the tabs in place.

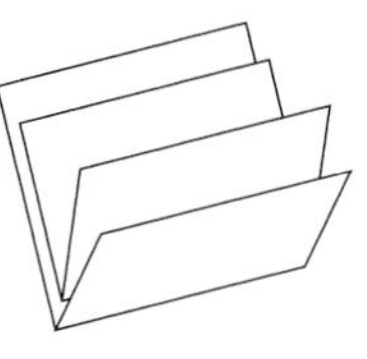

Step 3 Staple along the folded edge, or open and glue the papers together at the fold line.

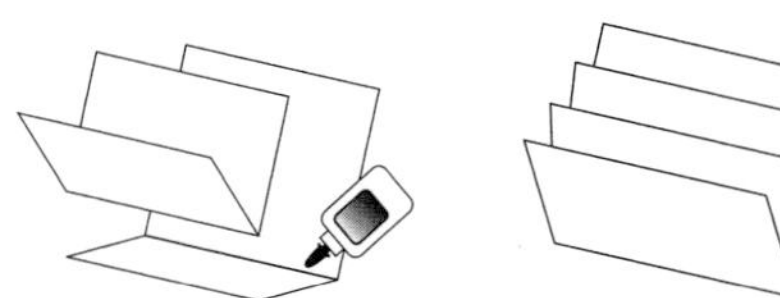

Variations

A Rotate the book so the fold is at the top or to the side.

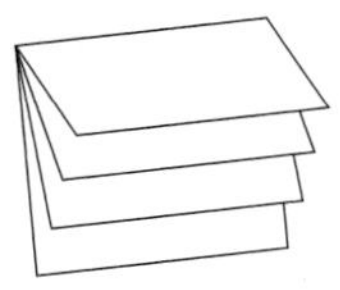

B Extend the book by using more than two sheets of paper.

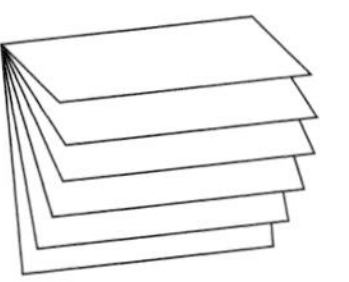

Envelope Foldable® By Dinah Zike

Step 1 Fold a sheet of paper into a *taco*. Cut off the tab at the top.

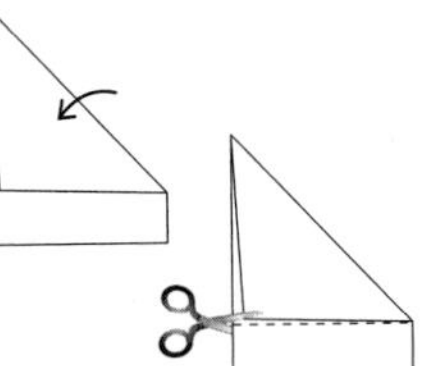

Step 2 Open the *taco* and fold it the opposite way making another *taco* and X-fold pattern on the sheet of paper.

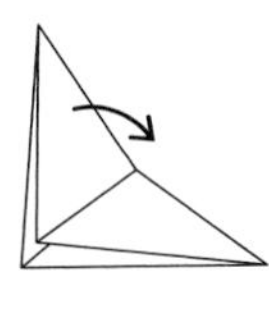

Step 3 Cut a map, illustration or diagram to fit the inside of the envelope.

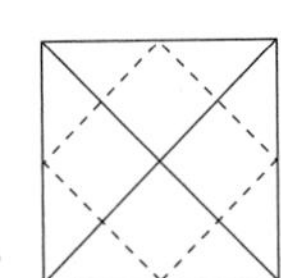

Step 4 Use the outside tabs for labels and inside tabs for writing information.

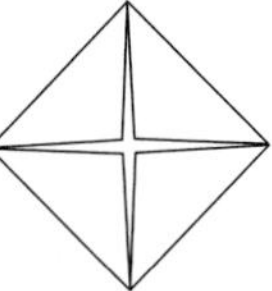

Variations

A Use 11″ × 17″ or 12″ × 18″ paper to make a large envelope.

B Cut off the points of the four tabs to make a window in the middle of the book.

Sentence Strip Foldable® By Dinah Zike

Step 1 Fold two sheets of paper in half vertically, like a *hamburger*.

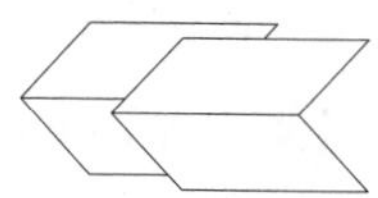

Step 2 Unfold and cut along fold lines making four half sheets.

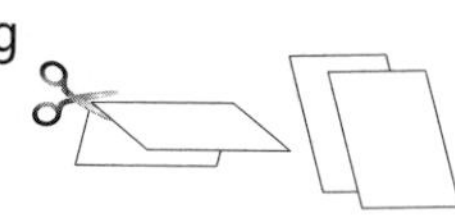

Step 3 Fold each half sheet in half horizontally, like a *hotdog*.

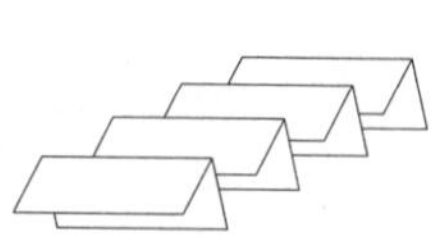

Step 4 Stack folded horizontal sheets evenly and staple together on the left side.

Step 5 Open the top flap of the first sentence strip and make a cut about 2 cm from the stapled edge to the fold line. This forms a flap that can be raisied and lowered. Repeat this step for each sentence strip.

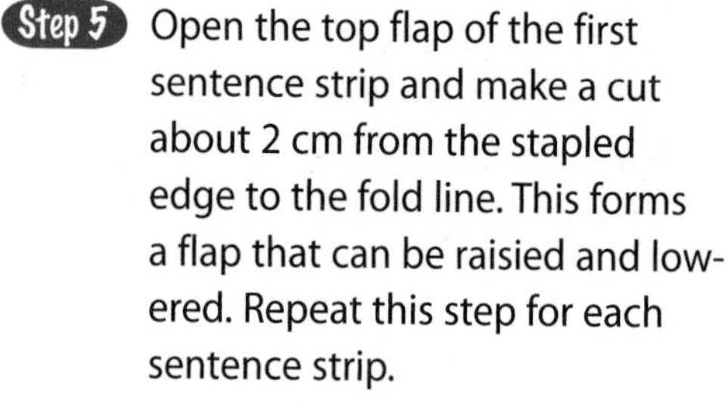

Variations

A Expand this book by using more than two sheets of paper.

B Use whole sheets of paper to make large books.

Pyramid Foldable® By Dinah Zike

Step 1 Fold a sheet of paper into a *taco*. Crease the fold line, but do not cut it off.

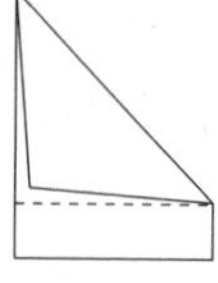

Step 2 Open the folded sheet and refold it like a *taco* in the opposite direction to create an X-fold pattern.

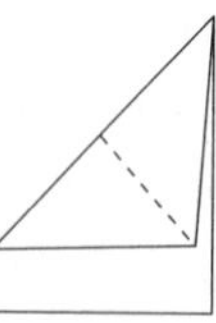

Step 3 Cut one fold line as shown, stopping at the center of the X-fold to make a flap.

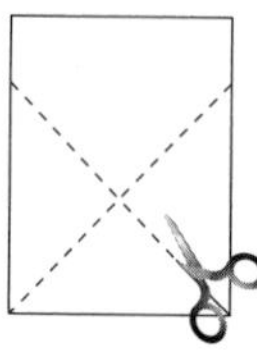

Step 4 Outline the fold lines of the X-fold. Label the three front sections and use the inside spaces for notes. Use the tab for the title.

Step 5 Glue the tab into a project book or notebook. Use the space under the pyramid for other information.

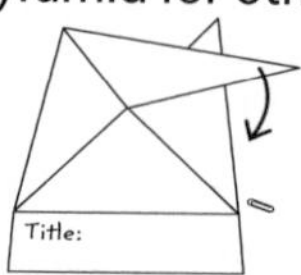

Step 6 To display the pyramid, fold the flap under and secure with a paper clip, if needed.

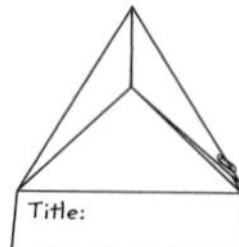

Single-Pocket or One-Pocket Foldable® By Dinah Zike

Step 1 Using a large piece of paper on a vertical axis, fold the bottom edge of the paper upwards, about 5 cm.

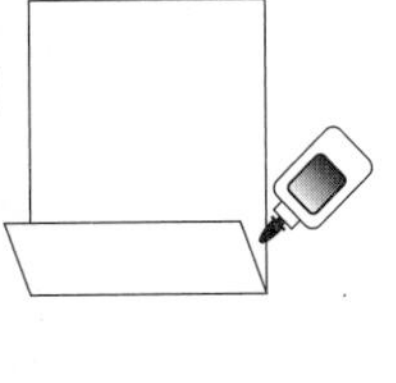

Step 2 Glue or staple the outer edges to make a large pocket.

PROJECT FORMAT
Use 11″ × 17″ or 12″ × 18″ paper and fold it vertically or horizontally to make a large pocket project.

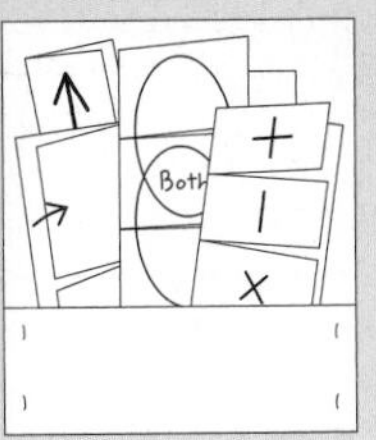

Variations

A Make the one-pocket project using the paper on the horizontal axis.

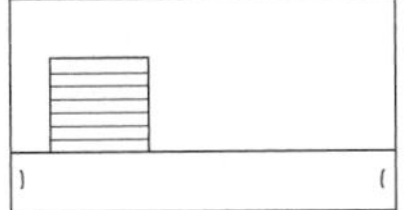

B To store materials securely inside, fold the top of the paper almost to the center, leaving about 2–4 cm between the paper edges. Slip the Foldables through the opening and under the top and bottom pockets.

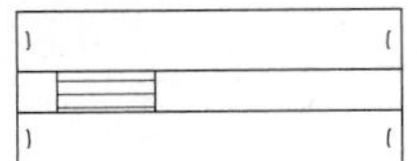

Multi-Tab Foldable® By Dinah Zike

Step 1 Fold a sheet of notebook paper in half like a *hotdog*.

Step 2 Open the paper and on one side cut every third line. This makes ten tabs on wide ruled notebook paper and twelve tabs on college ruled.

Step 3 Label the tabs on the front side and use the inside space for definitions, or other information.

Variation

A Make a tab for a title by folding the paper so the holes remain uncovered. This allows the notebook Foldable to be stored in a three-hole binder.

Science Skill Handbook
Math Skill Handbook
Foldables Handbook
Reference Handbook
Glossary/Glosario
Index

PERIODIC TABLE OF THE ELEMENTS

Element — Hydrogen
Atomic number — 1
Symbol — H
Atomic mass — 1.01
State of matter

Gas
Liquid
Solid
Synthetic

A column in the periodic table is called a **group.**

A row in the periodic table is called a **period.**

Period	1	2	3	4	5	6	7	8	9
1	Hydrogen 1 **H** 1.01								
2	Lithium 3 **Li** 6.94	Beryllium 4 **Be** 9.01							
3	Sodium 11 **Na** 22.99	Magnesium 12 **Mg** 24.31							
4	Potassium 19 **K** 39.10	Calcium 20 **Ca** 40.08	Scandium 21 **Sc** 44.96	Titanium 22 **Ti** 47.87	Vanadium 23 **V** 50.94	Chromium 24 **Cr** 52.00	Manganese 25 **Mn** 54.94	Iron 26 **Fe** 55.85	Cobalt 27 **Co** 58.93
5	Rubidium 37 **Rb** 85.47	Strontium 38 **Sr** 87.62	Yttrium 39 **Y** 88.91	Zirconium 40 **Zr** 91.22	Niobium 41 **Nb** 92.91	Molybdenum 42 **Mo** 95.96	Technetium 43 **Tc** (98)	Ruthenium 44 **Ru** 101.07	Rhodium 45 **Rh** 102.91
6	Cesium 55 **Cs** 132.91	Barium 56 **Ba** 137.33	Lanthanum 57 **La** 138.91	Hafnium 72 **Hf** 178.49	Tantalum 73 **Ta** 180.95	Tungsten 74 **W** 183.84	Rhenium 75 **Re** 186.21	Osmium 76 **Os** 190.23	Iridium 77 **Ir** 192.22
7	Francium 87 **Fr** (223)	Radium 88 **Ra** (226)	Actinium 89 **Ac** (227)	Rutherfordium 104 **Rf** (267)	Dubnium 105 **Db** (268)	Seaborgium 106 **Sg** (271)	Bohrium 107 **Bh** (272)	Hassium 108 **Hs** (270)	Meitnerium 109 **Mt** (276)

The number in parentheses is the mass number of the longest lived isotope for that element.

Lanthanide series	Cerium 58 **Ce** 140.12	Praseodymium 59 **Pr** 140.91	Neodymium 60 **Nd** 144.24	Promethium 61 **Pm** (145)	Samarium 62 **Sm** 150.36	Europium 63 **Eu** 151.96
Actinide series	Thorium 90 **Th** 232.04	Protactinium 91 **Pa** 231.04	Uranium 92 **U** 238.03	Neptunium 93 **Np** (237)	Plutonium 94 **Pu** (244)	Americium 95 **Am** (243)

Legend: Metal · Metalloid · Nonmetal · Recently discovered

10	11	12	13	14	15	16	17	18
								Helium 2 He 4.00
			Boron 5 B 10.81	Carbon 6 C 12.01	Nitrogen 7 N 14.01	Oxygen 8 O 16.00	Fluorine 9 F 19.00	Neon 10 Ne 20.18
			Aluminum 13 Al 26.98	Silicon 14 Si 28.09	Phosphorus 15 P 30.97	Sulfur 16 S 32.07	Chlorine 17 Cl 35.45	Argon 18 Ar 39.95
Nickel 28 Ni 58.69	Copper 29 Cu 63.55	Zinc 30 Zn 65.38	Gallium 31 Ga 69.72	Germanium 32 Ge 72.64	Arsenic 33 As 74.92	Selenium 34 Se 78.96	Bromine 35 Br 79.90	Krypton 36 Kr 83.80
Palladium 46 Pd 106.42	Silver 47 Ag 107.87	Cadmium 48 Cd 112.41	Indium 49 In 114.82	Tin 50 Sn 118.71	Antimony 51 Sb 121.76	Tellurium 52 Te 127.60	Iodine 53 I 126.90	Xenon 54 Xe 131.29
Platinum 78 Pt 195.08	Gold 79 Au 196.97	Mercury 80 Hg 200.59	Thallium 81 Tl 204.38	Lead 82 Pb 207.20	Bismuth 83 Bi 208.98	Polonium 84 Po (209)	Astatine 85 At (210)	Radon 86 Rn (222)
Darmstadtium 110 Ds (281)	Roentgenium 111 Rg (280)	Copernicium 112 Cn (285)	Ununtrium * 113 Uut (284)	Ununquadium * 114 Uuq (289)	Ununpentium * 115 Uup (288)	Ununhexium * 116 Uuh (293)		Ununoctium * 118 Uuo (294)

* The names and symbols for elements 113-116 and 118 are temporary. Final names will be selected when the elements' discoveries are verified.

Gadolinium 64 Gd 157.25	Terbium 65 Tb 158.93	Dysprosium 66 Dy 162.50	Holmium 67 Ho 164.93	Erbium 68 Er 167.26	Thulium 69 Tm 168.93	Ytterbium 70 Yb 173.05	Lutetium 71 Lu 174.97
Curium 96 Cm (247)	Berkelium 97 Bk (247)	Californium 98 Cf (251)	Einsteinium 99 Es (252)	Fermium 100 Fm (257)	Mendelevium 101 Md (258)	Nobelium 102 No (259)	Lawrencium 103 Lr (262)

Topographic Map Symbols

Topographic Map Symbols	
Primary highway, hard surface	Index contour
Secondary highway, hard surface	Supplementary contour
Light-duty road, hard or improved surface	Intermediate contour
Unimproved road	Depression contours
Railroad: single track	
Railroad: multiple track	Boundaries: national
Railroads in juxtaposition	State
	County, parish, municipal
Buildings	Civil township, precinct, town, barrio
cem Schools, church, and cemetery	Incorporated city, village, town, hamlet
Buildings (barn, warehouse, etc.)	Reservation, national or state
Wells other than water (labeled as to type)	Small park, cemetery, airport, etc.
Tanks: oil, water, etc. (labeled only if water)	Land grant
Located or landmark object; windmill	Township or range line, U.S. land survey
Open pit, mine, or quarry; prospect	
	Township or range line, approximate location
Marsh (swamp)	
Wooded marsh	Perennial streams
Woods or brushwood	Elevated aqueduct
Vineyard	Water well and spring
Land subject to controlled inundation	Small rapids
Submerged marsh	Large rapids
Mangrove	Intermittent lake
Orchard	Intermittent stream
Scrub	Aqueduct tunnel
Urban area	Glacier
	Small falls
x7369 Spot elevation	Large falls
670 Water elevation	Dry lake bed

Rocks

Rocks		
Rock Type	**Rock Name**	**Characteristics**
Igneous (intrusive)	Granite	Large mineral grains of quartz, feldspar, hornblende, and mica. Usually light in color.
	Diorite	Large mineral grains of feldspar, hornblende, and mica. Less quartz than granite. Intermediate in color.
	Gabbro	Large mineral grains of feldspar, augite, and olivine. No quartz. Dark in color.
Igneous (extrusive)	Rhyolite	Small mineral grains of quartz, feldspar, hornblende, and mica, or no visible grains. Light in color.
	Andesite	Small mineral grains of feldspar, hornblende, and mica or no visible grains. Intermediate in color.
	Basalt	Small mineral grains of feldspar, augite, and possibly olivine or no visible grains. No quartz. Dark in color.
	Obsidian	Glassy texture. No visible grains. Volcanic glass. Fracture looks like broken glass.
	Pumice	Frothy texture. Floats in water. Usually light in color.
Sedimentary (detrital)	Conglomerate	Coarse grained. Gravel or pebble-size grains.
	Sandstone	Sand-sized grains 1/16 to 2 mm.
	Siltstone	Grains are smaller than sand but larger than clay.
	Shale	Smallest grains. Often dark in color. Usually platy.
Sedimentary (chemical or organic)	Limestone	Major mineral is calcite. Usually forms in oceans and lakes. Often contains fossils.
	Coal	Forms in swampy areas. Compacted layers of organic material, mainly plant remains.
Sedimentary (chemical)	Rock Salt	Commonly forms by the evaporation of seawater.
Metamorphic (foliated)	Gneiss	Banding due to alternate layers of different minerals, of different colors. Parent rock often is granite.
	Schist	Parallel arrangement of sheetlike minerals, mainly micas. Forms from different parent rocks.
	Phyllite	Shiny or silky appearance. May look wrinkled. Common parent rocks are shale and slate.
	Slate	Harder, denser, and shinier than shale. Common parent rock is shale.
Metamorphic (nonfoliated)	Marble	Calcite or dolomite. Common parent rock is limestone.
	Soapstone	Mainly of talc. Soft with greasy feel.
	Quartzite	Hard with interlocking quartz crystals. Common parent rock is sandstone.

Minerals

Minerals					
Mineral (formula)	**Color**	**Streak**	**Hardness Pattern**	**Breakage Properties**	**Uses and Other**
Graphite (C)	black to gray	black to gray	1–1.5	basal cleavage (scales)	pencil lead, lubricants for locks, rods to control some small nuclear reactions, battery poles
Galena (PbS)	gray	gray to black	2.5	cubic cleavage perfect	source of lead, used for pipes, shields for X rays, fishing equipment sinkers
Hematite (Fe_2O_3)	black or reddish-brown	reddish-brown	5.5–6.5	irregular fracture	source of iron; converted to pig iron, made into steel
Magnetite (Fe_3O_4)	black	black	6	conchoidal fracture	source of iron, attracts a magnet
Pyrite (FeS_2)	light, brassy, yellow	greenish-black	6–6.5	uneven fracture	fool's gold
Talc ($Mg_3 Si_4O_{10} (OH)_2$)	white, greenish	white	1	cleavage in one direction	used for talcum powder, sculptures, paper, and tabletops
Gypsum ($CaSO_4{\cdot}2H_2O$)	colorless, gray, white, brown	white	2	basal cleavage	used in plaster of paris and dry wall for building construction
Sphalerite (ZnS)	brown, reddish-brown, greenish	light to dark brown	3.5–4	cleavage in six directions	main ore of zinc; used in paints, dyes, and medicine
Muscovite ($KAl_3Si_3 O_{10}(OH)_2$)	white, light gray, yellow, rose, green	colorless	2–2.5	basal cleavage	occurs in large, flexible plates; used as an insulator in electrical equipment, lubricant
Biotite ($K(Mg,Fe)_3 (AlSi_3O_{10}) (OH)_2$)	black to dark brown	colorless	2.5–3	basal cleavage	occurs in large, flexible plates
Halite (NaCl)	colorless, red, white, blue	colorless	2.5	cubic cleavage	salt; soluble in water; a preservative

Minerals

Minerals					
Mineral (formula)	**Color**	**Streak**	**Hardness**	**Breakage Pattern**	**Uses and Other Properties**
Calcite ($CaCO_3$)	colorless, white, pale blue	colorless, white	3	cleavage in three directions	fizzes when HCl is added; used in cements and other building materials
Dolomite ($CaMg(CO_3)_2$)	colorless, white, pink, green, gray, black	white	3.5–4	cleavage in three directions	concrete and cement; used as an ornamental building stone
Fluorite (CaF_2)	colorless, white, blue, green, red, yellow, purple	colorless	4	cleavage in four directions	used in the manufacture of optical equipment; glows under ultraviolet light
Hornblende ($(CaNa)_{2\text{-}3}(Mg,Al,Fe)_5\text{-}(Al,Si)_2Si_6O_{22}(OH)_2$)	green to black	gray to white	5–6	cleavage in two directions	will transmit light on thin edges; 6-sided cross section
Feldspar ($(KAlSi_3O_8)$ $(NaAlSi_3O_8)$, $(CaAl_2Si_2O_8)$)	colorless, white to gray, green	colorless	6	two cleavage planes meet at 90° angle	used in the manufacture of ceramics
Augite ($((Ca,Na)(Mg,Fe,Al)(Al,Si)_2O_6)$)	black	colorless	6	cleavage in two directions	square or 8-sided cross section
Olivine ($((Mg,Fe)_2SiO_4)$)	olive, green	none	6.5–7	conchoidal fracture	gemstones, refractory sand
Quartz (SiO_2)	colorless, various colors	none	7	conchoidal fracture	used in glass manufacture, electronic equipment, radios, computers, watches, gemstones

Weather Map Symbols

Sample Station Model

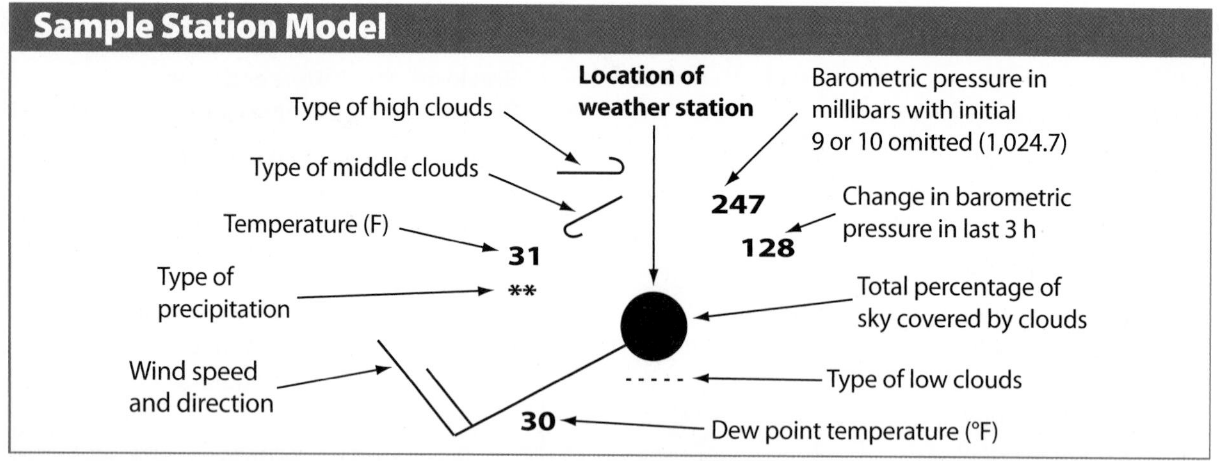

Sample Plotted Report at Each Station

Precipitation	Wind Speed and Direction	Sky Coverage	Some Types of High Clouds
Fog	0 calm	No cover	Scattered cirrus
Snow	1–2 knots	1/10 or less	Dense cirrus in patches
Rain	3–7 knots	2/10 to 3/10	Veil of cirrus covering entire sky
Thunderstorm	8–12 knots	4/10	Cirrus not covering entire sky
Drizzle	13–17 knots	–	
Showers	18–22 knots	6/10	
	23–27 knots	7/10	
	48–52 knots	Overcast with openings	
	1 knot = 1.852 km/h	Completely overcast	

Some Types of Middle Clouds	Some Types of Low Clouds	Fronts and Pressure Systems	
Thin altostratus layer	Cumulus of fair weather	H or High L or Low	Center of high- or low-pressure system
Thick altostratus layer	Stratocumulus		Cold front
Thin altostratus in patches	Fractocumulus of bad weather		Warm front
Thin altostratus in bands	Stratus of fair weather		Occluded front
			Stationary front

Use and Care of a Microscope

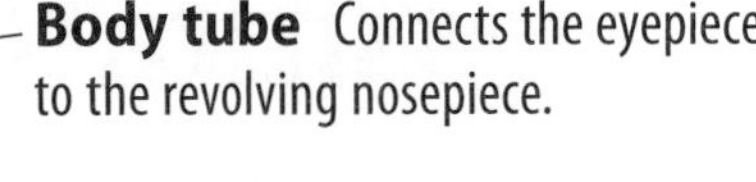

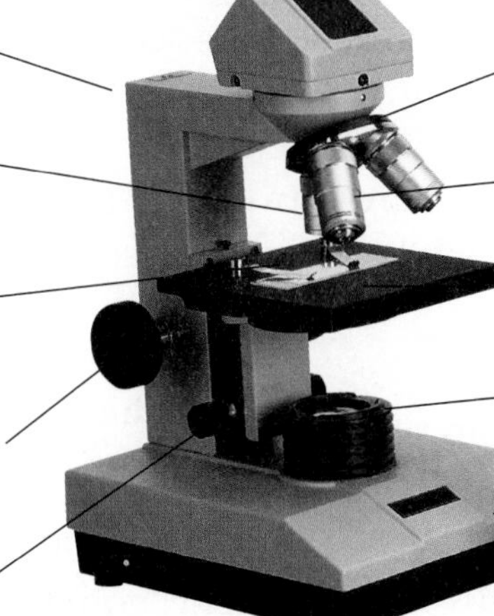
Eyepiece Contains magnifying lenses you look through.
Arm Supports the body tube.
Low-power objective Contains the lens with the lowest power magnification.
Stage clips Hold the microscope slide in place.
Coarse adjustment Focuses the image under low power.
Fine adjustment Sharpens the image under high magnification.
Body tube Connects the eyepiece to the revolving nosepiece.
Revolving nosepiece Holds and turns the objectives into viewing position.
High-power objective Contains the lens with the highest magnification.
Stage Supports the microscope slide.
Light source Provides light that passes upward through the diaphragm, the specimen, and the lenses.
Base Provides support for the microscope.

Caring for a Microscope

1. Always carry the microscope holding the arm with one hand and supporting the base with the other hand.
2. Don't touch the lenses with your fingers.
3. The coarse adjustment knob is used only when looking through the lowest-power objective lens. The fine adjustment knob is used when the high-power objective is in place.
4. Cover the microscope when you store it.

Using a Microscope

1. Place the microscope on a flat surface that is clear of objects. The arm should be toward you.
2. Look through the eyepiece. Adjust the diaphragm so light comes through the opening in the stage.
3. Place a slide on the stage so the specimen is in the field of view. Hold it firmly in place by using the stage clips.
4. Always focus with the coarse adjustment and the low-power objective lens first. After the object is in focus on low power, turn the nosepiece until the high-power objective is in place. Use ONLY the fine adjustment to focus with the high-power objective lens.

Making a Wet-Mount Slide

1. Carefully place the item you want to look at in the center of a clean, glass slide. Make sure the sample is thin enough for light to pass through.
2. Use a dropper to place one or two drops of water on the sample.
3. Hold a clean coverslip by the edges and place it at one edge of the water. Slowly lower the coverslip onto the water until it lies flat.
4. If you have too much water or a lot of air bubbles, touch the edge of a paper towel to the edge of the coverslip to draw off extra water and draw out unwanted air.

Diversity of Life: Classification of Living Organisms

A six-kingdom system of classification of organisms is used today. Two kingdoms—Kingdom Archaebacteria and Kingdom Eubacteria—contain organisms that do not have a nucleus and that lack membrane-bound structures in the cytoplasm of their cells. The members of the other four kingdoms have a cell or cells that contain a nucleus and structures in the cytoplasm, some of which are surrounded by membranes. These kingdoms are Kingdom Protista, Kingdom Fungi, Kingdom Plantae, and Kingdom Animalia.

Kingdom Archaebacteria

one-celled; some absorb food from their surroundings; some are photosynthetic; some are chemosynthetic; many are found in extremely harsh environments including salt ponds, hot springs, swamps, and deep-sea hydrothermal vents

Kingdom Eubacteria

one-celled; most absorb food from their surroundings; some are photosynthetic; some are chemosynthetic; many are parasites; many are round, spiral, or rod-shaped; some form colonies

Kingdom Protista

Phylum Euglenophyta one-celled; photosynthetic or take in food; most have one flagellum; euglenoids

Kingdom Eubacteria
Bacillus anthracis

Phylum Chlorophyta
Desmids

Phylum Bacillariophyta one-celled; photosynthetic; have unique double shells made of silica; diatoms

Phylum Dinoflagellata one-celled; photosynthetic; contain red pigments; have two flagella; dinoflagellates

Phylum Chlorophyta one-celled, many-celled, or colonies; photosynthetic; contain chlorophyll; live on land, in freshwater, or salt water; green algae

Phylum Rhodophyta most are many-celled; photosynthetic; contain red pigments; most live in deep, saltwater environments; red algae

Phylum Phaeophyta most are many-celled; photosynthetic; contain brown pigments; most live in saltwater environments; brown algae

Phylum Rhizopoda one-celled; take in food; are free-living or parasitic; move by means of pseudopods; amoebas

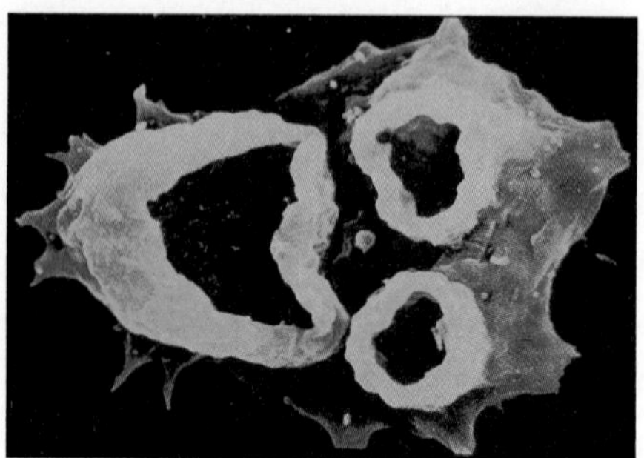

Amoeba

Phylum Zoomastigina one-celled; take in food; free-living or parasitic; have one or more flagella; zoomastigotes

Phylum Ciliophora one-celled; take in food; have large numbers of cilia; ciliates

Phylum Sporozoa one-celled; take in food; have no means of movement; are parasites in animals; sporozoans

Phylum Myxomycota
Slime mold

Phylum Oomycota
Phytophthora infestans

Phyla Myxomycota and Acrasiomycota one- or many-celled; absorb food; change form during life cycle; cellular and plasmodial slime molds

Phylum Oomycota many-celled; are either parasites or decomposers; live in freshwater or salt water; water molds, rusts and downy mildews

Kingdom Fungi

Phylum Zygomycota many-celled; absorb food; spores are produced in sporangia; zygote fungi; bread mold

Phylum Ascomycota one- and many-celled; absorb food; spores produced in asci; sac fungi; yeast

Phylum Basidiomycota many-celled; absorb food; spores produced in basidia; club fungi; mushrooms

Phylum Deuteromycota members with unknown reproductive structures; imperfect fungi; *Penicillium*

Phylum Mycophycota organisms formed by symbiotic relationship between an ascomycote or a basidiomycote and green alga or cyanobacterium; lichens

Lichens

Kingdom Plantae

Divisions Bryophyta (mosses), **Anthocerophyta** (hornworts), **Hepaticophyta** (liverworts), **Psilophyta** (whisk ferns) many-celled nonvascular plants; reproduce by spores produced in capsules; green; grow in moist, land environments

Division Lycophyta many-celled vascular plants; spores are produced in conelike structures; live on land; are photosynthetic; club mosses

Division Arthrophyta vascular plants; ribbed and jointed stems; scalelike leaves; spores produced in conelike structures; horsetails

Division Pterophyta vascular plants; leaves called fronds; spores produced in clusters of sporangia called sori; live on land or in water; ferns

Division Ginkgophyta deciduous trees; only one living species; have fan-shaped leaves with branching veins and fleshy cones with seeds; ginkgoes

Division Cycadophyta palmlike plants; have large, featherlike leaves; produces seeds in cones; cycads

Division Coniferophyta deciduous or evergreen; trees or shrubs; have needlelike or scalelike leaves; seeds produced in cones; conifers

Division Anthophyta
Tomato plant

Division Gnetophyta shrubs or woody vines; seeds are produced in cones; division contains only three genera; gnetum

Division Anthophyta dominant group of plants; flowering plants; have fruits with seeds

Kingdom Animalia

Phylum Porifera aquatic organisms that lack true tissues and organs; are asymmetrical and sessile; sponges

Phylum Cnidaria radially symmetrical organisms; have a digestive cavity with one opening; most have tentacles armed with stinging cells; live in aquatic environments singly or in colonies; includes jellyfish, corals, hydra, and sea anemones

Phylum Platyhelminthes bilaterally symmetrical worms; have flattened bodies; digestive system has one opening; parasitic and free-living species; flatworms

Division Bryophyta
Liverwort

Phylum Platyhelminthes
Flatworm

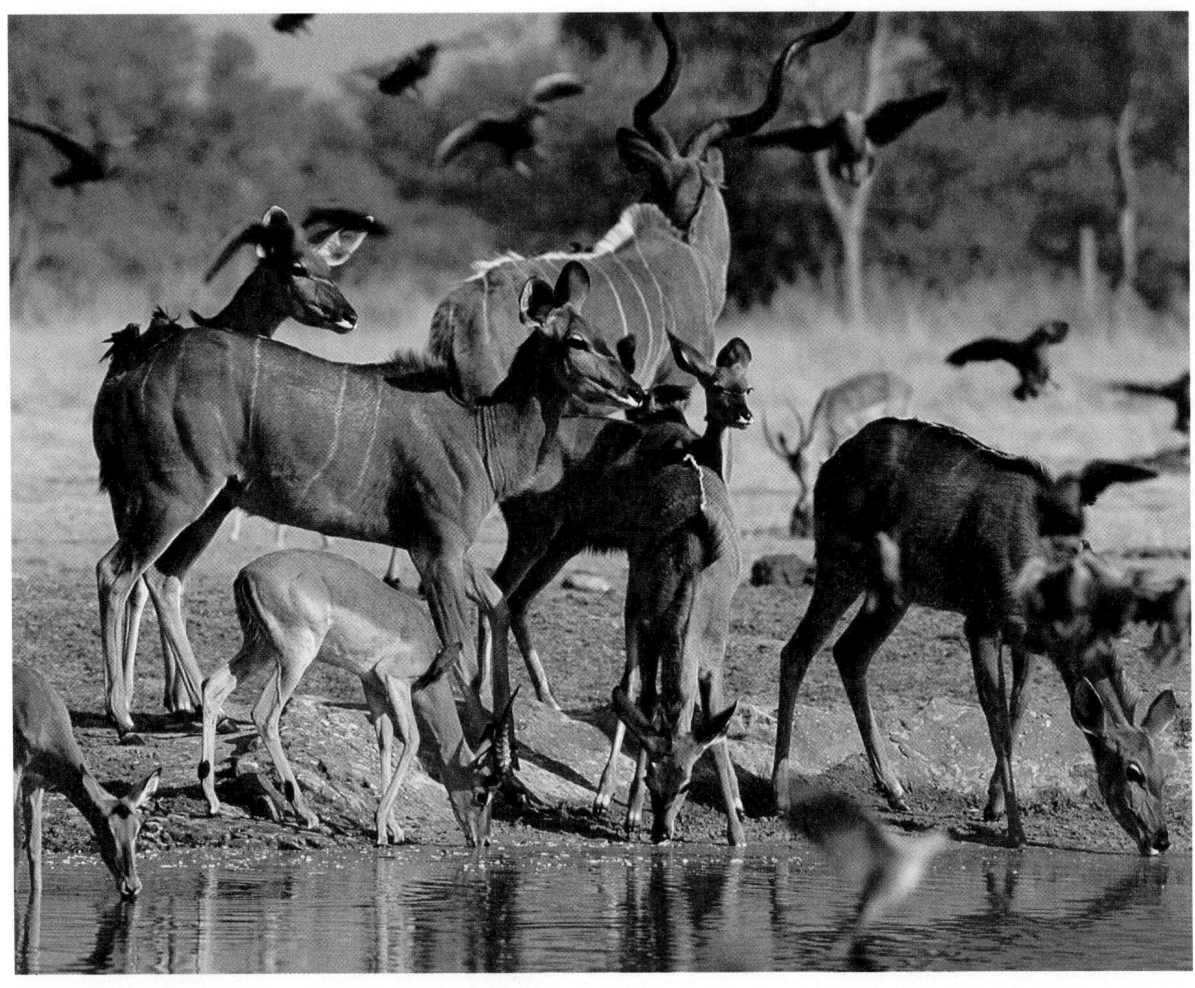

Phylum Chordata

Phylum Nematoda round, bilaterally symmetrical body; have digestive system with two openings; free-living forms and parasitic forms; roundworms

Phylum Mollusca soft-bodied animals, many with a hard shell and soft foot or footlike appendage; a mantle covers the soft body; aquatic and terrestrial species; includes clams, snails, squid, and octopuses

Phylum Annelida bilaterally symmetrical worms; have round, segmented bodies; terrestrial and aquatic species; includes earthworms, leeches, and marine polychaetes

Phylum Arthropoda largest animal group; have hard exoskeletons, segmented bodies, and pairs of jointed appendages; land and aquatic species; includes insects, crustaceans, and spiders

Phylum Echinodermata marine organisms; have spiny or leathery skin and a water-vascular system with tube feet; are radially symmetrical; includes sea stars, sand dollars, and sea urchins

Phylum Chordata organisms with internal skeletons and specialized body systems; most have paired appendages; all at some time have a notochord, nerve cord, gill slits, and a post-anal tail; include fish, amphibians, reptiles, birds, and mammals

Glossary/Glosario

Multilingual eGlossary

A science multilingual glossary is available on the science website. The glossary includes the following languages.

Arabic	Hmong	Tagalog
Bengali	Korean	Urdu
Chinese	Portuguese	Vietnamese
English	Russian	
Haitian Creole	Spanish	

Cómo usar el glosario en español:

1. Busca el término en inglés que desees encontrar.
2. El término en español, junto con la definición, se encuentran en la columna de la derecha.

Pronunciation Key

Use the following key to help you sound out words in the glossary.

a	back (BAK)	**ew**	food (FEWD)
ay	day (DAY)	**yoo**	pure (PYOOR)
ah	father (FAH thur)	**yew**	few (FYEW)
ow	flower (FLOW ur)	**uh**	comma (CAH muh)
ar	car (CAR)	**u (+ con)**	rub (RUB)
e	less (LES)	**sh**	shelf (SHELF)
ee	leaf (LEEF)	**ch**	nature (NAY chur)
ih	trip (TRIHP)	**g**	gift (GIHFT)
i (i + com + e)	idea (i DEE uh)	**j**	gem (JEM)
oh	go (GOH)	**ing**	sing (SING)
aw	soft (SAWFT)	**zh**	vision (VIH zhun)
or	orbit (OR buht)	**k**	cake (KAYK)
oy	coin (COYN)	**s**	seed, cent (SEED, SENT)
oo	foot (FOOT)	**z**	zone, raise (ZOHN, RAYZ)

English — A — Español

abyssal plains/adaptation — **planos abisales/adaptación**

abyssal plains: large, flat areas of the seafloor that extend across the deepest parts of ocean basins. (p. 270)

acid precipitation: precipitation that has a lower pH than that of normal rainwater (5.6). (pp. 215, 336)

activation energy: the minimum amount of energy needed to start a chemical reaction. (p. 170)

adaptation (a dap TAY shun): an inherited trait that increases an organism's chance of surviving and reproducing in a particular environment. (p. 443)

planos abisales: áreas extensas y planas del lecho marino que se extienden por las partes más profundas de las cuencas marinas. (pág. 270)

precipitación ácida: precipitación que tiene un pH más bajo que el del agua de la lluvia normal (5.6). (pág. 215, 336)

energía de activación: cantidad mínima de energía necesaria para iniciar una reacción química. (pág. 170)

adaptación: rasgo heredado que aumenta la oportunidad de un organismo de sobrevivir y reproducirse en su medioambiente. (pág. 443)

air mass: a large area of air that has uniform temperature, humidity, and pressure. (p. 240)

masa de aire: gran área de aire que tiene temperatura, humedad y presión uniformes. (pág. 240)

air pollution: the contamination of air by harmful substances including gases and smoke. (p. 214)

polución del aire: contaminación del aire por sustancias dañinas, como gases y humo. (pág. 214)

air pressure: the pressure that a column of air exerts on the air, or a surface, below it. (p. 232)

presión del aire: presión que una columna de aire ejerce sobre el aire o sobre la superficie debajo de ella. (pág. 232)

Air Quality Index (AQI): a scale that ranks levels of ozone and other air pollutants. (p. 339)

Índice de calidad del aire (ICA): escala que clasifica los niveles de ozono y de otros contaminantes del aire. (pág. 339)

alkali (AL kuh li) metal: an element in group 1 on the periodic table. (p. 89)

metal alcalino: elemento del grupo 1 de la tabla periódica. (pág. 89)

alkaline (AL kuh lun) earth metal: an element in group 2 on the periodic table. (p. 89)

metal alcalinotérreo: elemento del grupo 2 de la tabla periódica. (pág. 89)

allele (uh LEEL): a different form of a gene. (p. 400)

alelo: forma diferente de un gen. (pág. 400)

analogous (uh NAH luh gus) structures: body parts that perform a similar function but differ in structure. (p. 451)

estructuras análogas: partes del cuerpo que ejecutan una función similar pero tienen una estructura distinta. (pág. 451)

appendage: a structure, such as a leg or an arm, that extends from the central part of the body. (p. 479)

apéndice: estructura, como una pierna o un brazo, que se prolonga de la parte central del cuerpo. (pág. 479)

asexual reproduction: a type of reproduction in which one parent organism produces off-spring without meiosis and fertilization. (p. 369)

reproducción asexual: tipo de reproducción en la cual un organismo parental produce crías sin mitosis ni fertilización. (pág. 369)

asymmetry: a body plan in which an organism cannot be divided into any two parts that are nearly mirror images. (p. 469)

asimetría: plano corporal en el cual un organismo no se puede dividir en dos partes que sean casi imágenes al espejo una de otra. (pág. 469)

atmosphere (AT muh sfihr): a thin layer of gases surrounding Earth. (p. 189)

atmósfera: capa delgada de gases que rodean la Tierra. (pág. 189)

atom: a small particle that is the building block of matter. (p. 9)

átomo: partícula pequeña que es el componente básico de la materia. (pág. 9)

atomic number: the number of protons in an atom of an element. (p. 26)

número atómico: número de protones en el átomo de un elemento. (pág. 26)

B

bilateral symmetry: a body plan in which an organism can be divided into two parts that are nearly mirror images of each other. (p. 469)

simetría bilateral: plano corporal en el cual un organismo se puede dividir en dos partes que sean casi imágenes al espejo una de otra. (pág. 469)

biological evolution: the change over time in populations of related organisms. (p. 435)

evolución biológica: cambio a través del tiempo en las poblaciones de organismos relacionados. (pág. 435)

blizzard: a violent winter storm characterized by freezing temperatures, strong winds, and blowing snow. (p. 247)

Boyle's Law: the law that pressure of a gas increases if the volume decreases and pressure of a gas decreases if the volume increases, when temperature is constant. (p. 62)

brackish water: a mix of fresh water and sea water. (p. 269)

budding: the process during which a new organism grows by mitosis and cell division on the body of its parent. (p. 371)

ventisca: tormenta violenta de invierno caracterizada por temperaturas heladas, vientos fuertes, y nieve que sopla. (pág. 247)

Ley de Boyle: ley que afirma que la presión de un gas aumenta si el volumen disminuye y que la presión de un gas disminuye si el volumen aumenta, cuando la temperatura es constante. (pág. 62)

agua salobre: mezcla de agua dulce y agua de mar. (pág. 269)

germinación: proceso durante el cual un organismo nuevo crece por medio de mitosis y división celular en el cuerpo de su progenitor. (pág. 371)

C

camouflage (KAM uh flahj): an adaptation that enables a species to blend in with its environment. (p. 444)

carrying capacity: the largest number of individuals of one species that an ecosystem can support over time. (p. 312)

cast: a fossil copy of an organism made when a mold of the organism is filled with sediment or mineral deposits. (p. 431)

catalyst: a substance that increases reaction rate by lowering the activation energy of a reaction. (p. 172)

Charles's Law: the law the volume of a gas increases with increasing temperature, if the pressure is constant. (p. 63)

chemical bond: a force that holds two or more atoms together. (p. 118)

chemical equation: a description of a reaction using element symbols and chemical formulas. (p. 154)

chemical formula: a group of chemical symbols and numbers that represent the elements and the number of atoms of each element that make up a compound. (p. 130)

chemical reaction: a process in which atoms of one or more substances rearrange to form one or more new substances. (p. 151)

camuflaje: adaptación que permite a las especies mezclarse con su medioambiente. (pág. 444)

capacidad de carga: número mayor de individuos de una especie que un medioambiente puede mantener. (pág. 312)

contramolde: copia fósil de un organismo compuesto en un molde de el organismo está lleno de sedimentos o los depósitos de minerales. (pág. 431)

catalizador: sustancia que aumenta la velocidad de reacción al disminuir la energía de activación de una reacción. (pág. 172)

Ley de Charles: ley que afirma que el volumen de un gas aumenta cuando la temperatura aumenta, si la presión es constante. (pág. 63)

enlace químico: fuerza que mantiene unidos dos o más átomos. (pág. 118)

ecuación química: descripción de una reacción con símbolos de los elementos y fórmulas químicas. (pág. 154)

fórmula química: grupo de símbolos químicos y números que representan los elementos y el número de átomos de cada elemento que forman un compuesto. (pág. 130)

reacción química: proceso en el cual átomos de una o más sustancias se acomodan para formar una o más sustancias nuevas. (pág. 151)

chordate (KOR dat): an animal that has a notochord, a nerve cord, a tail, and structures called pharyngeal pouches at some point in its life. (p. 485)

cloning: a type of asexual reproduction performed in a laboratory that produces identical individuals from a cell or a cluster of cells taken from a multicellular organism. (p. 374)

codominance: an inheritance pattern in which both alleles can be observed in a phenotype. (p. 404)

coefficient: a number placed in front of an element symbol or chemical formula in an equation. (p. 158)

combustion: a chemical reaction in which a substance combines with oxygen and releases energy. (p. 164)

comparative anatomy: the study of similarities and differences among structures of living species. (p. 450)

compound: a substance containing atoms of two or more different elements chemically bonded together. (p. 12)

computer model: detailed computer programs that solve a set of complex mathematical formulas. (p. 254)

condensation: the change of state from a gas to a liquid. (p. 54)

conduction (kuhn DUK shun): the transfer of thermal energy due to collisions between particles. (p. 201)

constants: the factors in an experiment that remain the same. (p. NOS 19)

control group: the part of a controlled experiment that contains the same factors as the experimental group, but the independent variable is not changed. (p. NOS 19)

convection: the circulation of particles within a material caused by differences in thermal energy and density. (p. 201)

coral bleaching: the loss of color in corals that occurs when stressed corals expel the colorful algae that live in them. (p. 296)

cordado: animal que en algún momento de su vida tiene notocordio, cordón nervioso, cola y estructuras llamadas bolsas faríngeas. (pág. 485)

clonación: tipo de reproducción asexual realizada en un laboratorio que produce individuos idénticos a partir de una célula o grupo de células tomadas de un organismo pluricelular. (pág. 374)

condominante: patrón heredado en el cual los dos alelos se observan en un fenotipo. (pág. 404)

coeficiente: número colocado en frente del símbolo de un elemento o de una fórmula química en una ecuación. (pág. 158)

combustión: reacción química en la cual una sustancia se combina con oxígeno y libera energía. (pág. 164)

anatomía comparativa: estudio de las similitudes y diferencias entre las estructuras de las especies vivas. (pág. 450)

compuesto: sustancia que contiene átomos de dos o más elementos diferentes unidos químicamente. (pág. 12)

modelo de computadora: programas de computadora que resuelven un conjunto de fórmulas matemáticas complejas. (pág. 254)

condensación: cambio de estado gaseoso a líquido. (pág. 54)

conducción: transferencia de energía térmica debido a colisiones entre partículas. (pág. 201)

constantes: factores que no cambian en un experimento. (pág. NOS 19)

grupo de control: parte de un experimento controlado que contiene los mismos factores que el grupo experimental, pero la variable independiente no se cambia. (pág. NOS 19)

convección: circulación de partículas en el interior de un material causada por diferencias en la energía térmica y la densidad. (pág. 201)

blanqueamiento de coral: pérdida de color en los corales que ocurre cuando los corales estresados expelen las algas de color que viven en ellos. (pág. 296)

Coriolis effect: the movement of wind and water to the right or left that is caused by Earth's rotation. (p. 286)

covalent bond: a chemical bond formed when two atoms share one or more pairs of valence electrons. (p. 127)

critical thinking: comparing what you already know with information you are given in order to decide whether you agree with it. (p. NOS 8)

efecto Coriolis: movimiento del viento y del agua a la derecha o a la izquierda causado por la rotación de la Tierra. (pág. 286)

enlace covalente: enlace químico formado cuando dos átomos comparten uno o más pares de electrones de valencia. (pág. 127)

pensamiento crítico: comparación que se hace cuando se sabe algo acerca de información nueva, y se decide si se está o no de acuerdo con ella. (pág. NOS 8)

D

decomposition: a type of chemical reaction in which one compound breaks down and forms two or more substances. (p. 163)

deforestation: the removal of large areas of forests for human purposes. (p. 317)

dependent variable: the factor a scientist observes or measures during an experiment. (p. NOS 19)

deposition: the process of changing directly from a gas to a solid. (p. 54)

description: a spoken or written summary of an observation. (p. NOS 10)

desertification: the development of desertlike conditions due to human activities and/or climate change. (p. 318)

dew point: temperature at which air is fully saturated because of decreasing temperatures while holding the amount of moisture constant. (p. 233)

diploid: a cell that has pairs of chromosomes. (p. 358)

DNA: the abbreviation for deoxyribonucleic (dee AHK sih ri boh noo klee ihk) acid, an organism's genetic material. (p. 410)

dominant (DAH muh nunt) trait: a genetic factor that blocks another genetic factor. (p. 395)

Doppler radar: a specialized type of radar that can detect precipitation as well as the movement of small particles, which can be used to approximate wind speed. (p. 252)

descomposición: tipo de reacción química en la que un compuesto se descompone y forma dos o más sustancias. (pág. 163)

deforestación: eliminación de grandes áreas de bosques con propósitos humanos. (pág. 317)

variable dependiente: factor que el científico observa o mide durante un experimento. (pág. NOS 19)

deposición: proceso de cambiar directamente de gas a sólido. (pág. 54)

descripción: resumen oral o escrito de una observación. (pág. NOS 10)

desertificación: desarrollo de condiciones parecidas a las del desierto debido a actividades humanas y/o al cambio en el clima. (pág. 318)

punto de rocío: temperatura en la cual el aire está completamente saturado debido a la disminución en las temperaturas aunque mantiene constante la cantidad de humedad. (pág. 233)

diploide: célula que tiene pares de cromosomas. (pág. 358)

ADN: abreviatura para ácido desoxirribonucleico, material genético de un organismo. (pág. 410)

rasgo dominante: factor genético que bloquea otro factor genético. (pág. 395)

radar Dopler: tipo de radar especializado que detecta tanto la precipitación como el movimiento de partículas pequeñas, que se pueden usar para determinar la velocidad aproximada del viento. (pág. 252)

double-replacement reaction: a type of chemical reaction in which the negative ions in two compounds switch places, forming two new compounds. (p. 164)

ductility (duk TIH luh tee): the ability to be pulled into thin wires. (p. 88)

reacción de sustitución doble: tipo de reacción química en la que los iones negativos de dos compuestos intercambian lugares, para formar dos compuestos nuevos. (pág. 164)

ductilidad: capacidad para formar alambres delgados. (pág. 88)

E

egg: the female reproductive, or sex, cell; forms in an ovary. (p. 357)

electron: a negatively charged particle that occupies the space in an atom outside the nucleus. (p. 24)

electron cloud: the region surrounding an atom's nucleus where one or more electrons are most likely to be found. (p. 25)

electron dot diagram: a model that represents valence electrons in an atom as dots around the element's chemical symbol. (p. 121)

element: a substance that consists of only one type of atom. (p. 11)

embryology (em bree AH luh jee): the science of the development of embryos from fertilization to birth. (p. 452)

endothermic reaction: a chemical reaction that absorbs thermal energy. (p. 169)

enzyme: a catalyst that speeds up chemical reactions in living cells. (p. 172)

evaporation: the process of a liquid changing to a gas at the surface of the liquid. (p. 54)

exoskeleton: a thick, hard outer covering; protects and supports an animal's body. (p. 479)

exothermic reaction: a chemical reaction that releases thermal energy. (p. 169)

experimental group: the part of the controlled experiment used to study relationships among variables. (p. NOS 19)

explanation: an interpretation of observations. (p. NOS 10)

extinction (ihk STINGK shun): event that occurs when the last individual organism of a species dies. (p. 434)

óvulo: célula reproductiva femenina o sexual; forma en un ovario. (pág. 357)

electrón: partícula cargada negativamente que ocupa el espacio por fuera del núcleo de un átomo. (pág. 24)

nube de electrones: región que rodea el núcleo de un átomo en donde es más probable encontrar uno o más electrones. (pág. 25)

diagrama de puntos de Lewis: modelo que representa electrones de valencia en un átomo a manera de puntos alrededor del símbolo químico del elemento. (pág. 121)

elemento: sustancia que consiste de un sólo tipo de átomo. (pág. 11)

embriología: ciencia que trata el desarrollo de embriones desde la fertilización hasta el nacimiento. (pág. 452)

reacción endotérmica: reacción química que absorbe energía térmica. (pág. 169)

enzima: catalizador que acelera reacciones químicas en las células vivas. (pág. 172)

evaporación: proceso por el cual un líquido cambia a gas en la superficie de un líquido. (pág. 54)

exoesqueleto: cubierta externa, gruesa y dura; protege y soporta el cuerpo de un animal. (pág. 479)

reacción exotérmica: reacción química que libera energía térmica. (pág. 169)

grupo experimental: parte del experimento controlado que se usa para estudiar las relaciones entre las variables. (pág. NOS 19)

explicación: interpretación de las observaciones. (pág. NOS 10)

extinción: evento que ocurre cuando el último organismo individual de una especie muere. (pág. 434)

F

fertilization (fur tuh luh ZAY shun): a reproductive process in which a sperm joins with an egg. (p. 357)

fission: cell division that forms two genetically identical cells. (p. 370)

fossil record: record of all the fossils ever discovered on Earth. (p. 429)

front: a boundary between two air masses. (p. 242)

fertilización: proceso reproductivo en el cual un espermatozoide se une con un óvulo. (pág. 357)

fisión: división celular que forma dos células genéticamente idénticas. (pág. 370)

registro fósil: registro de todos los fósiles descubiertos en la Tierra. (pág. 429)

frente: límite entre dos masas de aire. (pág. 242)

G

gas: matter that has no definite volume and no definite shape. (p. 46)

gene (JEEN): a section of DNA on a chromosome that has genetic information for one trait. (p. 400)

genetics: the study of how traits are passed from parents to offspring. (p. 389)

genotype (JEE nuh tipe): the alleles of all the genes on an organism's chromosomes; controls an organism's phenotype. (p. 400)

geologic time scale: a chart that divides Earth's history into different time units based on changes in the rocks and fossils. (p. 433)

global warming: an increase in the average temperature of Earth's surface. (p. 337)

greenhouse effect: the natural process that occurs when certain gases in the atmosphere absorb and reradiate thermal energy from the Sun. (p. 338)

group: a column on the periodic table. (p. 82)

gyre: a large circular system of ocean currents. (p. 286)

gas: materia que no tiene volumen ni forma definidos. (pág. 46)

gen: parte del ADN en un cromosoma que contiene información genética para un rasgo. (pág. 400)

genética: estudio de cómo los rasgos pasan de los padres a los hijos. (pág. 389)

genotipo: de los alelos de todos los genes en los cromosomas de un organismo, los controles de fenotipo de un organismo. (pág. 400)

escala de tiempo geológico: tabla que divide la historia de la Tierra en diferentes unidades de tiempo, basado en los cambios en las rocas y fósiles. (pág. 433)

calentamiento global: incremento en la temperatura promedio de la superficie de la Tierra. (pág. 337)

efecto invernadero: proceso natural que ocurre cuando ciertos gases en la atmósfera absorben y vuelven a irradiar la energía térmica del Sol. (pág. 338)

grupo: columna en la tabla periódica. (pág. 82)

giro: sistema circular extenso de corrientes marinas. (pág. 286)

H

halogen (HA luh jun): an element in group 17 on the periodic table. (p. 97)

haploid: a cell that has only one chromosome from each pair. (p. 359)

harmful algal bloom: explosive growth of algae that harms organisms. (p. 295)

halógeno: elemento del grupo 17 de la tabla periódica. (pág. 97)

haploide: célula que tiene solamente un cromosoma de cada par. (pág. 359)

floración de algas nocivas: crecimiento explosivo de algas dañinas para los organismos. (pág. 295)

heredity (huh REH duh tee): the passing of traits from parents to offspring. (p. 389)

herencia: paso de rasgos de los padres a los hijos. (pág. 389)

heterogeneous mixture: a mixture in which substances are not evenly mixed. (p. 25)

mezcla heterogénea: mezcla en la cual las sustancias no están mezcladas de manera uniforme. (pág. 25)

heterozygous (he tuh roh ZI gus): a genotype in which the two alleles of a gene are different. (p. 401)

heterocigoto: genotipo en el cual los dos alelos de un gen son diferentes. (pág. 401)

high-pressure system: a large body of circulating air with high pressure at its center and lower pressure outside of the system. (p. 239)

sistema de alta presión: gran cuerpo de aire circulante con presión alta en el centro y presión más baja fuera del sistema. (pág. 239)

homogeneous mixture: a mixture in which two or more substances are evenly mixed but not bonded together. (p. 16)

mezcla homogénea: mezcla en la cual dos o más sustancias están mezcladas de manera uniforme, pero no están unidas químicamente. (pág. 16)

homologous (huh MAH luh gus) chromosomes: pairs of chromosomes that have genes for the same traits arranged in the same order. (p. 358)

cromosomas homólogos: pares de cromosomas que tienen genes de iguales rasgos dispuestos en el mismo orden. (pág. 358)

homologous (huh MAH luh gus) structures: body parts of organisms that are similar in structure and position but different in function. (p. 450)

estructuras homólogas: partes del cuerpo de los organismos que son similares en estructura y posición pero diferentes en función. (pág. 450)

homozygous (hoh muh ZI gus): a genotype in which the two alleles of a gene are the same. (p. 401)

homocigoto: genotipo en el cual los dos alelos de un gen son iguales. (pág. 401)

humidity (hyew MIH duh tee): the amount of water vapor in the air. (p. 232)

humedad: cantidad de vapor de agua en el aire. (pág. 232)

hurricane: an intense tropical storm with winds exceeding 119 km/h. (p. 246)

huracán: tormenta tropical intensa con vientos que exceden los 119 km/h. (pág. 246)

hypothesis: a possible explanation for an observation that can be tested by scientific investigations. (p. NOS 4)

hipótesis: explicación posible para una observación que puede ponerse a prueba en investigaciones científicas. (pág. NOS 4)

I

incomplete dominance: an inheritance pattern in which an offspring's phenotype is a combination of the parents' phenotypes. (p. 404)

dominancia incompleta: patrón heredado en el cual el fenotipo de un hijo es una combinación de los fenotipos de los padres. (pág. 404)

independent variable: the factor that is changed by the investigator to observe how it affects a dependent variable. (p. NOS 19)

variable independiente: factor que el investigador cambia para observar cómo afecta la variable dependiente. (pág. NOS 19)

inference: a logical explanation of an observation that is drawn from prior knowledge or experience. (p. NOS 4)

inferencia: explicación lógica de una observación que se obtiene a partir de conocimiento previo o experiencia. (pág. NOS 4)

inhibitor: a substance that slows, or even stops, a chemical reaction. (p. 172)

inhibidor: sustancia que disminuye, o incluso detiene, una reacción química. (pág. 172)

International System of Units (SI): the internationally accepted system of measurement. (p. NOS 10)

Sistema Internacional de Unidades (SI): sistema de medidas aceptado internacionalmente. (pág. NOS 10)

invertebrate (ihn VUR tuh brayt): an animal that does not have a backbone. (p. 468)

invertebrado: animal que no tiene columna vertebral. (pág. 468)

ion (I ahn): an atom that is no longer neutral because it has lost or gained valence electrons. (pp. 27, 134)

ión: átomo que no es neutro porque ha ganado o perdido electrones de valencia. (pág. 27, 134)

ionic bond: the attraction between positively and negatively charged ions in an ionic compound. (p. 136)

enlace iónico: atracción entre iones cargados positiva y negativamente en un compuesto iónico. (pág. 136)

ionosphere: a region within the mesosphere and thermosphere containing ions. (p. 193)

ionosfera: región entre la mesosfera y la termosfera que contiene iones. (pág. 193)

isobar: lines that connect all places on a map where pressure has the same value. (p. 253)

isobara: línea que conectan todos los lugares en un mapa donde la presión tiene el mismo valor. (pág. 253)

isotopes (I suh tohps): atoms of the same element that have different numbers of neutrons. (p. 27)

isótopos: átomos del mismo elemento que tienen diferente número de neutrones. (pág. 27)

J

jet stream: a narrow band of high winds located near the top of the troposphere. (p. 209)

corriente de chorro: banda angosta de vientos fuertes cerca de la parte superior de la troposfera. (pág. 209)

K

kinetic energy: energy due to motion. (p. 50)

energía cinética: energía debida al movimiento. (pág. 50)

kinetic molecular theory: an explanation of how particles in matter behave. (p. 60)

teoría cinética molecular: explicación de cómo se comportan las partículas en la materia. (pág. 60)

L

land breeze: a wind that blows from the land to the sea due to local temperature and pressure differences. (p. 210)

brisa terrestre: viento que sopla desde la tierra hacia el mar debido a diferencias en la temperatura local y la presión. (pág. 210)

law of conservation of mass: law that states that the total mass of the reactants before a chemical reaction is the same as the total mass of the products after the chemical reaction. (p. 156)

ley de la conservación de la masa: ley que plantea que la masa total de los reactivos antes de una reacción química es la misma que la masa total de los productos después de la reacción química. (pág. 156)

liquid: matter with a definite volume but no definite shape. (p. 44)

líquido: materia con volumen definido y forma indefinida. (pág. 44)

low-pressure system: a large body of circulating air with low pressure at its center and higher pressure outside of the system. (p. 239)

luster: the way a mineral reflects or absorbs light at its surface. (p. 87)

sistema baja presión: gran cuerpo de aire circulante con presión baja en el centro y presión más alta fuera del sistema. (pág. 239)

brillo: forma en que un mineral refleja o absorbe la luz en su superficie. (pág. 87)

M

malleability (ma lee uh BIH luh tee): the ability of a substance to be hammered or rolled into sheets. (p. 88)

marine: a term that refers to anything related to the oceans. (p. 294)

matter: anything that has mass and takes up space. (p. 9)

meiosis: a process in which one diploid cell divides to make four haploid sex cells. (p. 359)

metal: an element that is generally shiny, is easily pulled into wires or hammered into thin sheets, and is a good conductor of electricity and thermal energy. (p. 87)

metallic bond: a bond formed when many metal atoms share their pooled valence electrons. (p. 137)

metalloid (MEH tul oyd): an element that has physical and chemical properties of both metals and nonmetals. (p. 99)

mimicry (MIH mih kree): an adaptation in which one species looks like another species. (p. 444)

mixture: matter that can vary in composition. (p. 14)

mold: the impression of an organism in a rock. (p. 431)

molecule (MAH lih kyewl): two or more atoms that are held together by covalent bonds and act as a unit. (pp. 11, 128)

mutation (myew TAY shun): a permanent change in the sequence of DNA, or the nucleotides, in a gene or a chromosome. (p. 415)

maleabilidad: capacidad de una sustancia de martillarse o laminarse para formar hojas. (pág. 88)

marino: término que se refiere a todo lo relacionado con los océanos. (pág. 294)

materia: cualquier cosa que tiene masa y ocupa espacio. (pág. 9)

meiosis: proceso en el cual una célula diploide se divide para constituir cuatro células sexuales haploides. (pág. 359)

metal: elemento que generalmente es brillante, fácilmente puede estirarse para formar alambres o martillarse para formar hojas delgadas y es buen conductor de electricidad y energía térmica. (pág. 87)

enlace metálico: enlace formado cuando muchos átomos metálicos comparten su banco de electrones de valencia. (pág. 137)

metaloide: elemento que tiene las propiedades físicas y químicas de metales y no metales. (pág. 99)

mimetismo: una adaptación en el cual una especie se parece a otra especie. (pág. 444)

mezcla: materia que puede variar en composición. (pág. 14)

molde: impresión de un organismo en una roca. (pág. 431)

molécula: dos o más átomos que están unidos mediante enlaces covalentes y actúan como una unidad. (pág. 11, 128)

mutación: cambio permanente en la secuencia de ADN, de los nucleótidos, en un gen o en un cromosoma. (pág. 415)

N

naturalist: a person who studies plants and animals by observing them. (p. 439)

naturalista: persona que estudia las plantas y los animales por medio de la observación. (pág. 439)

natural selection: the process by which organisms with variations that help them survive in their environment live longer, compete better, and reproduce more than those that do not have the variations. (p. 442)

selección natural: proceso por el cual los organismos con variaciones que las ayudan a sobrevivir en sus medioambientes viven más, compiten mejor y se reproducen más que aquellas que no tienen esas variaciones. (pág. 442)

neap tide: the lowest tidal range that occurs when Earth, the Moon, and the Sun form a right angle. (p. 281)

marea muerta: rango de marea más bajo que ocurre cuando la Tierra, la Luna y el Sol forman un ángulo recto. (pág. 281)

neutron: a neutral particle in the nucleus of an atom. (p. 24)

neutrón: partícula neutra en el núcleo de un átomo. (pág. 24)

noble gas: an element in group 18 on the periodic table. (p. 98)

gas noble: elemento del grupo 18 de la tabla periódica. (pág. 98)

nonmetal: an element that has no metallic properties. (p. 95)

no metal: elemento que tiene propiedades no metálicas. (pág. 95)

nonpoint-source pollution: pollution from several widespread sources that cannot be traced back to a single location. (p. 329)

contaminación de fuente no puntual: contaminación de varias fuentes apartadas que no se pueden rastrear hasta una sola ubicación. (pág. 329)

notochord: a flexible, rod-shaped structure that supports the body of a developing chordate. (p. 485)

notocordio: estructura flexible con forma de varilla que soporta el cuerpo de un cordado en desarrollo. (pág. 485)

nucleotide (NEW klee uh tide): a molecule made of a nitrogen base, a sugar, and a phosphate group. (p. 411)

nucelótido: molécula constituida de una base de nitrógeno, azúcar y un grupo de fosfato. (pág. 411)

nucleus: the region in the center of an atom where most of an atom's mass and positive charge is concentrated. (p. 24)

núcleo: región en el centro de un átomo donde se concentra la mayor cantidad de masa y las cargas positivas. (pág. 24)

O

observation: the act of using one or more of your senses to gather information and take note of what occurs. (p. NOS 4)

observación: acción de usar uno o más sentidos para reunir información y tomar notar de lo que ocurre. (pág. NOS 4)

ocean current: a large volume of water flowing in a certain direction. (p. 285)

corriente oceánica: gran cantidad de agua que fluye en cierta dirección. (pág. 285)

ozone layer: the area of the stratosphere with a high concentration of ozone. (p. 192)

capa de ozono: área de la estratosfera con gran concentración de ozono. (pág. 192)

P

particulate (par TIH kyuh lut) matter: the mix of both solid and liquid particles in the air. (pp. 216, 336)

partículas en suspensión: mezcla de partículas tanto sólidas como líquidas en el aire. (pág. 216, 336)

percent error: the expression of error as a percentage of the accepted value. (p. NOS 13)

error porcentual: expresión del error como porcentaje del valor aceptado. (pág. NOS 13)

period: a row on the periodic table. (p. 82)

período: hilera en la tabla periódica. (pág. 82)

periodic table: a chart of the elements arranged into rows and columns according to their physical and chemical properties. (p. 77)

phenotype (FEE nuh tipe): how a trait appears or is expressed. (p. 400)

photochemical smog: air pollution that forms from the interaction between chemicals in the air and sunlight. (pp. 215, 335)

point-source pollution: pollution from a single source that can be identified. (p. 328)

polar easterlies: cold winds that blow from the east to the west near the North Pole and South Pole. (p. 209)

polar molecule: a molecule with a slight negative charge in one area and a slight positive charge in another area. (p. 129)

polygenic inheritance: an inheritance pattern in which multiple genes determine the phenotype of a trait. (p. 405)

population: all the organisms of the same species that live in the same area at the same time. (p. 311)

precipitation: water, in liquid or solid form, that falls from the atmosphere. (p. 235)

prediction: a statement of what will happen next in a sequence of events. (p. NOS 4)

pressure: the amount of force per unit area applied to an object's surface. (p. 61)

product: a substance produced by a chemical reaction. (p. 155)

proton: a positively charged particle in the nucleus of an atom. (p. 24)

Punnett square: a model that is used to show the probability of all possible genotypes and phenotypes of offspring. (p. 402)

tabla periódica: cuadro en que los elementos están organizados en hileras y columnas según sus propiedades físicas y químicas. (pág. 77)

fenotipo: forma como aparece o se expresa un rasgo. (pág. 400)

smog fotoquímico: polución del aire que se forma de la interacción entre los químicos en el aire y la luz solar. (pág. 215, 335)

contaminación de fuente puntual: contaminación de una sola fuente que se puede identificar. (pág. 328)

brisas polares: vientos fríos que soplan del este al oeste cerca del Polo Norte y del Polo Sur. (pág. 209)

molécula polar: molécula con carga ligeramente negativa en una parte y ligeramente positiva en otra. (pág. 129)

herencia poligénica: patrón de herencia en el cual genes múltiples determinan el fenotipo de un rasgo. (pág. 405)

población: todos los organismos de la misma especie que viven en la misma área al mismo tiempo. (pág. 311)

precipitación: agua, de forma líquida o sólida, que cae de la atmósfera. (pág. 235)

predicción: afirmación de lo que ocurrirá después en una secuencia de eventos. (pág. NOS 4)

presión: cantidad de fuerza por unidad de área aplicada a la superficie de un objeto. (pág. 61)

producto: sustancia producida por una reacción química. (pág. 155)

protón: partícula cargada positivamente en el núcleo de un átomo. (pág. 24)

cuadro de Punnett: modelo que se utiliza para demostrar la probabilidad de que todos los genotipos y fenotipos posibles de cría. (pág. 402)

Q

qualitative data: the use of words to describe what is observed in an experiment. (p. NOS 19)

quantitative data: the use of numbers to describe what is observed in an experiment. (p. NOS 19)

datos cualitativos: uso de palabras para describir lo que se observa en un experimento. (pág. NOS 19)

datos cuantitativos: uso de números para describir lo que se observa en un experimento. (pág. NOS 19)

Science Skill Handbook
Math Skill Handbook
Foldables Handbook
Reference Handbook
Glossary/Glosario
Index

R

radial symmetry: a body plan in which an organism can be divided into two parts that are nearly mirror images of each other anywhere through its central axis. (p. 469)

simetría radial: plano corporal en el cual un organismo se puede dividir en dos partes para que sean casi imágenes al espejo una de la otra, en cualquier parte del eje axial. (pág. 469)

radiation: the transfer of thermal energy by electromagnetic waves. (p. 198)

radiación: transferencia de energía térmica mediante ondas electromagnéticas. (pág. 198)

reactant: a starting substance in a chemical reaction. (p. 155)

reactivo: sustancia inicial en una reacción química. (pág. 155)

recessive (rih SE sihv) trait: a genetic factor that is blocked by the presence of a dominant factor. (p. 395)

rasgo recesivo: factor genético boqueado por la presencia de un factor dominante. (pág. 395)

reclamation: a process in which mined land must be recovered with soil and replanted with vegetation. (p. 322)

recuperación: proceso por el cual las tierras explotadas se deben recubrir con suelo y se deben replantar con vegetación. (pág. 322)

reforestation: process of planting trees to replace trees that have been cut or burned down. (p. 322)

reforestación: proceso de siembra de árboles para reemplazar los árboles que se han cortado o quemado. (pág. 322)

regeneration: a type of asexual reproduction that occurs when an offspring grows from a piece of its parent. (p. 372)

regeneración: tipo de reproducción asexual que ocurre cuando un organismo se origina de una parte de su progenitor. (pág. 372)

relative humidity: the amount of water vapor present in the air compared to the maximum amount of water vapor the air could contain at that temperature. (p. 233)

humedad relativa: cantidad de vapor de agua presente en el aire comparada con la cantidad máxima de vapor de agua que el aire podría contener en esa temperatura. (pág. 233)

replication: the process of copying a DNA molecule to make another DNA molecule. (p. 412)

replicación: proceso por el cual se copia una molécula de ADN para hacer otra molécula de ADN. (pág. 412)

RNA: ribonucleic acid, a type of nucleic acid that carries the code for making proteins from the nucleus to the cytoplasm. (p. 413)

ARN: ácido ribonucleico, un tipo de ácido nucléico que contiene el código para hacer proteínas del núcleo para el citoplasma. (pág. 413)

S

salinity: a measure of the mass of dissolved salts in a mass of water. (p. 269)

salinidad: medida de la masa de sales disueltas en una masa de agua. (pág. 269)

science: the investigation and exploration of natural events and of the new information that results from those investigations. (p. NOS 2)

ciencia: investigación y exploración de eventos naturales y la información nueva que resulta de dichas investigaciones. (pág. NOS 2)

scientific law: a rule that describes a pattern in nature. (p. NOS 7)

ley científica: regla que describe un patrón en la naturaleza. (pág. NOS 7)

scientific literacy: having knowledge of scientific concepts and being able to use that knowledge in your everyday life. (p. NOS 8)

scientific notation: a method of writing or displaying very small or very large numbers. (p. NOS 13)

scientific theory: an explanation of observations or events that is based on knowledge gained from many observations and investigations. (p. NOS 7)

sea breeze: a wind that blows from the sea to the land due to local temperature and pressure differences. (p. 210)

sea level: the average level of the ocean's surface at any given time. (p. 280)

seawater: water from a sea or ocean that has an average salinity of 35 ppt. (p. 269)

selective breeding: the selection and breeding of organisms for desired traits. (p. 445)

semiconductor: a substance that conducts electricity at high temperatures but not at low temperatures. (p. 99)

sexual reproduction: type of reproduction in which the genetic material from two different cells—a sperm and an egg—combine, producing an offspring. (p. 357)

single-replacement reaction: a type of chemical reaction in which one element replaces another element in a compound. (p. 164)

solid: matter that has a definite shape and a definite volume. (p. 43)

sperm: a male reproductive, or sex, cell; forms in a testis. (p. 357)

spring tide: the largest tidal range that occurs when Earth, the Moon, and the Sun form a straight line. (p. 281)

stability: whether circulating air motions will be strong or weak. (p. 202)

stratosphere (STRA tuh sfihr): the atmospheric layer directly above the troposphere. (p. 192)

sublimation: the process of changing directly from a solid to a gas. (p. 54)

saber científico: tener conocimiento de conceptos científicos y ser capaz de usarlo en la vida diaria. (pág. NOS 8)

notación científica: método para escribir o expresar números muy pequeños o muy grandes. (pág. NOS 13)

teoría científica: explicación de las observaciones y los eventos basada en conocimiento obtenido en muchas observaciones e investigaciones. (pág. NOS 7)

brisa marina: viento que sopla del mar hacia la tierra debido a diferencias en la temperatura local y la presión. (pág. 210)

nivel del mar: promedio del nivel de la superficie del océano en algún momento dado. (pág. 280)

agua de mar: agua del mar o del océano que tiene una salinidad promedio de 35 ppt. (pág. 269)

cría selectiva: selección y la cría de organismos para las características deseadas. (pág. 445)

semiconductor: sustancia que conduce electricidad a altas temperaturas, pero no a bajas temperaturas. (pág. 99)

reproducción sexual: tipo de reproducción en la cual el material genético de dos células diferentes de un espermatozoide y un óvulo se combinan, produciendo una cría. (pág. 357)

reacción de sustitución sencilla: tipo de reacción química en la que un elemento reemplaza a otro en un compuesto. (pág. 164)

sólido: materia con forma y volumen definidos. (pág. 43)

esperma: célula reproductora masculina o sexual; forma en un testículo. (pág. 357)

marea de primavera: rango de marea más alto que ocurre cuando la Tierra, la Luna y el Sol forman una línea recta. (pág. 281)

estabilidad: condición en la que los movimientos del aire circulante pueden ser fuertes o débiles. (pág. 202)

estratosfera: capa atmosférica justo arriba de la troposfera. (pág. 192)

sublimación: proceso de cambiar directamente de sólido a gas. (pág. 54)

substance: matter with a composition that is always the same. (p. 10)

surface report: a description of a set of weather measurements made on Earth's surface. (p. 251)

surface tension: the uneven forces acting on the particles on the surface of a liquid. (p. 45)

synthesis (SIHN thuh sus): a type of chemical reaction in which two or more substances combine and form one compound. (p. 163)

sustancia: materia cuya composición es siempre la misma. (pág. 10)

informe de superficie: descripción de un conjunto de mediciones del tiempo realizadas en la superficie de la Tierra. (pág. 251)

tensión superficial: fuerzas desiguales que actúan sobre las partículas en la superficie de un líquido. (pág. 45)

síntesis: tipo de reacción química en el que dos o más sustancias se combinan y forman un compuesto. (pág. 163)

T

technology: the practical use of scientific knowledge, especially for industrial or commercial use. (p. NOS 6)

temperature: the measure of the average kinetic energy of the particles in a material. (p. 50)

temperature inversion: a temperature increase as altitude increases in the troposphere. (p. 203)

thermal energy: the sum of the kinetic energy and the potential energy of the particles that make up an object. (p. 51)

tidal range: the difference in water level between a high tide and a low tide. (p. 280)

tide: the periodic rise and fall of the ocean's surface caused by gravitational force between Earth and the Moon, and Earth and the Sun. (p. 280)

tornado: a violent, whirling column of air in contact with the ground. (p. 245)

trace fossil: the preserved evidence of the activity of an organism. (p. 431)

trade winds: steady winds that flow from east to west between 30°N latitude and 30°S latitude. (p. 209)

transcription: the process of making mRNA from DNA. (p. 413)

transition element: an element in groups 3–12 on the periodic table. (p. 90)

translation: the process of making a protein from RNA. (p. 414)

troposphere (TRO puh sfihr): the atmospheric layer closest to Earth's surface. (p. 192)

tecnología: uso práctico del conocimiento científico, especialmente para empleo industrial o comercial. (pág. NOS 6)

temperatura: medida de la energía cinética promedio de las partículas de un material. (pág. 50)

inversión de temperatura: aumento de la temperatura en la troposfera a medida que aumenta la altitud. (pág. 203)

energía térmica: suma de la energía cinética y potencial de las partículas que forman un objeto. (pág. 51)

rango de marea: diferencia en el nivel de agua entre una marea alta y una marea baja. (pág. 280)

marea: ascenso y descenso periódico de la superficie del océano causados por la fuerza gravitacional entre la Tierra y la Luna, y la Tierra y el Sol. (pág. 280)

tornado: columna de aire violenta y rotativa en contacto con el suelo. (pág. 245)

traza fósil: evidencia conservada de la actividad de un organismo. (pág. 431)

vientos alisios: vientos constantes que soplan del este al oeste entre 30°N de latitud y 30°S de latitud. (pág. 209)

transcripción: proceso por el cual se hace mARN de ADN. (pág. 413)

elemento de transición: elemento de los grupos 3–12 de la tabla periódica. (pág. 90)

traslación: proceso por el cual se hacen proteínas a partir de ARN. (pág. 414)

troposfera: capa atmosférica más cercana a la Tierra. (pág. 192)

tsunami: a wave that forms when an ocean disturbance suddenly moves a large volume of water. (p. 279)

tsunami: ola que se forma cuando una alteración en el océano mueve repentinamente una gran cantidad de agua. (pág. 279)

U

upper-air report: a description of wind, temperature, and humidity conditions above Earth's surface. (p. 251)

upwelling: the vertical movement of water toward the ocean's surface. (p. 287)

urban sprawl: the development of land for houses and other buildings near a city. (p. 320)

informe del aire superior: descripción de las condiciones del viento, de la temperatura y de la humedad por encima de la superficie de la Tierra. (pág. 251)

surgencia: movimiento vertical del agua hacia la superficie del océano. (pág. 287)

expansión urbana: urbanización de tierra para viviendas y otras construcciones cerca de la ciudad. (pág. 320)

V

valence electron: the outermost electron of an atom that participates in chemical bonding. (p. 120)

vapor: the gas state of a substance that is normally a solid or a liquid at room temperature. (p. 46)

vaporization: the change in state from a liquid to a gas. (p. 53)

variable: any factor that can have more than one value. (p. NOS 19)

variation (ver ee AY shun): a slight difference in an inherited trait among individual members of a species. (p. 441)

vegetative reproduction: a form of asexual reproduction in which offspring grow from a part of a parent plant. (p. 373)

vertebrate (VUR tuh brayt): an animal with a backbone. (p. 468)

vestigial (veh STIH jee ul) structure: body part that has lost its original function through evolution. (p. 451)

viscosity (vihs KAW sih tee): a measurement of a liquid's resistance to flow. (p. 44)

electrón de valencia: electrón más externo de un átomo que participa en el enlace químico. (pág. 120)

vapor: estado gaseoso de una sustancia que normalmente es sólida o líquida a temperatura ambiente. (pág. 46)

vaporización: cambio de estado líquido a gaseoso. (pág. 53)

variable: cualquier factor que tenga más de un valor. (pág. NOS 19)

variación: ligera diferencia en un rasgo hereditario entre los miembros individuales de una especie. (pág. 441)

reproducción vegetativa: forma de reproducción asexual en la cual el organismo se origina a partir de una planta parental. (pág. 373)

vertebrado: animal con columna vertebral. (pág. 468)

estructura vestigial: parte del cuerpo que a través de la evolución perdió la función original. (pág. 451)

viscosidad: medida de la resistencia de un líquido a fluir. (pág. 44)

water cycle: the series of natural processes by which water continually moves throughout the hydrosphere. (p. 235)

water vapor: water in its gaseous form. (p. 190)

ciclo del agua: serie de procesos naturales por los que el cual el agua se mueve continuamente en toda la hidrosfera. (pág. 235)

vapor de agua: agua en forma gaseosa. (pág. 190)

weather: the atmospheric conditions, along with short-term changes, of a certain place at a certain time. (p. 231)

westerlies: steady winds that flow from west to east between latitudes 30°N and 60°N, and 30°S and 60°S. (p. 209)

wind: the movement of air from areas of high pressure to areas of low pressure. (p. 207)

tiempo atmosférico: condiciones atmosféricas, junto con cambios a corto plazo, de un lugar determinado a una hora determinada. (pág. 231)

vientos del oeste: vientos constantes que soplan de oeste a este entre latitudes 30° N y 60° N, y 30° S y 60° S. (pág. 209)

viento: movimiento del aire desde áreas de alta presión hasta áreas de baja presión. (pág. 207)

Z

zygote (ZI goht): the new cell that forms when a sperm cell fertilizes an egg cell. (p. 357)

zigoto: célula nueva que se forma cuando un espermatozoide fecunda un óvulo. (pág. 357)

Index

Italic numbers = illustration/photo **Bold numbers = vocabulary term**
lab = indicates entry is used in a lab on this page

A

H

I

N

Credits

339 Nancy Ney/Getty Images; **340** (l)Toru Hanai/Reuters/CORBIS, (r)AP Images; **341** (t)Getty Images, (b)AP Images; **342** (t to b)(2)Macmillan/McGraw-Hill, (3)Hutchings Photography/Digital Light Source, (4)(5)(6)Macmillan/McGraw-Hill, (7)Hutchings Photography/Digital Light Source, (8)The Mcgraw-Hill Companies; **343** Mark Scheuern/Alamy; **344** (t)Doug Menuez/Getty Images, (b)AP Images; **347** Grant Faint/Getty Images; **352** (t)Wayne R Bilenduke/Getty Images; **354–355** Bill Coster/Getty Images; **356** Science Pictures Ltd./Photo Researchers; **357** Hutchings Photography/Digital Light Source; **360–361** Ed Reschke/Peter Arnold, Inc.; **362** (t)(c)Nature's Images/Photo Researchers, (b)Jeremy West/Getty Images; **364** (l)Rob Walls/Alamy, (r)Nigel Cattlin/Alamy; **365** (tl)Stockbyte/Getty Images, (tr)Craig Lovell/CORBIS, (c)Piotr & Irena Kolasa/Alamy, (bl)image100/SuperStock, (br)Wally Eberhart/Visuals Unlimited/Getty Images; **366** Bill Coster/Getty Images; **367** (bl)Greg Broussard, (bkgd) David Thompson/Photolibrary; **368** Dr. Brad Mogen/Visuals Unlimited; **369** Horizons Companies; **370** CNRI/Photo Researchers; **371** Biophoto Associates/Photo Researchers; **373** (l)sciencephotos/Alamy, (t)Wally Eberhart/Visuals Unlimited, (r)DEA/G.CIGOLINI/Getty Images, (b)Jerome Wexler/Photo Researchers; **375** Roslin Institute; **376** Mark Steinmetz; **377** (t)Dr. Brad Mogen/Visuals Unlimited, (c)Roslin Institute (b)Mark Steinmetz, **378–379** Hutchings Photography/Digital Light Source; **380** (t)Science Pictures Ltd./Photo Researchers, (b)CNRI/Photo Researchers; **383** Bill Coster/Getty Images; **386–387** Tom and Pat Leeson; **388** Nigel Cattlin/Visuals Unlimited; **389** (cr)Getty Images, (bl)(br)The McGraw-Hill Companies; **390** Wally Eberhart/Visuals Unlimited; **392** DEA PICTURE LIBRARY/Photolibrary; **393** (l)DEA PICTURE LIBRARY/Photolibrary, (r)WILDLIFE/Peter Arnold, Inc.; **396** (t)Tom and Pat Leesson, (bl)DEA PICTURE LIBRARY/Photolibrary, (br)WILDLIFE/Peter Arnold, Inc.; **397** (t)Pixtal/age Fotostock, (c)World History Archive/age Fotostock, (b)Tek Image/Photo Researchers, (bkgd)Jason Reed/Getty Images; **398** (l to r, t to b)Getty Images, (2)Getty Images, (3)Punchstock, (4)CORBIS, (5)(6)(7)(8)(9)Getty Images, (10)CMCD/Getty Images, (11)(12)CORBIS; **399** (t)Richard Hutchings/Digital Light Source; **400** (b)Biophoto Associates/Photo Researchers; **401** (t)Martin Shields/Photo Researchers, (b)Martin Shields/Photo Researchers; **403** (l)Maya Barnes/The Image Works, (r)Bill Aron/PhotoEdit, **404** (l)Peter Smithers/CORBIS, (tr)Geoff Bryant/Photo Researchers, (c)Bill Ross/CORBIS, (bl)J. Schwanke/Alamy, (bc)(br)Yann Arthus-Bertrand/CORBIS; **405** Chris Clinton/Getty Images; **406** (tl)Picture Net/Corbis, (tr)June Green/Alamy Images, (c)Carolyn A. McKeone/Photo Researchers, (bl)(br)Hania Arensten-Berdys/www.gardensafari.net; **407** Chris Clinton/Getty Images; **408** (l)(r)Kristina Yu/Exploratorium Store; **409** PHOTOTAKE Inc./Alamy, (tl)Geoff du Feu/Alamy, (tr)Ken Karp/McGraw-Hill Companies, (cl)Glow Images/Getty Images; **410–418** Hutchings Photography/Digital Light Source; **419** (tl)Hutchings Photography/Digital Light Source, (tr)The McGraw-Hill Companies, (bl);(br)Hutchings Photography/Digital Light Source; **420** DEA PICTURE LIBRARY/Photolibrary, (cl)WILDLIFE/Peter Arnold, Inc; **423** Tom and Pat Leesson; **426–427** William Osborn/Minden Pictures; **428** Florida Museum of Natural History photo by Eric Zamora © 2008; **429** Hutchings Photography/Digital Light Source; **430** (l)B.A.E. Inc./Alamy, (r)The Natural History Museum/Alamy; **431** (l)Mark Steinmetz, (c)Tom Bean/CORBIS, (r)Dorling Kindersely/Getty Images; **435** Hutchings Photography/Digital Light Source; **436** Dorling Kindersely/Getty Images; **437** Getty Images, (t)Ryan McVay/Getty Images, (c)C Squared Studios/Getty Images, (b)Richard Broadwell/Alamy, (2)Tim O'Hara/Corbis, C Squared Studios/Getty Images; **438** DLILLC/CORBIS; **439** Hutchings Photography/Digital Light Source; **440** (l)Jeffrey Greenberg/Photo Researchers, (c)David Hosking/Alamy, (r)Mark Jones/Photolibrary; **441** Chip Clark; **443** (l)Carey Alan & Sandy/Photolibrary, (c)Robert Shantz/Alamy, (r)Stan Osolinski/Photolibrary; **444** (l)Paul Sutherland/National Geographic/Getty Images, (t)NHPA/Photoshot, (r)Kay Nietfeld/dpa/CORBIS, (b)Mitsuhiko Imamori/Minden Pictures; **445** (l)ARCO/D. Usher/age Fotostock, (t)Photodisc/Getty Images, (r)Joe Blossom/NHPA/Photoshot, (b)Hutchings Photo[illegible] Light Source, Joseph Van Os/Getty Images; **446** (t)Mark [illegible]brary, (tc)Chip Clar, (b)Don Mammoser/Bruce Coleman, Inc./P[illegible] Paul Sutherland/National Geographic/Getty Images; **447** (t)D[illegible]er-Cook, (b)B. Rosemary Grant/AP Images, (bkgd)Skan9/Ge[illegible] **448** Joseph Van Os/Getty Images; **449** Hutchings Photography/D[illegible] Source; **454** T. Daeschler/The Academy of Natural Sciences/VIREO; [illegible]GS, (br)Mary Plage/Photolibrary, (t to b)Hutchings Photograp[illegible] Light Source, (2)(3)(4)Macmillan/McGraw-Hill, (5)Richard Hutc[illegible] Digital Light Source); **458** Mark Steinmetz]; **461** William Osbor[illegible]n Pictures; **464–465** Gary Bell/Getty Images; **466** Darrell Gulin/Getty [illegible]; **467** (t)Hutchings Photography/Digital Light Source, (b)John Canc[illegible]Alamy; **468** Geoff Brightling/Getty Images; **469** (l)Brand X Pictures/Pu[illegible]tock; (c)Paul Nicklen/National Geographic/Getty Images; (r)To[illegible]/Tom Stack & Associates; **470** (c)Francesco Rovero, (b)Frank Gree[illegible]Getty Images; **472** (t)John Cancalosi/Alamy, (b)Paul Nicklen/Nat[illegible] Geographic/Getty Images; **473** (c)The McGraw-Hill Companies/Barry [illegible]er, photographer, (inset)N. Simmons/American Museum of Nat[illegible] History, (bkgd)age fotostock/SuperStock; **474** Matthew Oldfield, Scubazoo/Photo Researchers; **475** Hutchings Photography/Digital Light Source; **477** (t)James H Robinson/Photo Researchers, (b)Sinclair Stammers/Photo Researchers; **478** (t)Ingram Publishing/Alamy, (b)Doug Perrine/SeaPics.com; **480** (t)Ingram Publishing/Alamy, (c)Hutchings Photography/Digital Light Source, (b)Jeremy Woodhouse/Getty Images; **482** (t)Ingram Publishing/Alamy, (b)Jeremy Woodhouse/Getty Images; **483** (l to r, t to b)C Squared Studios/Getty Images, (1)Siede Preis/Getty Images, (2)Brand X Pictures/PunchStock, (3)John Foxx/Alamy, (4)Photodisc/Getty Images, (5)Creatas/PunchStock, (6)Hutchings Photography/Digital Light Source, (7)Siede Preis/Getty Images, (8)Brand X Pictures/PunchStock, (9)Siede Preis/Getty Images; **484** FRANS LANTING/National Geographic Stock; **485** Hutchings Photography/Digital Light Source; **486** Pacific Stock/SuperStock; **488** (inset)Daniel Heuclin/NHPA/Photoshot, (bkgd)JH Pete Carmichael/Getty Images; **490** Steve Kaufman/CORBIS; **491** (t)Daniel Heuclin/NHPA/Photoshot, (c)Steve Kaufman/CORBIS, (b)Dave Watts/Tom Stack & Associates; **492** (t)(c)Macmillan/McGraw-Hill, (b)Hutchings Photography/Digital Light Source; **493** Hutchings Photography/Digital Light Source; **494** (t)John Cancalosi/Alamy, (b)Doug Perrine/SeaPics.com; **496** (l)Frederic Pacorel/Getty Images, (r)IT Stock Free/Alamy; **497** (l)Ingram Publishing/Alamy, (c)David Fleetham/Visuals Unlimited/Getty Images, (r)Gary Bell/Getty Images; **SR-0–SR-1** (bkgd)Gallo Images - Neil Overy/Getty Images; **SR-2** Hutchings Photography/Digital Light Source; **SR-6** Michell D. Bridwell/PhotoEdit; **SR-7** (t)The McGraw-Hill Companies, (b)Dominic Oldershaw; **SR-8** StudiOhio; **SR-9** Timothy Fuller; **SR-10** Aaron Haupt; **SR-12** KS Studios; **SR-13–SR-47** Matt Meadows; **SR-48** Stephen Durr, (c)NIBSC/Photo Researchers, Inc., (r)Science VU/Drs. D.T. John & T.B. Cole/Visuals Unlimited, Inc.; **SR-49** (t)Mark Steinmetz, (r)Andrew Syred/Science Photo Library/Photo Researchers, (br)Rich Brommer; **SR-50** David Fleetham/Visuals Unlimited/Getty Images, (l)Lynn Keddie/Photolibrary; (tr)G.R. Roberts; **SR-51** Gallo Images/CORBIS.

Credits

McGraw-Hill, (7)(8) Hutchings Photography/Di [illegible] ce, (9)Macmillan/McGraw-Hill; 141 Hutchings Ph [illegible] tal Light Source; 145 altrendo images/Getty Images; [illegible] d) Anton Luhr/ Photolibrary; 150 Darwin Dale/Photo Resea [illegible] 154; 151 Hutchings Photography/Digital Light Sourc [illegible] alty-Free/CORBIS, (tr)Charles D. Winters/Photo Researchers, I [illegible] on Scientific Films/ photolibrary.com, (cr)sciencephotos/Alam [illegible] X Pictures, (br)Dante Fenolio/Photo Researchers, Inc.; 155 Hut [illegible] tography/Digital Light Source; 156 Hutchings Photography/Dig [illegible] Source; 160 The McGraw-Hill Companies; 161 sciencephotos/Ala [illegible] AP Photo/Greg Campbell; 163 (t)Charles D. Winters/Photo Resea [illegible] Inc., (b)The McGraw-Hill Companies, Inc./Jacques Cornell photo [illegible] her, (t)The McGraw-Hill Companies, Inc./Stephen Frisch, phot [illegible] (c)sciencephotos/Alamy, (b)Park Dale/Alamy; 165 The McGraw [illegible] Companies, Inc./Stephen Frisch, photographer; 166 Joel Sartore/N [illegible] Geographic/Getty Images; 167 Brand X Pictures/PunchStock; [illegible] McGraw-Hill Companies, (tc)Brand X Pictures/PunchSt [illegible] (tr)Tet [illegible] Images/Getty Images, (bl)The McGraw-Hill Companies, (bc [illegible] alty-Free/CORBIS, (br)Alexis Grattier/Getty Images; 172 Hutchings Photography/Digital Light Source; 174 (t to b)(2)Hutchings Photography/Digital Light Source, (3)(4)Macmillan/McGraw-Hill, (5)Hutchings Photography/Digital Light Source; 175 Hutchings Photography/Digital Light Source; 176 Park Dale/Alamy; 179 Anton Luhr/ Photolibrary; 186–187 Daniel H. Bailey/Alamy; 187 (t to b)James Brunker/ Alamy; 187 (3)CORBIS, (4)MICHAEL S. YAMASHITA/National Geographic Image Collection; 188 CORBIS; 189–190 Hutchings Photography/Digital Light Source; 191 (t)PhotoLink/Getty Images, (b)C. Sherburne/PhotoLink/ Getty Images; 193 Per Breiehagen/Getty Images; 194 CORBIS; 195 (t)PhotoLink/Getty Images, (l)Per Breiehagen/Getty Images, (r)Hutchings Photography/Digital Light Source; 196 (t)American Museum of Natural History, (b)Pedro Guzman, (bkgd)PhotoLink/Getty Images; 197 John King/ Alamy; 198 Hutchings Photography/Digital Light Source; 199 Eric James/ Alamy; 202 (t)C. Sherburne/PhotoLink/Getty Images, (b)James Brunker/ Alamy; 204 Eric James/Alamy; 205 (r)(t to b)Hutchings Photography/Digital Light Source, (2)Macmillan/McGraw-Hill, (3)(4)(5)(6)(7)Hutchings Photography/Digital Light Source, (8)Macmillan/McGraw-Hill, (9)(10)(11) Hutchings Photography/Digital Light Source; 206 Lester Lefkowitz/Getty Images; 207 Hutchings Photography/Digital Light Source; 209 (t)CORBIS, (b)Hutchings Photography/Digital Light Source; 211 Lester Lefkowitz/Getty Images; 212 (t to b)(2)Hutchings Photography/Digital Light Source, (3)(4)Macmillan/McGraw-Hill, (5)Hutchings Photography/Digital Light Source; 213 Reuters/CORBIS; 214 C. Sherburne/PhotoLink/Getty Images; 215 MICHAEL S. YAMASHITA/National Geographic Image Collection; 218 (t to b)Digital Vision Ltd./SuperStock, (2)Masterfile, (3)Creatas/PictureQuest, (4)C. Sherburne/PhotoLink/Getty Images; 219 (t)C. Sherburne/PhotoLink/ Getty Images, (b)MICHAEL S. YAMASHITA/National Geographic Image Collection; 220 (r)(t to b)Hutchings Photography/Digital Light Source, (2)Macmillan/McGraw-Hill, (3)Hutchings Photography/Digital Light Source, (4)Macmillan/McGraw-Hill, (5)(6)(7)(8)(9)Hutchings Photography/Digital Light Source; 221 Hutchings Photography/Digital Light Source; 222 (t)PhotoLink/Getty Images, (b)C. Sherburne/PhotoLink/Getty Images; 224 supershoot/Alamy; 225 Daniel H. Bailey/Alamy; 228–229 George Frey/ Getty Images; 230 Peter de Clercq/Alamy; 231 Hutchings Photography/ Digital Light Source; 232 (l)Jan Tadeusz/Alamy, (r)matthias engelien/ Alamy; 234 (l)WIN-Initiative/Getty Images; 236 (t)WIN-Initiative/Getty Images, (c)MIMOTITO/Getty Images, (r)age fotostock/SuperStock, (b)Jan Tadeusz/Alamy; 237 (t)NASA/Jeff Schmaltz, MODIS Land Rapid Response Team, (b)Jocelyn Augustino/FEMA; 238 Kyle Niemi/U.S. Coast Guard via Getty Images; 239–241 Hutchings Photography/Digital Light Source; 244 (l)Amazon-Images/Alamy, (c)Roger Coulam/Alamy, (r)mediacolor's/Alamy; 245 Eric Nguyen/CORBIS; 246 StockTrek/Getty Images; 247 AP Photo/Dick Blume, Syracuse Newspapers; 248 Eric Nguyen/CORBIS; 250 Gene Rhoden/ Visuals Unlimited; 251 Hutchings Photography/Digital Light Source; 252 National Oceanic and Atmospheric Administration (NOAA); 254 Dennis MacDonald/Alamy; 255 (t)National Oceanic and Atmospheric Administration (NOAA); 255 (b)Dennis MacDonald/Alamy; 256 (t to b) Aaron Haupt, (2)(3)(4)(5)Hutchings Photography/Digital Light Source; 258 (t)Peter de Clercq/Alamy, (c)AP Photo/Dick Blume, Syracuse Newspapers, (b)matthias engelien/Alamy; 261 George Frey/Getty Images; 264–265 Frank Krahmer/Getty Images; 266 DAVID DOUBILET/National Geographic Stock; 267 (t)Hutchings Photography/Digital Light Source, (b)Image by Reto Stockli, NASA/Goddard Space Flight Center. Enhancements by Robert Simmon.; 268 (t)Steve Kaufman/CORBIS, (b)Pixtal/SuperStock; 269 Hutchings Photography/Digital Light Source; 271 (t)Arnulf Husmo/Getty Images, (c)KAZUHIRO NOGI/AFP/Getty Images, (b)Peter Ryan/Photo Researchers, Inc.; 272 (tl)Guillen Photography/UW/USA/Gulf of Mexico/ Alamy, (tr)David Fleetham/Getty Images, (b)Brandon Cole Marine Photography/Alamy; 274 (t)Steve Kaufman/CORBIS, (b)Brandon Cole Marine Photography/Alamy; 275 (c)Susan Humphris, (r)American Museum of Natural History, (bkgd)Ralph White/CORBIS; 276 Brian Bielmann; 277 Hutchings Photography/Digital Light Source; 280–282 Bill Brooks/Alamy; 284 (inset) NASA, (bkgd) Jacques Descloitres, MODIS Rapid Response Team, NASA/GSFC; 285 (t)Hutchings Photography/Digital Light Source, (b)Peter Sterling/Getty Images; 289 Hutchings Photography/Digital Light Source; 291 (t)Hutchings Photography/Digital Light Source, (c)(b)The McGraw-Hill Companies, Inc./Jill Braaten, photographer; 292 Chris Cheadle/age fotostock; 293 T. O'Keefe/PhotoLink/Getty Images; 294 (t)Matt Cramer, (b)NASA; 295 (tl)LOOK Die Bildagentur der Fotografen GmbH/Alamy, (tr)Visuals Unlimited/CORBIS, (b)JLP/CORBIS; 296 (tl)Darryl Leniuk/Getty Images, (b)Timothy G. Laman/National Geographic/Getty Images; 297 (t)Steve Allen/Brand X/CORBIS, (b)National Geographic Society; 298 STEVE GSCHMEISSNER/SCIENCE PHOTO LIBRARY; 299 (tl)JLP/CORBIS, (cl)Timothy G. Laman/National Geographic/Getty Images, (bl)STEVE GSCHMEISSNER/ SCIENCE PHOTO LIBRARY, (br)Steve Allen/Brand X/CORBIS; 300 (t to b) Macmillan/McGraw-Hill, (2)Heimir Harðar/Peter Arnold Inc., (3)Biospho to/ Swann Christopher/Peter Arnold Inc., (4)FLIP NICKLIN/MINDEN PICTURES/ National Geographic Stock, (5)Digital Vision/PunchStock; 301 PATRICIO ROBLES GIL/MINDEN PICTURES/National Geographic Stock; 302 (t)DAVID DOUBILET/National Geographic Stock, (cl)Jacques Descloitres, MODIS Rapid Response Team, NASA/GSFC, (cr)Brian Bielmann, (b)Timothy G. Laman/ National Geographic/Getty Images; 304 Bill Brooks/Alamy; 305 Frank Krahmer/Getty Images; 308–309 Grant Faint/Getty Images; 310 Data courtesy Marc Imhoff of NASA GSFC and Christopher Elvidge of NOAA NGDC. Image by Craig Mayhew and Robert Simmon, NASA; 311 (t)Hutchings Photography/Digital Light Source, (b)Douglas McLaughlin; 313 Jeff Greenberg/Alamy; 314 (t)Douglas McLaughlin, (b)Jeff Greenberg/Alamy; 315 Hutchings Photography/Digital Light Source; 316 Jason Hawkes/ CORBIS; 317 (t)Hutchings Photography/Digital Light Source, (b)Steven Weinberg/Getty Images; 319 (t)Beth Wald/Getty Images, (b)Hutchings Photography/Digital Light Source; 320 (l)Aerial Photography Copyright Province of Nova Scotia, (r)Aerial Photography Copyright Province of Nova Scotia; 322 (t)Karl Weatherly/Getty Images, (bl)(br)Indiana DNR; 323 (t)Doug Menuez/Getty Images, (c)Lester Lefkowitz/CORBIS, (b)Wave Royalty Free/Alamy; 324 (t)Steven Weinberg/Getty Images, (c)Aerial Photography Copyright Province of Nova Scotia, (b)Jeff Greenberg/Alamy; 325 (r)Alain Choisnet/Getty Images, (t to b)The McGraw-Hill Companies, (2)Hutchings Photography/Digital Light Source, (3)Macmillan/McGraw-Hill, (4)Hutchings Photography/Digital Light Source; 326 Noah Clayton/Getty Images; 327 Hutchings Photography/Digital Light Source; 330 AP Images; 331 (l)Adrian Weinbrecht/PhotoLibrary, (r)David Young-Wolff/PhotoEdit; 332 (t)Noah Clayton/Getty Images, (b)David Young-Wolff/PhotoEdit; 333 Bo Zaunders/ CORBIS; 334 Fritz Hoffmann/CORBIS; 335 (t)Hutchings Photography/Digital Light Source; 336 SIMON FRASER/SCIENCE PHOTO LIBRARY, (b)Getty Images;

Credits

Art Acknowledgments: MCA+, Argosy, Cindy Shaw, Mapping Specialists Ltd.

Photo Credits

Cover Russell Burden/Photolibrary; **ix** (b)Fancy Photography/Veer; **vii** Ransom Studios; **NOS 2–3** NASA - digital version copyright/Science Faction/CORBIS; **NOS 4** (inset)SMC Images/Getty Images, (bkgd)Popperfoto/Getty Images; **NOS 5** (t)Maria Stenzel/Getty, (c)Stephen Alvarez/Getty Images, (b)Science Source/Photo Researchers, Inc.; **NOS 6** Martyn Chillmaid/photolibrary.com; **NOS 7** NASA; **NOS 9** (t)Andy Sacks/Getty Images, (c)NASA, H. Ford (JHU), G. Illingworth (UCSC/LO), M.Clampin (STScI), G. Hartig (STScI), the ACS Science Team, and ESA, (b)Michael Rosenfeld/Science Faction/Corbis; **NOS 10** StockShot/Alamy; **NOS 11** Michael Newman/PhotoEdit; **NOS 12** (tr) Photo by Lynn Betts, USDA Natural Resources Conservation Service; **NOS 13** (t) Annie Griffiths Belt/CORBIS, (b)Getty Images; **NOS 14** Tim Wright/CORBIS; **NOS 15** Hutchings Photography/Digital Light Source; **NOS 16** Hutchings Photography/Digital Light Source; **NOS 18** (tl)Matt Meadows, (tr)ASP/YPP/age footstock, (bl)Blair Seitz/photolibrary.com, (br)The McGraw-Hill Companies, Inc./Louis Rosenstock, photographer; **NOS 19** (t)The McGraw-Hill Companies, (c)photostock1/Alamy, (b)Blend Images/Alamy; **NOS 20** (tl)The McGraw-Hill Companies, (tr) Hutchings Photography/Digital Light Source, (bl)(br)The McGraw-Hill Companies; **NOS 21** (t to b)Hutchings Photography, (2)Macmillan/McGraw-Hill, (4)Hutchings Photography/Digital Light Source, (5)Carlos Casariego/Getty Image; **NOS 22** MANDEL NGAN/AFP/Getty Images; **NOS 23** Brian Stevenson/Getty Images; **NOS 24** AP Photo/NTSB, (t)Hisham Ibrahim/Getty Images, (bl)Bordner Aerials; **NOS 25** AP Photo/The Minnesota Daily, Stacy Bengs; **NOS 26** LARRY DOWNING/Reuters/Landov; **NOS 27** Plus Pix/age footstock; **NOS 28** ASSOCIATED PRESS; **NOS 30** (3)Macmillan/McGraw-Hill (others)Hutchings Photography/Digital Light Source; **NOS 31** Hutchings Photography/Digital Light Source; **NOS 33** (l)Andy Sacks/Getty Images, (r)NASA - digital version copyright/Science Faction/Corbis; **4** Reuters/Corbis, (tl)Jochen Tack/photolibrary.com, (c)adrian davies/Alamy, (r)Oleksiy Maksymenko/Alamy, (bl)Biophoto Associates/Photo Researchers, Inc.; **5** (l)John W. van de Lindt/Colorado State University, (tl)Dennis Kunkel Microscopy, Inc./Visuals Unlimited, Inc., (r)Daniel Cox/O.H. Hinsdale Research Laboratory/Oregon State University, (r)PhotoAlto/PunchStock, (b)Pacific Marine Environmental Laboratory/NOAA, (bl)Amanda Hall/Robert Harding World Imagery/Getty Images; **6–7** Visions LLC/Photolibrary; **8** Getty Images; **9** Hutchings Photography/Digital Light Source; **10** (l)Bill Curtsinger/Getty Images, (cl)CORBIS, (cr)Jose Luis Pelaez/Getty Images, (r)Sagel & Kranefeld/Corbis; **12** Hutchings Photography/Digital Light Source; **13** (t)Simon Fraser/Photo Researchers, Inc., (c)EIGHTFISH/Getty Images, (b)Philip Evans/Getty Images; **14** Hutchings Photography/Digital Light Source; **15** Conny Fridh/Getty Images, (l)imagebroker/Alamy, (c)Mark Steinmetz; **16** (t)Hutchings Photography/Digital Light Source, (bl)C Squared Studios/Getty Images, (bc)Steve Allen/Brand X Pictures/Alamy, (br)The Mcgraw-Hill Companies; **18** Hutchings Photography/Digital Light Source, (r)Andy Crawford and Tim Ridley/Getty Images; **20** (t)Sagel & Kranefeld/Corbis, (c)Mark Steinmetz, (b)C Squared Studios/Getty Images; **21** (inset)sciencephotos/Alamy, (bkgd)Charles Smith/Corbis; **22** Bryan F. Peterson/CORBIS; **23** Hutchings Photography/Digital Light Source; **25** (l)Anna Yu/Getty Images, (r)Stocktrek/age footstock; **29** Anna Yu/Getty Images; **30** (4)Macmillan/McGraw-Hill, (others) (r)Hutchings Photography/Digital Light Source, Hutchings Photography/Digital Light Source; **31** Hutchings Photography/Digital Light Source, **32** Steve Allen/Brand X Pictures/Alamy, **35** Visions LLC/Photolibrary, **38–39** Gregor M. Schmid/CORBIS, **40** Atlantide Phototravel/Corbis, **41** Hutchings Photography/Digital Light Source, **43** (t)Royalty Free/Corbis (c)Steve Hamblin/Alamy (b)The McGraw-Hill Companies, **44** (t)Vito Palmisano/Getty Images (b)creativ collection/age fotostock, **45** (l)Mauritius/SuperStock (r)Hutchings Photography/Digital Light Source **46** Alberto Coto/Getty Images, **48** (t)Finley - StockFood Munich, (b)The McGraw-Hill Companies, (bkgd)Michael Rosenfeld/Getty Images; **49** Alaska Stock/age footstock; **50–53** Hutchings Photography/Digital Light Source; **54** (l)Charles D. Winters/Photo Researchers, Inc., (r)Jean du Boisberranger/Getty Images; **56** Hutchings Photography/Digital Light Source; **57** (t)Alaska Stock/age fotostock, (c)Hutchings Photography/Digital Light Source, (bl)Jean du Boisberranger/Getty Images, (br)Charles D. Winters/Photo Researchers, Inc.; **58** Hutchings Photography/Digital Light Source; **59** Check Six/Getty Images; **60–67** Hutchings Photography/Digital Light Source; **71** Gregor M. Schmid/CORBIS; **74–75** Jim Reed/Science Faction/Getty Images; **76** P.J. Stewart/Photo Researchers, Inc.; **77** Hutchings Photography/Digital Light Source; **79** (tl)DEA/A.RIZZI/De Agostini Picture Library/Getty Images, (tr)Astrid & Hanns-Frieder Michler/Photo Researchers, Inc., (cl)Visuals Unlimited/Ken Lucas/Getty Images, (cr)Richard Treptow/Photo Researchers, Inc., (bl)CORBIS (br)ImageState/Alamy; **82** (l)David J. Green/Alamy, (c)WILDLIFE/Peter Arnold Inc., (r)Mark Schneider/Visuals Unlimited/Getty Images; **83** (l)LBNL/Photo Researchers, Inc., (c)Boyer/Roger Viollet/Getty Images, (r)ullstein bild/Peter Arnold, Inc.; **85** Hutchings Photography/Digital Light Source; **86** Paul Katz/photolibrary.com; **87** Hutchings Photography/Digital Light Source; **88** (tl)The McGraw-Hill Companies, (tc)Paul Katz/Getty Images, (tr)Egyptian National Museum, Cairo, Egypt, Photo © Boltin Picture Library/The Bridgeman Art Library International, (bl)NASA, (bc)Hutchings Photography/Digital Light Source, (br)Charles Stirling/Alamy; **89** (l)The McGraw-Hill Companies, Inc./Stephen Frisch, photographer, (c)sciencephotos/Alamy, (r)Martyn Chillmaid/Oxford Scientific (OSF)/photolibrary.com; **90** (l)Royalty-Free/CORBIS, (cl)Dr. Parvinder Sethi, (cr)Joel Arem/Photo Researchers, Inc., (r)Ingram Publishing/SuperStock; **91** Hutchings Photography/Digital Light Source; **92** (t)Egyptian National Museum, Cairo, Egypt, Photo © Boltin Picture Library/The Bridgeman Art Library International, (c)The McGraw-Hill Companies, Inc./Stephen Frisch, photographer, (b)Paul Katz/Getty Images; **93** Jeff Hunter/Getty Images; **94** E.O. Lawrence Berkely National Laboratory, University of California, U.S. Department of Energy; **95** Hutchings Photography/Digital Light Source; **96** (tl)Ted Foxx/Alamy, (tr)Richard Treptow/Photo Researchers, Inc., (c)Hutchings Photography/Digital Light Source, (bl)Photodisc/Getty Images, (br)Charles D. Winters/Photo Researchers, Inc.; **97** sciencephotos/Alamy; **98** NASA-JPL; **99** (l)Ingemar Aourell/Getty Images, (cl)Don Farrall/Getty Images, (cr)Gabe Palmer/Alamy, (r)Henrik Sorensen/Getty Images; **100** (t)PhotoLink/Getty Images, (b)Hutchings Photography/Digital Light Source; **101** (t)Richard Treptow/Photo Researchers, Inc., (c)sciencephotos/Alamy, (b)PhotoLink/Getty Images; **102–103** Hutchings Photography/Digital Light Source; **104** (t)David J. Green/Alamy, (b)Mark Schneider/Visuals Unlimited/Getty Images; **107** Jim Reed/Science Faction/Getty Images; **112** (t)PARIS PIERCE/Alamy, (c)University Library, Leipzig, Germany/Archives Charmet/The Bridgeman Art Library, (b)British Library, London, UK/© British Library Board. All Rights Reserved/The Bridgeman Art Library; **113** ACE STOCK LIMITED/Alamy; **114–115** altrendo images/Getty Images; **116** Douglas Fisher/Alamy; **117–122** Hutchings Photography/Digital Light Source; **124** (t)Popperfoto/Getty Images, (c)Underwood & Underwood/CORBIS, (bl)John Meyer, (br)Ilene MacDonald/Alamy; **125** Gazimal/Getty Images; **126–130** Hutchings Photography/Digital Light Source; **132** (l)Macmillan/McGraw-Hill, (r)Hutchings Photography/Digital Light Source; **133** Brent Winebrenner/Photolibrary.com; **134** Hutchings Photography/Digital Light Source; **138** (t)Photodisc/Getty Images, (c)C Squared Studios/Getty Images, (b)Jennifer Martine/Jupiter Images; **140** (tr)(cr)(bl)Macmillan/McGraw-Hill, (br)(t to b)(2)Hutchings Photography/Digital Light Source, (3)Macmillan/McGraw-Hill, (4) Hutchings Photography/Digital Light Source, (5)(6)Macmillan/